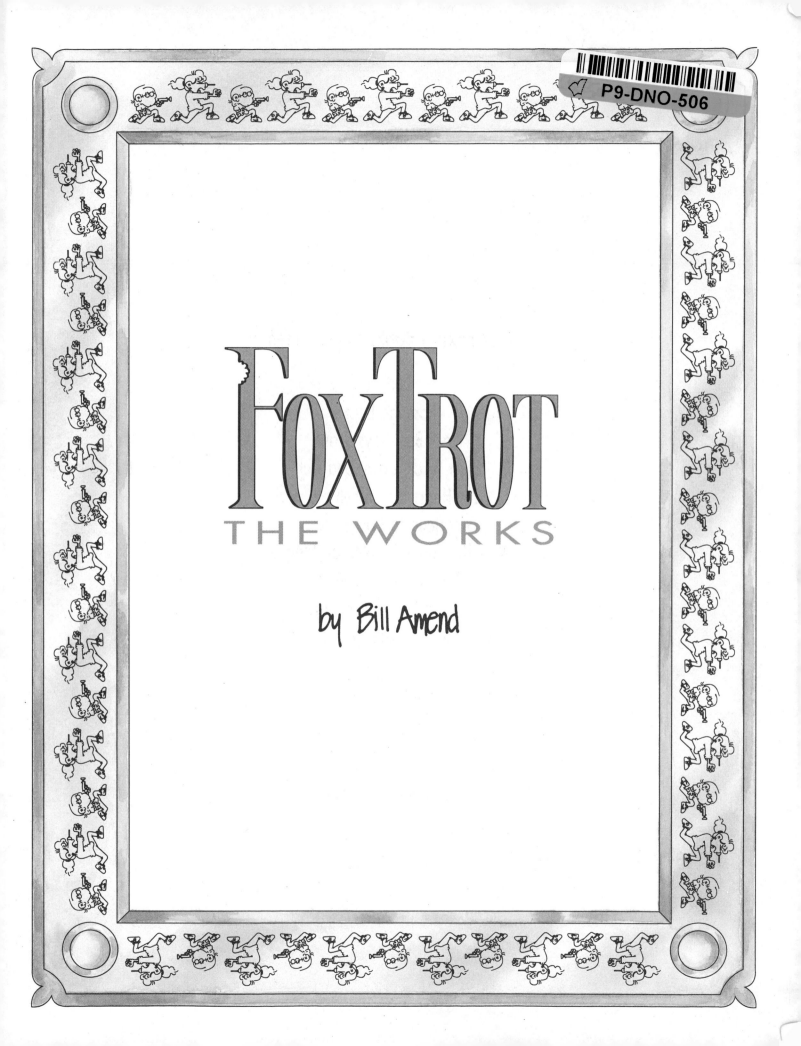

FoxTrot

THE WORKS

by Bill Amend

Other FoxTrot Books by Bill Amend

FoxTrot
Pass the Loot
Black Bart Says Draw
Eight Yards, Down and Out
Bury My Heart at Fun-Fun Mountain
Say Hello to Cactus Flats
May The Force Be With Us, Please
Take Us To Your Mall
The Return Of The Lone Iguana
At Least This Place Sells T-Shirts

Anthology

FoxTrot: *en masse*
Wildly FoxTrot
Enormously FoxTrot

THE WORKS

by Bill Amend

Andrews and McMeel　　　A Universal Press Syndicate Company　　　**Kansas City**

FoxTrot is syndicated internationally by Universal Press Syndicate.

FoxTrot: The Works copyright © 1990 by Universal Press Syndicate. All rights reserved. Printed in the United States of America. No part of this book may be reproduced in any manner whatsoever without written permission except in the context of reviews. For information write Andrews and McMeel, a Universal Press Syndicate Company, 4520 Main Street, Kansas City, Missouri 64111.

ISBN: 0-8362-1848-5

Library of Congress Catalog Card **Number: 90-82677**

First Printing, August 1990
Fifth Printing, February 1997

To Jake, Lee, and Sue,
who put me in my place

Preface

The first comic strip I can remember reading as a child was Ernie Bushmiller's Nancy. While I cannot for the life of me recall whether or not I found the strip to be entertaining, I do remember taking a peculiar fascination with young Nancy's hair.

It was unusual hair, to say the least. Imagine a football helmet made out of black Astroturf and you have a pretty fair approximation of this otherwise apparently normal child's coiffure.

What would it look like soaking wet? How about in a 50 mph wind? Did it feel as bristly as it looked? Did she, or for that matter could she, ever comb it? And did she arrive at the breakfast table each morning with a pillow stuck to the back of the head?

These are reasonable questions to ask, and I'm sure that I pondered them at great length. But what sticks in my mind today were my first and most spontaneous thoughts upon seeing this prickly do: What fun it must be to draw this. Never mind the tedium. I imagined this Bushmiller fellow saving those little spikes of hair as the last thing to ink—sort of the dessert or reward waiting at the end of a day's work.

Like most adults, my youthful zeal has tempered a bit with age and I can't honestly say that the thought of drawing Nancy's hair day after day does for me quite what it used to. That's probably a good thing, although the image of Roger Fox in a Nancy wig does raise interesting possibilities.

What has remained, however, is a personal definition of drawing as something fun. As the title of this book is meant to suggest, producing a half-decent daily comic strip involves a tremendous amount of work. Much of it boring and repetitive, and all of it seemingly due yesterday. Deadlines loom everywhere and the pressure to be "funny" never lets up. If I *didn't* find drawing a joy, I certainly wouldn't be doing this for a living. At the very least, I'd hire myself an assistant.

Drawing a comic strip *is* fun. Never mind the tedium. Words to live by. Let's hope they don't kill me.

Cartoons have the wonderful ability to appeal to readers of all ages. It's something I try to keep in mind. Because when I was but a boy of seven, a strip reached out to me. In a way that Mr. Bushmiller probably knew firsthand.

——BILL AMEND

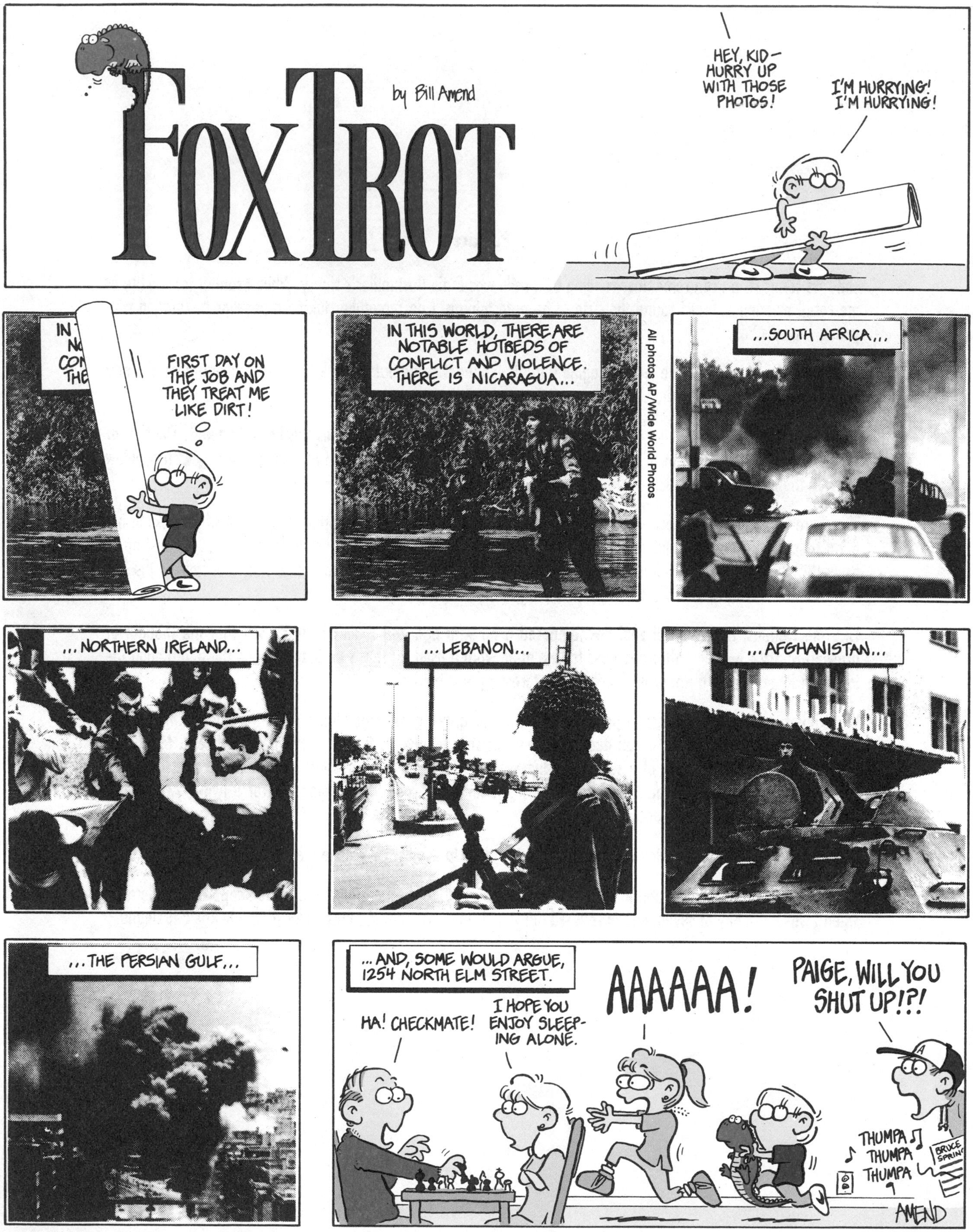
FOXTROT
by Bill Amend
HEY, KID— HURRY UP WITH THOSE PHOTOS!
I'M HURRYING! I'M HURRYING!
FIRST DAY ON THE JOB AND THEY TREAT ME LIKE DIRT!
IN THIS WORLD, THERE ARE NOTABLE HOTBEDS OF CONFLICT AND VIOLENCE. THERE IS NICARAGUA...
All photos AP/Wide World Photos
...SOUTH AFRICA...
...NORTHERN IRELAND...
...LEBANON...
...AFGHANISTAN...
...THE PERSIAN GULF...
...AND, SOME WOULD ARGUE, 1254 NORTH ELM STREET.
HA! CHECKMATE!
I HOPE YOU ENJOY SLEEPING ALONE.
AAAAAA!
PAIGE, WILL YOU SHUT UP!?!
THUMPA THUMPA THUMPA
AMEND

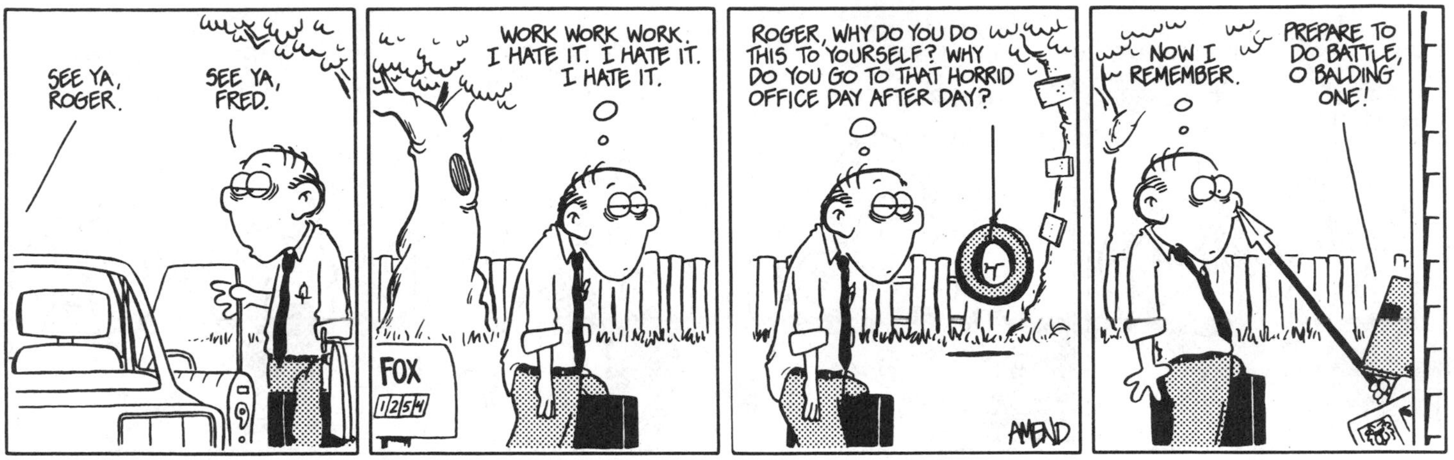
SEE YA, ROGER.
SEE YA, FRED.
WORK WORK WORK. I HATE IT. I HATE IT. I HATE IT.
FOX
ROGER, WHY DO YOU DO THIS TO YOURSELF? WHY DO YOU GO TO THAT HORRID OFFICE DAY AFTER DAY?
AMEND
NOW I REMEMBER.
PREPARE TO DO BATTLE, O BALDING ONE!

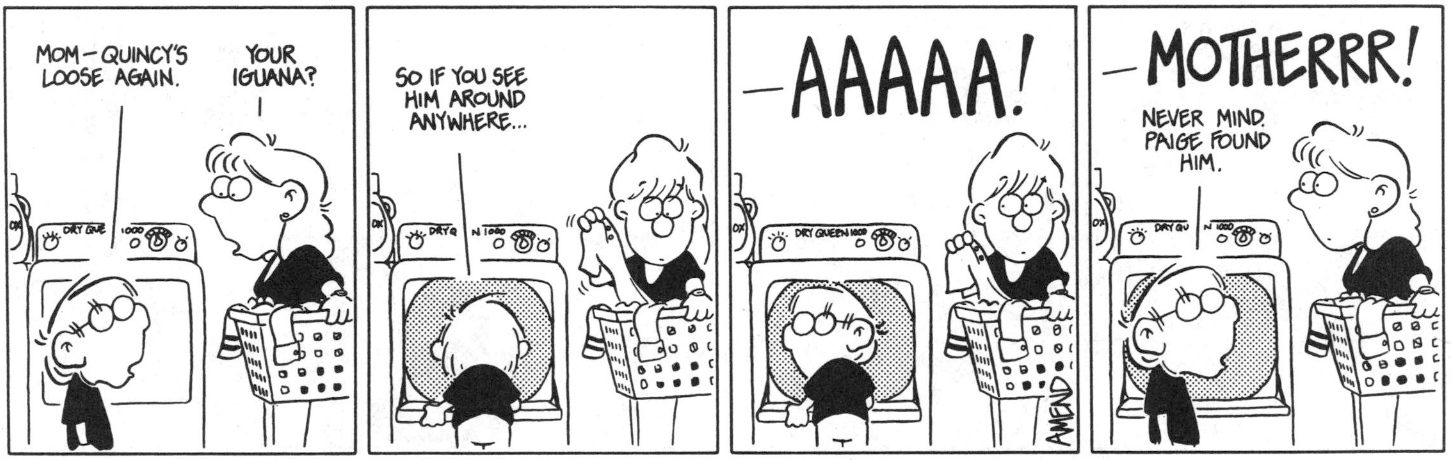
MOM–QUINCY'S LOOSE AGAIN.
YOUR IGUANA?
SO IF YOU SEE HIM AROUND ANYWHERE...
–AAAAA!
AMEND
–MOTHERRR!
NEVER MIND. PAIGE FOUND HIM.

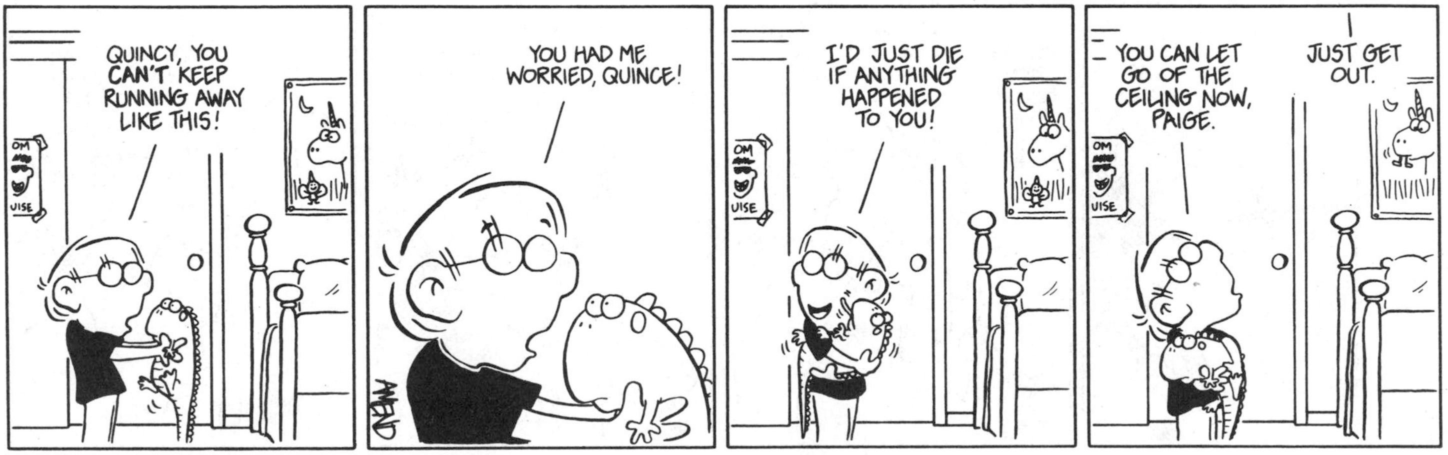
QUINCY, YOU CAN'T KEEP RUNNING AWAY LIKE THIS!
YOU HAD ME WORRIED, QUINCE!
I'D JUST DIE IF ANYTHING HAPPENED TO YOU!
YOU CAN LET GO OF THE CEILING NOW, PAIGE.
JUST GET OUT.

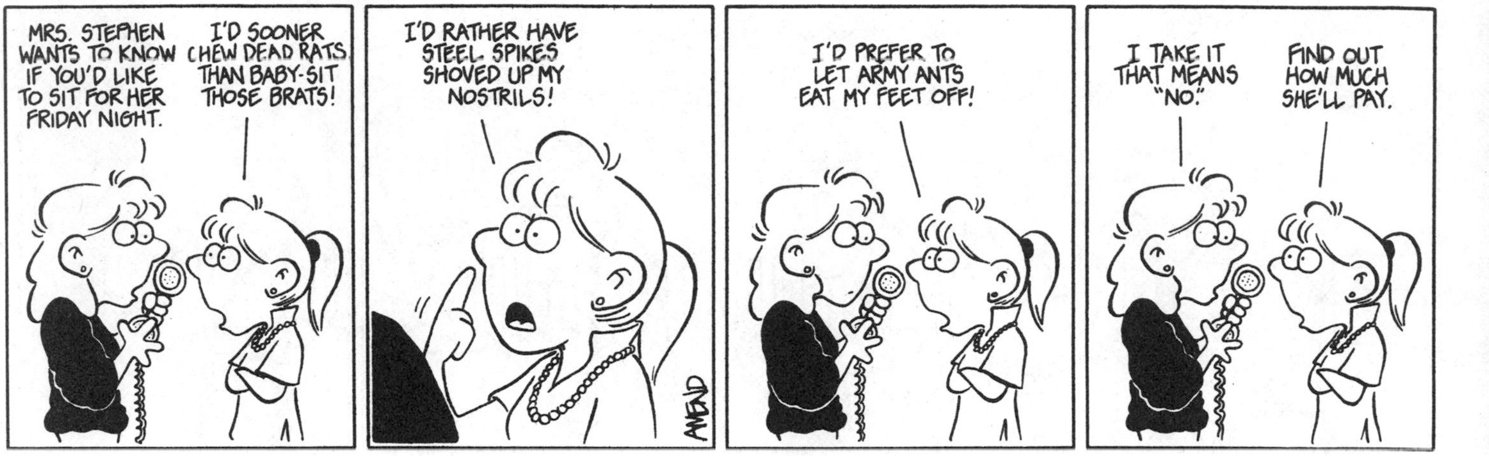
MRS. STEPHEN WANTS TO KNOW IF YOU'D LIKE TO SIT FOR HER FRIDAY NIGHT.
I'D SOONER CHEW DEAD RATS THAN BABY-SIT THOSE BRATS!
I'D RATHER HAVE STEEL SPIKES SHOVED UP MY NOSTRILS!
AMEND
I'D PREFER TO LET ARMY ANTS EAT MY FEET OFF!
I TAKE IT THAT MEANS "NO."
FIND OUT HOW MUCH SHE'LL PAY.

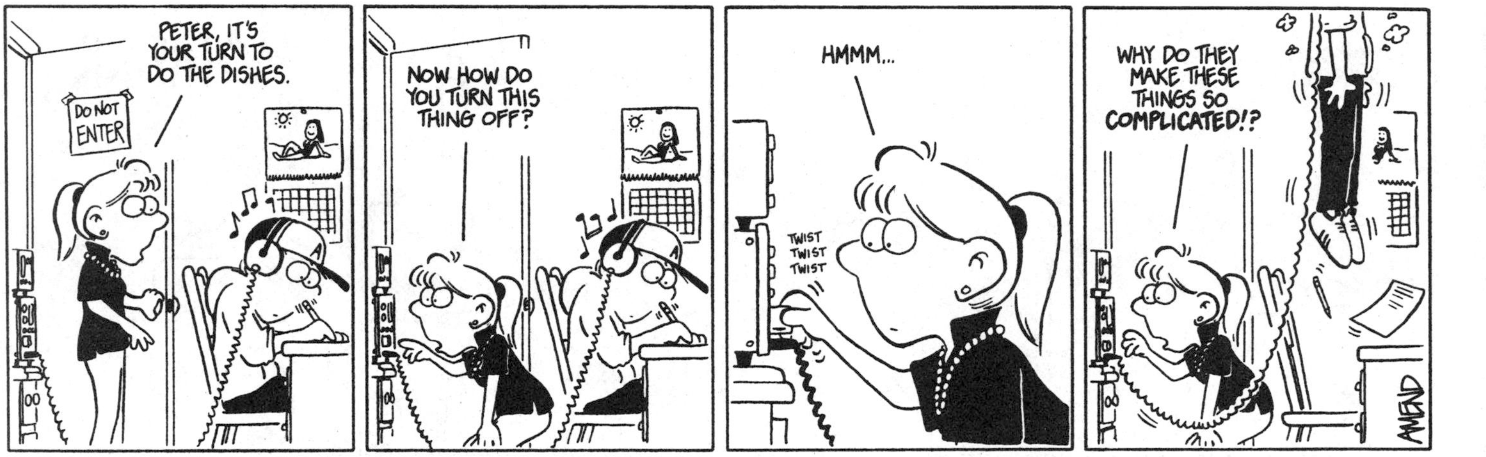
PETER, IT'S YOUR TURN TO DO THE DISHES.
DO NOT ENTER
NOW HOW DO YOU TURN THIS THING OFF?
HMMM...
TWIST TWIST TWIST
WHY DO THEY MAKE THESE THINGS SO **COMPLICATED!?**
AMEND

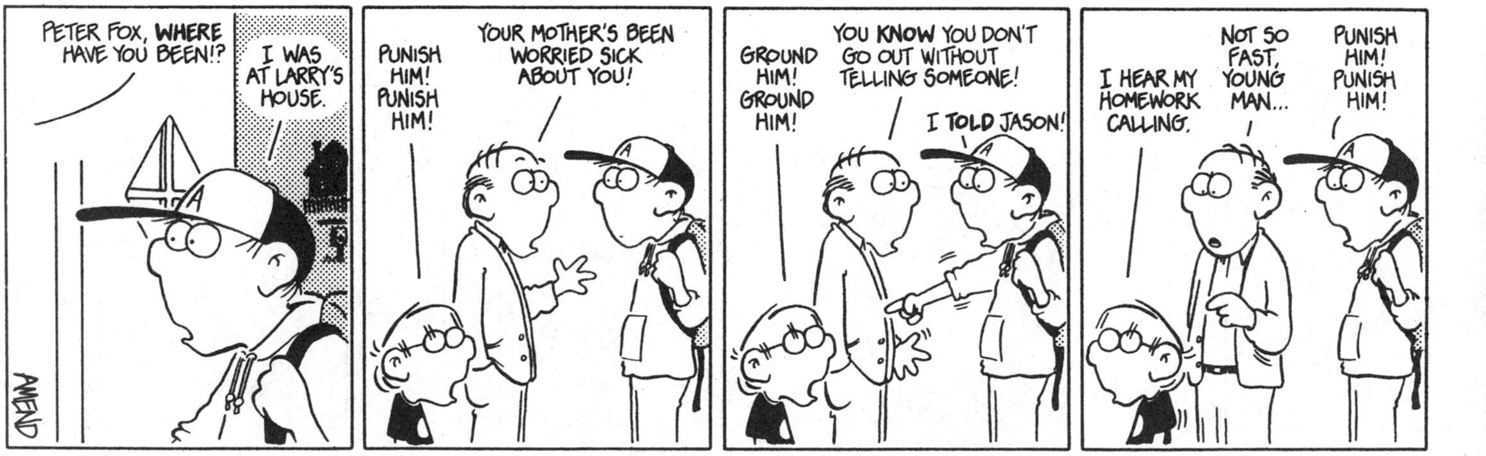
PETER FOX, **WHERE** HAVE YOU BEEN!?
I WAS AT LARRY'S HOUSE.
AMEND
PUNISH HIM! PUNISH HIM!
YOUR MOTHER'S BEEN WORRIED SICK ABOUT YOU!
GROUND HIM! GROUND HIM!
YOU **KNOW** YOU DON'T GO OUT WITHOUT TELLING SOMEONE!
I **TOLD** JASON!
I HEAR MY HOMEWORK CALLING.
NOT SO FAST, YOUNG MAN...
PUNISH HIM! PUNISH HIM!

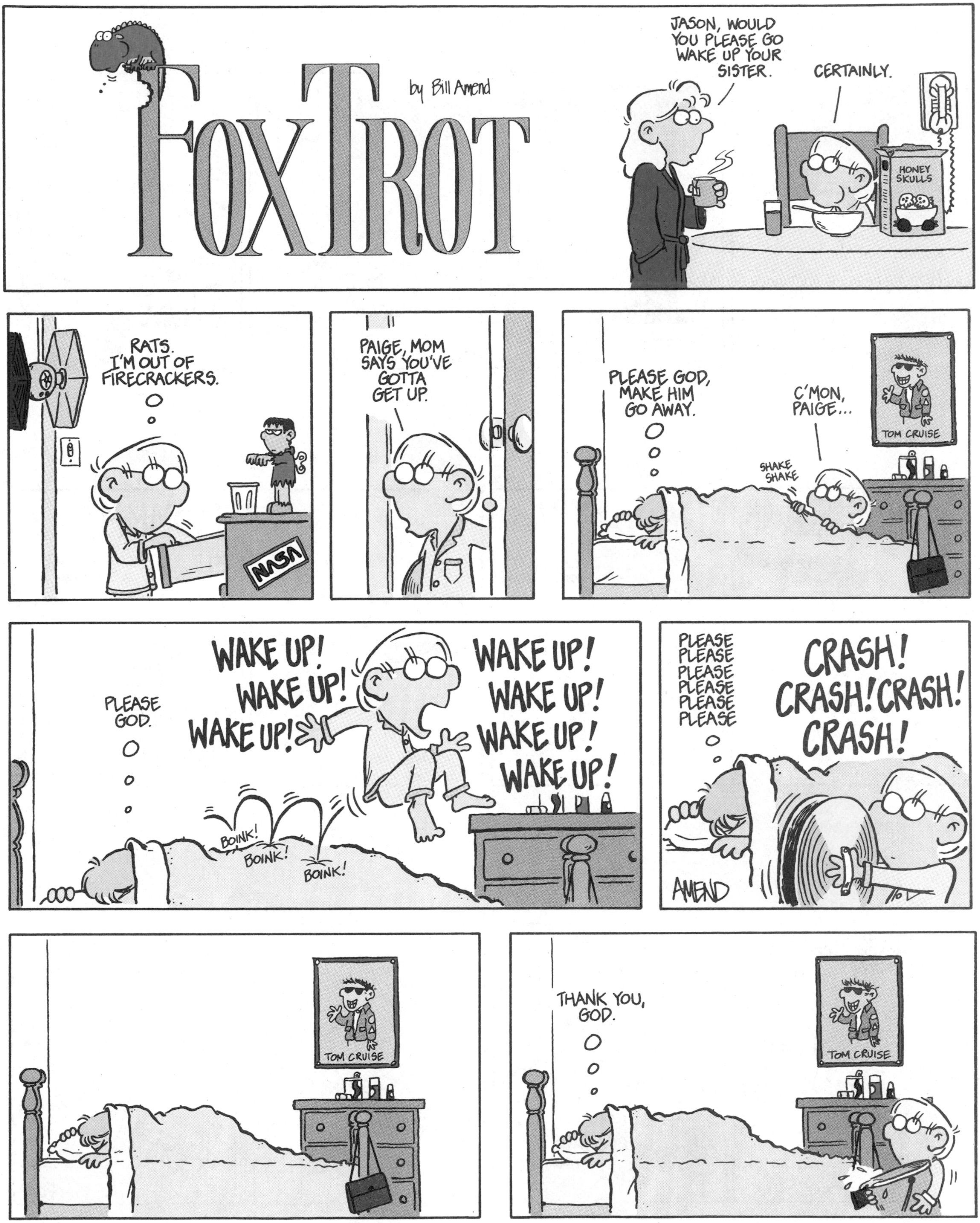
FOXTROT
by Bill Amend
JASON, WOULD YOU PLEASE GO WAKE UP YOUR SISTER.
CERTAINLY.
HONEY SKULLS
RATS. I'M OUT OF FIRECRACKERS.
NASA
PAIGE, MOM SAYS YOU'VE GOTTA GET UP.
PLEASE GOD, MAKE HIM GO AWAY.
C'MON, PAIGE...
SHAKE SHAKE
TOM CRUISE
PLEASE GOD.
WAKE UP! WAKE UP! WAKE UP!
WAKE UP! WAKE UP! WAKE UP! WAKE UP!
BOINK! BOINK! BOINK!
PLEASE PLEASE PLEASE PLEASE PLEASE PLEASE
CRASH! CRASH! CRASH! CRASH!
AMEND
TOM CRUISE
THANK YOU, GOD.
TOM CRUISE

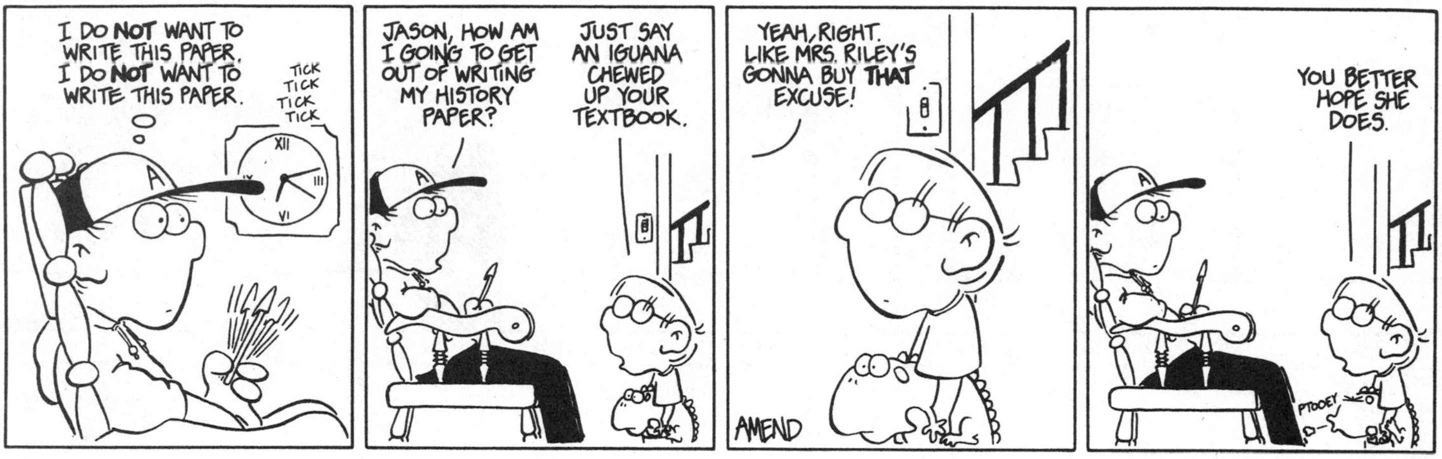
I DO **NOT** WANT TO WRITE THIS PAPER. I DO **NOT** WANT TO WRITE THIS PAPER.
TICK TICK TICK TICK
JASON, HOW AM I GOING TO GET OUT OF WRITING MY HISTORY PAPER?
JUST SAY AN IGUANA CHEWED UP YOUR TEXTBOOK.
YEAH, RIGHT. LIKE MRS. RILEY'S GONNA BUY **THAT** EXCUSE!
AMEND
YOU BETTER HOPE SHE DOES.
PTOOEY

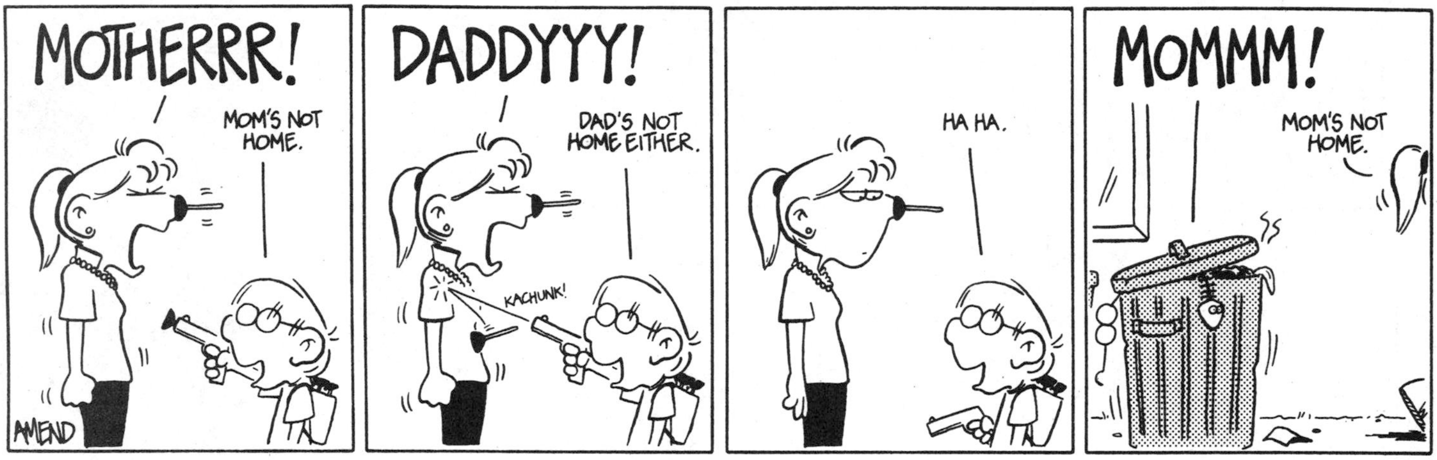
MOTHERRR!
MOM'S NOT HOME.
AMEND
DADDYYY!
DAD'S NOT HOME EITHER.
KACHUNK!
HA HA.
MOMMM!
MOM'S NOT HOME.

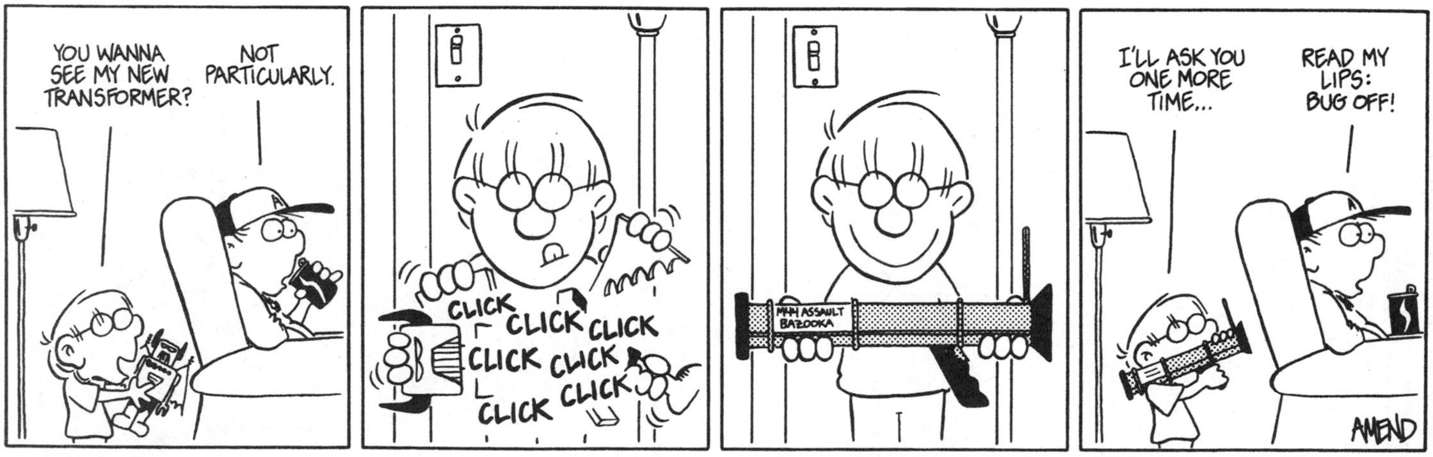
YOU WANNA SEE MY NEW TRANSFORMER?
NOT PARTICULARLY.
CLICK CLICK CLICK CLICK CLICK CLICK CLICK
ASSAULT BAZOOKA
I'LL ASK YOU ONE MORE TIME...
READ MY LIPS: BUG OFF!
AMEND

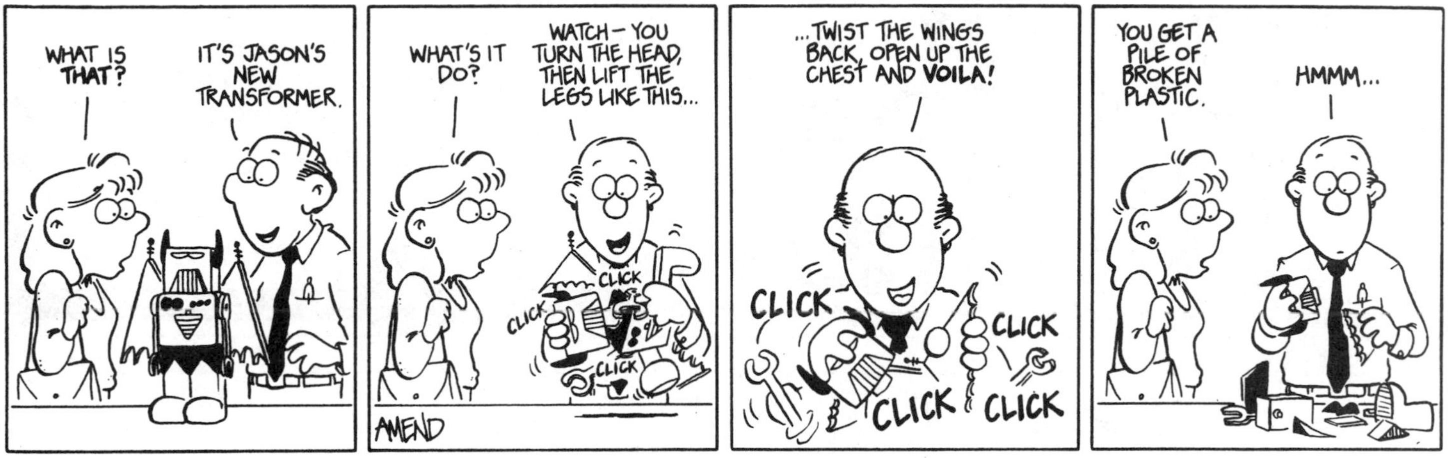
WHAT IS THAT?
IT'S JASON'S NEW TRANSFORMER.
WHAT'S IT DO?
WATCH—YOU TURN THE HEAD, THEN LIFT THE LEGS LIKE THIS...
CLICK CLICK CLICK CLICK
...TWIST THE WINGS BACK, OPEN UP THE CHEST AND VOILA!
CLICK CLICK CLICK CLICK
YOU GET A PILE OF BROKEN PLASTIC.
HMMM...
AMEND

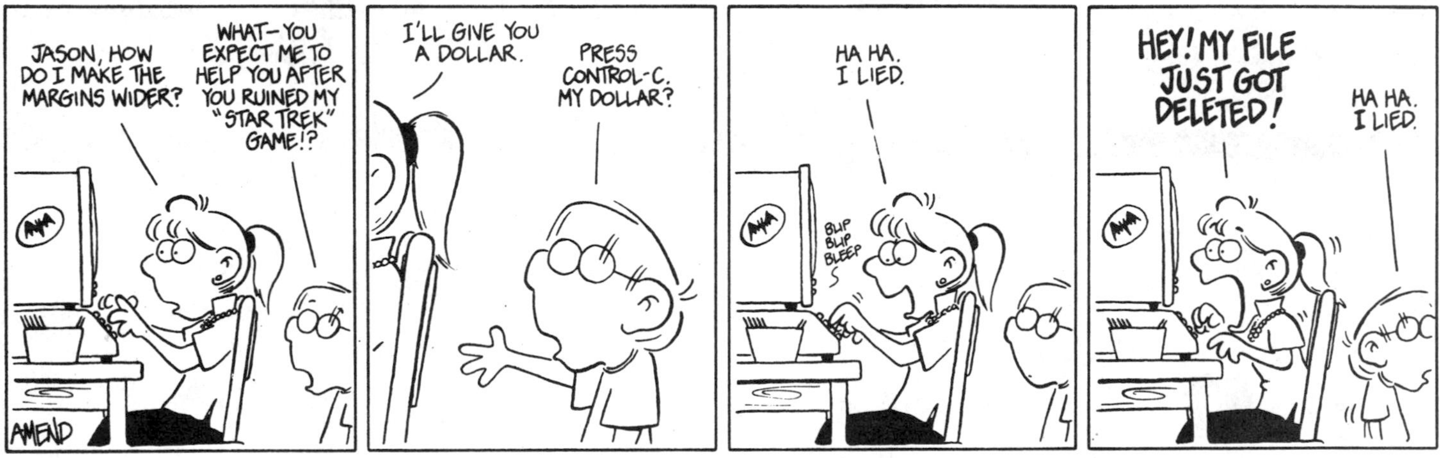
JASON, HOW DO I MAKE THE MARGINS WIDER?
WHAT—YOU EXPECT ME TO HELP YOU AFTER YOU RUINED MY "STAR TREK" GAME!?
I'LL GIVE YOU A DOLLAR.
PRESS CONTROL-C. MY DOLLAR?
HA HA. I LIED.
BLIP BLIP BLEEP
HEY! MY FILE JUST GOT DELETED!
HA HA. I LIED.
AMEND

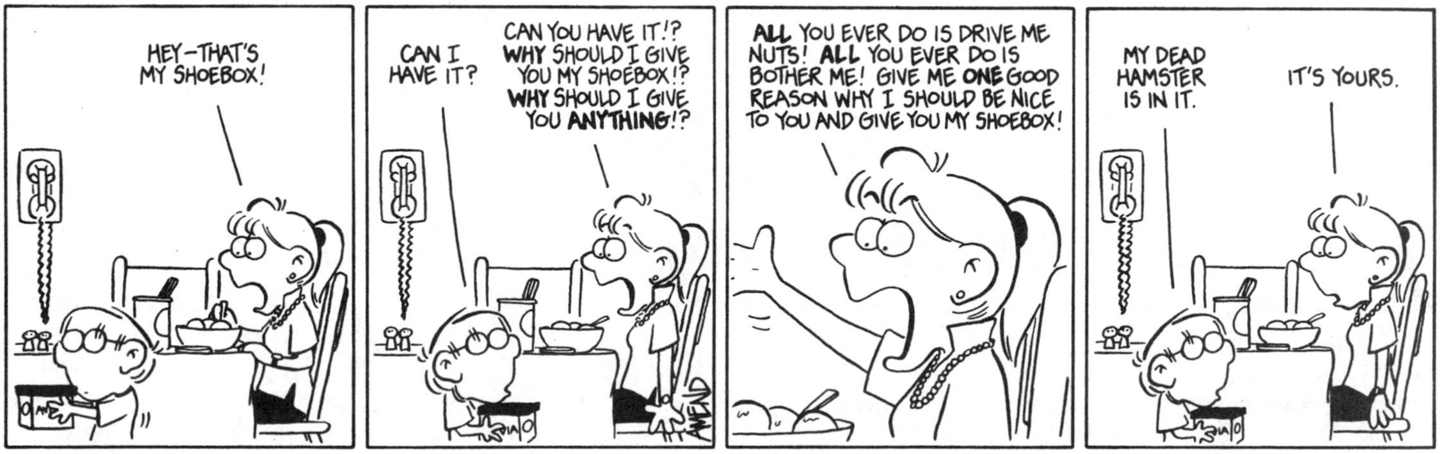
HEY—THAT'S MY SHOEBOX!
CAN I HAVE IT?
CAN YOU HAVE IT!? WHY SHOULD I GIVE YOU MY SHOEBOX!? WHY SHOULD I GIVE YOU ANYTHING!?
ALL YOU EVER DO IS DRIVE ME NUTS! ALL YOU EVER DO IS BOTHER ME! GIVE ME ONE GOOD REASON WHY I SHOULD BE NICE TO YOU AND GIVE YOU MY SHOEBOX!
MY DEAD HAMSTER IS IN IT.
IT'S YOURS.
AMEND

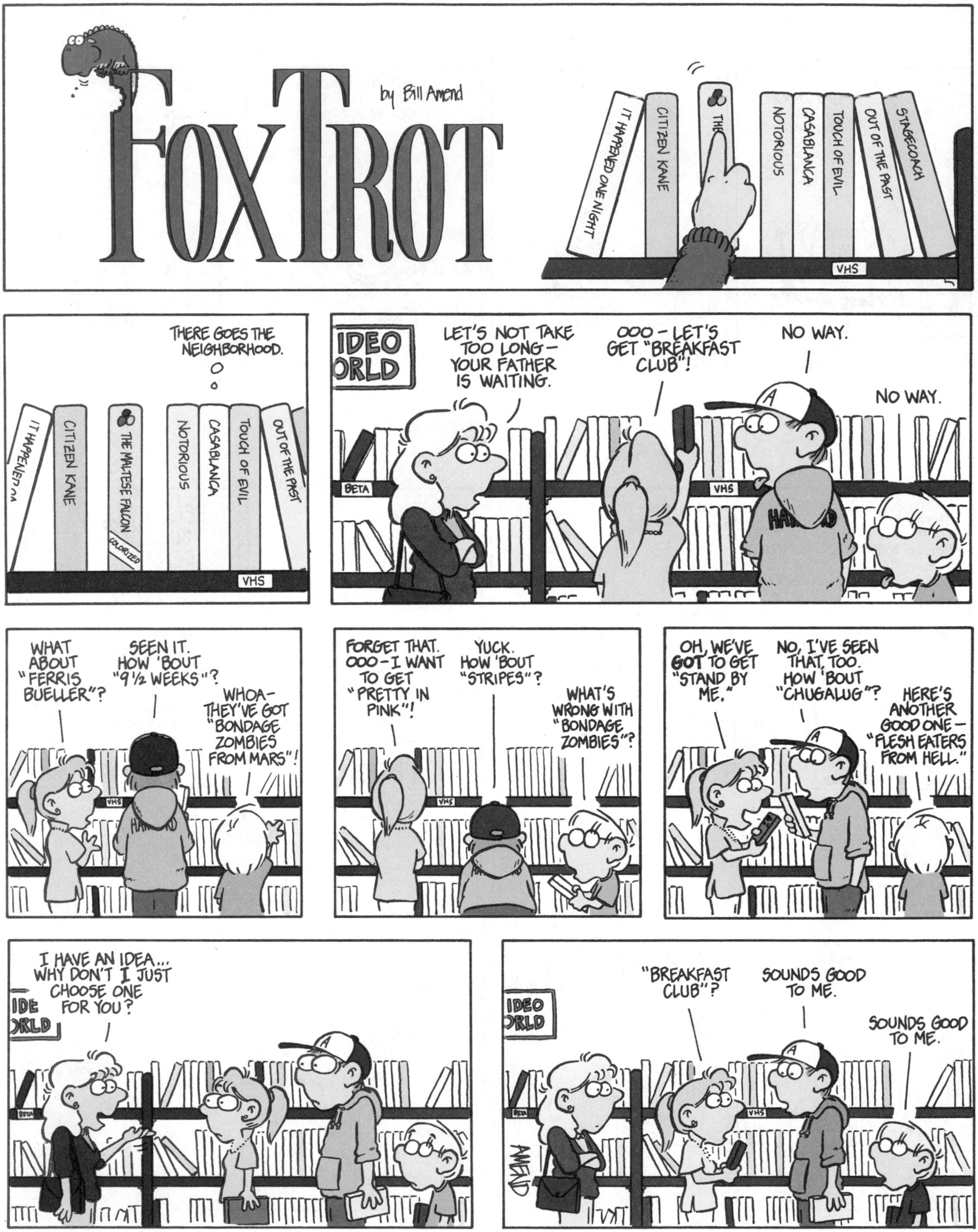
FoxTrot
by Bill Amend
IT HAPPENED ONE NIGHT
CITIZEN KANE
NOTORIOUS
CASABLANCA
TOUCH OF EVIL
OUT OF THE PAST
STAGECOACH
VHS
THERE GOES THE NEIGHBORHOOD.
THE MALTESE FALCON
COLORIZED
IDEO
ORLD
LET'S NOT TAKE TOO LONG— YOUR FATHER IS WAITING.
OOO—LET'S GET "BREAKFAST CLUB"!
NO WAY.
NO WAY.
WHAT ABOUT "FERRIS BUELLER"?
SEEN IT. HOW 'BOUT "9½ WEEKS"?
WHOA—THEY'VE GOT "BONDAGE ZOMBIES FROM MARS"!
FORGET THAT. OOO—I WANT TO GET "PRETTY IN PINK"!
YUCK. HOW 'BOUT "STRIPES"?
WHAT'S WRONG WITH "BONDAGE ZOMBIES"?
OH, WE'VE GOT TO GET "STAND BY ME."
NO, I'VE SEEN THAT, TOO. HOW 'BOUT "CHUGALUG"?
HERE'S ANOTHER GOOD ONE—"FLESH EATERS FROM HELL."
I HAVE AN IDEA... WHY DON'T I JUST CHOOSE ONE FOR YOU?
"BREAKFAST CLUB"?
SOUNDS GOOD TO ME.
SOUNDS GOOD TO ME.
AMEND

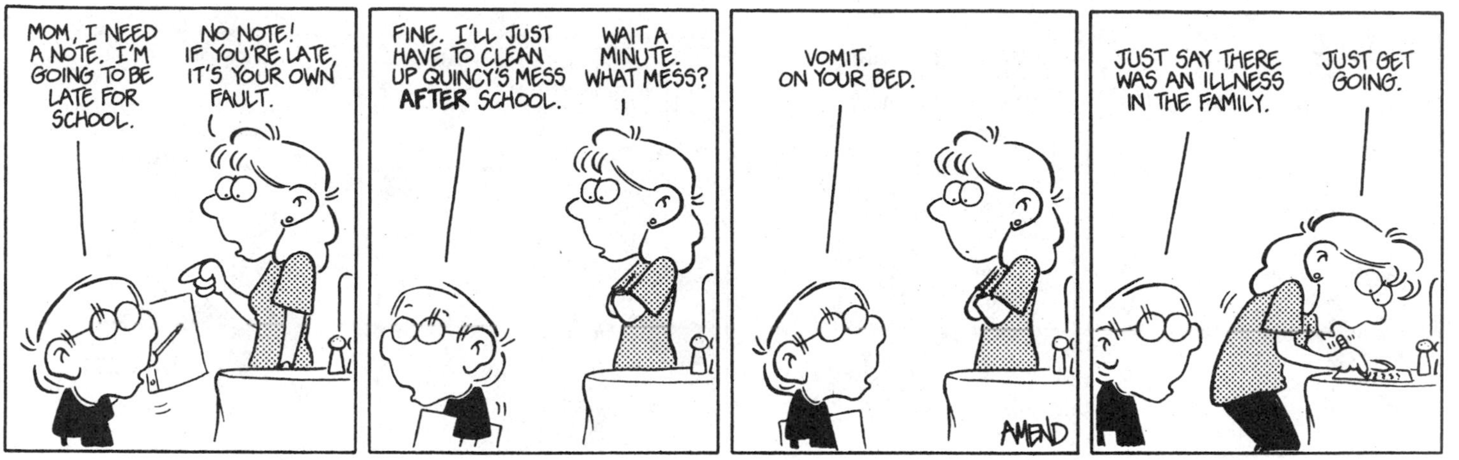
MOM, I NEED A NOTE. I'M GOING TO BE LATE FOR SCHOOL.
NO NOTE! IF YOU'RE LATE, IT'S YOUR OWN FAULT.
FINE. I'LL JUST HAVE TO CLEAN UP QUINCY'S MESS **AFTER** SCHOOL.
WAIT A MINUTE. WHAT MESS?
VOMIT. ON YOUR BED.
AMEND
JUST SAY THERE WAS AN ILLNESS IN THE FAMILY.
JUST GET GOING.

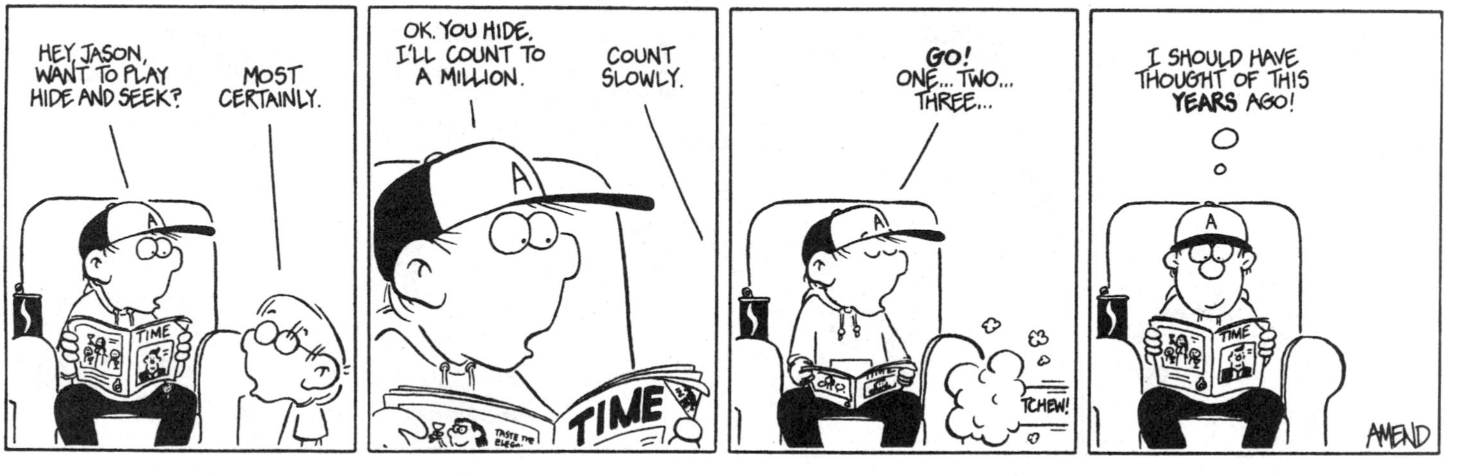
HEY, JASON, WANT TO PLAY HIDE AND SEEK?
MOST CERTAINLY.
TIME
OK. YOU HIDE. I'LL COUNT TO A MILLION.
COUNT SLOWLY.
TIME
GO! ONE... TWO... THREE...
TCHEW!
I SHOULD HAVE THOUGHT OF THIS **YEARS** AGO!
TIME
AMEND

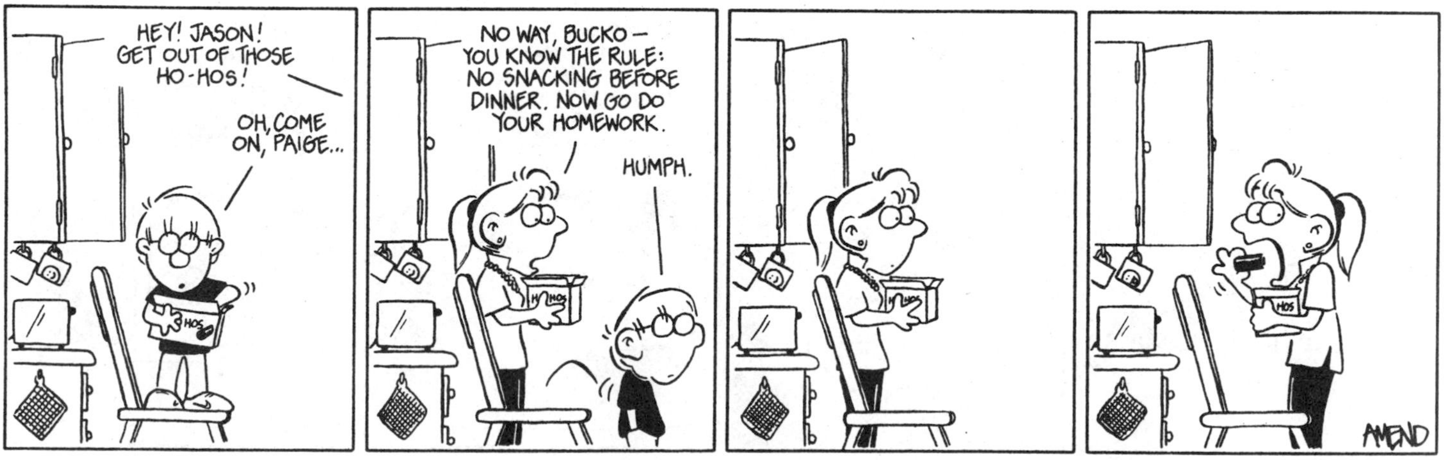
HEY! JASON! GET OUT OF THOSE HO-HOS!
OH, COME ON, PAIGE...
NO WAY, BUCKO — YOU KNOW THE RULE: NO SNACKING BEFORE DINNER. NOW GO DO YOUR HOMEWORK.
HUMPH.
AMEND

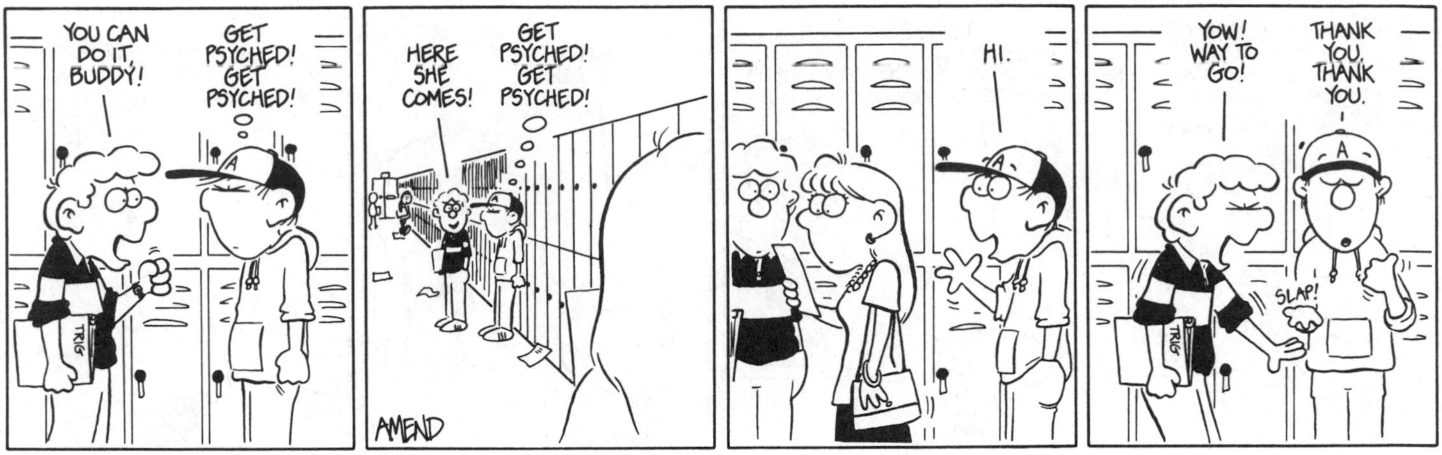
YOU CAN DO IT, BUDDY!
GET PSYCHED! GET PSYCHED!
TRIG
HERE SHE COMES!
GET PSYCHED! GET PSYCHED!
AMEND
HI.
YOW! WAY TO GO!
THANK YOU. THANK YOU.
SLAP!
TRIG

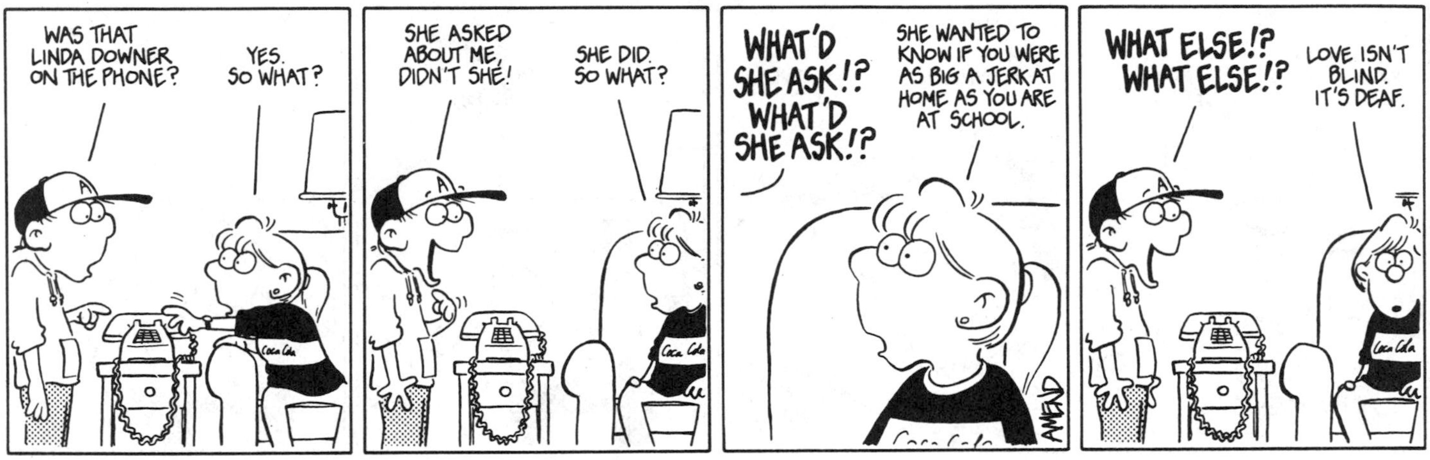
WAS THAT LINDA DOWNER ON THE PHONE?
YES. SO WHAT?
Coca Cola
SHE ASKED ABOUT ME, DIDN'T SHE!
SHE DID. SO WHAT?
Coca Cola
WHAT'D SHE ASK!? WHAT'D SHE ASK!?
SHE WANTED TO KNOW IF YOU WERE AS BIG A JERK AT HOME AS YOU ARE AT SCHOOL.
AMEND
WHAT ELSE!? WHAT ELSE!?
LOVE ISN'T BLIND. IT'S DEAF.
Coca Cola

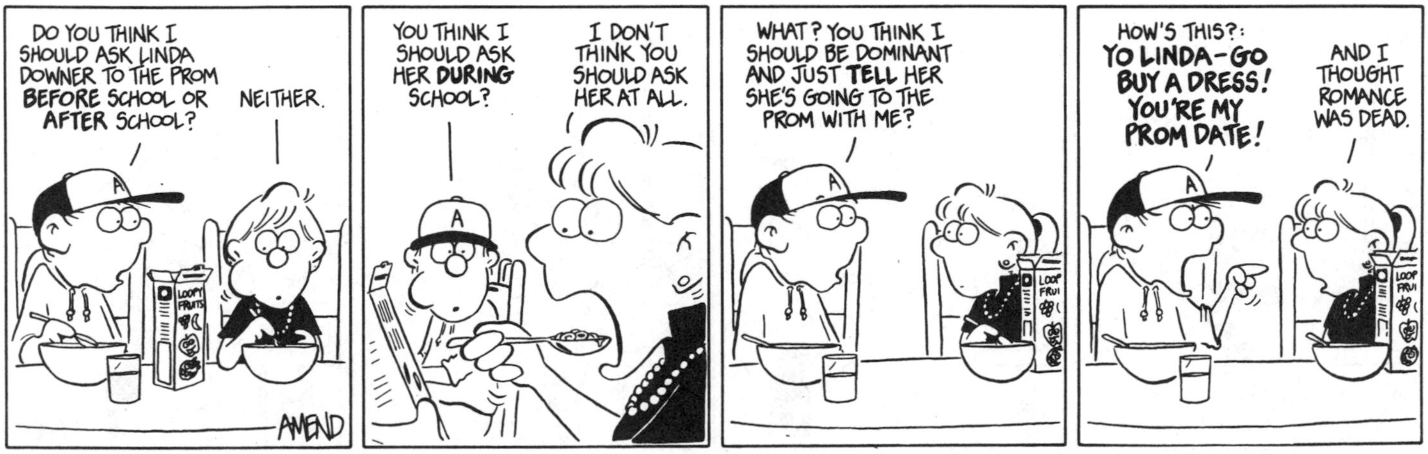
DO YOU THINK I SHOULD ASK LINDA DOWNER TO THE PROM BEFORE SCHOOL OR AFTER SCHOOL?
NEITHER.
LOOPY FRUITS
AMEND
YOU THINK I SHOULD ASK HER DURING SCHOOL?
I DON'T THINK YOU SHOULD ASK HER AT ALL.
WHAT? YOU THINK I SHOULD BE DOMINANT AND JUST TELL HER SHE'S GOING TO THE PROM WITH ME?
HOW'S THIS?: YO LINDA-GO BUY A DRESS! YOU'RE MY PROM DATE!
AND I THOUGHT ROMANCE WAS DEAD.

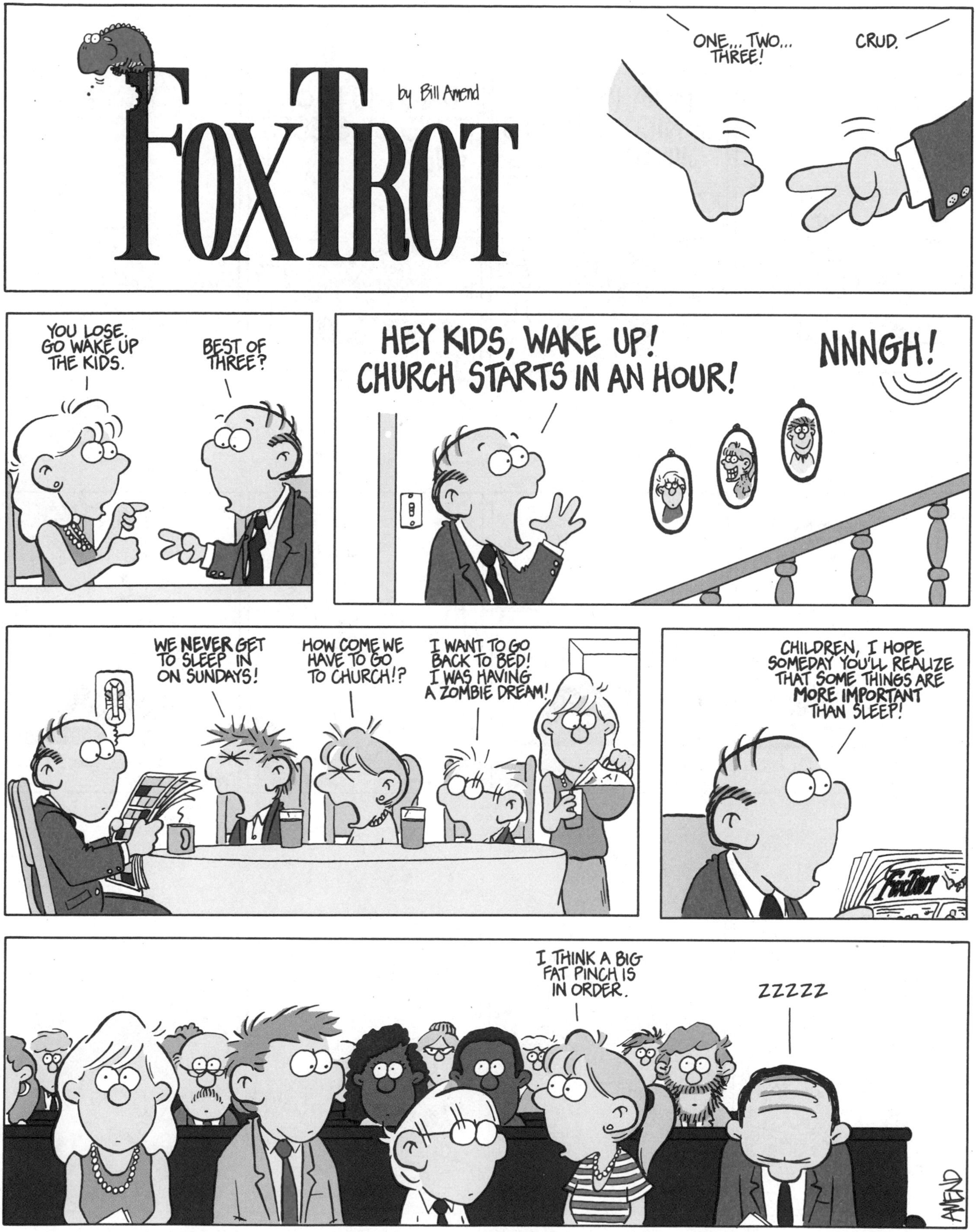
FoxTrot
by Bill Amend
ONE... TWO... THREE!
CRUD.
YOU LOSE. GO WAKE UP THE KIDS.
BEST OF THREE?
HEY KIDS, WAKE UP! CHURCH STARTS IN AN HOUR!
NNNGH!
WE NEVER GET TO SLEEP IN ON SUNDAYS!
HOW COME WE HAVE TO GO TO CHURCH!?
I WANT TO GO BACK TO BED! I WAS HAVING A ZOMBIE DREAM!
CHILDREN, I HOPE SOMEDAY YOU'LL REALIZE THAT SOME THINGS ARE MORE IMPORTANT THAN SLEEP!
I THINK A BIG FAT PINCH IS IN ORDER.
ZZZZZ
AMEND

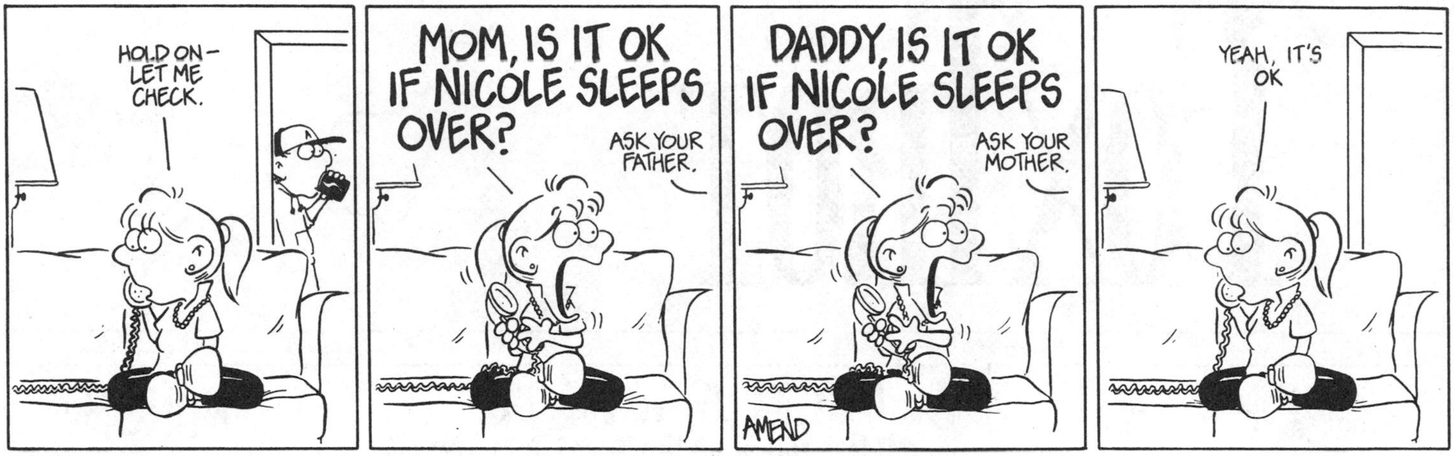
HOLD ON—
LET ME
CHECK.
MOM, IS IT OK
IF NICOLE SLEEPS
OVER?
ASK YOUR
FATHER.
DADDY, IS IT OK
IF NICOLE SLEEPS
OVER?
ASK YOUR
MOTHER.
AMEND
YEAH, IT'S
OK

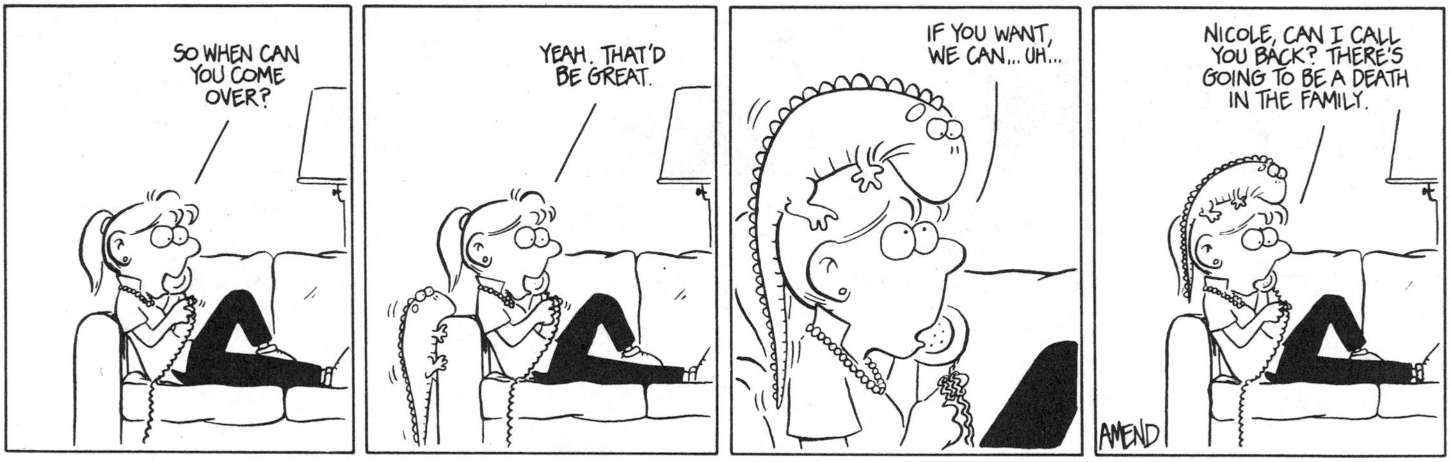
SO WHEN CAN
YOU COME
OVER?
YEAH. THAT'D
BE GREAT.
IF YOU WANT,
WE CAN... UH...
NICOLE, CAN I CALL
YOU BACK? THERE'S
GOING TO BE A DEATH
IN THE FAMILY.
AMEND

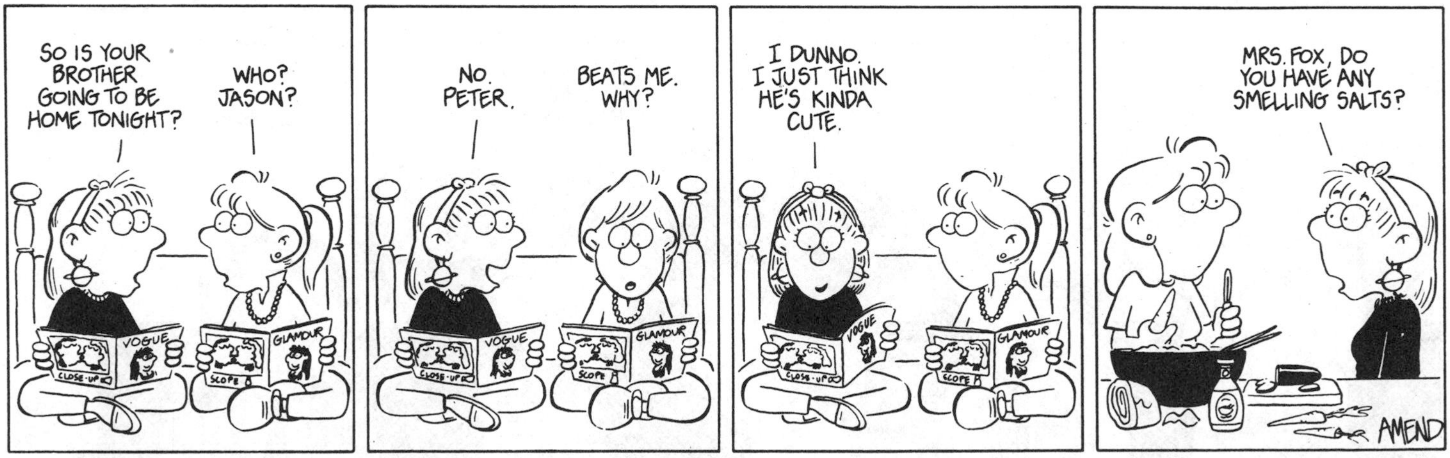
SO IS YOUR
BROTHER
GOING TO BE
HOME TONIGHT?
WHO?
JASON?
VOGUE
CLOSE-UP
GLAMOUR
SCOPE
NO.
PETER.
BEATS ME.
WHY?
I DUNNO.
I JUST THINK
HE'S KINDA
CUTE.
MRS. FOX, DO
YOU HAVE ANY
SMELLING SALTS?
AMEND

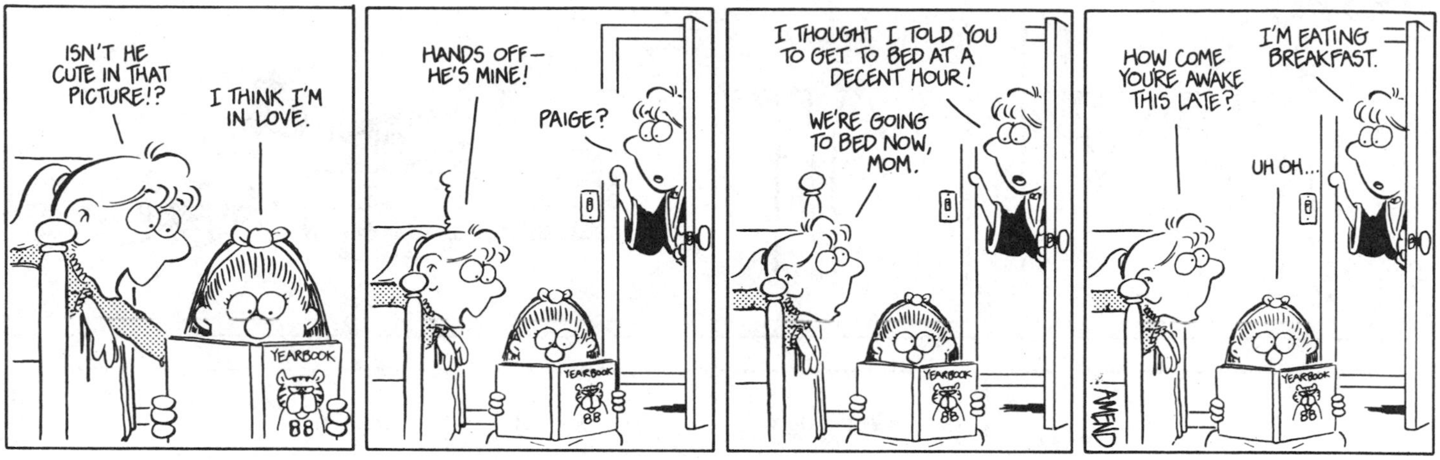
ISN'T HE CUTE IN THAT PICTURE!?
I THINK I'M IN LOVE.
YEARBOOK
BB
HANDS OFF— HE'S MINE!
PAIGE?
YEARBOOK
BB
I THOUGHT I TOLD YOU TO GET TO BED AT A DECENT HOUR!
WE'RE GOING TO BED NOW, MOM.
YEARBOOK
HOW COME YOU'RE AWAKE THIS LATE?
I'M EATING BREAKFAST.
UH OH...
YEARBOOK
AMEND

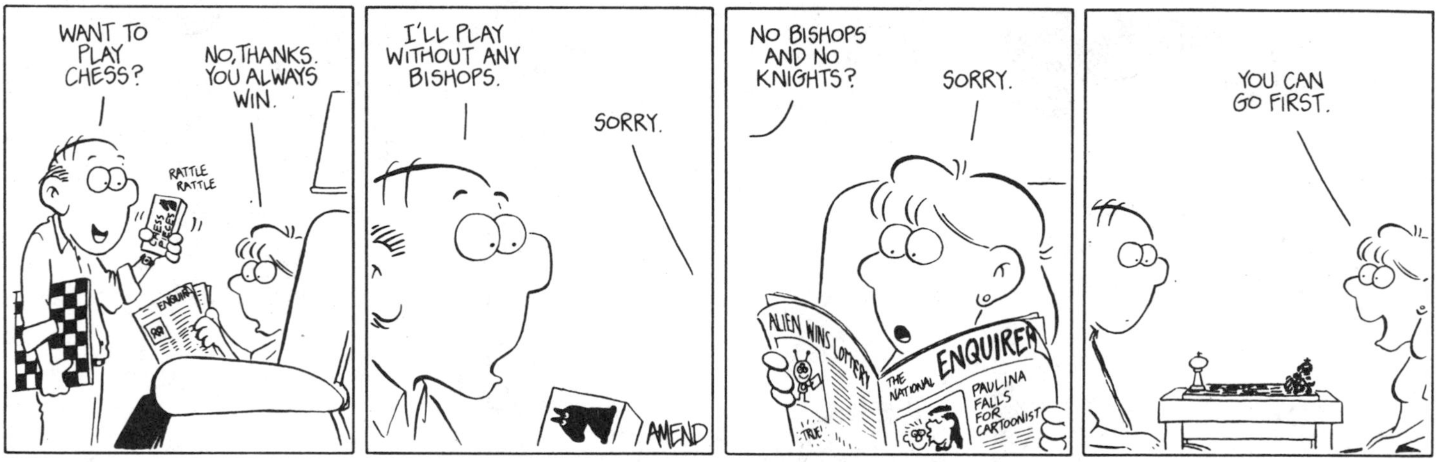
WANT TO PLAY CHESS?
NO, THANKS. YOU ALWAYS WIN.
RATTLE RATTLE
CHESS PIECES
ENQUIRER
I'LL PLAY WITHOUT ANY BISHOPS.
SORRY.
AMEND
NO BISHOPS AND NO KNIGHTS?
SORRY.
ALIEN WINS LOTTERY
TRUE!
THE NATIONAL ENQUIRER
PAULINA FALLS FOR CARTOONIST
YOU CAN GO FIRST.

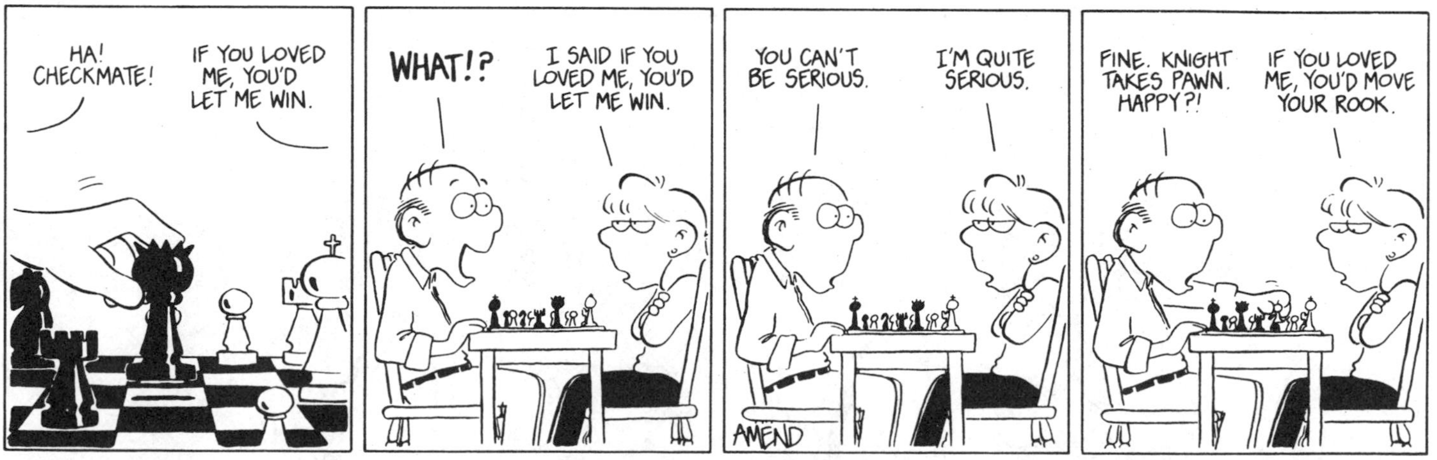
HA! CHECKMATE!
IF YOU LOVED ME, YOU'D LET ME WIN.
WHAT!?
I SAID IF YOU LOVED ME, YOU'D LET ME WIN.
YOU CAN'T BE SERIOUS.
I'M QUITE SERIOUS.
AMEND
FINE. KNIGHT TAKES PAWN. HAPPY?!
IF YOU LOVED ME, YOU'D MOVE YOUR ROOK.

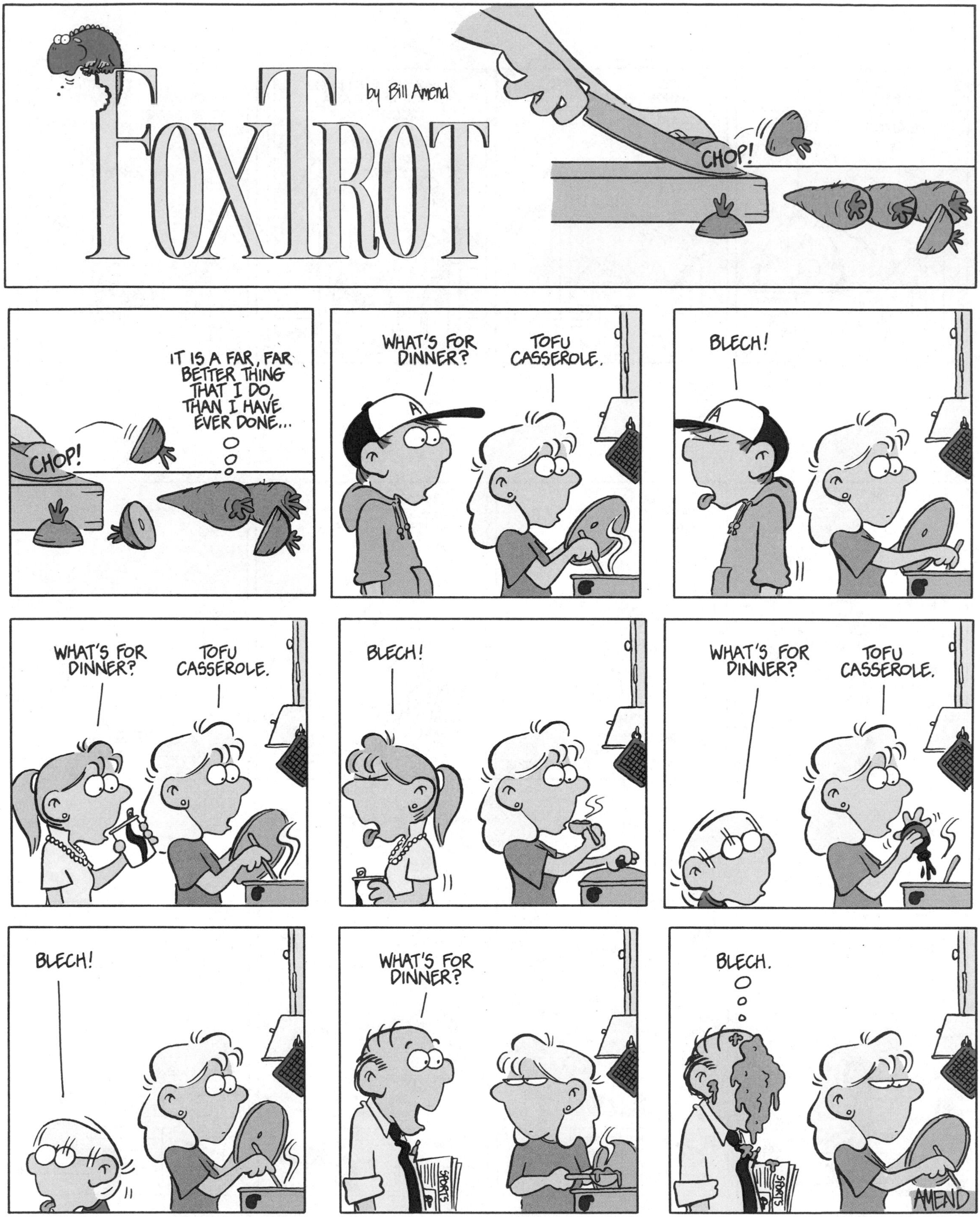
FOXTROT
by Bill Amend
CHOP!
CHOP!
IT IS A FAR, FAR BETTER THING THAT I DO, THAN I HAVE EVER DONE...
WHAT'S FOR DINNER?
TOFU CASSEROLE.
BLECH!
WHAT'S FOR DINNER?
TOFU CASSEROLE.
BLECH!
WHAT'S FOR DINNER?
TOFU CASSEROLE.
BLECH!
WHAT'S FOR DINNER?
BLECH.
SPORTS
AMEND

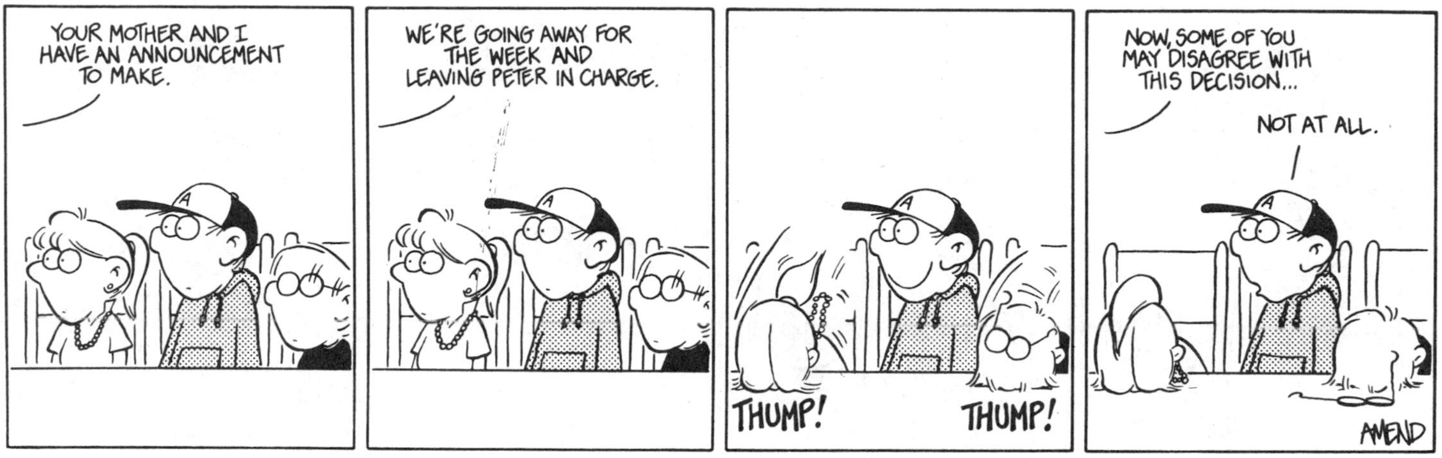
YOUR MOTHER AND I HAVE AN ANNOUNCEMENT TO MAKE.
WE'RE GOING AWAY FOR THE WEEK AND LEAVING PETER IN CHARGE.
THUMP!
THUMP!
NOW, SOME OF YOU MAY DISAGREE WITH THIS DECISION...
NOT AT ALL.
AMEND

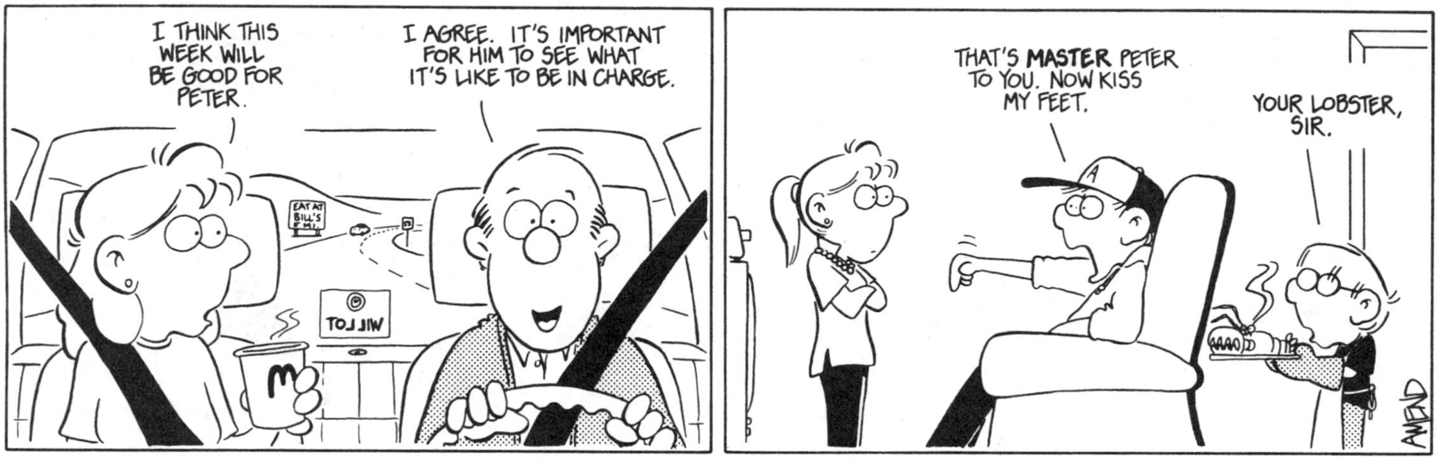
I THINK THIS WEEK WILL BE GOOD FOR PETER.
I AGREE. IT'S IMPORTANT FOR HIM TO SEE WHAT IT'S LIKE TO BE IN CHARGE.
THAT'S **MASTER** PETER TO YOU. NOW KISS MY FEET.
YOUR LOBSTER, SIR.
AMEND

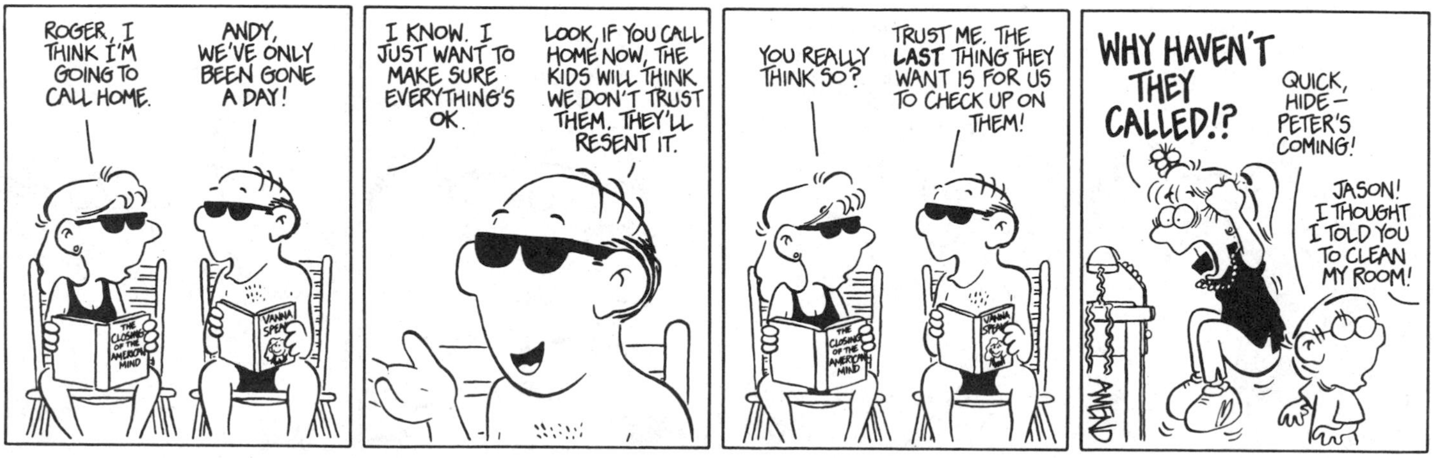
ROGER, I THINK I'M GOING TO CALL HOME.
ANDY, WE'VE ONLY BEEN GONE A DAY!
I KNOW. I JUST WANT TO MAKE SURE EVERYTHING'S OK.
LOOK, IF YOU CALL HOME NOW, THE KIDS WILL THINK WE DON'T TRUST THEM. THEY'LL RESENT IT.
YOU REALLY THINK SO?
TRUST ME. THE **LAST** THING THEY WANT IS FOR US TO CHECK UP ON THEM!
WHY HAVEN'T THEY CALLED!?
QUICK, HIDE— PETER'S COMING!
JASON! I THOUGHT I TOLD YOU TO CLEAN MY ROOM!
AMEND

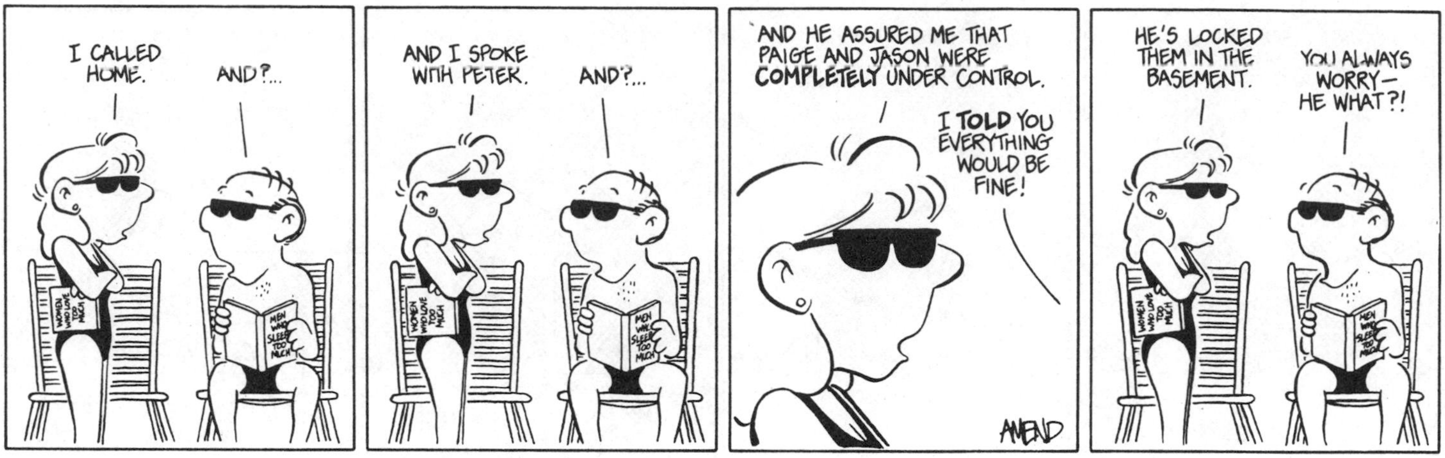
I CALLED HOME.
AND?...
AND I SPOKE WITH PETER.
AND?...
AND HE ASSURED ME THAT PAIGE AND JASON WERE **COMPLETELY** UNDER CONTROL.
I **TOLD** YOU EVERYTHING WOULD BE FINE!
AMEND
HE'S LOCKED THEM IN THE BASEMENT.
YOU ALWAYS WORRY— HE WHAT?!

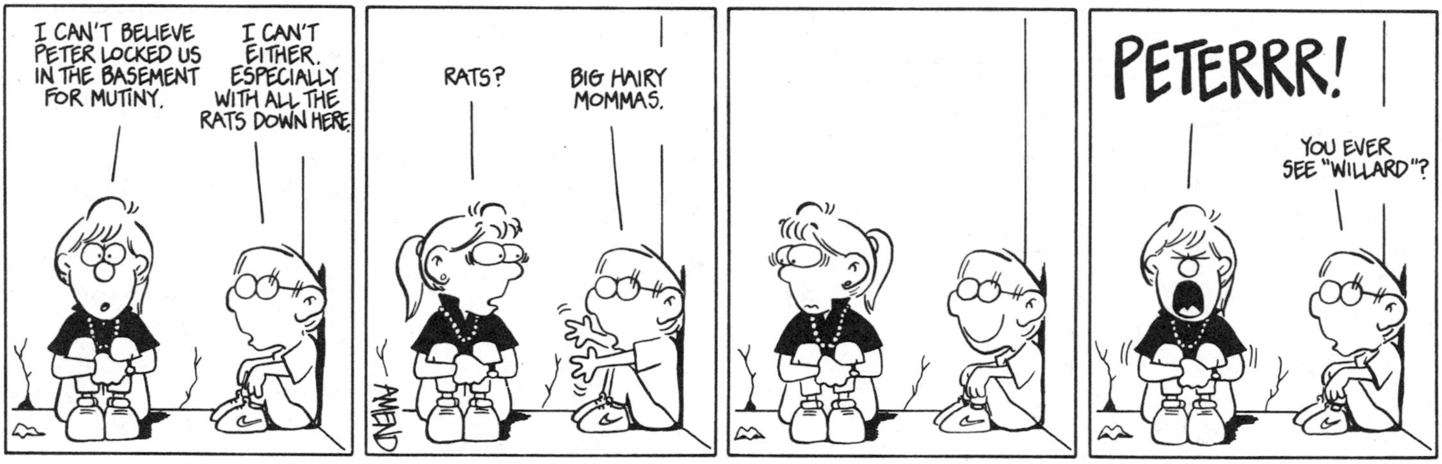
I CAN'T BELIEVE PETER LOCKED US IN THE BASEMENT FOR MUTINY.
I CAN'T EITHER. ESPECIALLY WITH ALL THE RATS DOWN HERE.
RATS?
BIG HAIRY MOMMAS.
AMEND
PETERRR!
YOU EVER SEE "WILLARD"?

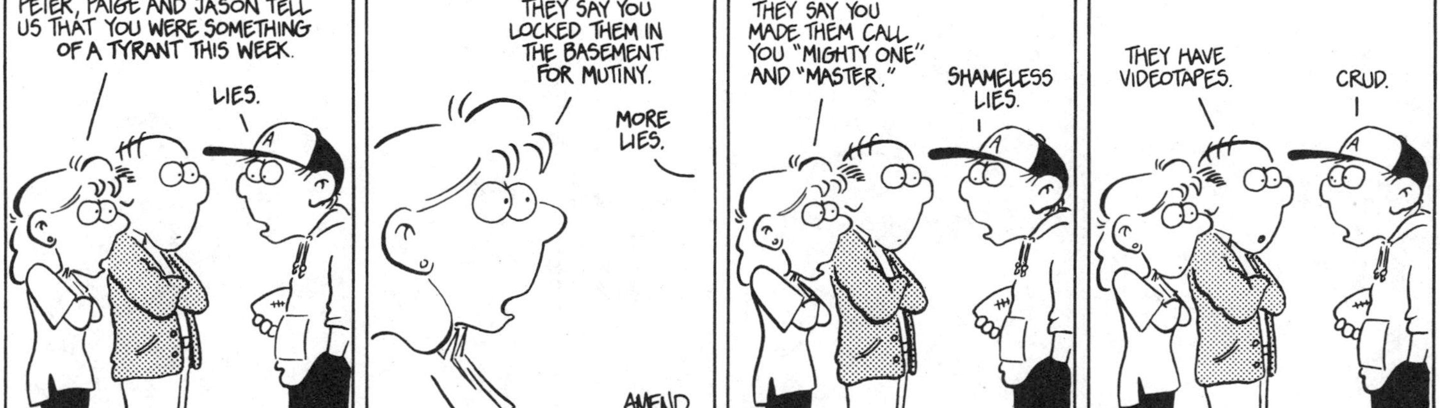
PETER, PAIGE AND JASON TELL US THAT YOU WERE SOMETHING OF A TYRANT THIS WEEK.
LIES.
THEY SAY YOU LOCKED THEM IN THE BASEMENT FOR MUTINY.
MORE LIES.
AMEND
THEY SAY YOU MADE THEM CALL YOU "MIGHTY ONE" AND "MASTER."
SHAMELESS LIES.
THEY HAVE VIDEOTAPES.
CRUD.

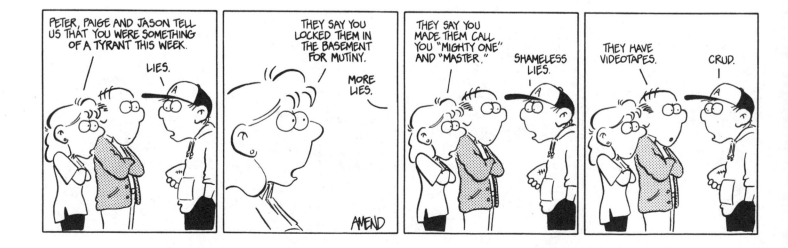

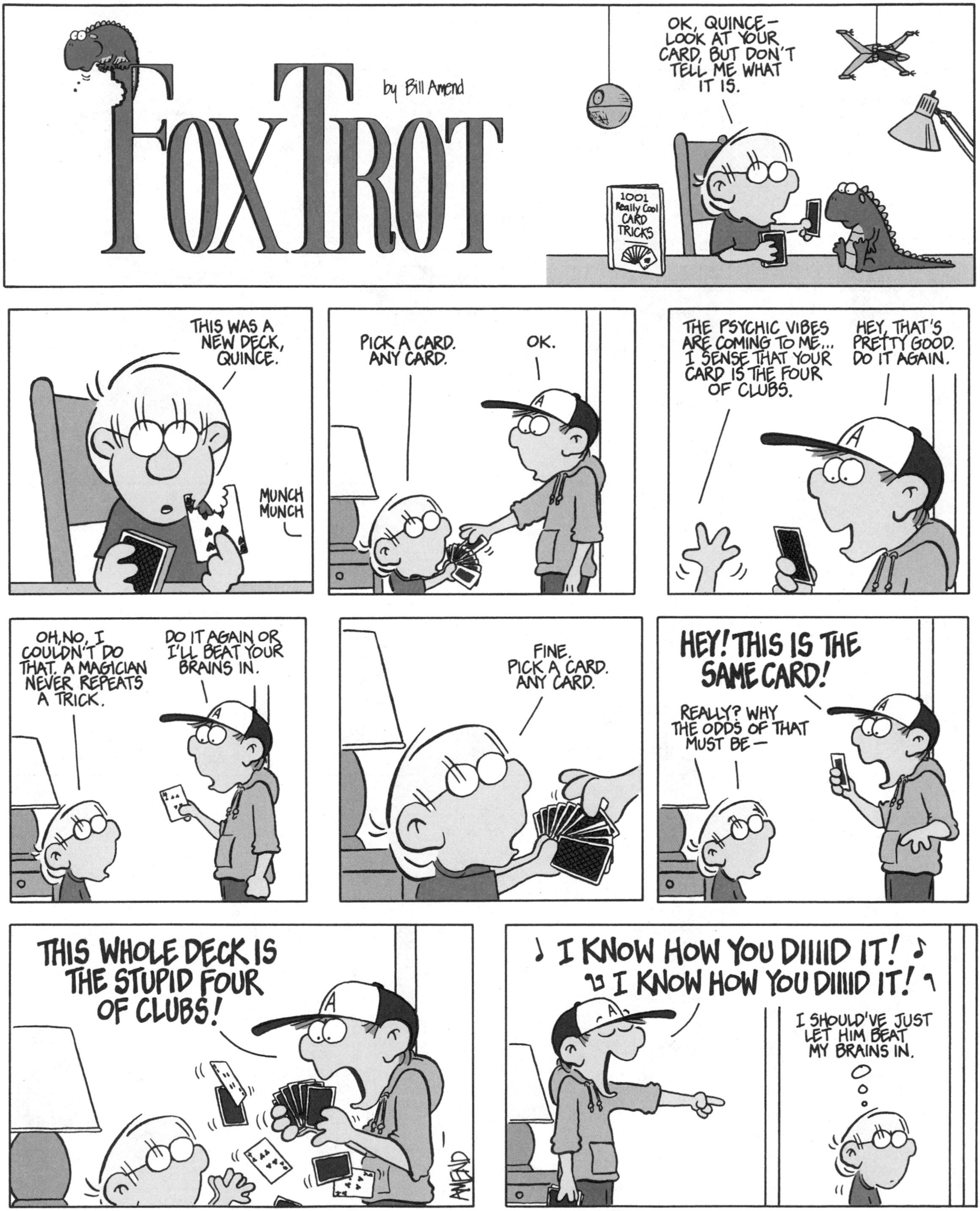

FoxTrot
by Bill Amend
OK, QUINCE— LOOK AT YOUR CARD, BUT DON'T TELL ME WHAT IT IS.
1001 Really Cool CARD TRICKS
THIS WAS A NEW DECK, QUINCE.
MUNCH MUNCH
PICK A CARD. ANY CARD.
OK.
THE PSYCHIC VIBES ARE COMING TO ME... I SENSE THAT YOUR CARD IS THE FOUR OF CLUBS.
HEY, THAT'S PRETTY GOOD. DO IT AGAIN.
OH, NO, I COULDN'T DO THAT. A MAGICIAN NEVER REPEATS A TRICK.
DO IT AGAIN OR I'LL BEAT YOUR BRAINS IN.
FINE. PICK A CARD. ANY CARD.
HEY! THIS IS THE SAME CARD!
REALLY? WHY THE ODDS OF THAT MUST BE—
THIS WHOLE DECK IS THE STUPID FOUR OF CLUBS!
AMEND
I KNOW HOW YOU DIIIID IT!
I KNOW HOW YOU DIIIID IT!
I SHOULD'VE JUST LET HIM BEAT MY BRAINS IN.

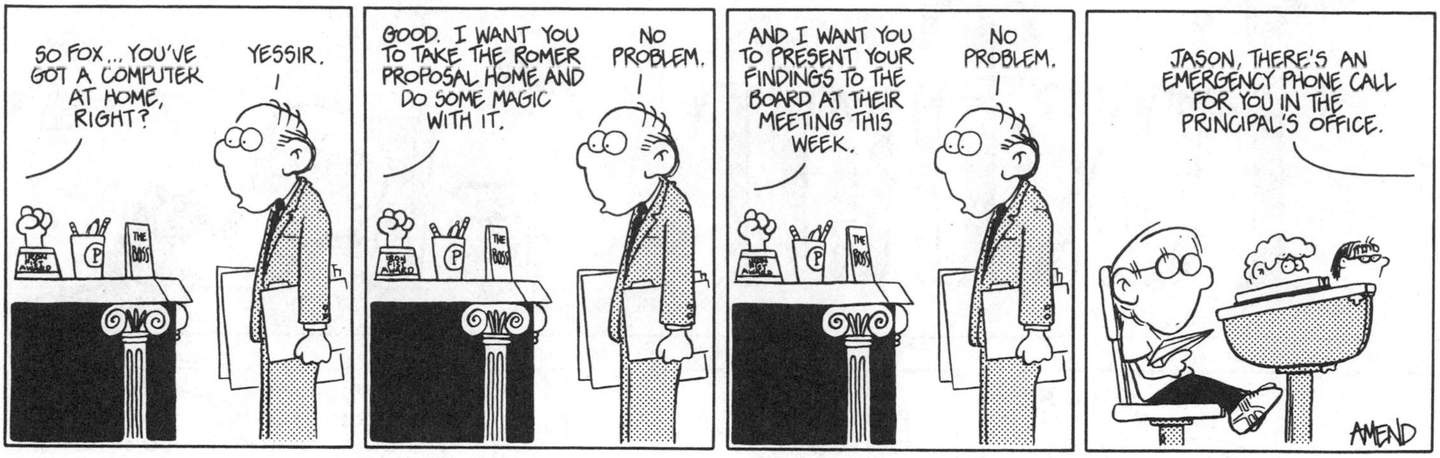
SO FOX... YOU'VE GOT A COMPUTER AT HOME, RIGHT?
YESSIR.
GOOD. I WANT YOU TO TAKE THE ROMER PROPOSAL HOME AND DO SOME MAGIC WITH IT.
NO PROBLEM.
AND I WANT YOU TO PRESENT YOUR FINDINGS TO THE BOARD AT THEIR MEETING THIS WEEK.
NO PROBLEM.
JASON, THERE'S AN EMERGENCY PHONE CALL FOR YOU IN THE PRINCIPAL'S OFFICE.
AMEND

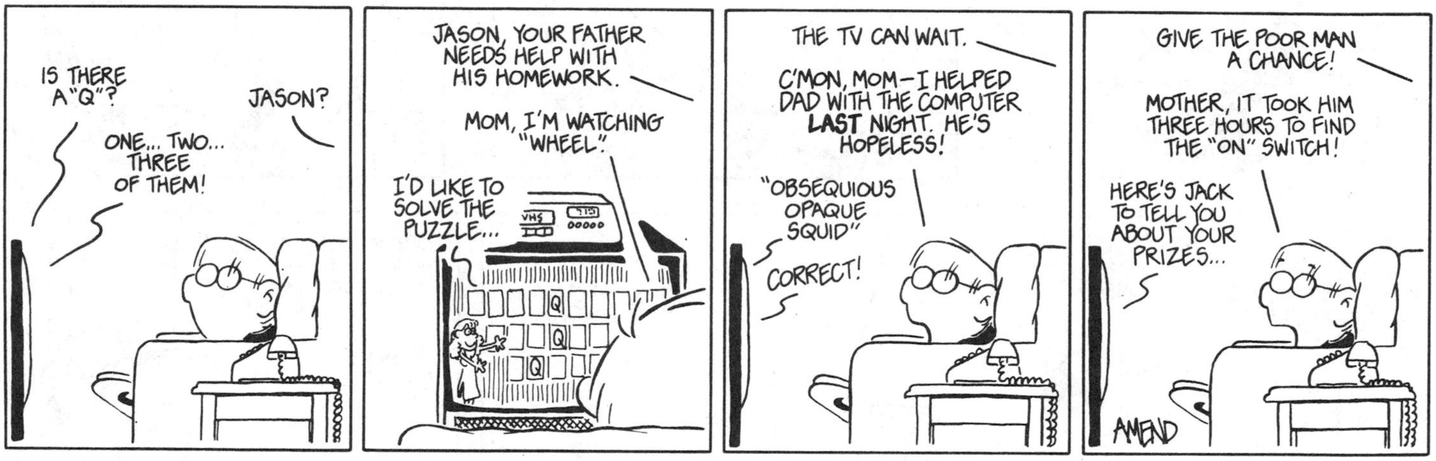
IS THERE A "Q"?
ONE... TWO... THREE OF THEM!
JASON?
JASON, YOUR FATHER NEEDS HELP WITH HIS HOMEWORK.
MOM, I'M WATCHING "WHEEL."
I'D LIKE TO SOLVE THE PUZZLE...
THE TV CAN WAIT.
C'MON, MOM–I HELPED DAD WITH THE COMPUTER **LAST** NIGHT. HE'S HOPELESS!
"OBSEQUIOUS OPAQUE SQUID"
CORRECT!
GIVE THE POOR MAN A CHANCE!
MOTHER, IT TOOK HIM THREE HOURS TO FIND THE "ON" SWITCH!
HERE'S JACK TO TELL YOU ABOUT YOUR PRIZES...
AMEND

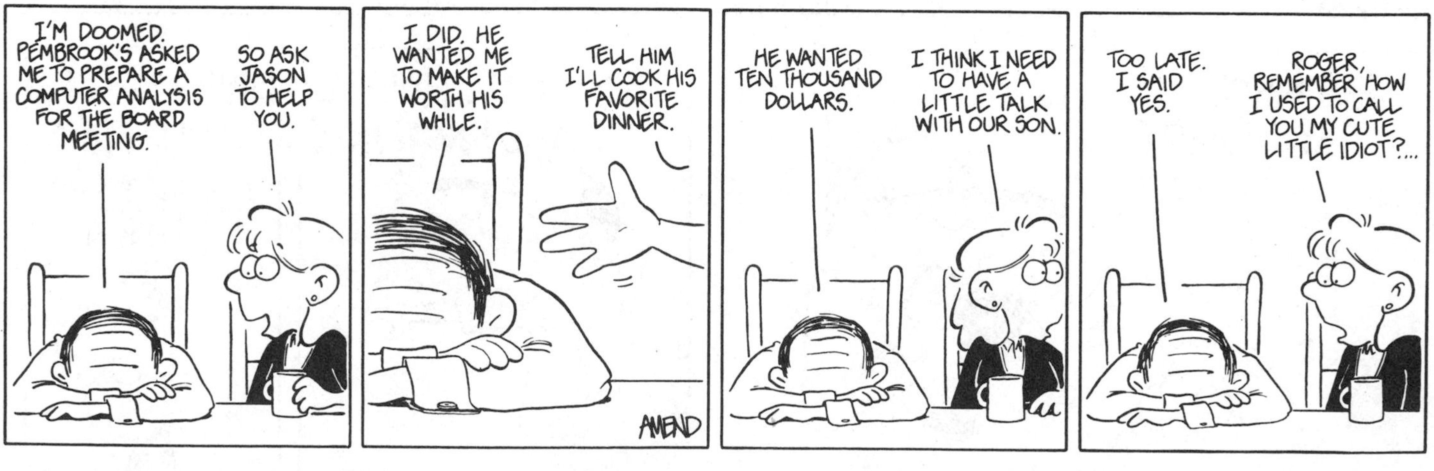
I'M DOOMED. PEMBROOK'S ASKED ME TO PREPARE A COMPUTER ANALYSIS FOR THE BOARD MEETING.
SO ASK JASON TO HELP YOU.
I DID. HE WANTED ME TO MAKE IT WORTH HIS WHILE.
TELL HIM I'LL COOK HIS FAVORITE DINNER.
HE WANTED TEN THOUSAND DOLLARS.
I THINK I NEED TO HAVE A LITTLE TALK WITH OUR SON.
TOO LATE. I SAID YES.
ROGER, REMEMBER HOW I USED TO CALL YOU MY CUTE LITTLE IDIOT?...
AMEND

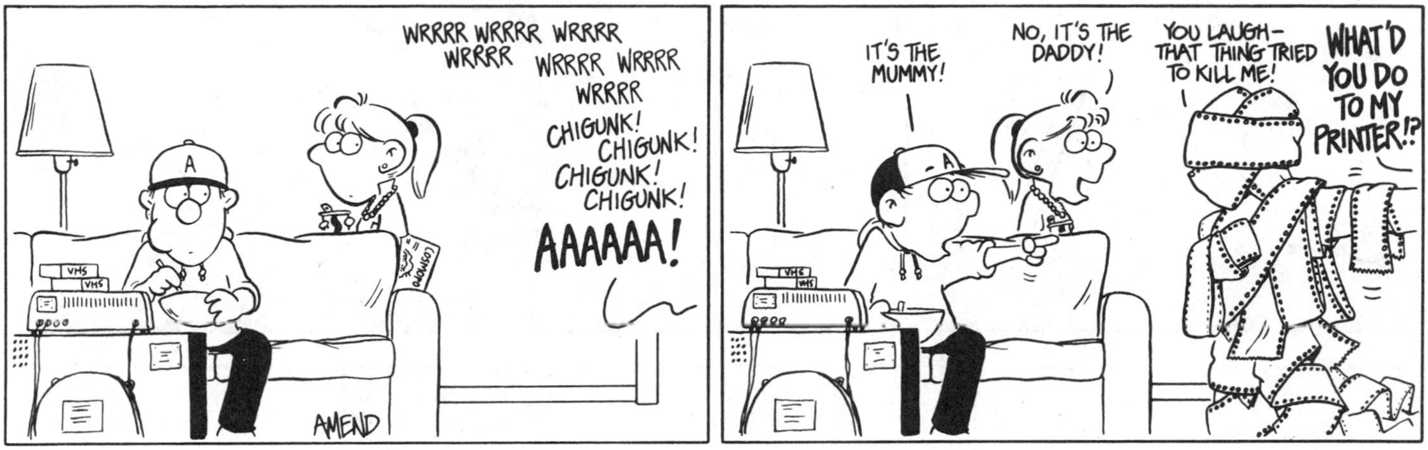
WRRRR WRRRR WRRRR
WRRRR WRRRR WRRRR
WRRRR
CHIGUNK! CHIGUNK!
CHIGUNK! CHIGUNK!
AAAAAA!
AMEND
IT'S THE MUMMY!
NO, IT'S THE DADDY!
YOU LAUGH— THAT THING TRIED TO KILL ME!
WHAT'D YOU DO TO MY PRINTER!?

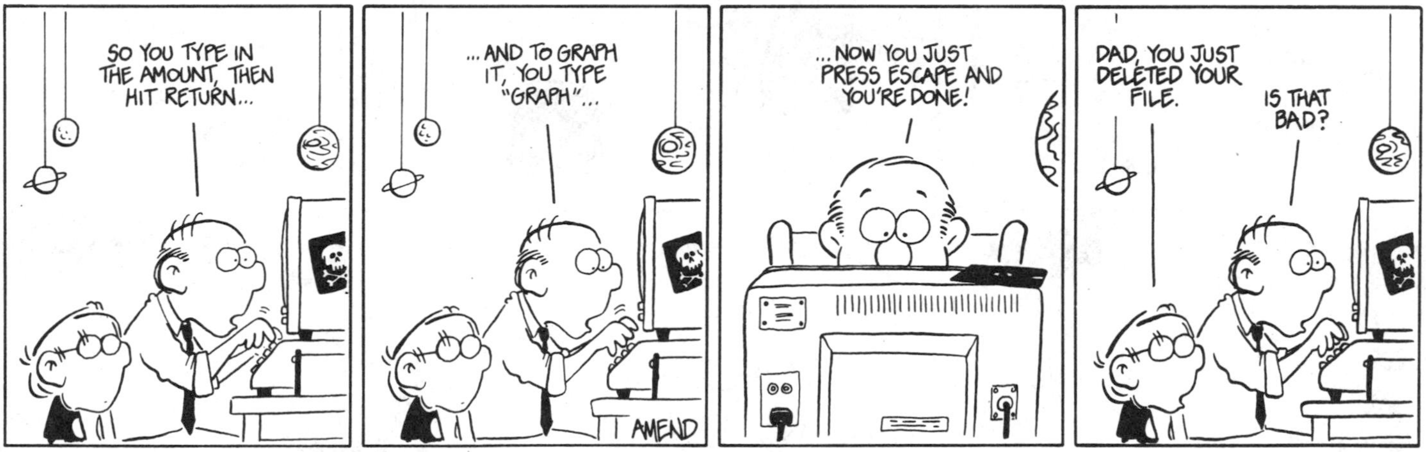
SO YOU TYPE IN THE AMOUNT, THEN HIT RETURN...
...AND TO GRAPH IT, YOU TYPE "GRAPH"...
AMEND
...NOW YOU JUST PRESS ESCAPE AND YOU'RE DONE!
DAD, YOU JUST DELETED YOUR FILE.
IS THAT BAD?

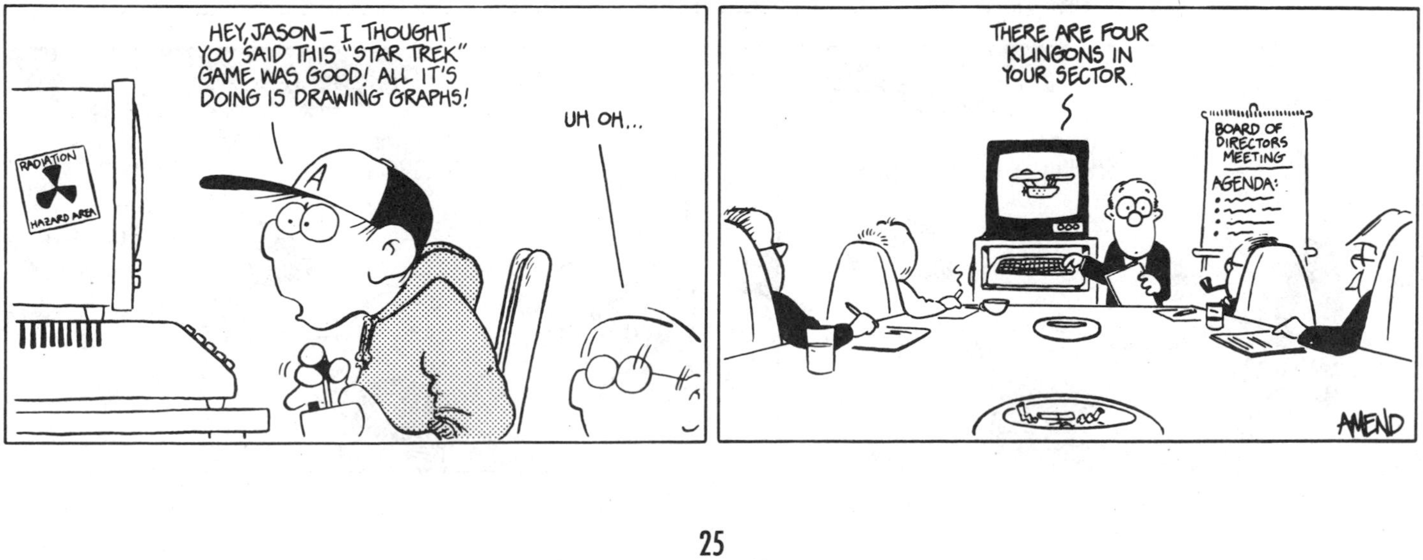
HEY, JASON— I THOUGHT YOU SAID THIS "STAR TREK" GAME WAS GOOD! ALL IT'S DOING IS DRAWING GRAPHS!
RADIATION HAZARD AREA
UH OH...
THERE ARE FOUR KLINGONS IN YOUR SECTOR.
BOARD OF DIRECTORS MEETING
AGENDA:
AMEND

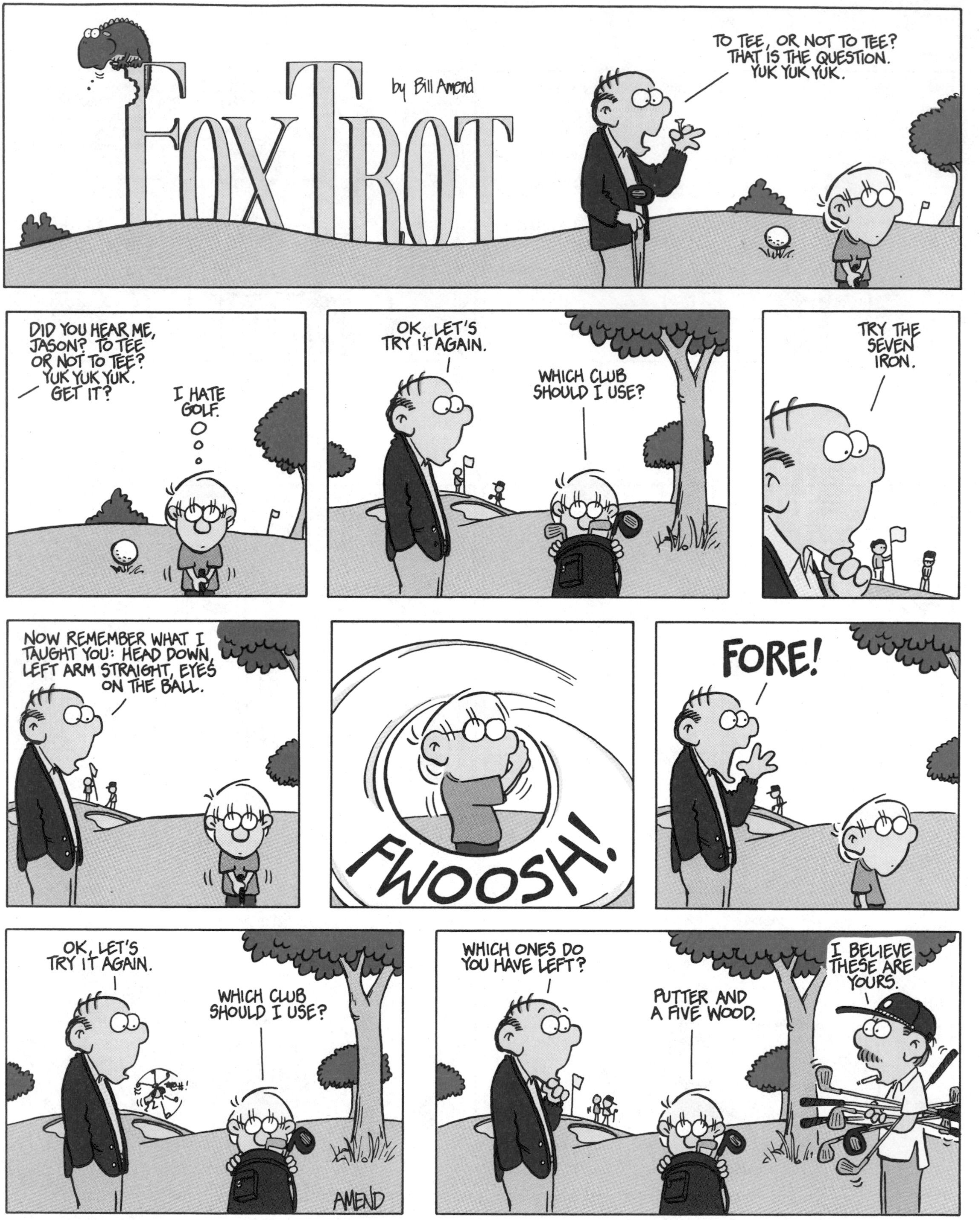
FOXTROT
by Bill Amend
TO TEE, OR NOT TO TEE? THAT IS THE QUESTION. YUK YUK YUK.
DID YOU HEAR ME, JASON? TO TEE OR NOT TO TEE? YUK YUK YUK. GET IT?
I HATE GOLF.
OK, LET'S TRY IT AGAIN.
WHICH CLUB SHOULD I USE?
TRY THE SEVEN IRON.
NOW REMEMBER WHAT I TAUGHT YOU: HEAD DOWN, LEFT ARM STRAIGHT, EYES ON THE BALL.
FWOOSH!
FORE!
OK, LET'S TRY IT AGAIN.
WHICH CLUB SHOULD I USE?
WHICH ONES DO YOU HAVE LEFT?
PUTTER AND A FIVE WOOD.
I BELIEVE THESE ARE YOURS.
AMEND

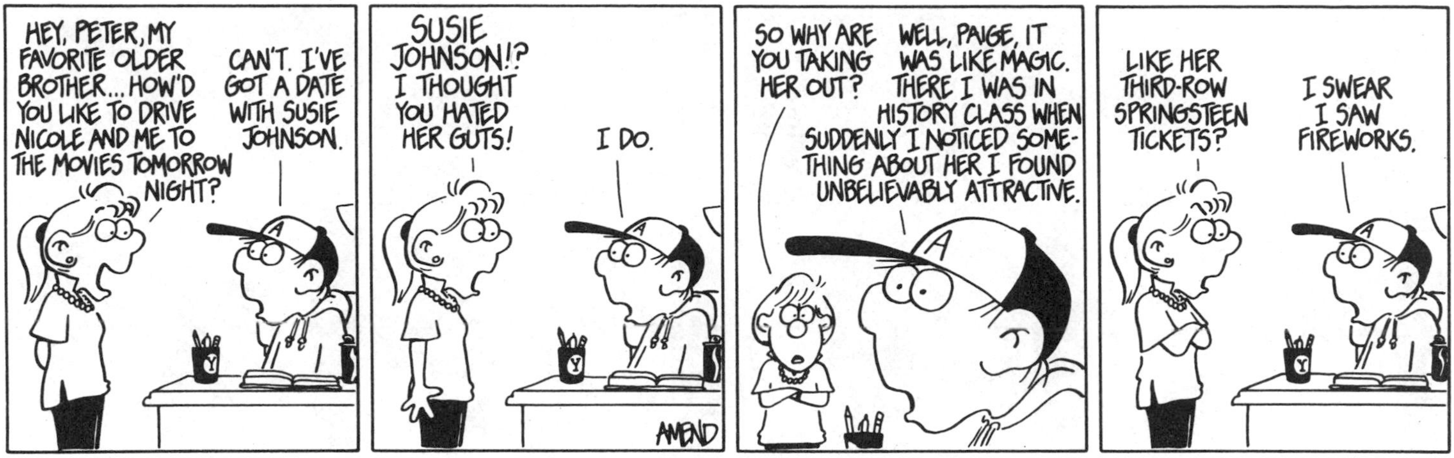
HEY, PETER, MY FAVORITE OLDER BROTHER... HOW'D YOU LIKE TO DRIVE NICOLE AND ME TO THE MOVIES TOMORROW NIGHT?
CAN'T. I'VE GOT A DATE WITH SUSIE JOHNSON.
SUSIE JOHNSON!? I THOUGHT YOU HATED HER GUTS!
I DO.
AMEND
SO WHY ARE YOU TAKING HER OUT?
WELL, PAIGE, IT WAS LIKE MAGIC. THERE I WAS IN HISTORY CLASS WHEN SUDDENLY I NOTICED SOMETHING ABOUT HER I FOUND UNBELIEVABLY ATTRACTIVE.
LIKE HER THIRD-ROW SPRINGSTEEN TICKETS?
I SWEAR I SAW FIREWORKS.

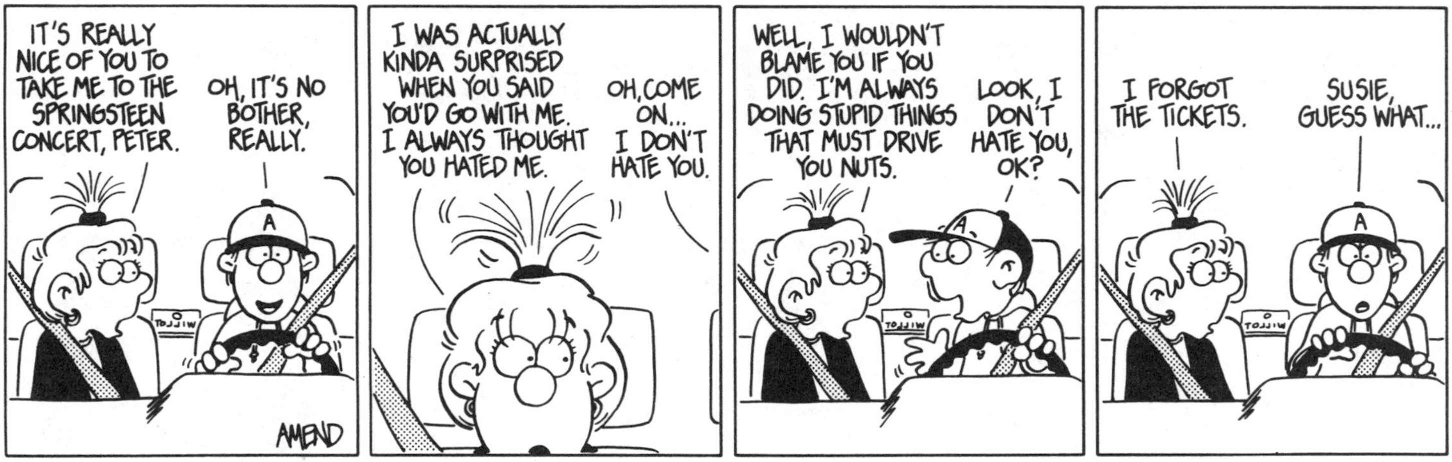
IT'S REALLY NICE OF YOU TO TAKE ME TO THE SPRINGSTEEN CONCERT, PETER.
OH, IT'S NO BOTHER, REALLY.
AMEND
I WAS ACTUALLY KINDA SURPRISED WHEN YOU SAID YOU'D GO WITH ME. I ALWAYS THOUGHT YOU HATED ME.
OH, COME ON... I DON'T HATE YOU.
WELL, I WOULDN'T BLAME YOU IF YOU DID. I'M ALWAYS DOING STUPID THINGS THAT MUST DRIVE YOU NUTS.
LOOK, I DON'T HATE YOU, OK?
I FORGOT THE TICKETS.
SUSIE, GUESS WHAT...

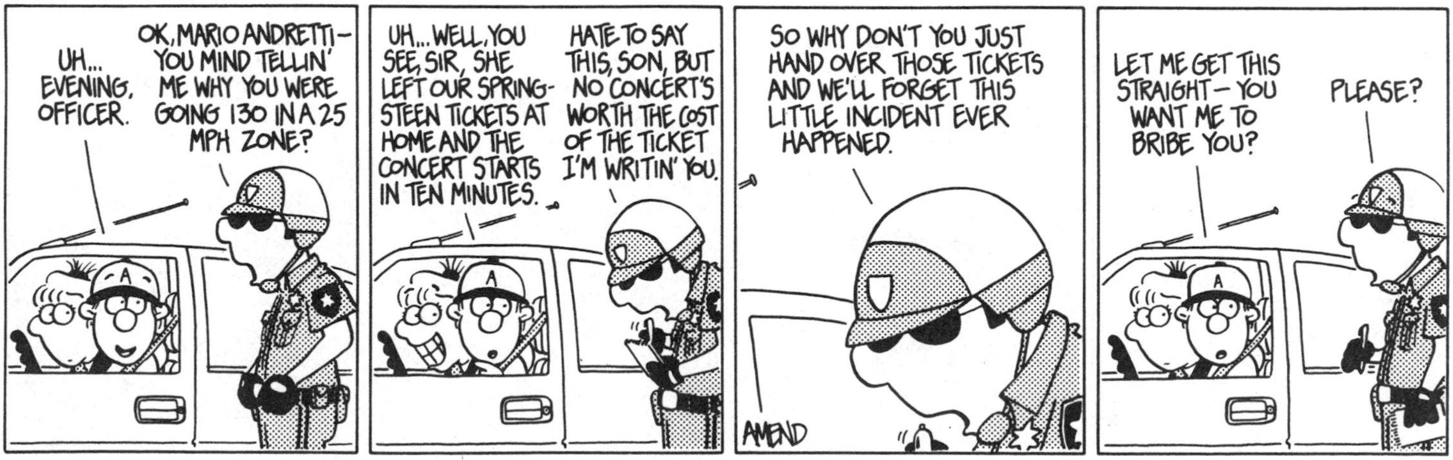
UH... EVENING, OFFICER.
OK, MARIO ANDRETTI— YOU MIND TELLIN' ME WHY YOU WERE GOING 130 IN A 25 MPH ZONE?
UH... WELL, YOU SEE, SIR, SHE LEFT OUR SPRINGSTEEN TICKETS AT HOME AND THE CONCERT STARTS IN TEN MINUTES.
HATE TO SAY THIS, SON, BUT NO CONCERT'S WORTH THE COST OF THE TICKET I'M WRITIN' YOU.
SO WHY DON'T YOU JUST HAND OVER THOSE TICKETS AND WE'LL FORGET THIS LITTLE INCIDENT EVER HAPPENED.
AMEND
LET ME GET THIS STRAIGHT— YOU WANT ME TO BRIBE YOU?
PLEASE?

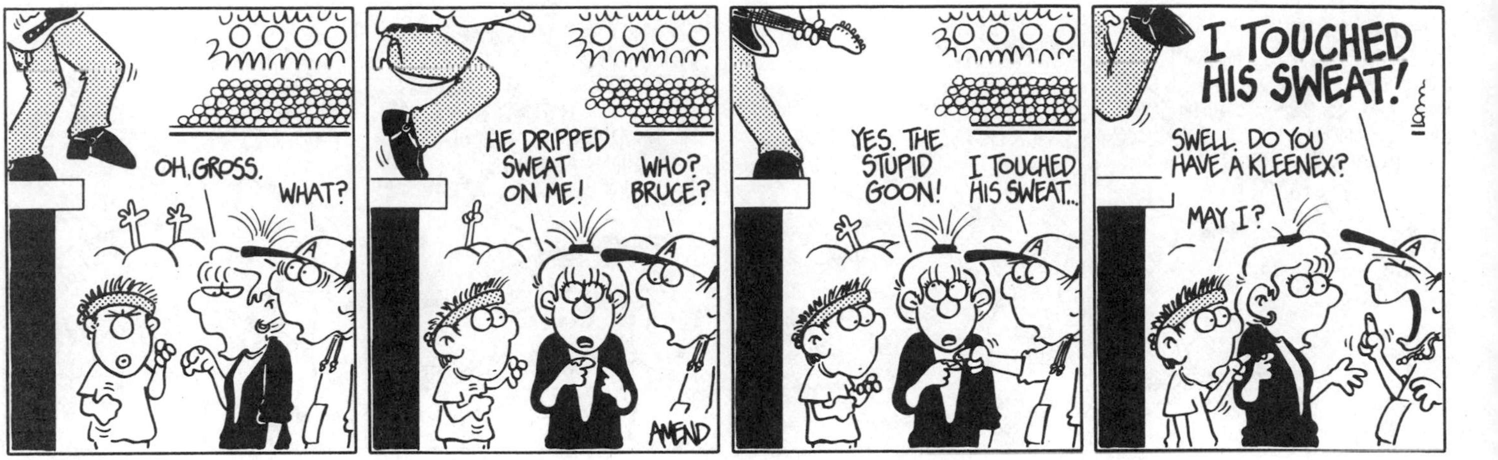
OH, GROSS.
WHAT?
HE DRIPPED SWEAT ON ME!
WHO? BRUCE?
AMEND
YES. THE STUPID GOON!
I TOUCHED HIS SWEAT...
MAY I?
SWELL. DO YOU HAVE A KLEENEX?
I TOUCHED HIS SWEAT!

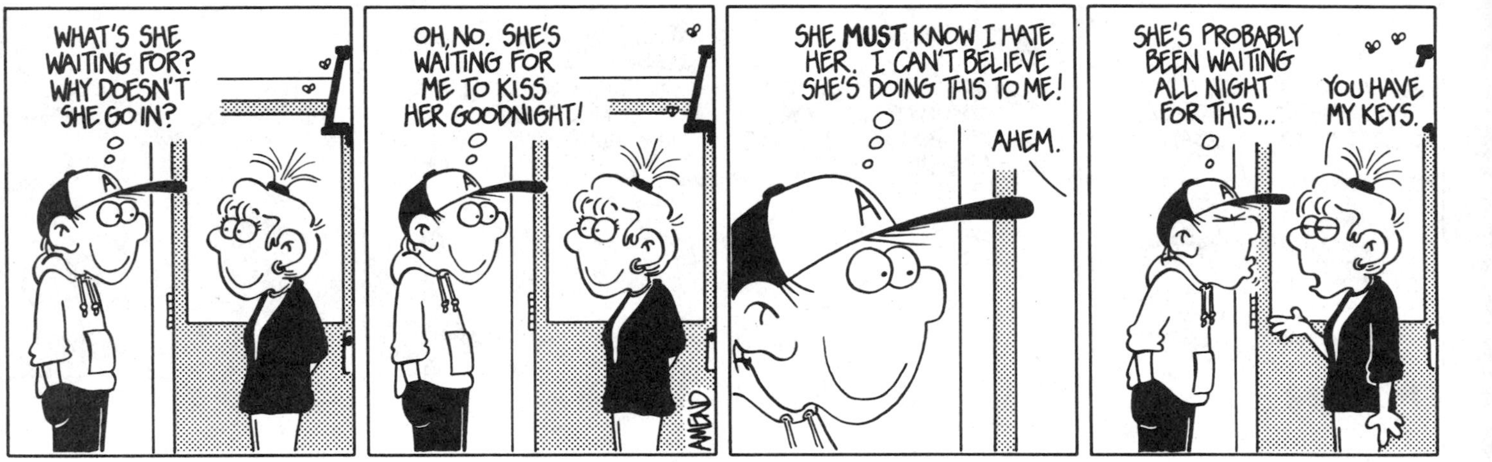
WHAT'S SHE WAITING FOR? WHY DOESN'T SHE GO IN?
OH, NO. SHE'S WAITING FOR ME TO KISS HER GOODNIGHT!
AMEND
SHE MUST KNOW I HATE HER. I CAN'T BELIEVE SHE'S DOING THIS TO ME!
AHEM.
SHE'S PROBABLY BEEN WAITING ALL NIGHT FOR THIS...
YOU HAVE MY KEYS.

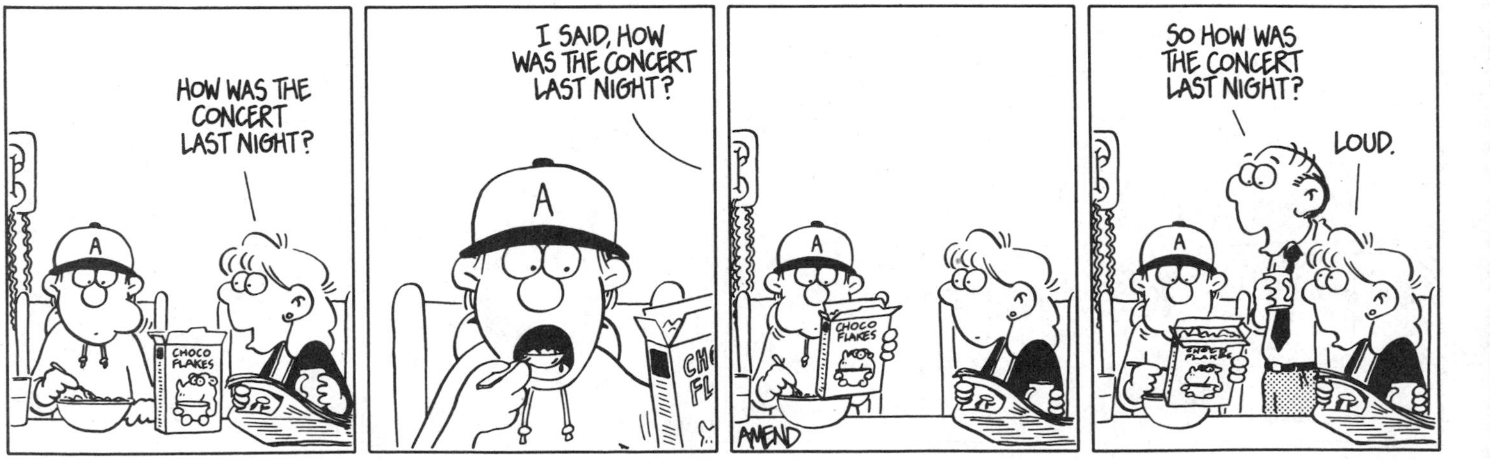
HOW WAS THE CONCERT LAST NIGHT?
CHOCO FLAKES
I SAID, HOW WAS THE CONCERT LAST NIGHT?
AMEND
SO HOW WAS THE CONCERT LAST NIGHT?
LOUD.

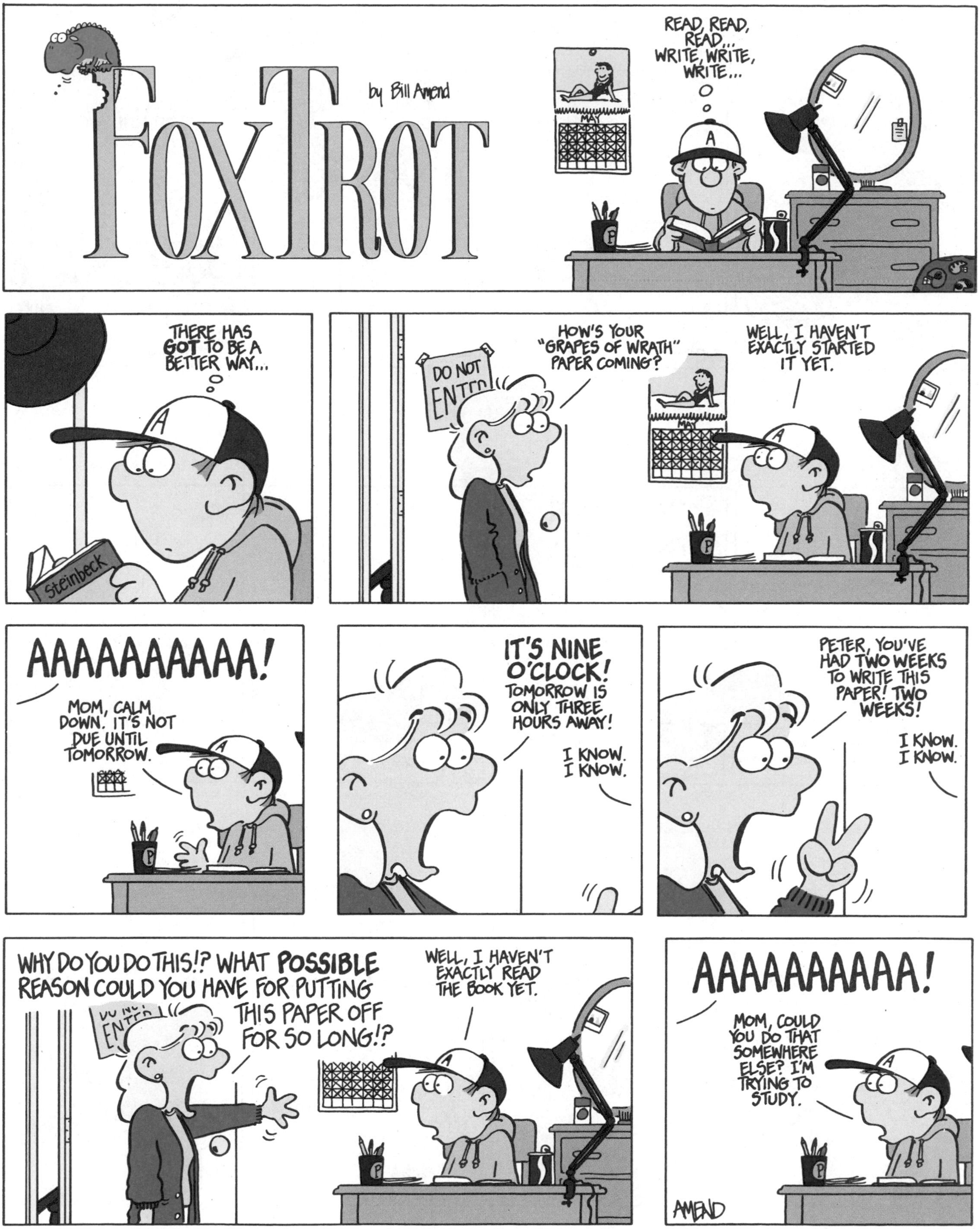
FoxTrot
by Bill Amend
READ, READ, READ... WRITE, WRITE, WRITE...
MAY
THERE HAS GOT TO BE A BETTER WAY...
Steinbeck
DO NOT ENTER
HOW'S YOUR "GRAPES OF WRATH" PAPER COMING?
WELL, I HAVEN'T EXACTLY STARTED IT YET.
MAY
AAAAAAAAAA!
MOM, CALM DOWN. IT'S NOT DUE UNTIL TOMORROW.
IT'S NINE O'CLOCK! TOMORROW IS ONLY THREE HOURS AWAY!
I KNOW. I KNOW.
PETER, YOU'VE HAD TWO WEEKS TO WRITE THIS PAPER! TWO WEEKS!
I KNOW. I KNOW.
WHY DO YOU DO THIS!? WHAT POSSIBLE REASON COULD YOU HAVE FOR PUTTING THIS PAPER OFF FOR SO LONG!?
WELL, I HAVEN'T EXACTLY READ THE BOOK YET.
AAAAAAAAAA!
MOM, COULD YOU DO THAT SOMEWHERE ELSE? I'M TRYING TO STUDY.
AMEND

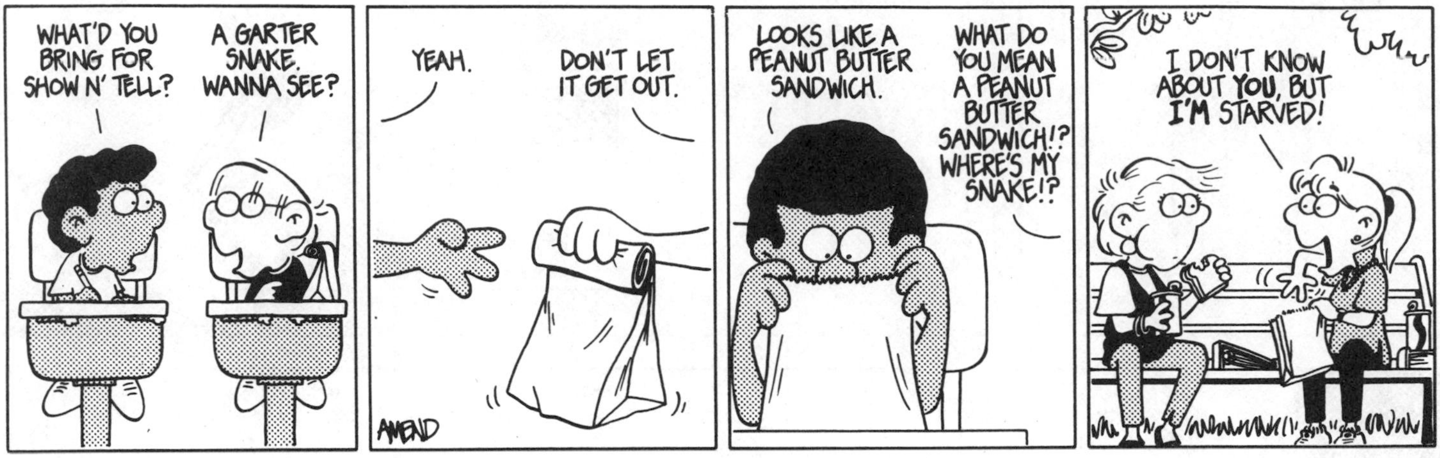
WHAT'D YOU BRING FOR SHOW N' TELL?
A GARTER SNAKE. WANNA SEE?
YEAH.
DON'T LET IT GET OUT.
AMEND
LOOKS LIKE A PEANUT BUTTER SANDWICH.
WHAT DO YOU MEAN A PEANUT BUTTER SANDWICH!? WHERE'S MY SNAKE!?
I DON'T KNOW ABOUT YOU, BUT I'M STARVED!

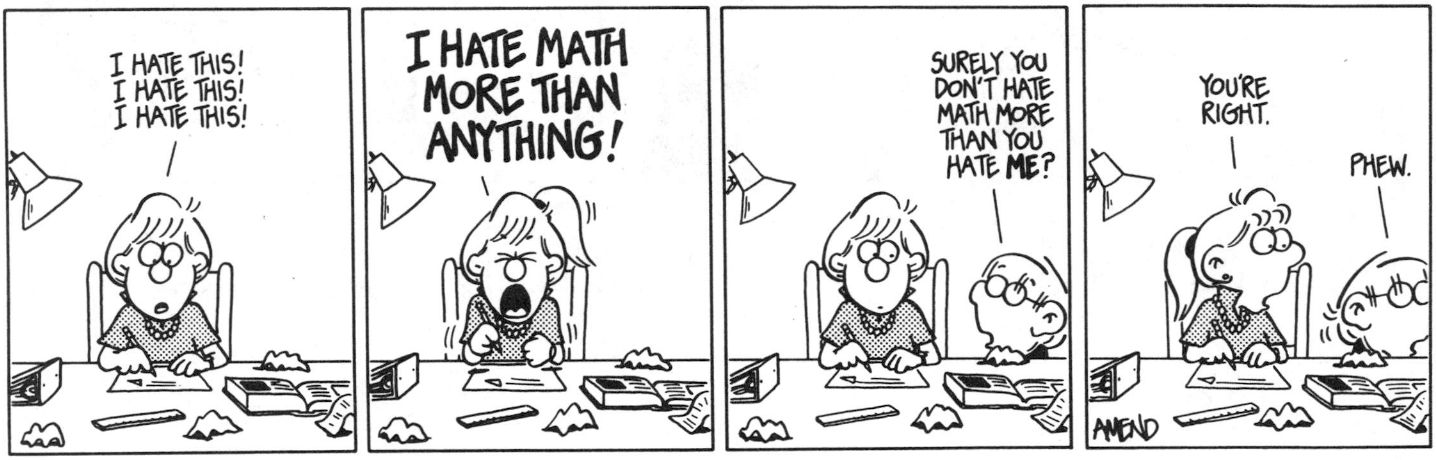
I HATE THIS! I HATE THIS! I HATE THIS!
I HATE MATH MORE THAN ANYTHING!
SURELY YOU DON'T HATE MATH MORE THAN YOU HATE ME?
YOU'RE RIGHT.
PHEW.
AMEND

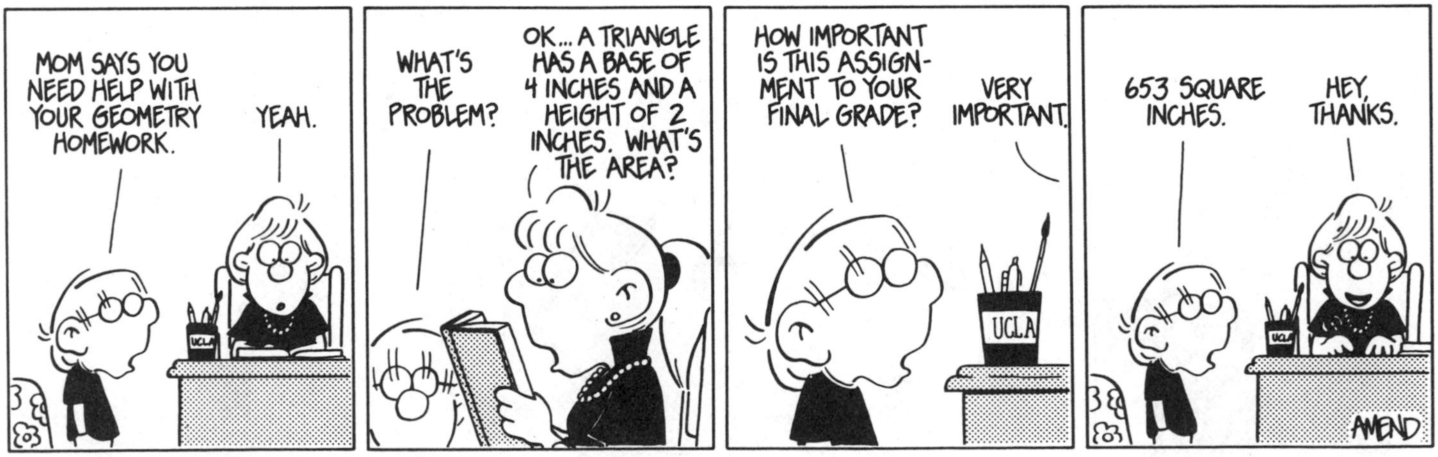
MOM SAYS YOU NEED HELP WITH YOUR GEOMETRY HOMEWORK.
YEAH.
UCLA
WHAT'S THE PROBLEM?
OK... A TRIANGLE HAS A BASE OF 4 INCHES AND A HEIGHT OF 2 INCHES. WHAT'S THE AREA?
HOW IMPORTANT IS THIS ASSIGNMENT TO YOUR FINAL GRADE?
VERY IMPORTANT.
UCLA
653 SQUARE INCHES.
HEY, THANKS.
UCLA
AMEND

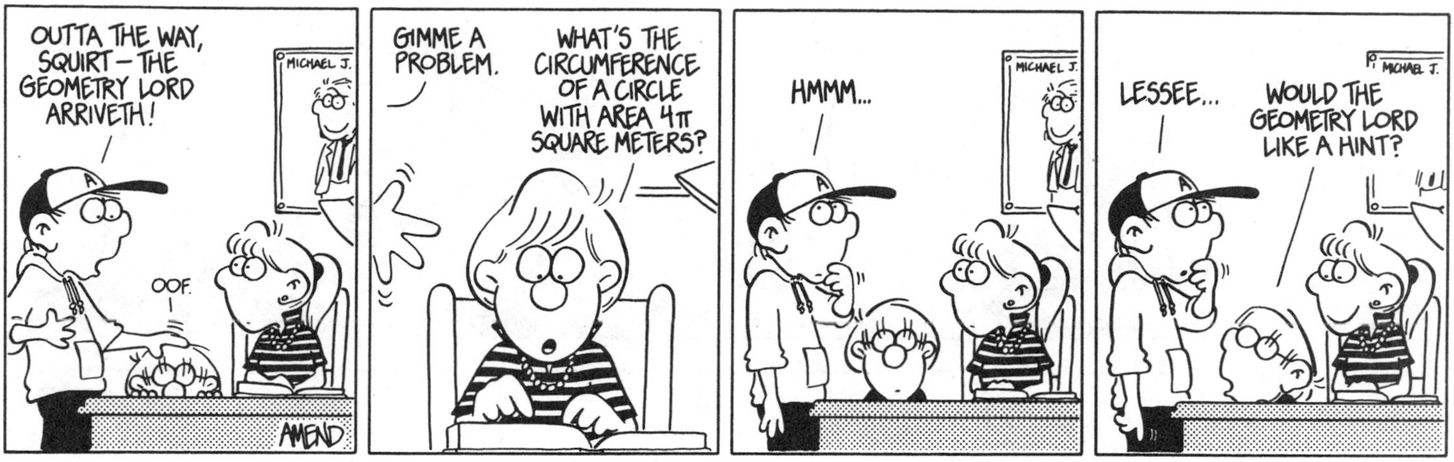
OUTTA THE WAY, SQUIRT — THE GEOMETRY LORD ARRIVETH!
OOF.
MICHAEL J.
GIMME A PROBLEM.
WHAT'S THE CIRCUMFERENCE OF A CIRCLE WITH AREA 4π SQUARE METERS?
HMMM...
MICHAEL J.
LESSEE...
WOULD THE GEOMETRY LORD LIKE A HINT?
MICHAEL J.
AMEND

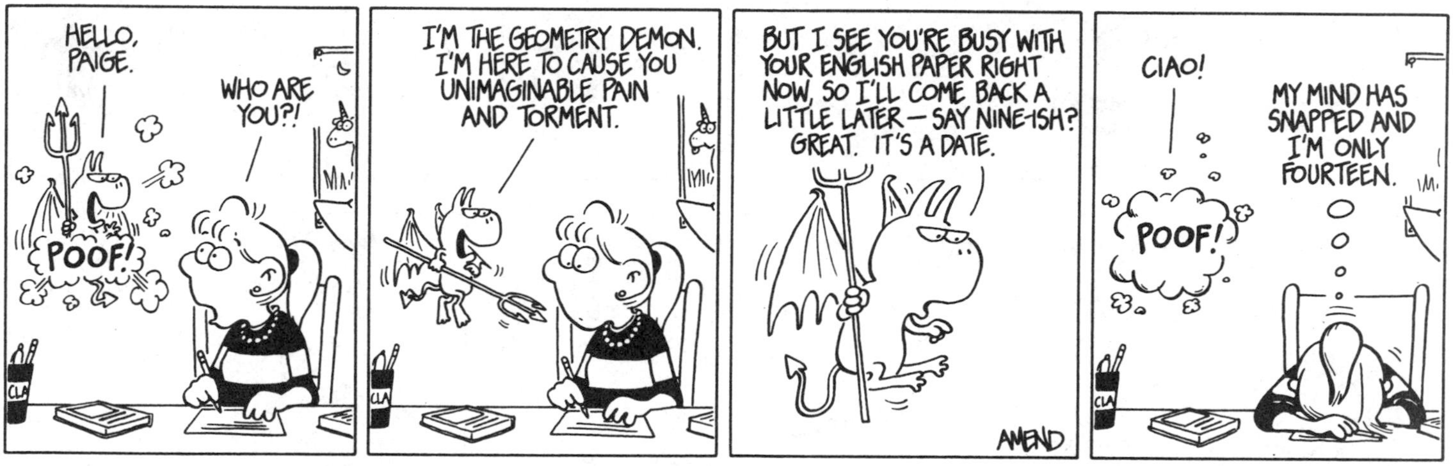
HELLO, PAIGE.
POOF!
WHO ARE YOU?!
I'M THE GEOMETRY DEMON. I'M HERE TO CAUSE YOU UNIMAGINABLE PAIN AND TORMENT.
BUT I SEE YOU'RE BUSY WITH YOUR ENGLISH PAPER RIGHT NOW, SO I'LL COME BACK A LITTLE LATER — SAY NINE-ISH? GREAT. IT'S A DATE.
AMEND
CIAO!
POOF!
MY MIND HAS SNAPPED AND I'M ONLY FOURTEEN.

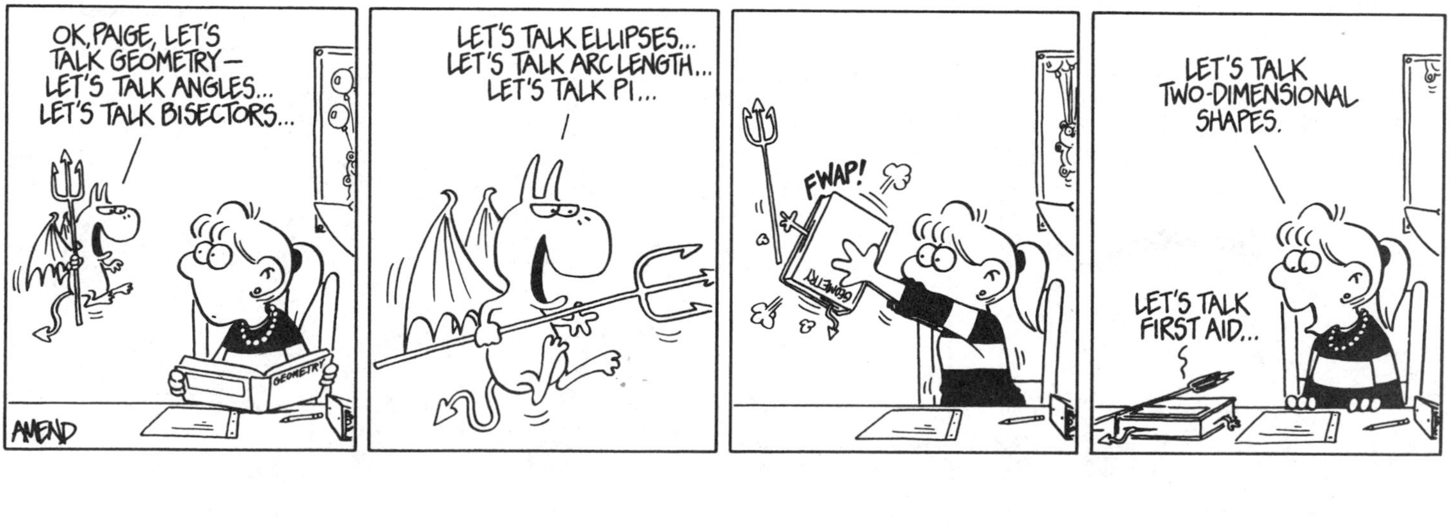
OK, PAIGE, LET'S TALK GEOMETRY — LET'S TALK ANGLES... LET'S TALK BISECTORS...
GEOMETRY
AMEND
LET'S TALK ELLIPSES... LET'S TALK ARC LENGTH... LET'S TALK PI...
FWAP!
GEOMETRY
LET'S TALK TWO-DIMENSIONAL SHAPES.
LET'S TALK FIRST AID...

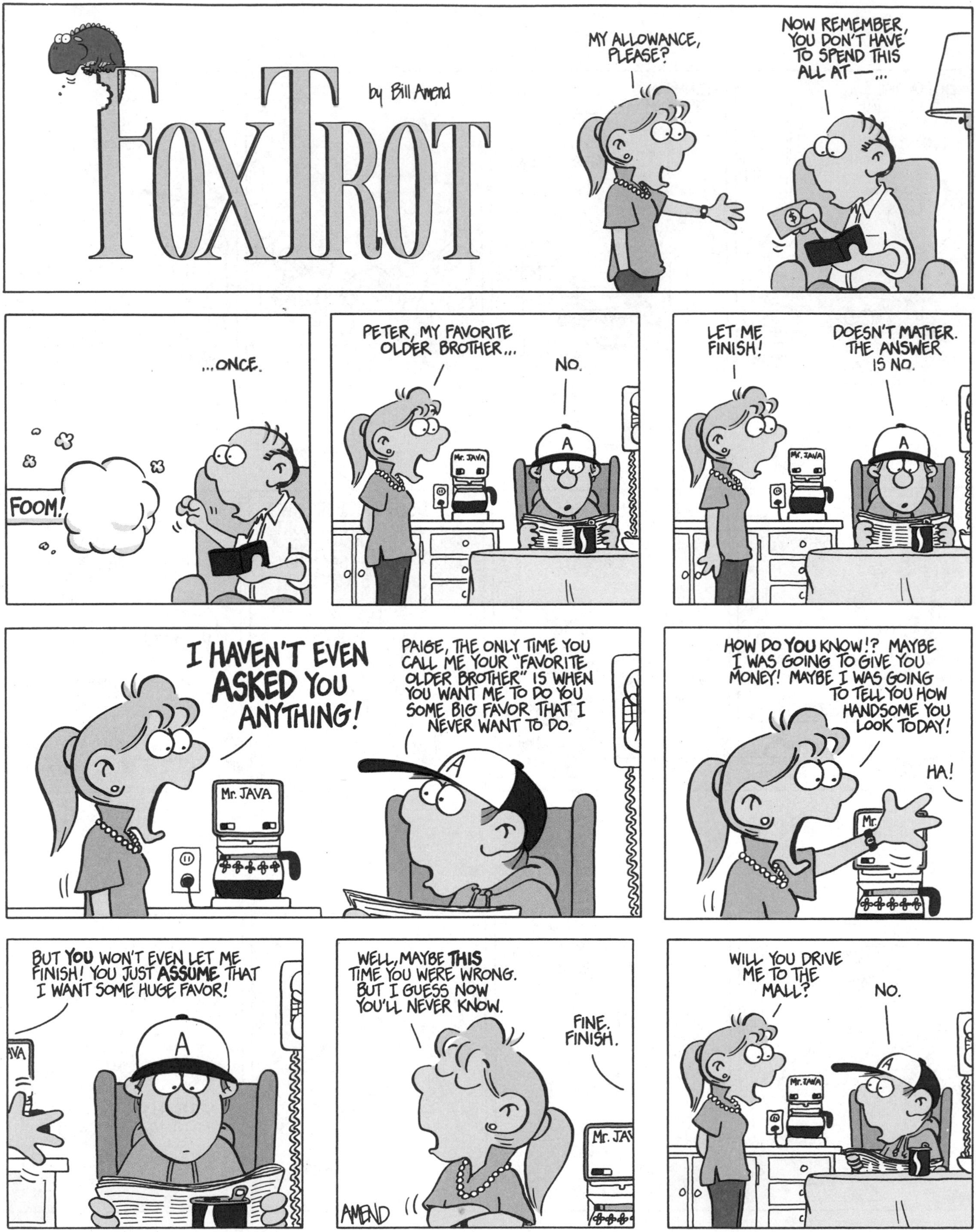
FOXTROT
by Bill Amend
MY ALLOWANCE, PLEASE?
NOW REMEMBER, YOU DON'T HAVE TO SPEND THIS ALL AT —...
...ONCE.
FOOM!
PETER, MY FAVORITE OLDER BROTHER...
NO.
LET ME FINISH!
DOESN'T MATTER. THE ANSWER IS NO.
I HAVEN'T EVEN ASKED YOU ANYTHING!
PAIGE, THE ONLY TIME YOU CALL ME YOUR "FAVORITE OLDER BROTHER" IS WHEN YOU WANT ME TO DO YOU SOME BIG FAVOR THAT I NEVER WANT TO DO.
HOW DO YOU KNOW!? MAYBE I WAS GOING TO GIVE YOU MONEY! MAYBE I WAS GOING TO TELL YOU HOW HANDSOME YOU LOOK TODAY!
HA!
BUT YOU WON'T EVEN LET ME FINISH! YOU JUST ASSUME THAT I WANT SOME HUGE FAVOR!
WELL, MAYBE THIS TIME YOU WERE WRONG. BUT I GUESS NOW YOU'LL NEVER KNOW.
FINE. FINISH.
WILL YOU DRIVE ME TO THE MALL?
NO.
AMEND

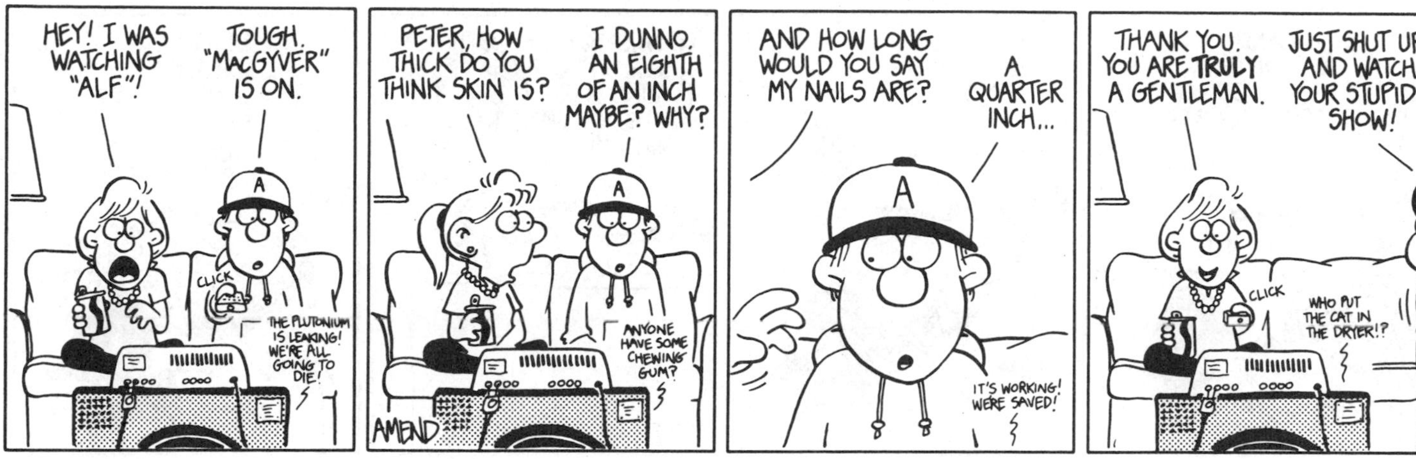
HEY! I WAS WATCHING "ALF"!
TOUGH. "MacGYVER" IS ON.
CLICK
THE PLUTONIUM IS LEAKING! WE'RE ALL GOING TO DIE!
PETER, HOW THICK DO YOU THINK SKIN IS?
I DUNNO. AN EIGHTH OF AN INCH MAYBE? WHY?
ANYONE HAVE SOME CHEWING GUM?
AMEND
AND HOW LONG WOULD YOU SAY MY NAILS ARE?
A QUARTER INCH...
IT'S WORKING! WE'RE SAVED!
THANK YOU. YOU ARE **TRULY** A GENTLEMAN.
JUST SHUT UP AND WATCH YOUR STUPID SHOW!
CLICK
WHO PUT THE CAT IN THE DRYER!?

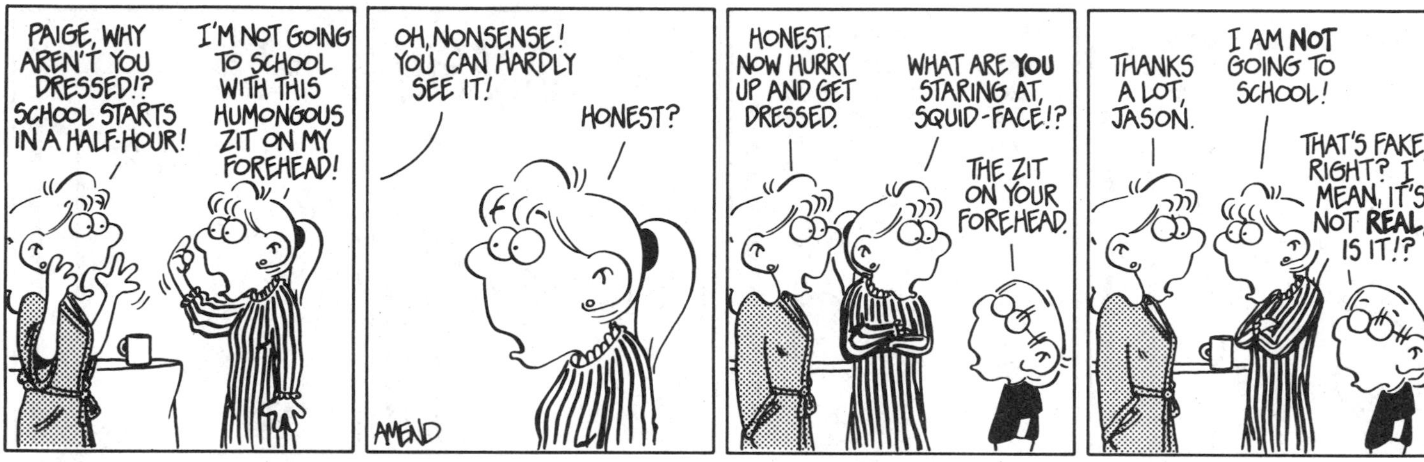
PAIGE, WHY AREN'T YOU DRESSED!? SCHOOL STARTS IN A HALF-HOUR!
I'M NOT GOING TO SCHOOL WITH THIS HUMONGOUS ZIT ON MY FOREHEAD!
OH, NONSENSE! YOU CAN HARDLY SEE IT!
HONEST?
AMEND
HONEST. NOW HURRY UP AND GET DRESSED.
WHAT ARE **YOU** STARING AT, SQUID-FACE!?
THE ZIT ON YOUR FOREHEAD.
THANKS A LOT, JASON.
I AM **NOT** GOING TO SCHOOL!
THAT'S FAKE, RIGHT? I MEAN, IT'S NOT **REAL**, IS IT!?

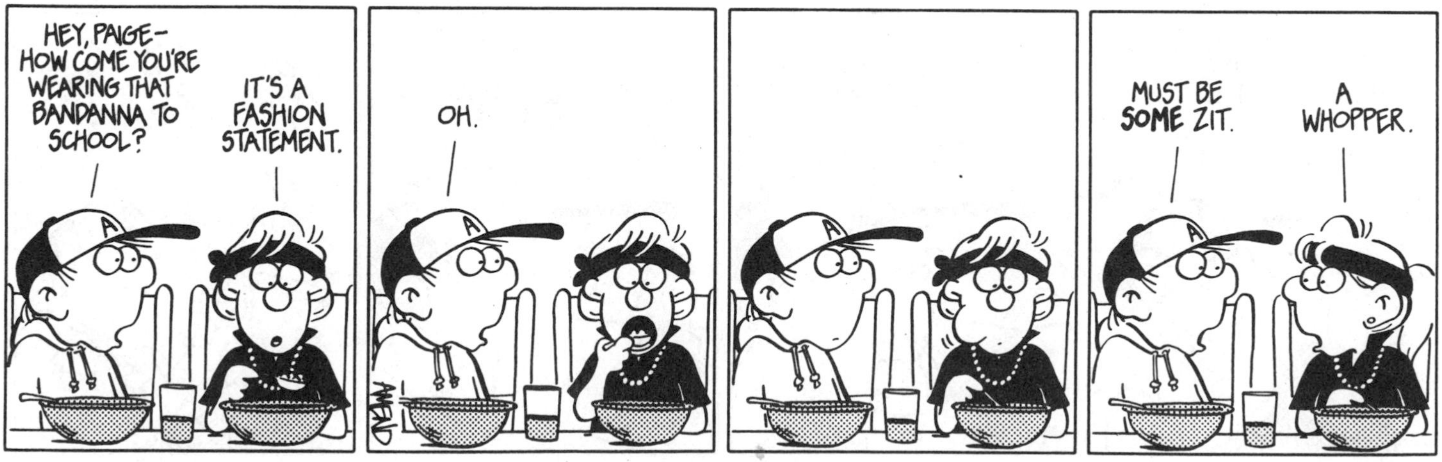
HEY, PAIGE- HOW COME YOU'RE WEARING THAT BANDANNA TO SCHOOL?
IT'S A FASHION STATEMENT.
AMEND
OH.
MUST BE **SOME** ZIT.
A WHOPPER.

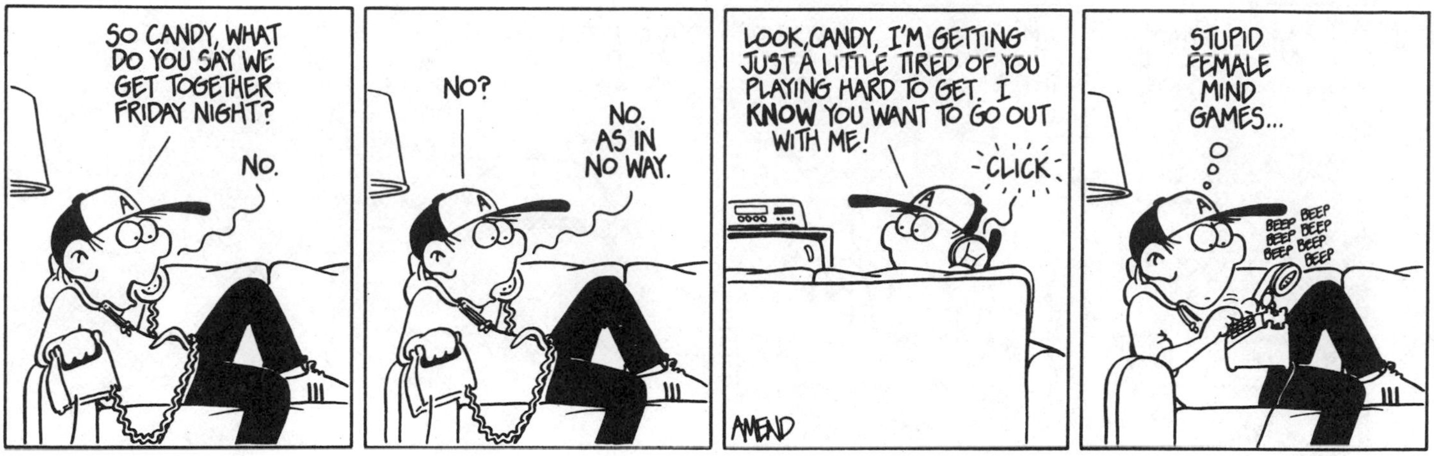
SO CANDY, WHAT DO YOU SAY WE GET TOGETHER FRIDAY NIGHT?
NO.
NO?
NO. AS IN NO WAY.
LOOK, CANDY, I'M GETTING JUST A LITTLE TIRED OF YOU PLAYING HARD TO GET. I KNOW YOU WANT TO GO OUT WITH ME!
CLICK
AMEND
STUPID FEMALE MIND GAMES...
BEEP BEEP BEEP BEEP BEEP BEEP BEEP BEEP

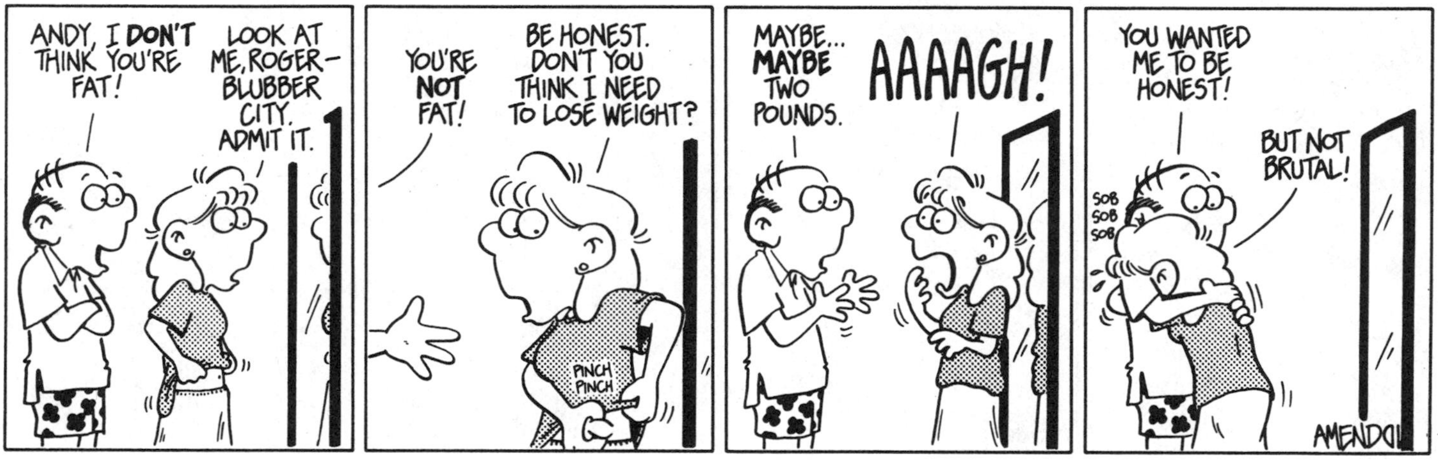
ANDY, I DON'T THINK YOU'RE FAT!
LOOK AT ME, ROGER— BLUBBER CITY. ADMIT IT.
YOU'RE NOT FAT!
BE HONEST. DON'T YOU THINK I NEED TO LOSE WEIGHT?
PINCH PINCH
MAYBE... MAYBE TWO POUNDS.
AAAAGH!
YOU WANTED ME TO BE HONEST!
SOB SOB SOB
BUT NOT BRUTAL!
AMEND

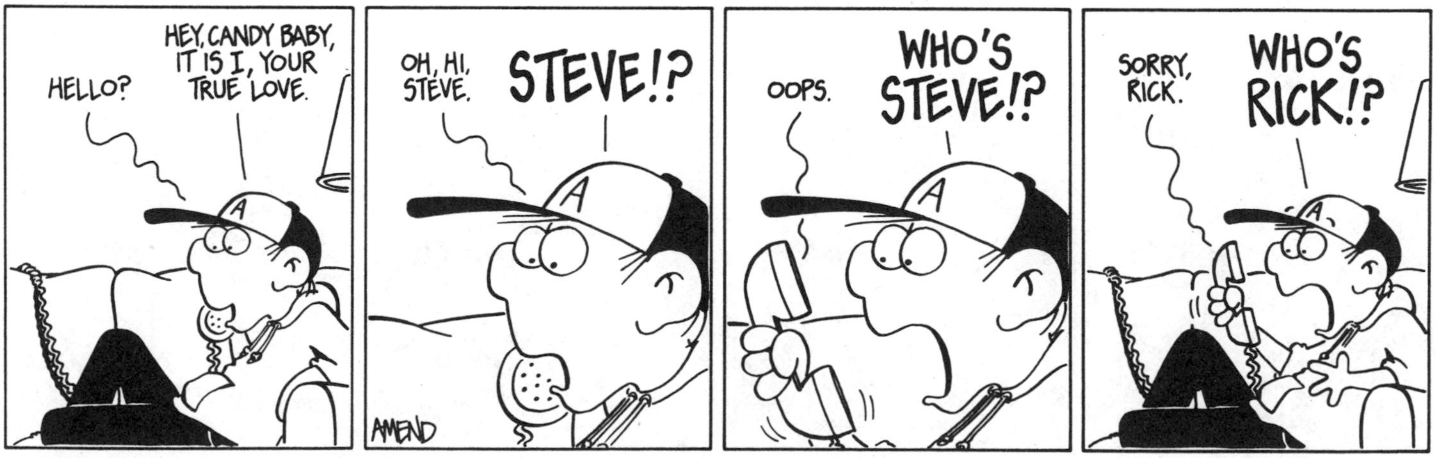
HELLO?
HEY, CANDY BABY, IT IS I, YOUR TRUE LOVE.
OH, HI, STEVE.
STEVE!?
AMEND
OOPS.
WHO'S STEVE!?
SORRY, RICK.
WHO'S RICK!?

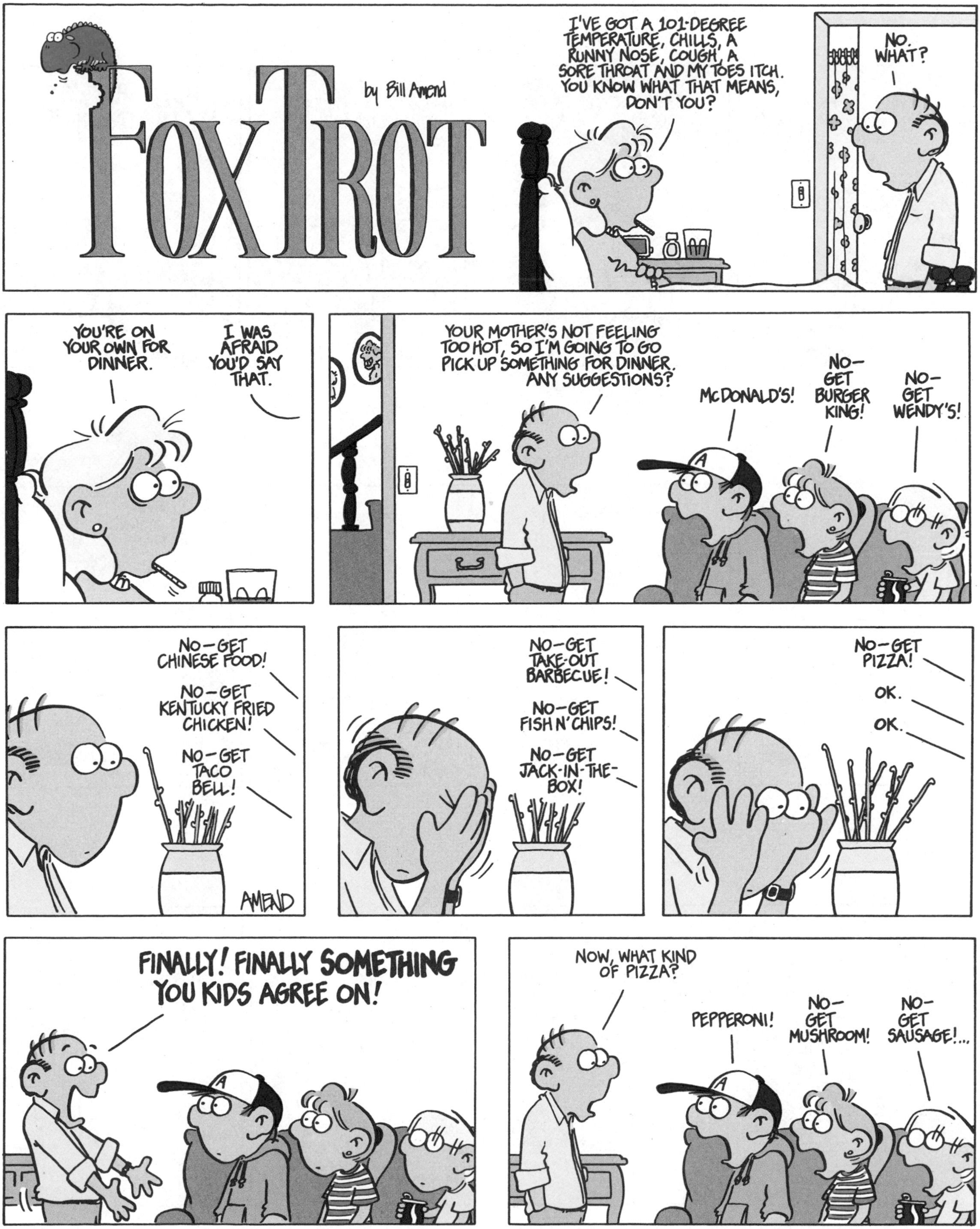
FOXTROT
by Bill Amend
I'VE GOT A 101-DEGREE TEMPERATURE, CHILLS, A RUNNY NOSE, COUGH, A SORE THROAT AND MY TOES ITCH. YOU KNOW WHAT THAT MEANS, DON'T YOU?
NO. WHAT?
YOU'RE ON YOUR OWN FOR DINNER.
I WAS AFRAID YOU'D SAY THAT.
YOUR MOTHER'S NOT FEELING TOO HOT, SO I'M GOING TO GO PICK UP SOMETHING FOR DINNER. ANY SUGGESTIONS?
McDONALD'S!
NO- GET BURGER KING!
NO- GET WENDY'S!
NO-GET CHINESE FOOD!
NO-GET KENTUCKY FRIED CHICKEN!
NO-GET TACO BELL!
AMEND
NO-GET TAKE-OUT BARBECUE!
NO-GET FISH N' CHIPS!
NO-GET JACK-IN-THE-BOX!
NO-GET PIZZA!
OK.
OK.
FINALLY! FINALLY SOMETHING YOU KIDS AGREE ON!
NOW, WHAT KIND OF PIZZA?
PEPPERONI!
NO- GET MUSHROOM!
NO- GET SAUSAGE!...

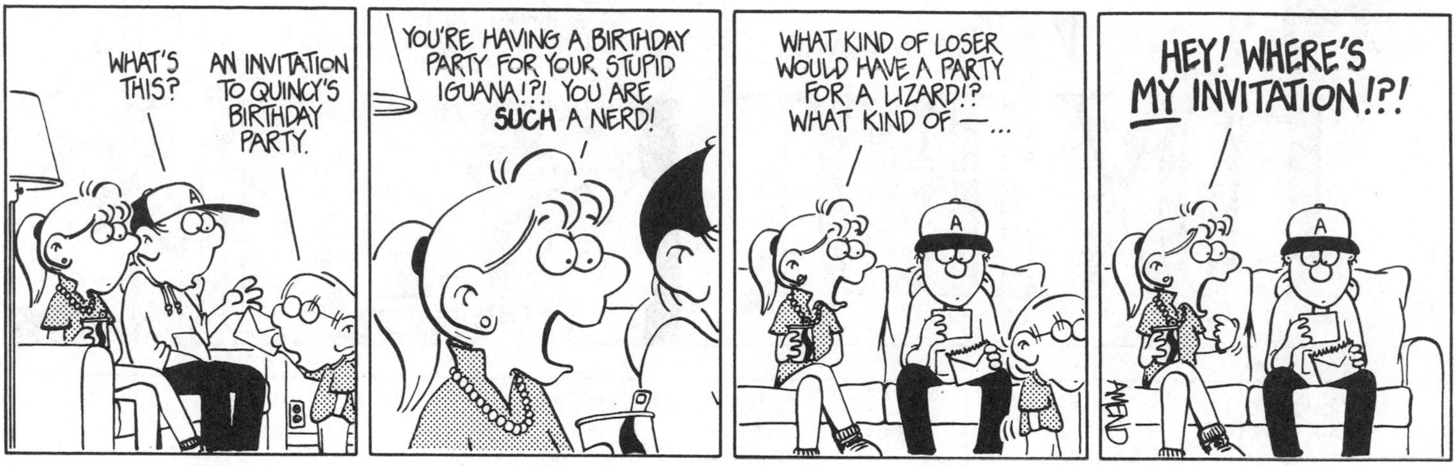
WHAT'S THIS?
AN INVITATION TO QUINCY'S BIRTHDAY PARTY.
YOU'RE HAVING A BIRTHDAY PARTY FOR YOUR STUPID IGUANA!?! YOU ARE SUCH A NERD!
WHAT KIND OF LOSER WOULD HAVE A PARTY FOR A LIZARD!? WHAT KIND OF —...
HEY! WHERE'S MY INVITATION!?!
AMEND

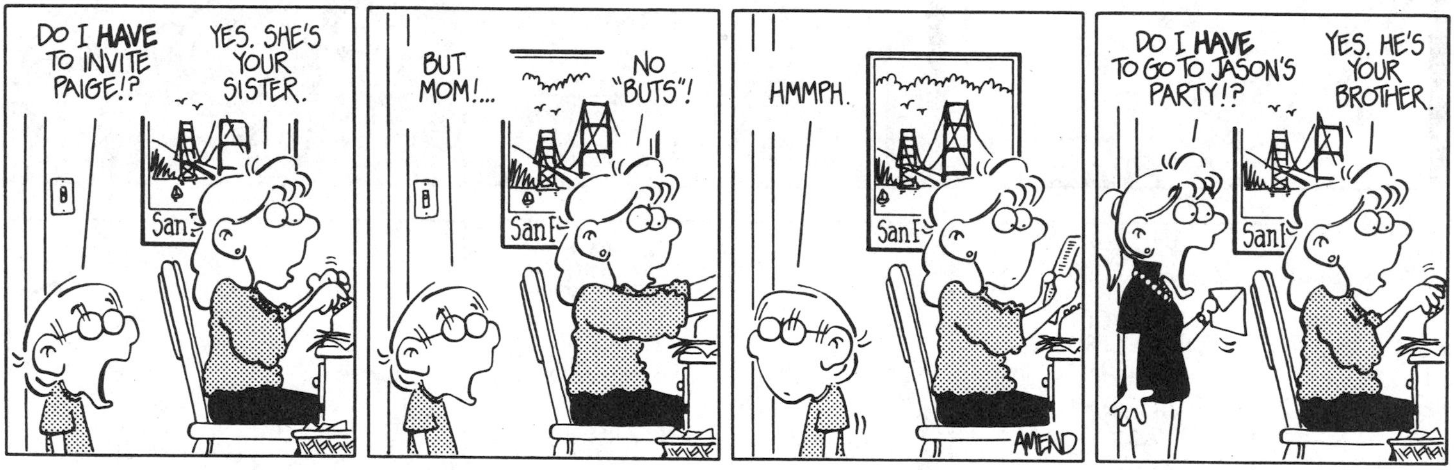
DO I HAVE TO INVITE PAIGE!?
YES. SHE'S YOUR SISTER.
BUT MOM!...
NO "BUTS"!
HMMPH.
AMEND
DO I HAVE TO GO TO JASON'S PARTY!?
YES. HE'S YOUR BROTHER.

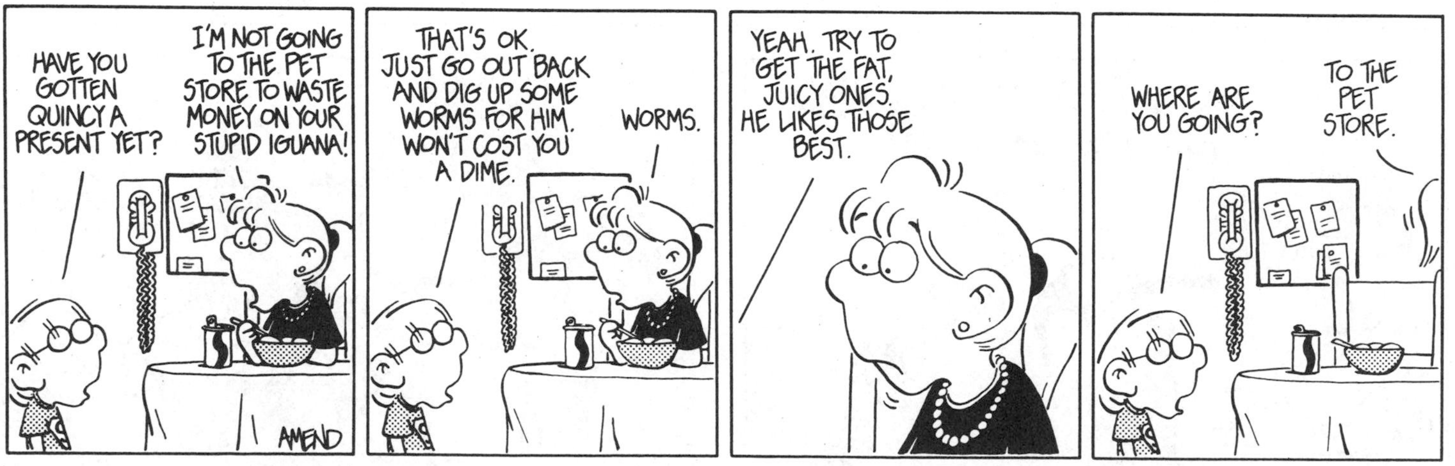
HAVE YOU GOTTEN QUINCY A PRESENT YET?
I'M NOT GOING TO THE PET STORE TO WASTE MONEY ON YOUR STUPID IGUANA!
AMEND
THAT'S OK. JUST GO OUT BACK AND DIG UP SOME WORMS FOR HIM. WON'T COST YOU A DIME.
WORMS.
YEAH. TRY TO GET THE FAT, JUICY ONES. HE LIKES THOSE BEST.
WHERE ARE YOU GOING?
TO THE PET STORE.

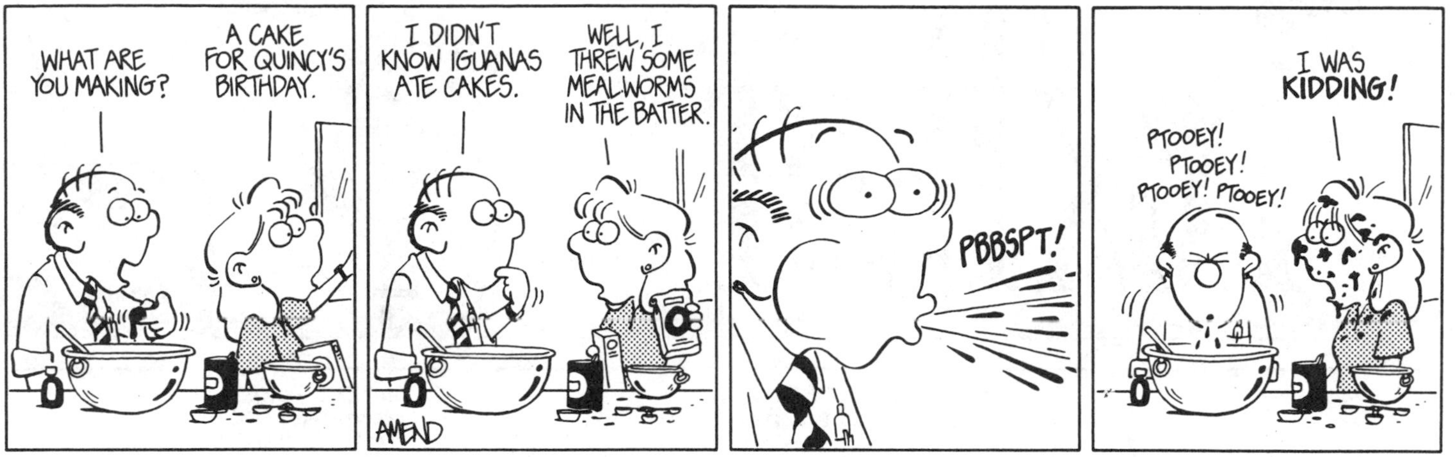
WHAT ARE YOU MAKING?
A CAKE FOR QUINCY'S BIRTHDAY.
I DIDN'T KNOW IGUANAS ATE CAKES.
WELL, I THREW SOME MEALWORMS IN THE BATTER.
AMEND
PBBSPT!
PTOOEY! PTOOEY! PTOOEY! PTOOEY!
I WAS **KIDDING!**

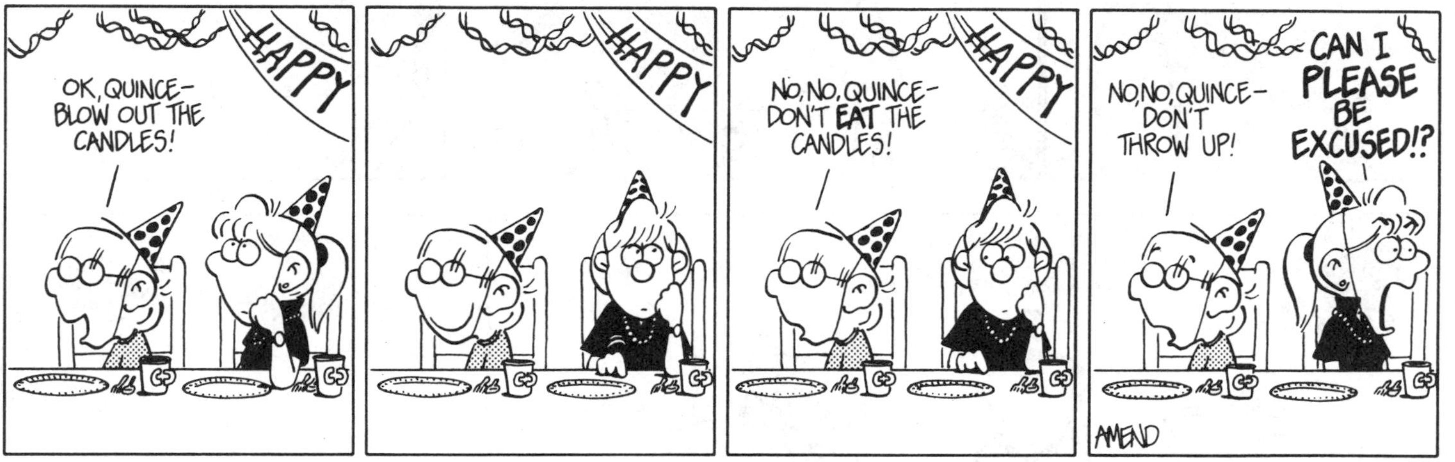
HAPPY
OK, QUINCE- BLOW OUT THE CANDLES!
HAPPY
HAPPY
NO, NO, QUINCE- DON'T **EAT** THE CANDLES!
NO, NO, QUINCE- DON'T THROW UP!
CAN I **PLEASE** BE **EXCUSED!?**
AMEND

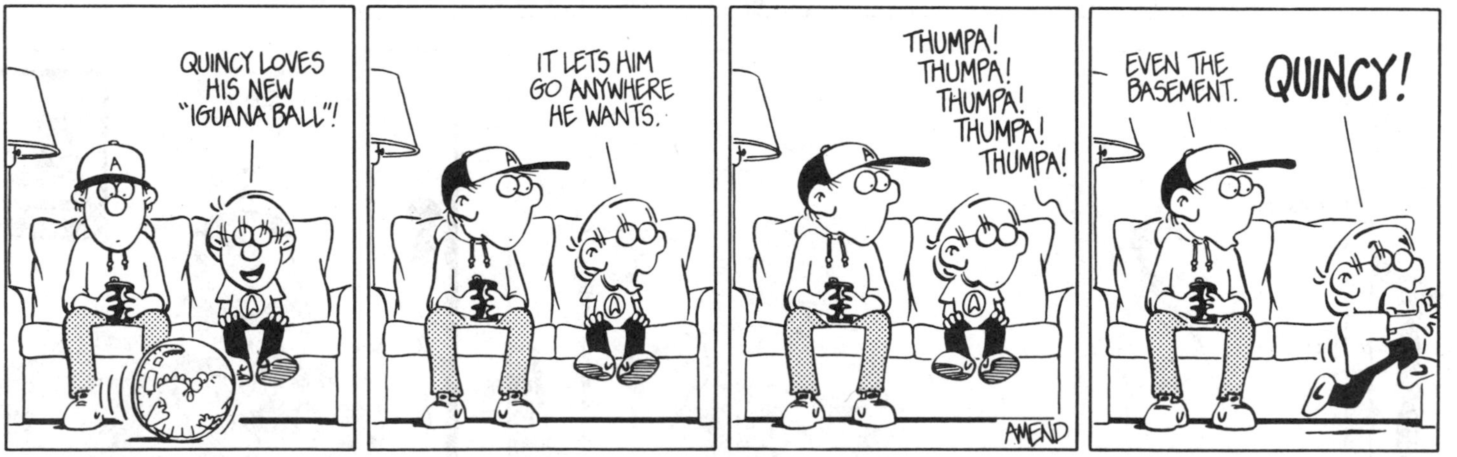
QUINCY LOVES HIS NEW "IGUANA BALL"!
IT LETS HIM GO ANYWHERE HE WANTS.
THUMPA! THUMPA! THUMPA! THUMPA! THUMPA!
AMEND
EVEN THE BASEMENT.
QUINCY!

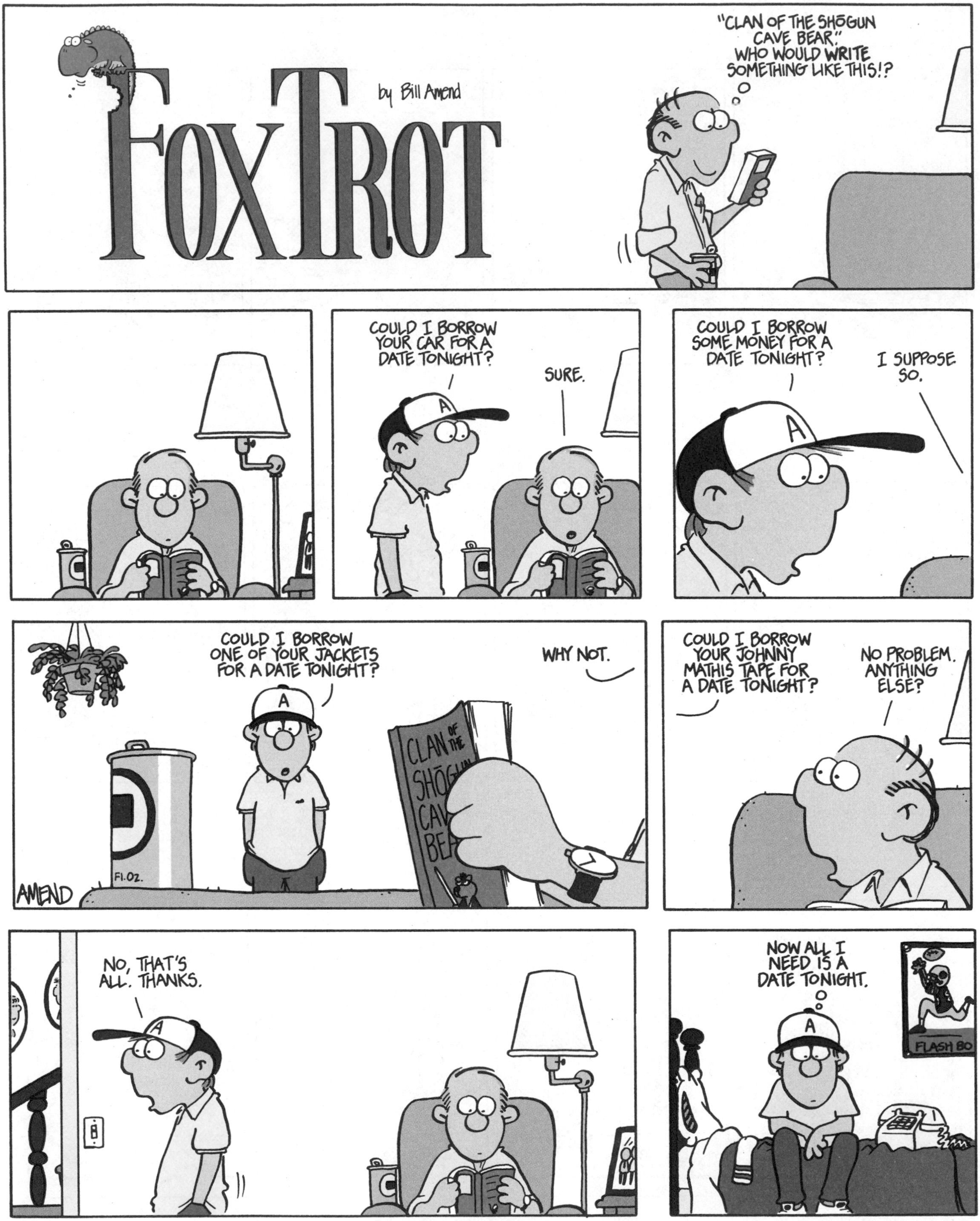
FoxTrot
by Bill Amend
"CLAN OF THE SHŌGUN CAVE BEAR." WHO WOULD WRITE SOMETHING LIKE THIS!?
COULD I BORROW YOUR CAR FOR A DATE TONIGHT?
SURE.
COULD I BORROW SOME MONEY FOR A DATE TONIGHT?
I SUPPOSE SO.
COULD I BORROW ONE OF YOUR JACKETS FOR A DATE TONIGHT?
WHY NOT.
AMEND
COULD I BORROW YOUR JOHNNY MATHIS TAPE FOR A DATE TONIGHT?
NO PROBLEM. ANYTHING ELSE?
NO, THAT'S ALL. THANKS.
NOW ALL I NEED IS A DATE TONIGHT.

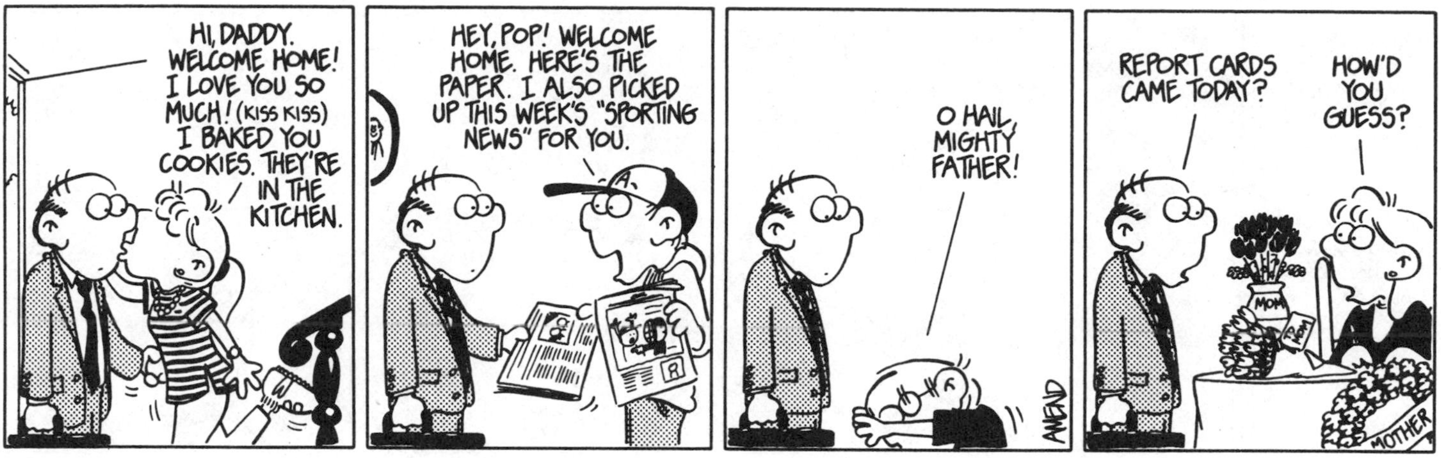
HI, DADDY. WELCOME HOME! I LOVE YOU SO MUCH! (KISS KISS) I BAKED YOU COOKIES. THEY'RE IN THE KITCHEN.
HEY, POP! WELCOME HOME. HERE'S THE PAPER. I ALSO PICKED UP THIS WEEK'S "SPORTING NEWS" FOR YOU.
O HAIL, MIGHTY FATHER!
REPORT CARDS CAME TODAY?
HOW'D YOU GUESS?
MOM
MOTHER

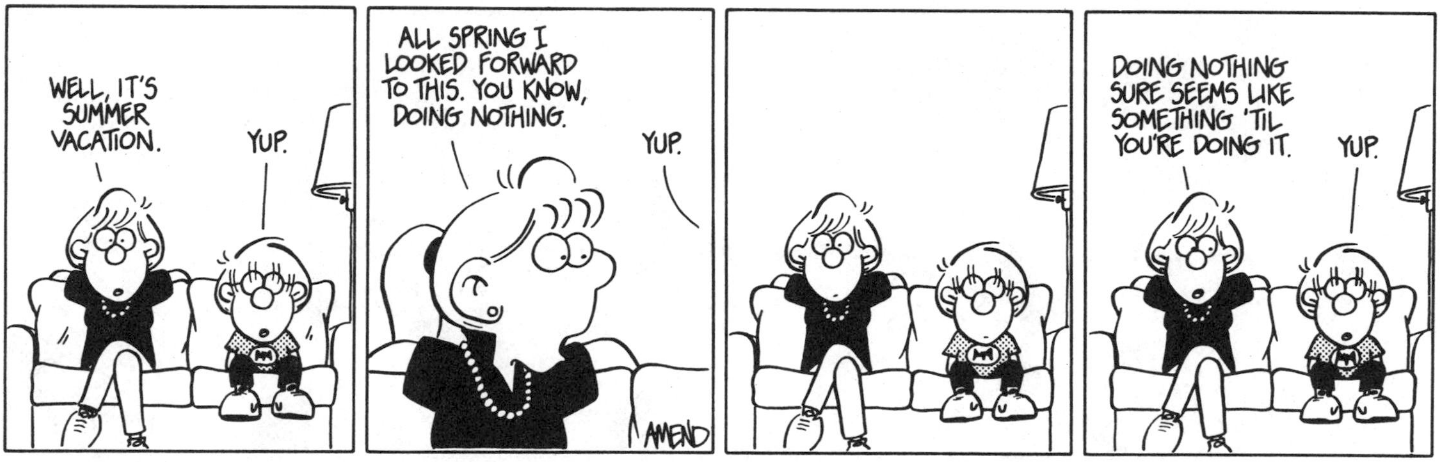
WELL, IT'S SUMMER VACATION.
YUP.
ALL SPRING I LOOKED FORWARD TO THIS. YOU KNOW, DOING NOTHING.
YUP.
DOING NOTHING SURE SEEMS LIKE SOMETHING 'TIL YOU'RE DOING IT.
YUP.

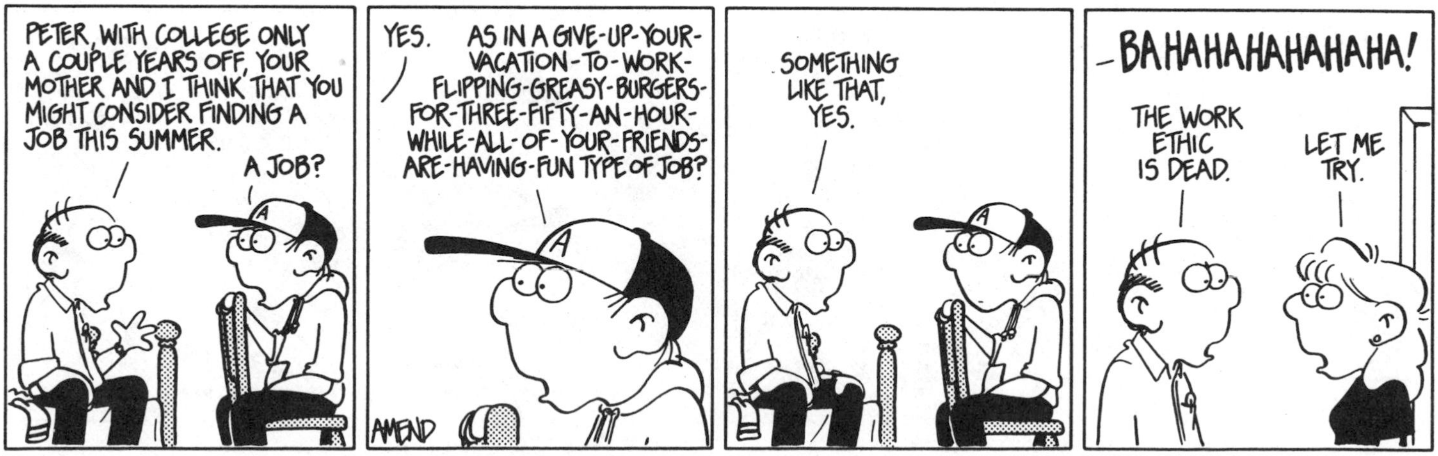
PETER, WITH COLLEGE ONLY A COUPLE YEARS OFF, YOUR MOTHER AND I THINK THAT YOU MIGHT CONSIDER FINDING A JOB THIS SUMMER.
A JOB?
YES.
AS IN A GIVE-UP-YOUR-VACATION-TO-WORK-FLIPPING-GREASY-BURGERS-FOR-THREE-FIFTY-AN-HOUR-WHILE-ALL-OF-YOUR-FRIENDS-ARE-HAVING-FUN TYPE OF JOB?
SOMETHING LIKE THAT, YES.
BAHAHAHAHAHAHA!
THE WORK ETHIC IS DEAD.
LET ME TRY.

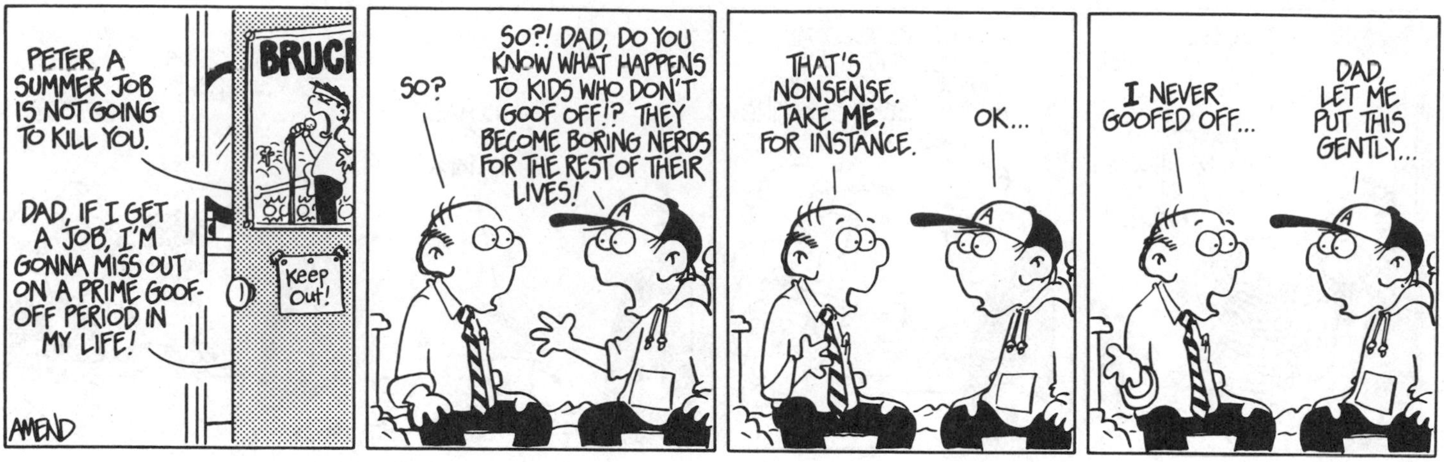
PETER, A SUMMER JOB IS NOT GOING TO KILL YOU.
DAD, IF I GET A JOB, I'M GONNA MISS OUT ON A PRIME GOOF-OFF PERIOD IN MY LIFE!
BRUCE
Keep Out!
AMEND
SO?
SO?! DAD, DO YOU KNOW WHAT HAPPENS TO KIDS WHO DON'T GOOF OFF!? THEY BECOME BORING NERDS FOR THE REST OF THEIR LIVES!
THAT'S NONSENSE. TAKE ME, FOR INSTANCE.
OK...
I NEVER GOOFED OFF...
DAD, LET ME PUT THIS GENTLY...

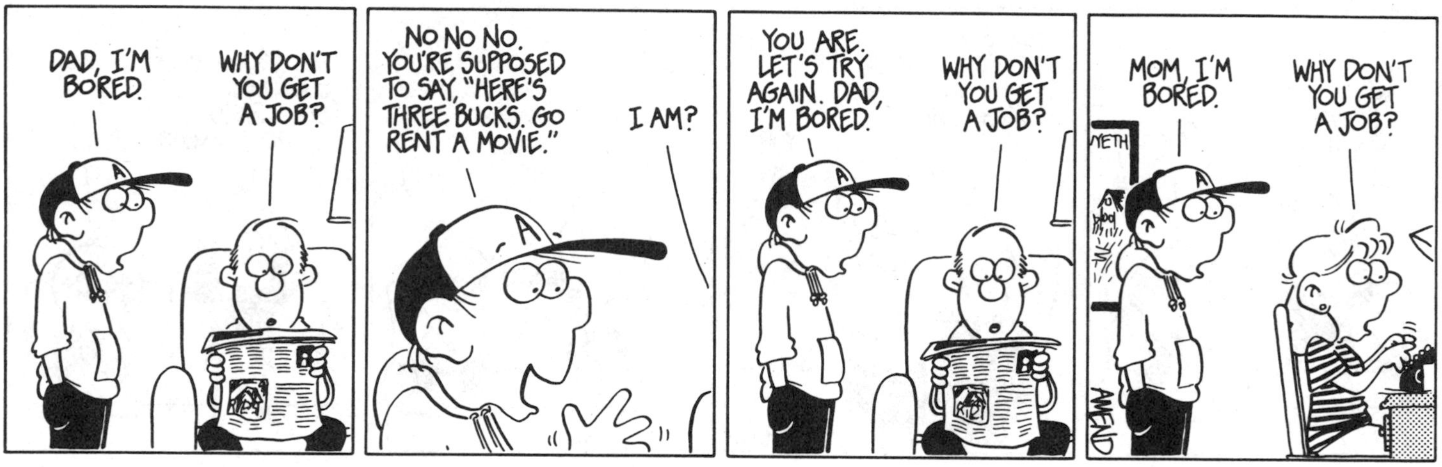
DAD, I'M BORED.
WHY DON'T YOU GET A JOB?
NO NO NO. YOU'RE SUPPOSED TO SAY, "HERE'S THREE BUCKS. GO RENT A MOVIE."
I AM?
YOU ARE. LET'S TRY AGAIN. DAD, I'M BORED.
WHY DON'T YOU GET A JOB?
MOM, I'M BORED.
WHY DON'T YOU GET A JOB?
AMEND

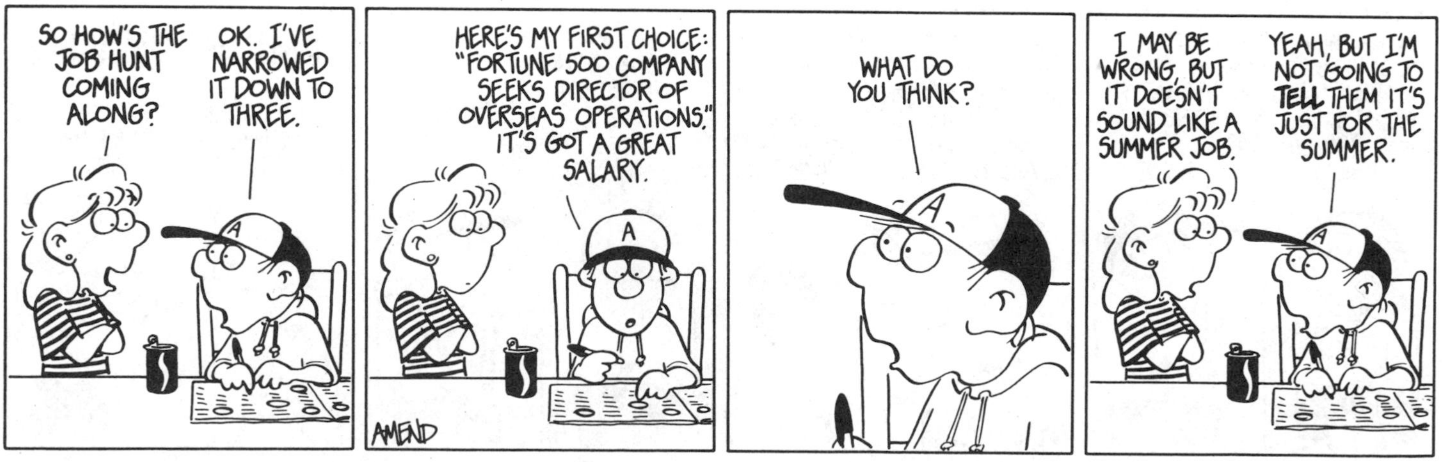
SO HOW'S THE JOB HUNT COMING ALONG?
OK. I'VE NARROWED IT DOWN TO THREE.
HERE'S MY FIRST CHOICE: "FORTUNE 500 COMPANY SEEKS DIRECTOR OF OVERSEAS OPERATIONS." IT'S GOT A GREAT SALARY.
AMEND
WHAT DO YOU THINK?
I MAY BE WRONG, BUT IT DOESN'T SOUND LIKE A SUMMER JOB.
YEAH, BUT I'M NOT GOING TO TELL THEM IT'S JUST FOR THE SUMMER.

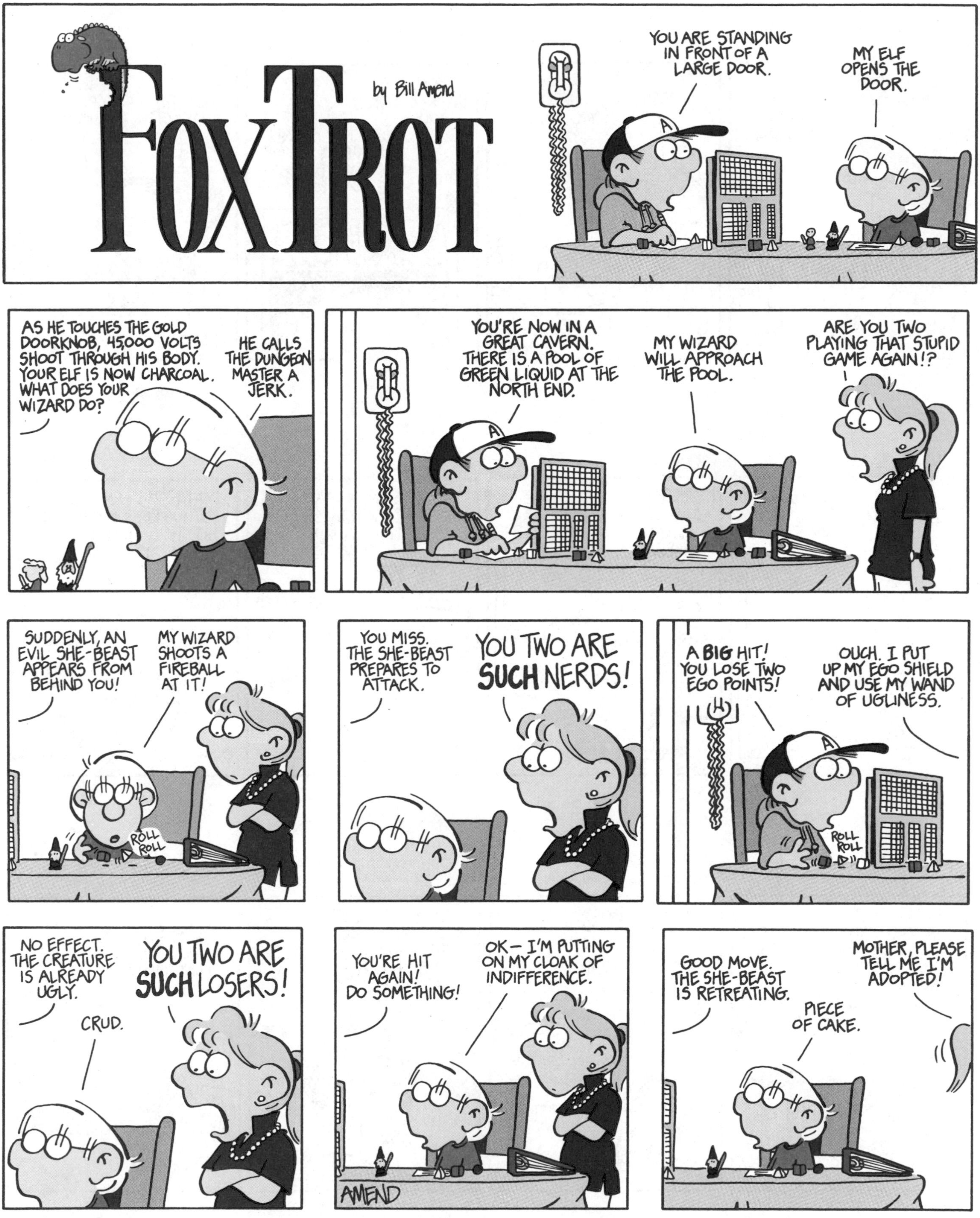
FoxTrot
by Bill Amend
YOU ARE STANDING IN FRONT OF A LARGE DOOR.
MY ELF OPENS THE DOOR.
AS HE TOUCHES THE GOLD DOORKNOB, 45,000 VOLTS SHOOT THROUGH HIS BODY. YOUR ELF IS NOW CHARCOAL. WHAT DOES YOUR WIZARD DO?
HE CALLS THE DUNGEON MASTER A JERK.
YOU'RE NOW IN A GREAT CAVERN. THERE IS A POOL OF GREEN LIQUID AT THE NORTH END.
MY WIZARD WILL APPROACH THE POOL.
ARE YOU TWO PLAYING THAT STUPID GAME AGAIN!?
SUDDENLY, AN EVIL SHE-BEAST APPEARS FROM BEHIND YOU!
MY WIZARD SHOOTS A FIREBALL AT IT!
ROLL ROLL
YOU MISS. THE SHE-BEAST PREPARES TO ATTACK.
YOU TWO ARE SUCH NERDS!
A BIG HIT! YOU LOSE TWO EGO POINTS!
OUCH. I PUT UP MY EGO SHIELD AND USE MY WAND OF UGLINESS.
ROLL ROLL
NO EFFECT. THE CREATURE IS ALREADY UGLY.
YOU TWO ARE SUCH LOSERS!
CRUD.
YOU'RE HIT AGAIN! DO SOMETHING!
OK— I'M PUTTING ON MY CLOAK OF INDIFFERENCE.
AMEND
GOOD MOVE. THE SHE-BEAST IS RETREATING.
MOTHER, PLEASE TELL ME I'M ADOPTED!
PIECE OF CAKE.

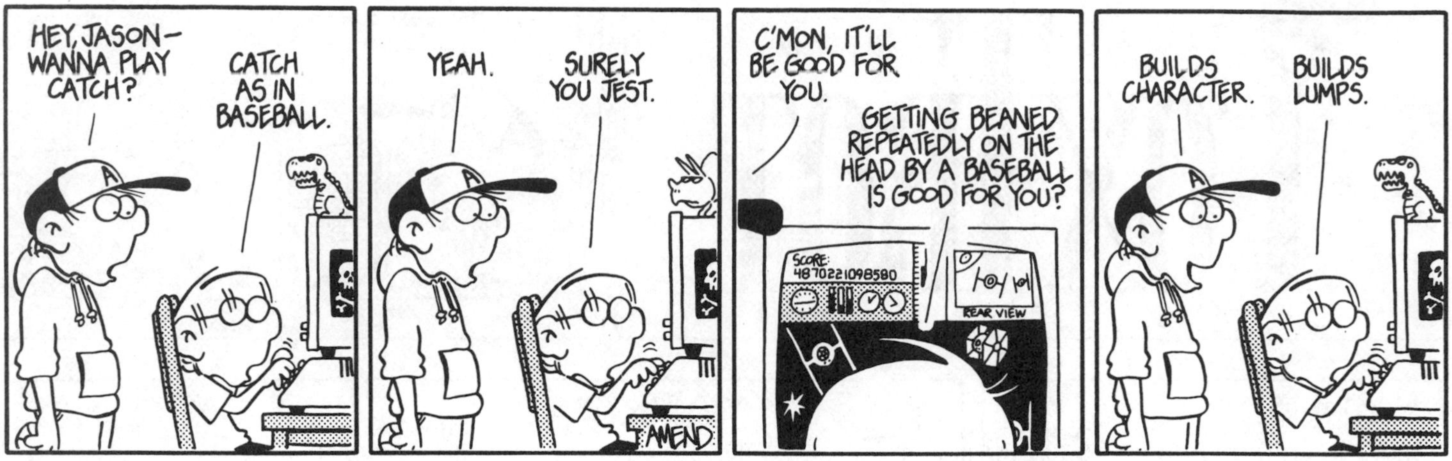
HEY, JASON—WANNA PLAY CATCH?
CATCH AS IN BASEBALL.
YEAH.
SURELY YOU JEST.
C'MON, IT'LL BE GOOD FOR YOU.
GETTING BEANED REPEATEDLY ON THE HEAD BY A BASEBALL IS GOOD FOR YOU?
SCORE: 4870221098580
REAR VIEW
AMEND
BUILDS CHARACTER.
BUILDS LUMPS.

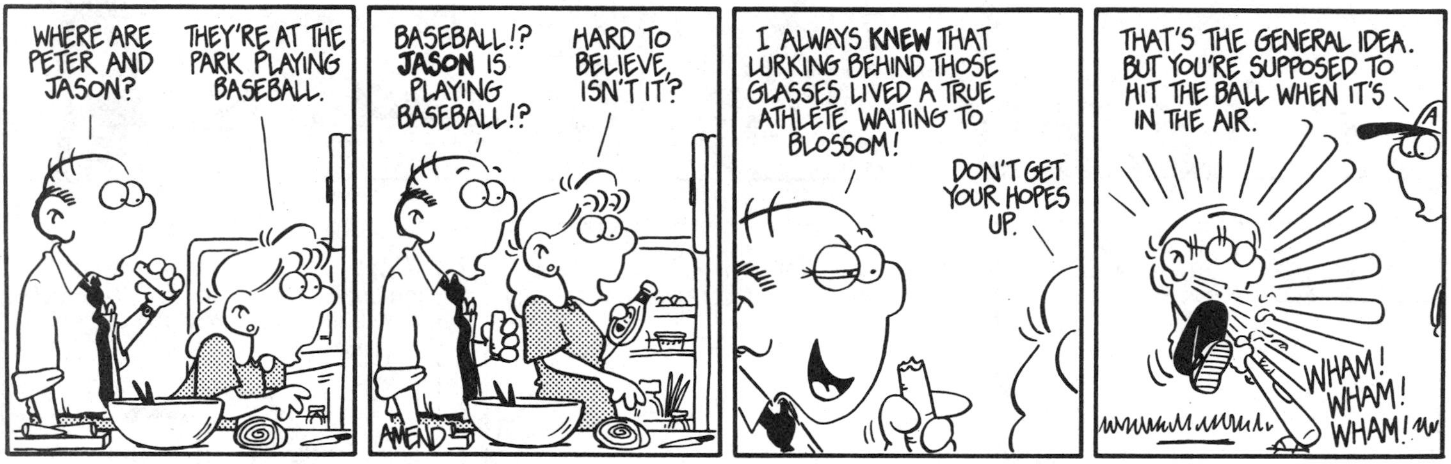
WHERE ARE PETER AND JASON?
THEY'RE AT THE PARK PLAYING BASEBALL.
BASEBALL!? JASON IS PLAYING BASEBALL!?
HARD TO BELIEVE, ISN'T IT?
AMEND
I ALWAYS KNEW THAT LURKING BEHIND THOSE GLASSES LIVED A TRUE ATHLETE WAITING TO BLOSSOM!
DON'T GET YOUR HOPES UP.
THAT'S THE GENERAL IDEA. BUT YOU'RE SUPPOSED TO HIT THE BALL WHEN IT'S IN THE AIR.
WHAM! WHAM! WHAM!

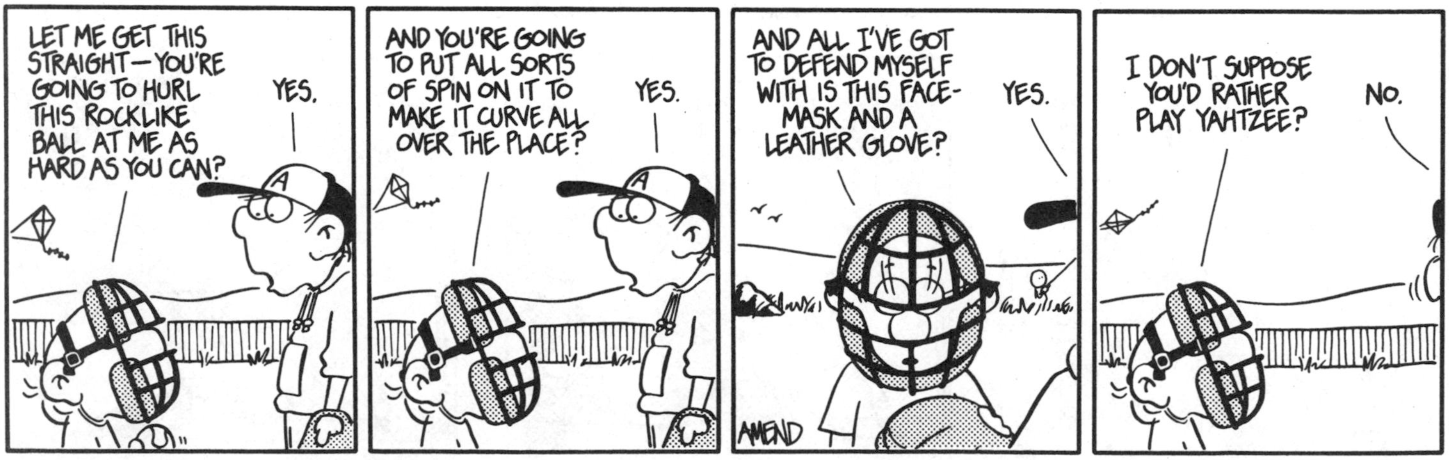
LET ME GET THIS STRAIGHT—YOU'RE GOING TO HURL THIS ROCKLIKE BALL AT ME AS HARD AS YOU CAN?
YES.
AND YOU'RE GOING TO PUT ALL SORTS OF SPIN ON IT TO MAKE IT CURVE ALL OVER THE PLACE?
YES.
AND ALL I'VE GOT TO DEFEND MYSELF WITH IS THIS FACE-MASK AND A LEATHER GLOVE?
YES.
AMEND
I DON'T SUPPOSE YOU'D RATHER PLAY YAHTZEE?
NO.

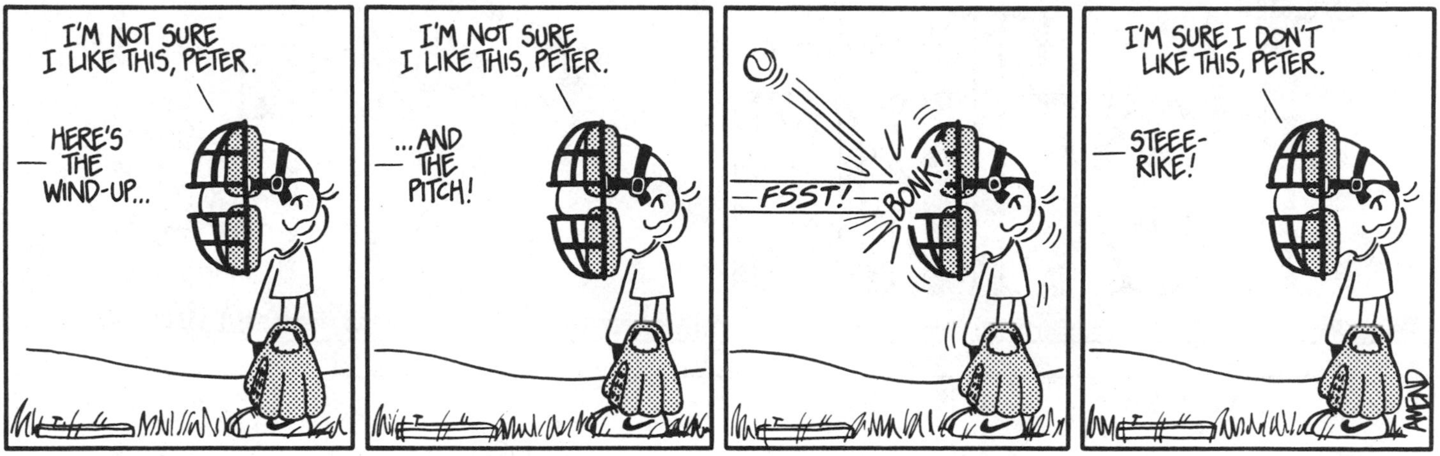
I'M NOT SURE I LIKE THIS, PETER.
HERE'S THE WIND-UP...
I'M NOT SURE I LIKE THIS, PETER.
...AND THE PITCH!
FSST!
BONK!
I'M SURE I DON'T LIKE THIS, PETER.
STEEE-RIKE!
AMEND

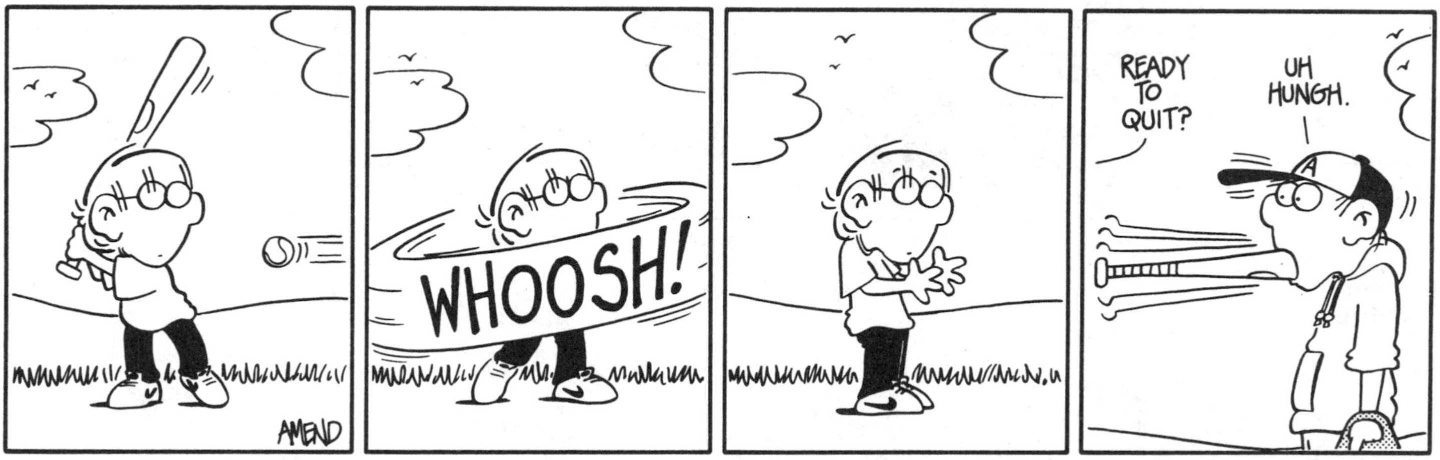
AMEND
WHOOSH!
READY TO QUIT?
UH HUNGH.

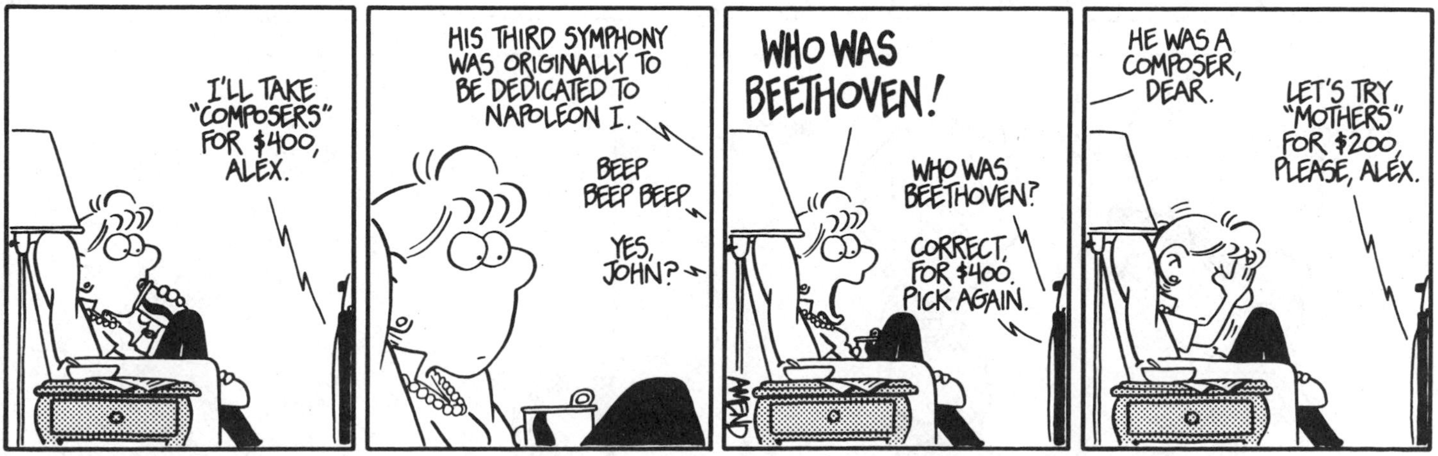
I'LL TAKE "COMPOSERS" FOR $400, ALEX.
HIS THIRD SYMPHONY WAS ORIGINALLY TO BE DEDICATED TO NAPOLEON I.
BEEP BEEP BEEP
YES, JOHN?
WHO WAS BEETHOVEN!
WHO WAS BEETHOVEN?
CORRECT, FOR $400. PICK AGAIN.
AMEND
HE WAS A COMPOSER, DEAR.
LET'S TRY "MOTHERS" FOR $200, PLEASE, ALEX.

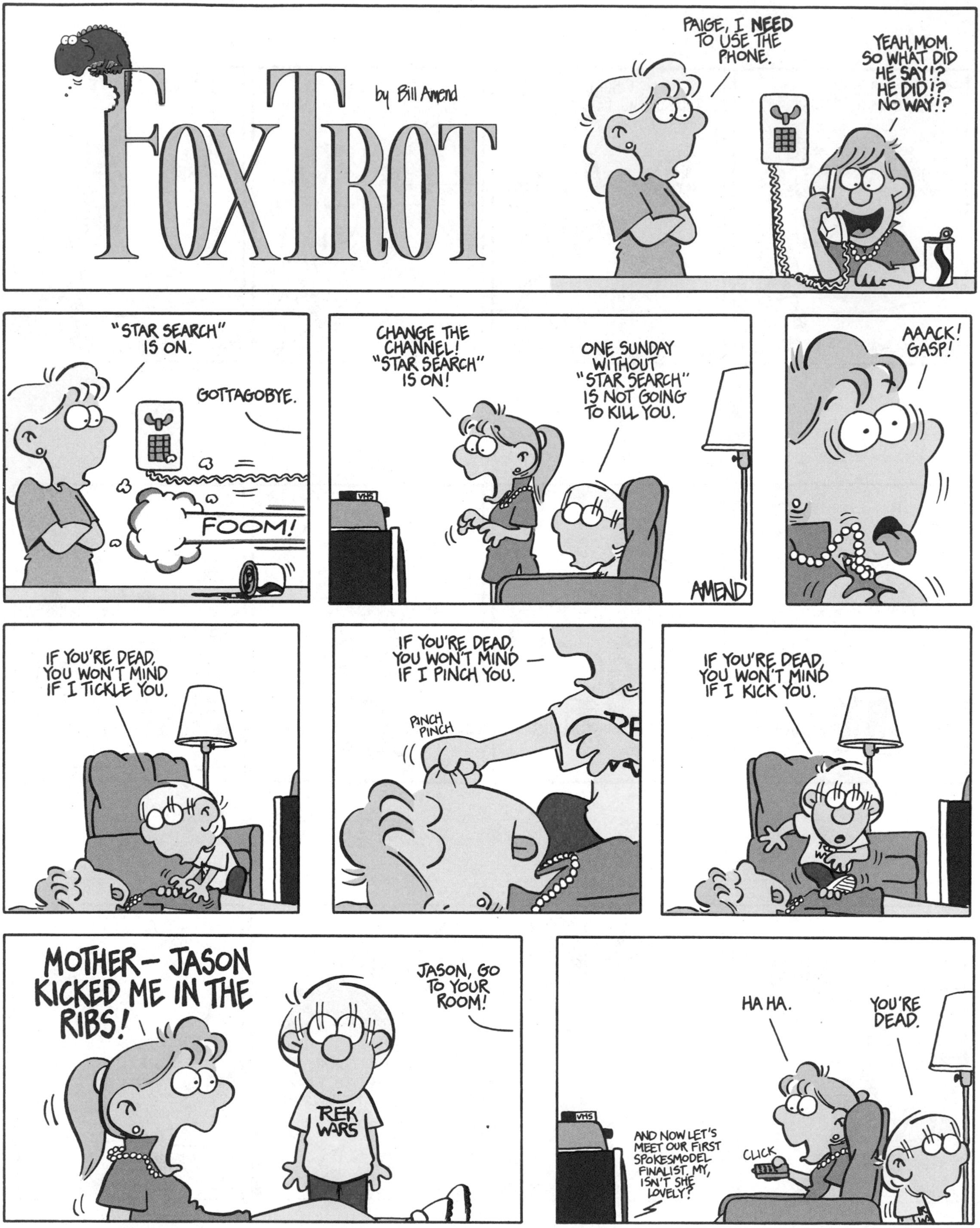
FoxTrot
by Bill Amend
PAIGE, I NEED TO USE THE PHONE.
YEAH, MOM. SO WHAT DID HE SAY!? HE DID!? NO WAY!?
"STAR SEARCH" IS ON.
GOTTAGOBYE.
FOOM!
CHANGE THE CHANNEL! "STAR SEARCH" IS ON!
ONE SUNDAY WITHOUT "STAR SEARCH" IS NOT GOING TO KILL YOU.
VHS
AMEND
AAACK! GASP!
IF YOU'RE DEAD, YOU WON'T MIND IF I TICKLE YOU.
IF YOU'RE DEAD, YOU WON'T MIND IF I PINCH YOU.
PINCH PINCH
IF YOU'RE DEAD, YOU WON'T MIND IF I KICK YOU.
MOTHER— JASON KICKED ME IN THE RIBS!
JASON, GO TO YOUR ROOM!
REK WARS
HA HA.
YOU'RE DEAD.
VHS
AND NOW LET'S MEET OUR FIRST SPOKESMODEL FINALIST. MY, ISN'T SHE LOVELY?
CLICK

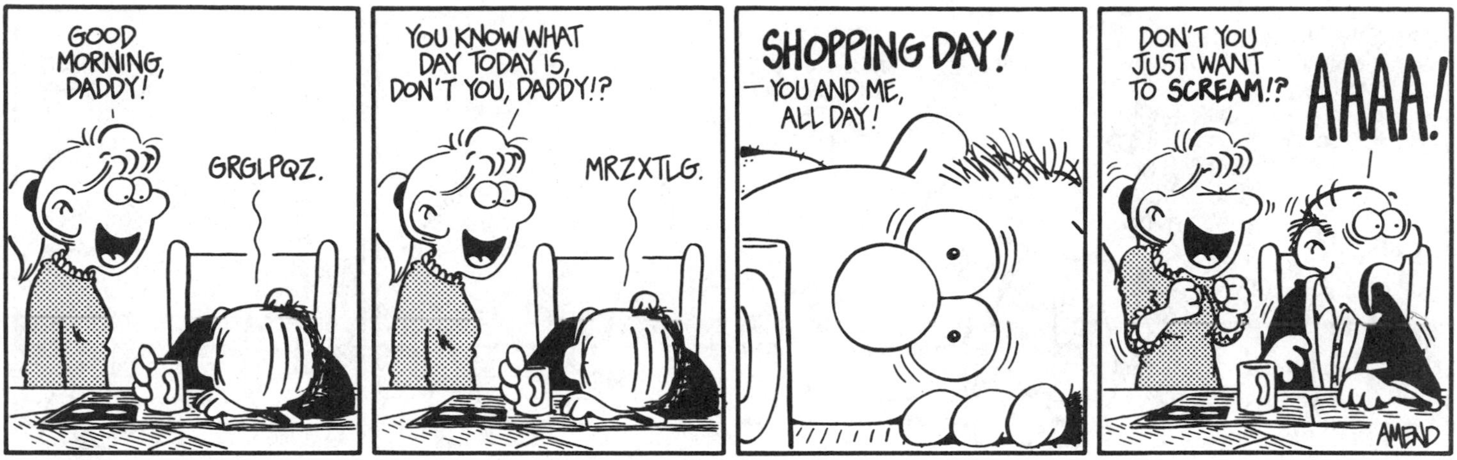
GOOD MORNING, DADDY!
GRGLPQZ.
YOU KNOW WHAT DAY TODAY IS, DON'T YOU, DADDY!?
MRZXTLG.
SHOPPING DAY!
YOU AND ME, ALL DAY!
DON'T YOU JUST WANT TO SCREAM!?
AAAA!
AMEND

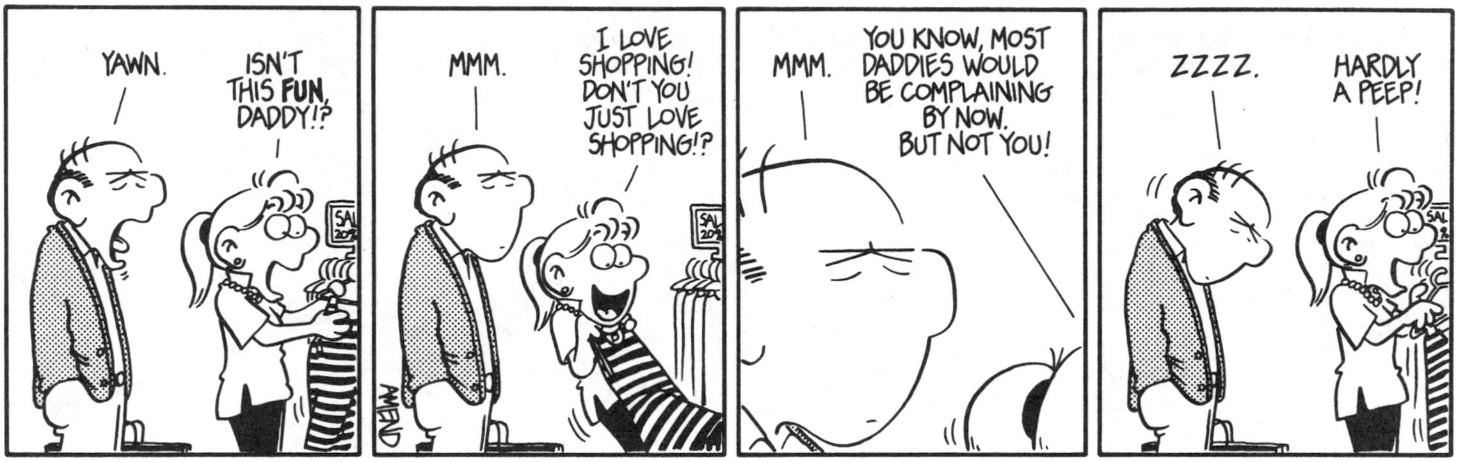
YAWN.
ISN'T THIS FUN, DADDY!?
MMM.
I LOVE SHOPPING! DON'T YOU JUST LOVE SHOPPING!?
AMEND
MMM.
YOU KNOW, MOST DADDIES WOULD BE COMPLAINING BY NOW. BUT NOT YOU!
ZZZZ.
HARDLY A PEEP!

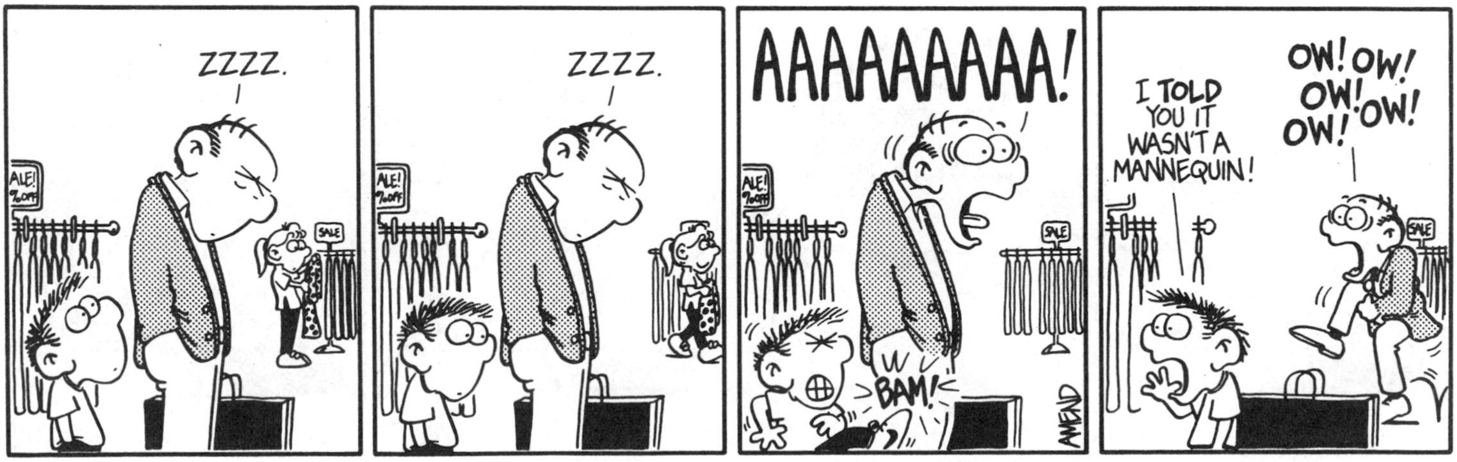
ZZZZ.
ZZZZ.
AAAAAAAAA!
BAM!
AMEND
I TOLD YOU IT WASN'T A MANNEQUIN!
OW! OW! OW! OW! OW!

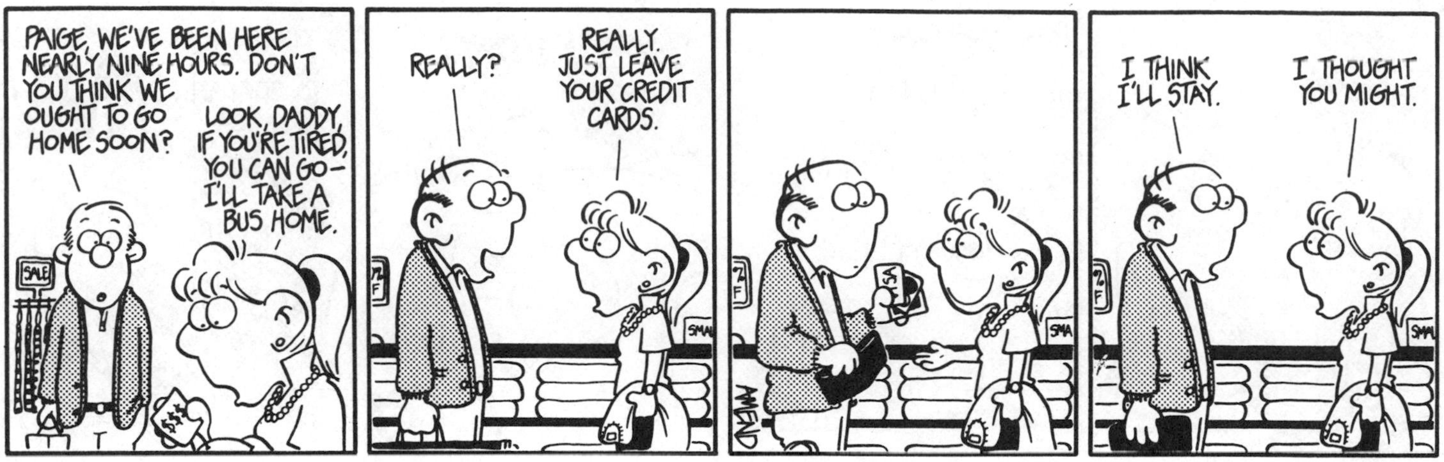
PAIGE, WE'VE BEEN HERE NEARLY NINE HOURS. DON'T YOU THINK WE OUGHT TO GO HOME SOON?
LOOK, DADDY, IF YOU'RE TIRED, YOU CAN GO– I'LL TAKE A BUS HOME.
SALE
REALLY?
REALLY. JUST LEAVE YOUR CREDIT CARDS.
AMEND
I THINK I'LL STAY.
I THOUGHT YOU MIGHT.

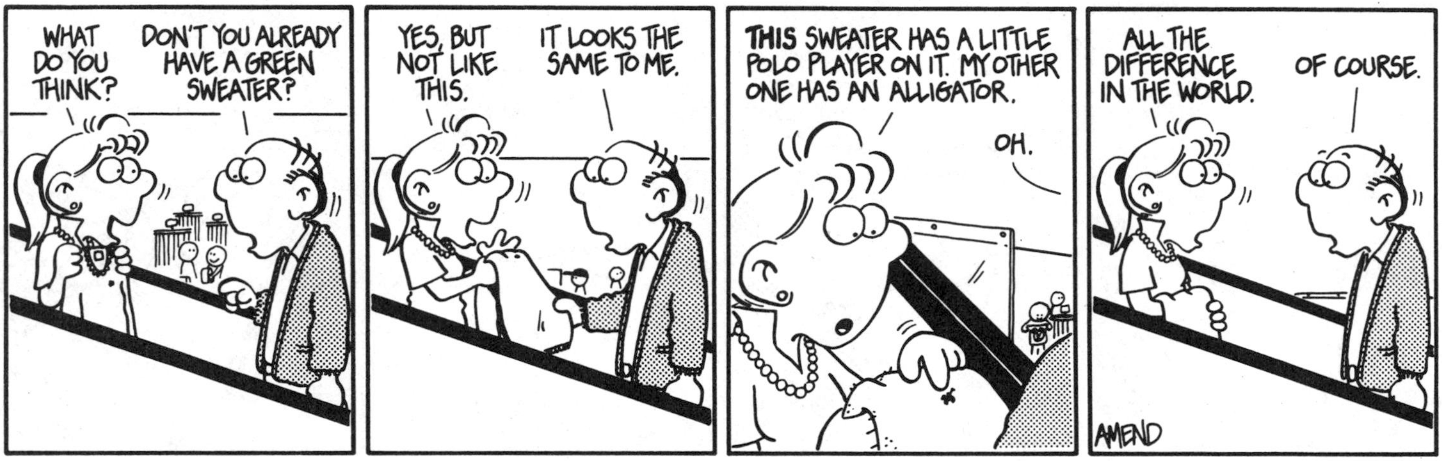
WHAT DO YOU THINK?
DON'T YOU ALREADY HAVE A GREEN SWEATER?
YES, BUT NOT LIKE THIS.
IT LOOKS THE SAME TO ME.
THIS SWEATER HAS A LITTLE POLO PLAYER ON IT. MY OTHER ONE HAS AN ALLIGATOR.
OH.
ALL THE DIFFERENCE IN THE WORLD.
OF COURSE.
AMEND

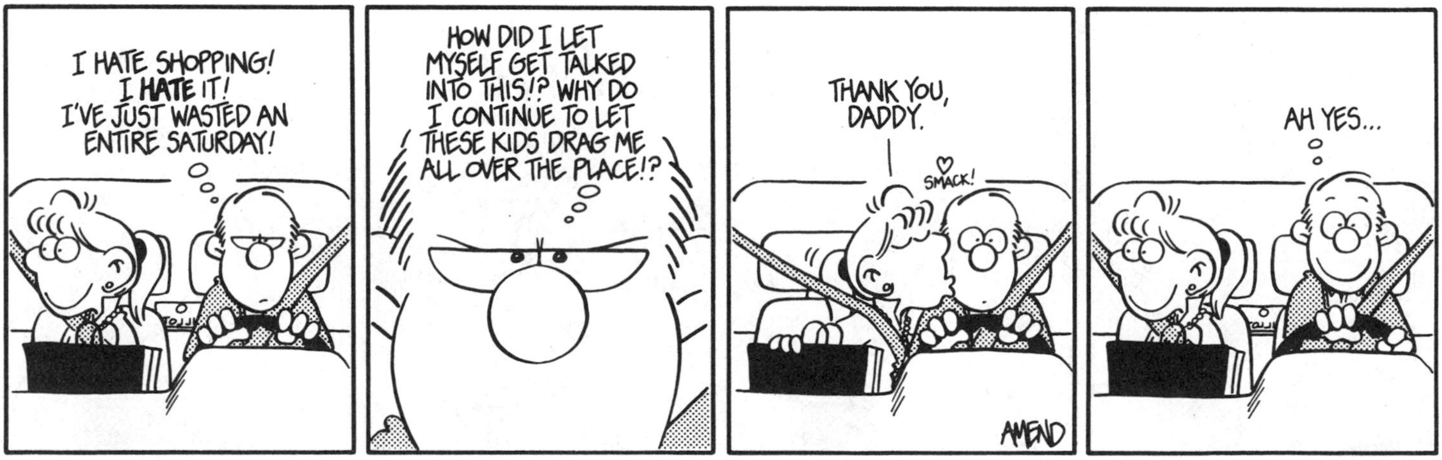
I HATE SHOPPING! I HATE IT! I'VE JUST WASTED AN ENTIRE SATURDAY!
HOW DID I LET MYSELF GET TALKED INTO THIS!? WHY DO I CONTINUE TO LET THESE KIDS DRAG ME ALL OVER THE PLACE!?
THANK YOU, DADDY.
SMACK!
AMEND
AH YES...

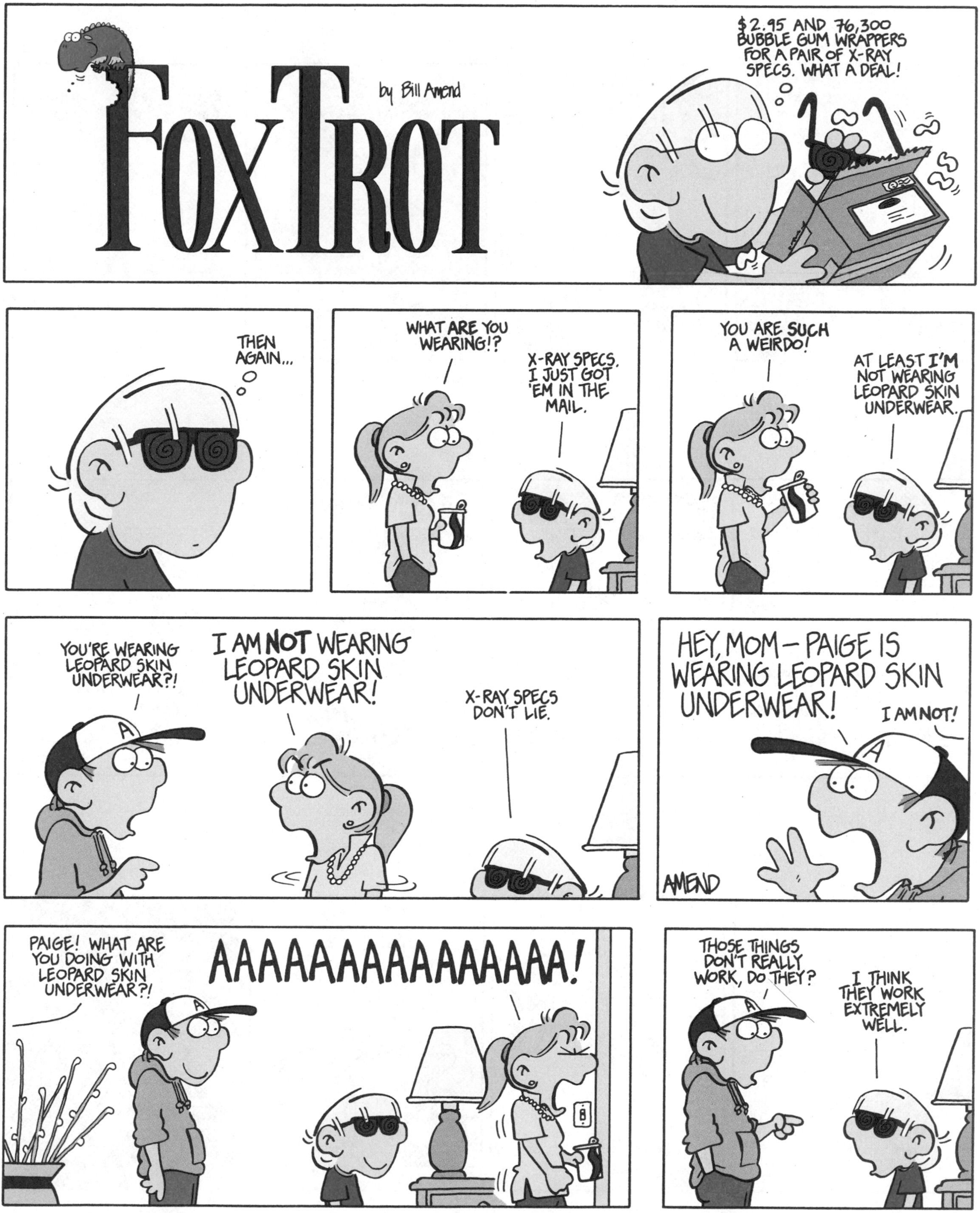
FoxTrot
by Bill Amend
$2.95 AND 76,300 BUBBLE GUM WRAPPERS FOR A PAIR OF X-RAY SPECS. WHAT A DEAL!
THEN AGAIN...
WHAT ARE YOU WEARING!?
X-RAY SPECS. I JUST GOT 'EM IN THE MAIL.
YOU ARE SUCH A WEIRDO!
AT LEAST I'M NOT WEARING LEOPARD SKIN UNDERWEAR.
YOU'RE WEARING LEOPARD SKIN UNDERWEAR?!
I AM NOT WEARING LEOPARD SKIN UNDERWEAR!
X-RAY SPECS DON'T LIE.
HEY, MOM – PAIGE IS WEARING LEOPARD SKIN UNDERWEAR!
I AM NOT!
AMEND
PAIGE! WHAT ARE YOU DOING WITH LEOPARD SKIN UNDERWEAR?!
AAAAAAAAAAAAAAA!
THOSE THINGS DON'T REALLY WORK, DO THEY?
I THINK THEY WORK EXTREMELY WELL.

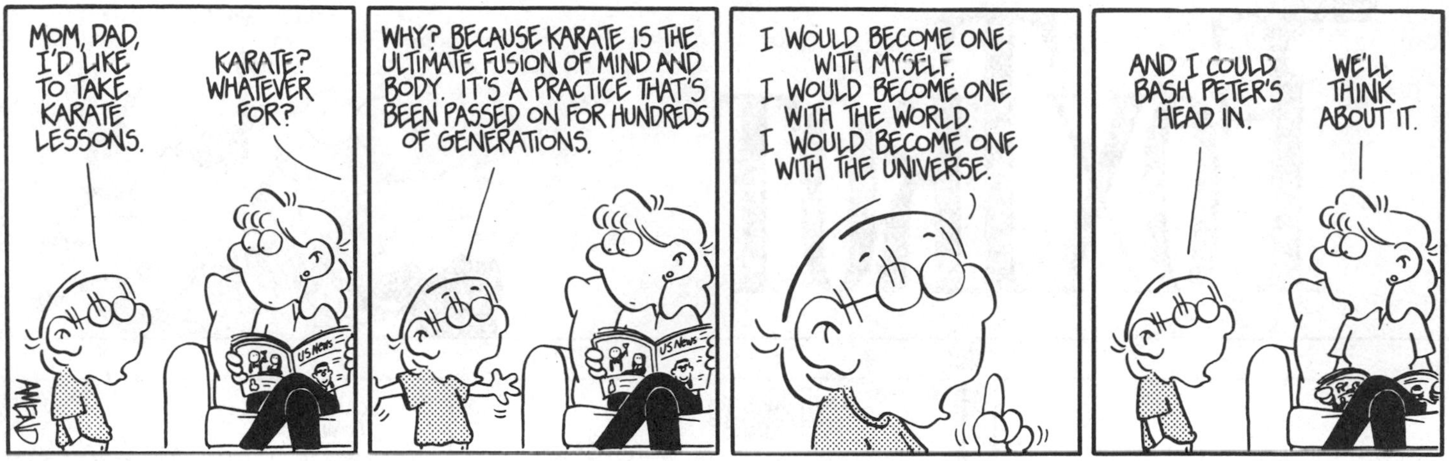
MOM, DAD, I'D LIKE TO TAKE KARATE LESSONS.
KARATE? WHATEVER FOR?
AMEND
US NEWS
WHY? BECAUSE KARATE IS THE ULTIMATE FUSION OF MIND AND BODY. IT'S A PRACTICE THAT'S BEEN PASSED ON FOR HUNDREDS OF GENERATIONS.
US NEWS
I WOULD BECOME ONE WITH MYSELF. I WOULD BECOME ONE WITH THE WORLD. I WOULD BECOME ONE WITH THE UNIVERSE.
AND I COULD BASH PETER'S HEAD IN.
WE'LL THINK ABOUT IT.

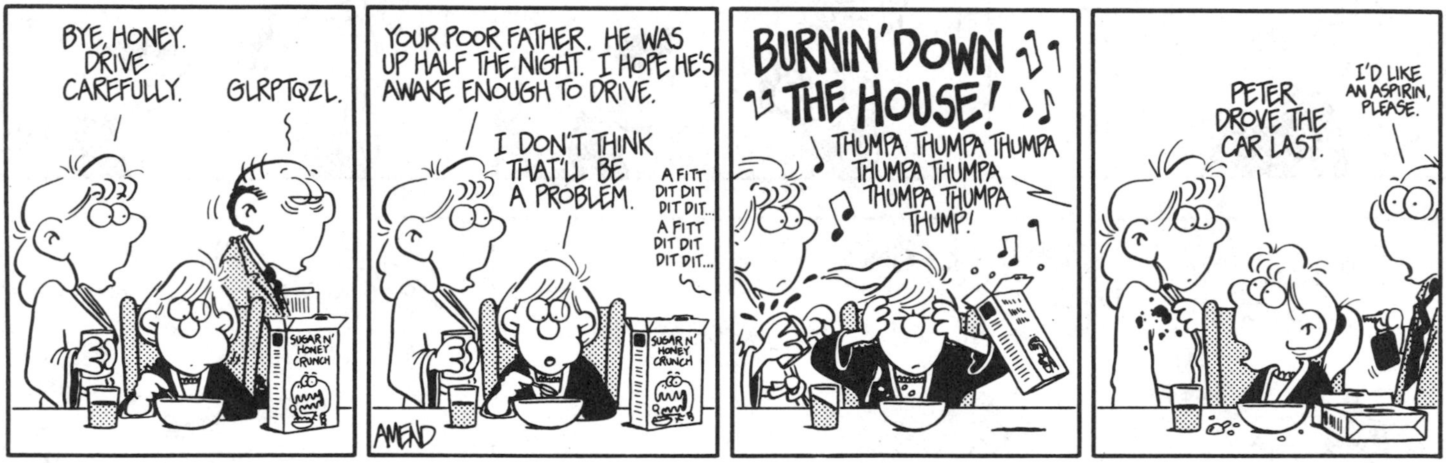
BYE, HONEY. DRIVE CAREFULLY.
GLRPTQZL.
SUGAR N' HONEY CRUNCH
YOUR POOR FATHER. HE WAS UP HALF THE NIGHT. I HOPE HE'S AWAKE ENOUGH TO DRIVE.
I DON'T THINK THAT'LL BE A PROBLEM.
A FITT DIT DIT DIT DIT... A FITT DIT DIT DIT DIT...
SUGAR N' HONEY CRUNCH
AMEND
BURNIN' DOWN THE HOUSE!
THUMPA THUMPA THUMPA THUMPA THUMPA THUMPA THUMPA THUMP!
PETER DROVE THE CAR LAST.
I'D LIKE AN ASPIRIN, PLEASE.

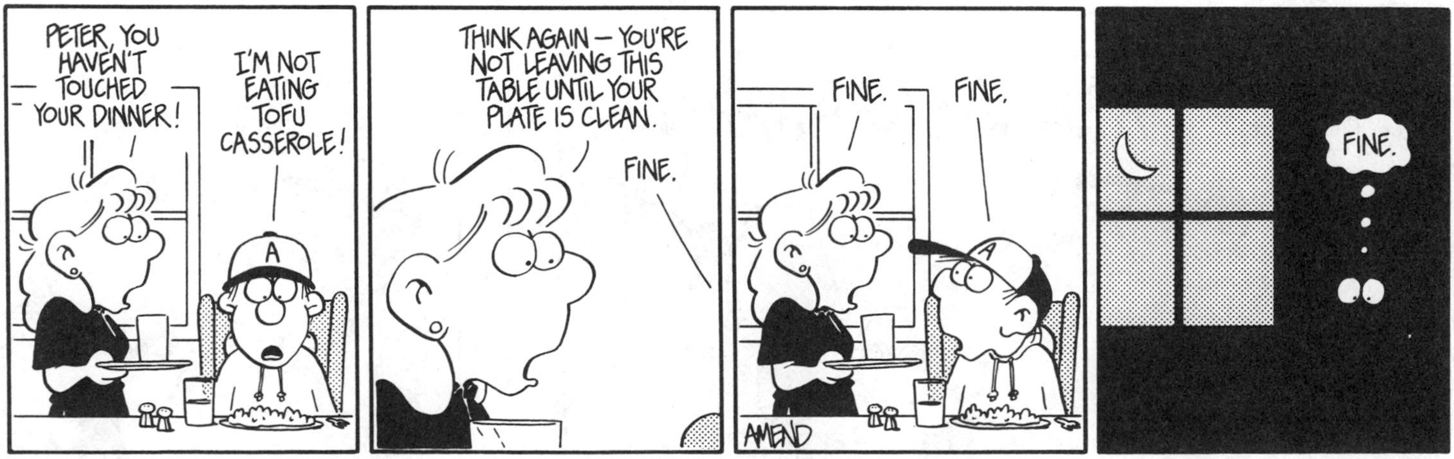
PETER, YOU HAVEN'T TOUCHED YOUR DINNER!
I'M NOT EATING TOFU CASSEROLE!
THINK AGAIN — YOU'RE NOT LEAVING THIS TABLE UNTIL YOUR PLATE IS CLEAN.
FINE.
FINE.
FINE.
AMEND
FINE.

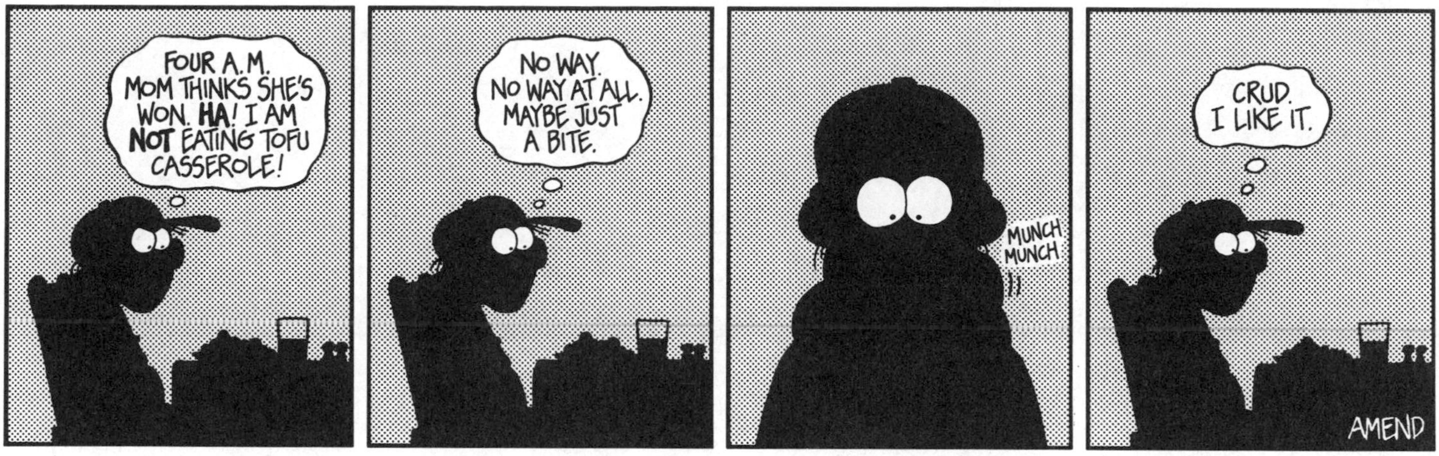
FOUR A.M. MOM THINKS SHE'S WON. HA! I AM NOT EATING TOFU CASSEROLE!
NO WAY. NO WAY AT ALL. MAYBE JUST A BITE.
MUNCH MUNCH
CRUD. I LIKE IT.
AMEND

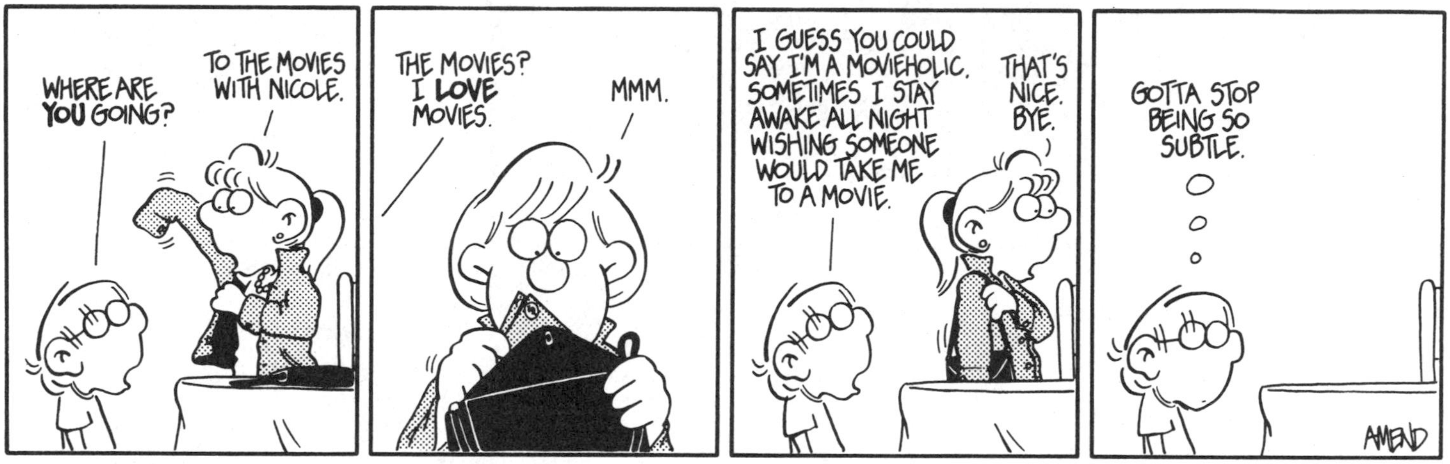
WHERE ARE YOU GOING?
TO THE MOVIES WITH NICOLE.
THE MOVIES? I LOVE MOVIES.
MMM.
I GUESS YOU COULD SAY I'M A MOVIEHOLIC. SOMETIMES I STAY AWAKE ALL NIGHT WISHING SOMEONE WOULD TAKE ME TO A MOVIE.
THAT'S NICE. BYE.
GOTTA STOP BEING SO SUBTLE.
AMEND

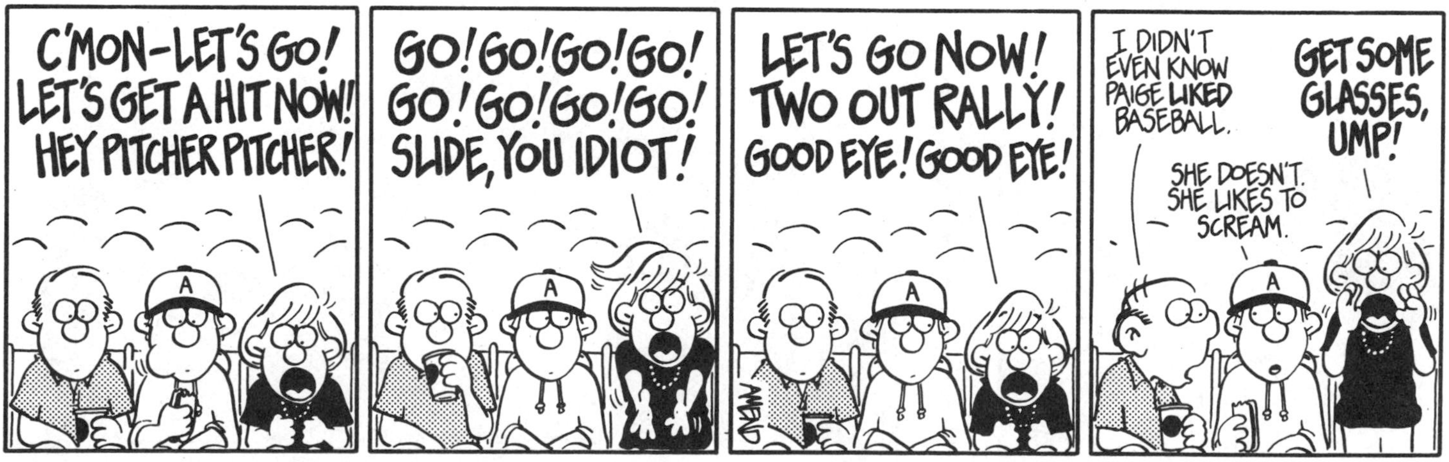
C'MON-LET'S GO! LET'S GET A HIT NOW! HEY PITCHER PITCHER!
GO! GO! GO! GO! GO! GO! GO! GO! SLIDE, YOU IDIOT!
LET'S GO NOW! TWO OUT RALLY! GOOD EYE! GOOD EYE!
I DIDN'T EVEN KNOW PAIGE LIKED BASEBALL.
SHE DOESN'T. SHE LIKES TO SCREAM.
GET SOME GLASSES, UMP!

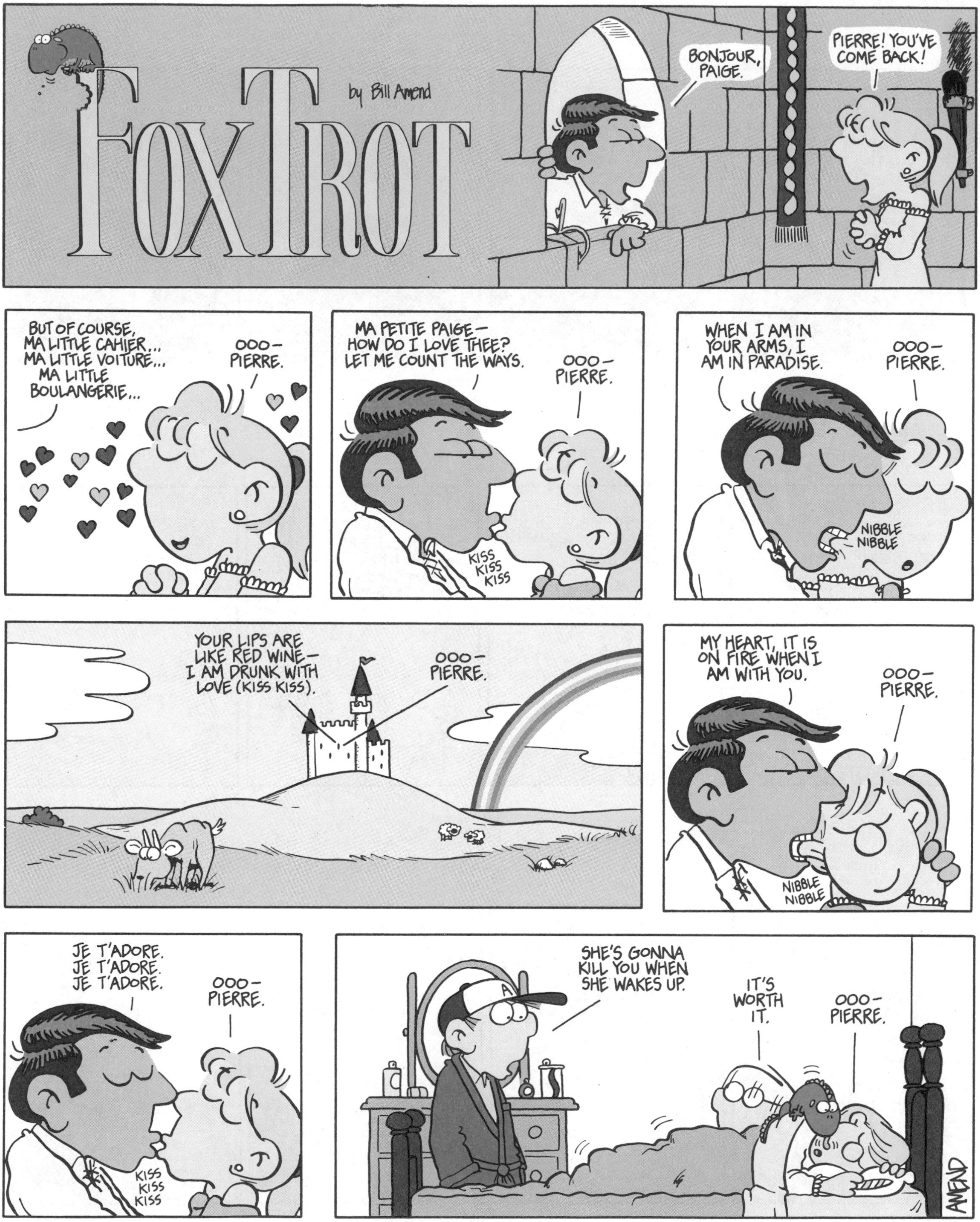
FoxTrot
by Bill Amend
BONJOUR, PAIGE.
PIERRE! YOU'VE COME BACK!
BUT OF COURSE, MA LITTLE CAHIER... MA LITTLE VOITURE... MA LITTLE BOULANGERIE...
OOO- PIERRE.
MA PETITE PAIGE— HOW DO I LOVE THEE? LET ME COUNT THE WAYS.
OOO- PIERRE.
KISS KISS KISS
WHEN I AM IN YOUR ARMS, I AM IN PARADISE.
OOO- PIERRE.
NIBBLE NIBBLE
YOUR LIPS ARE LIKE RED WINE— I AM DRUNK WITH LOVE (KISS KISS).
OOO- PIERRE.
MY HEART, IT IS ON FIRE WHEN I AM WITH YOU.
OOO- PIERRE.
NIBBLE NIBBLE
JE T'ADORE. JE T'ADORE. JE T'ADORE.
OOO- PIERRE.
KISS KISS KISS
SHE'S GONNA KILL YOU WHEN SHE WAKES UP.
IT'S WORTH IT.
OOO- PIERRE.
AMEND

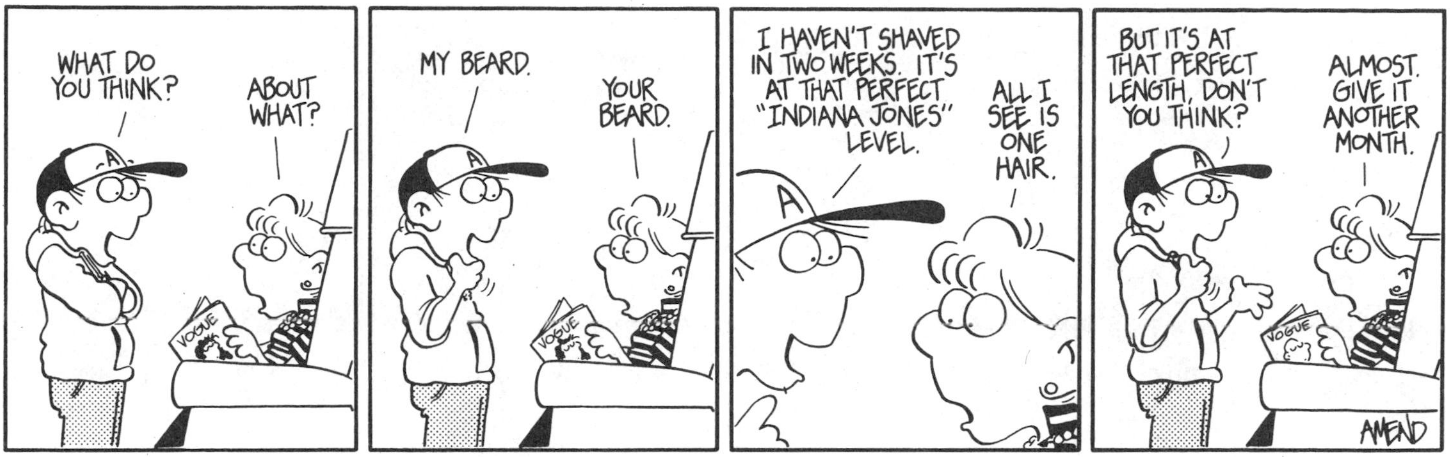
WHAT DO YOU THINK?
ABOUT WHAT?
MY BEARD.
YOUR BEARD.
I HAVEN'T SHAVED IN TWO WEEKS. IT'S AT THAT PERFECT "INDIANA JONES" LEVEL.
ALL I SEE IS ONE HAIR.
BUT IT'S AT THAT PERFECT LENGTH, DON'T YOU THINK?
ALMOST. GIVE IT ANOTHER MONTH.
VOGUE
AMEND

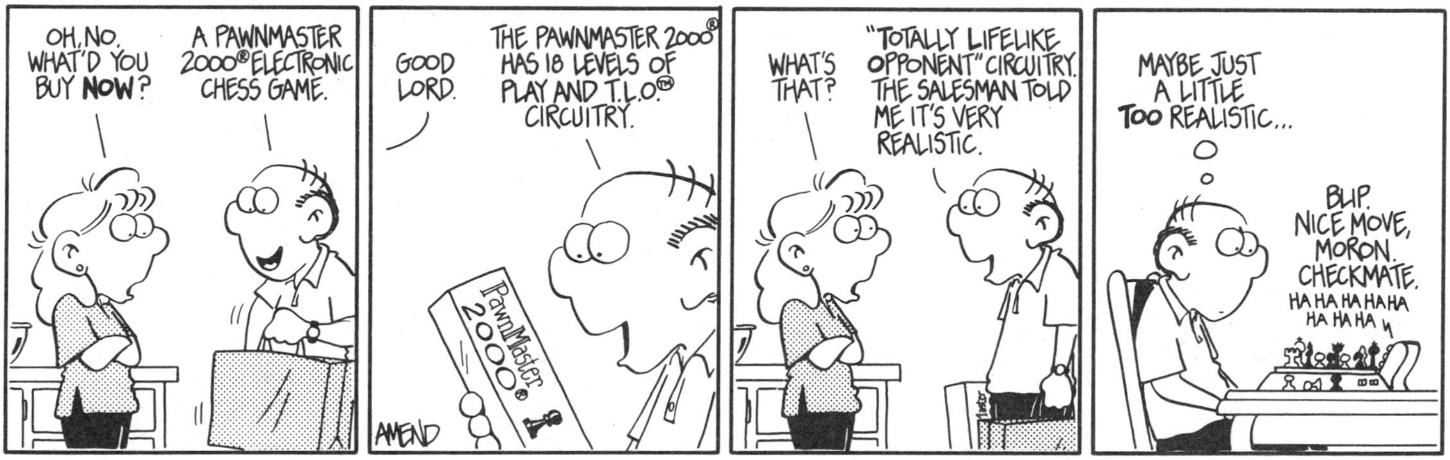
OH, NO. WHAT'D YOU BUY **NOW**?
A PAWNMASTER 2000® ELECTRONIC CHESS GAME.
GOOD LORD.
THE PAWNMASTER 2000® HAS 18 LEVELS OF PLAY AND T.L.O.™ CIRCUITRY.
PawnMaster 2000®
AMEND
WHAT'S THAT?
"TOTALLY LIFELIKE OPPONENT" CIRCUITRY. THE SALESMAN TOLD ME IT'S VERY REALISTIC.
MAYBE JUST A LITTLE **TOO** REALISTIC...
BLIP. NICE MOVE, MORON. CHECKMATE.
HA HA HA HA HA HA HA HA

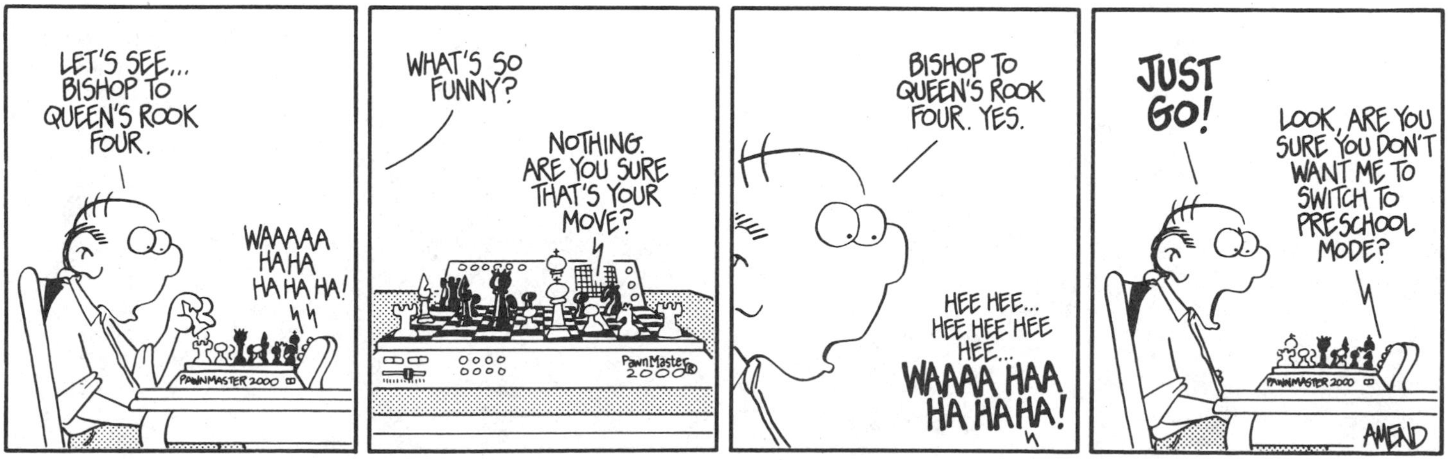
LET'S SEE... BISHOP TO QUEEN'S ROOK FOUR.
WAAAAA HA HA HA HA HA!
PAWNMASTER 2000
WHAT'S SO FUNNY?
NOTHING. ARE YOU SURE THAT'S YOUR MOVE?
PawnMaster 2000®
BISHOP TO QUEEN'S ROOK FOUR. YES.
HEE HEE... HEE HEE HEE HEE...
WAAAA HAA HA HA HA!
JUST GO!
LOOK, ARE YOU SURE YOU DON'T WANT ME TO SWITCH TO PRESCHOOL MODE?
PAWNMASTER 2000
AMEND

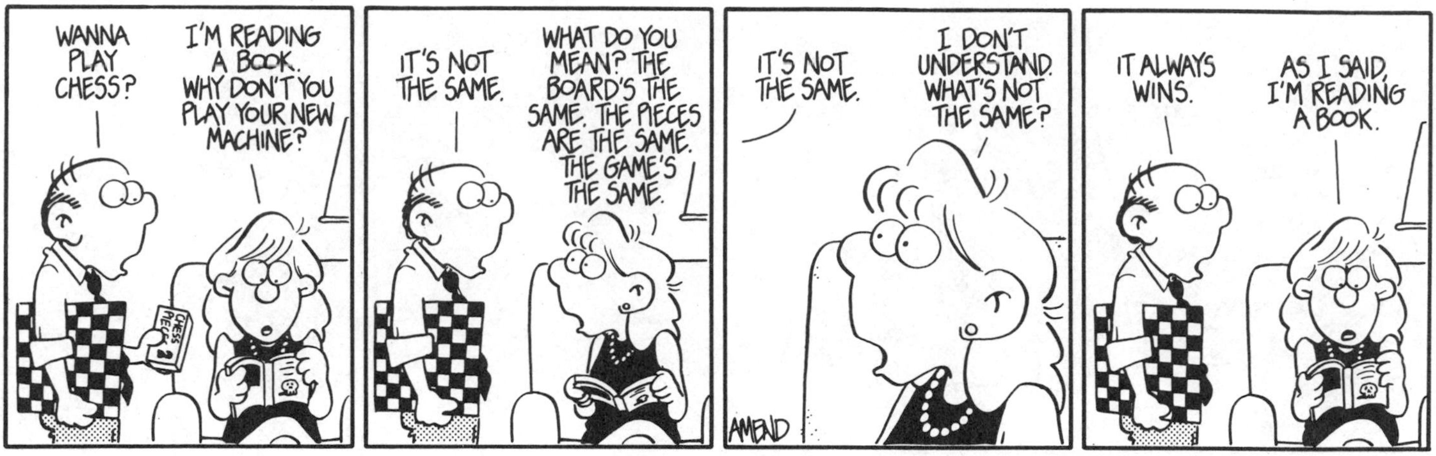
WANNA PLAY CHESS?
I'M READING A BOOK. WHY DON'T YOU PLAY YOUR NEW MACHINE?
CHESS PIECE 2
IT'S NOT THE SAME.
WHAT DO YOU MEAN? THE BOARD'S THE SAME. THE PIECES ARE THE SAME. THE GAME'S THE SAME.
IT'S NOT THE SAME.
I DON'T UNDERSTAND. WHAT'S NOT THE SAME?
AMEND
IT ALWAYS WINS.
AS I SAID, I'M READING A BOOK.

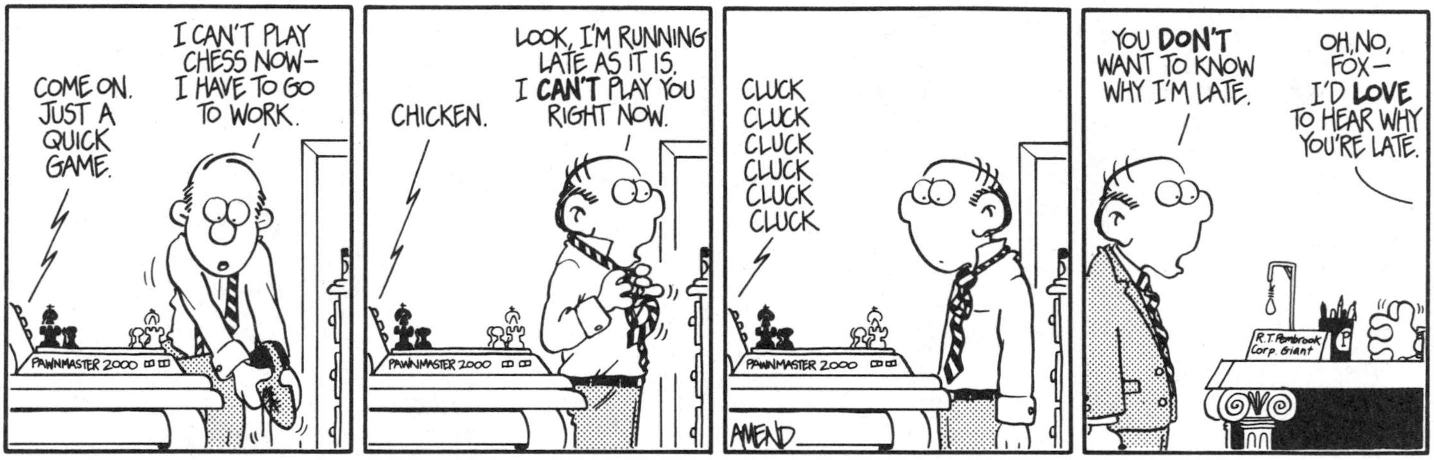
COME ON. JUST A QUICK GAME.
I CAN'T PLAY CHESS NOW– I HAVE TO GO TO WORK.
PAWNMASTER 2000
CHICKEN.
LOOK, I'M RUNNING LATE AS IT IS. I **CAN'T** PLAY YOU RIGHT NOW.
PAWNMASTER 2000
CLUCK CLUCK CLUCK CLUCK CLUCK CLUCK
PAWNMASTER 2000
AMEND
YOU **DON'T** WANT TO KNOW WHY I'M LATE.
OH, NO, FOX– I'D **LOVE** TO HEAR WHY YOU'RE LATE.
R.T. Pembrook Corp. Giant

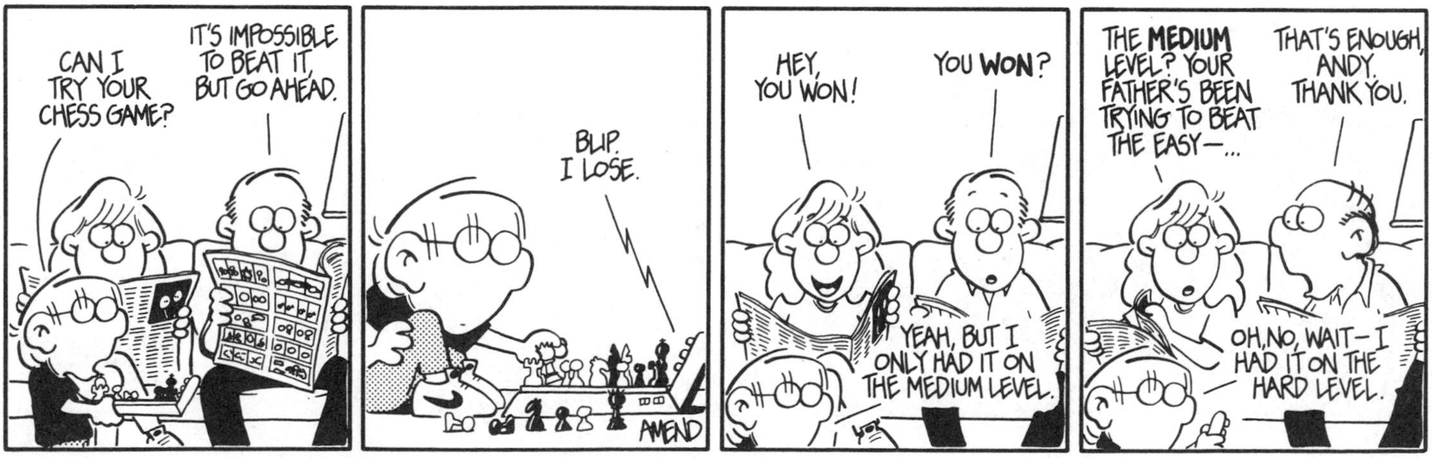
CAN I TRY YOUR CHESS GAME?
IT'S IMPOSSIBLE TO BEAT IT, BUT GO AHEAD.
BLIP. I LOSE.
AMEND
HEY, YOU WON!
YOU **WON**?
YEAH, BUT I ONLY HAD IT ON THE MEDIUM LEVEL.
THE **MEDIUM** LEVEL? YOUR FATHER'S BEEN TRYING TO BEAT THE EASY–...
THAT'S ENOUGH, ANDY. THANK YOU.
OH, NO, WAIT– I HAD IT ON THE HARD LEVEL.

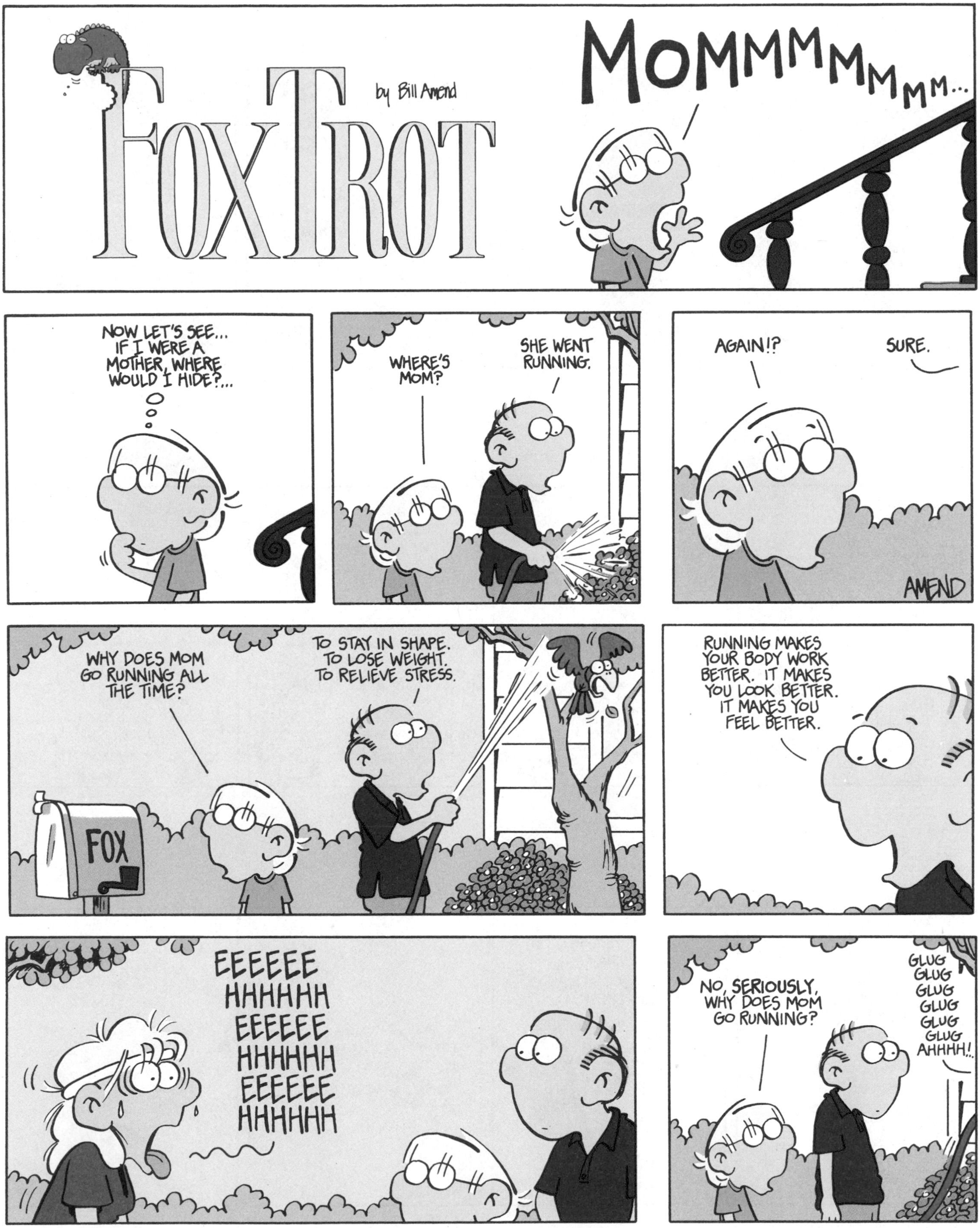
FoxTrot
by Bill Amend
MOMMMMMMMM...
NOW LET'S SEE... IF I WERE A MOTHER, WHERE WOULD I HIDE?...
WHERE'S MOM?
SHE WENT RUNNING.
AGAIN!?
SURE.
AMEND
WHY DOES MOM GO RUNNING ALL THE TIME?
TO STAY IN SHAPE. TO LOSE WEIGHT. TO RELIEVE STRESS.
FOX
RUNNING MAKES YOUR BODY WORK BETTER. IT MAKES YOU LOOK BETTER. IT MAKES YOU FEEL BETTER.
EEEEEE HHHHHH EEEEEE HHHHHH EEEEEE HHHHHH
NO, SERIOUSLY, WHY DOES MOM GO RUNNING?
GLUG GLUG GLUG GLUG GLUG GLUG AHHHH!!

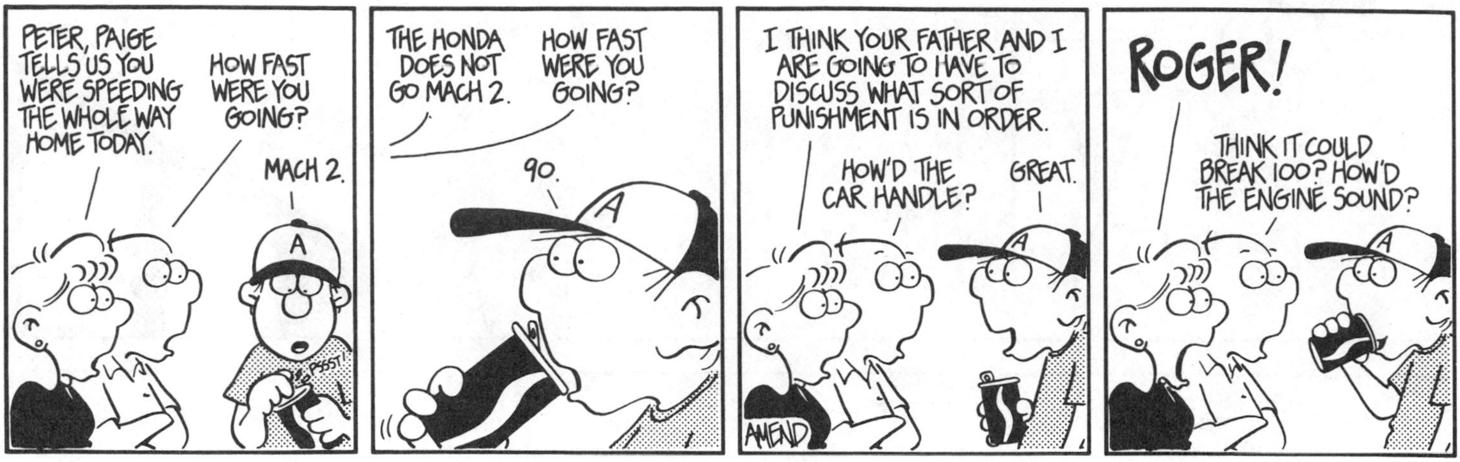
PETER, PAIGE TELLS US YOU WERE SPEEDING THE WHOLE WAY HOME TODAY.
HOW FAST WERE YOU GOING?
MACH 2.
PSSST!
THE HONDA DOES NOT GO MACH 2.
HOW FAST WERE YOU GOING?
90.
I THINK YOUR FATHER AND I ARE GOING TO HAVE TO DISCUSS WHAT SORT OF PUNISHMENT IS IN ORDER.
HOW'D THE CAR HANDLE?
GREAT.
AMEND
ROGER!
THINK IT COULD BREAK 100? HOW'D THE ENGINE SOUND?

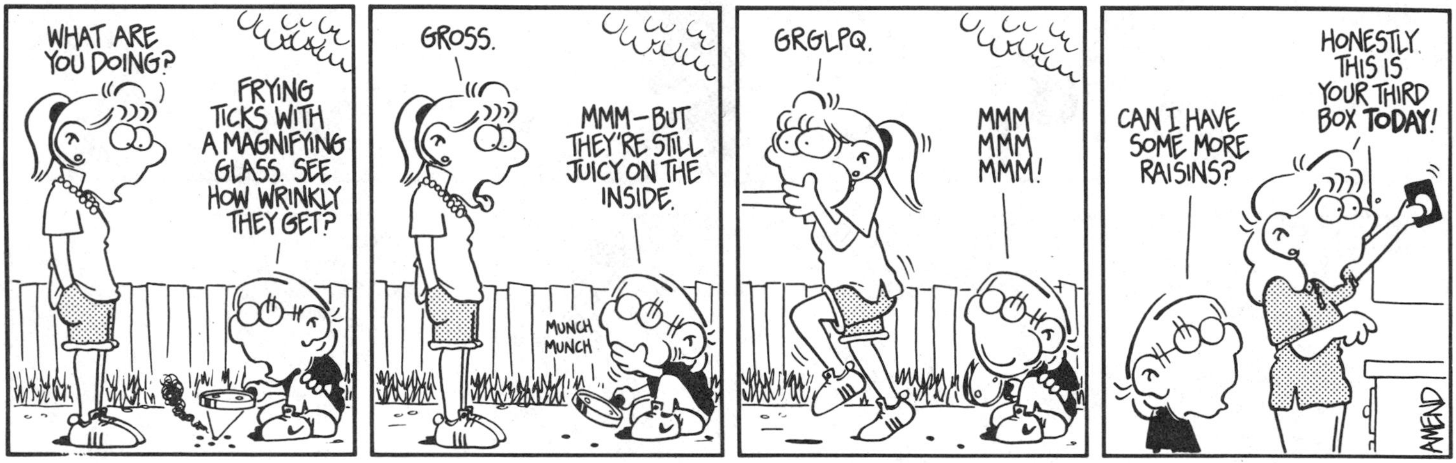
WHAT ARE YOU DOING?
FRYING TICKS WITH A MAGNIFYING GLASS. SEE HOW WRINKLY THEY GET?
GROSS.
MMM—BUT THEY'RE STILL JUICY ON THE INSIDE.
MUNCH MUNCH
GRGLPQ.
MMM MMM MMM!
CAN I HAVE SOME MORE RAISINS?
HONESTLY. THIS IS YOUR THIRD BOX TODAY!
AMEND

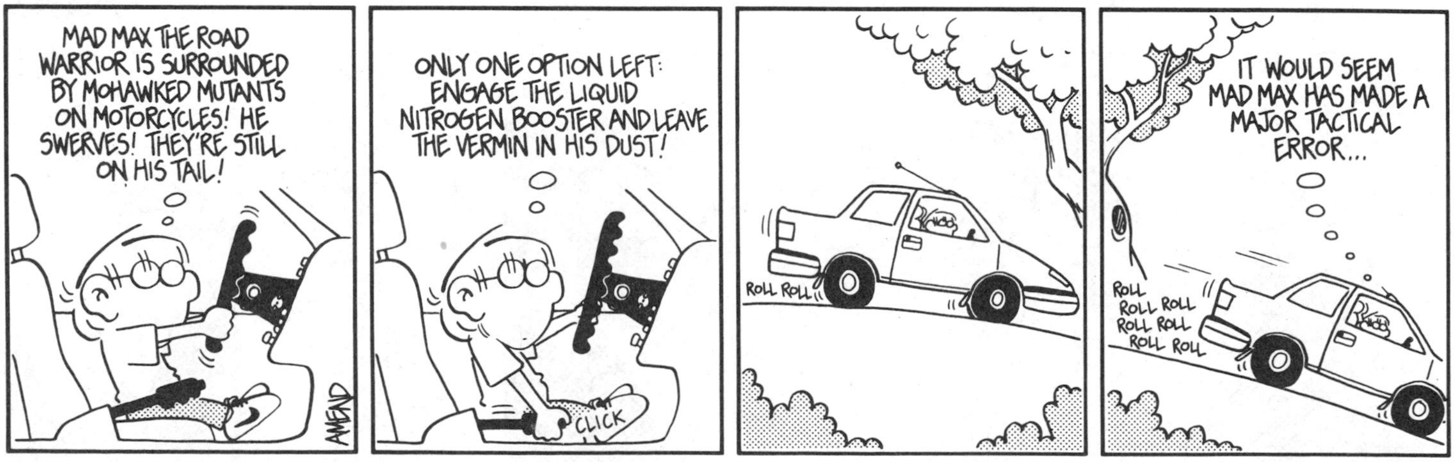
MAD MAX THE ROAD WARRIOR IS SURROUNDED BY MOHAWKED MUTANTS ON MOTORCYCLES! HE SWERVES! THEY'RE STILL ON HIS TAIL!
AMEND
ONLY ONE OPTION LEFT: ENGAGE THE LIQUID NITROGEN BOOSTER AND LEAVE THE VERMIN IN HIS DUST!
CLICK
ROLL ROLL
IT WOULD SEEM MAD MAX HAS MADE A MAJOR TACTICAL ERROR...
ROLL ROLL ROLL ROLL ROLL ROLL ROLL

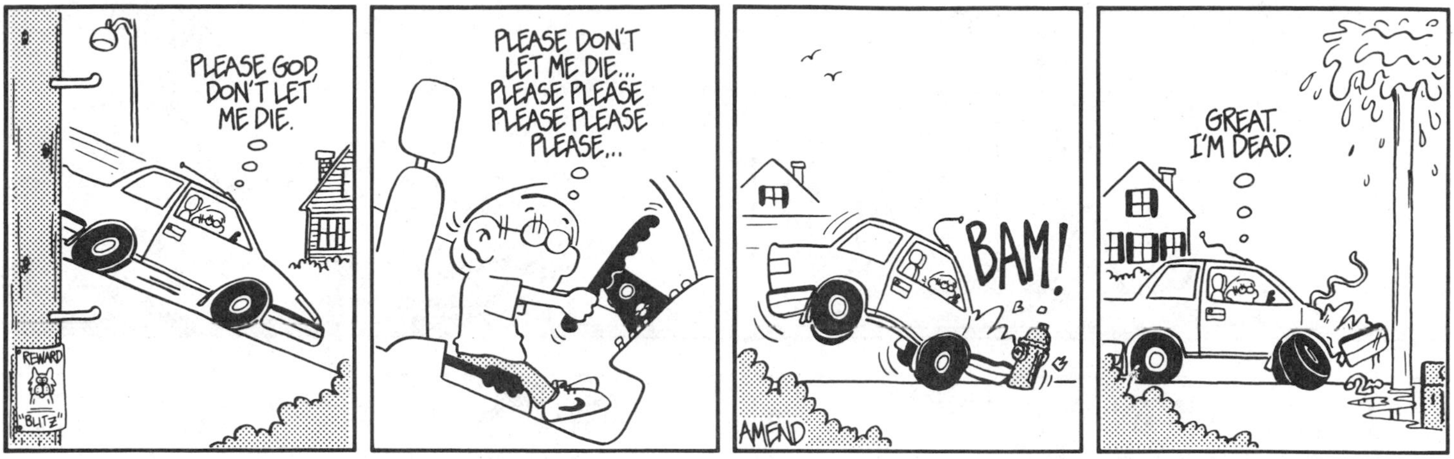
PLEASE GOD DON'T LET ME DIE.
REWARD "BLITZ"
PLEASE DON'T LET ME DIE... PLEASE PLEASE PLEASE PLEASE PLEASE...
BAM!
AMEND
GREAT. I'M DEAD.

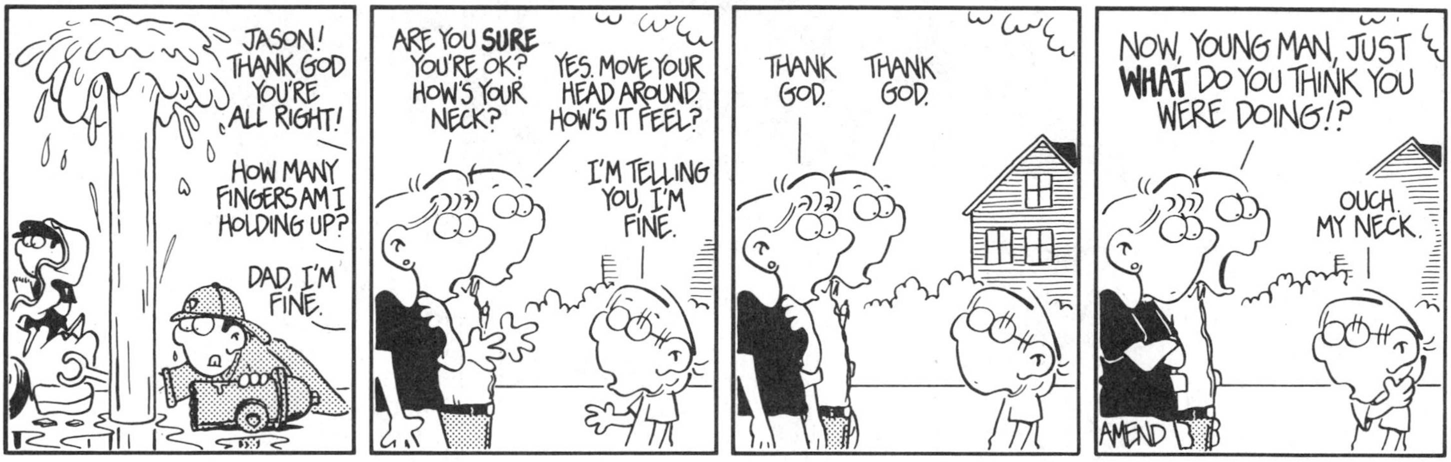
JASON! THANK GOD YOU'RE ALL RIGHT!
HOW MANY FINGERS AM I HOLDING UP?
DAD, I'M FINE.
ARE YOU SURE YOU'RE OK? HOW'S YOUR NECK?
YES. MOVE YOUR HEAD AROUND. HOW'S IT FEEL?
I'M TELLING YOU, I'M FINE.
THANK GOD.
THANK GOD.
NOW, YOUNG MAN, JUST WHAT DO YOU THINK YOU WERE DOING!?
OUCH. MY NECK.
AMEND

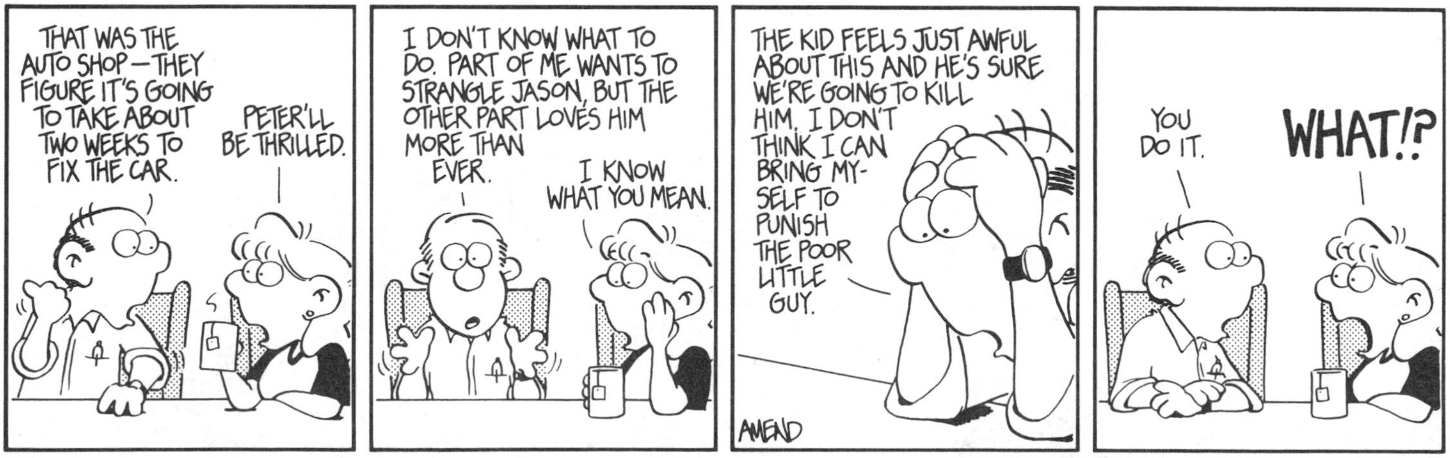
THAT WAS THE AUTO SHOP—THEY FIGURE IT'S GOING TO TAKE ABOUT TWO WEEKS TO FIX THE CAR.
PETER'LL BE THRILLED.
I DON'T KNOW WHAT TO DO. PART OF ME WANTS TO STRANGLE JASON, BUT THE OTHER PART LOVES HIM MORE THAN EVER.
I KNOW WHAT YOU MEAN.
THE KID FEELS JUST AWFUL ABOUT THIS AND HE'S SURE WE'RE GOING TO KILL HIM. I DON'T THINK I CAN BRING MYSELF TO PUNISH THE POOR LITTLE GUY.
AMEND
YOU DO IT.
WHAT!?

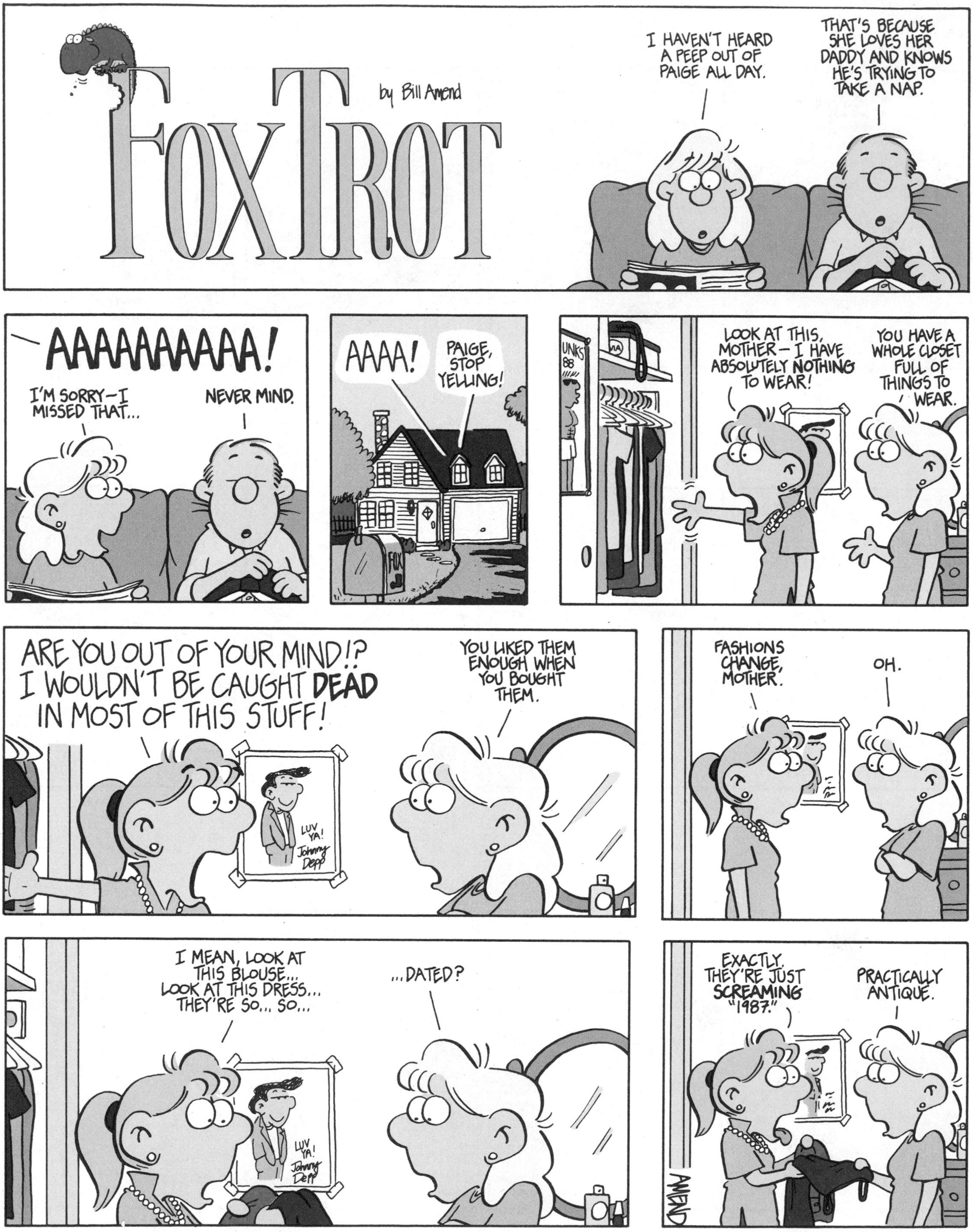
FOXTROT
by Bill Amend
I HAVEN'T HEARD A PEEP OUT OF PAIGE ALL DAY.
THAT'S BECAUSE SHE LOVES HER DADDY AND KNOWS HE'S TRYING TO TAKE A NAP.
AAAAAAAAAA!
I'M SORRY—I MISSED THAT...
NEVER MIND.
AAAA!
PAIGE, STOP YELLING!
FOX
LOOK AT THIS, MOTHER—I HAVE ABSOLUTELY NOTHING TO WEAR!
YOU HAVE A WHOLE CLOSET FULL OF THINGS TO WEAR.
ARE YOU OUT OF YOUR MIND!? I WOULDN'T BE CAUGHT DEAD IN MOST OF THIS STUFF!
LUV YA! Johnny Depp
YOU LIKED THEM ENOUGH WHEN YOU BOUGHT THEM.
FASHIONS CHANGE, MOTHER.
OH.
I MEAN, LOOK AT THIS BLOUSE... LOOK AT THIS DRESS... THEY'RE SO... SO...
LUV YA! Johnny Depp
...DATED?
EXACTLY. THEY'RE JUST SCREAMING "1987."
PRACTICALLY ANTIQUE.
AMEND

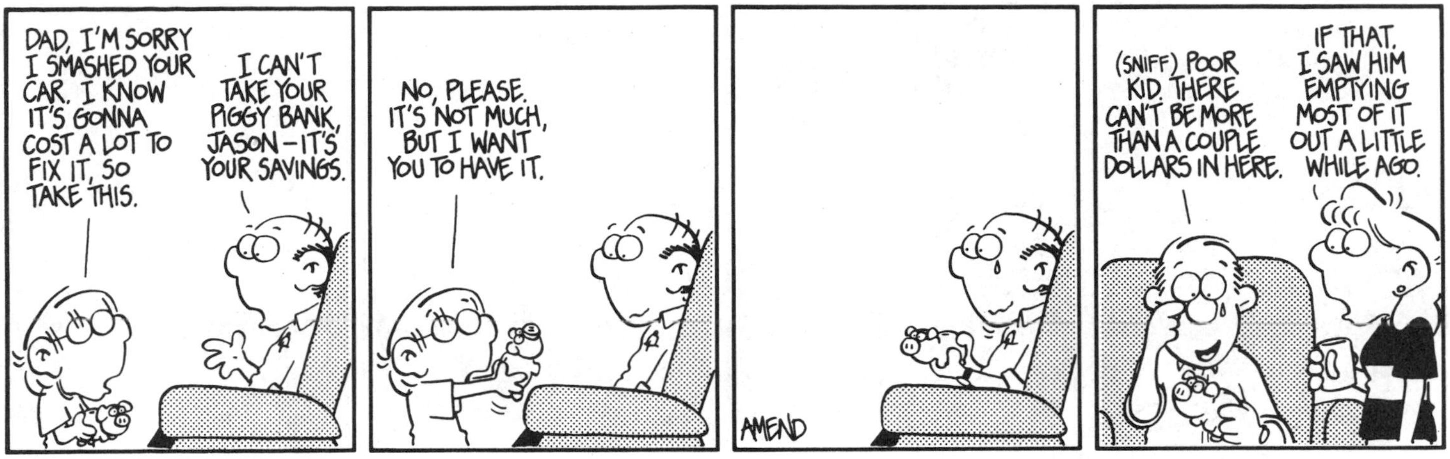
DAD, I'M SORRY I SMASHED YOUR CAR. I KNOW IT'S GONNA COST A LOT TO FIX IT, SO TAKE THIS.
I CAN'T TAKE YOUR PIGGY BANK, JASON – IT'S YOUR SAVINGS.
NO, PLEASE. IT'S NOT MUCH, BUT I WANT YOU TO HAVE IT.
AMEND
(SNIFF) POOR KID. THERE CAN'T BE MORE THAN A COUPLE DOLLARS IN HERE.
IF THAT. I SAW HIM EMPTYING MOST OF IT OUT A LITTLE WHILE AGO.

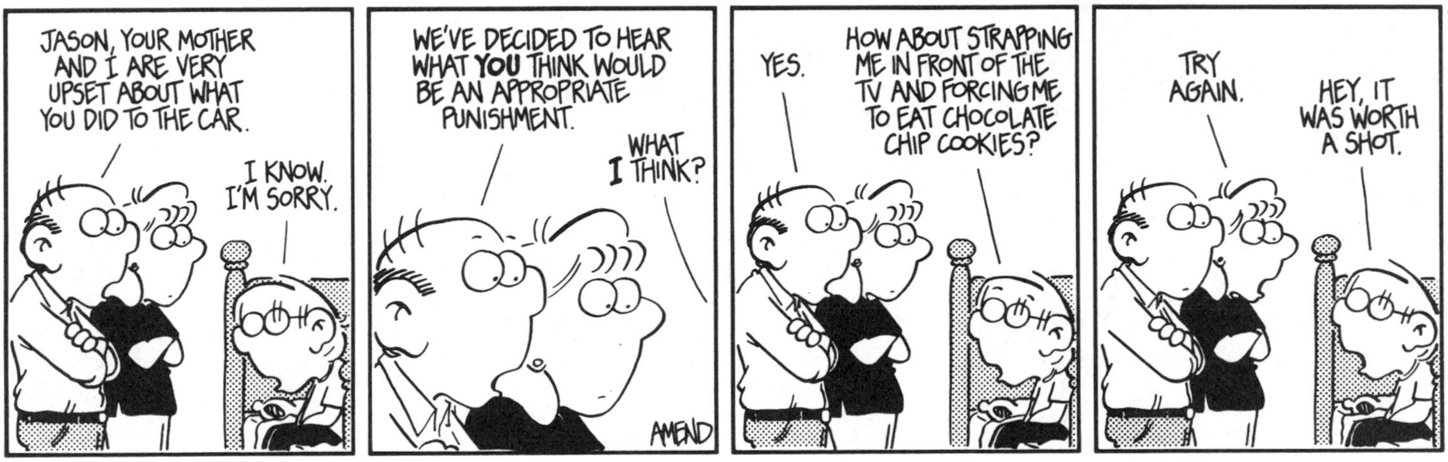
JASON, YOUR MOTHER AND I ARE VERY UPSET ABOUT WHAT YOU DID TO THE CAR.
I KNOW. I'M SORRY.
WE'VE DECIDED TO HEAR WHAT **YOU** THINK WOULD BE AN APPROPRIATE PUNISHMENT.
WHAT **I** THINK?
AMEND
YES.
HOW ABOUT STRAPPING ME IN FRONT OF THE TV AND FORCING ME TO EAT CHOCOLATE CHIP COOKIES?
TRY AGAIN.
HEY, IT WAS WORTH A SHOT.

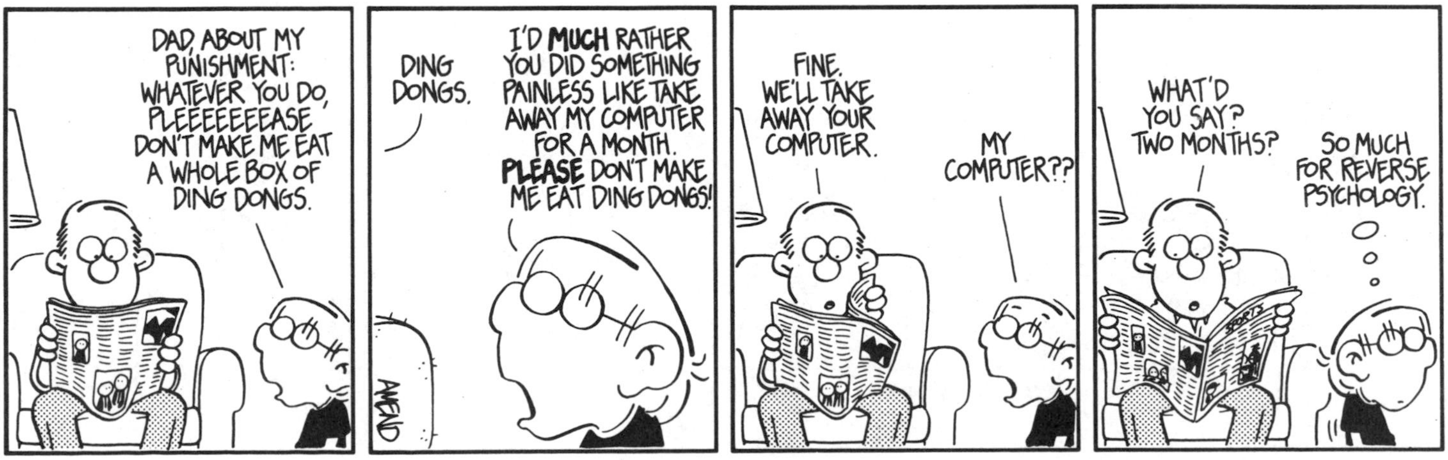
DAD, ABOUT MY PUNISHMENT: WHATEVER YOU DO, PLEEEEEEEASE DON'T MAKE ME EAT A WHOLE BOX OF DING DONGS.
DING DONGS.
I'D **MUCH** RATHER YOU DID SOMETHING PAINLESS LIKE TAKE AWAY MY COMPUTER FOR A MONTH. **PLEASE** DON'T MAKE ME EAT DING DONGS!
AMEND
FINE. WE'LL TAKE AWAY YOUR COMPUTER.
MY COMPUTER??
WHAT'D YOU SAY? TWO MONTHS?
SO MUCH FOR REVERSE PSYCHOLOGY.

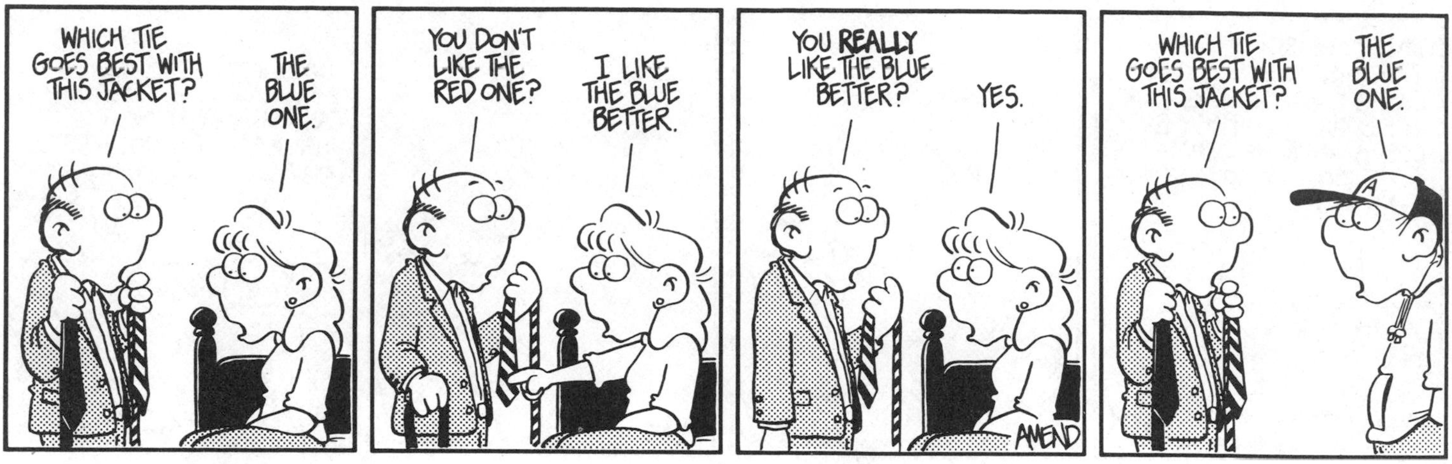
WHICH TIE GOES BEST WITH THIS JACKET?
THE BLUE ONE.
YOU DON'T LIKE THE RED ONE?
I LIKE THE BLUE BETTER.
YOU REALLY LIKE THE BLUE BETTER?
YES.
AMEND
WHICH TIE GOES BEST WITH THIS JACKET?
THE BLUE ONE.

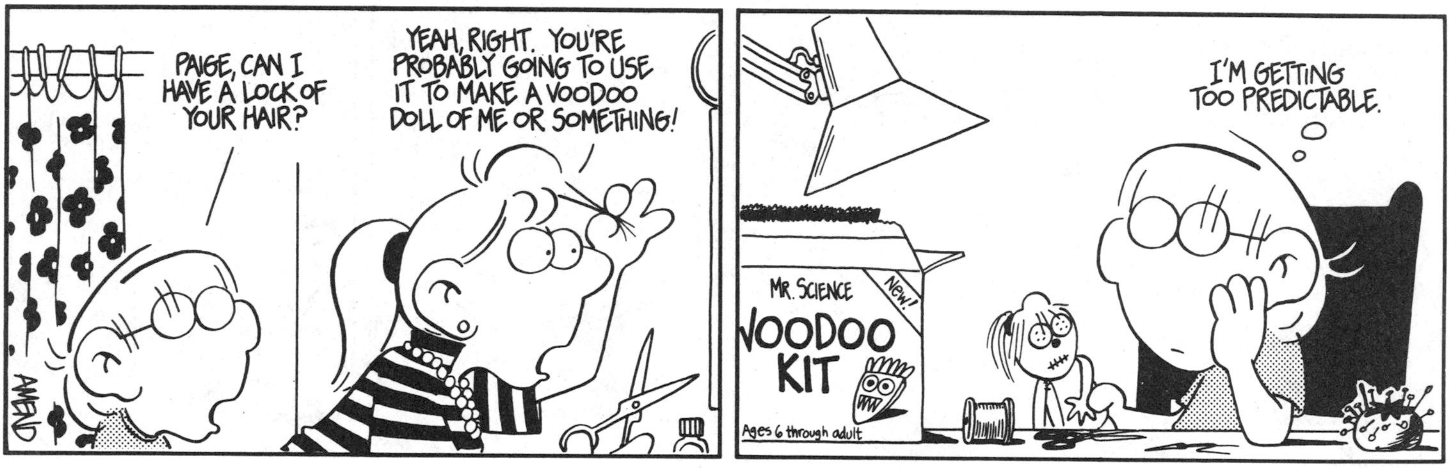
PAIGE, CAN I HAVE A LOCK OF YOUR HAIR?
YEAH, RIGHT. YOU'RE PROBABLY GOING TO USE IT TO MAKE A VOODOO DOLL OF ME OR SOMETHING!
AMEND
I'M GETTING TOO PREDICTABLE.
MR. SCIENCE
New!
VOODOO KIT
Ages 6 through adult

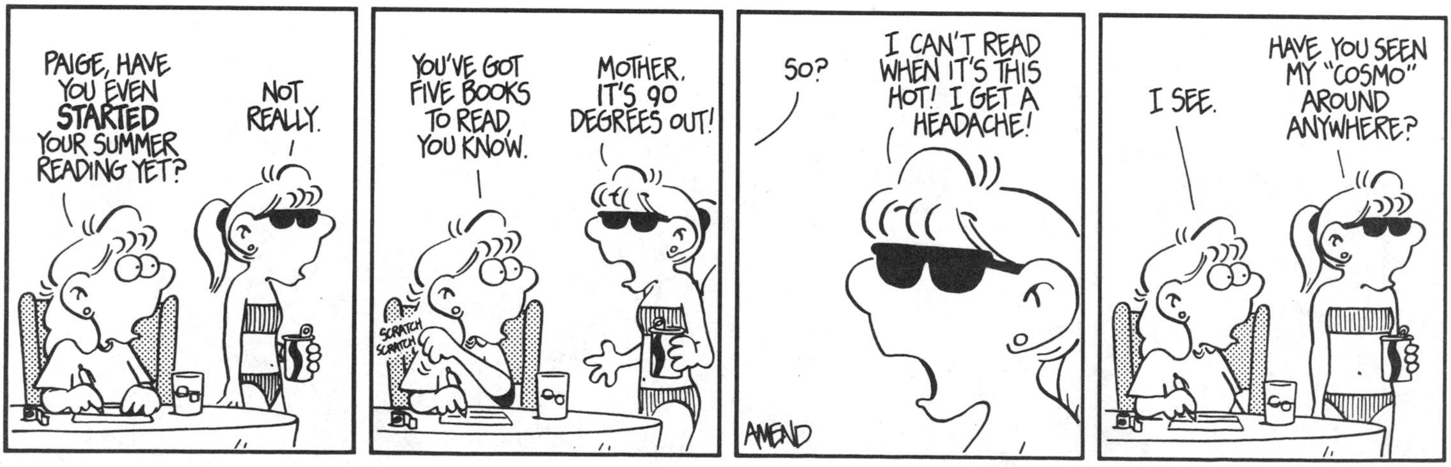
PAIGE, HAVE YOU EVEN STARTED YOUR SUMMER READING YET?
NOT REALLY.
YOU'VE GOT FIVE BOOKS TO READ, YOU KNOW.
MOTHER, IT'S 90 DEGREES OUT!
SCRATCH SCRATCH
SO?
I CAN'T READ WHEN IT'S THIS HOT! I GET A HEADACHE!
AMEND
I SEE.
HAVE YOU SEEN MY "COSMO" AROUND ANYWHERE?

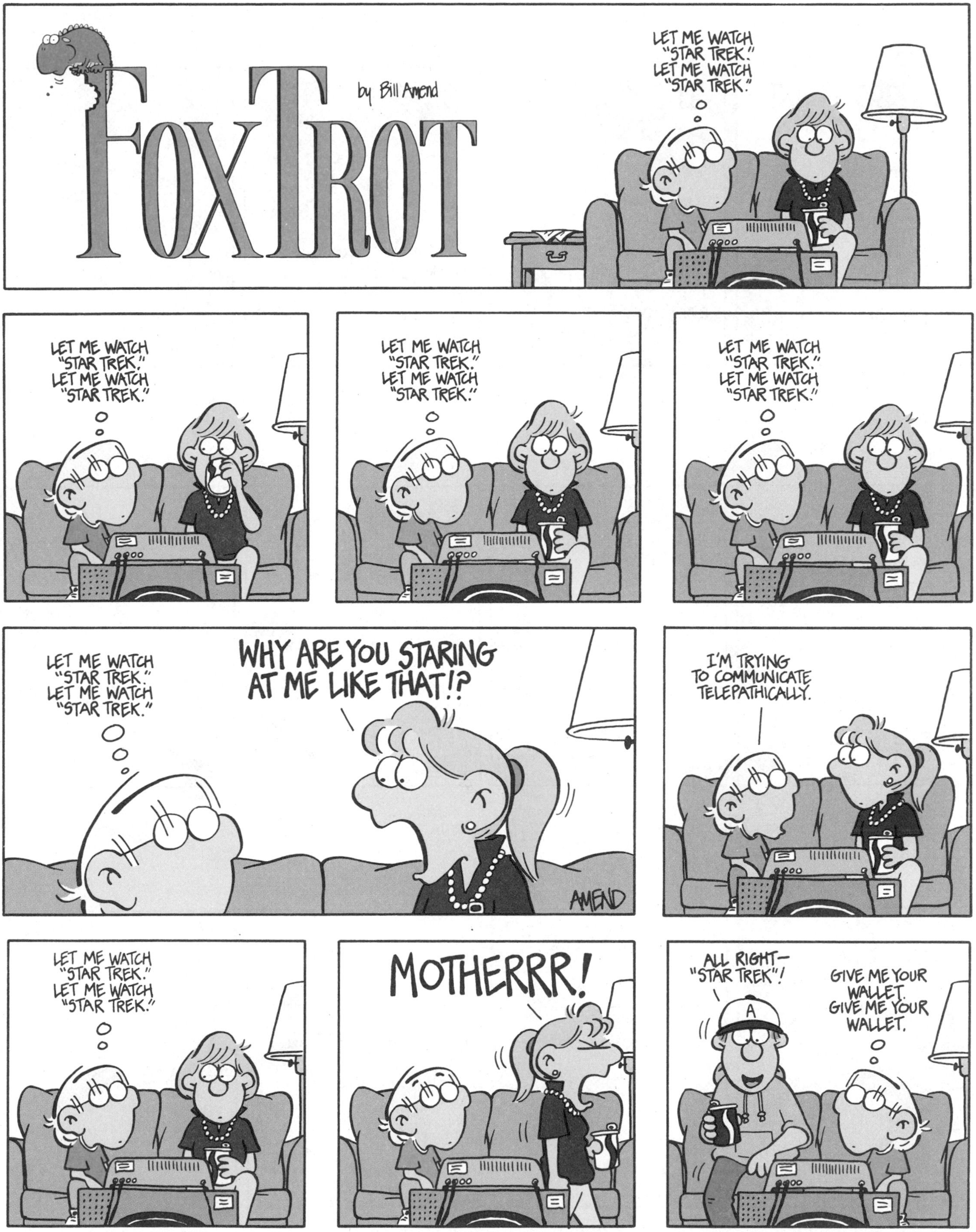
FoxTrot
by Bill Amend
LET ME WATCH "STAR TREK." LET ME WATCH "STAR TREK."
LET ME WATCH "STAR TREK." LET ME WATCH "STAR TREK."
LET ME WATCH "STAR TREK." LET ME WATCH "STAR TREK."
LET ME WATCH "STAR TREK." LET ME WATCH "STAR TREK."
LET ME WATCH "STAR TREK." LET ME WATCH "STAR TREK."
WHY ARE YOU STARING AT ME LIKE THAT!?
AMEND
I'M TRYING TO COMMUNICATE TELEPATHICALLY.
LET ME WATCH "STAR TREK." LET ME WATCH "STAR TREK."
MOTHERRR!
ALL RIGHT— "STAR TREK"!
GIVE ME YOUR WALLET. GIVE ME YOUR WALLET.

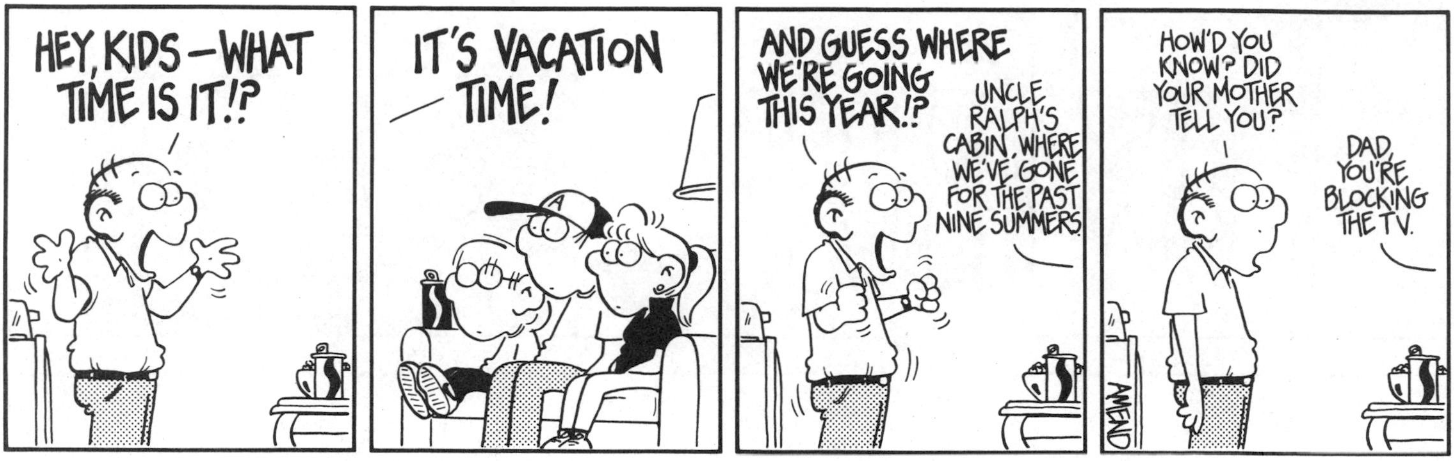
HEY, KIDS—WHAT TIME IS IT!?
IT'S VACATION TIME!
AND GUESS WHERE WE'RE GOING THIS YEAR!?
UNCLE RALPH'S CABIN, WHERE WE'VE GONE FOR THE PAST NINE SUMMERS.
HOW'D YOU KNOW? DID YOUR MOTHER TELL YOU?
DAD, YOU'RE BLOCKING THE T.V.
AMEND

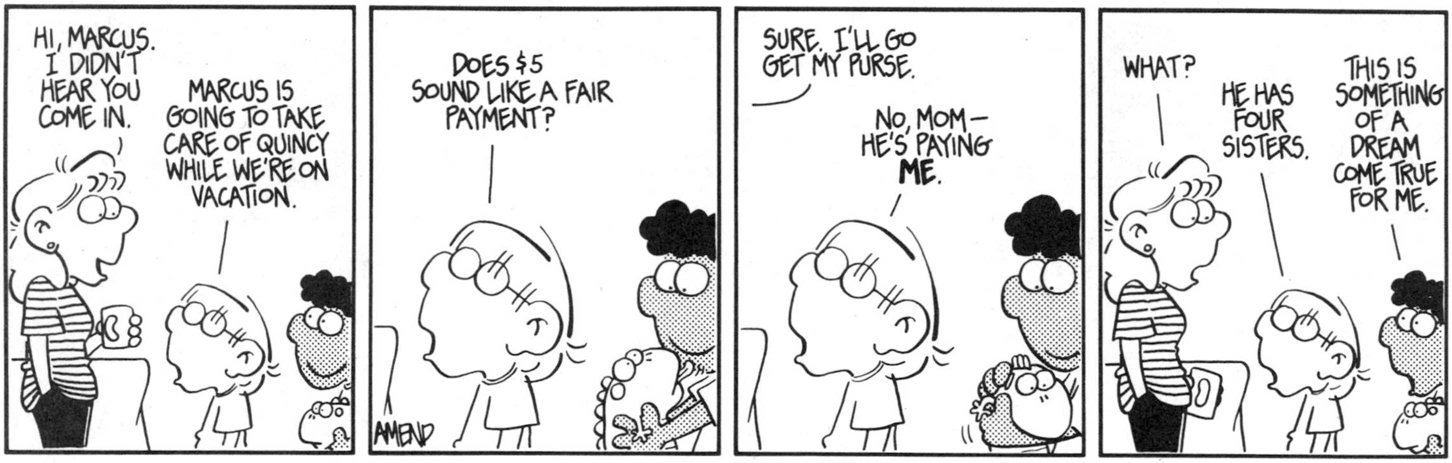
HI, MARCUS. I DIDN'T HEAR YOU COME IN.
MARCUS IS GOING TO TAKE CARE OF QUINCY WHILE WE'RE ON VACATION.
DOES $5 SOUND LIKE A FAIR PAYMENT?
AMEND
SURE. I'LL GO GET MY PURSE.
NO, MOM—HE'S PAYING **ME**.
WHAT?
HE HAS FOUR SISTERS.
THIS IS SOMETHING OF A DREAM COME TRUE FOR ME.

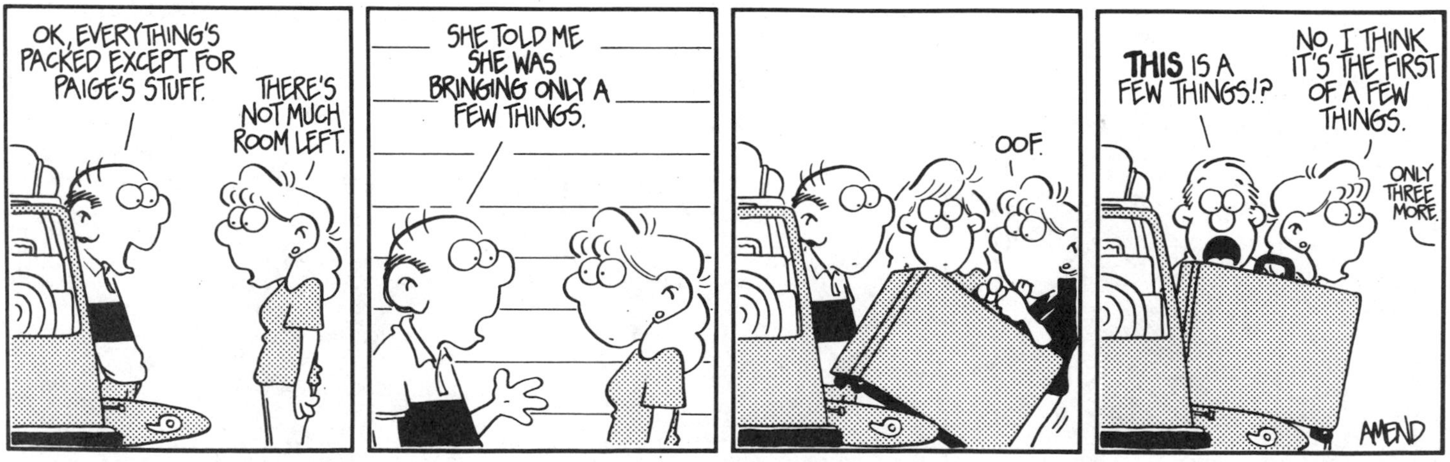
OK, EVERYTHING'S PACKED EXCEPT FOR PAIGE'S STUFF.
THERE'S NOT MUCH ROOM LEFT.
SHE TOLD ME SHE WAS BRINGING ONLY A FEW THINGS.
OOF.
THIS IS A FEW THINGS!?
NO, I THINK IT'S THE FIRST OF A FEW THINGS.
ONLY THREE MORE.
AMEND

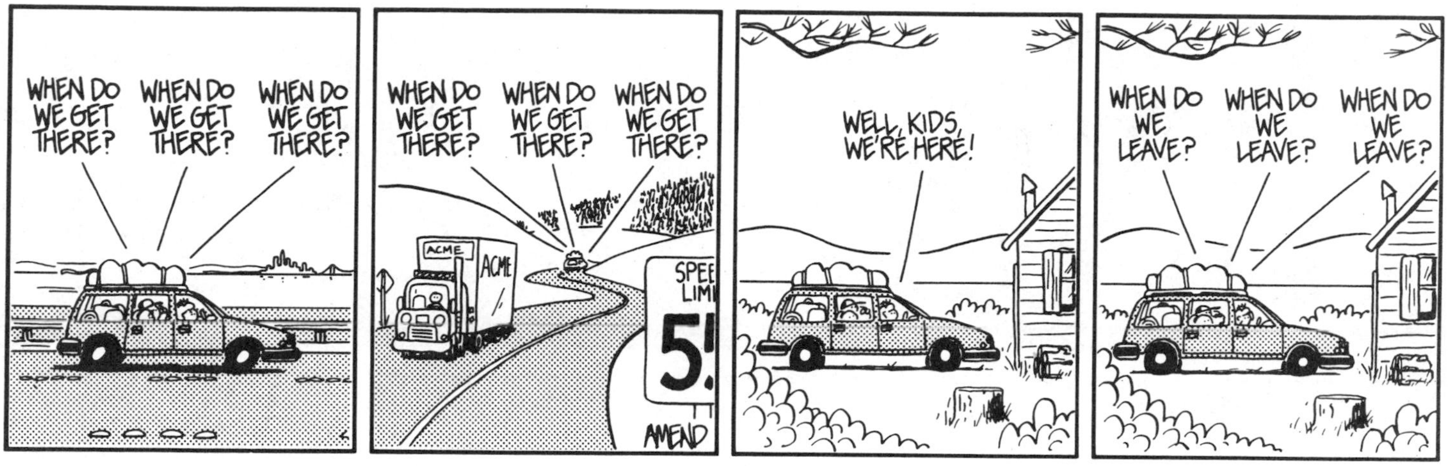
WHEN DO WE GET THERE?
WHEN DO WE GET THERE?
WHEN DO WE GET THERE?
WHEN DO WE GET THERE?
WHEN DO WE GET THERE?
WHEN DO WE GET THERE?
ACME
ACME
AMEND
WELL, KIDS, WE'RE HERE!
WHEN DO WE LEAVE?
WHEN DO WE LEAVE?
WHEN DO WE LEAVE?

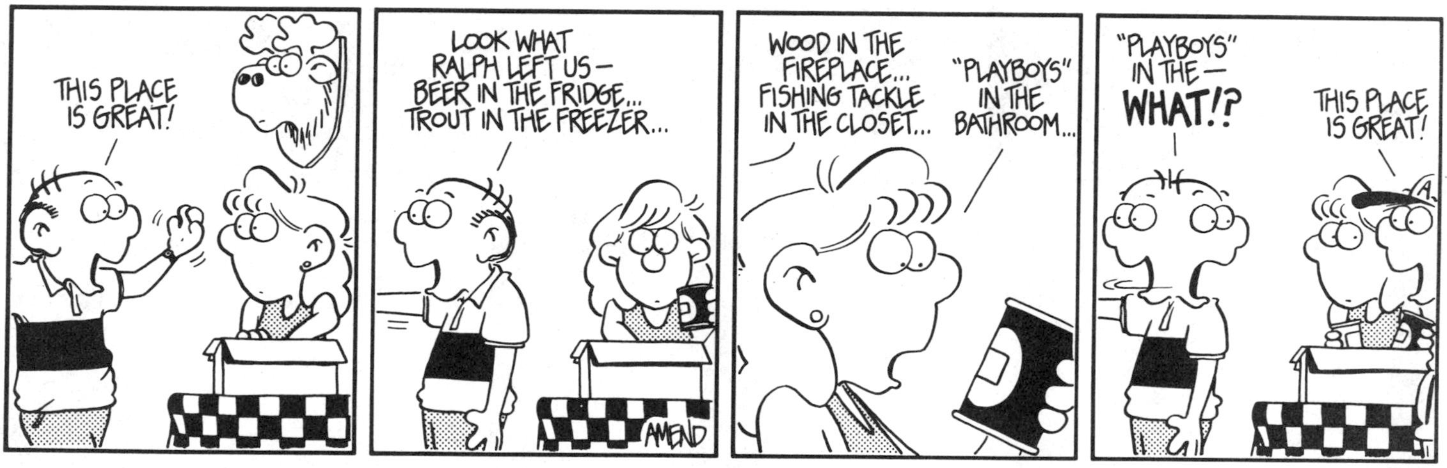
THIS PLACE IS GREAT!
LOOK WHAT RALPH LEFT US— BEER IN THE FRIDGE... TROUT IN THE FREEZER...
AMEND
WOOD IN THE FIREPLACE... FISHING TACKLE IN THE CLOSET...
"PLAYBOYS" IN THE BATHROOM...
"PLAYBOYS" IN THE— WHAT!?
THIS PLACE IS GREAT!

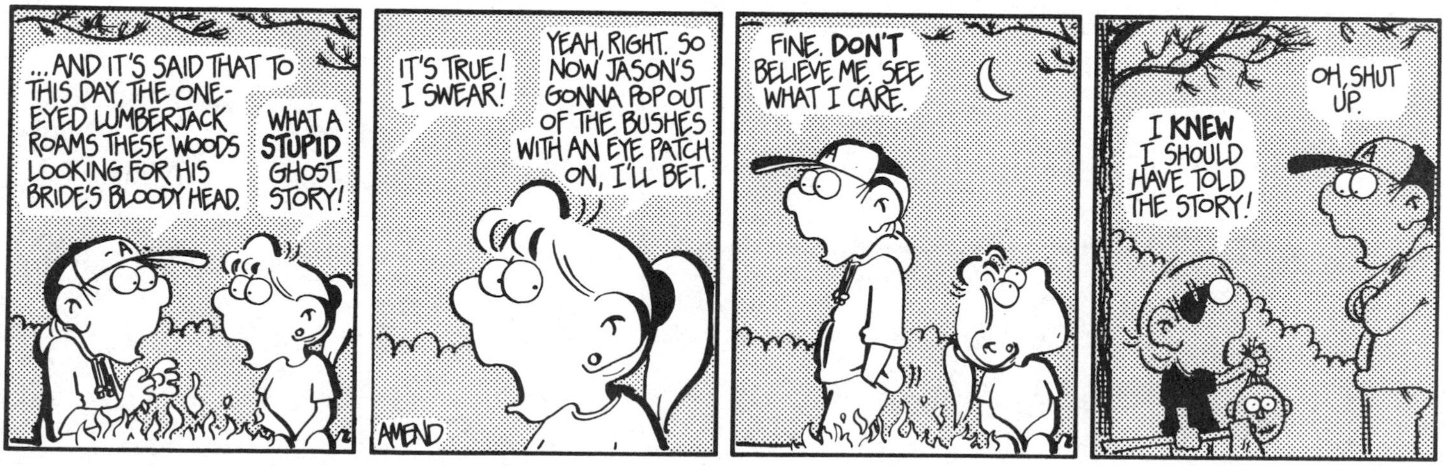
...AND IT'S SAID THAT TO THIS DAY, THE ONE-EYED LUMBERJACK ROAMS THESE WOODS LOOKING FOR HIS BRIDE'S BLOODY HEAD.
WHAT A STUPID GHOST STORY!
IT'S TRUE! I SWEAR!
YEAH, RIGHT. SO NOW JASON'S GONNA POP OUT OF THE BUSHES WITH AN EYE PATCH ON, I'LL BET.
AMEND
FINE. DON'T BELIEVE ME. SEE WHAT I CARE.
I KNEW I SHOULD HAVE TOLD THE STORY!
OH, SHUT UP.

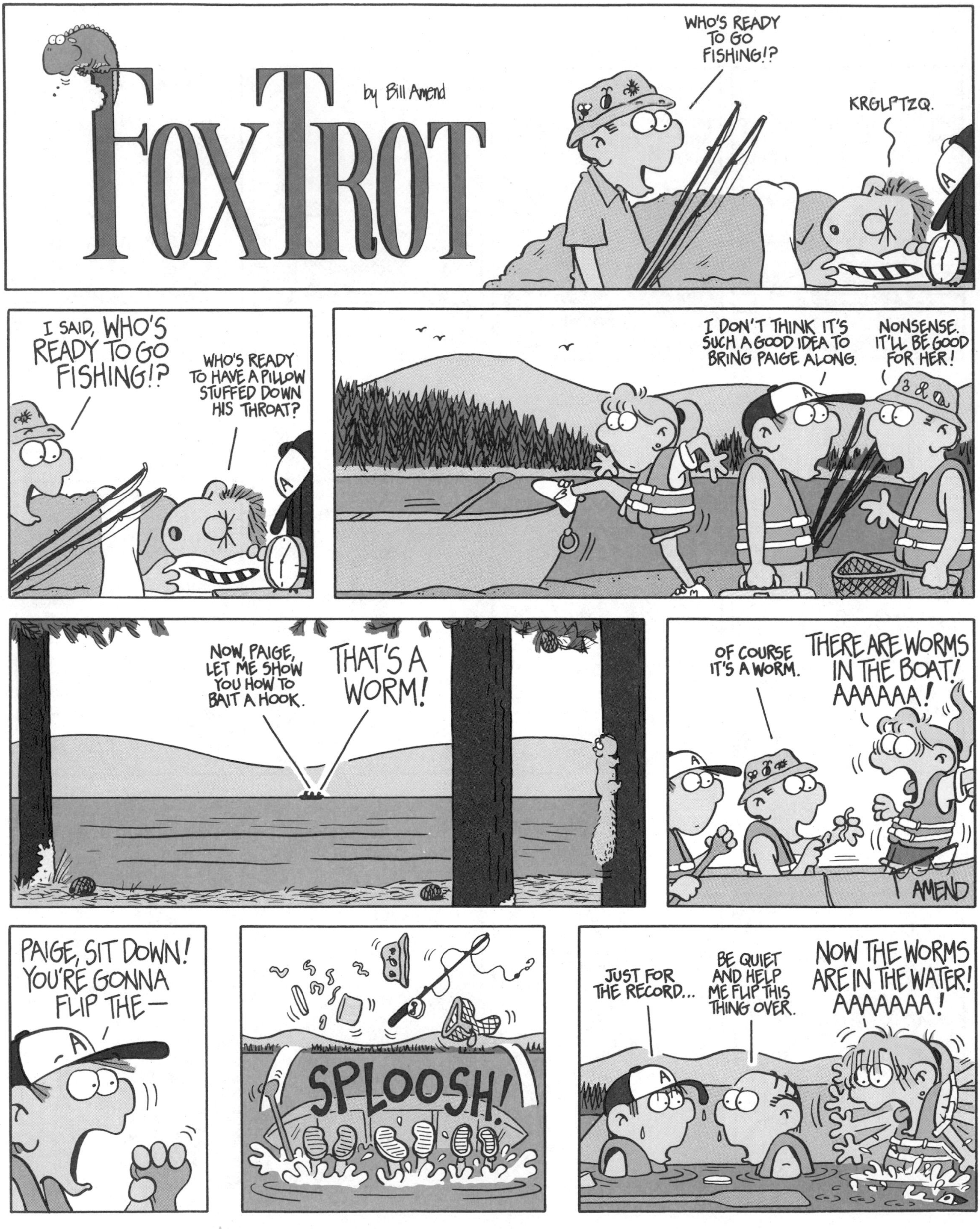
FoxTrot
by Bill Amend
WHO'S READY TO GO FISHING!?
KRGLPTZQ.
I SAID, WHO'S READY TO GO FISHING!?
WHO'S READY TO HAVE A PILLOW STUFFED DOWN HIS THROAT?
I DON'T THINK IT'S SUCH A GOOD IDEA TO BRING PAIGE ALONG.
NONSENSE. IT'LL BE GOOD FOR HER!
NOW, PAIGE, LET ME SHOW YOU HOW TO BAIT A HOOK.
THAT'S A WORM!
OF COURSE IT'S A WORM.
THERE ARE WORMS IN THE BOAT! AAAAAA!
AMEND
PAIGE, SIT DOWN! YOU'RE GONNA FLIP THE—
SPLOOSH!
JUST FOR THE RECORD...
BE QUIET AND HELP ME FLIP THIS THING OVER.
NOW THE WORMS ARE IN THE WATER! AAAAAAA!

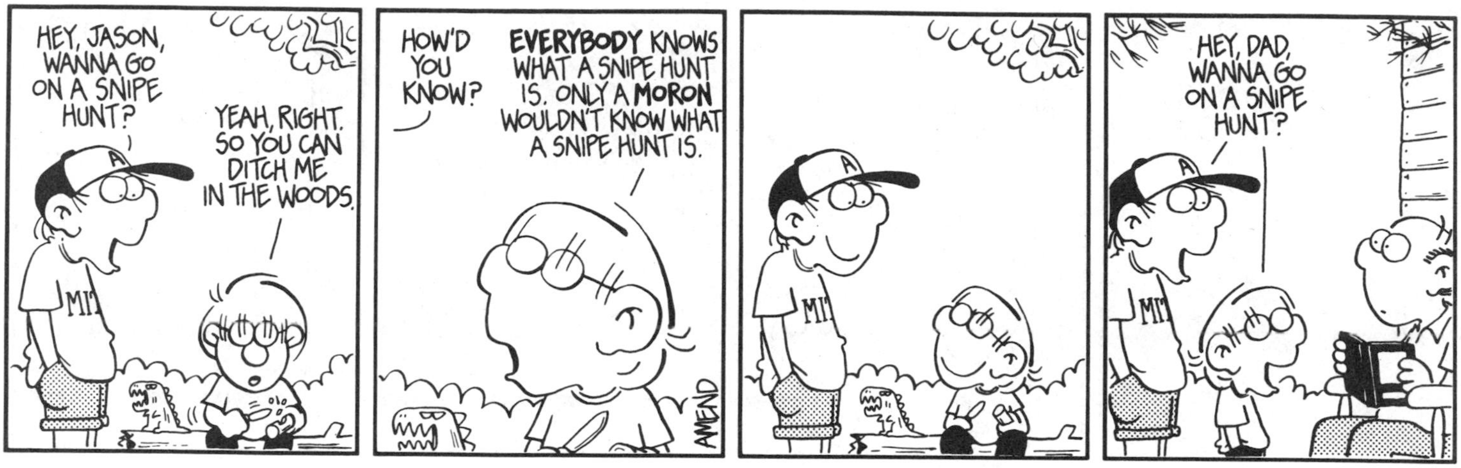
HEY, JASON, WANNA GO ON A SNIPE HUNT?
YEAH, RIGHT. SO YOU CAN DITCH ME IN THE WOODS.
HOW'D YOU KNOW?
EVERYBODY KNOWS WHAT A SNIPE HUNT IS. ONLY A MORON WOULDN'T KNOW WHAT A SNIPE HUNT IS.
AMEND
HEY, DAD, WANNA GO ON A SNIPE HUNT?

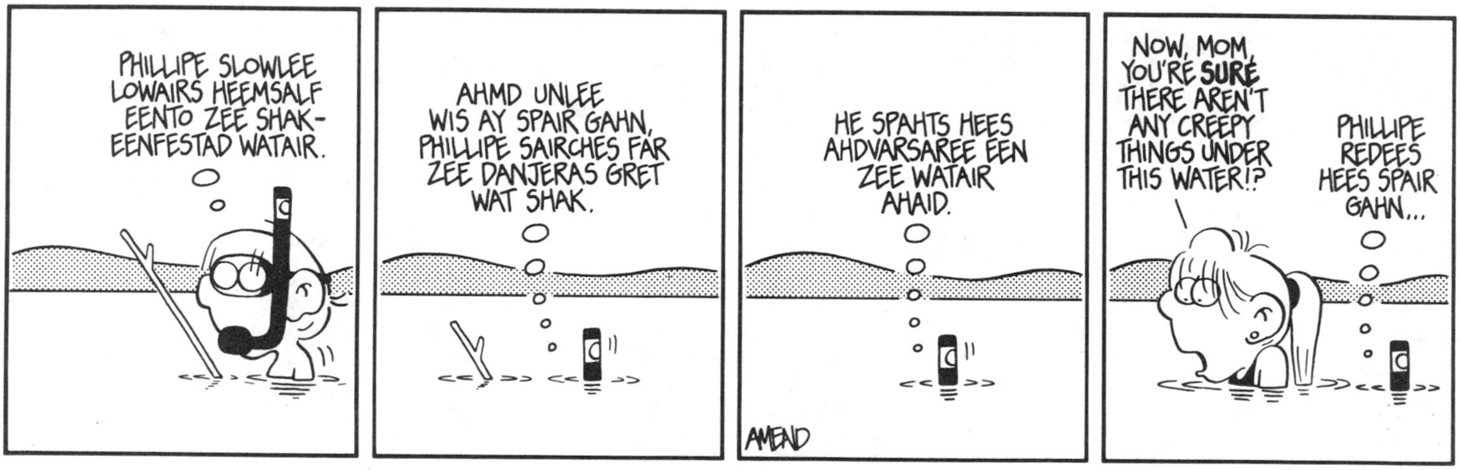
PHILLIPE SLOWLEE LOWAIRS HEEMSALF EENTO ZEE SHAK-EENFESTAD WATAIR.
AHMD UNLEE WIS AY SPAIR GAHN, PHILLIPE SAIRCHES FAR ZEE DANJERAS GRET WAT SHAK.
HE SPAHTS HEES AHDVARSAREE EEN ZEE WATAIR AHAID.
AMEND
NOW, MOM, YOU'RE SURE THERE AREN'T ANY CREEPY THINGS UNDER THIS WATER!?
PHILLIPE REDEES HEES SPAIR GAHN...

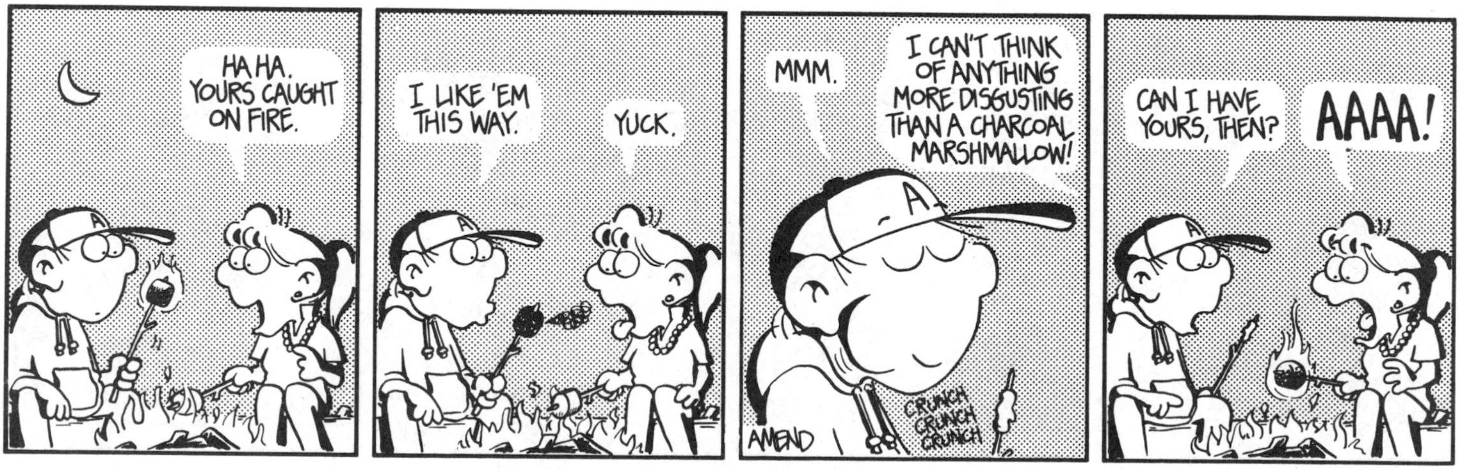
HA HA. YOURS CAUGHT ON FIRE.
I LIKE 'EM THIS WAY.
YUCK.
MMM.
I CAN'T THINK OF ANYTHING MORE DISGUSTING THAN A CHARCOAL MARSHMALLOW!
CRUNCH CRUNCH CRUNCH
AMEND
CAN I HAVE YOURS, THEN?
AAAA!

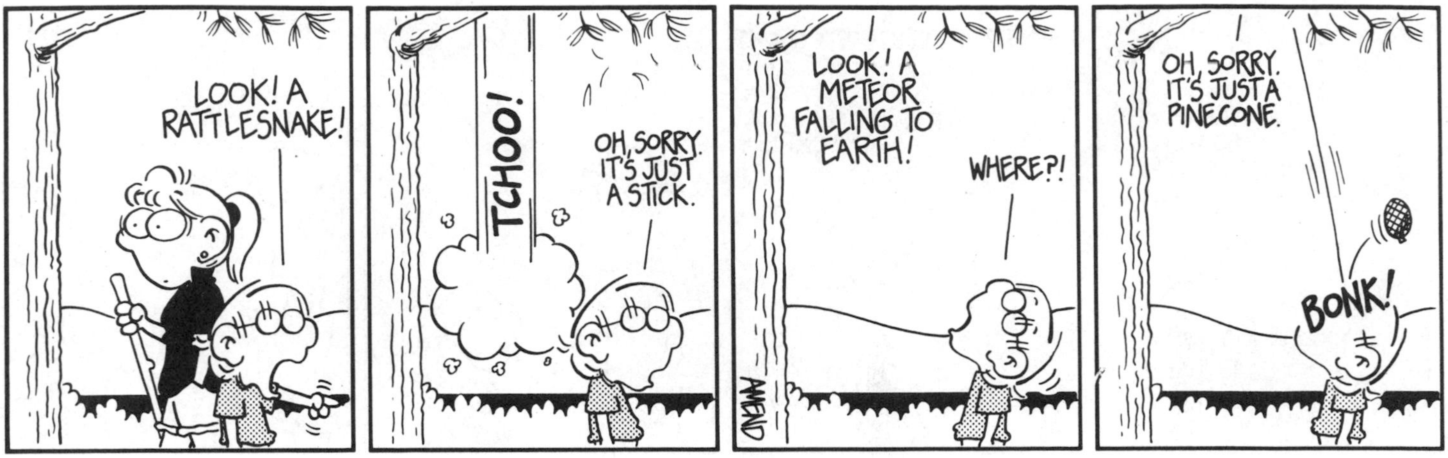
LOOK! A RATTLESNAKE!
TCHOO!
OH, SORRY. IT'S JUST A STICK.
AMEND
LOOK! A METEOR FALLING TO EARTH!
WHERE?!
OH, SORRY. IT'S JUST A PINECONE.
BONK!

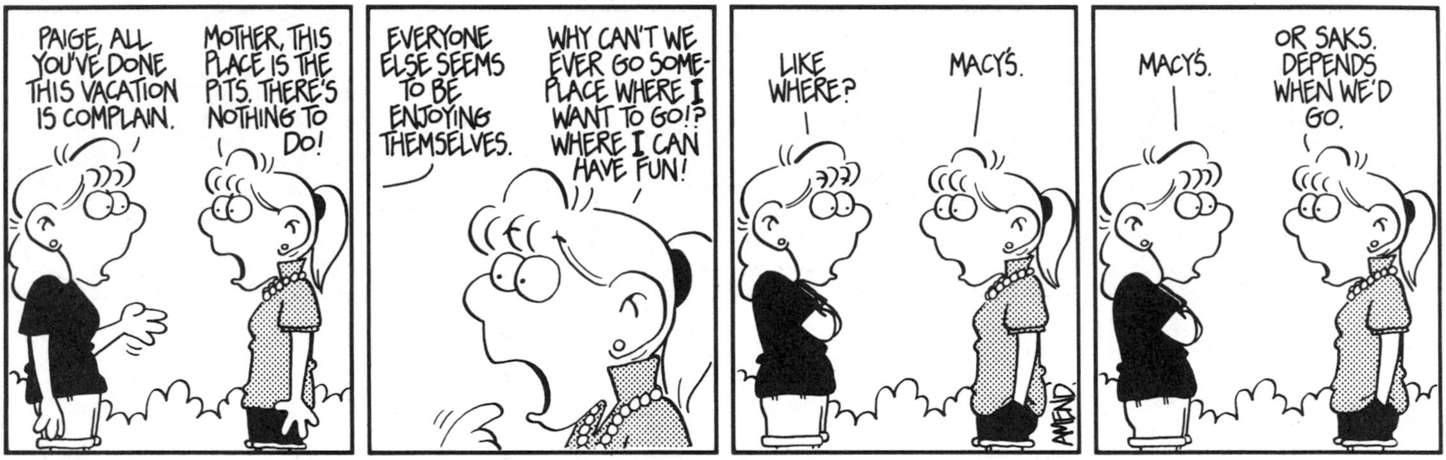
PAIGE, ALL YOU'VE DONE THIS VACATION IS COMPLAIN.
MOTHER, THIS PLACE IS THE PITS. THERE'S NOTHING TO DO!
EVERYONE ELSE SEEMS TO BE ENJOYING THEMSELVES.
WHY CAN'T WE EVER GO SOME-PLACE WHERE I WANT TO GO!? WHERE I CAN HAVE FUN!
LIKE WHERE?
MACY'S.
AMEND
MACY'S.
OR SAKS. DEPENDS WHEN WE'D GO.

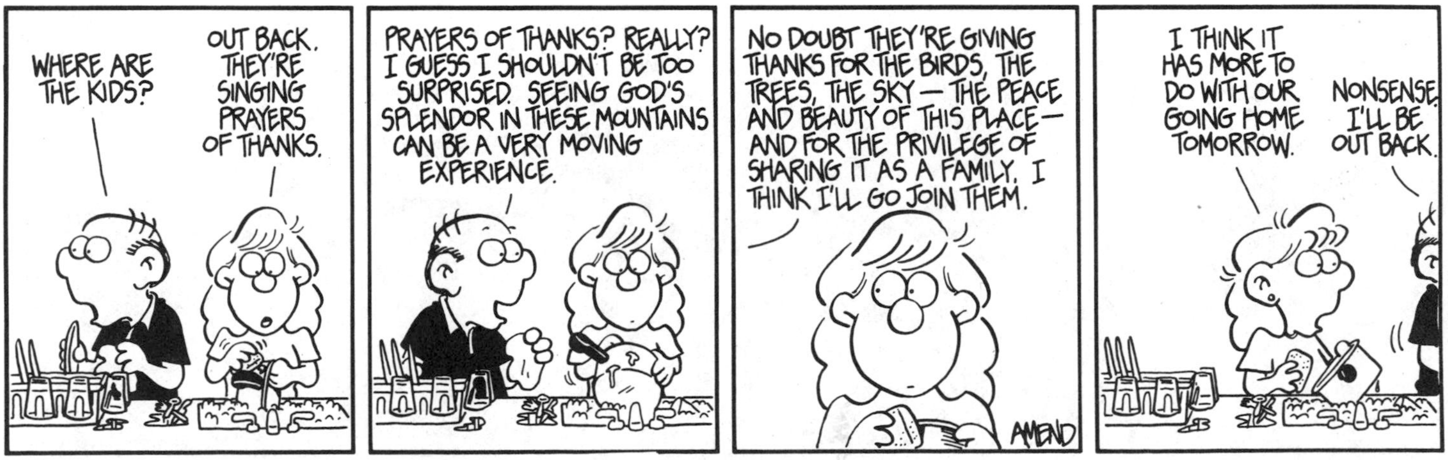
WHERE ARE THE KIDS?
OUT BACK. THEY'RE SINGING PRAYERS OF THANKS.
PRAYERS OF THANKS? REALLY? I GUESS I SHOULDN'T BE TOO SURPRISED. SEEING GOD'S SPLENDOR IN THESE MOUNTAINS CAN BE A VERY MOVING EXPERIENCE.
NO DOUBT THEY'RE GIVING THANKS FOR THE BIRDS, THE TREES, THE SKY — THE PEACE AND BEAUTY OF THIS PLACE — AND FOR THE PRIVILEGE OF SHARING IT AS A FAMILY. I THINK I'LL GO JOIN THEM.
AMEND
I THINK IT HAS MORE TO DO WITH OUR GOING HOME TOMORROW.
NONSENSE. I'LL BE OUT BACK.

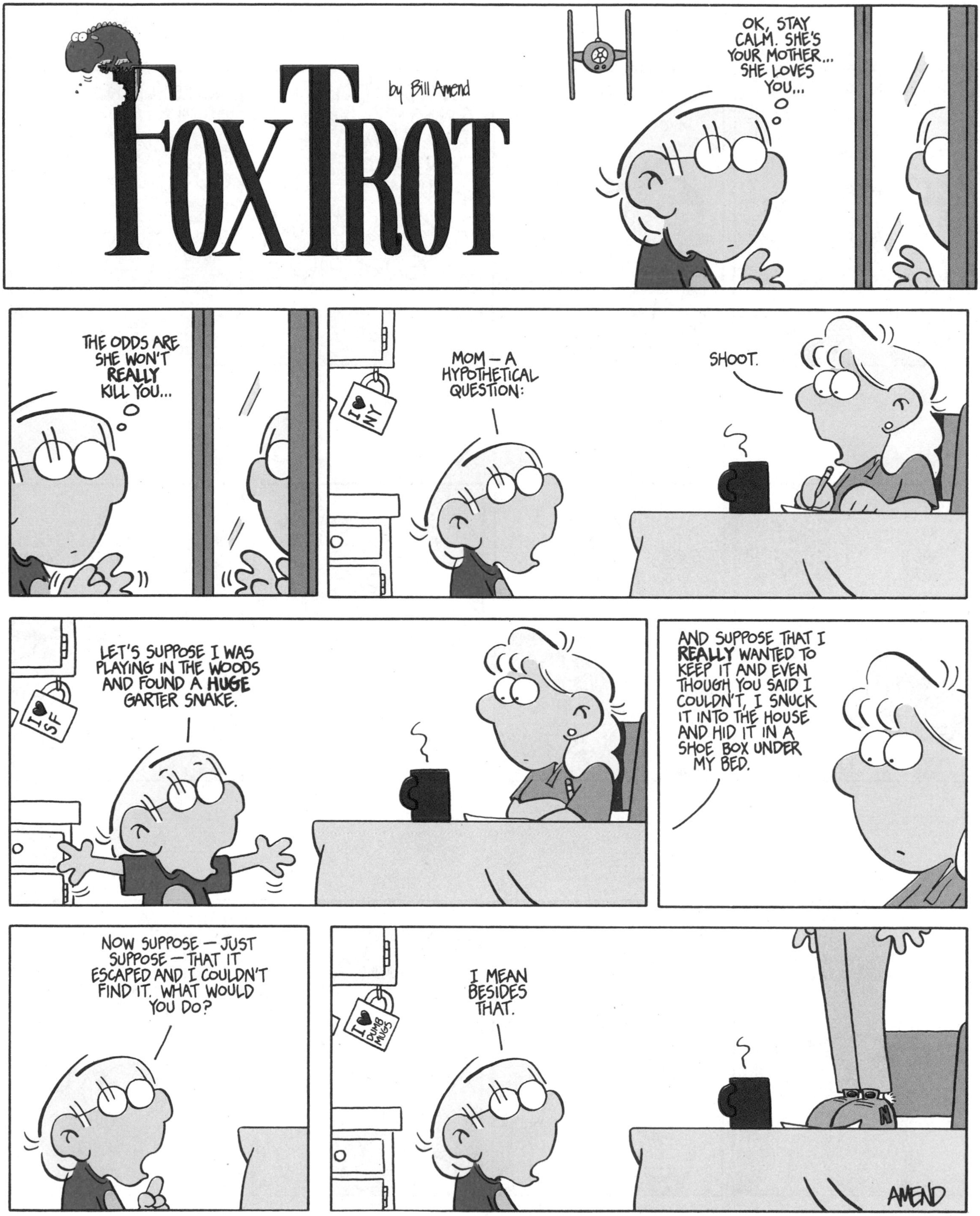
FOXTROT
by Bill Amend
OK, STAY CALM. SHE'S YOUR MOTHER... SHE LOVES YOU...
THE ODDS ARE SHE WON'T REALLY KILL YOU...
MOM — A HYPOTHETICAL QUESTION:
SHOOT.
I ♥ NY
LET'S SUPPOSE I WAS PLAYING IN THE WOODS AND FOUND A HUGE GARTER SNAKE.
I ♥ SF
AND SUPPOSE THAT I REALLY WANTED TO KEEP IT AND EVEN THOUGH YOU SAID I COULDN'T, I SNUCK IT INTO THE HOUSE AND HID IT IN A SHOE BOX UNDER MY BED.
NOW SUPPOSE — JUST SUPPOSE — THAT IT ESCAPED AND I COULDN'T FIND IT. WHAT WOULD YOU DO?
I MEAN BESIDES THAT.
I ♥ DUMB MUGS
AMEND

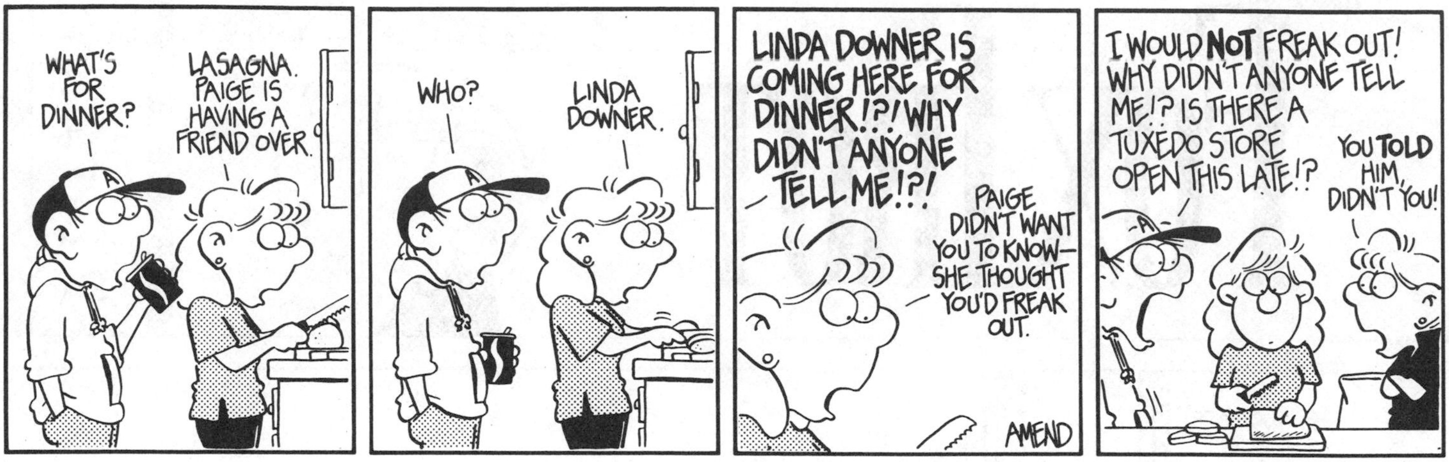
WHAT'S FOR DINNER?
LASAGNA. PAIGE IS HAVING A FRIEND OVER.
WHO?
LINDA DOWNER.
LINDA DOWNER IS COMING HERE FOR DINNER!?! WHY DIDN'T ANYONE TELL ME!?!
PAIGE DIDN'T WANT YOU TO KNOW—SHE THOUGHT YOU'D FREAK OUT.
AMEND
I WOULD NOT FREAK OUT! WHY DIDN'T ANYONE TELL ME!? IS THERE A TUXEDO STORE OPEN THIS LATE!?
YOU TOLD HIM, DIDN'T YOU!

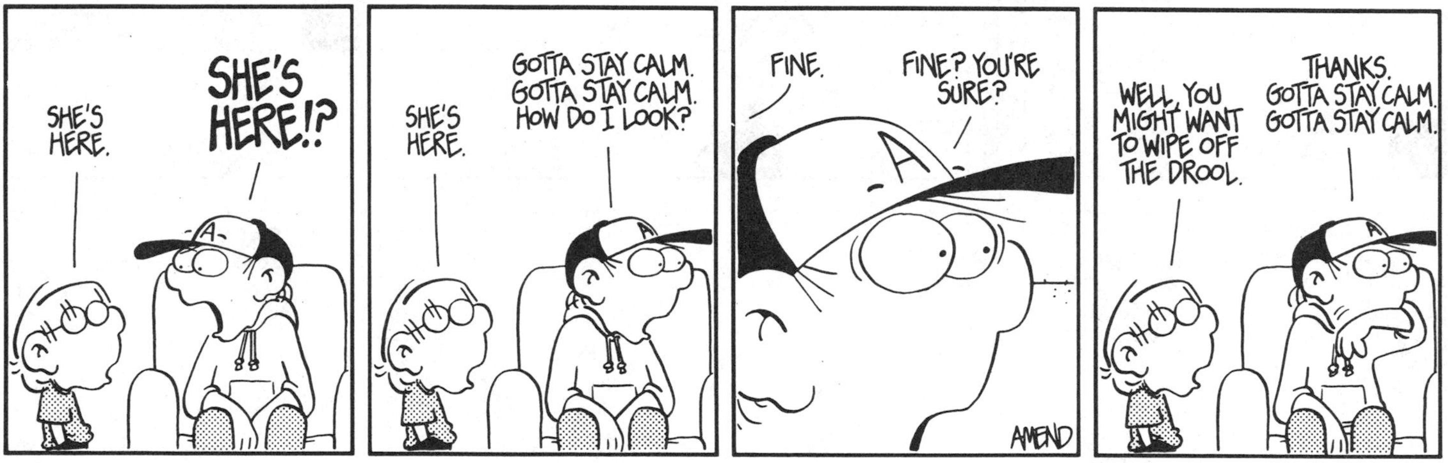
SHE'S HERE.
SHE'S HERE!?
SHE'S HERE.
GOTTA STAY CALM. GOTTA STAY CALM. HOW DO I LOOK?
FINE.
FINE? YOU'RE SURE?
AMEND
WELL, YOU MIGHT WANT TO WIPE OFF THE DROOL.
THANKS. GOTTA STAY CALM. GOTTA STAY CALM.

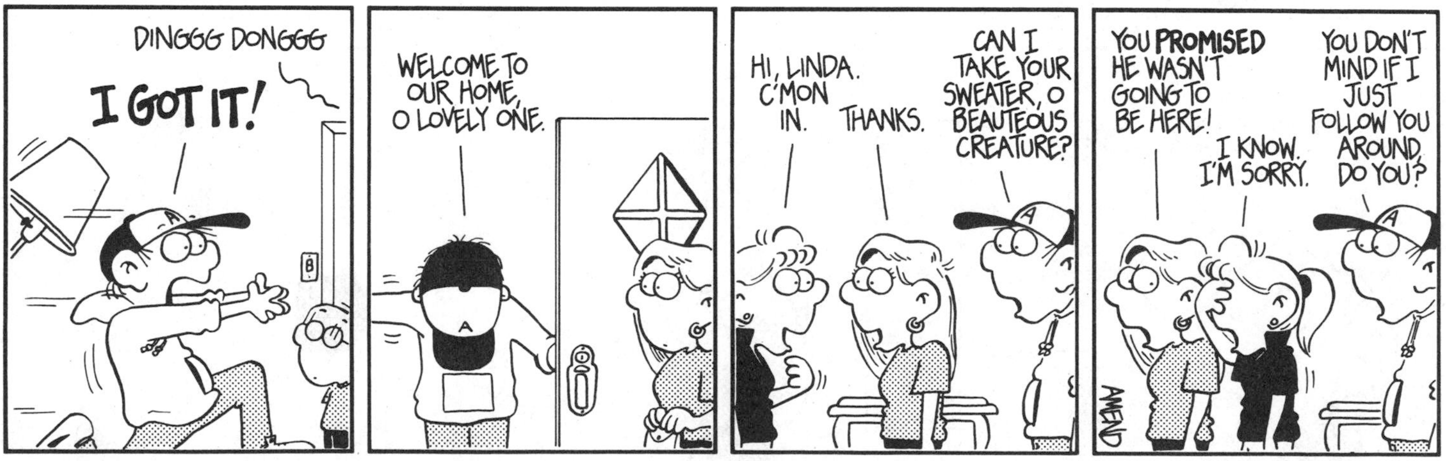
DINGGG DONGGG
I GOT IT!
WELCOME TO OUR HOME, O LOVELY ONE.
HI, LINDA. C'MON IN.
THANKS.
CAN I TAKE YOUR SWEATER, O BEAUTEOUS CREATURE?
YOU PROMISED HE WASN'T GOING TO BE HERE!
I KNOW. I'M SORRY.
YOU DON'T MIND IF I JUST FOLLOW YOU AROUND, DO YOU?
AMEND

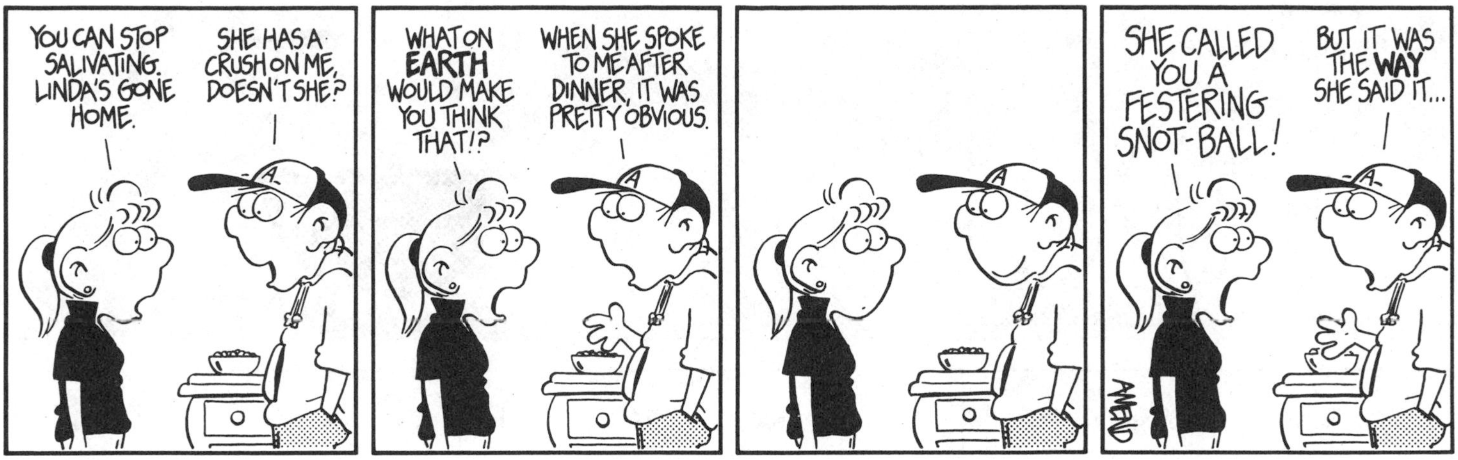
YOU CAN STOP SALIVATING. LINDA'S GONE HOME.
SHE HAS A CRUSH ON ME, DOESN'T SHE?
WHAT ON EARTH WOULD MAKE YOU THINK THAT!?
WHEN SHE SPOKE TO ME AFTER DINNER, IT WAS PRETTY OBVIOUS.
SHE CALLED YOU A FESTERING SNOT-BALL!
BUT IT WAS THE WAY SHE SAID IT...
AMEND

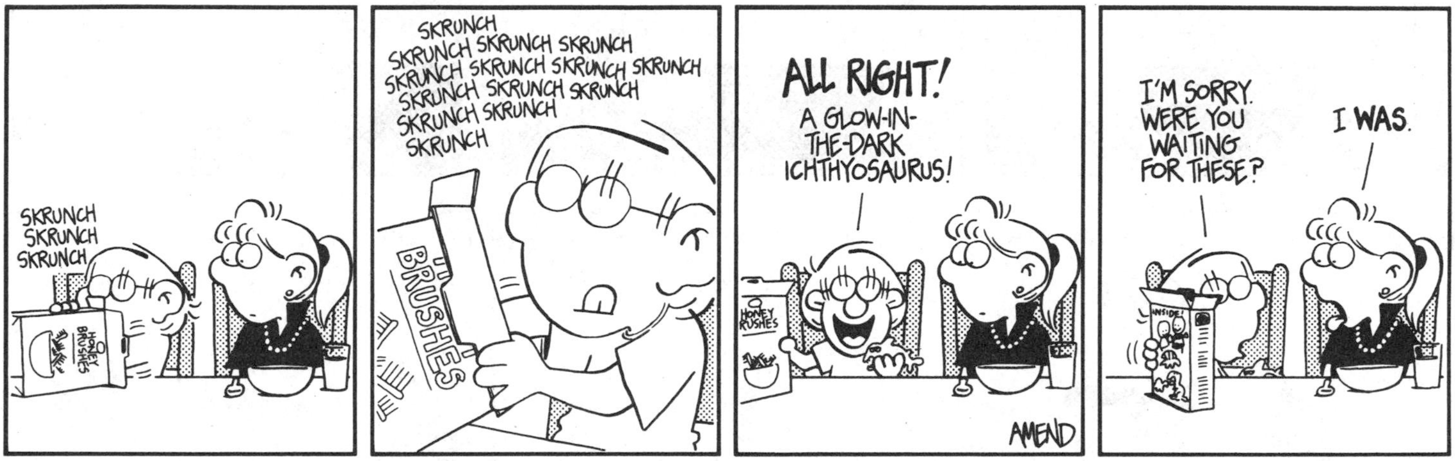
SKRUNCH SKRUNCH SKRUNCH
HONEY BRUSHES
SKRUNCH
SKRUNCH SKRUNCH SKRUNCH
SKRUNCH SKRUNCH SKRUNCH SKRUNCH
SKRUNCH SKRUNCH SKRUNCH
SKRUNCH SKRUNCH
SKRUNCH
BRUSHES
ALL RIGHT! A GLOW-IN-THE-DARK ICHTHYOSAURUS!
HONEY BRUSHES
AMEND
I'M SORRY. WERE YOU WAITING FOR THESE?
I WAS.
INSIDE

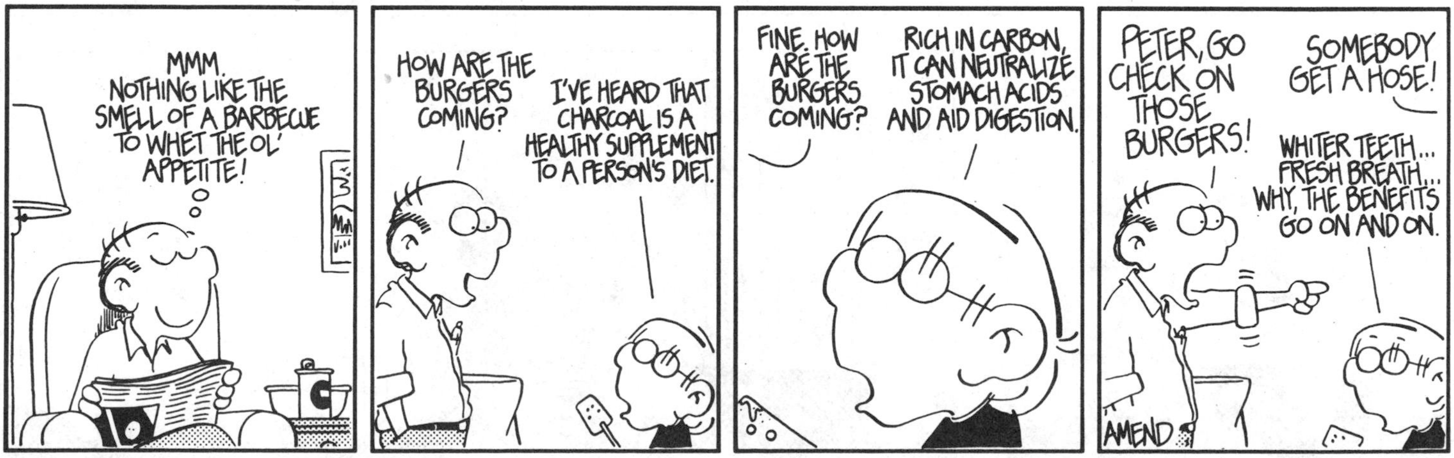
MMM. NOTHING LIKE THE SMELL OF A BARBECUE TO WHET THE OL' APPETITE!
HOW ARE THE BURGERS COMING?
I'VE HEARD THAT CHARCOAL IS A HEALTHY SUPPLEMENT TO A PERSON'S DIET.
FINE. HOW ARE THE BURGERS COMING?
RICH IN CARBON, IT CAN NEUTRALIZE STOMACH ACIDS AND AID DIGESTION.
PETER, GO CHECK ON THOSE BURGERS!
SOMEBODY GET A HOSE!
WHITER TEETH... FRESH BREATH... WHY, THE BENEFITS GO ON AND ON.
AMEND

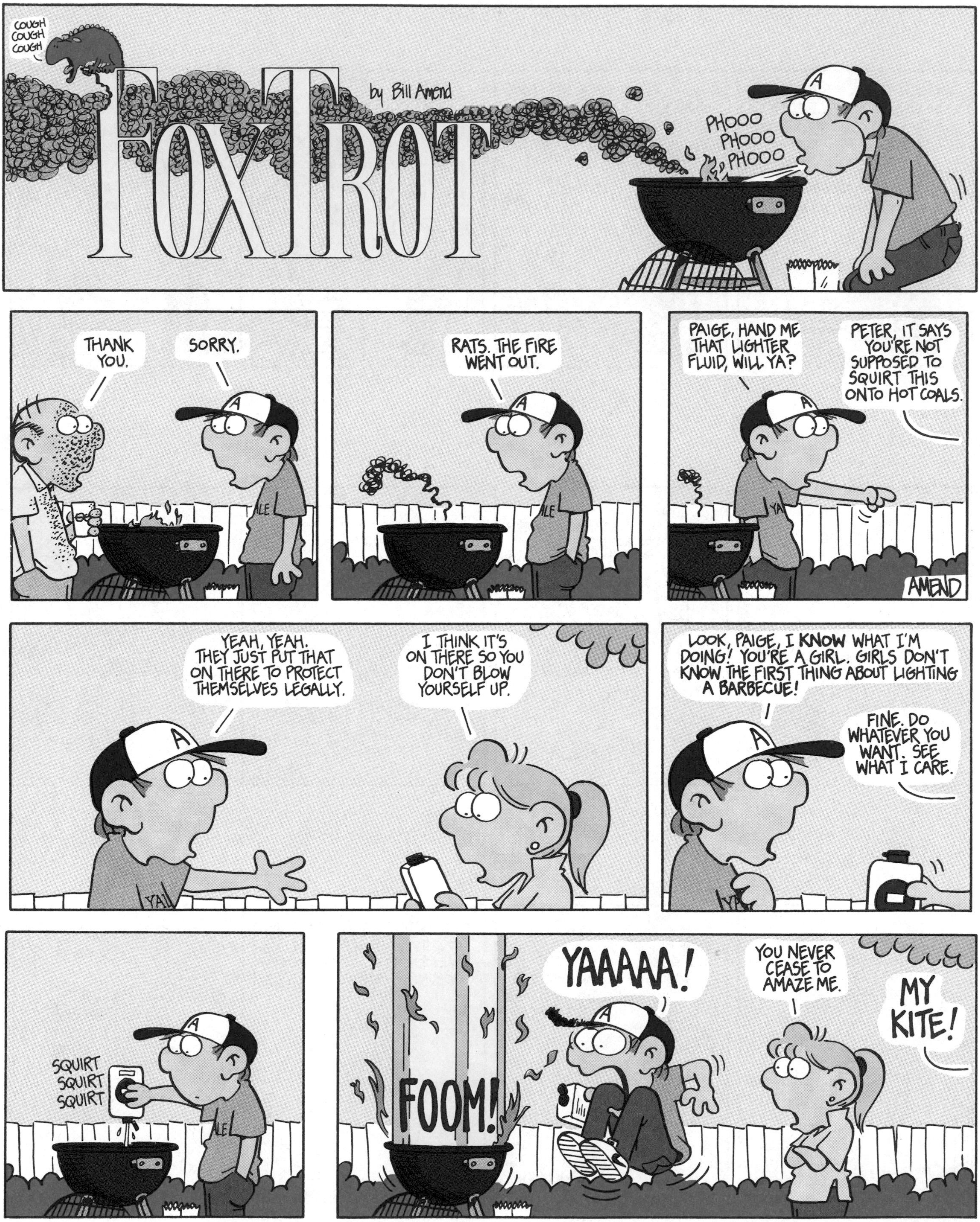
COUGH COUGH COUGH
FOXTROT
by Bill Amend
PHOOO PHOOO PHOOO
THANK YOU.
SORRY.
RATS. THE FIRE WENT OUT.
PAIGE, HAND ME THAT LIGHTER FLUID, WILL YA?
PETER, IT SAYS YOU'RE NOT SUPPOSED TO SQUIRT THIS ONTO HOT COALS.
AMEND
YEAH, YEAH. THEY JUST PUT THAT ON THERE TO PROTECT THEMSELVES LEGALLY.
I THINK IT'S ON THERE SO YOU DON'T BLOW YOURSELF UP.
LOOK, PAIGE, I KNOW WHAT I'M DOING! YOU'RE A GIRL. GIRLS DON'T KNOW THE FIRST THING ABOUT LIGHTING A BARBECUE!
FINE. DO WHATEVER YOU WANT. SEE WHAT I CARE.
SQUIRT SQUIRT SQUIRT
FOOM!
YAAAAA!
YOU NEVER CEASE TO AMAZE ME.
MY KITE!

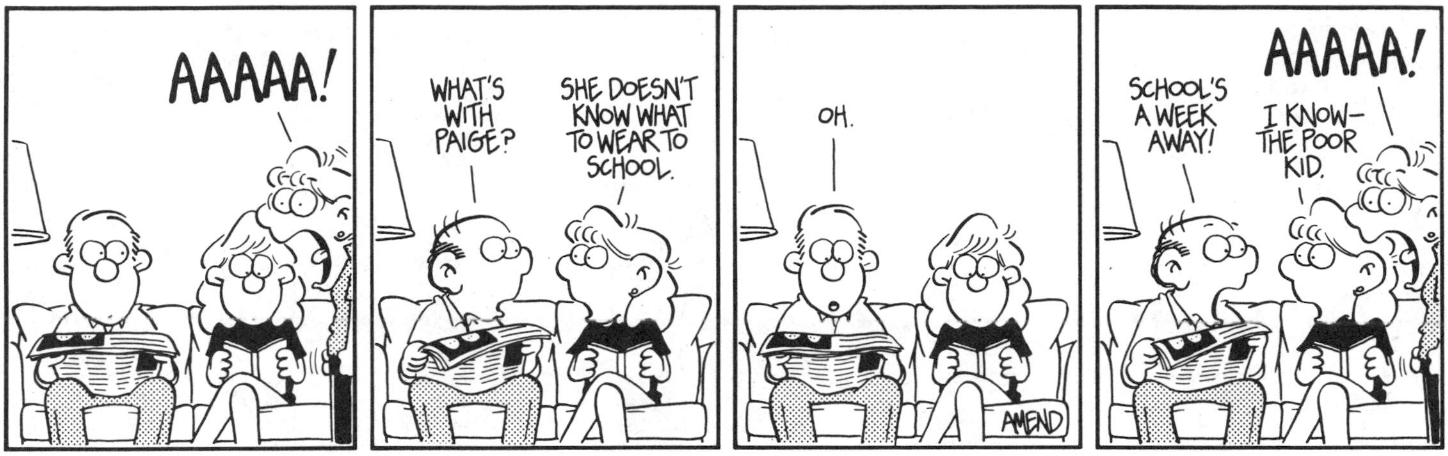
AAAAA!
WHAT'S WITH PAIGE?
SHE DOESN'T KNOW WHAT TO WEAR TO SCHOOL.
OH.
AMEND
SCHOOL'S A WEEK AWAY!
I KNOW— THE POOR KID.
AAAAA!

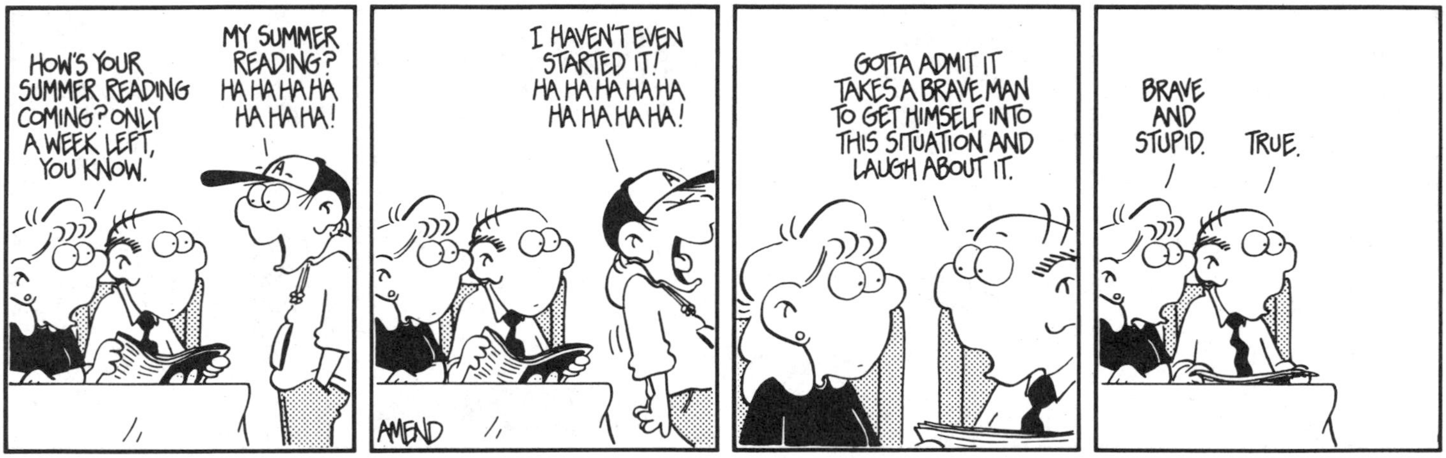
HOW'S YOUR SUMMER READING COMING? ONLY A WEEK LEFT, YOU KNOW.
MY SUMMER READING? HA HA HA HA HA HA HA!
I HAVEN'T EVEN STARTED IT! HA HA HA HA HA HA HA HA HA!
AMEND
GOTTA ADMIT IT TAKES A BRAVE MAN TO GET HIMSELF INTO THIS SITUATION AND LAUGH ABOUT IT.
BRAVE AND STUPID.
TRUE.

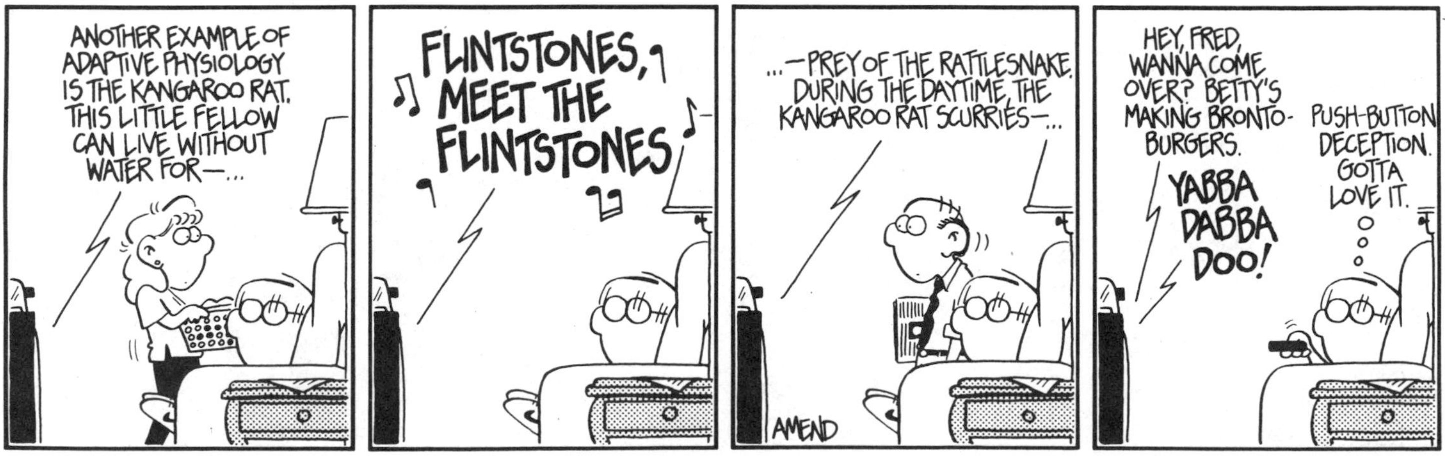
ANOTHER EXAMPLE OF ADAPTIVE PHYSIOLOGY IS THE KANGAROO RAT. THIS LITTLE FELLOW CAN LIVE WITHOUT WATER FOR—...
FLINTSTONES, MEET THE FLINTSTONES
...—PREY OF THE RATTLESNAKE. DURING THE DAYTIME, THE KANGAROO RAT SCURRIES—...
AMEND
HEY, FRED, WANNA COME OVER? BETTY'S MAKING BRONTO-BURGERS.
YABBA DABBA DOO!
PUSH-BUTTON DECEPTION. GOTTA LOVE IT.

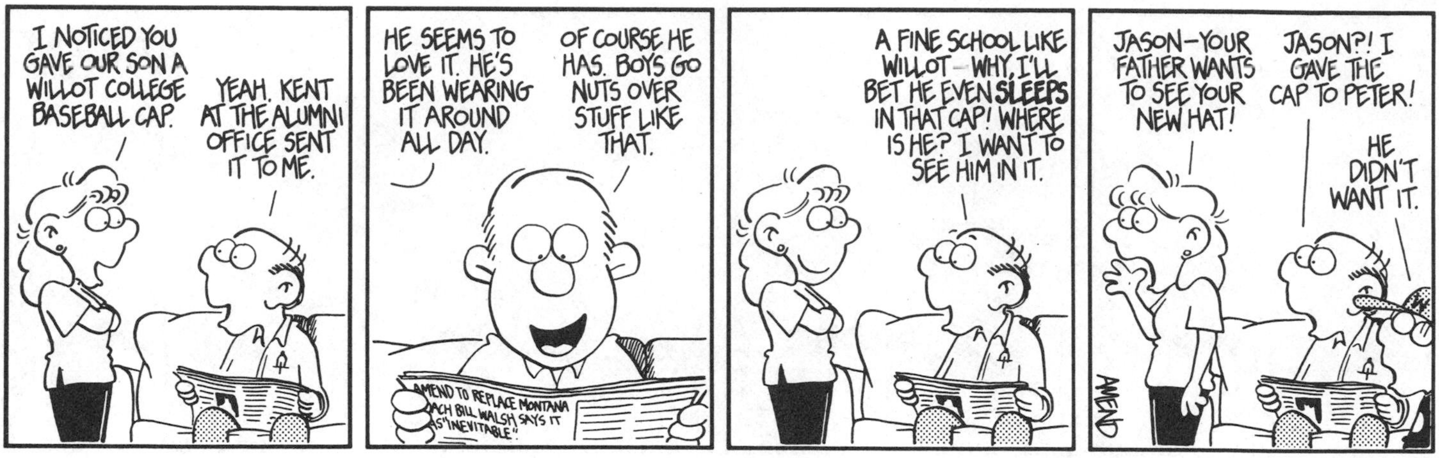
I NOTICED YOU GAVE OUR SON A WILLOT COLLEGE BASEBALL CAP.
YEAH. KENT AT THE ALUMNI OFFICE SENT IT TO ME.
HE SEEMS TO LOVE IT. HE'S BEEN WEARING IT AROUND ALL DAY.
OF COURSE HE HAS. BOYS GO NUTS OVER STUFF LIKE THAT.
AMEND TO REPLACE MONTANA
ACH BILL WALSH SAYS IT
AS "INEVITABLE."
A FINE SCHOOL LIKE WILLOT—WHY, I'LL BET HE EVEN **SLEEPS** IN THAT CAP! WHERE IS HE? I WANT TO SEE HIM IN IT.
JASON—YOUR FATHER WANTS TO SEE YOUR NEW HAT!
JASON?! I GAVE THE CAP TO PETER!
HE DIDN'T WANT IT.
AMEND

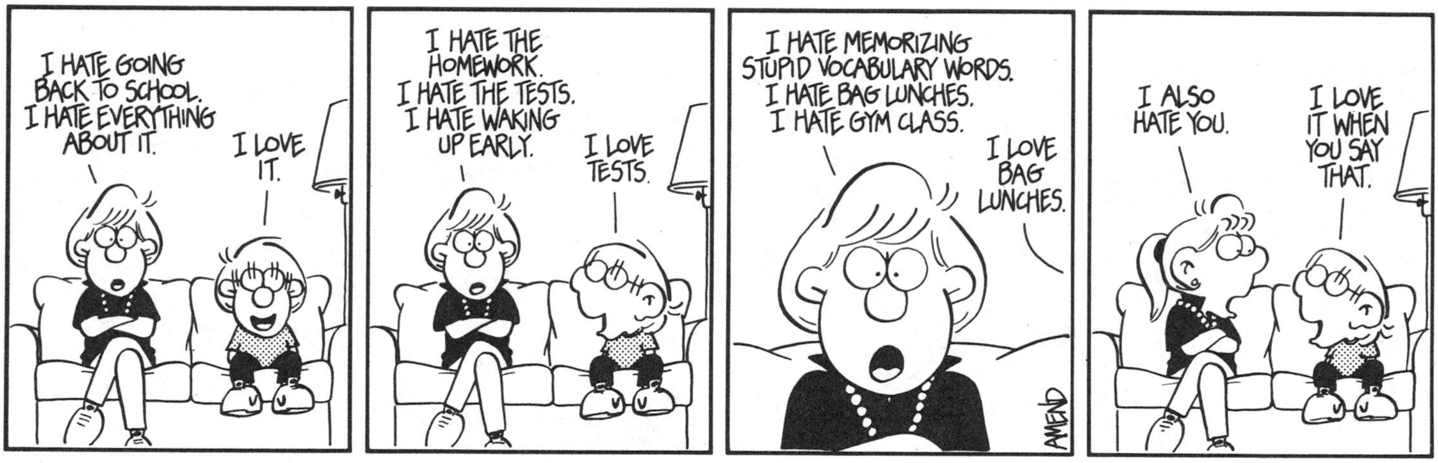
I HATE GOING BACK TO SCHOOL. I HATE EVERYTHING ABOUT IT.
I LOVE IT.
I HATE THE HOMEWORK. I HATE THE TESTS. I HATE WAKING UP EARLY.
I LOVE TESTS.
I HATE MEMORIZING STUPID VOCABULARY WORDS. I HATE BAG LUNCHES. I HATE GYM CLASS.
I LOVE BAG LUNCHES.
AMEND
I ALSO HATE YOU.
I LOVE IT WHEN YOU SAY THAT.

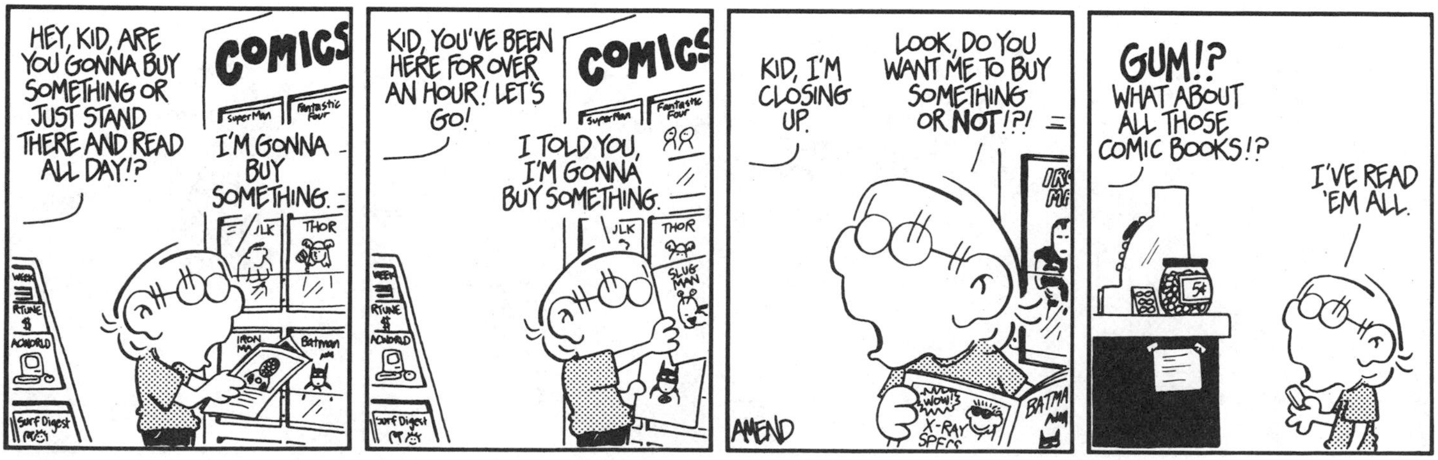
HEY, KID, ARE YOU GONNA BUY SOMETHING OR JUST STAND THERE AND READ ALL DAY!?
COMICS
I'M GONNA BUY SOMETHING.
KID, YOU'VE BEEN HERE FOR OVER AN HOUR! LET'S GO!
I TOLD YOU, I'M GONNA BUY SOMETHING.
KID, I'M CLOSING UP.
LOOK, DO YOU WANT ME TO BUY SOMETHING OR **NOT**!?!
AMEND
GUM!? WHAT ABOUT ALL THOSE COMIC BOOKS!?
I'VE READ 'EM ALL.

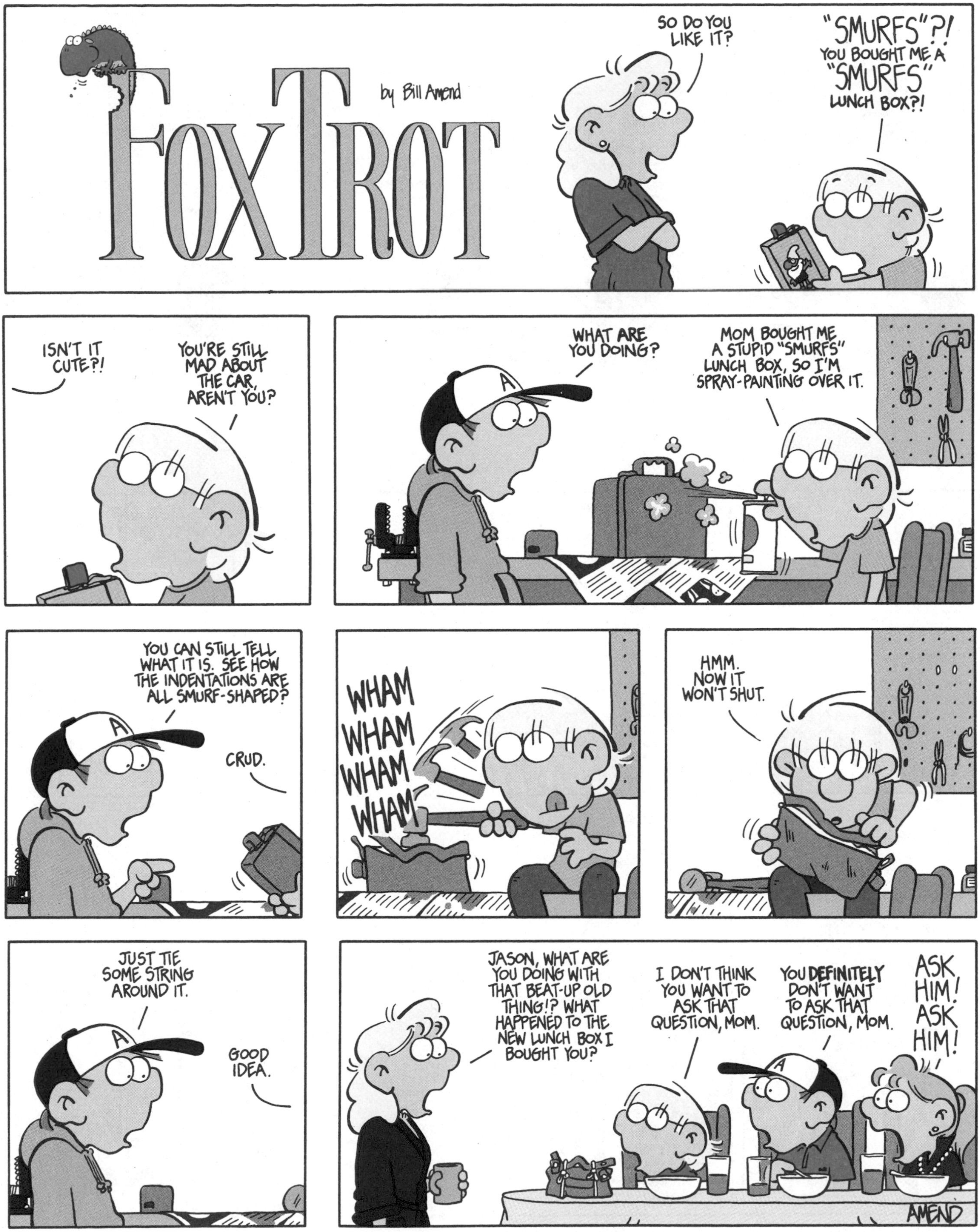
FoxTrot
by Bill Amend
SO DO YOU LIKE IT?
"SMURFS"?! YOU BOUGHT ME A "SMURFS" LUNCH BOX?!
ISN'T IT CUTE?!
YOU'RE STILL MAD ABOUT THE CAR, AREN'T YOU?
WHAT ARE YOU DOING?
MOM BOUGHT ME A STUPID "SMURFS" LUNCH BOX, SO I'M SPRAY-PAINTING OVER IT.
YOU CAN STILL TELL WHAT IT IS. SEE HOW THE INDENTATIONS ARE ALL SMURF-SHAPED?
CRUD.
WHAM WHAM WHAM WHAM
HMM. NOW IT WON'T SHUT.
JUST TIE SOME STRING AROUND IT.
GOOD IDEA.
JASON, WHAT ARE YOU DOING WITH THAT BEAT-UP OLD THING!? WHAT HAPPENED TO THE NEW LUNCH BOX I BOUGHT YOU?
I DON'T THINK YOU WANT TO ASK THAT QUESTION, MOM.
YOU DEFINITELY DON'T WANT TO ASK THAT QUESTION, MOM.
ASK HIM! ASK HIM!
AMEND

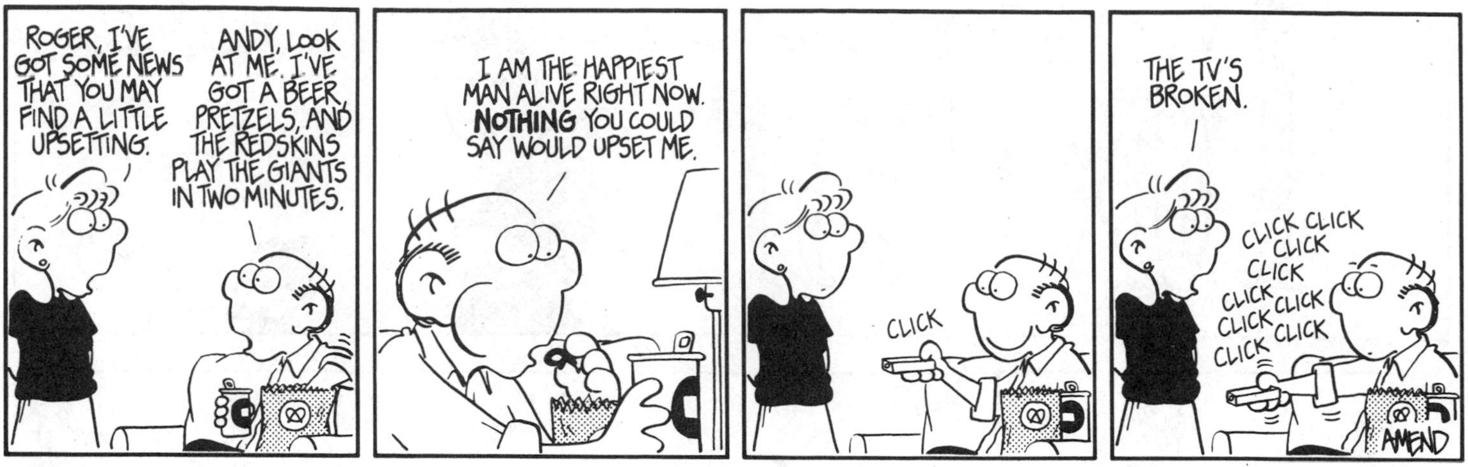
ROGER, I'VE GOT SOME NEWS THAT YOU MAY FIND A LITTLE UPSETTING.
ANDY, LOOK AT ME. I'VE GOT A BEER, PRETZELS, AND THE REDSKINS PLAY THE GIANTS IN TWO MINUTES.
I AM THE HAPPIEST MAN ALIVE RIGHT NOW. NOTHING YOU COULD SAY WOULD UPSET ME.
CLICK
THE TV'S BROKEN.
CLICK CLICK CLICK CLICK CLICK CLICK CLICK CLICK CLICK CLICK
AMEND

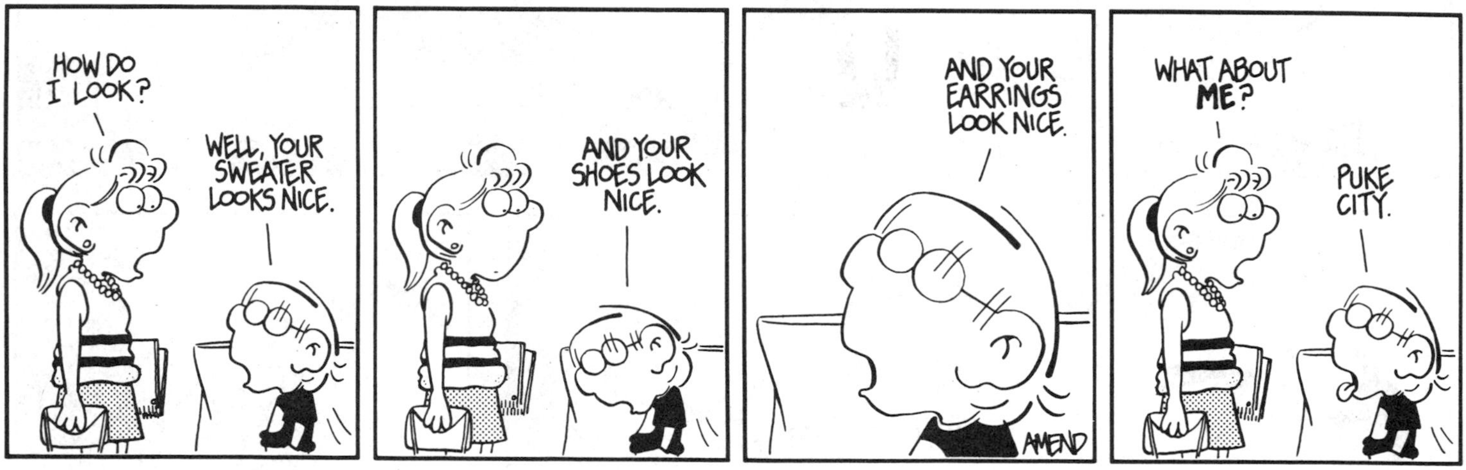
HOW DO I LOOK?
WELL, YOUR SWEATER LOOKS NICE.
AND YOUR SHOES LOOK NICE.
AND YOUR EARRINGS LOOK NICE.
AMEND
WHAT ABOUT ME?
PUKE CITY.

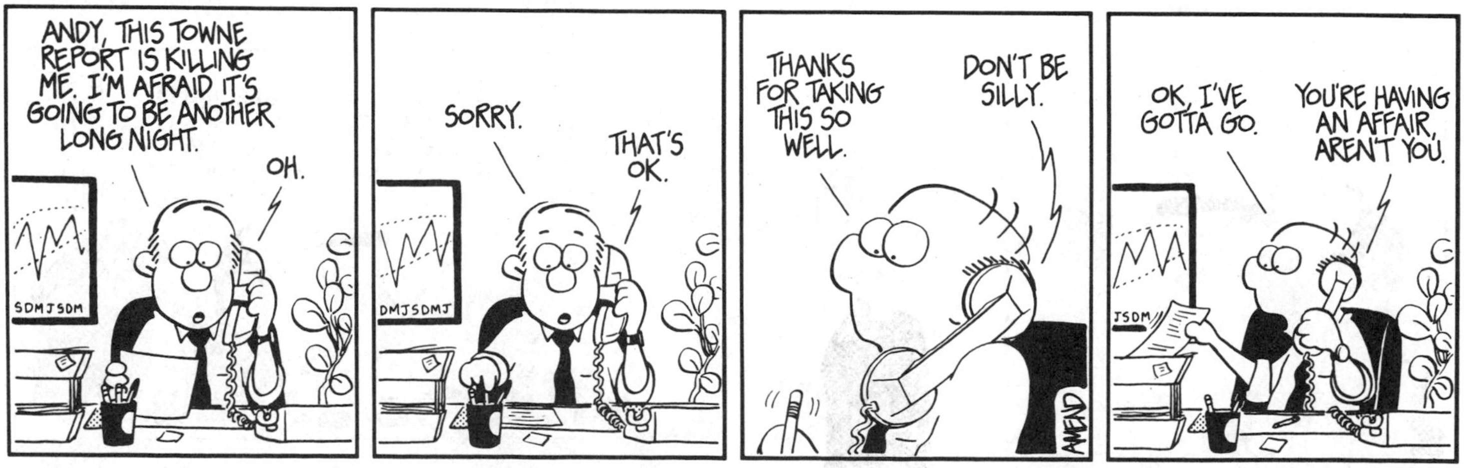
ANDY, THIS TOWNE REPORT IS KILLING ME. I'M AFRAID IT'S GOING TO BE ANOTHER LONG NIGHT.
OH.
SDMJSDM
SORRY.
THAT'S OK.
DMJSDMJ
THANKS FOR TAKING THIS SO WELL.
DON'T BE SILLY.
AMEND
OK, I'VE GOTTA GO.
YOU'RE HAVING AN AFFAIR, AREN'T YOU.
JSDM

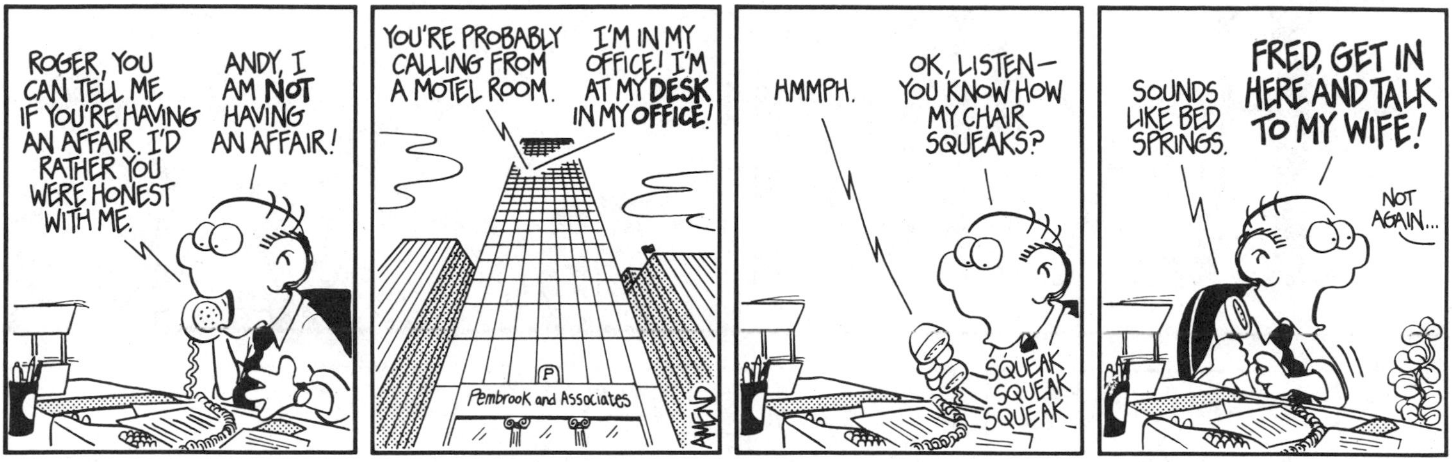
ROGER, YOU CAN TELL ME IF YOU'RE HAVING AN AFFAIR. I'D RATHER YOU WERE HONEST WITH ME.
ANDY, I AM **NOT** HAVING AN AFFAIR!
YOU'RE PROBABLY CALLING FROM A MOTEL ROOM.
I'M IN MY OFFICE! I'M AT MY **DESK** IN MY **OFFICE**!
Pembrook and Associates
AMEND
HMMPH.
OK, LISTEN— YOU KNOW HOW MY CHAIR SQUEAKS?
SQUEAK SQUEAK SQUEAK
SOUNDS LIKE BED SPRINGS.
FRED, GET IN HERE AND TALK TO MY WIFE!
NOT AGAIN...

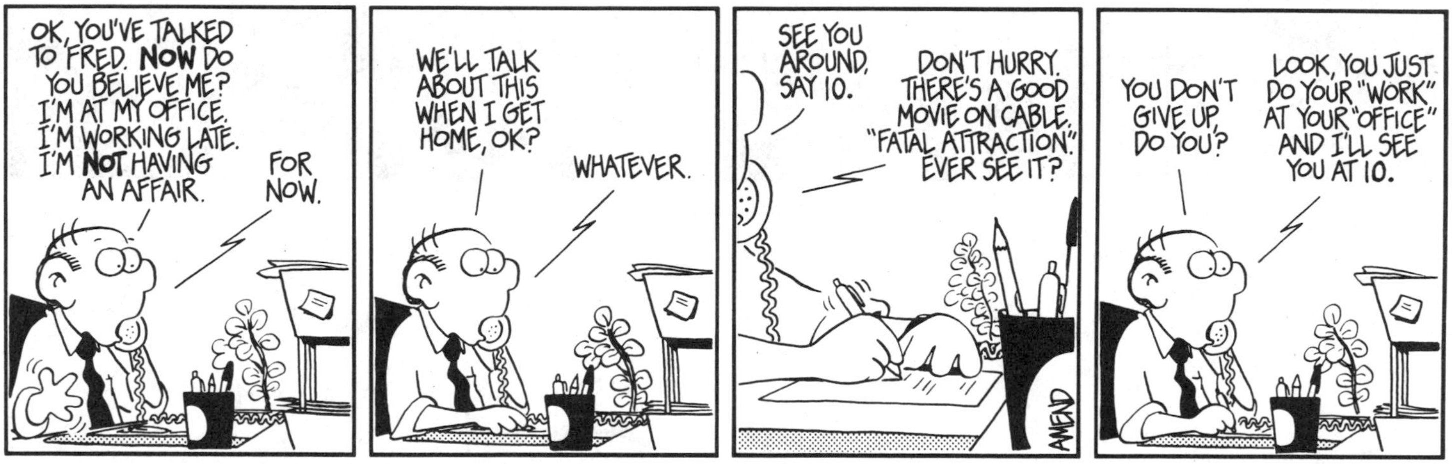
OK, YOU'VE TALKED TO FRED. **NOW** DO YOU BELIEVE ME? I'M AT MY OFFICE. I'M WORKING LATE. I'M **NOT** HAVING AN AFFAIR.
FOR NOW.
WE'LL TALK ABOUT THIS WHEN I GET HOME, OK?
WHATEVER.
SEE YOU AROUND, SAY 10.
DON'T HURRY. THERE'S A GOOD MOVIE ON CABLE. "FATAL ATTRACTION." EVER SEE IT?
AMEND
YOU DON'T GIVE UP, DO YOU?
LOOK, YOU JUST DO YOUR "WORK" AT YOUR "OFFICE" AND I'LL SEE YOU AT 10.

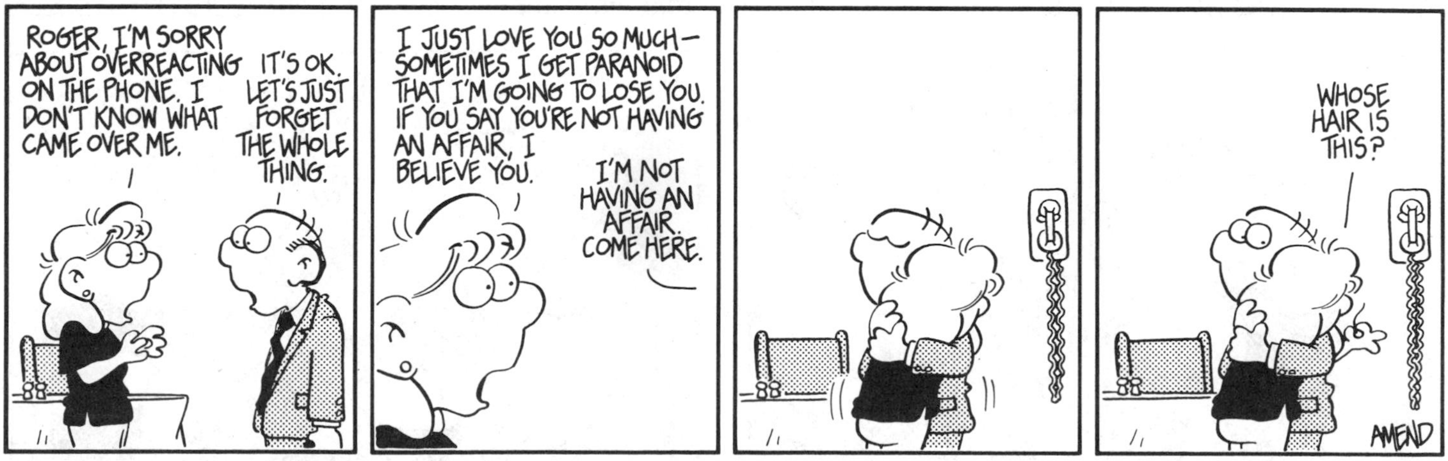
ROGER, I'M SORRY ABOUT OVERREACTING ON THE PHONE. I DON'T KNOW WHAT CAME OVER ME.
IT'S OK. LET'S JUST FORGET THE WHOLE THING.
I JUST LOVE YOU SO MUCH— SOMETIMES I GET PARANOID THAT I'M GOING TO LOSE YOU. IF YOU SAY YOU'RE NOT HAVING AN AFFAIR, I BELIEVE YOU.
I'M NOT HAVING AN AFFAIR. COME HERE.
WHOSE HAIR IS THIS?
AMEND

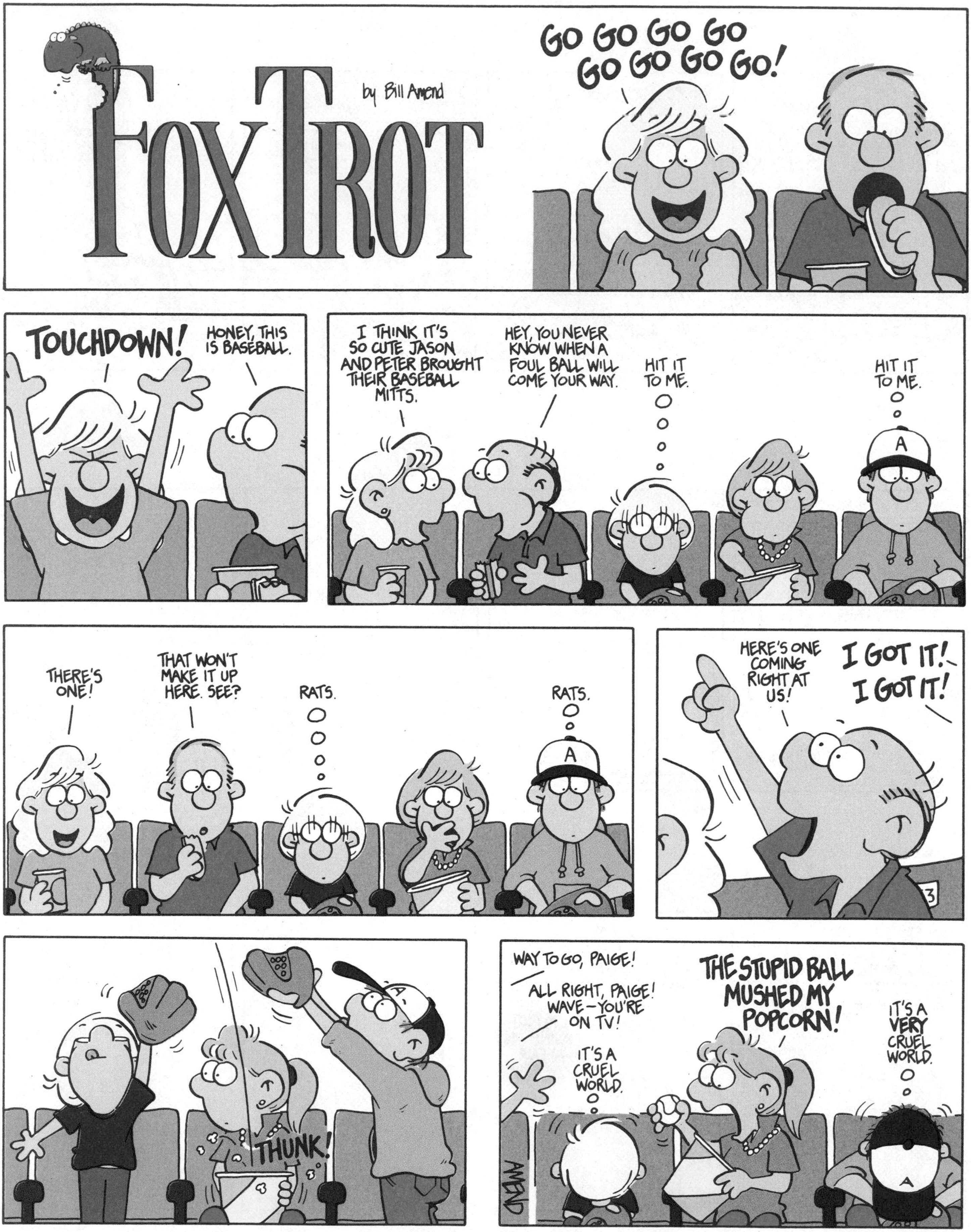
FoxTrot
by Bill Amend
GO GO GO GO GO GO GO GO!
TOUCHDOWN!
HONEY, THIS IS BASEBALL.
I THINK IT'S SO CUTE JASON AND PETER BROUGHT THEIR BASEBALL MITTS.
HEY, YOU NEVER KNOW WHEN A FOUL BALL WILL COME YOUR WAY.
HIT IT TO ME.
HIT IT TO ME.
THERE'S ONE!
THAT WON'T MAKE IT UP HERE. SEE?
RATS.
RATS.
HERE'S ONE COMING RIGHT AT US!
I GOT IT! I GOT IT!
THUNK!
WAY TO GO, PAIGE!
ALL RIGHT, PAIGE! WAVE–YOU'RE ON TV!
IT'S A CRUEL WORLD.
THE STUPID BALL MUSHED MY POPCORN!
IT'S A VERY CRUEL WORLD.
AMEND

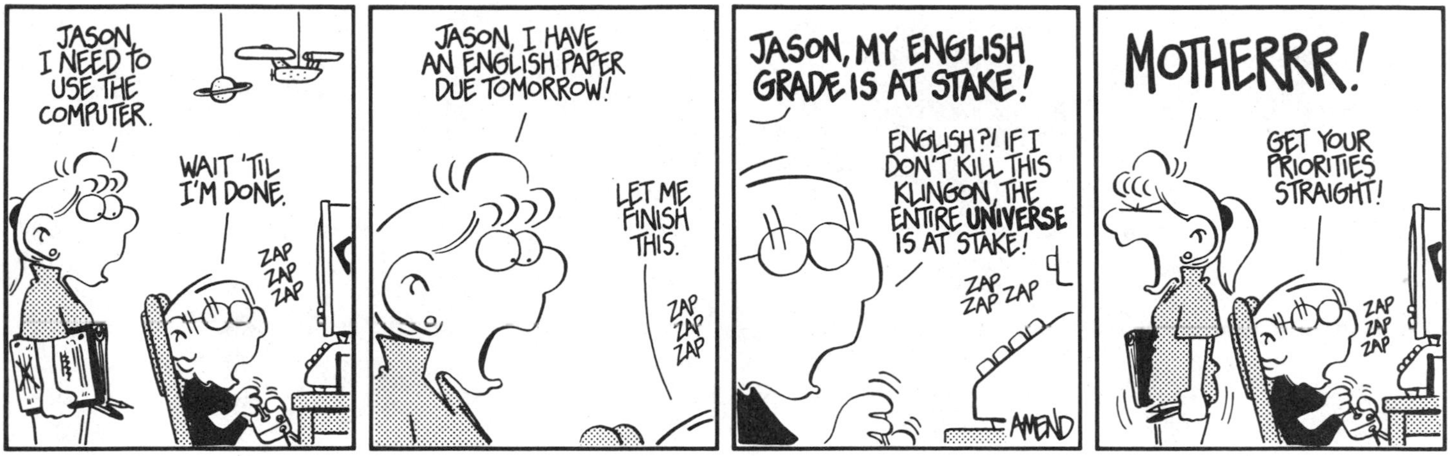
JASON, I NEED TO USE THE COMPUTER.
WAIT 'TIL I'M DONE.
ZAP ZAP ZAP
JASON, I HAVE AN ENGLISH PAPER DUE TOMORROW!
LET ME FINISH THIS.
ZAP ZAP ZAP
JASON, MY ENGLISH GRADE IS AT STAKE!
ENGLISH?! IF I DON'T KILL THIS KLINGON, THE ENTIRE UNIVERSE IS AT STAKE!
ZAP ZAP ZAP
AMEND
MOTHERRR!
GET YOUR PRIORITIES STRAIGHT!
ZAP ZAP ZAP

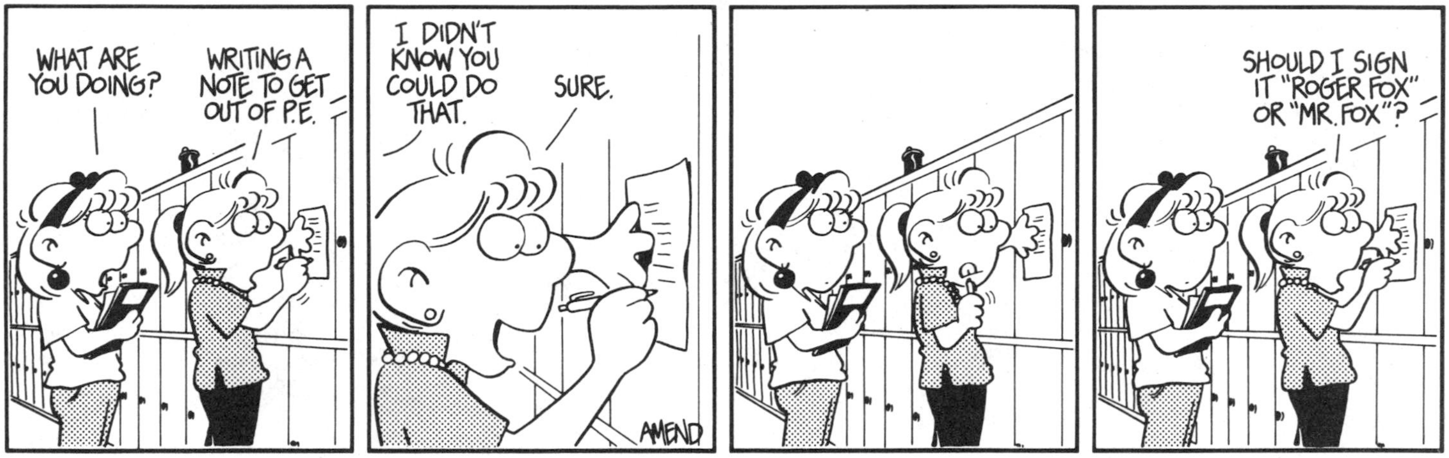
WHAT ARE YOU DOING?
WRITING A NOTE TO GET OUT OF P.E.
I DIDN'T KNOW YOU COULD DO THAT.
SURE.
AMEND
SHOULD I SIGN IT "ROGER FOX" OR "MR. FOX"?

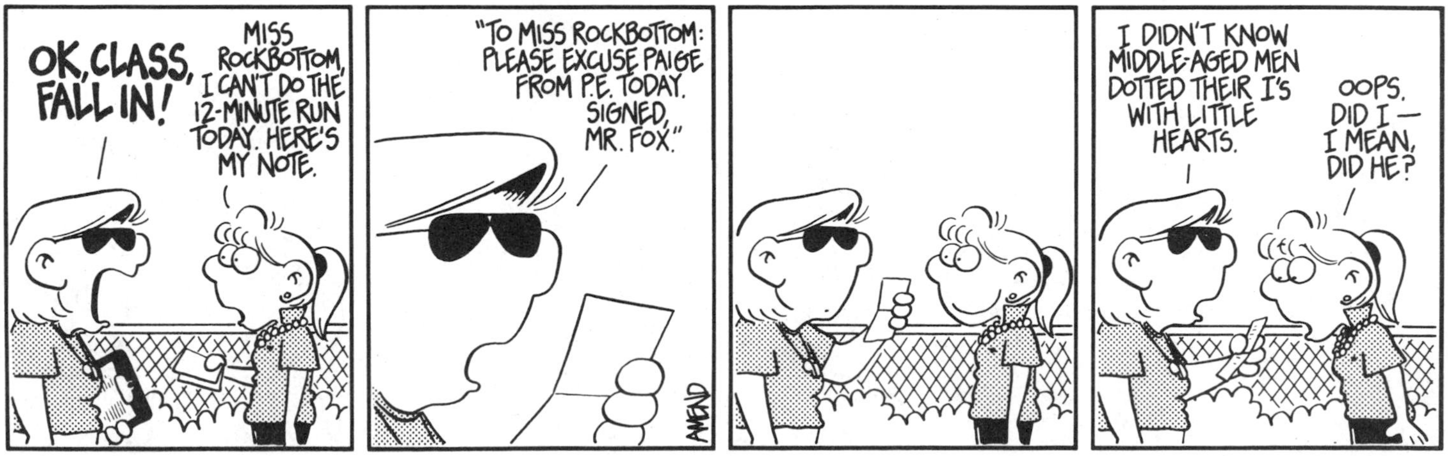
OK, CLASS, FALL IN!
MISS ROCKBOTTOM, I CAN'T DO THE 12-MINUTE RUN TODAY. HERE'S MY NOTE.
"TO MISS ROCKBOTTOM: PLEASE EXCUSE PAIGE FROM P.E. TODAY. SIGNED, MR. FOX."
AMEND
I DIDN'T KNOW MIDDLE-AGED MEN DOTTED THEIR I'S WITH LITTLE HEARTS.
OOPS. DID I — I MEAN, DID HE?

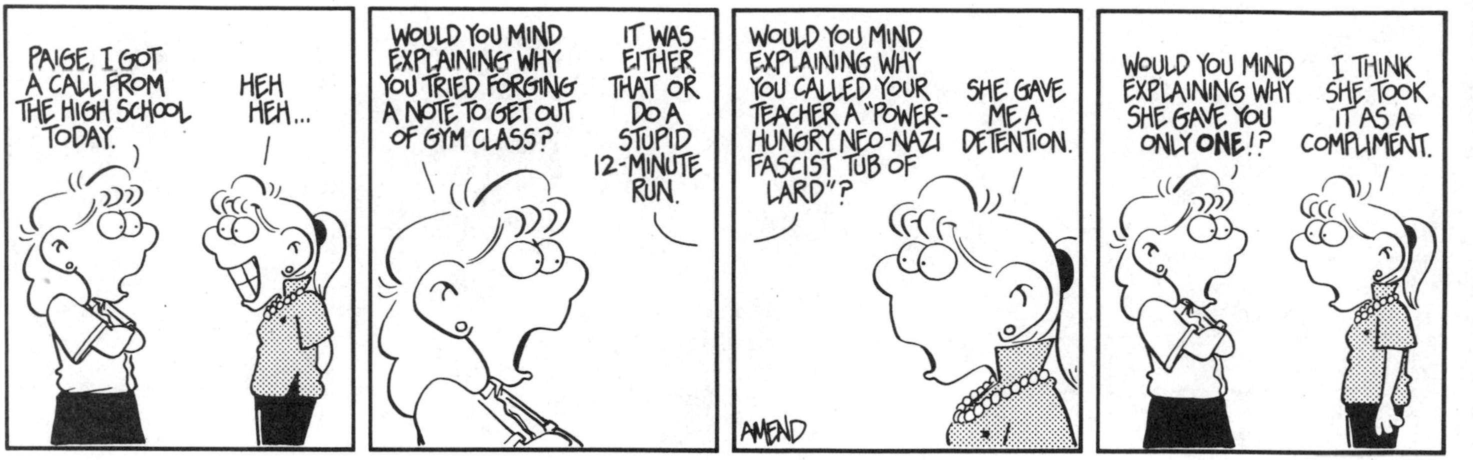
PAIGE, I GOT A CALL FROM THE HIGH SCHOOL TODAY.
HEH HEH...
WOULD YOU MIND EXPLAINING WHY YOU TRIED FORGING A NOTE TO GET OUT OF GYM CLASS?
IT WAS EITHER THAT OR DO A STUPID 12-MINUTE RUN.
WOULD YOU MIND EXPLAINING WHY YOU CALLED YOUR TEACHER A "POWER-HUNGRY NEO-NAZI FASCIST TUB OF LARD"?
SHE GAVE ME A DETENTION.
AMEND
WOULD YOU MIND EXPLAINING WHY SHE GAVE YOU ONLY **ONE**!?
I THINK SHE TOOK IT AS A COMPLIMENT.

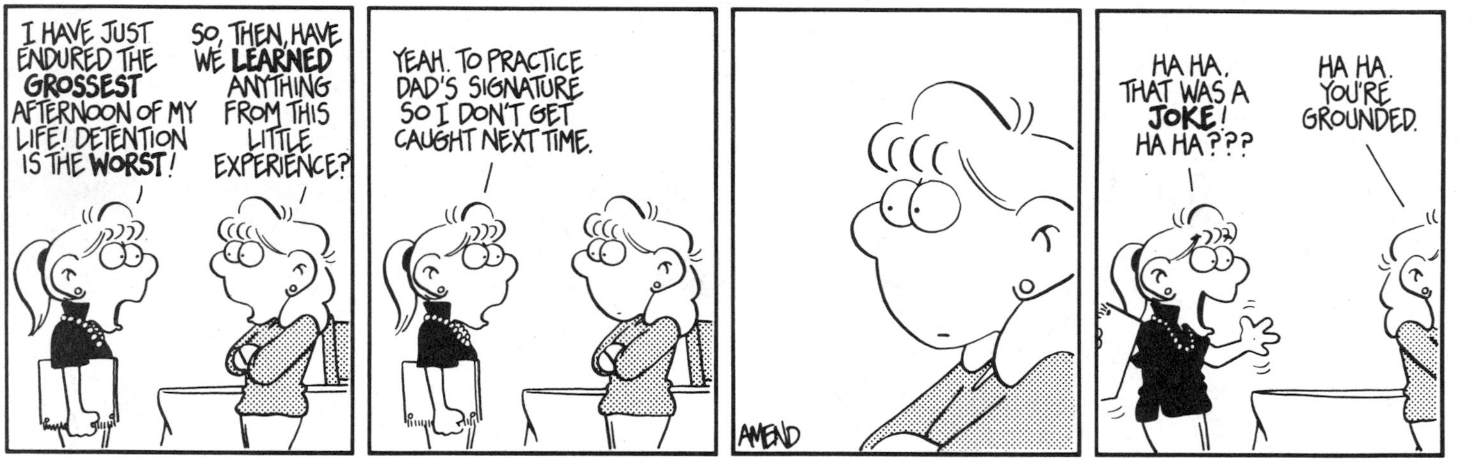
I HAVE JUST ENDURED THE **GROSSEST** AFTERNOON OF MY LIFE! DETENTION IS THE **WORST**!
SO, THEN, HAVE WE **LEARNED** ANYTHING FROM THIS LITTLE EXPERIENCE?
YEAH. TO PRACTICE DAD'S SIGNATURE SO I DON'T GET CAUGHT NEXT TIME.
AMEND
HA HA, THAT WAS A **JOKE**! HA HA???
HA HA. YOU'RE GROUNDED.

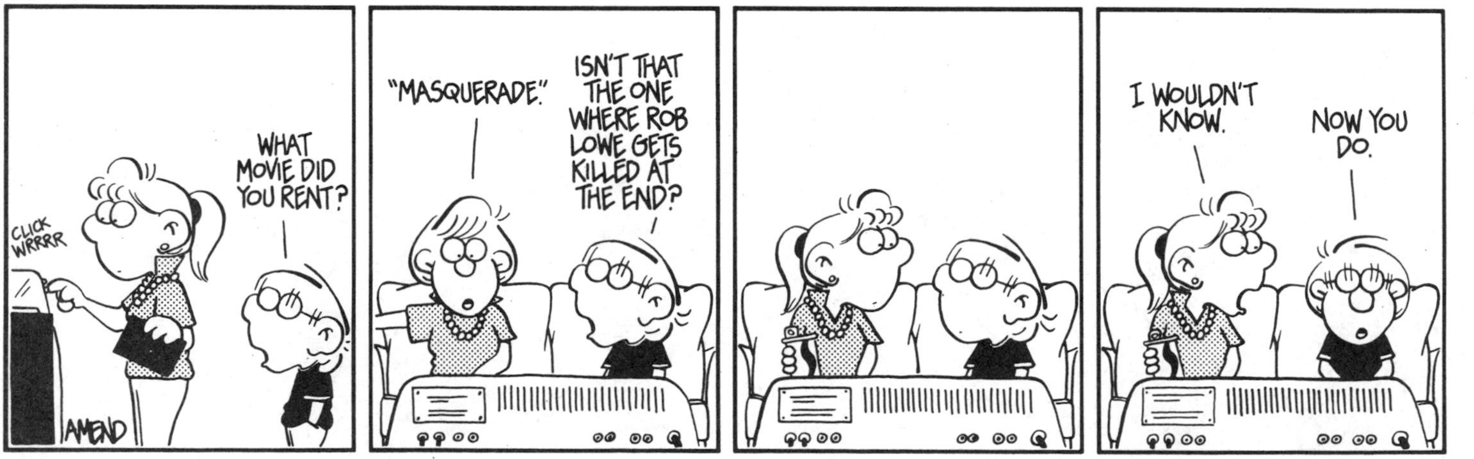
CLICK WRRRR
WHAT MOVIE DID YOU RENT?
AMEND
"MASQUERADE."
ISN'T THAT THE ONE WHERE ROB LOWE GETS KILLED AT THE END?
I WOULDN'T KNOW.
NOW YOU DO.

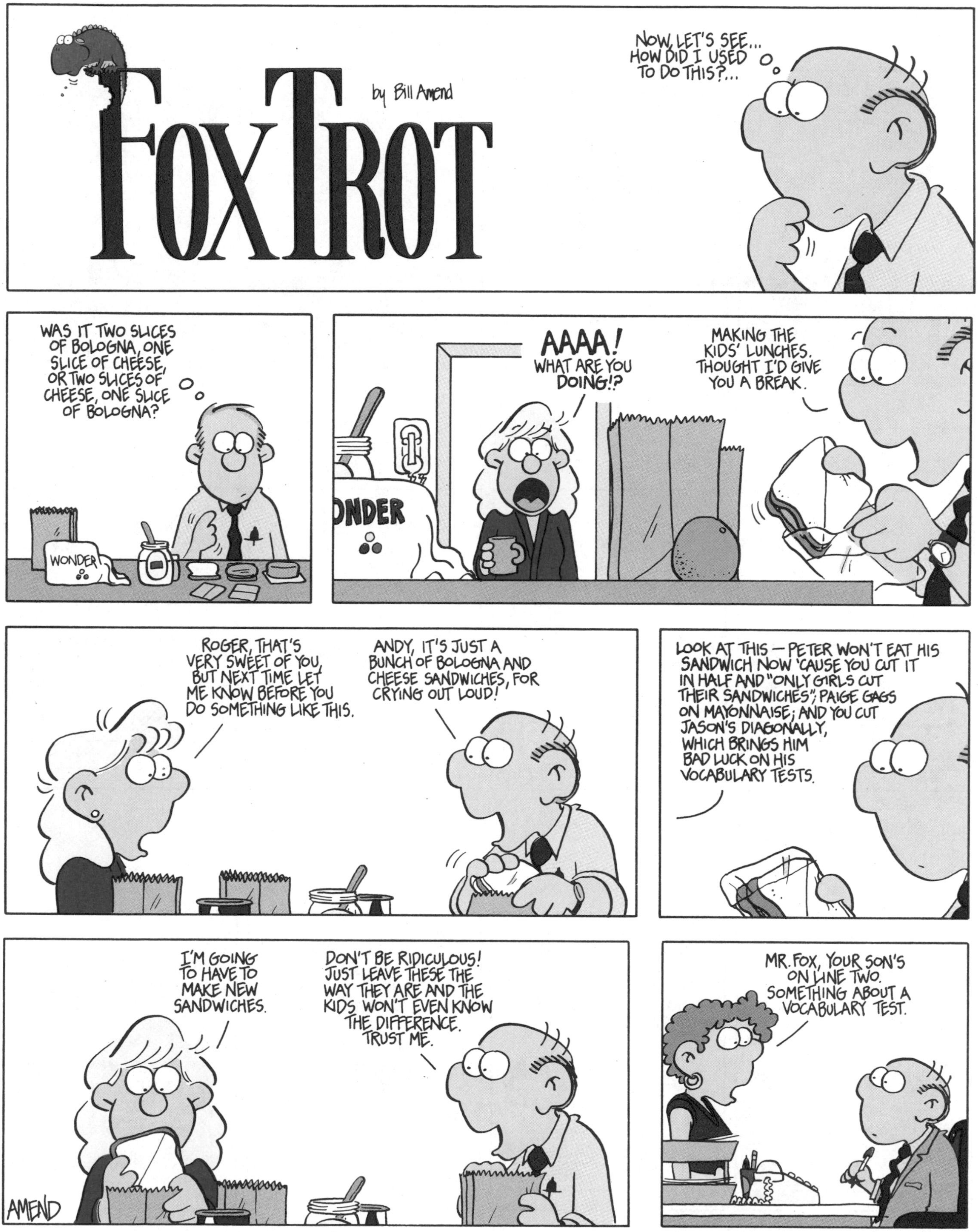
FoxTrot
by Bill Amend
NOW, LET'S SEE... HOW DID I USED TO DO THIS?...
WAS IT TWO SLICES OF BOLOGNA, ONE SLICE OF CHEESE, OR TWO SLICES OF CHEESE, ONE SLICE OF BOLOGNA?
WONDER
AAAA! WHAT ARE YOU DOING!?
MAKING THE KIDS' LUNCHES. THOUGHT I'D GIVE YOU A BREAK.
ROGER, THAT'S VERY SWEET OF YOU, BUT NEXT TIME LET ME KNOW BEFORE YOU DO SOMETHING LIKE THIS.
ANDY, IT'S JUST A BUNCH OF BOLOGNA AND CHEESE SANDWICHES, FOR CRYING OUT LOUD!
LOOK AT THIS — PETER WON'T EAT HIS SANDWICH NOW 'CAUSE YOU CUT IT IN HALF AND "ONLY GIRLS CUT THEIR SANDWICHES"; PAIGE GAGS ON MAYONNAISE; AND YOU CUT JASON'S DIAGONALLY, WHICH BRINGS HIM BAD LUCK ON HIS VOCABULARY TESTS.
I'M GOING TO HAVE TO MAKE NEW SANDWICHES.
DON'T BE RIDICULOUS! JUST LEAVE THESE THE WAY THEY ARE AND THE KIDS WON'T EVEN KNOW THE DIFFERENCE. TRUST ME.
AMEND
MR. FOX, YOUR SON'S ON LINE TWO. SOMETHING ABOUT A VOCABULARY TEST.

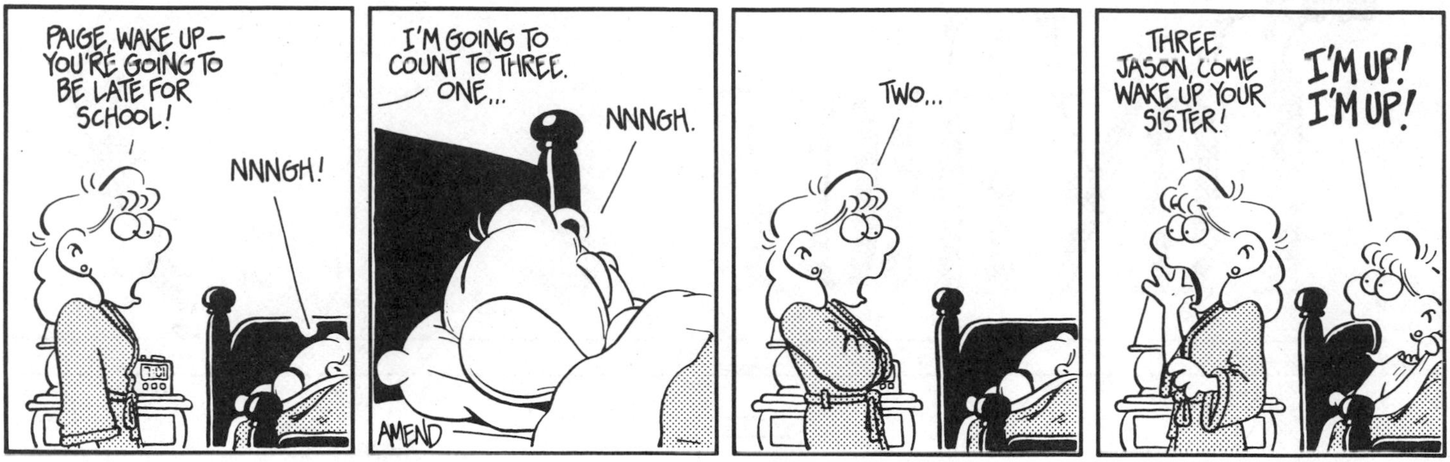
PAIGE, WAKE UP— YOU'RE GOING TO BE LATE FOR SCHOOL!
NNNGH!
I'M GOING TO COUNT TO THREE. ONE,...
NNNGH.
AMEND
TWO,...
THREE. JASON, COME WAKE UP YOUR SISTER!
I'M UP! I'M UP!

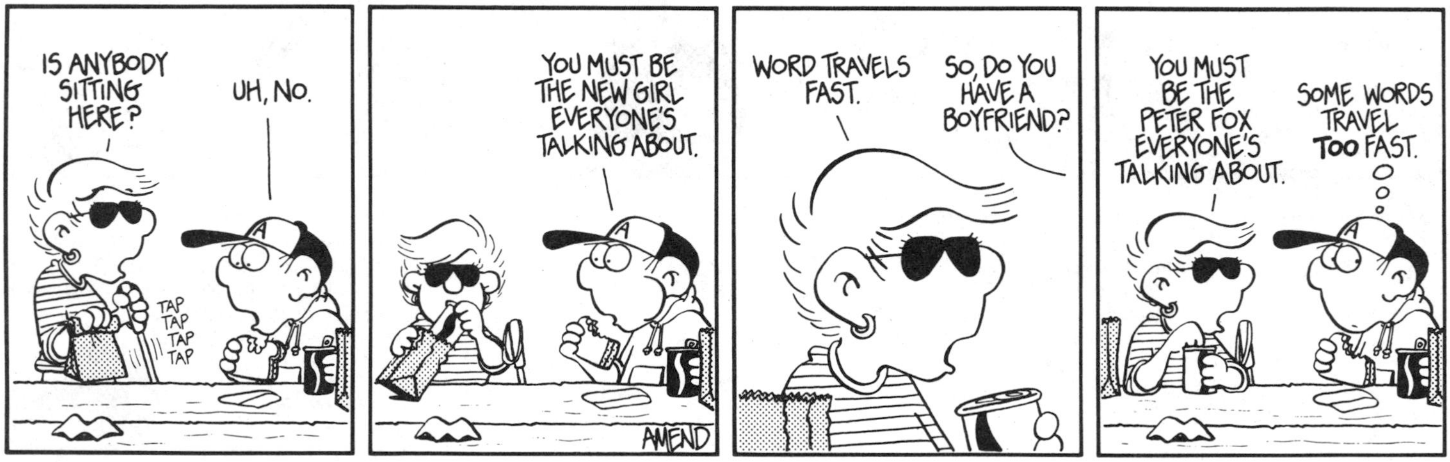
IS ANYBODY SITTING HERE?
UH, NO.
TAP TAP TAP TAP
YOU MUST BE THE NEW GIRL EVERYONE'S TALKING ABOUT.
AMEND
WORD TRAVELS FAST.
SO, DO YOU HAVE A BOYFRIEND?
YOU MUST BE THE PETER FOX EVERYONE'S TALKING ABOUT.
SOME WORDS TRAVEL **TOO** FAST.

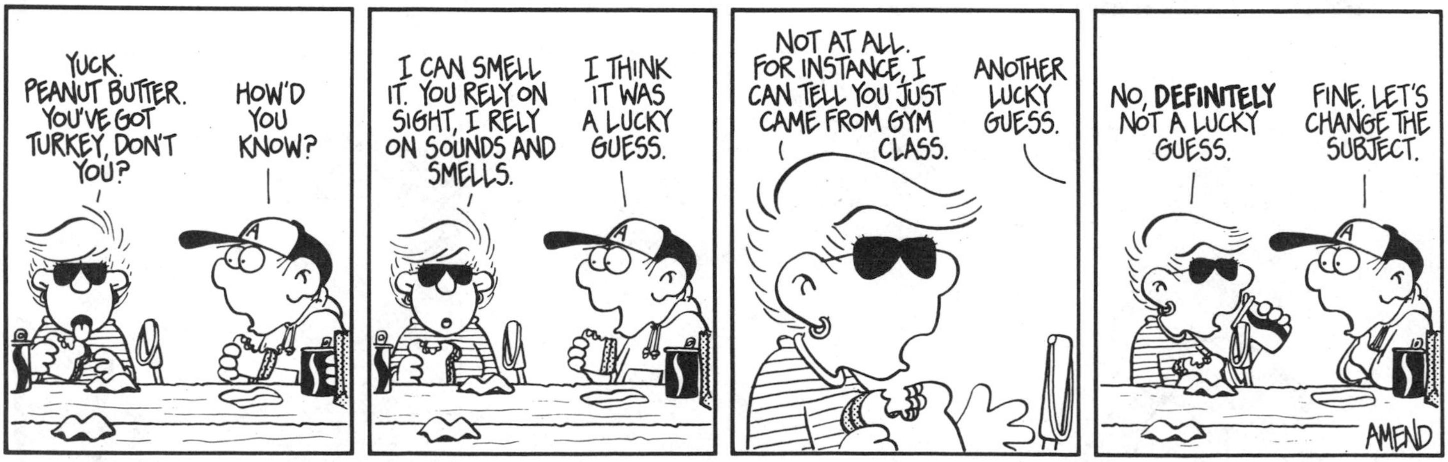
YUCK. PEANUT BUTTER. YOU'VE GOT TURKEY, DON'T YOU?
HOW'D YOU KNOW?
I CAN SMELL IT. YOU RELY ON SIGHT, I RELY ON SOUNDS AND SMELLS.
I THINK IT WAS A LUCKY GUESS.
NOT AT ALL. FOR INSTANCE, I CAN TELL YOU JUST CAME FROM GYM CLASS.
ANOTHER LUCKY GUESS.
NO, **DEFINITELY** NOT A LUCKY GUESS.
FINE. LET'S CHANGE THE SUBJECT.
AMEND

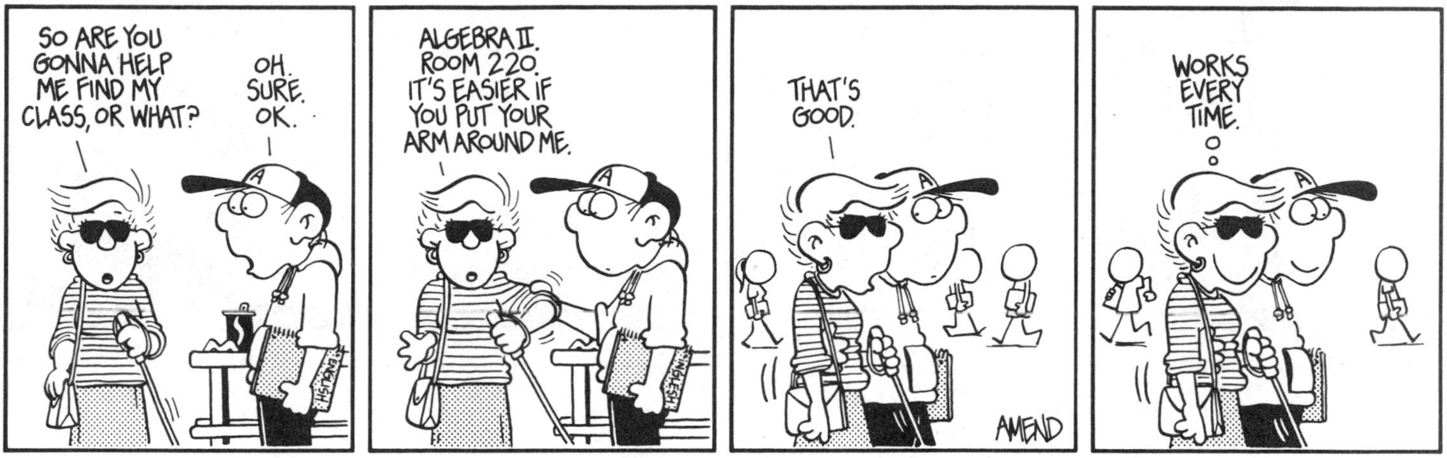

SO ARE YOU GONNA HELP ME FIND MY CLASS, OR WHAT?
OH. SURE. OK.
ENGLISH
ALGEBRA II. ROOM 220. IT'S EASIER IF YOU PUT YOUR ARM AROUND ME.
ENGLISH
THAT'S GOOD.
AMEND
WORKS EVERY TIME.

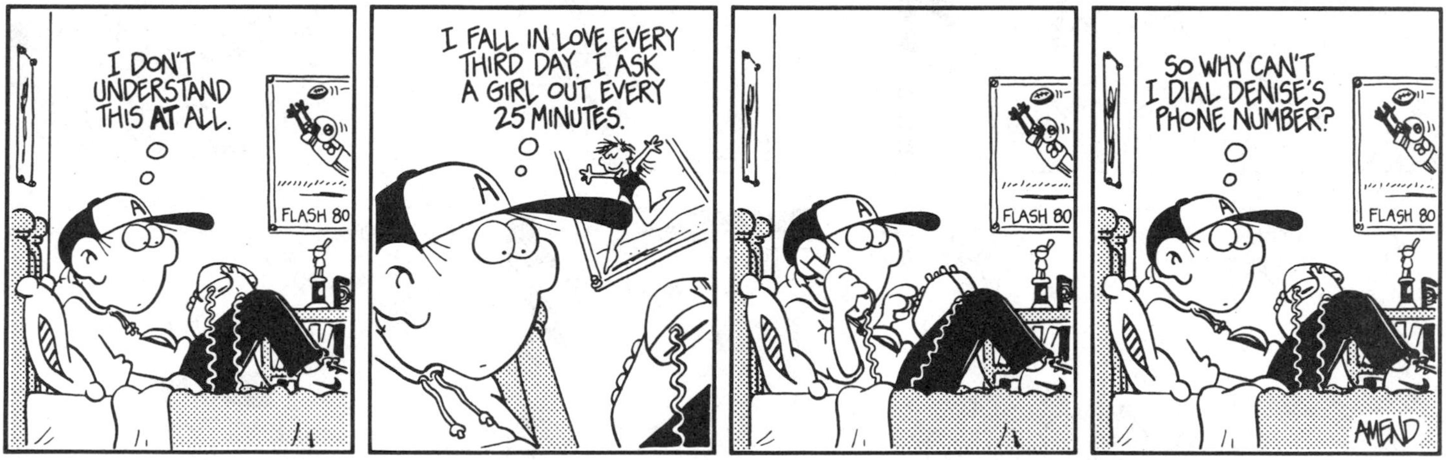

I DON'T UNDERSTAND THIS AT ALL.
FLASH 80
I FALL IN LOVE EVERY THIRD DAY. I ASK A GIRL OUT EVERY 25 MINUTES.
FLASH 80
SO WHY CAN'T I DIAL DENISE'S PHONE NUMBER?
FLASH 80
AMEND

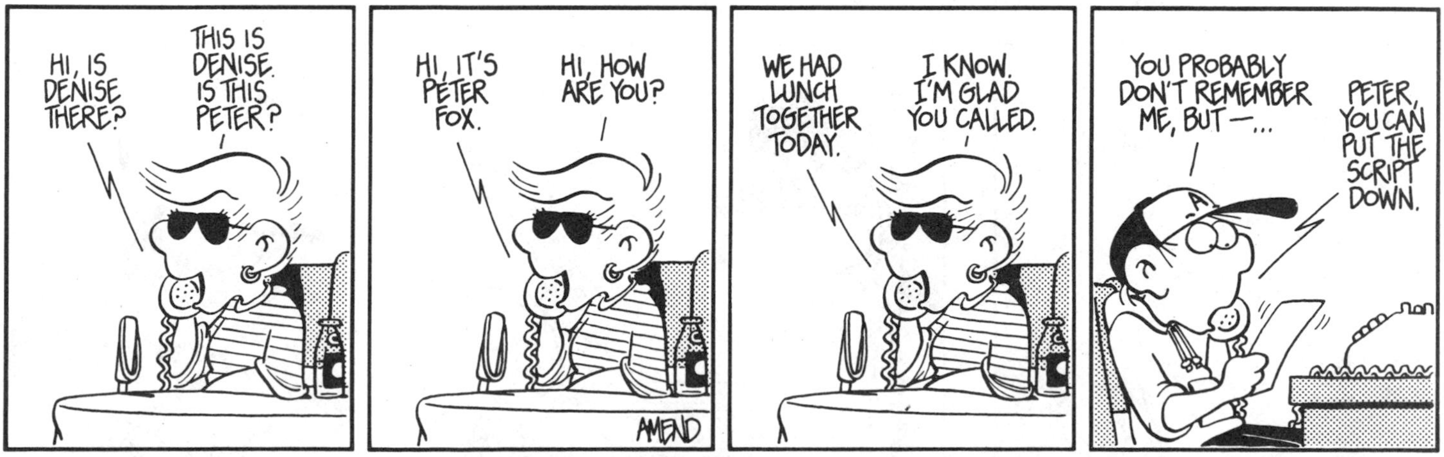

HI, IS DENISE THERE?
THIS IS DENISE. IS THIS PETER?
HI, IT'S PETER FOX.
HI, HOW ARE YOU?
AMEND
WE HAD LUNCH TOGETHER TODAY.
I KNOW. I'M GLAD YOU CALLED.
YOU PROBABLY DON'T REMEMBER ME, BUT—...
PETER, YOU CAN PUT THE SCRIPT DOWN.

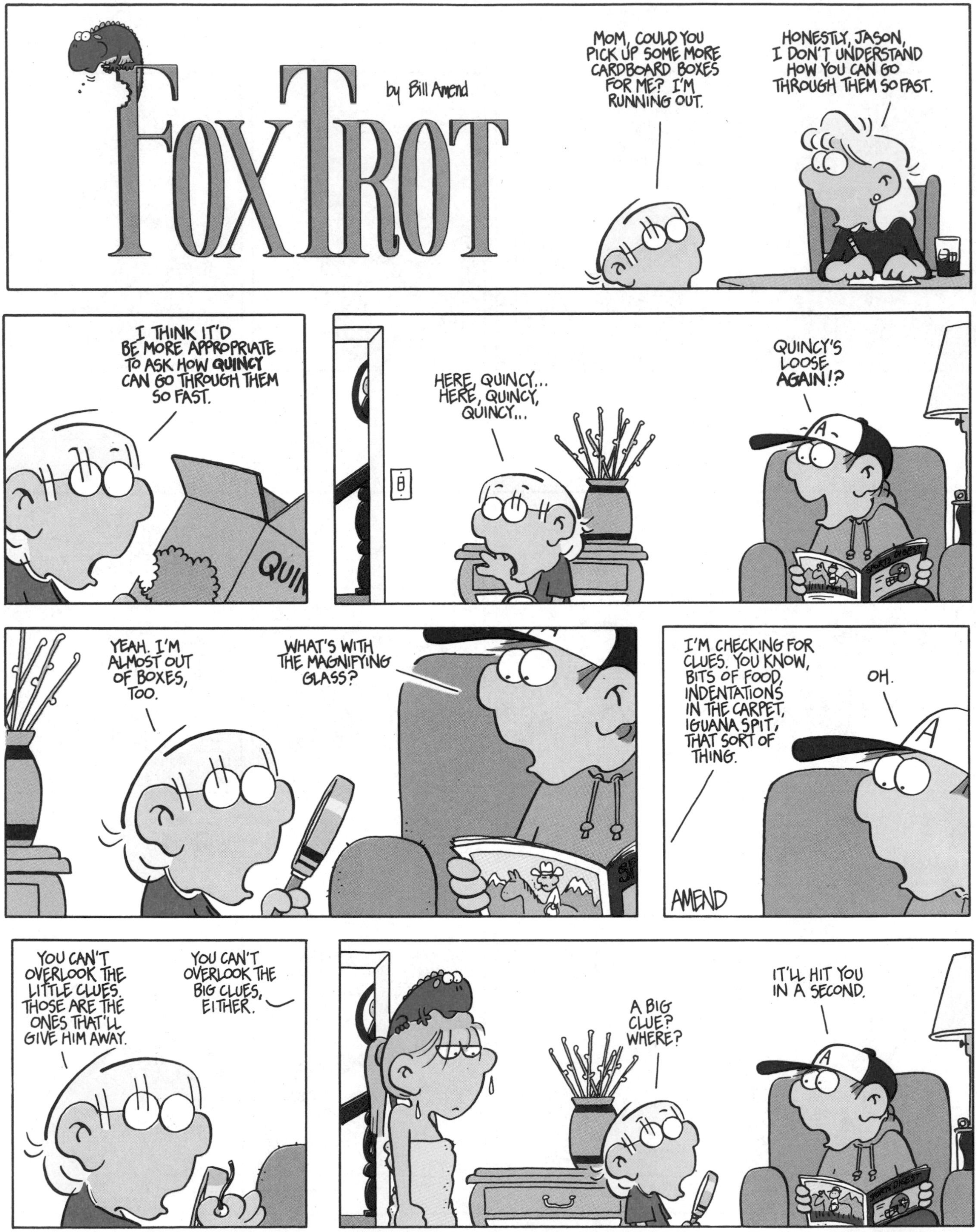
FoxTrot
by Bill Amend
MOM, COULD YOU PICK UP SOME MORE CARDBOARD BOXES FOR ME? I'M RUNNING OUT.
HONESTLY, JASON, I DON'T UNDERSTAND HOW YOU CAN GO THROUGH THEM SO FAST.
I THINK IT'D BE MORE APPROPRIATE TO ASK HOW QUINCY CAN GO THROUGH THEM SO FAST.
QUIN
HERE, QUINCY... HERE, QUINCY, QUINCY...
QUINCY'S LOOSE AGAIN!?
YEAH. I'M ALMOST OUT OF BOXES, TOO.
WHAT'S WITH THE MAGNIFYING GLASS?
I'M CHECKING FOR CLUES. YOU KNOW, BITS OF FOOD, INDENTATIONS IN THE CARPET, IGUANA SPIT, THAT SORT OF THING.
OH.
AMEND
YOU CAN'T OVERLOOK THE LITTLE CLUES. THOSE ARE THE ONES THAT'LL GIVE HIM AWAY.
YOU CAN'T OVERLOOK THE BIG CLUES, EITHER.
A BIG CLUE? WHERE?
IT'LL HIT YOU IN A SECOND.

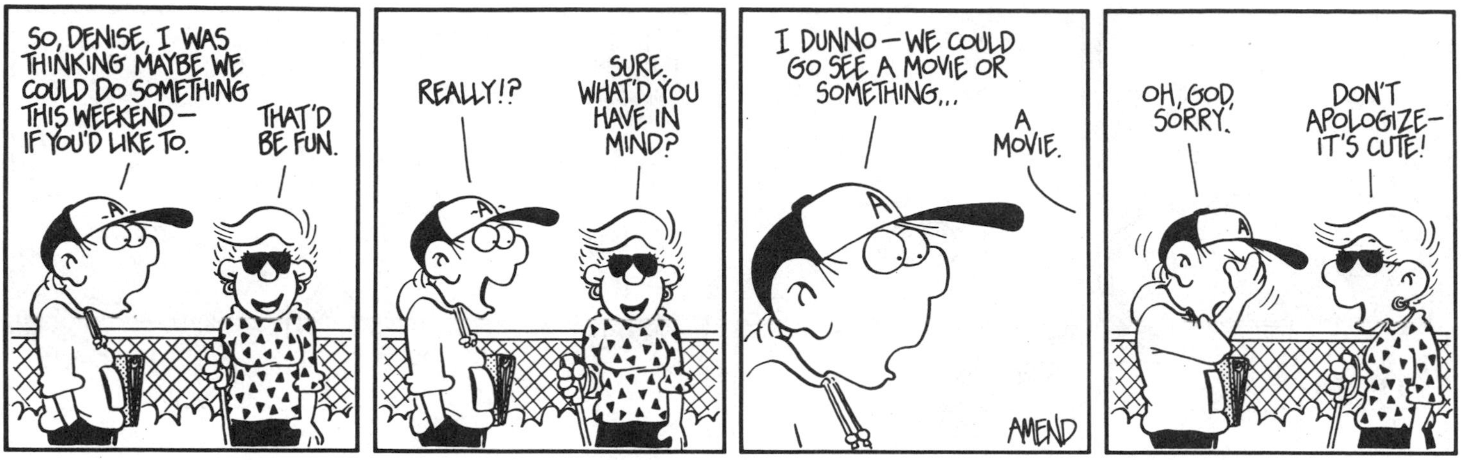
SO, DENISE, I WAS THINKING MAYBE WE COULD DO SOMETHING THIS WEEKEND— IF YOU'D LIKE TO.
THAT'D BE FUN.
REALLY!?
SURE. WHAT'D YOU HAVE IN MIND?
I DUNNO—WE COULD GO SEE A MOVIE OR SOMETHING...
A MOVIE.
AMEND
OH, GOD, SORRY.
DON'T APOLOGIZE— IT'S CUTE!

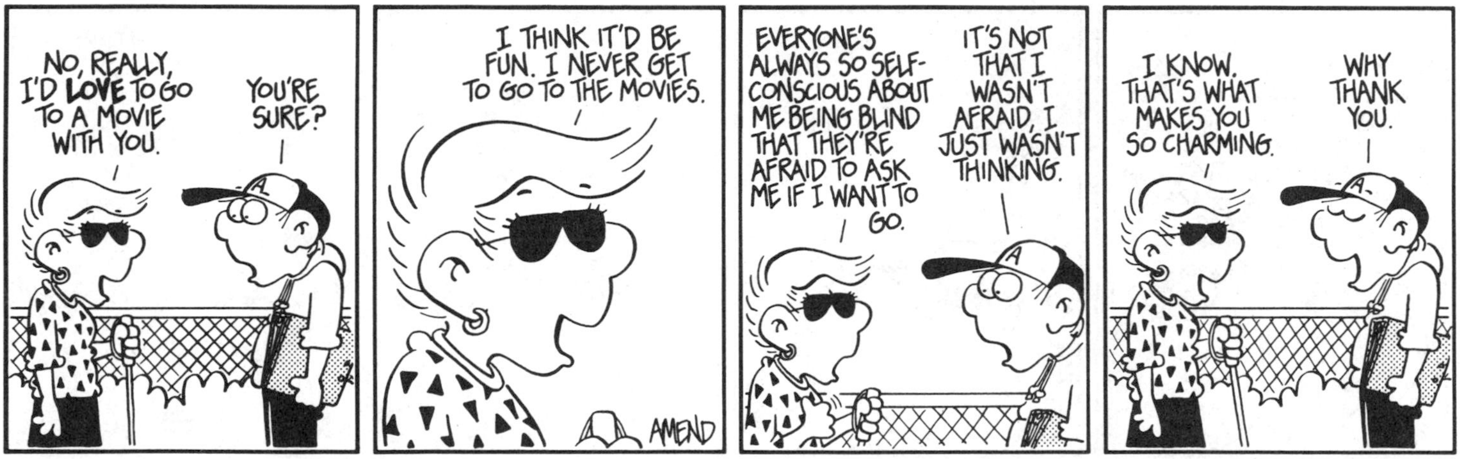
NO, REALLY, I'D **LOVE** TO GO TO A MOVIE WITH YOU.
YOU'RE SURE?
I THINK IT'D BE FUN. I NEVER GET TO GO TO THE MOVIES.
AMEND
EVERYONE'S ALWAYS SO SELF-CONSCIOUS ABOUT ME BEING BLIND THAT THEY'RE AFRAID TO ASK ME IF I WANT TO GO.
IT'S NOT THAT I WASN'T AFRAID, I JUST WASN'T THINKING.
I KNOW. THAT'S WHAT MAKES YOU SO CHARMING.
WHY THANK YOU.

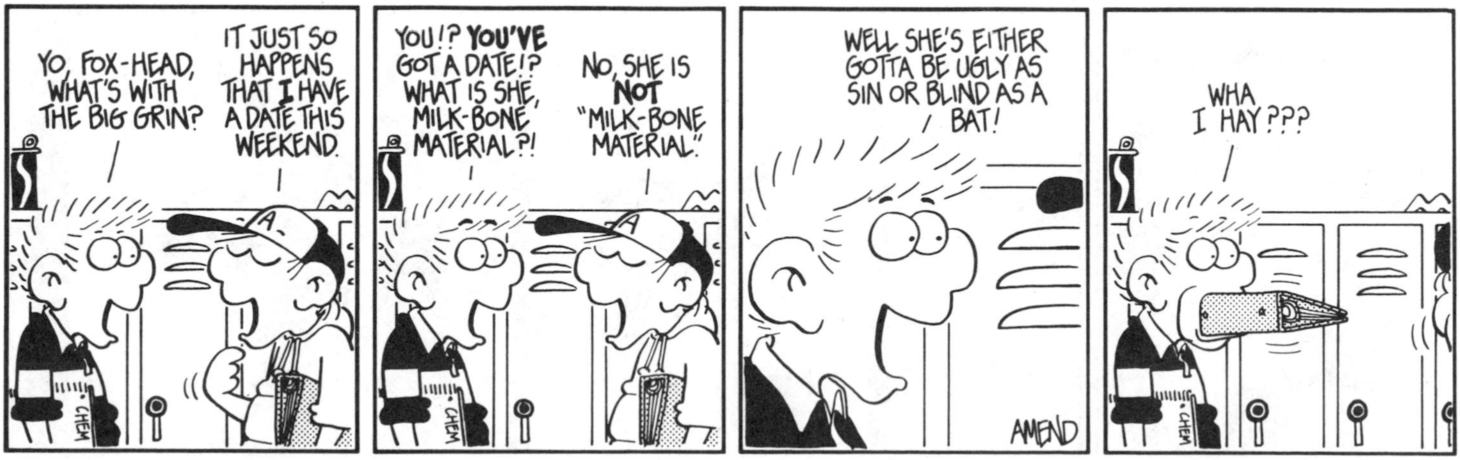
YO, FOX-HEAD, WHAT'S WITH THE BIG GRIN?
IT JUST SO HAPPENS THAT **I** HAVE A DATE THIS WEEKEND.
CHEM
YOU!? **YOU'VE** GOT A DATE!? WHAT IS SHE, MILK-BONE MATERIAL?!
NO, SHE IS **NOT** "MILK-BONE MATERIAL."
WELL SHE'S EITHER GOTTA BE UGLY AS SIN OR BLIND AS A BAT!
AMEND
WHA I HAY???

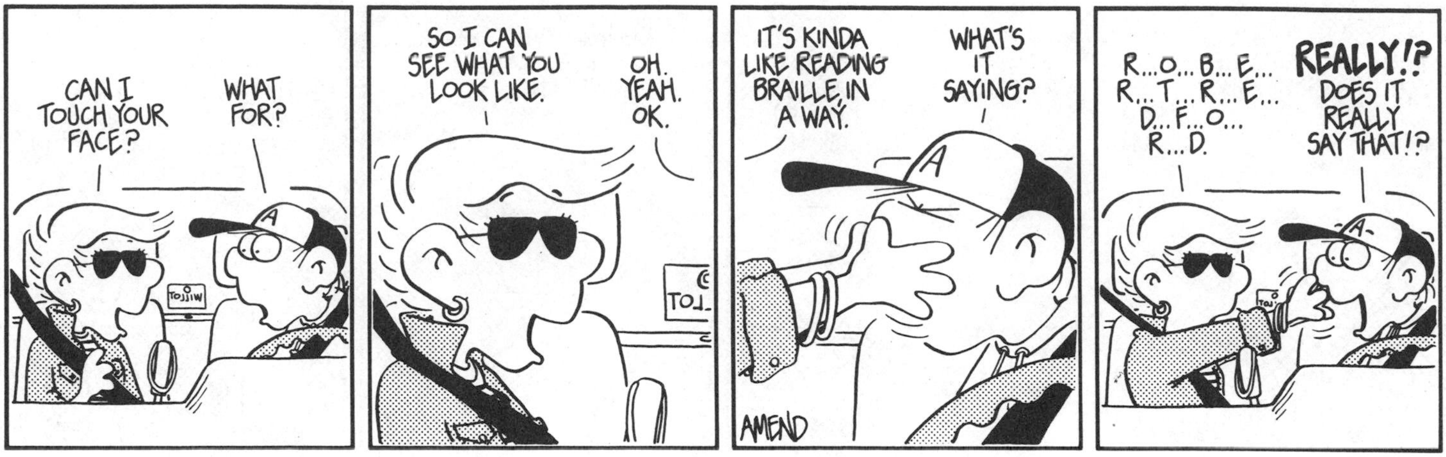
CAN I TOUCH YOUR FACE?
WHAT FOR?
SO I CAN SEE WHAT YOU LOOK LIKE.
OH. YEAH. OK.
IT'S KINDA LIKE READING BRAILLE, IN A WAY.
WHAT'S IT SAYING?
AMEND
R...O...B...E... R...T...R...E... D...F...O... R...D.
REALLY!? DOES IT REALLY SAY THAT!?

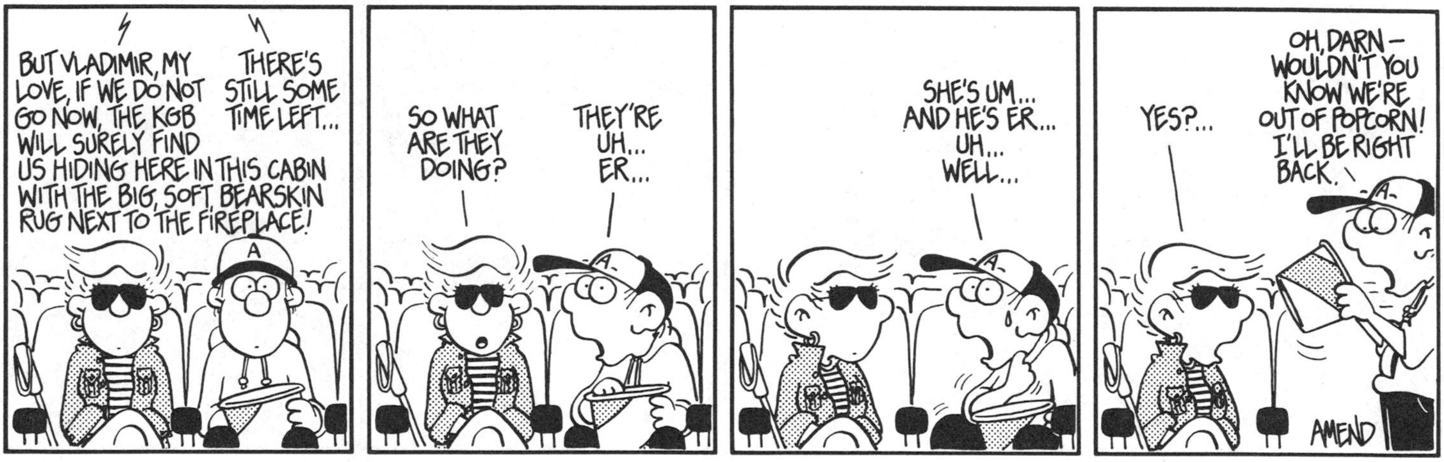
BUT VLADIMIR, MY LOVE, IF WE DO NOT GO NOW, THE KGB WILL SURELY FIND US HIDING HERE IN THIS CABIN WITH THE BIG, SOFT BEARSKIN RUG NEXT TO THE FIREPLACE!
THERE'S STILL SOME TIME LEFT...
SO WHAT ARE THEY DOING?
THEY'RE UH... ER...
SHE'S UM... AND HE'S ER... UH... WELL...
YES?...
OH, DARN — WOULDN'T YOU KNOW WE'RE OUT OF POPCORN! I'LL BE RIGHT BACK.
AMEND

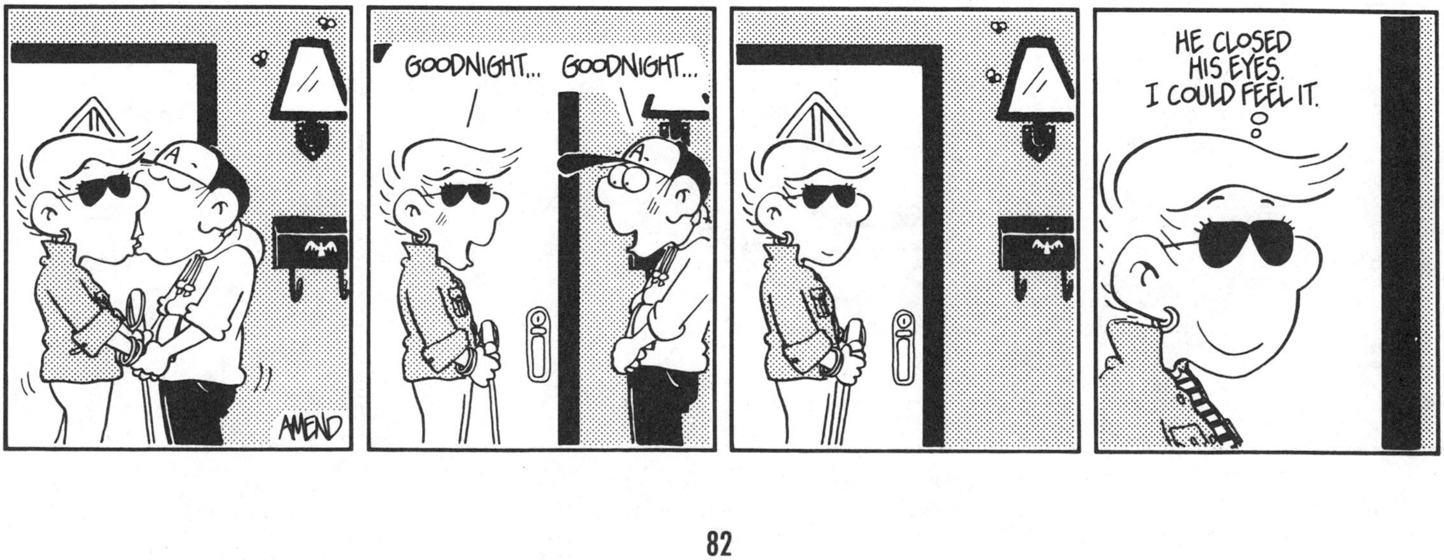
AMEND
GOODNIGHT...
GOODNIGHT...
HE CLOSED HIS EYES. I COULD FEEL IT.

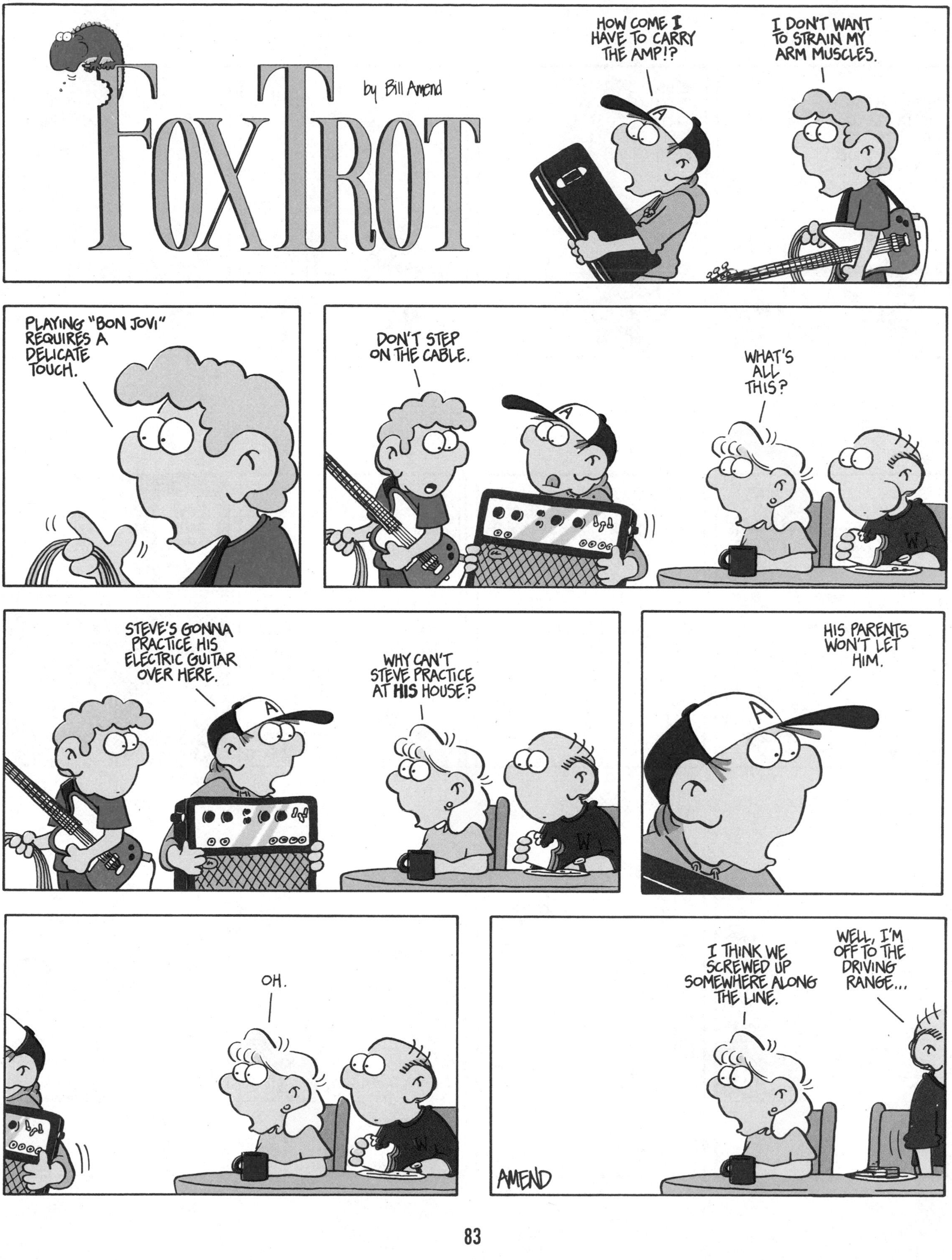
FoxTrot
by Bill Amend
HOW COME I HAVE TO CARRY THE AMP!?
I DON'T WANT TO STRAIN MY ARM MUSCLES.
PLAYING "BON JOVI" REQUIRES A DELICATE TOUCH.
DON'T STEP ON THE CABLE.
WHAT'S ALL THIS?
STEVE'S GONNA PRACTICE HIS ELECTRIC GUITAR OVER HERE.
WHY CAN'T STEVE PRACTICE AT HIS HOUSE?
HIS PARENTS WON'T LET HIM.
OH.
I THINK WE SCREWED UP SOMEWHERE ALONG THE LINE.
WELL, I'M OFF TO THE DRIVING RANGE...
AMEND

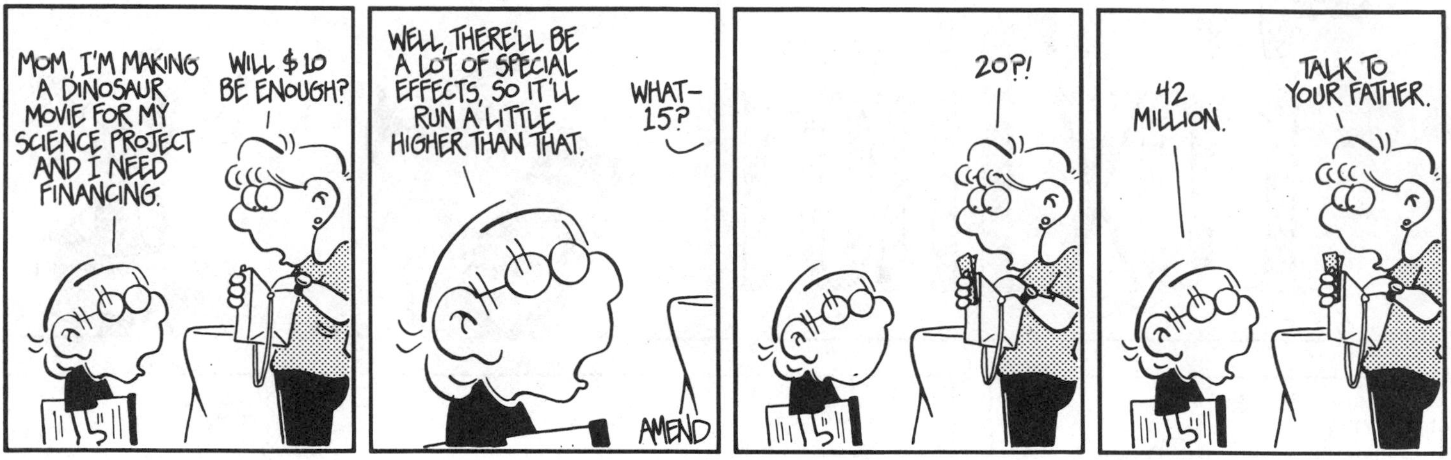
MOM, I'M MAKING A DINOSAUR MOVIE FOR MY SCIENCE PROJECT AND I NEED FINANCING.
WILL $10 BE ENOUGH?
WELL, THERE'LL BE A LOT OF SPECIAL EFFECTS, SO IT'LL RUN A LITTLE HIGHER THAN THAT.
WHAT- 15?
20?!
42 MILLION.
TALK TO YOUR FATHER.
AMEND

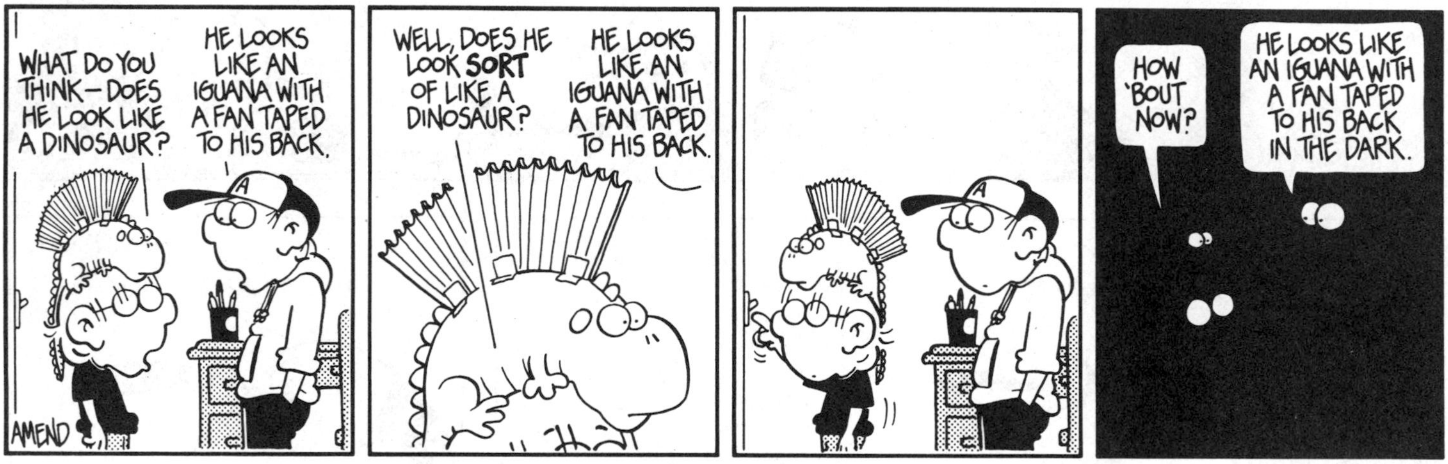
WHAT DO YOU THINK-DOES HE LOOK LIKE A DINOSAUR?
HE LOOKS LIKE AN IGUANA WITH A FAN TAPED TO HIS BACK.
AMEND
WELL, DOES HE LOOK **SORT** OF LIKE A DINOSAUR?
HE LOOKS LIKE AN IGUANA WITH A FAN TAPED TO HIS BACK.
HOW 'BOUT NOW?
HE LOOKS LIKE AN IGUANA WITH A FAN TAPED TO HIS BACK IN THE DARK.

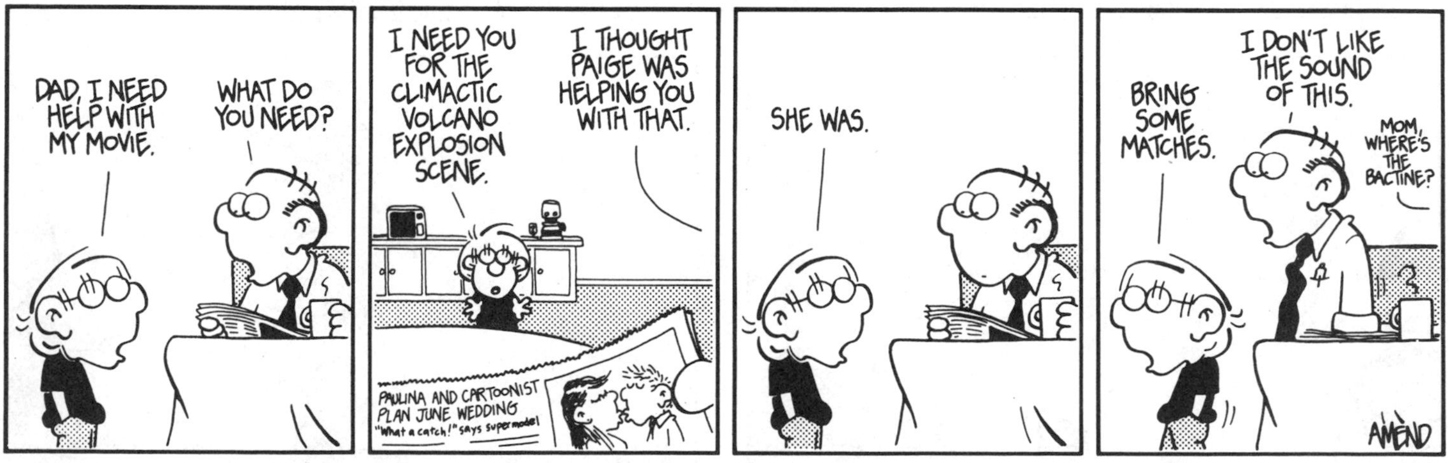
DAD, I NEED HELP WITH MY MOVIE.
WHAT DO YOU NEED?
I NEED YOU FOR THE CLIMACTIC VOLCANO EXPLOSION SCENE.
I THOUGHT PAIGE WAS HELPING YOU WITH THAT.
PAULINA AND CARTOONIST PLAN JUNE WEDDING
"What a catch!" says supermodel
SHE WAS.
BRING SOME MATCHES.
I DON'T LIKE THE SOUND OF THIS.
MOM, WHERE'S THE BACTINE?
AMEND

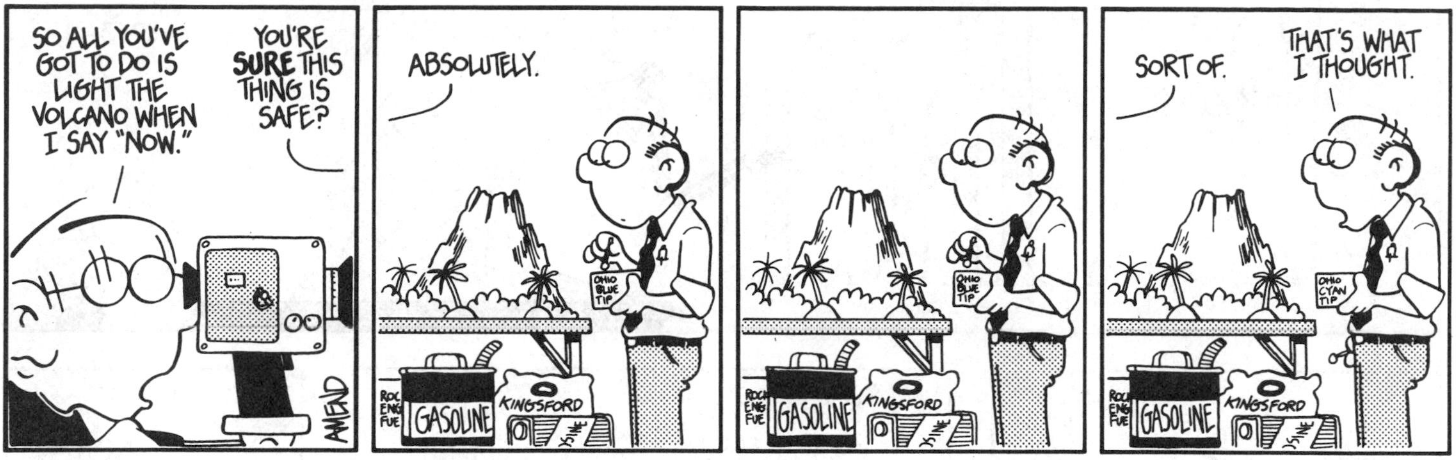
SO ALL YOU'VE GOT TO DO IS LIGHT THE VOLCANO WHEN I SAY "NOW."
YOU'RE **SURE** THIS THING IS SAFE?
AMEND
ABSOLUTELY.
OHIO BLUE TIP
GASOLINE
KINGSFORD
SORT OF.
THAT'S WHAT I THOUGHT.
OHIO CYAN TIP

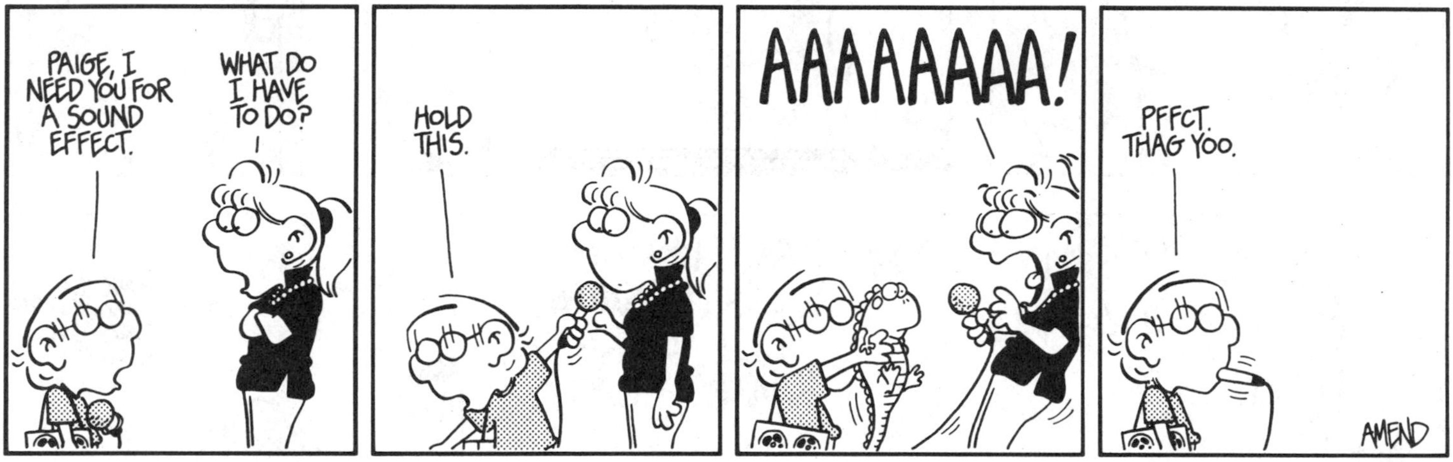
PAIGE, I NEED YOU FOR A SOUND EFFECT.
WHAT DO I HAVE TO DO?
HOLD THIS.
AAAAAAAA!
PFFCT. THAG YOO.
AMEND

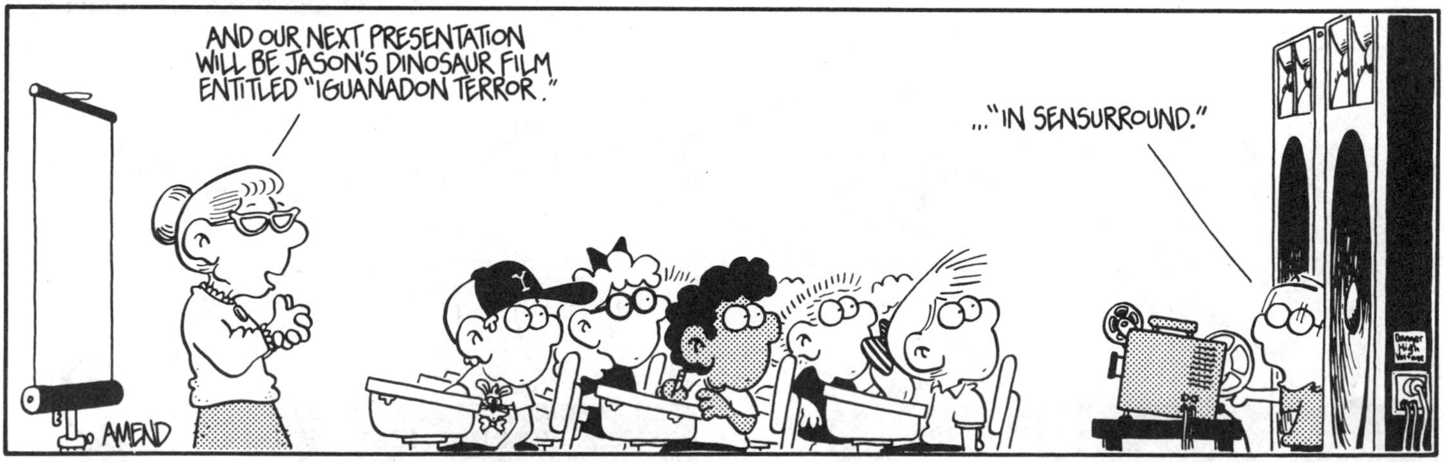
AND OUR NEXT PRESENTATION WILL BE JASON'S DINOSAUR FILM ENTITLED "IGUANADON TERROR."
..."IN SENSURROUND."
AMEND

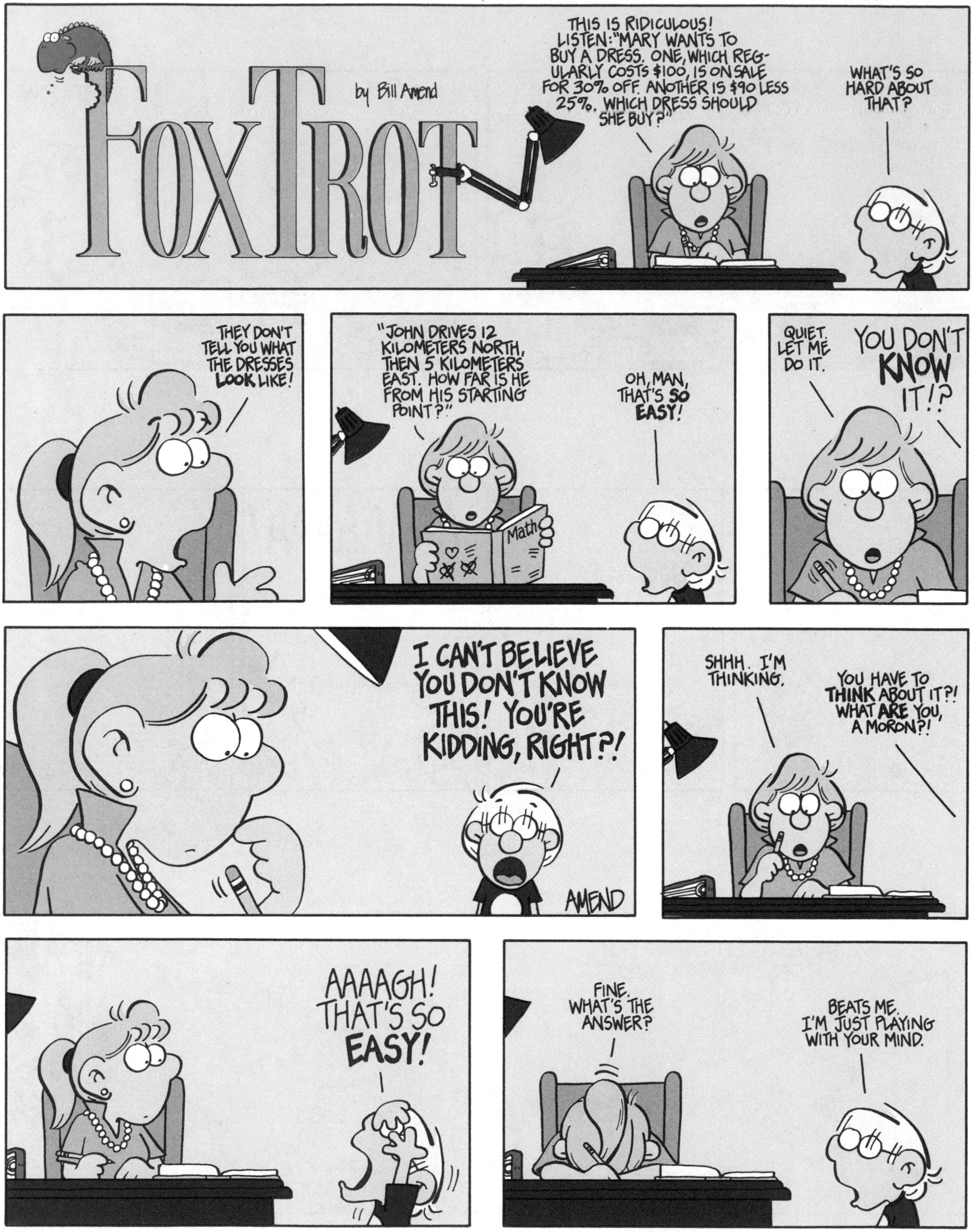
FoxTrot
by Bill Amend
THIS IS RIDICULOUS! LISTEN: "MARY WANTS TO BUY A DRESS. ONE, WHICH REGULARLY COSTS $100, IS ON SALE FOR 30% OFF. ANOTHER IS $90 LESS 25%. WHICH DRESS SHOULD SHE BUY?"
WHAT'S SO HARD ABOUT THAT?
THEY DON'T TELL YOU WHAT THE DRESSES LOOK LIKE!
"JOHN DRIVES 12 KILOMETERS NORTH, THEN 5 KILOMETERS EAST. HOW FAR IS HE FROM HIS STARTING POINT?"
Math
OH, MAN, THAT'S SO EASY!
QUIET. LET ME DO IT.
YOU DON'T KNOW IT!?
I CAN'T BELIEVE YOU DON'T KNOW THIS! YOU'RE KIDDING, RIGHT?!
AMEND
SHHH. I'M THINKING.
YOU HAVE TO THINK ABOUT IT?! WHAT ARE YOU, A MORON?!
AAAAGH! THAT'S SO EASY!
FINE. WHAT'S THE ANSWER?
BEATS ME. I'M JUST PLAYING WITH YOUR MIND.

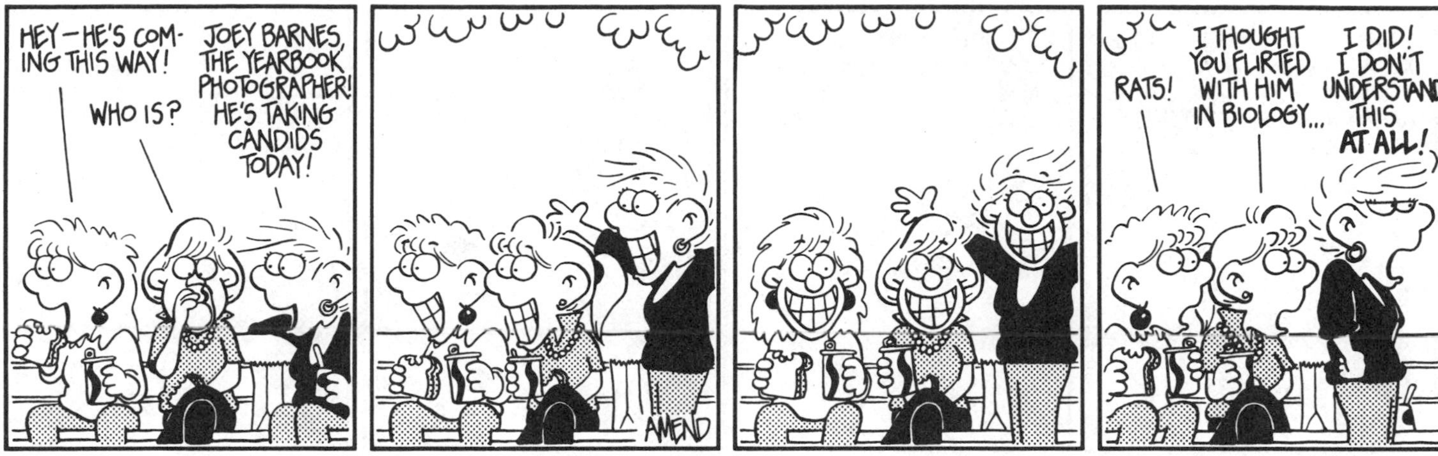
HEY—HE'S COMING THIS WAY!
WHO IS?
JOEY BARNES, THE YEARBOOK PHOTOGRAPHER! HE'S TAKING CANDIDS TODAY!
AMEND
RATS!
I THOUGHT YOU FLIRTED WITH HIM IN BIOLOGY...
I DID! I DON'T UNDERSTAND THIS AT ALL!

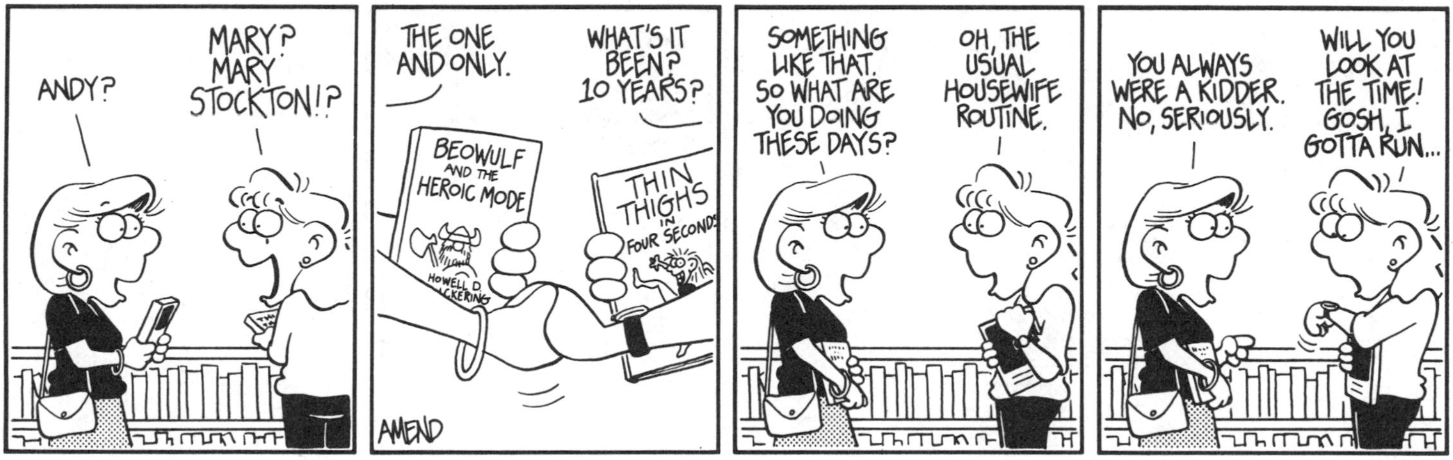
ANDY?
MARY? MARY STOCKTON!?
THE ONE AND ONLY.
WHAT'S IT BEEN? 10 YEARS?
BEOWULF AND THE HEROIC MODE
THIN THIGHS IN FOUR SECONDS
AMEND
SOMETHING LIKE THAT. SO WHAT ARE YOU DOING THESE DAYS?
OH, THE USUAL HOUSEWIFE ROUTINE.
YOU ALWAYS WERE A KIDDER. NO, SERIOUSLY.
WILL YOU LOOK AT THE TIME! GOSH, I GOTTA RUN...

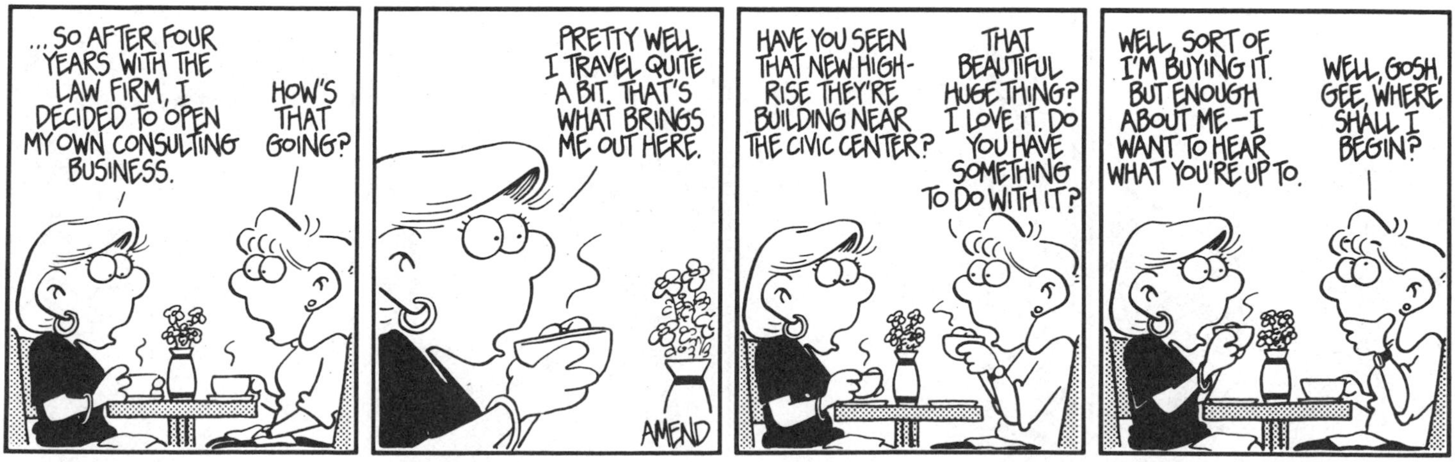
...SO AFTER FOUR YEARS WITH THE LAW FIRM, I DECIDED TO OPEN MY OWN CONSULTING BUSINESS.
HOW'S THAT GOING?
PRETTY WELL. I TRAVEL QUITE A BIT. THAT'S WHAT BRINGS ME OUT HERE.
AMEND
HAVE YOU SEEN THAT NEW HIGH-RISE THEY'RE BUILDING NEAR THE CIVIC CENTER?
THAT BEAUTIFUL HUGE THING? I LOVE IT. DO YOU HAVE SOMETHING TO DO WITH IT?
WELL, SORT OF. I'M BUYING IT. BUT ENOUGH ABOUT ME—I WANT TO HEAR WHAT YOU'RE UP TO.
WELL, GOSH, GEE, WHERE SHALL I BEGIN?

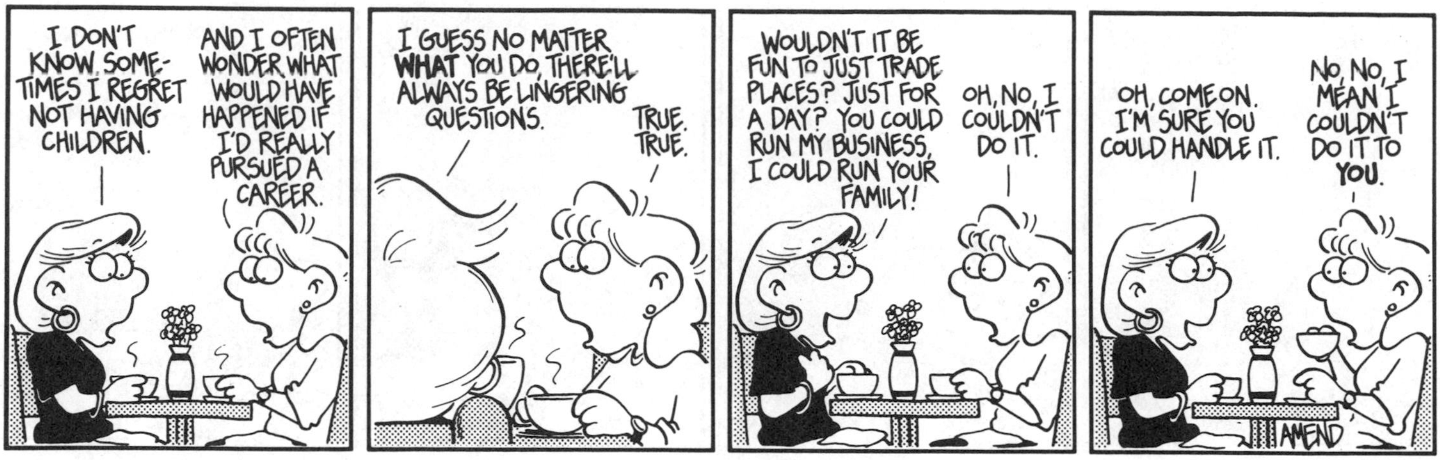
I DON'T KNOW. SOMETIMES I REGRET NOT HAVING CHILDREN.
AND I OFTEN WONDER WHAT WOULD HAVE HAPPENED IF I'D REALLY PURSUED A CAREER.
I GUESS NO MATTER **WHAT** YOU DO, THERE'LL ALWAYS BE LINGERING QUESTIONS.
TRUE. TRUE.
WOULDN'T IT BE FUN TO JUST TRADE PLACES? JUST FOR A DAY? YOU COULD RUN MY BUSINESS, I COULD RUN YOUR FAMILY!
OH, NO, I COULDN'T DO IT.
OH, COME ON. I'M SURE YOU COULD HANDLE IT.
NO, NO, I MEAN I COULDN'T DO IT TO **YOU**.
AMEND

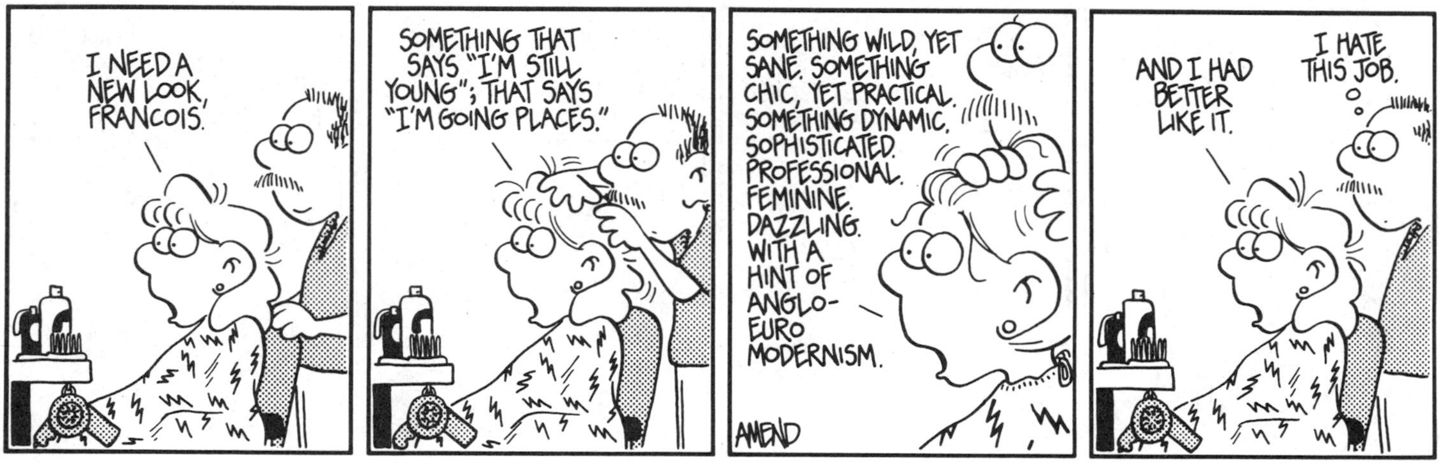
I NEED A NEW LOOK, FRANCOIS.
SOMETHING THAT SAYS "I'M STILL YOUNG"; THAT SAYS "I'M GOING PLACES."
SOMETHING WILD, YET SANE. SOMETHING CHIC, YET PRACTICAL. SOMETHING DYNAMIC. SOPHISTICATED. PROFESSIONAL. FEMININE. DAZZLING. WITH A HINT OF ANGLO-EURO MODERNISM.
AMEND
AND I HAD BETTER LIKE IT.
I HATE THIS JOB.

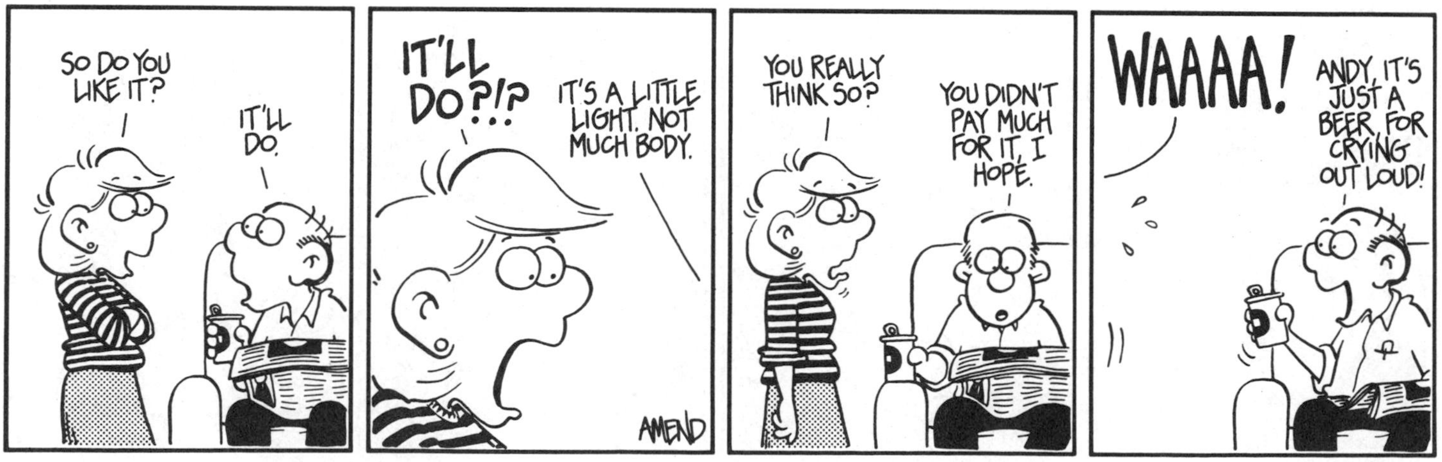
SO DO YOU LIKE IT?
IT'LL DO.
IT'LL DO?!?...
IT'S A LITTLE LIGHT. NOT MUCH BODY.
AMEND
YOU REALLY THINK SO?
YOU DIDN'T PAY MUCH FOR IT, I HOPE.
WAAAA!
ANDY, IT'S JUST A BEER, FOR CRYING OUT LOUD!

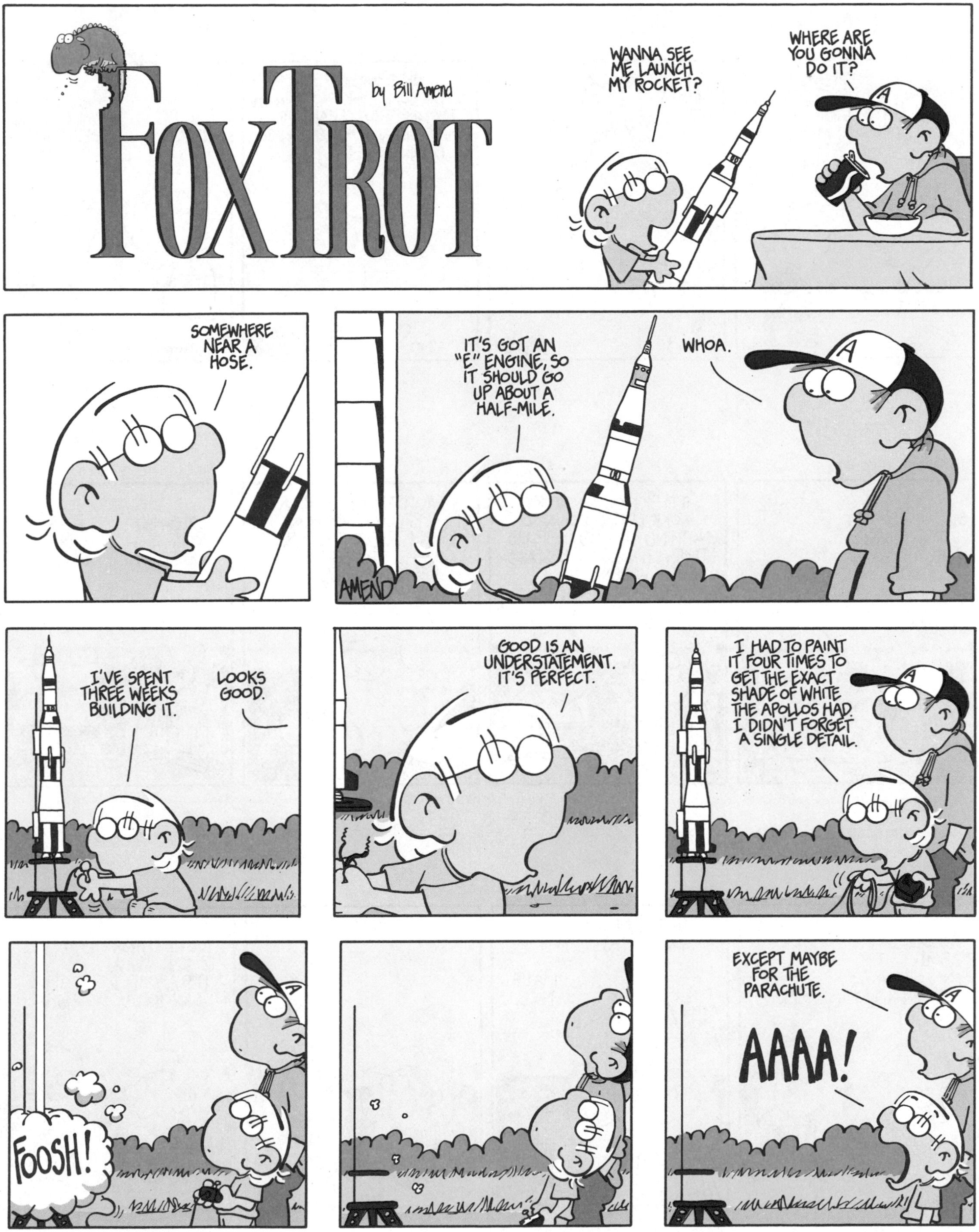
FoxTrot
by Bill Amend
WANNA SEE ME LAUNCH MY ROCKET?
WHERE ARE YOU GONNA DO IT?
SOMEWHERE NEAR A HOSE.
IT'S GOT AN "E" ENGINE, SO IT SHOULD GO UP ABOUT A HALF-MILE.
WHOA.
AMEND
I'VE SPENT THREE WEEKS BUILDING IT.
LOOKS GOOD.
GOOD IS AN UNDERSTATEMENT. IT'S PERFECT.
I HAD TO PAINT IT FOUR TIMES TO GET THE EXACT SHADE OF WHITE THE APOLLOS HAD. I DIDN'T FORGET A SINGLE DETAIL.
FOOSH!
EXCEPT MAYBE FOR THE PARACHUTE.
AAAA!

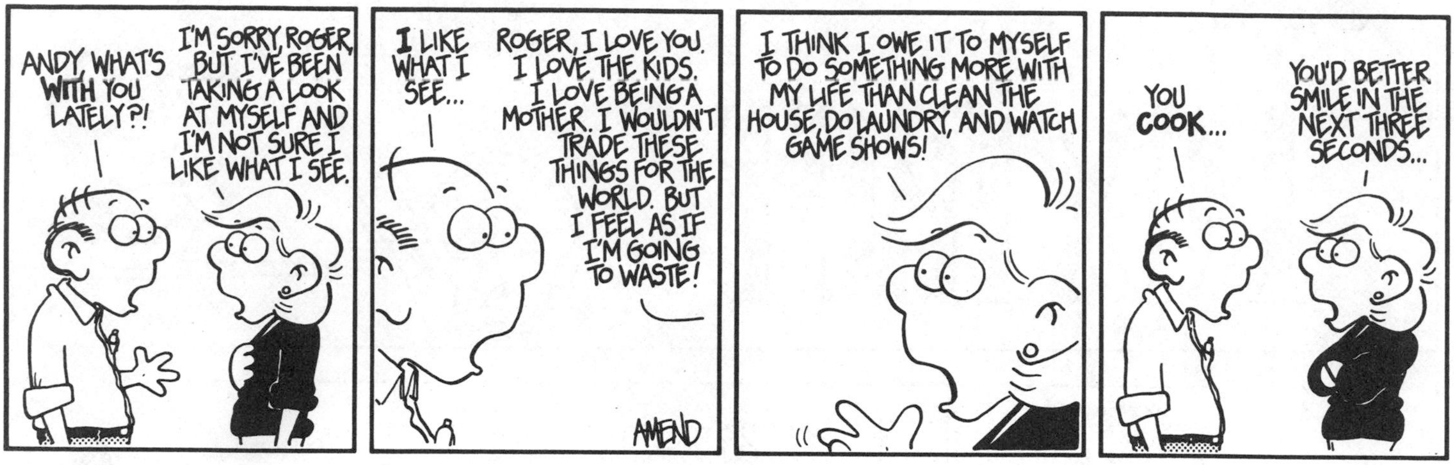
ANDY, WHAT'S **WITH** YOU LATELY?!
I'M SORRY, ROGER, BUT I'VE BEEN TAKING A LOOK AT MYSELF AND I'M NOT SURE I LIKE WHAT I SEE.
I LIKE WHAT I SEE...
ROGER, I LOVE YOU. I LOVE THE KIDS. I LOVE BEING A MOTHER. I WOULDN'T TRADE THESE THINGS FOR THE WORLD. BUT I FEEL AS IF I'M GOING TO WASTE!
AMEND
I THINK I OWE IT TO MYSELF TO DO SOMETHING MORE WITH MY LIFE THAN CLEAN THE HOUSE, DO LAUNDRY, AND WATCH GAME SHOWS!
YOU **COOK**...
YOU'D BETTER SMILE IN THE NEXT THREE SECONDS...

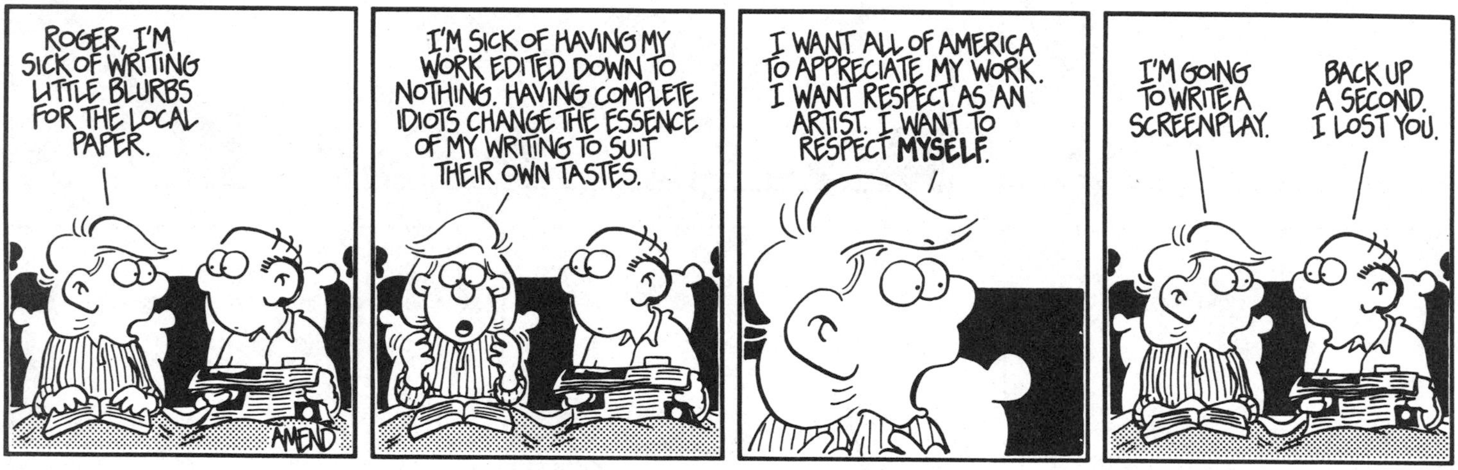
ROGER, I'M SICK OF WRITING LITTLE BLURBS FOR THE LOCAL PAPER.
AMEND
I'M SICK OF HAVING MY WORK EDITED DOWN TO NOTHING. HAVING COMPLETE IDIOTS CHANGE THE ESSENCE OF MY WRITING TO SUIT THEIR OWN TASTES.
I WANT ALL OF AMERICA TO APPRECIATE MY WORK. I WANT RESPECT AS AN ARTIST. I WANT TO RESPECT **MYSELF**.
I'M GOING TO WRITE A SCREENPLAY.
BACK UP A SECOND. I LOST YOU.

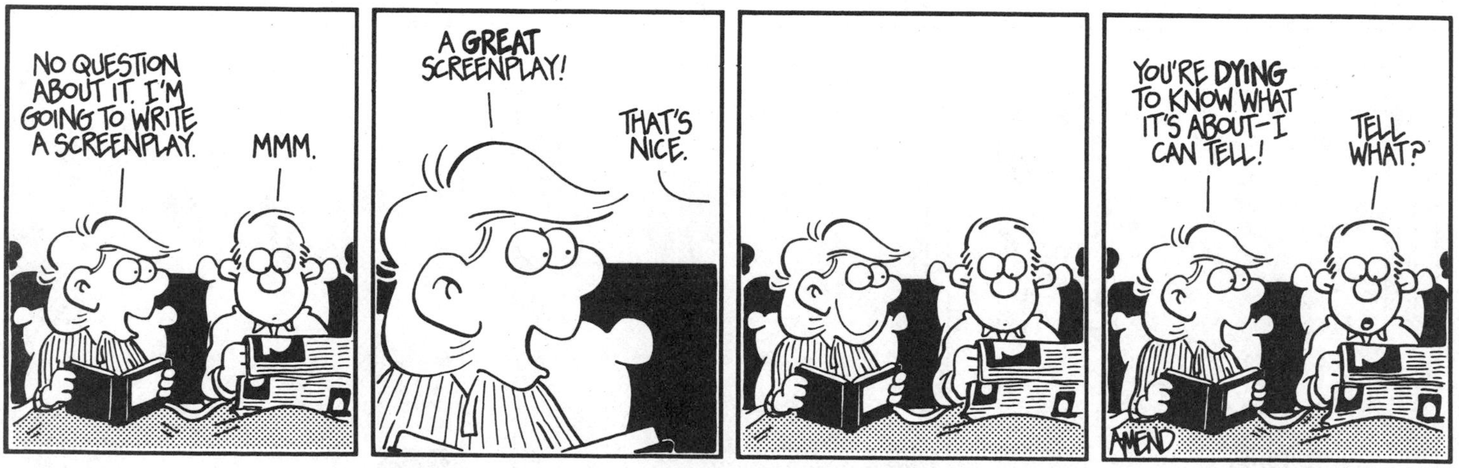
NO QUESTION ABOUT IT. I'M GOING TO WRITE A SCREENPLAY.
MMM.
A **GREAT** SCREENPLAY!
THAT'S NICE.
YOU'RE **DYING** TO KNOW WHAT IT'S ABOUT—I CAN TELL!
TELL WHAT?
AMEND

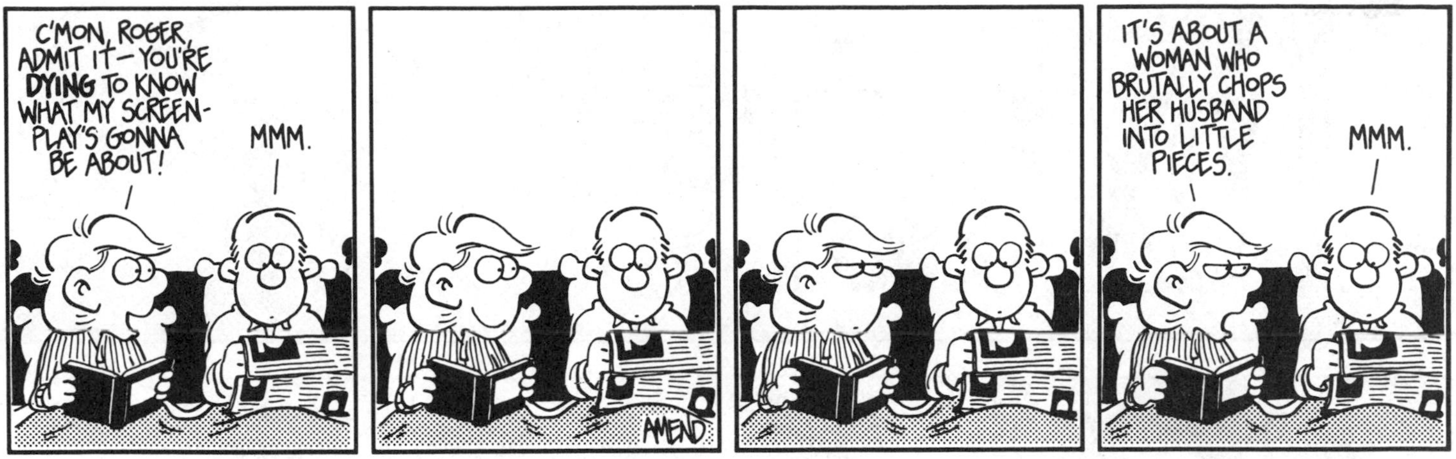
C'MON, ROGER, ADMIT IT—YOU'RE **DYING** TO KNOW WHAT MY SCREEN-PLAY'S GONNA BE ABOUT!
MMM.
IT'S ABOUT A WOMAN WHO BRUTALLY CHOPS HER HUSBAND INTO LITTLE PIECES.
MMM.
AMEND

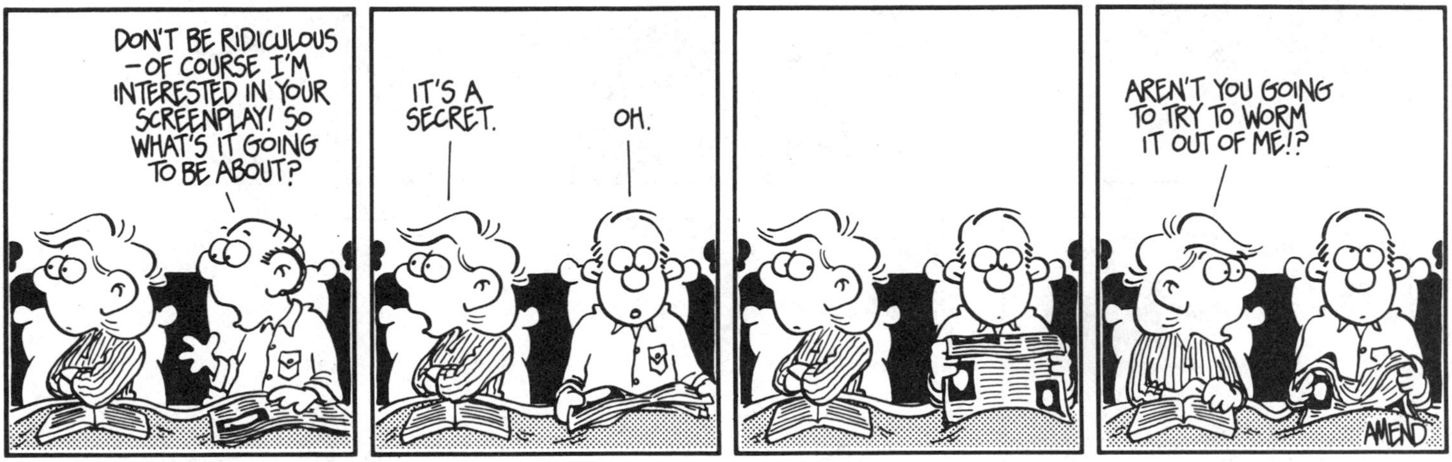
DON'T BE RIDICULOUS—OF COURSE I'M INTERESTED IN YOUR SCREENPLAY! SO WHAT'S IT GOING TO BE ABOUT?
IT'S A SECRET.
OH.
AREN'T YOU GOING TO TRY TO WORM IT OUT OF ME!?
AMEND

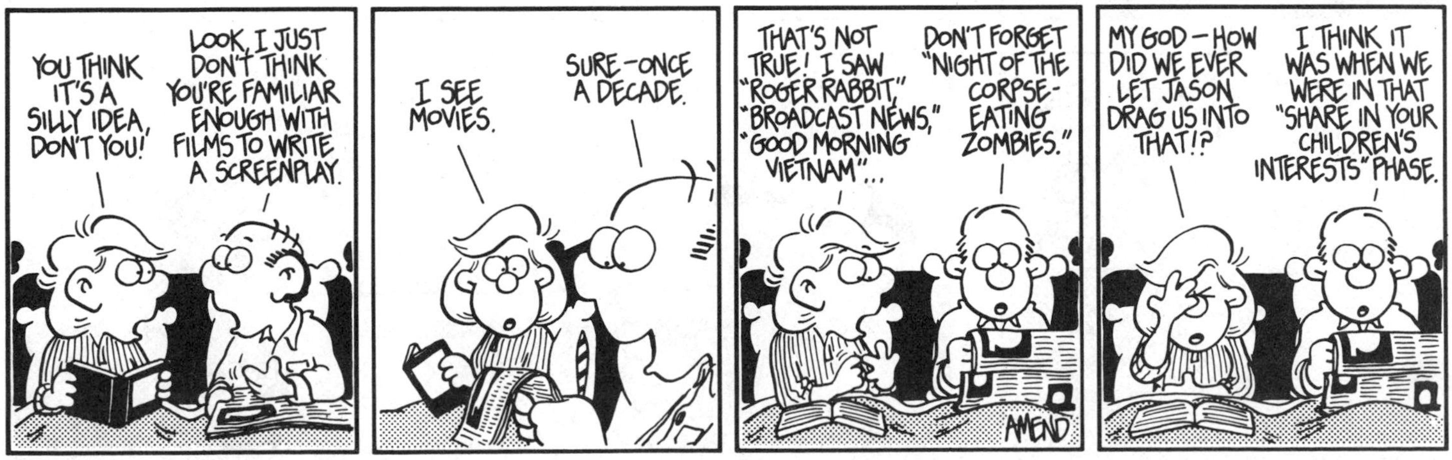
YOU THINK IT'S A SILLY IDEA, DON'T YOU!
LOOK, I JUST DON'T THINK YOU'RE FAMILIAR ENOUGH WITH FILMS TO WRITE A SCREENPLAY.
I SEE MOVIES.
SURE—ONCE A DECADE.
THAT'S NOT TRUE! I SAW "ROGER RABBIT," "BROADCAST NEWS," "GOOD MORNING VIETNAM"...
DON'T FORGET "NIGHT OF THE CORPSE-EATING ZOMBIES."
AMEND
MY GOD—HOW DID WE EVER LET JASON DRAG US INTO THAT!?
I THINK IT WAS WHEN WE WERE IN THAT "SHARE IN YOUR CHILDREN'S INTERESTS" PHASE.

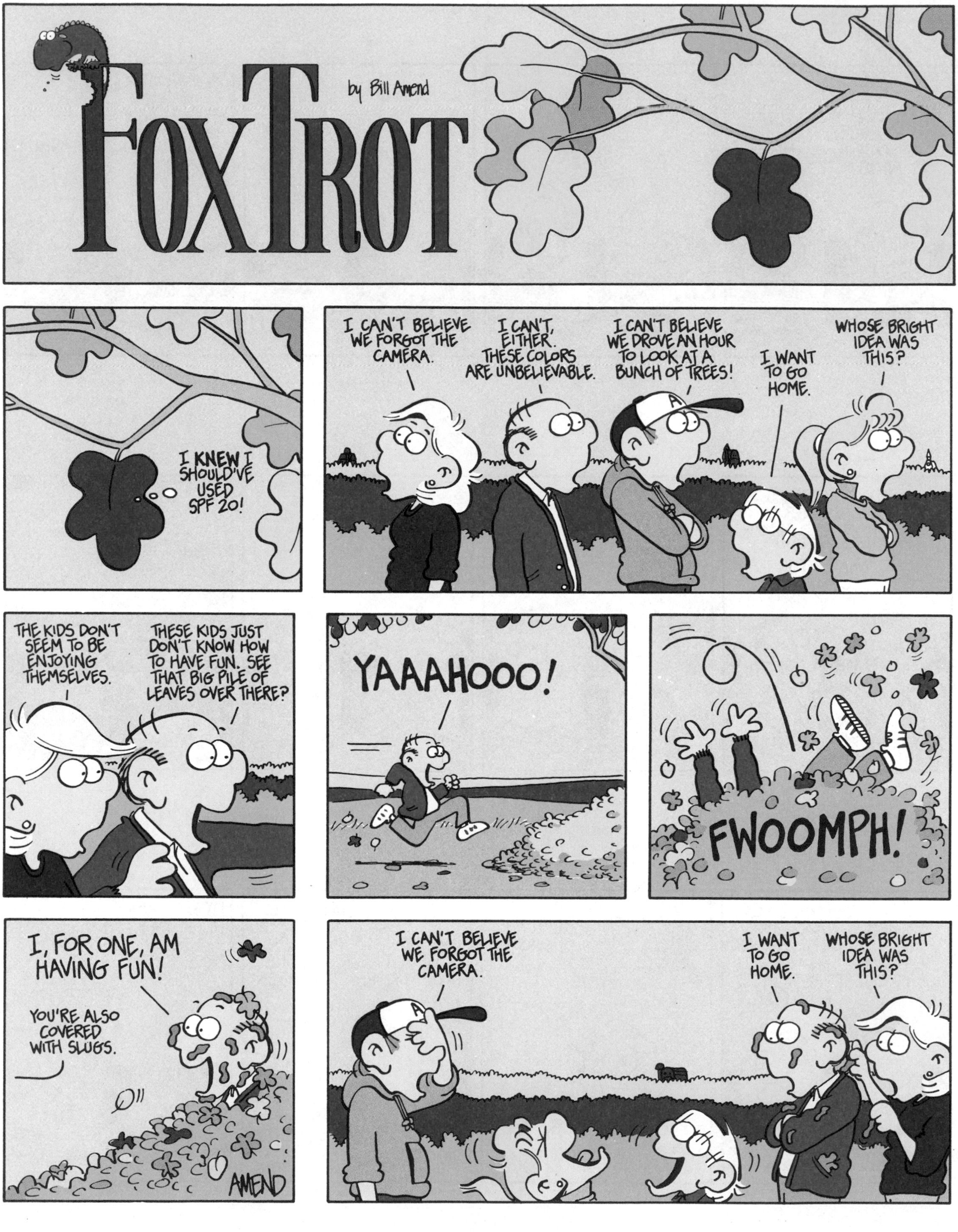
FOXTROT
by Bill Amend
I KNEW I SHOULD'VE USED SPF 20!
I CAN'T BELIEVE WE FORGOT THE CAMERA.
I CAN'T, EITHER. THESE COLORS ARE UNBELIEVABLE.
I CAN'T BELIEVE WE DROVE AN HOUR TO LOOK AT A BUNCH OF TREES!
I WANT TO GO HOME.
WHOSE BRIGHT IDEA WAS THIS?
THE KIDS DON'T SEEM TO BE ENJOYING THEMSELVES.
THESE KIDS JUST DON'T KNOW HOW TO HAVE FUN. SEE THAT BIG PILE OF LEAVES OVER THERE?
YAAAHOOO!
FWOOMPH!
I, FOR ONE, AM HAVING FUN!
YOU'RE ALSO COVERED WITH SLUGS.
AMEND
I CAN'T BELIEVE WE FORGOT THE CAMERA.
I WANT TO GO HOME.
WHOSE BRIGHT IDEA WAS THIS?

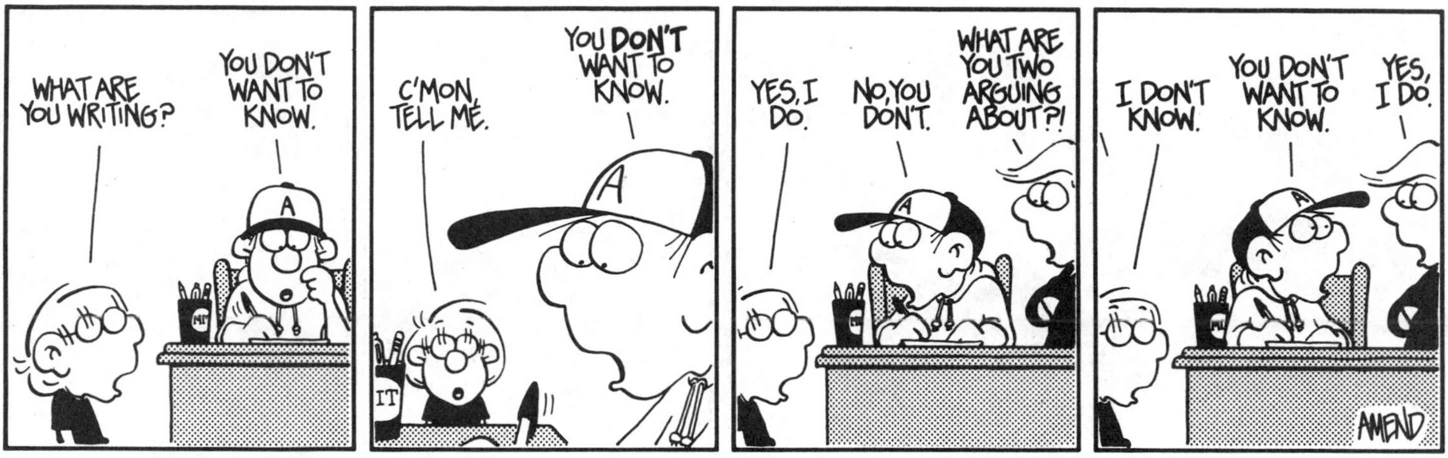
WHAT ARE YOU WRITING?
YOU DON'T WANT TO KNOW.
C'MON, TELL ME.
YOU DON'T WANT TO KNOW.
YES, I DO.
NO, YOU DON'T.
WHAT ARE YOU TWO ARGUING ABOUT?!
I DON'T KNOW.
YOU DON'T WANT TO KNOW.
YES, I DO.
AMEND

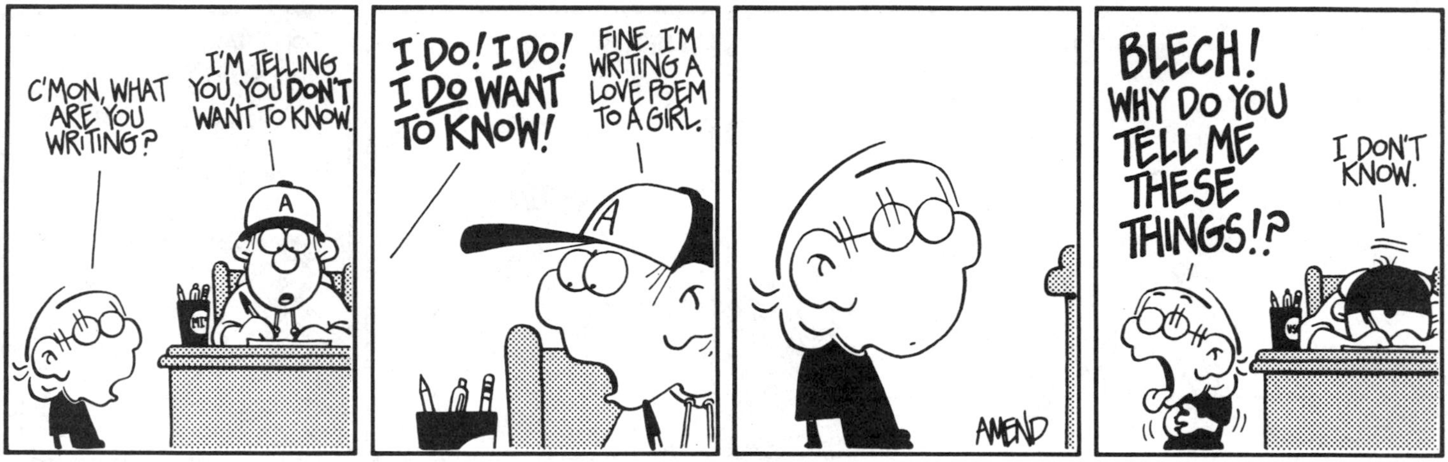
C'MON, WHAT ARE YOU WRITING?
I'M TELLING YOU, YOU DON'T WANT TO KNOW.
I DO! I DO! I DO WANT TO KNOW!
FINE. I'M WRITING A LOVE POEM TO A GIRL.
AMEND
BLECH! WHY DO YOU TELL ME THESE THINGS!?
I DON'T KNOW.

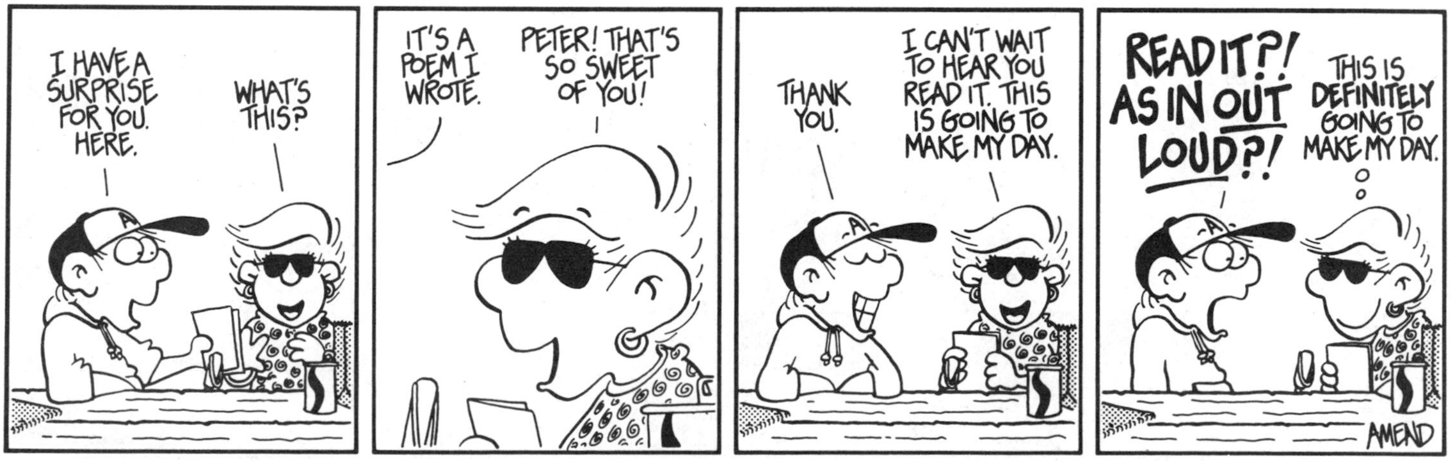
I HAVE A SURPRISE FOR YOU. HERE.
WHAT'S THIS?
IT'S A POEM I WROTE.
PETER! THAT'S SO SWEET OF YOU!
THANK YOU.
I CAN'T WAIT TO HEAR YOU READ IT. THIS IS GOING TO MAKE MY DAY.
READ IT?! AS IN OUT LOUD?!
THIS IS DEFINITELY GOING TO MAKE MY DAY.
AMEND

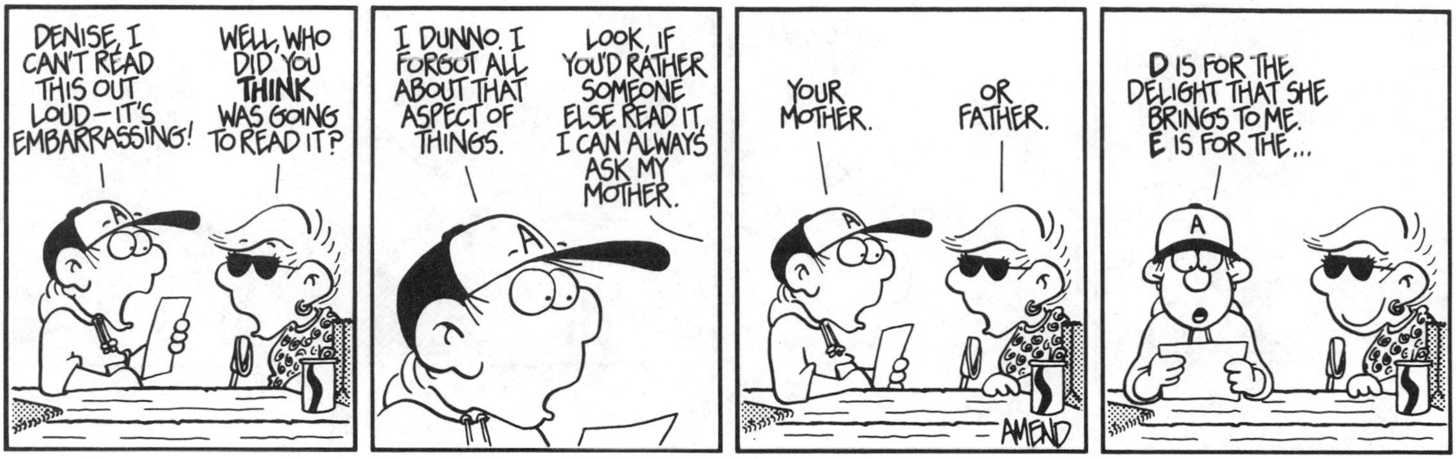
DENISE, I CAN'T READ THIS OUT LOUD—IT'S EMBARRASSING!
WELL, WHO DID YOU **THINK** WAS GOING TO READ IT?
I DUNNO. I FORGOT ALL ABOUT THAT ASPECT OF THINGS.
LOOK, IF YOU'D RATHER SOMEONE ELSE READ IT, I CAN ALWAYS ASK MY MOTHER.
YOUR MOTHER.
OR FATHER.
AMEND
D IS FOR THE DELIGHT THAT SHE BRINGS TO ME. **E** IS FOR THE...

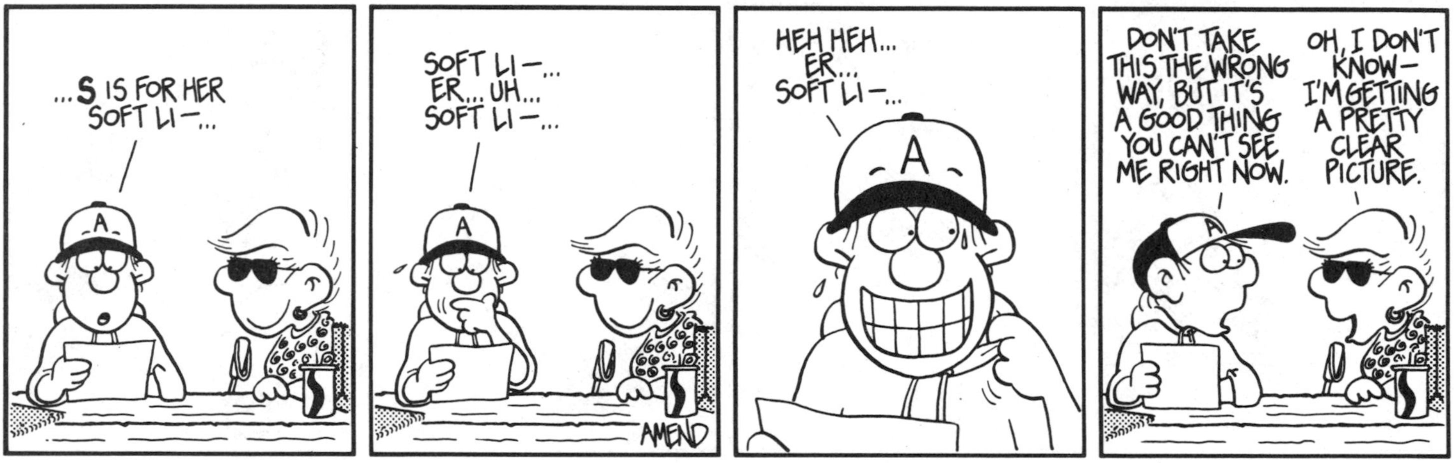
...**S** IS FOR HER SOFT LI—...
SOFT LI—... ER... UH... SOFT LI—...
AMEND
HEH HEH... ER... SOFT LI—...
DON'T TAKE THIS THE WRONG WAY, BUT IT'S A GOOD THING YOU CAN'T SEE ME RIGHT NOW.
OH, I DON'T KNOW—I'M GETTING A PRETTY CLEAR PICTURE.

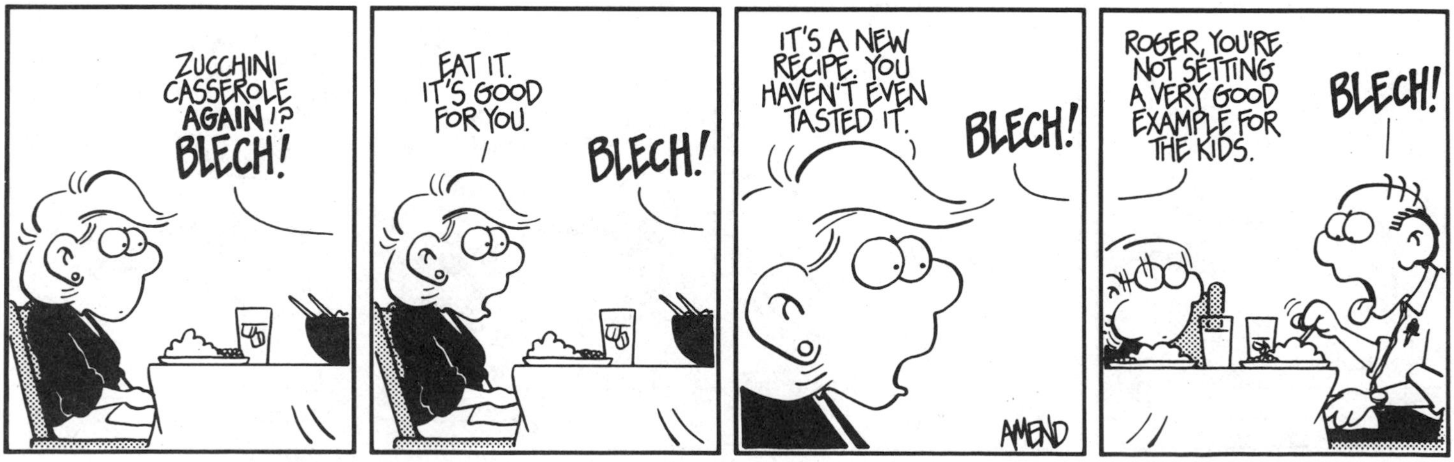
ZUCCHINI CASSEROLE **AGAIN**!? BLECH!
EAT IT. IT'S GOOD FOR YOU.
BLECH!
IT'S A NEW RECIPE. YOU HAVEN'T EVEN TASTED IT.
BLECH!
AMEND
ROGER, YOU'RE NOT SETTING A VERY GOOD EXAMPLE FOR THE KIDS.
BLECH!

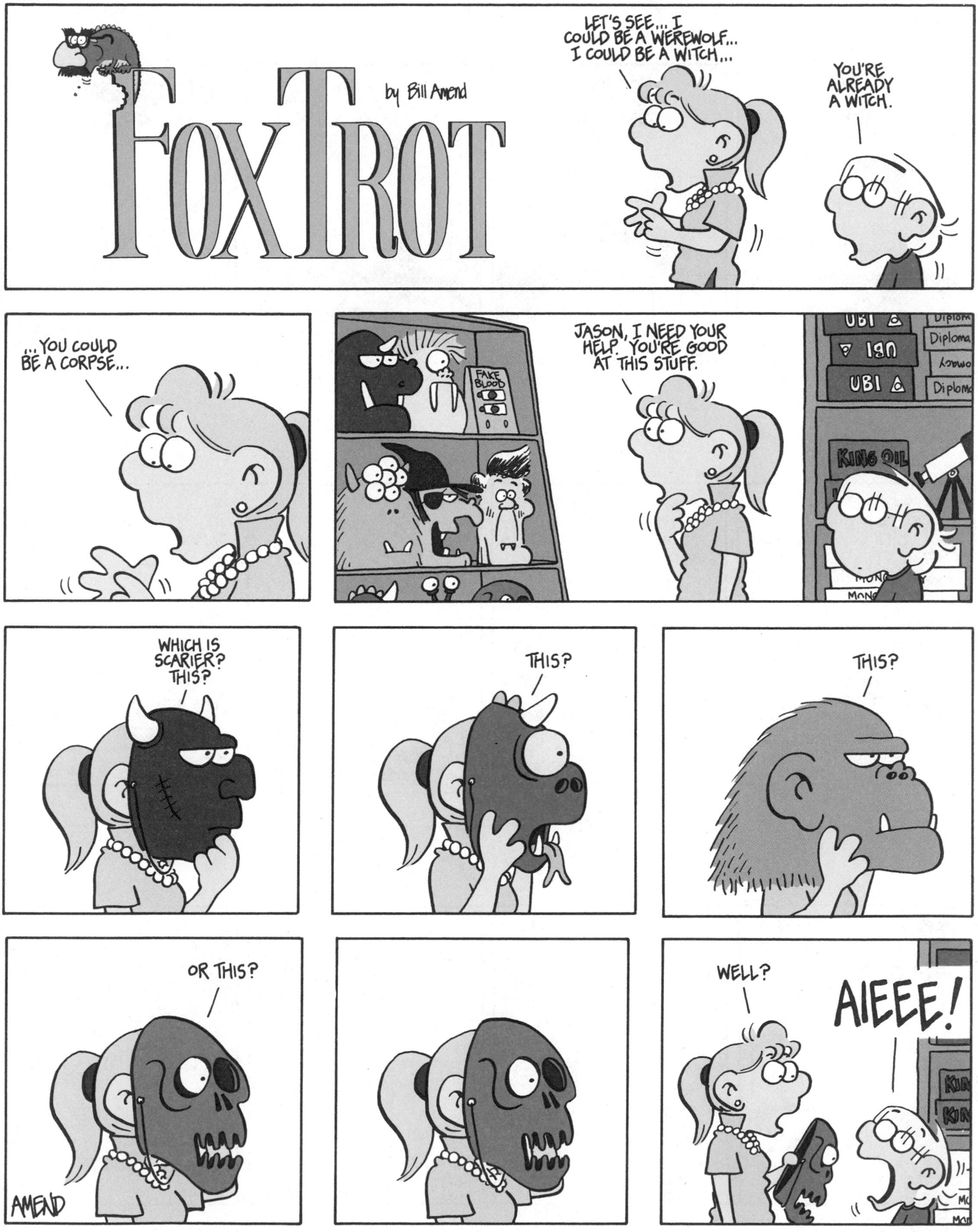
FoxTrot
by Bill Amend
LET'S SEE... I COULD BE A WEREWOLF... I COULD BE A WITCH...
YOU'RE ALREADY A WITCH.
...YOU COULD BE A CORPSE...
FAKE BLOOD
JASON, I NEED YOUR HELP. YOU'RE GOOD AT THIS STUFF.
UBI
KING OIL
WHICH IS SCARIER? THIS?
THIS?
THIS?
OR THIS?
AMEND
WELL?
AIEEE!

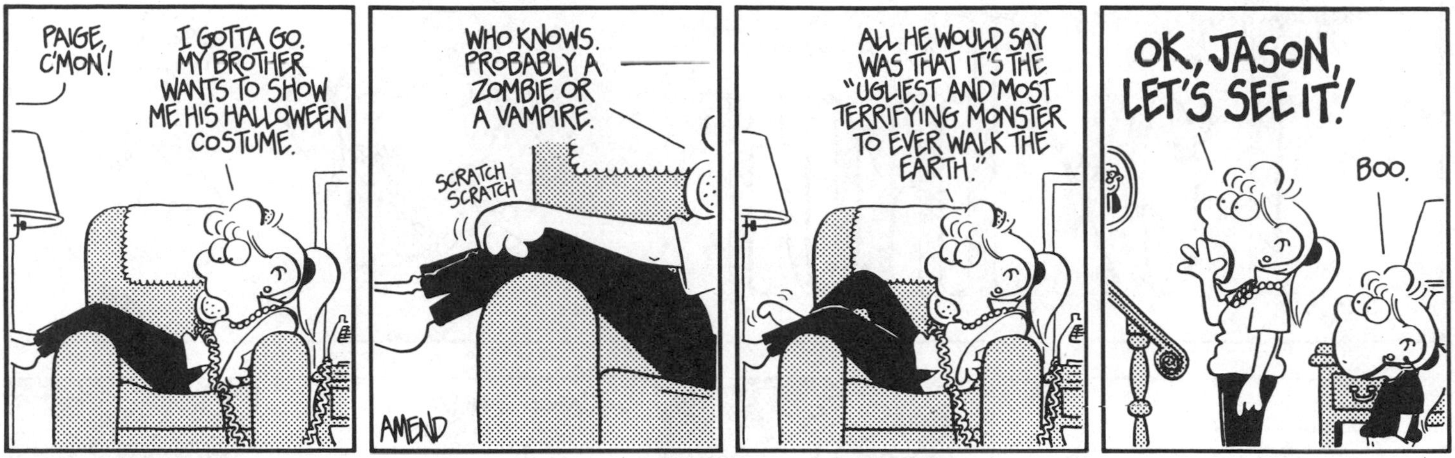
PAIGE, C'MON!
I GOTTA GO. MY BROTHER WANTS TO SHOW ME HIS HALLOWEEN COSTUME.
WHO KNOWS. PROBABLY A ZOMBIE OR A VAMPIRE.
SCRATCH SCRATCH
AMEND
ALL HE WOULD SAY WAS THAT IT'S THE "UGLIEST AND MOST TERRIFYING MONSTER TO EVER WALK THE EARTH."
OK, JASON, LET'S SEE IT!
BOO.

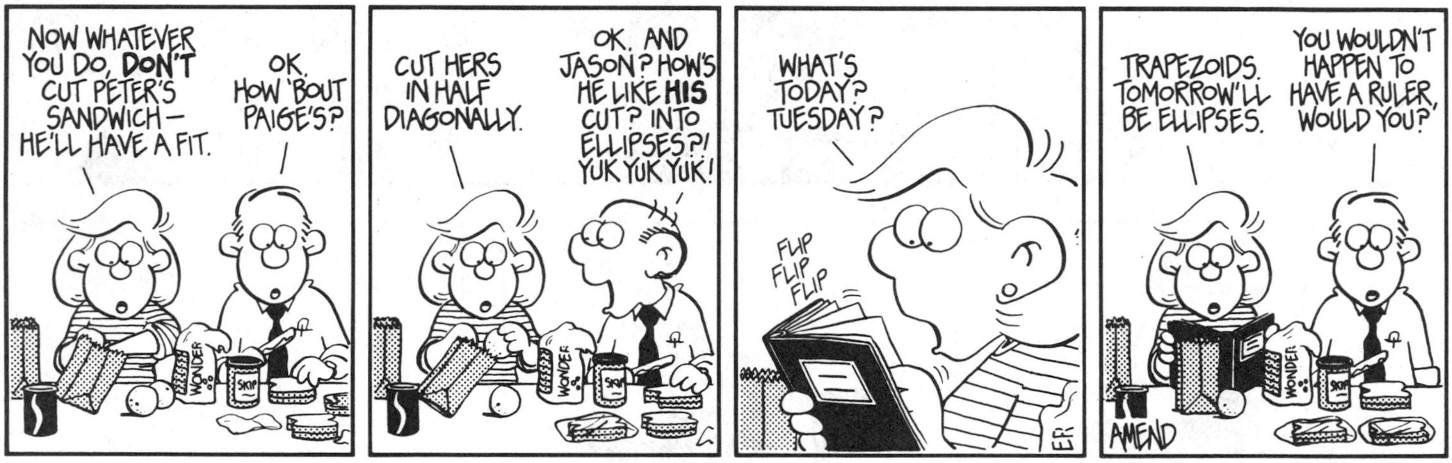
NOW WHATEVER YOU DO, **DON'T** CUT PETER'S SANDWICH— HE'LL HAVE A FIT.
OK. HOW 'BOUT PAIGE'S?
WONDER
SKIP
CUT HERS IN HALF DIAGONALLY.
OK. AND JASON? HOW'S HE LIKE **HIS** CUT? INTO ELLIPSES?! YUK YUK YUK!
WHAT'S TODAY? TUESDAY?
FLIP FLIP FLIP
TRAPEZOIDS. TOMORROW'LL BE ELLIPSES.
YOU WOULDN'T HAPPEN TO HAVE A RULER, WOULD YOU?
AMEND

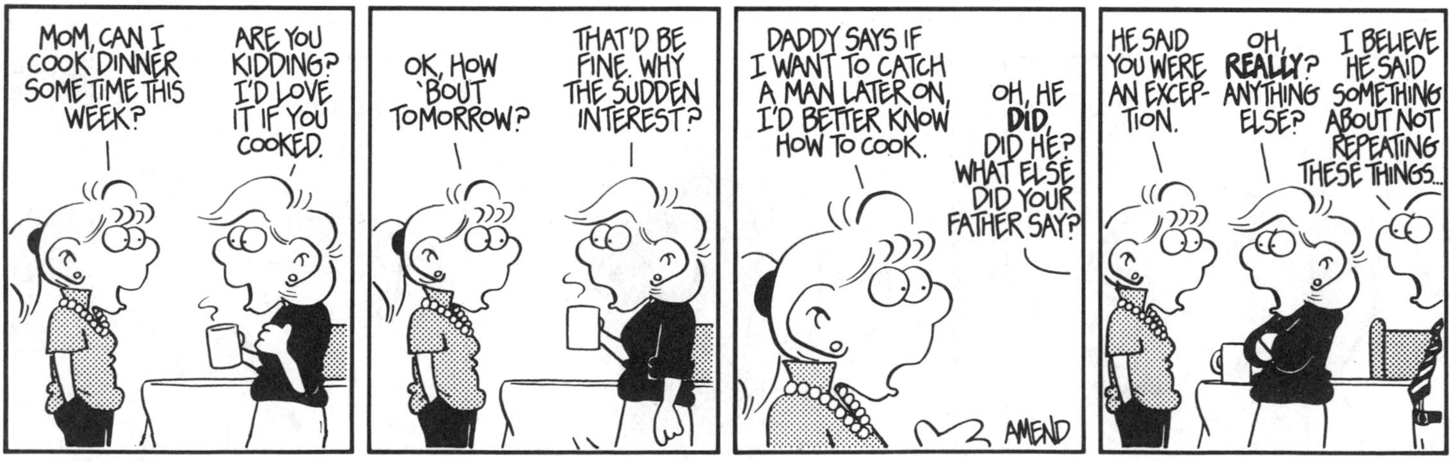
MOM, CAN I COOK DINNER SOME TIME THIS WEEK?
ARE YOU KIDDING? I'D LOVE IT IF YOU COOKED.
OK, HOW 'BOUT TOMORROW?
THAT'D BE FINE. WHY THE SUDDEN INTEREST?
DADDY SAYS IF I WANT TO CATCH A MAN LATER ON, I'D BETTER KNOW HOW TO COOK.
OH, HE **DID**, DID HE? WHAT ELSE DID YOUR FATHER SAY?
AMEND
HE SAID YOU WERE AN EXCEPTION.
OH, **REALLY**? ANYTHING ELSE?
I BELIEVE HE SAID SOMETHING ABOUT NOT REPEATING THESE THINGS...

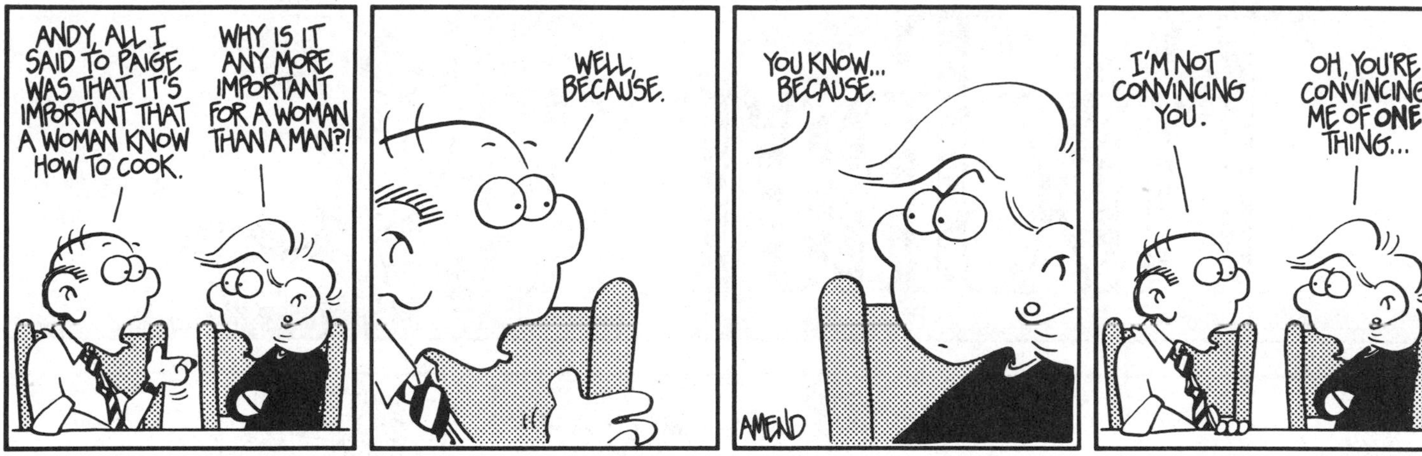
ANDY, ALL I SAID TO PAIGE WAS THAT IT'S IMPORTANT THAT A WOMAN KNOW HOW TO COOK.
WHY IS IT ANY MORE IMPORTANT FOR A WOMAN THAN A MAN?!
WELL, BECAUSE.
YOU KNOW... BECAUSE.
AMEND
I'M NOT CONVINCING YOU.
OH, YOU'RE CONVINCING ME OF ONE THING...

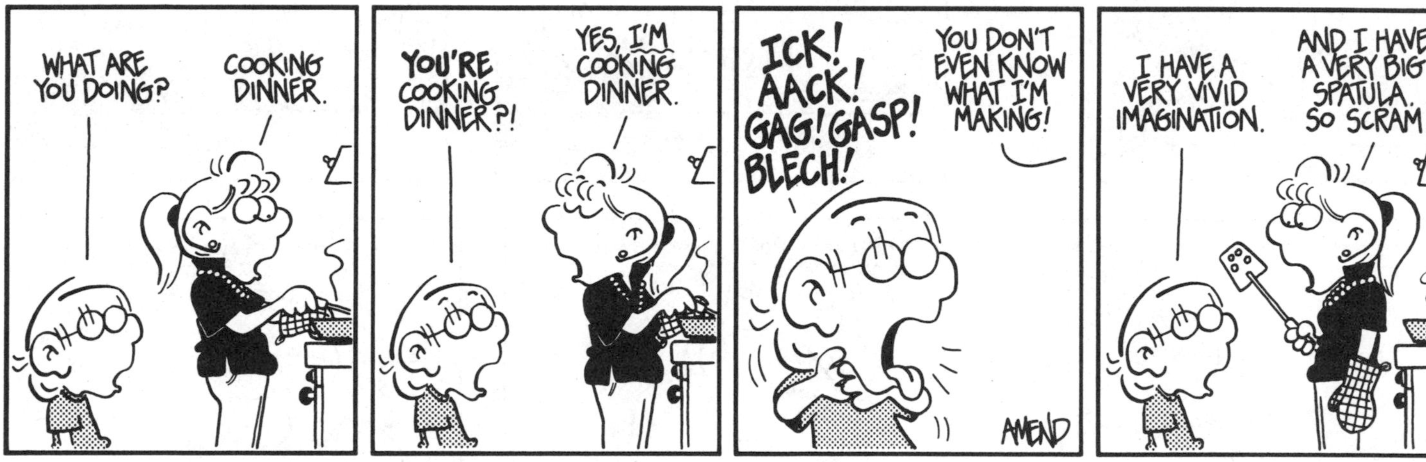
WHAT ARE YOU DOING?
COOKING DINNER.
YOU'RE COOKING DINNER?!
YES, I'M COOKING DINNER.
ICK! AACK! GAG! GASP! BLECH!
YOU DON'T EVEN KNOW WHAT I'M MAKING!
AMEND
I HAVE A VERY VIVID IMAGINATION.
AND I HAVE A VERY BIG SPATULA. SO SCRAM!

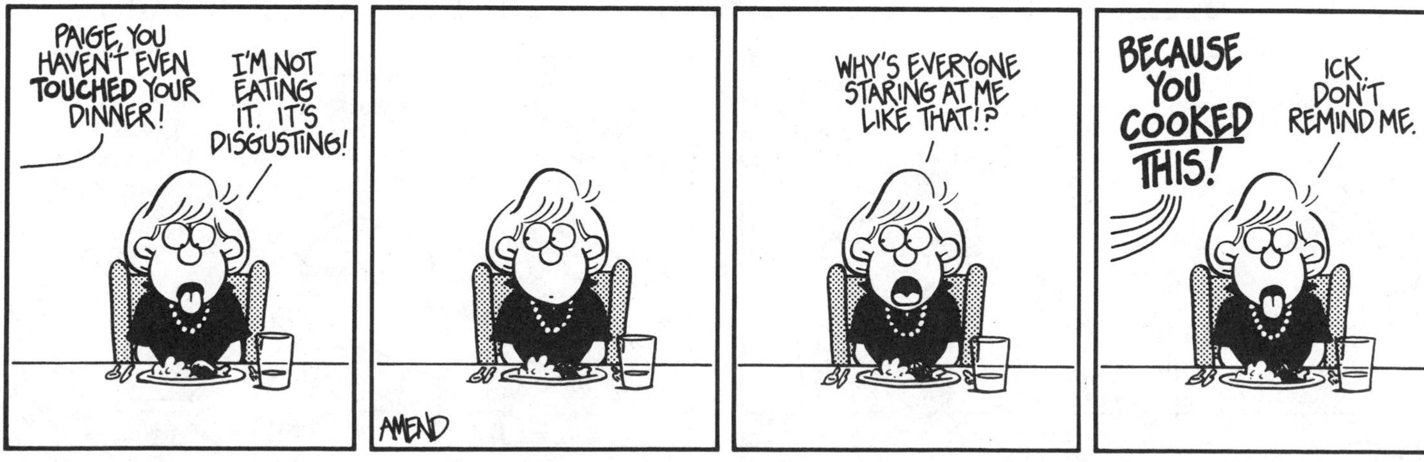
PAIGE, YOU HAVEN'T EVEN TOUCHED YOUR DINNER!
I'M NOT EATING IT. IT'S DISGUSTING!
AMEND
WHY'S EVERYONE STARING AT ME LIKE THAT!?
BECAUSE YOU COOKED THIS!
ICK. DON'T REMIND ME.

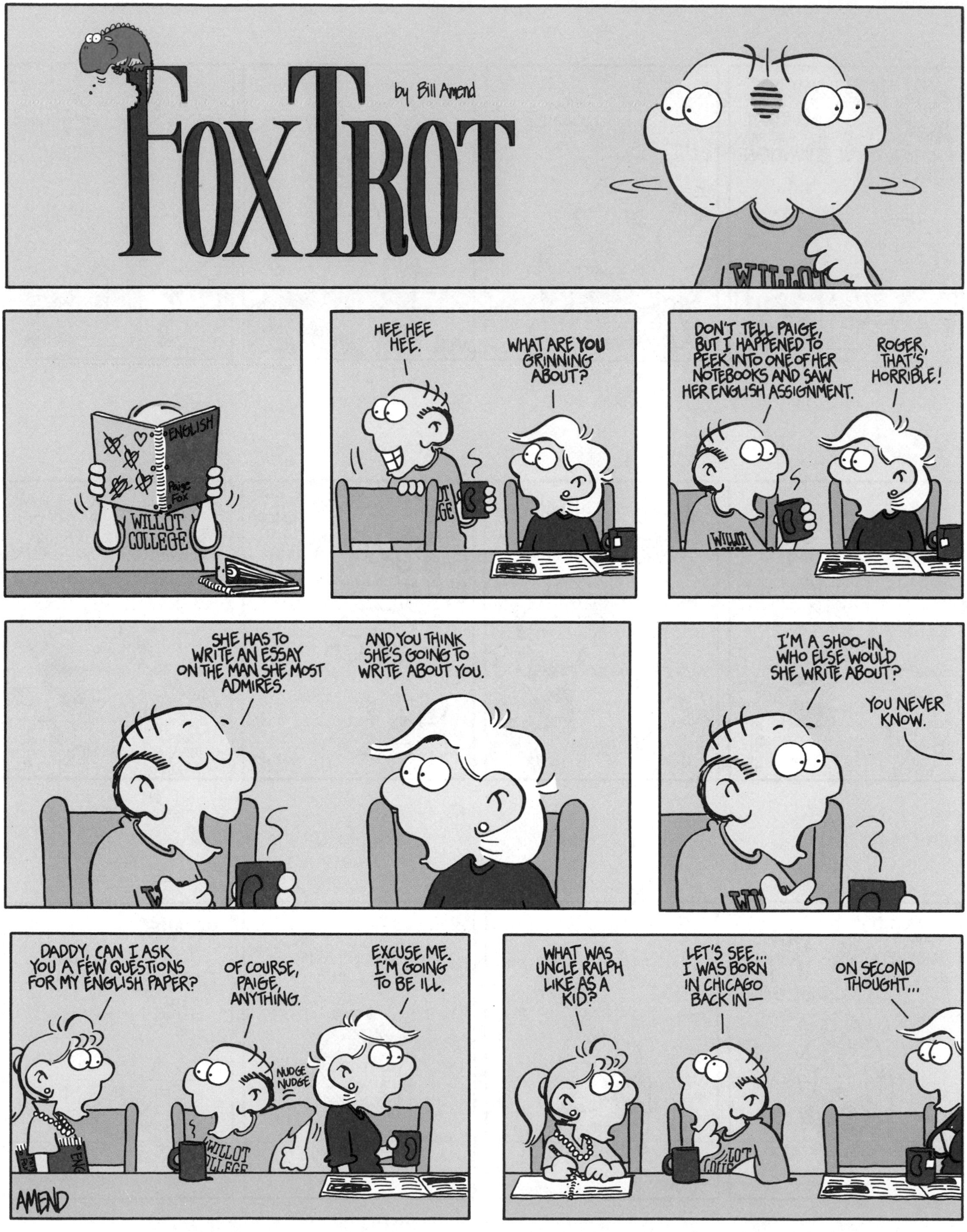
FoxTrot
by Bill Amend
WILLOT
ENGLISH
Paige Fox
WILLOT COLLEGE
HEE HEE HEE.
WHAT ARE YOU GRINNING ABOUT?
DON'T TELL PAIGE, BUT I HAPPENED TO PEEK INTO ONE OF HER NOTEBOOKS AND SAW HER ENGLISH ASSIGNMENT.
ROGER, THAT'S HORRIBLE!
SHE HAS TO WRITE AN ESSAY ON THE MAN SHE MOST ADMIRES.
AND YOU THINK SHE'S GOING TO WRITE ABOUT YOU.
I'M A SHOO-IN. WHO ELSE WOULD SHE WRITE ABOUT?
YOU NEVER KNOW.
DADDY, CAN I ASK YOU A FEW QUESTIONS FOR MY ENGLISH PAPER?
OF COURSE, PAIGE, ANYTHING.
EXCUSE ME. I'M GOING TO BE ILL.
NUDGE NUDGE
WILLOT COLLEGE
AMEND
WHAT WAS UNCLE RALPH LIKE AS A KID?
LET'S SEE... I WAS BORN IN CHICAGO BACK IN—
ON SECOND THOUGHT...

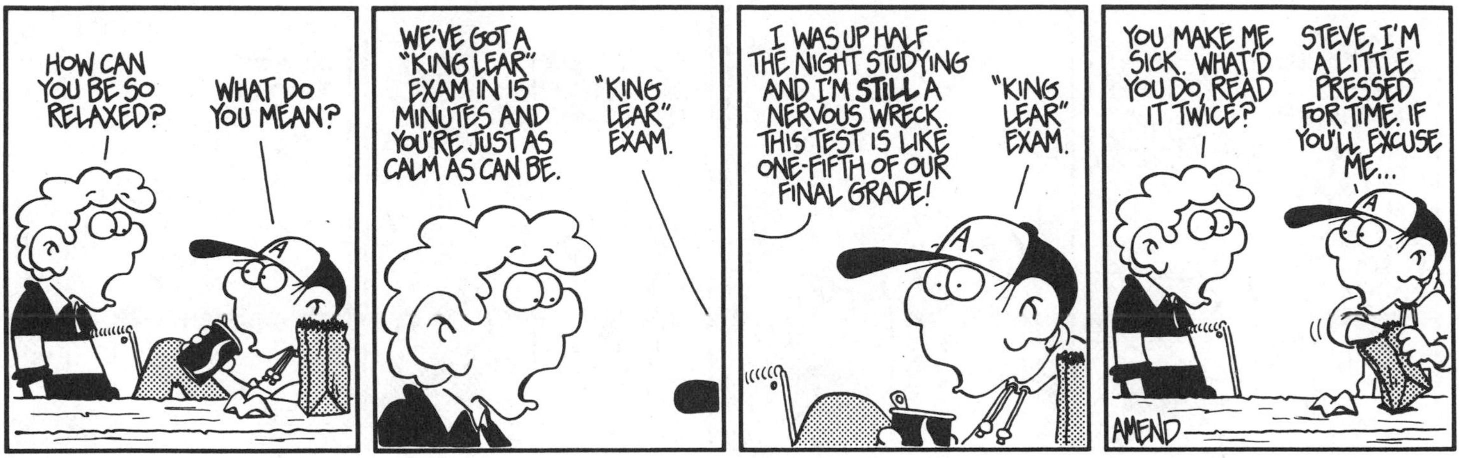
HOW CAN YOU BE SO RELAXED?
WHAT DO YOU MEAN?
WE'VE GOT A "KING LEAR" EXAM IN 15 MINUTES AND YOU'RE JUST AS CALM AS CAN BE.
"KING LEAR" EXAM.
I WAS UP HALF THE NIGHT STUDYING AND I'M **STILL** A NERVOUS WRECK. THIS TEST IS LIKE ONE-FIFTH OF OUR FINAL GRADE!
"KING LEAR" EXAM.
YOU MAKE ME SICK. WHAT'D YOU DO, READ IT TWICE?
STEVE, I'M A LITTLE PRESSED FOR TIME. IF YOU'LL EXCUSE ME...
AMEND

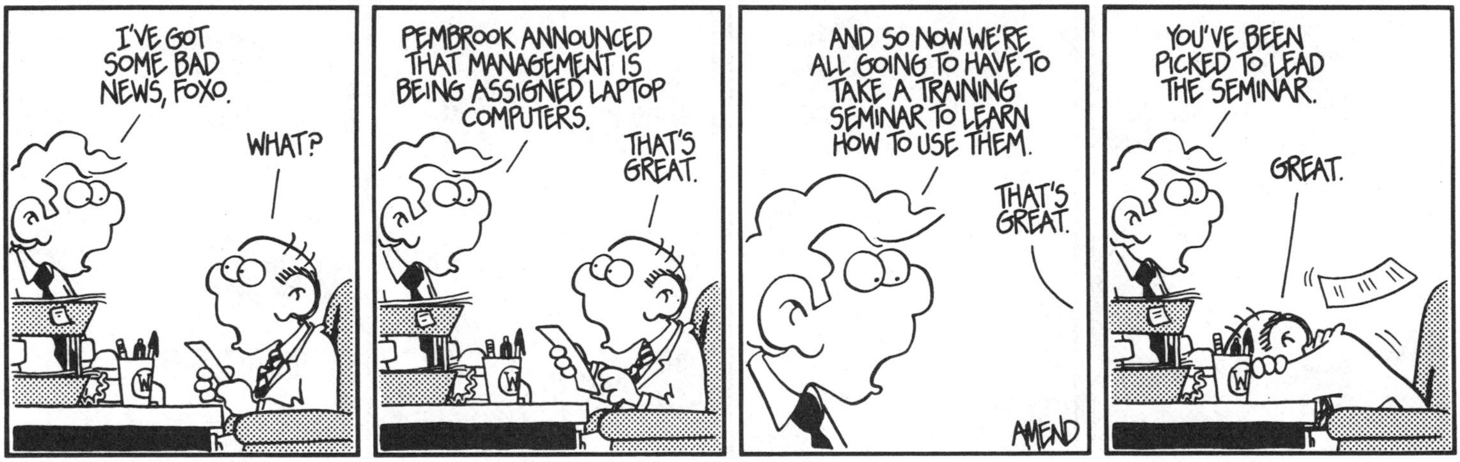
I'VE GOT SOME BAD NEWS, FOXO.
WHAT?
PEMBROOK ANNOUNCED THAT MANAGEMENT IS BEING ASSIGNED LAPTOP COMPUTERS.
THAT'S GREAT.
AND SO NOW WE'RE ALL GOING TO HAVE TO TAKE A TRAINING SEMINAR TO LEARN HOW TO USE THEM.
THAT'S GREAT.
AMEND
YOU'VE BEEN PICKED TO LEAD THE SEMINAR.
GREAT.

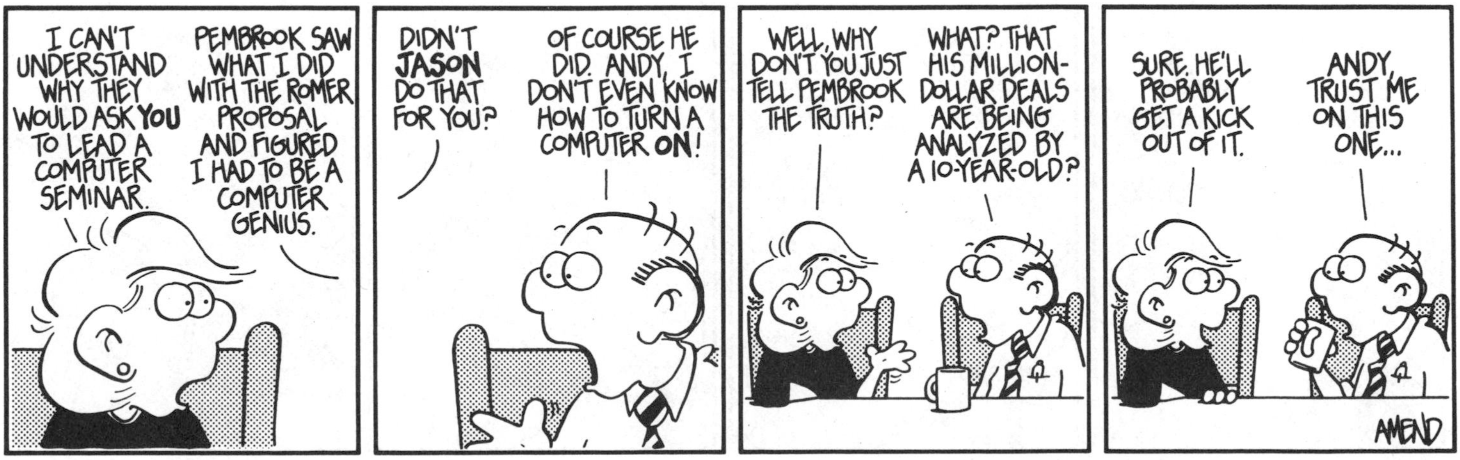
I CAN'T UNDERSTAND WHY THEY WOULD ASK **YOU** TO LEAD A COMPUTER SEMINAR.
PEMBROOK SAW WHAT I DID WITH THE ROMER PROPOSAL AND FIGURED I HAD TO BE A COMPUTER GENIUS.
DIDN'T **JASON** DO THAT FOR YOU?
OF COURSE HE DID. ANDY, I DON'T EVEN KNOW HOW TO TURN A COMPUTER **ON**!
WELL, WHY DON'T YOU JUST TELL PEMBROOK THE TRUTH?
WHAT? THAT HIS MILLION-DOLLAR DEALS ARE BEING ANALYZED BY A 10-YEAR-OLD?
SURE. HE'LL PROBABLY GET A KICK OUT OF IT.
ANDY, TRUST ME ON THIS ONE...
AMEND

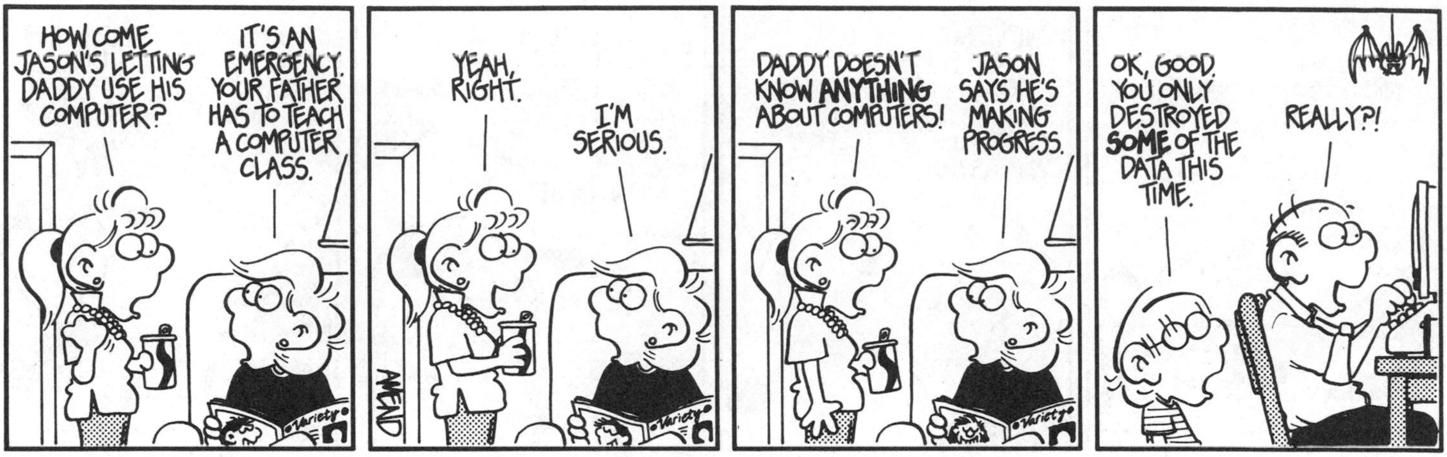
HOW COME JASON'S LETTING DADDY USE HIS COMPUTER?
IT'S AN EMERGENCY. YOUR FATHER HAS TO TEACH A COMPUTER CLASS.
YEAH, RIGHT.
I'M SERIOUS.
DADDY DOESN'T KNOW ANYTHING ABOUT COMPUTERS!
JASON SAYS HE'S MAKING PROGRESS.
OK, GOOD. YOU ONLY DESTROYED SOME OF THE DATA THIS TIME.
REALLY?!
AMEND

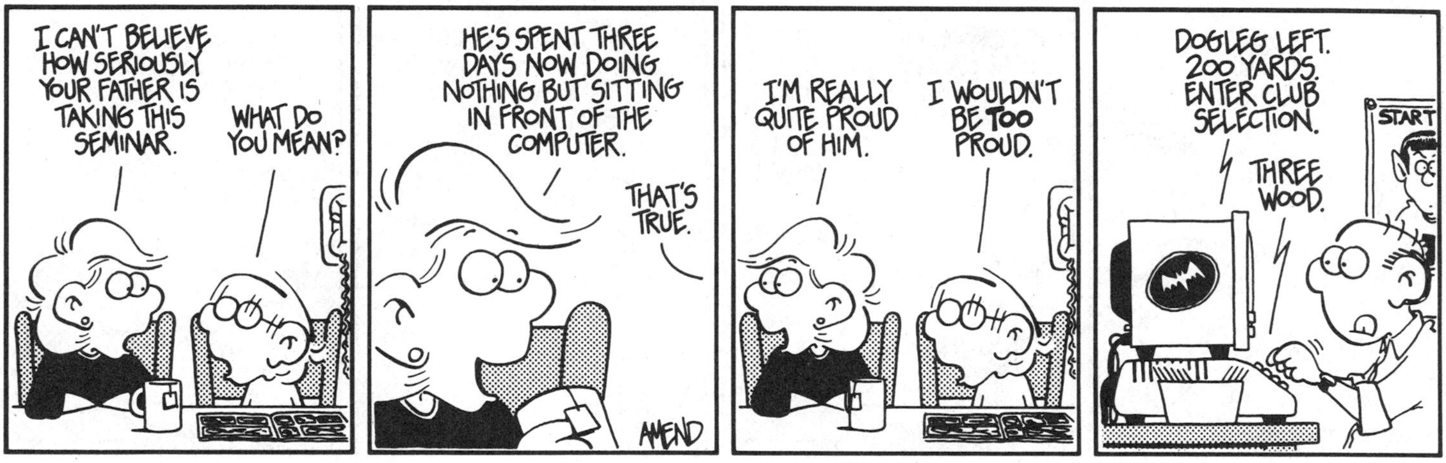
I CAN'T BELIEVE HOW SERIOUSLY YOUR FATHER IS TAKING THIS SEMINAR.
WHAT DO YOU MEAN?
HE'S SPENT THREE DAYS NOW DOING NOTHING BUT SITTING IN FRONT OF THE COMPUTER.
THAT'S TRUE.
AMEND
I'M REALLY QUITE PROUD OF HIM.
I WOULDN'T BE TOO PROUD.
DOGLEG LEFT. 200 YARDS. ENTER CLUB SELECTION.
THREE WOOD.
START

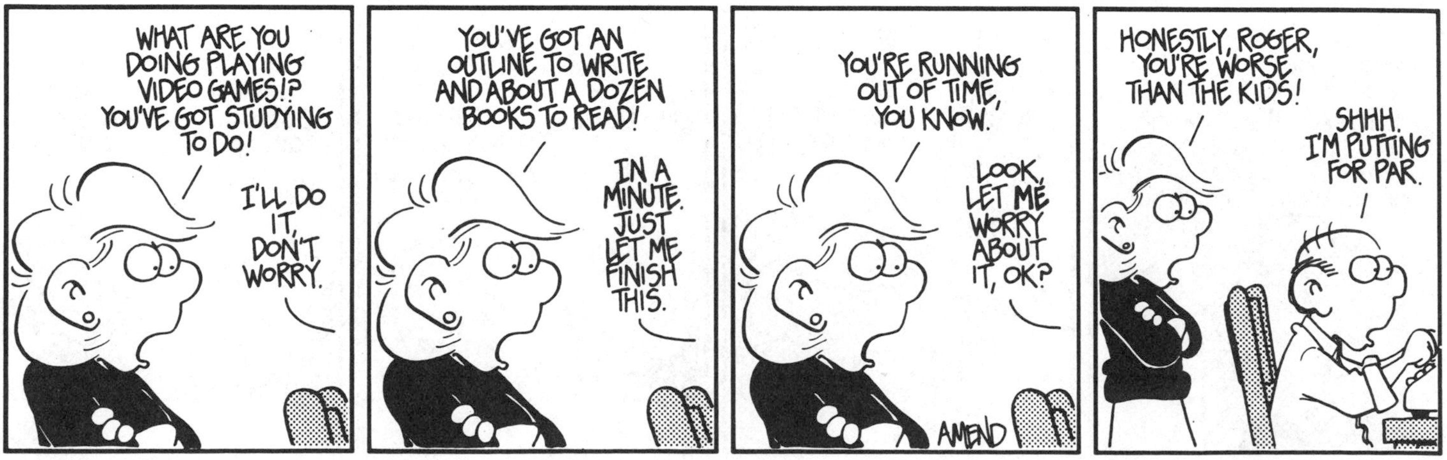
WHAT ARE YOU DOING PLAYING VIDEO GAMES!? YOU'VE GOT STUDYING TO DO!
I'LL DO IT, DON'T WORRY.
YOU'VE GOT AN OUTLINE TO WRITE AND ABOUT A DOZEN BOOKS TO READ!
IN A MINUTE. JUST LET ME FINISH THIS.
YOU'RE RUNNING OUT OF TIME, YOU KNOW.
LOOK, LET ME WORRY ABOUT IT, OK?
AMEND
HONESTLY, ROGER, YOU'RE WORSE THAN THE KIDS!
SHHH. I'M PUTTING FOR PAR.

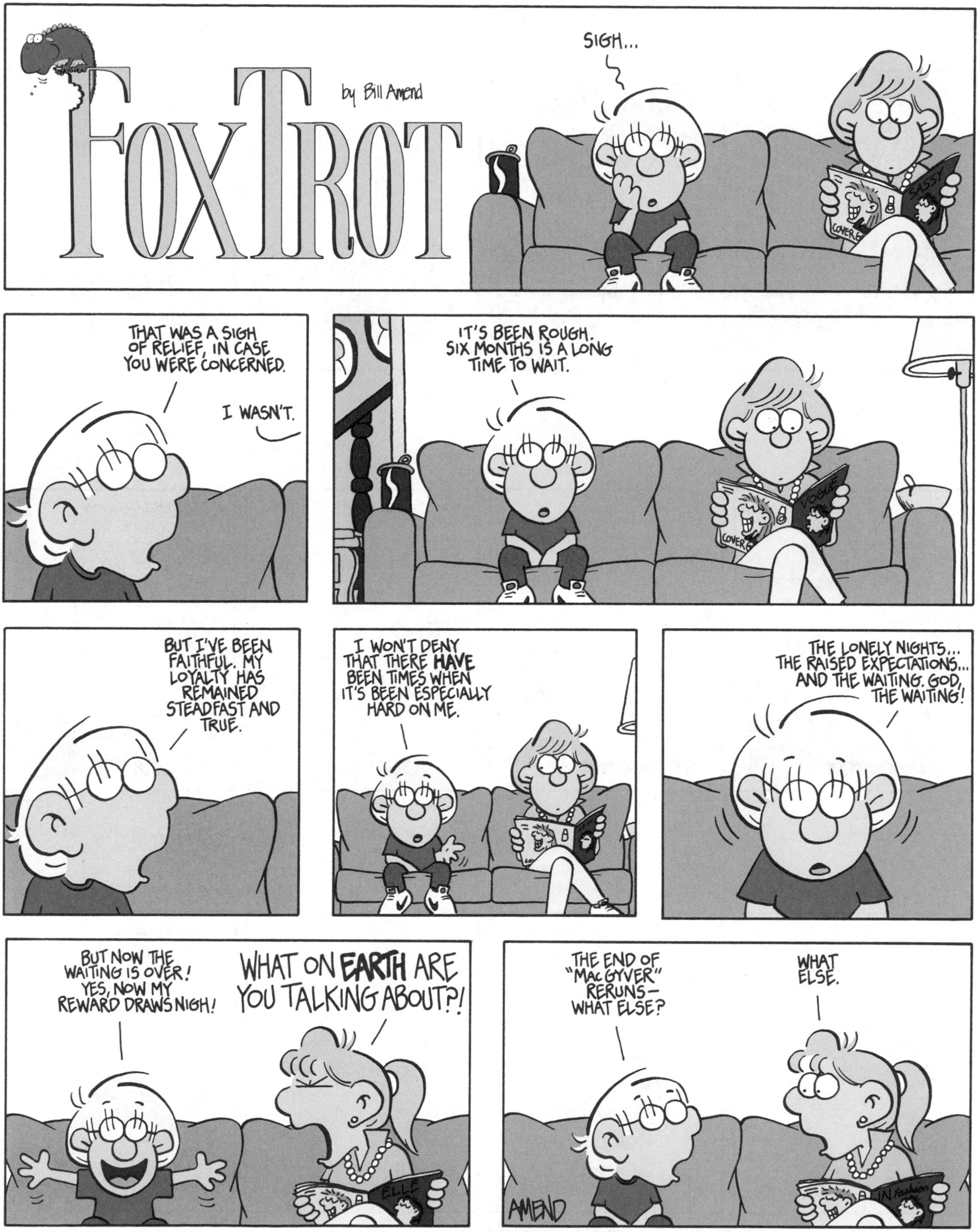
FoxTrot
by Bill Amend
SIGH...
THAT WAS A SIGH OF RELIEF, IN CASE YOU WERE CONCERNED.
I WASN'T.
IT'S BEEN ROUGH. SIX MONTHS IS A LONG TIME TO WAIT.
BUT I'VE BEEN FAITHFUL. MY LOYALTY HAS REMAINED STEADFAST AND TRUE.
I WON'T DENY THAT THERE **HAVE** BEEN TIMES WHEN IT'S BEEN ESPECIALLY HARD ON ME.
THE LONELY NIGHTS... THE RAISED EXPECTATIONS... AND THE WAITING. GOD, THE WAITING!
BUT NOW THE WAITING IS OVER! YES, NOW MY REWARD DRAWS NIGH!
WHAT ON **EARTH** ARE YOU TALKING ABOUT?!
THE END OF "MacGYVER" RERUNS— WHAT ELSE?
WHAT ELSE.
AMEND

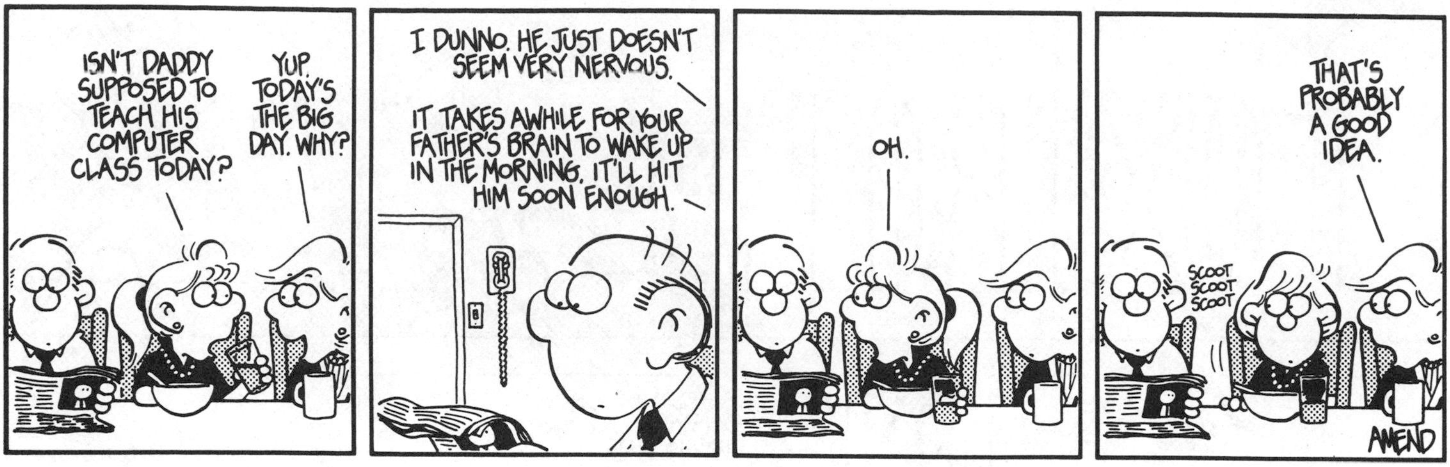
ISN'T DADDY SUPPOSED TO TEACH HIS COMPUTER CLASS TODAY?
YUP. TODAY'S THE BIG DAY. WHY?
I DUNNO. HE JUST DOESN'T SEEM VERY NERVOUS.
IT TAKES AWHILE FOR YOUR FATHER'S BRAIN TO WAKE UP IN THE MORNING. IT'LL HIT HIM SOON ENOUGH.
OH.
SCOOT SCOOT SCOOT
THAT'S PROBABLY A GOOD IDEA.
AMEND

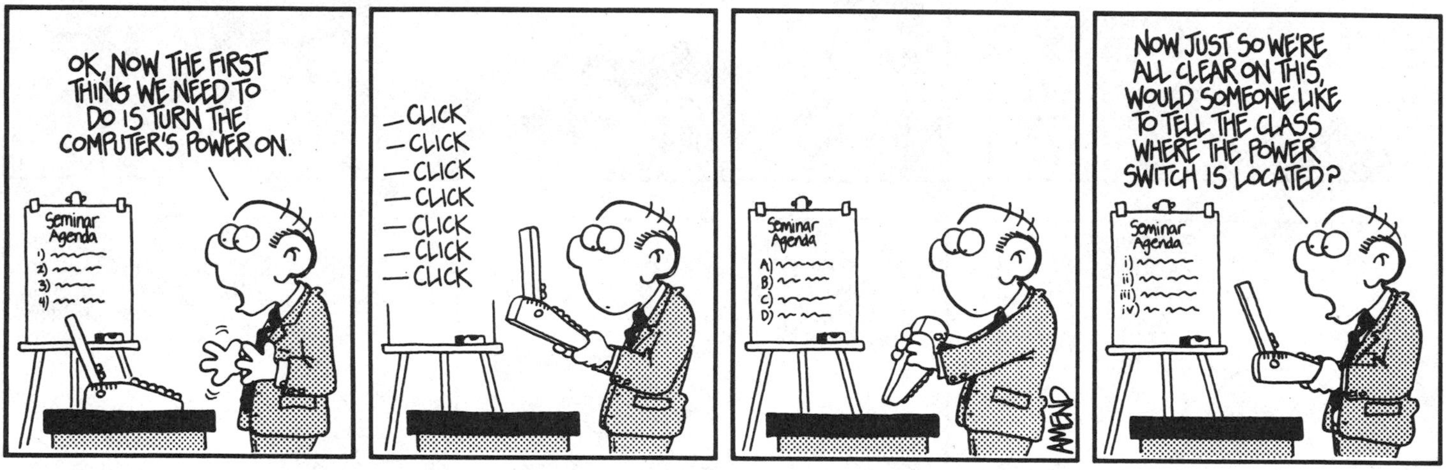
OK, NOW THE FIRST THING WE NEED TO DO IS TURN THE COMPUTER'S POWER ON.
Seminar Agenda
CLICK
CLICK
CLICK
CLICK
CLICK
CLICK
CLICK
Seminar Agenda
AMEND
NOW JUST SO WE'RE ALL CLEAR ON THIS, WOULD SOMEONE LIKE TO TELL THE CLASS WHERE THE POWER SWITCH IS LOCATED?
Seminar Agenda

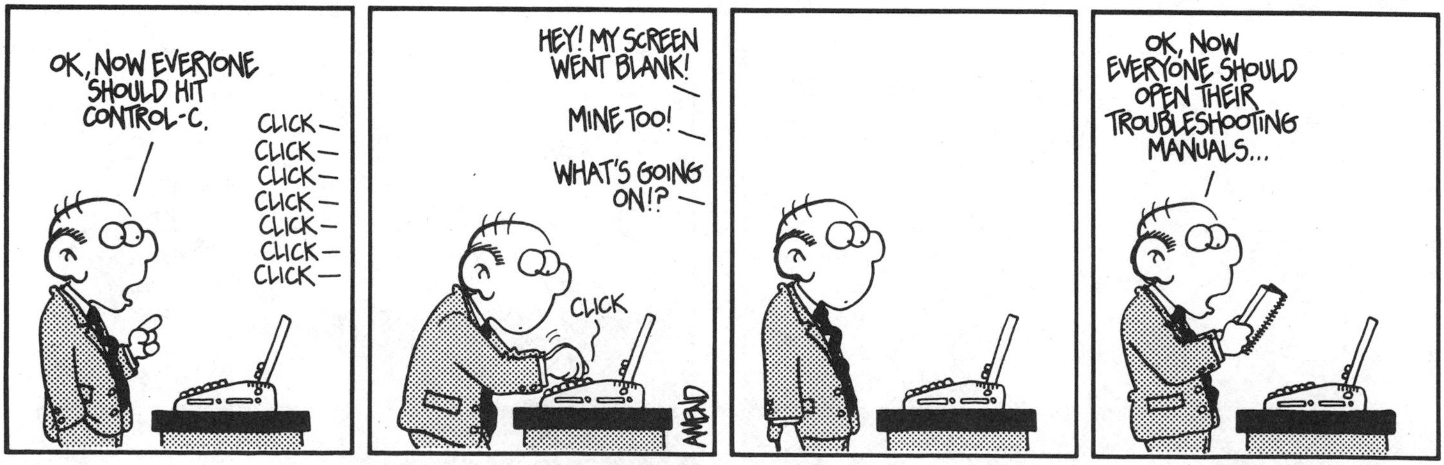
OK, NOW EVERYONE SHOULD HIT CONTROL-C.
CLICK
CLICK
CLICK
CLICK
CLICK
CLICK
CLICK
HEY! MY SCREEN WENT BLANK!
MINE TOO!
WHAT'S GOING ON!?
CLICK
AMEND
OK, NOW EVERYONE SHOULD OPEN THEIR TROUBLESHOOTING MANUALS...

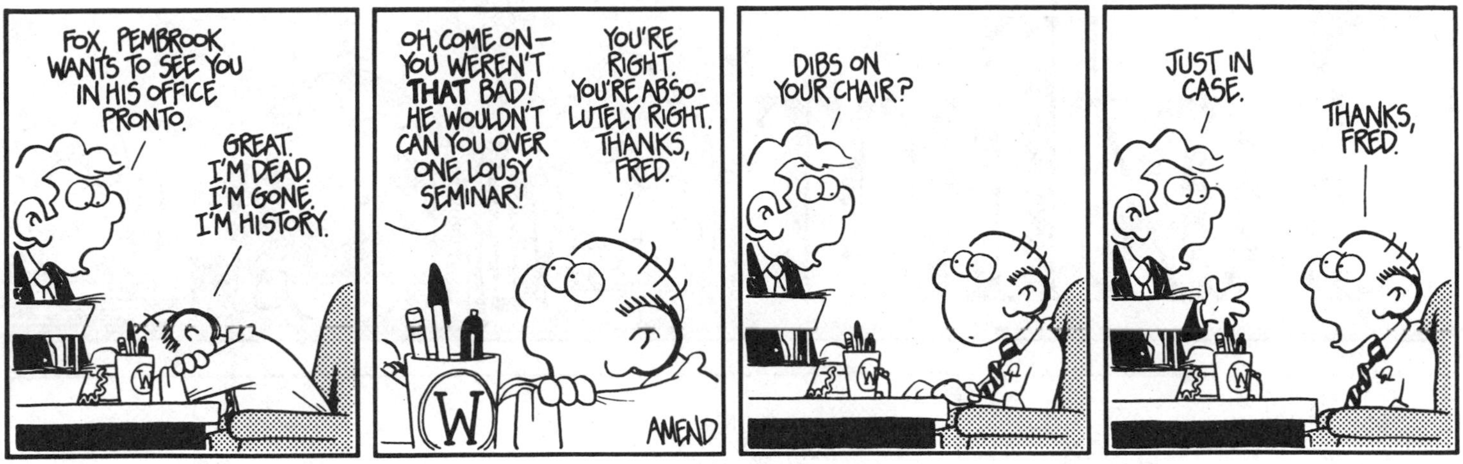
FOX, PEMBROOK WANTS TO SEE YOU IN HIS OFFICE PRONTO.
GREAT. I'M DEAD. I'M GONE. I'M HISTORY.
OH, COME ON– YOU WEREN'T **THAT** BAD! HE WOULDN'T CAN YOU OVER ONE LOUSY SEMINAR!
YOU'RE RIGHT. YOU'RE ABSO-LUTELY RIGHT. THANKS, FRED.
AMEND
DIBS ON YOUR CHAIR?
JUST IN CASE.
THANKS, FRED.

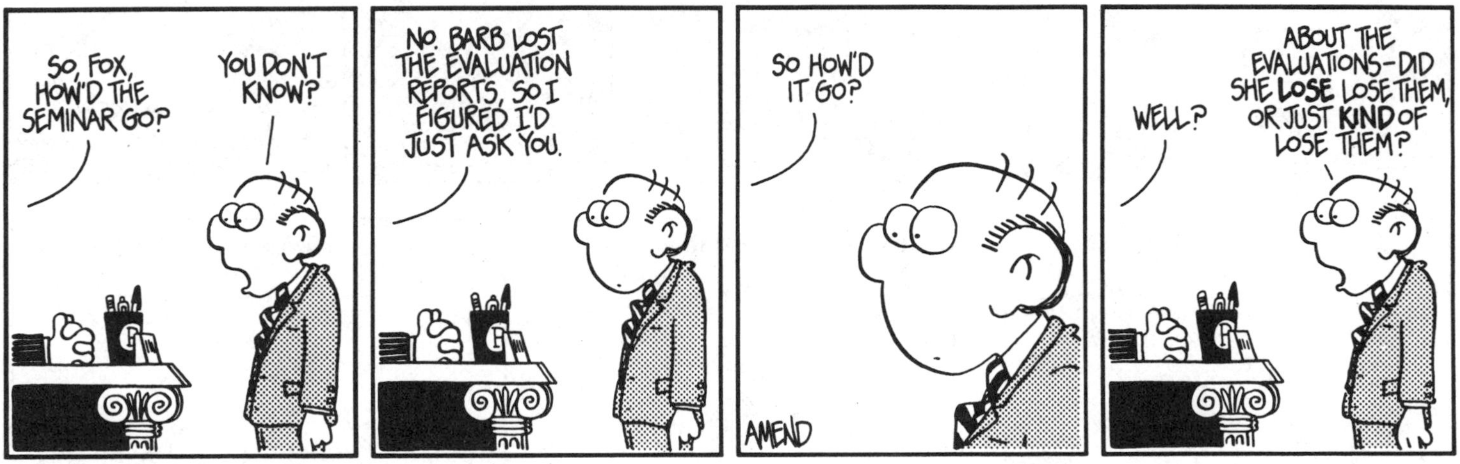
SO, FOX, HOW'D THE SEMINAR GO?
YOU DON'T KNOW?
NO. BARB LOST THE EVALUATION REPORTS, SO I FIGURED I'D JUST ASK YOU.
SO HOW'D IT GO?
AMEND
WELL?
ABOUT THE EVALUATIONS–DID SHE **LOSE** LOSE THEM, OR JUST **KIND** OF LOSE THEM?

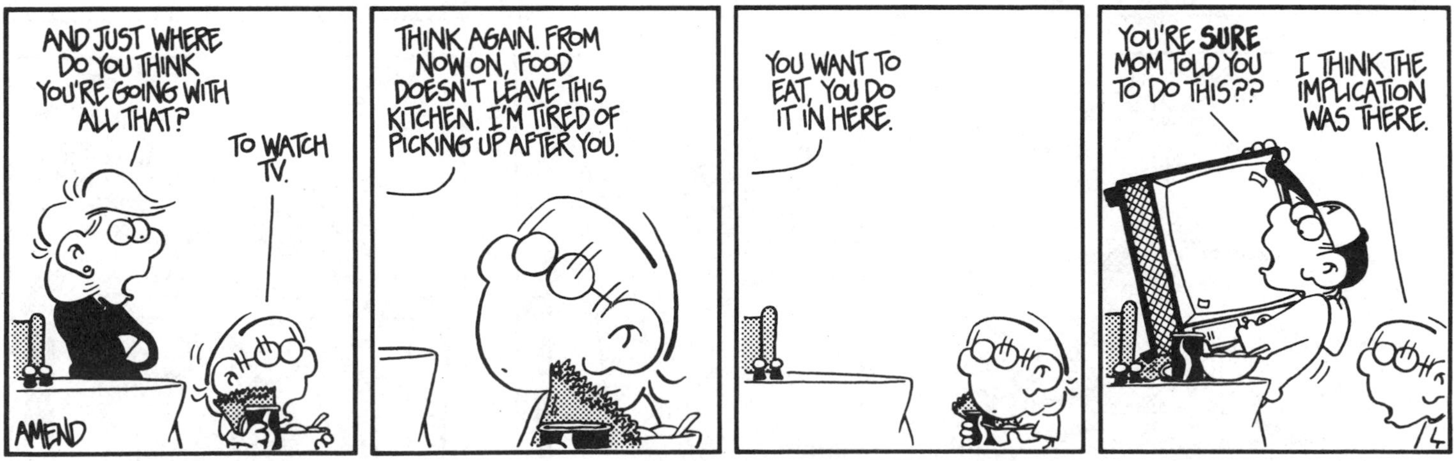
AND JUST WHERE DO YOU THINK YOU'RE GOING WITH ALL THAT?
TO WATCH TV.
AMEND
THINK AGAIN. FROM NOW ON, FOOD DOESN'T LEAVE THIS KITCHEN. I'M TIRED OF PICKING UP AFTER YOU.
YOU WANT TO EAT, YOU DO IT IN HERE.
YOU'RE **SURE** MOM TOLD YOU TO DO THIS??
I THINK THE IMPLICATION WAS THERE.

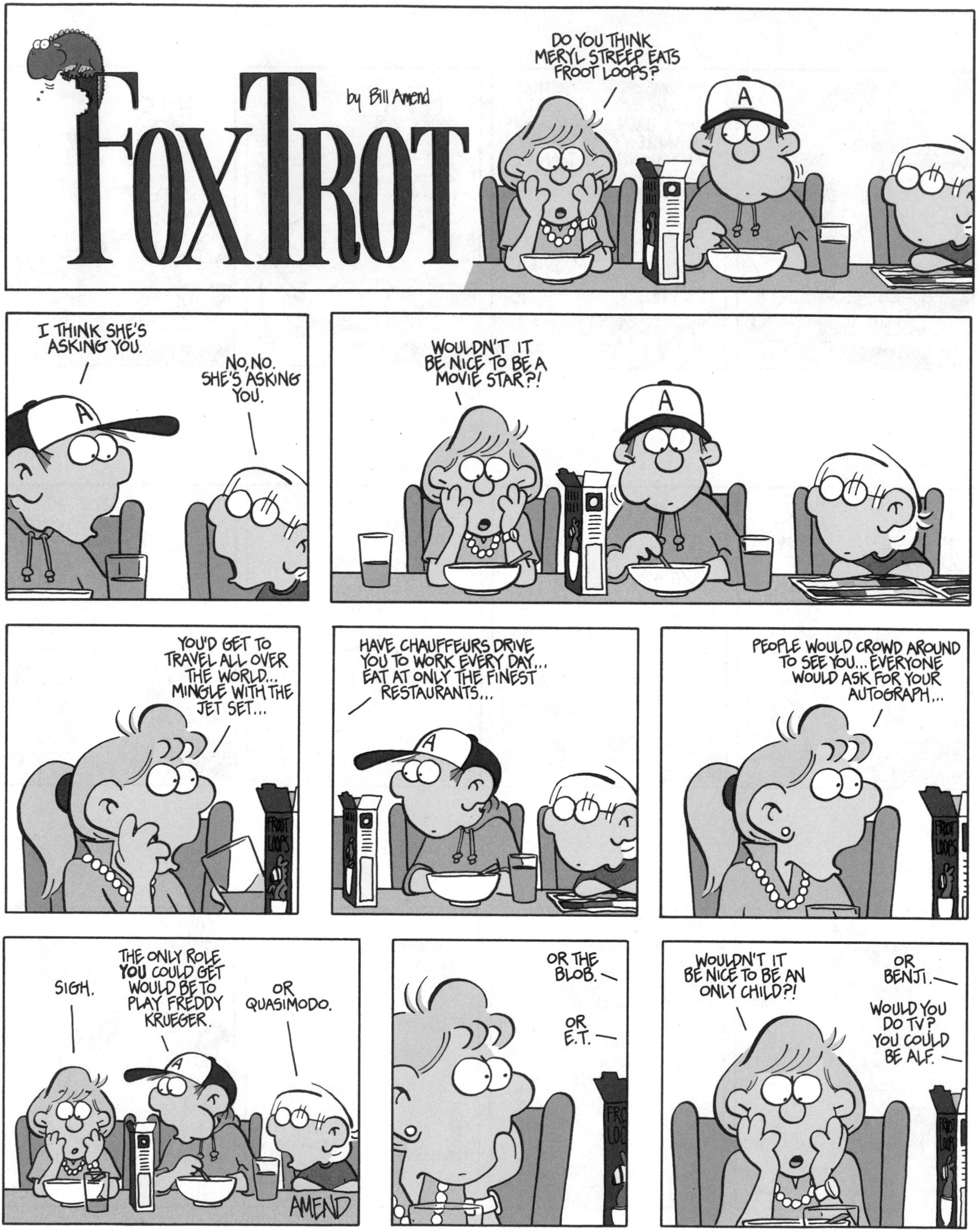
FoxTrot
by Bill Amend
DO YOU THINK MERYL STREEP EATS FROOT LOOPS?
I THINK SHE'S ASKING YOU.
NO, NO. SHE'S ASKING YOU.
WOULDN'T IT BE NICE TO BE A MOVIE STAR?!
YOU'D GET TO TRAVEL ALL OVER THE WORLD... MINGLE WITH THE JET SET...
HAVE CHAUFFEURS DRIVE YOU TO WORK EVERY DAY... EAT AT ONLY THE FINEST RESTAURANTS...
PEOPLE WOULD CROWD AROUND TO SEE YOU... EVERYONE WOULD ASK FOR YOUR AUTOGRAPH...
SIGH.
THE ONLY ROLE YOU COULD GET WOULD BE TO PLAY FREDDY KRUEGER.
OR QUASIMODO.
OR THE BLOB.
OR E.T.
WOULDN'T IT BE NICE TO BE AN ONLY CHILD?!
OR BENJI.
WOULD YOU DO TV? YOU COULD BE ALF.
AMEND

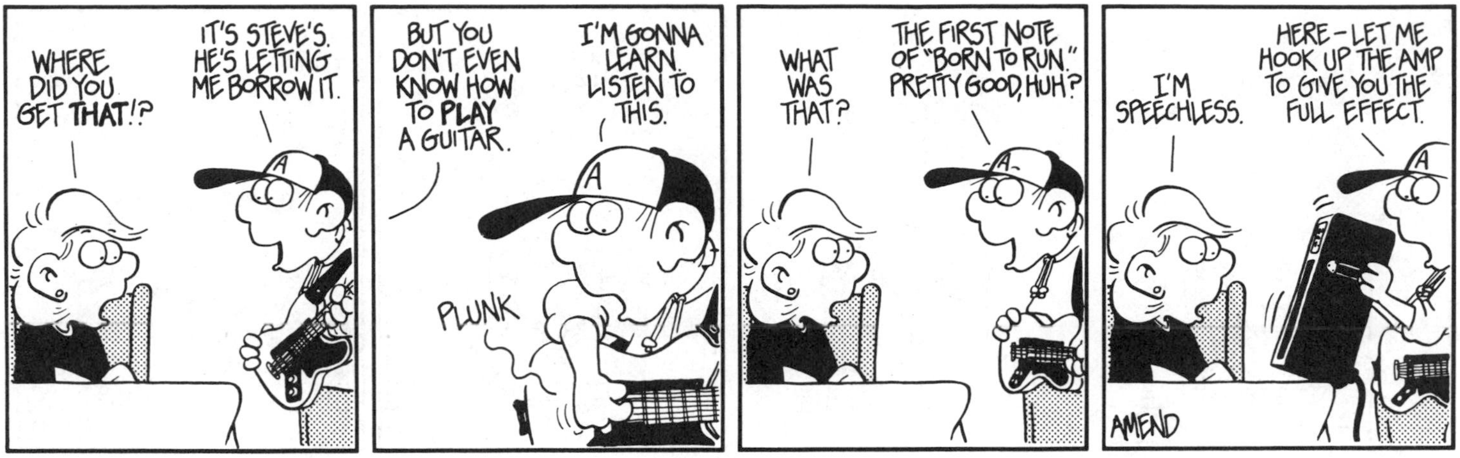
WHERE DID YOU GET **THAT**!?
IT'S STEVE'S. HE'S LETTING ME BORROW IT.
BUT YOU DON'T EVEN KNOW HOW TO **PLAY** A GUITAR.
I'M GONNA LEARN. LISTEN TO THIS.
PLUNK
WHAT WAS THAT?
THE FIRST NOTE OF "BORN TO RUN." PRETTY GOOD, HUH?
I'M SPEECHLESS.
HERE – LET ME HOOK UP THE AMP TO GIVE YOU THE FULL EFFECT.
AMEND

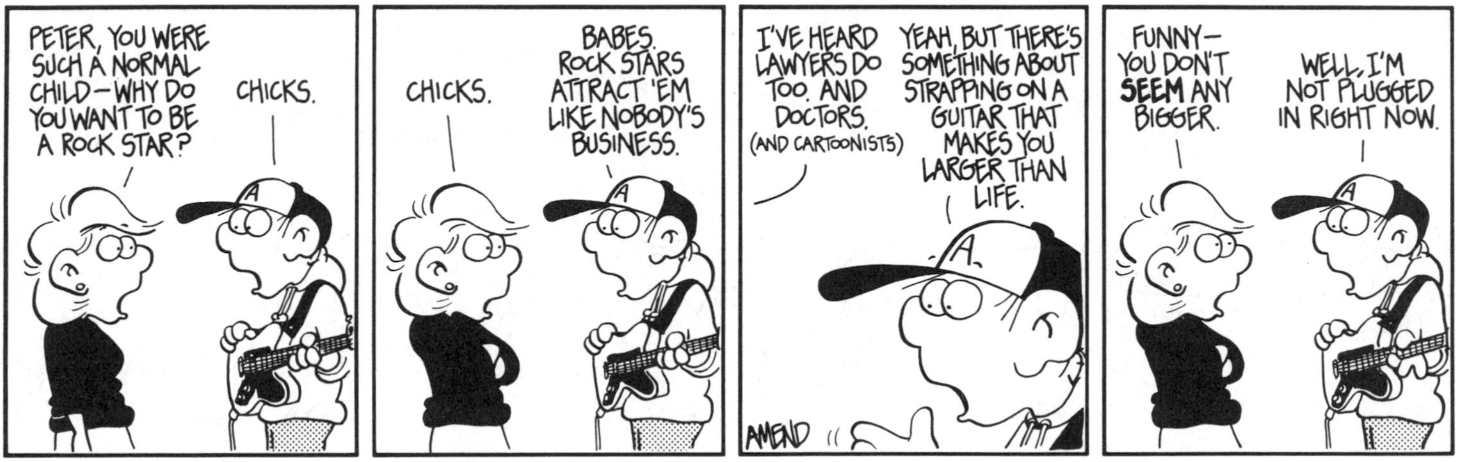
PETER, YOU WERE SUCH A NORMAL CHILD – WHY DO YOU WANT TO BE A ROCK STAR?
CHICKS.
CHICKS.
BABES. ROCK STARS ATTRACT 'EM LIKE NOBODY'S BUSINESS.
I'VE HEARD LAWYERS DO TOO. AND DOCTORS.
(AND CARTOONISTS)
YEAH, BUT THERE'S SOMETHING ABOUT STRAPPING ON A GUITAR THAT MAKES YOU LARGER THAN LIFE.
AMEND
FUNNY – YOU DON'T **SEEM** ANY BIGGER.
WELL, I'M NOT PLUGGED IN RIGHT NOW.

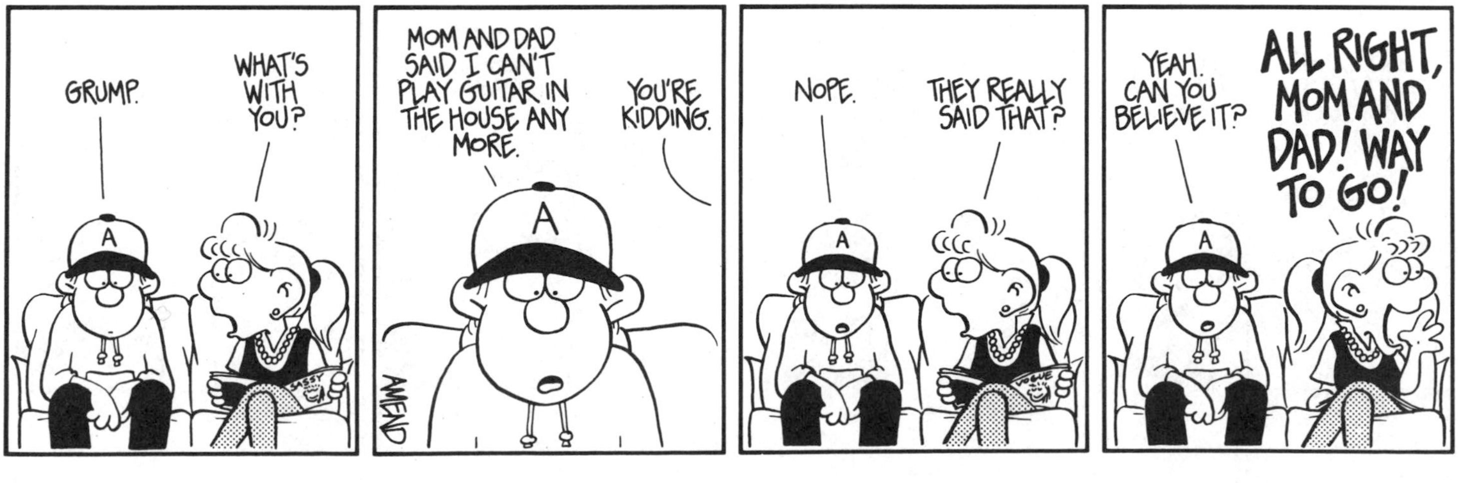
GRUMP.
WHAT'S WITH YOU?
MOM AND DAD SAID I CAN'T PLAY GUITAR IN THE HOUSE ANY MORE.
YOU'RE KIDDING.
AMEND
NOPE.
THEY REALLY SAID THAT?
YEAH. CAN YOU BELIEVE IT?
ALL RIGHT, MOM AND DAD! WAY TO GO!

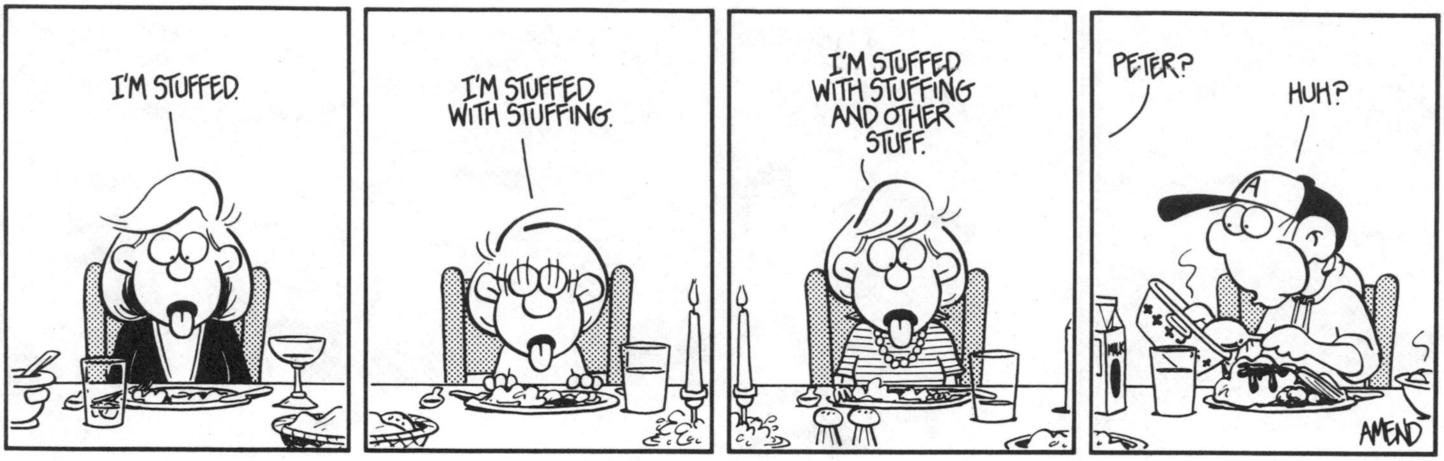
I'M STUFFED.
I'M STUFFED WITH STUFFING.
I'M STUFFED WITH STUFFING AND OTHER STUFF.
PETER?
HUH?
MILK
AMEND

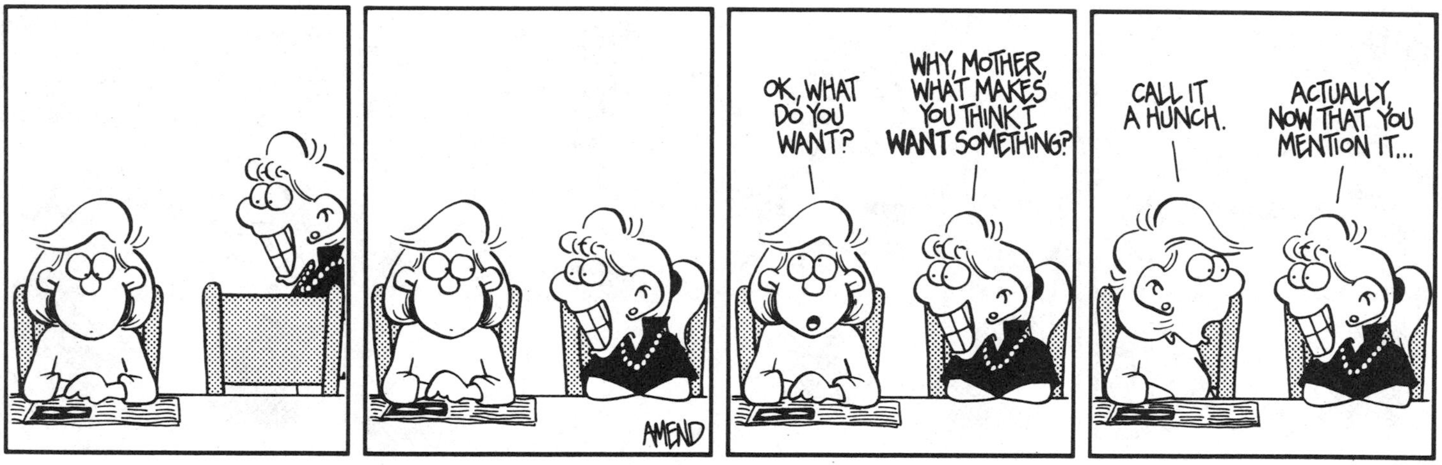
AMEND
OK, WHAT DO YOU WANT?
WHY, MOTHER, WHAT MAKES YOU THINK I **WANT** SOMETHING?
CALL IT A HUNCH.
ACTUALLY, NOW THAT YOU MENTION IT...

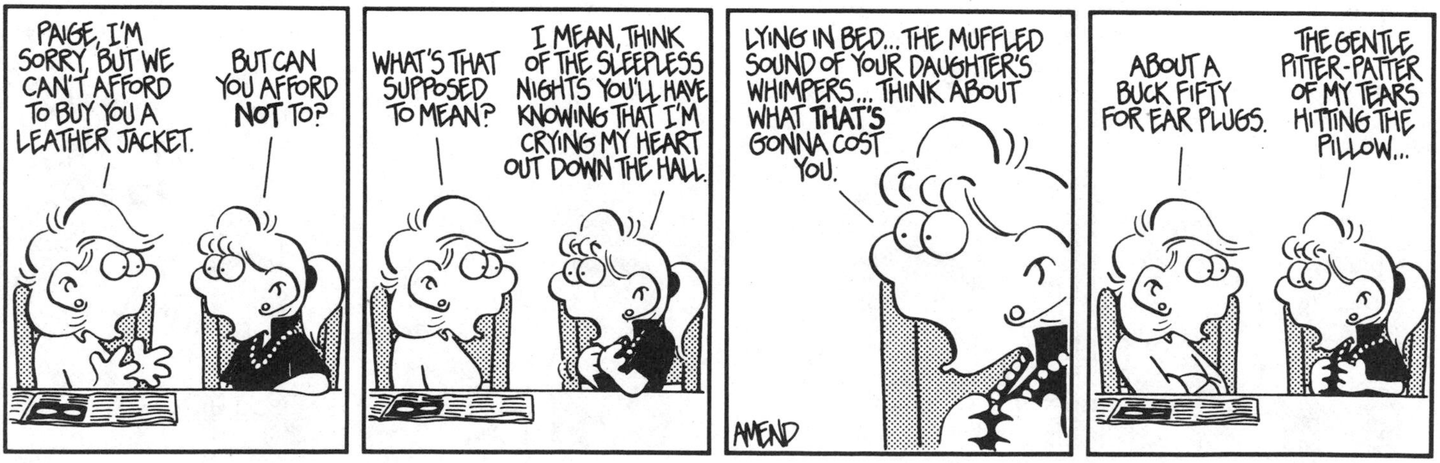
PAIGE, I'M SORRY, BUT WE CAN'T AFFORD TO BUY YOU A LEATHER JACKET.
BUT CAN YOU AFFORD **NOT** TO?
WHAT'S THAT SUPPOSED TO MEAN?
I MEAN, THINK OF THE SLEEPLESS NIGHTS YOU'LL HAVE KNOWING THAT I'M CRYING MY HEART OUT DOWN THE HALL.
LYING IN BED... THE MUFFLED SOUND OF YOUR DAUGHTER'S WHIMPERS... THINK ABOUT WHAT **THAT'S** GONNA COST YOU.
AMEND
ABOUT A BUCK FIFTY FOR EAR PLUGS.
THE GENTLE PITTER-PATTER OF MY TEARS HITTING THE PILLOW...

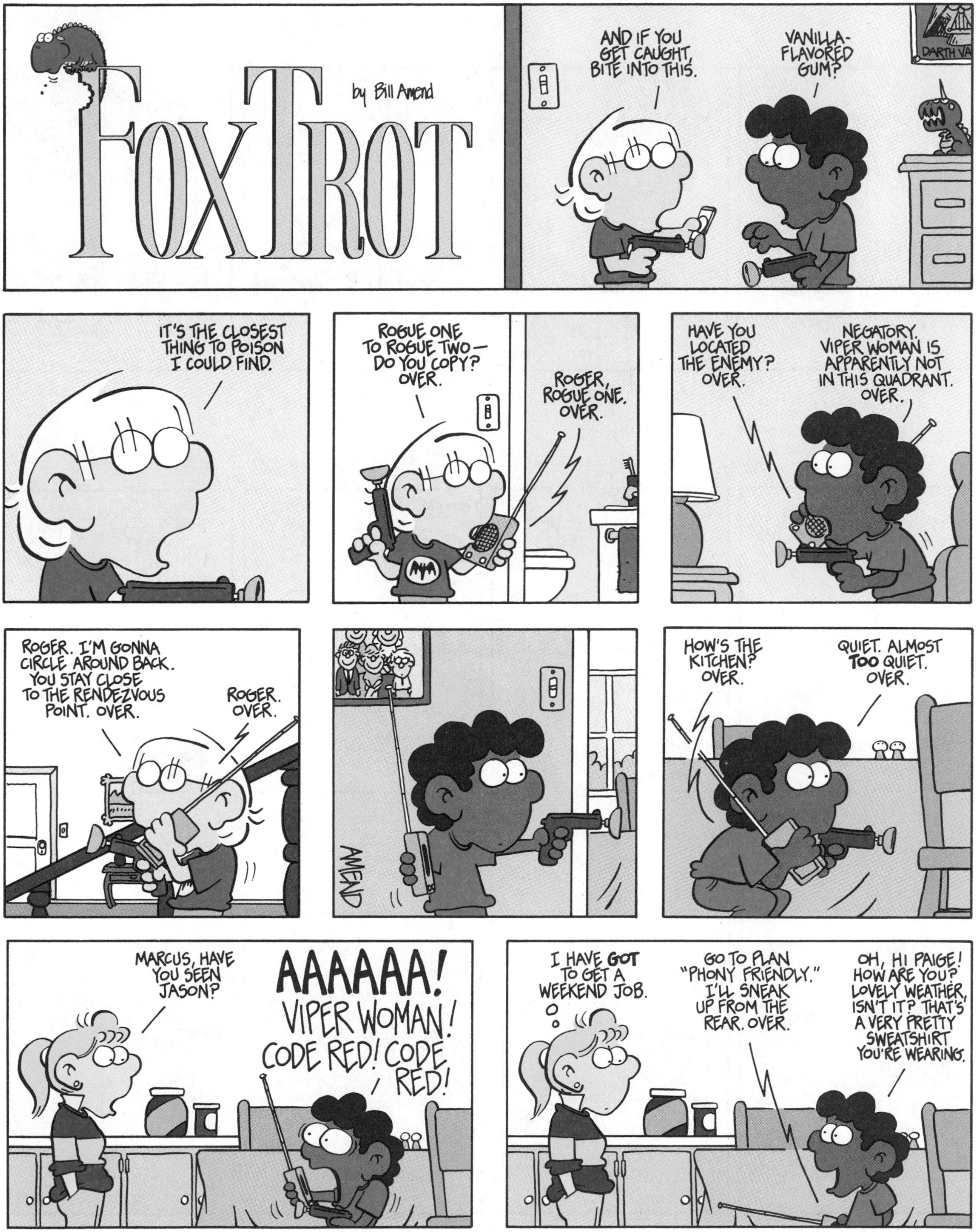
FoxTrot
by Bill Amend
AND IF YOU GET CAUGHT, BITE INTO THIS.
VANILLA-FLAVORED GUM?
DARTH VA
IT'S THE CLOSEST THING TO POISON I COULD FIND.
ROGUE ONE TO ROGUE TWO— DO YOU COPY? OVER.
ROGER, ROGUE ONE. OVER.
HAVE YOU LOCATED THE ENEMY? OVER.
NEGATORY. VIPER WOMAN IS APPARENTLY NOT IN THIS QUADRANT. OVER.
ROGER. I'M GONNA CIRCLE AROUND BACK. YOU STAY CLOSE TO THE RENDEZVOUS POINT. OVER.
ROGER. OVER.
AMEND
HOW'S THE KITCHEN? OVER.
QUIET. ALMOST **TOO** QUIET. OVER.
MARCUS, HAVE YOU SEEN JASON?
AAAAAA! VIPER WOMAN! CODE RED! CODE RED!
I HAVE **GOT** TO GET A WEEKEND JOB.
GO TO PLAN "PHONY FRIENDLY." I'LL SNEAK UP FROM THE REAR. OVER.
OH, HI PAIGE! HOW ARE YOU? LOVELY WEATHER, ISN'T IT? THAT'S A VERY PRETTY SWEATSHIRT YOU'RE WEARING.

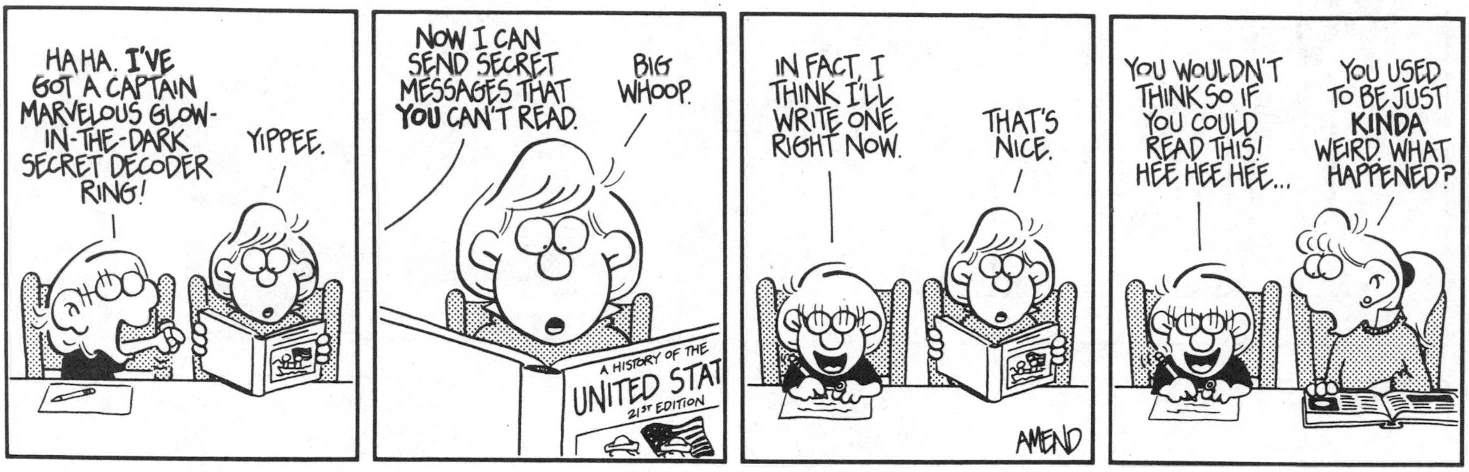

HA HA. I'VE GOT A CAPTAIN MARVELOUS GLOW-IN-THE-DARK SECRET DECODER RING!
YIPPEE.
NOW I CAN SEND SECRET MESSAGES THAT YOU CAN'T READ.
BIG WHOOP.
A HISTORY OF THE UNITED STAT
21ST EDITION
IN FACT, I THINK I'LL WRITE ONE RIGHT NOW.
THAT'S NICE.
AMEND
YOU WOULDN'T THINK SO IF YOU COULD READ THIS! HEE HEE HEE...
YOU USED TO BE JUST KINDA WEIRD. WHAT HAPPENED?

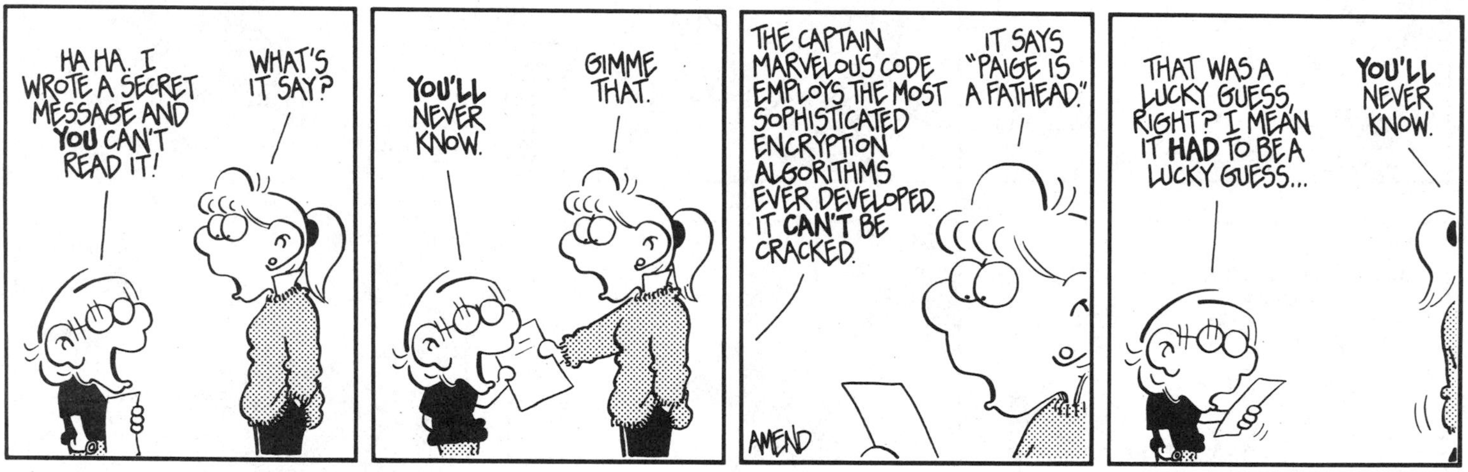

HA HA. I WROTE A SECRET MESSAGE AND YOU CAN'T READ IT!
WHAT'S IT SAY?
YOU'LL NEVER KNOW.
GIMME THAT.
THE CAPTAIN MARVELOUS CODE EMPLOYS THE MOST SOPHISTICATED ENCRYPTION ALGORITHMS EVER DEVELOPED. IT CAN'T BE CRACKED.
IT SAYS "PAIGE IS A FATHEAD."
AMEND
THAT WAS A LUCKY GUESS, RIGHT? I MEAN IT HAD TO BE A LUCKY GUESS...
YOU'LL NEVER KNOW.

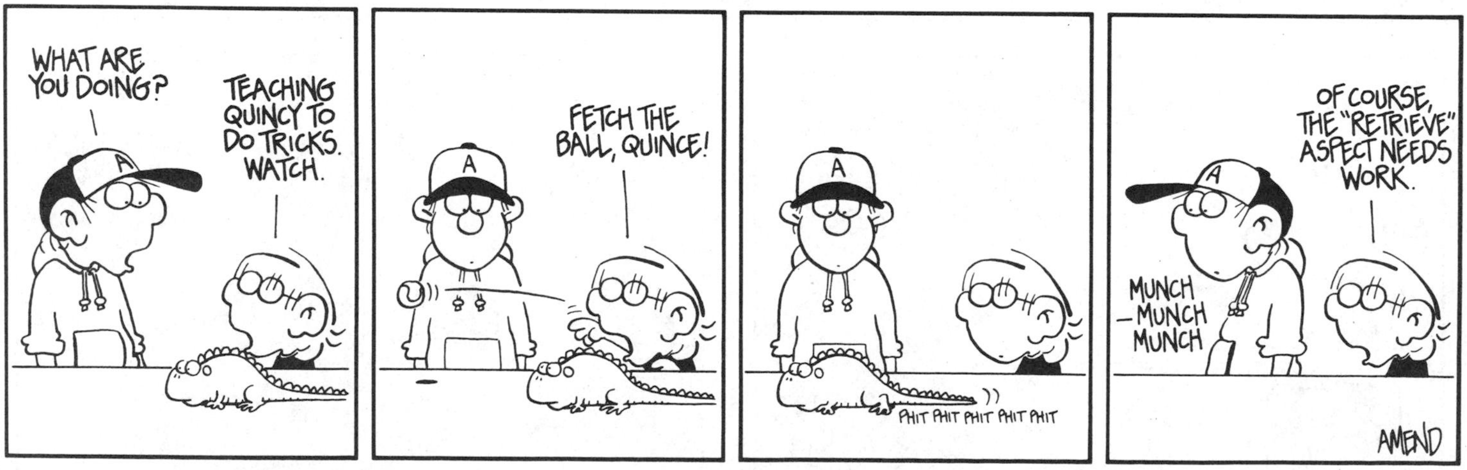

WHAT ARE YOU DOING?
TEACHING QUINCY TO DO TRICKS. WATCH.
FETCH THE BALL, QUINCE!
PHIT PHIT PHIT PHIT PHIT
MUNCH MUNCH MUNCH
OF COURSE, THE "RETRIEVE" ASPECT NEEDS WORK.
AMEND

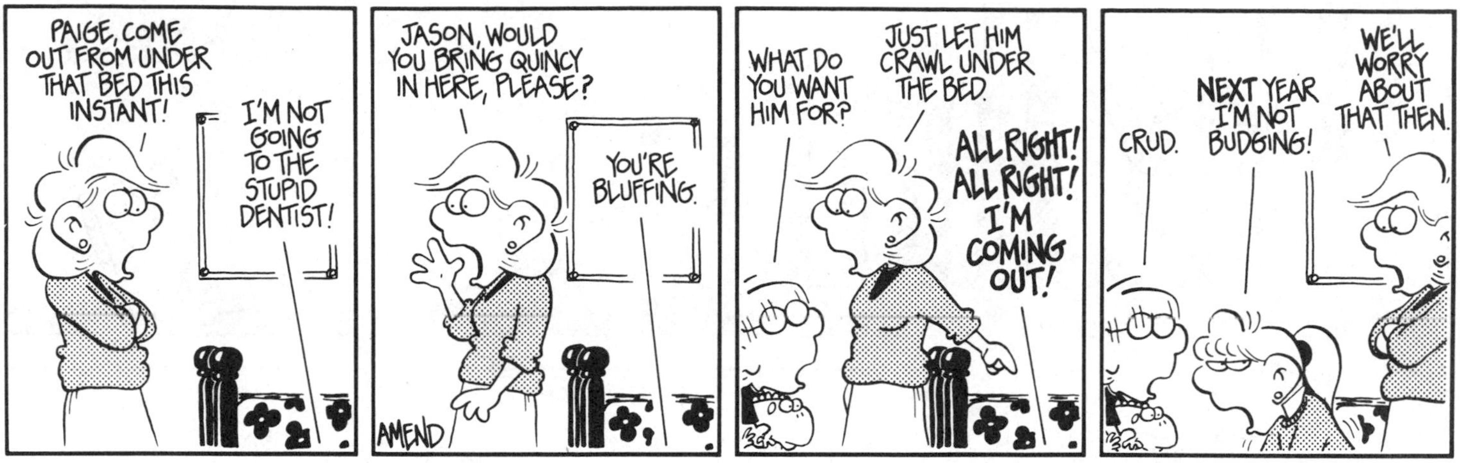
PAIGE, COME OUT FROM UNDER THAT BED THIS INSTANT!
I'M NOT GOING TO THE STUPID DENTIST!
JASON, WOULD YOU BRING QUINCY IN HERE, PLEASE?
YOU'RE BLUFFING.
AMEND
WHAT DO YOU WANT HIM FOR?
JUST LET HIM CRAWL UNDER THE BED.
ALL RIGHT! ALL RIGHT! I'M COMING OUT!
CRUD.
NEXT YEAR I'M NOT BUDGING!
WE'LL WORRY ABOUT THAT THEN.

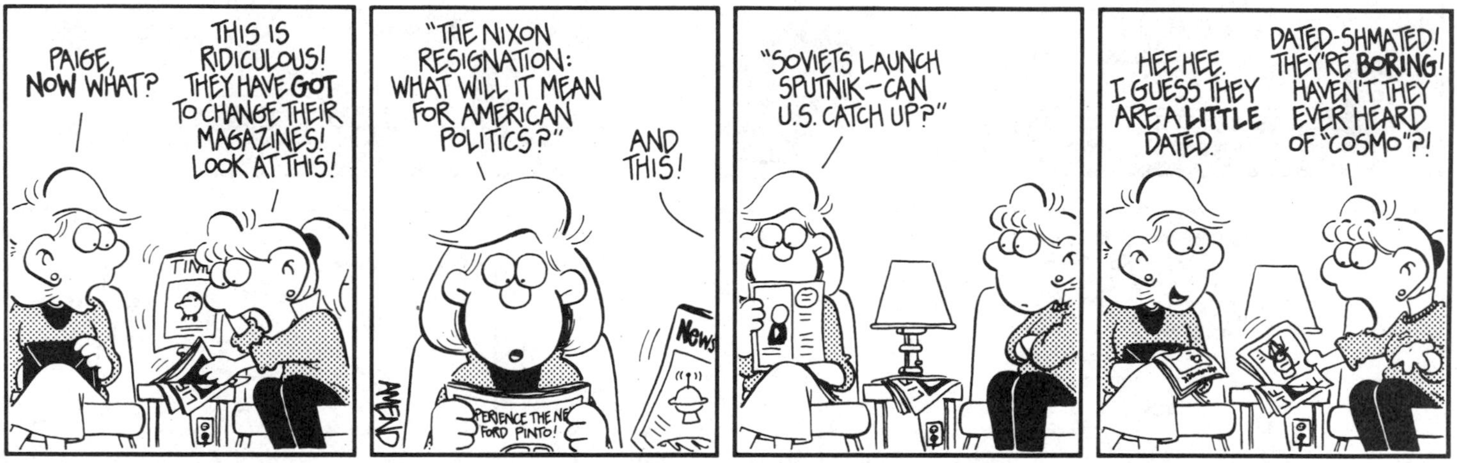
PAIGE, NOW WHAT?
THIS IS RIDICULOUS! THEY HAVE GOT TO CHANGE THEIR MAGAZINES! LOOK AT THIS!
"THE NIXON RESIGNATION: WHAT WILL IT MEAN FOR AMERICAN POLITICS?"
AND THIS!
AMEND
News
"SOVIETS LAUNCH SPUTNIK—CAN U.S. CATCH UP?"
HEE HEE. I GUESS THEY ARE A LITTLE DATED.
DATED-SHMATED! THEY'RE BORING! HAVEN'T THEY EVER HEARD OF "COSMO"?!

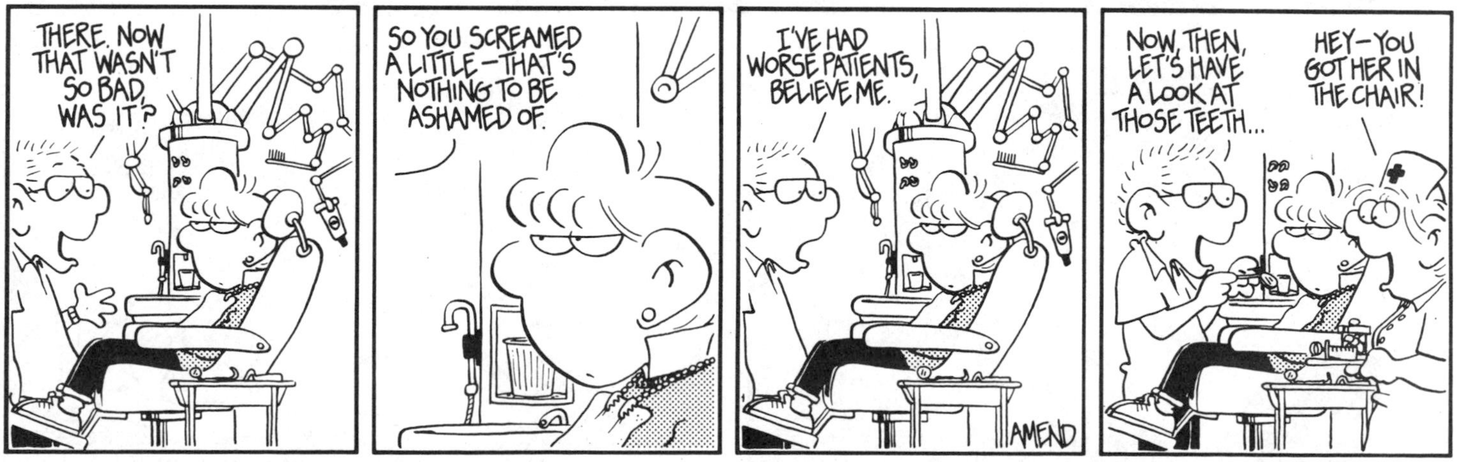
THERE. NOW THAT WASN'T SO BAD, WAS IT?
SO YOU SCREAMED A LITTLE—THAT'S NOTHING TO BE ASHAMED OF.
I'VE HAD WORSE PATIENTS, BELIEVE ME.
AMEND
NOW, THEN, LET'S HAVE A LOOK AT THOSE TEETH...
HEY—YOU GOT HER IN THE CHAIR!

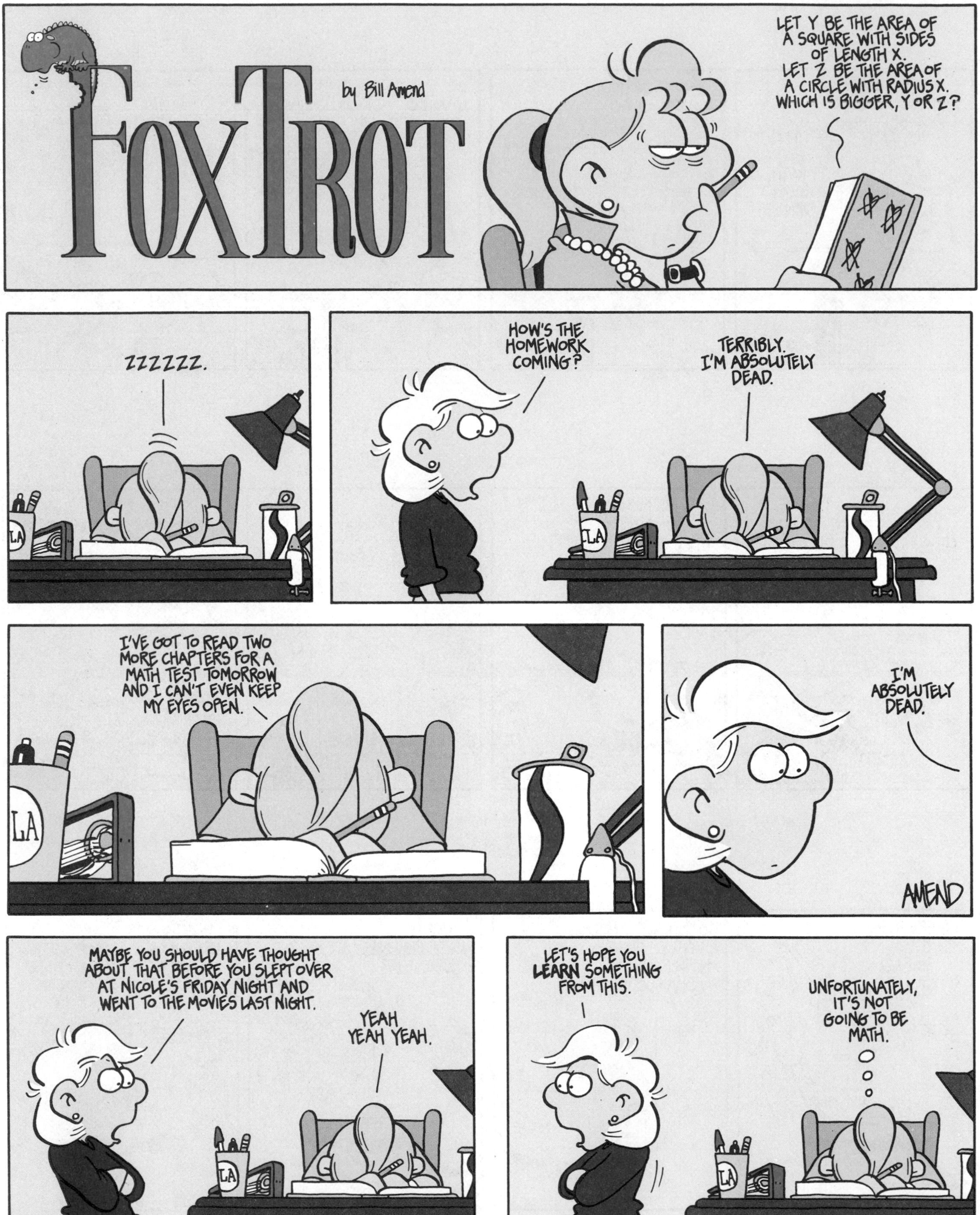
FoxTrot
by Bill Amend
LET Y BE THE AREA OF A SQUARE WITH SIDES OF LENGTH X. LET Z BE THE AREA OF A CIRCLE WITH RADIUS X. WHICH IS BIGGER, Y OR Z?
ZZZZZZ.
HOW'S THE HOMEWORK COMING?
TERRIBLY. I'M ABSOLUTELY DEAD.
I'VE GOT TO READ TWO MORE CHAPTERS FOR A MATH TEST TOMORROW AND I CAN'T EVEN KEEP MY EYES OPEN.
I'M ABSOLUTELY DEAD.
AMEND
MAYBE YOU SHOULD HAVE THOUGHT ABOUT THAT BEFORE YOU SLEPT OVER AT NICOLE'S FRIDAY NIGHT AND WENT TO THE MOVIES LAST NIGHT.
YEAH YEAH YEAH.
LET'S HOPE YOU **LEARN** SOMETHING FROM THIS.
UNFORTUNATELY, IT'S NOT GOING TO BE MATH.

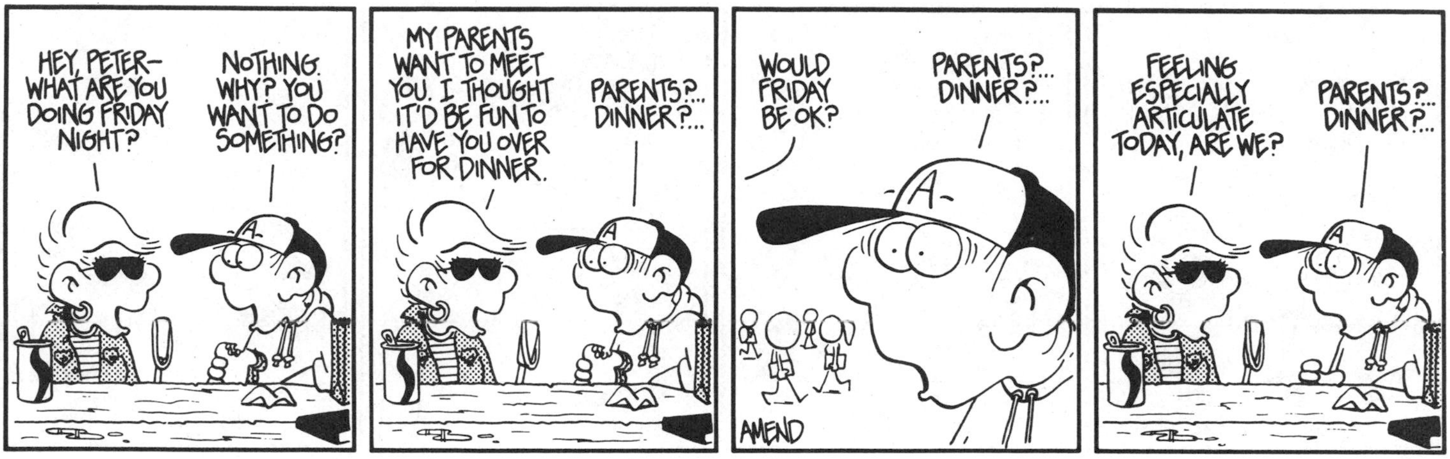
HEY, PETER- WHAT ARE YOU DOING FRIDAY NIGHT?
NOTHING. WHY? YOU WANT TO DO SOMETHING?
MY PARENTS WANT TO MEET YOU. I THOUGHT IT'D BE FUN TO HAVE YOU OVER FOR DINNER.
PARENTS?... DINNER?...
WOULD FRIDAY BE OK?
PARENTS?... DINNER?...
AMEND
FEELING ESPECIALLY ARTICULATE TODAY, ARE WE?
PARENTS?... DINNER?...

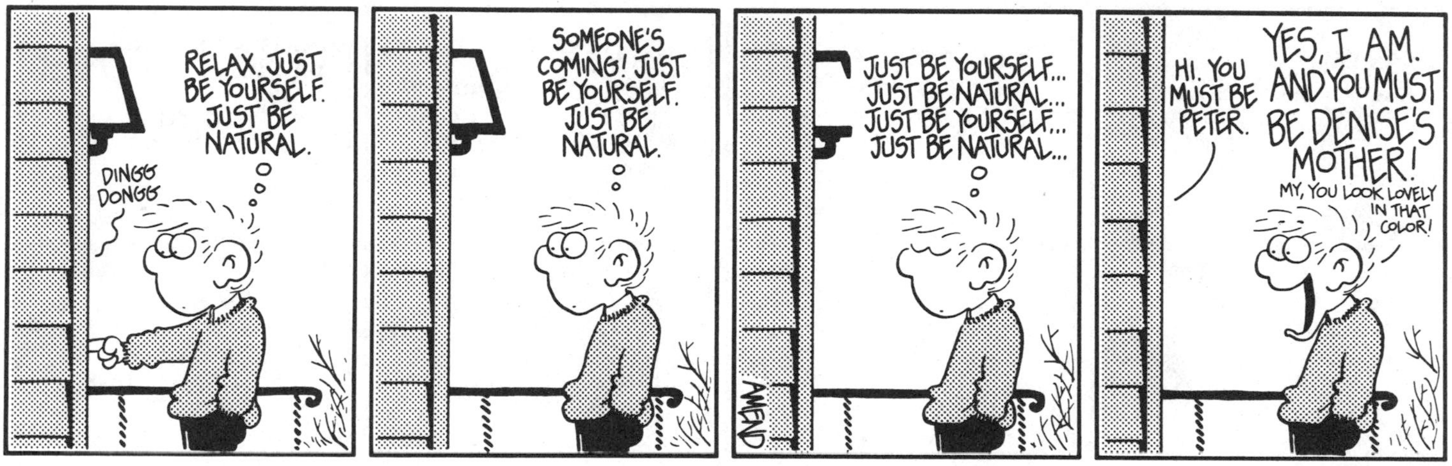
RELAX. JUST BE YOURSELF. JUST BE NATURAL.
DINGG DONGG
SOMEONE'S COMING! JUST BE YOURSELF. JUST BE NATURAL.
JUST BE YOURSELF... JUST BE NATURAL... JUST BE YOURSELF... JUST BE NATURAL...
AMEND
HI. YOU MUST BE PETER.
YES, I AM. AND YOU MUST BE DENISE'S MOTHER!
MY, YOU LOOK LOVELY IN THAT COLOR!

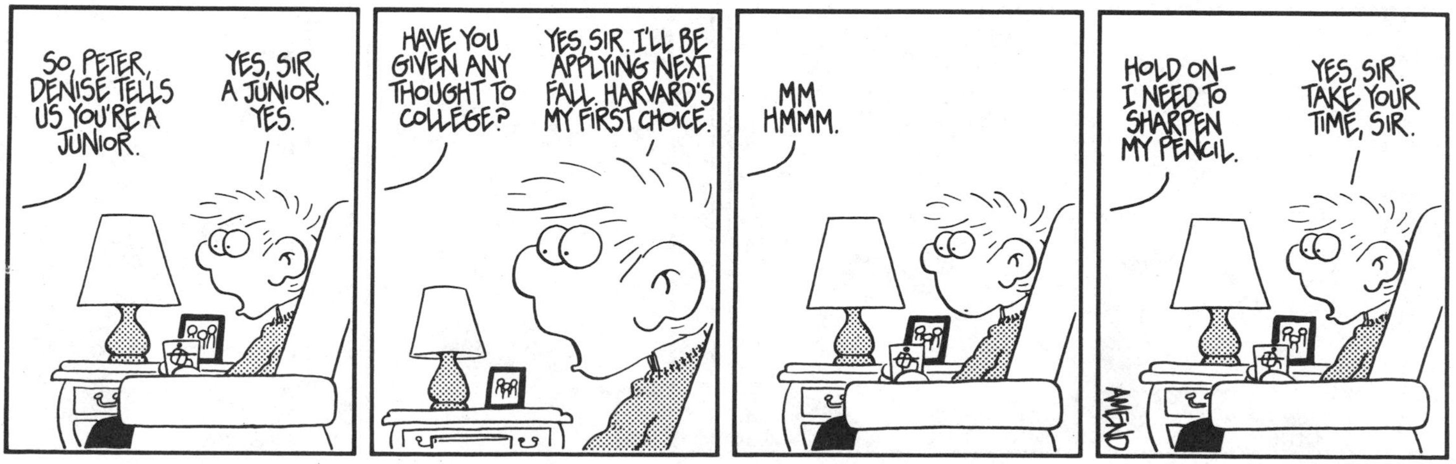
SO, PETER, DENISE TELLS US YOU'RE A JUNIOR.
YES, SIR, A JUNIOR. YES.
HAVE YOU GIVEN ANY THOUGHT TO COLLEGE?
YES, SIR. I'LL BE APPLYING NEXT FALL. HARVARD'S MY FIRST CHOICE.
MM HMMM.
HOLD ON- I NEED TO SHARPEN MY PENCIL.
YES, SIR. TAKE YOUR TIME, SIR.
AMEND

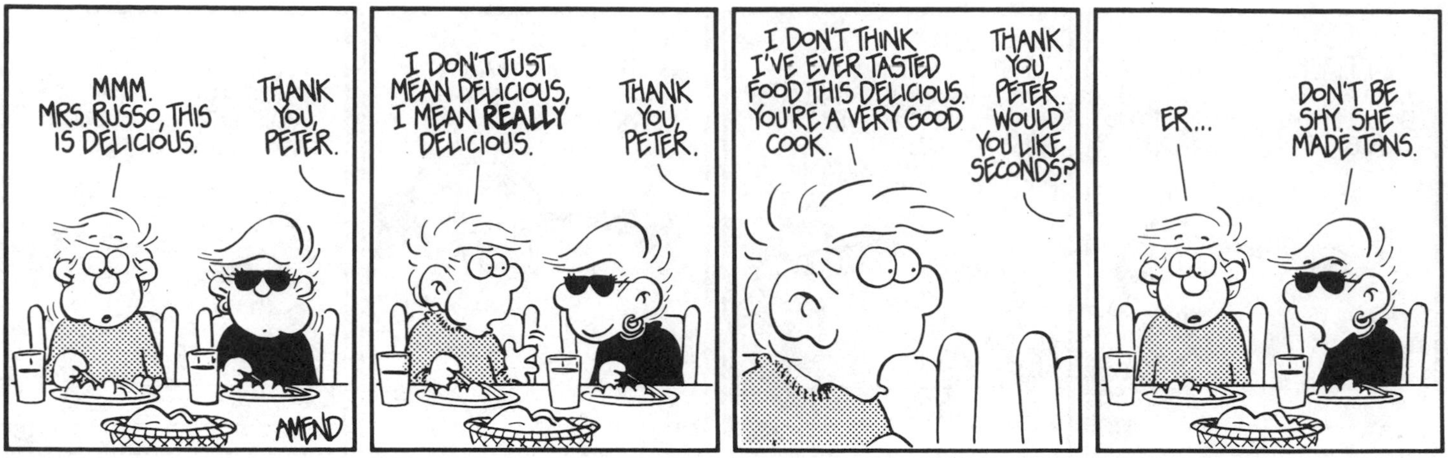
MMM. MRS. RUSSO, THIS IS DELICIOUS.
THANK YOU, PETER.
I DON'T JUST MEAN DELICIOUS, I MEAN **REALLY** DELICIOUS.
THANK YOU, PETER.
I DON'T THINK I'VE EVER TASTED FOOD THIS DELICIOUS. YOU'RE A VERY GOOD COOK.
THANK YOU, PETER. WOULD YOU LIKE SECONDS?
ER...
DON'T BE SHY. SHE MADE TONS.
AMEND

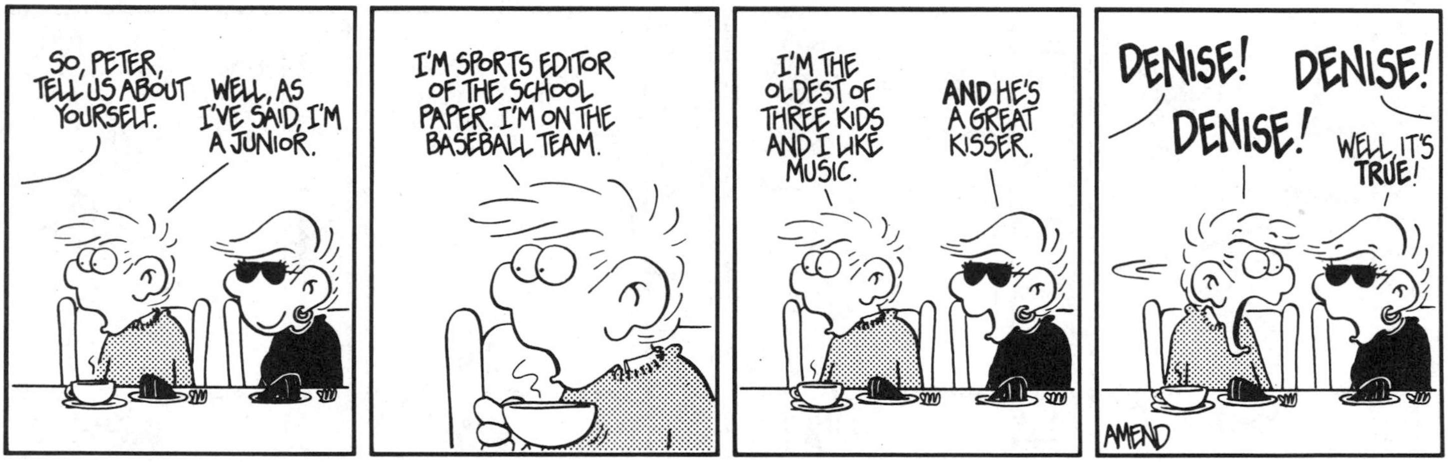
SO, PETER, TELL US ABOUT YOURSELF.
WELL, AS I'VE SAID, I'M A JUNIOR.
I'M SPORTS EDITOR OF THE SCHOOL PAPER. I'M ON THE BASEBALL TEAM.
I'M THE OLDEST OF THREE KIDS AND I LIKE MUSIC.
AND HE'S A GREAT KISSER.
DENISE!
DENISE!
DENISE!
WELL, IT'S **TRUE**!
AMEND

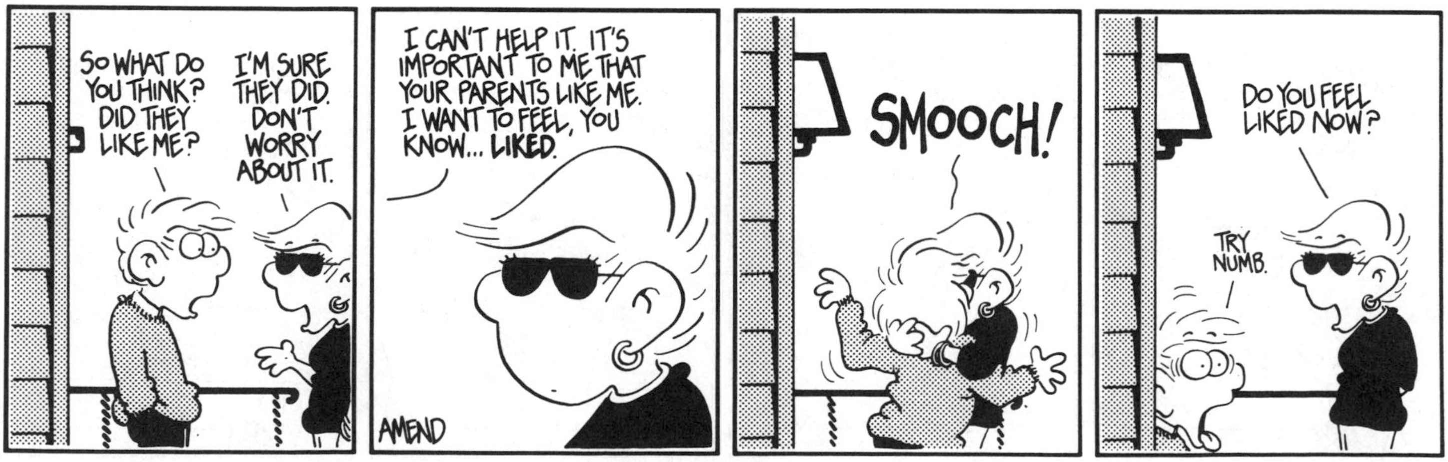
SO WHAT DO YOU THINK? DID THEY LIKE ME?
I'M SURE THEY DID. DON'T WORRY ABOUT IT.
I CAN'T HELP IT. IT'S IMPORTANT TO ME THAT YOUR PARENTS LIKE ME. I WANT TO FEEL, YOU KNOW... **LIKED**.
AMEND
SMOOCH!
DO YOU FEEL LIKED NOW?
TRY NUMB.

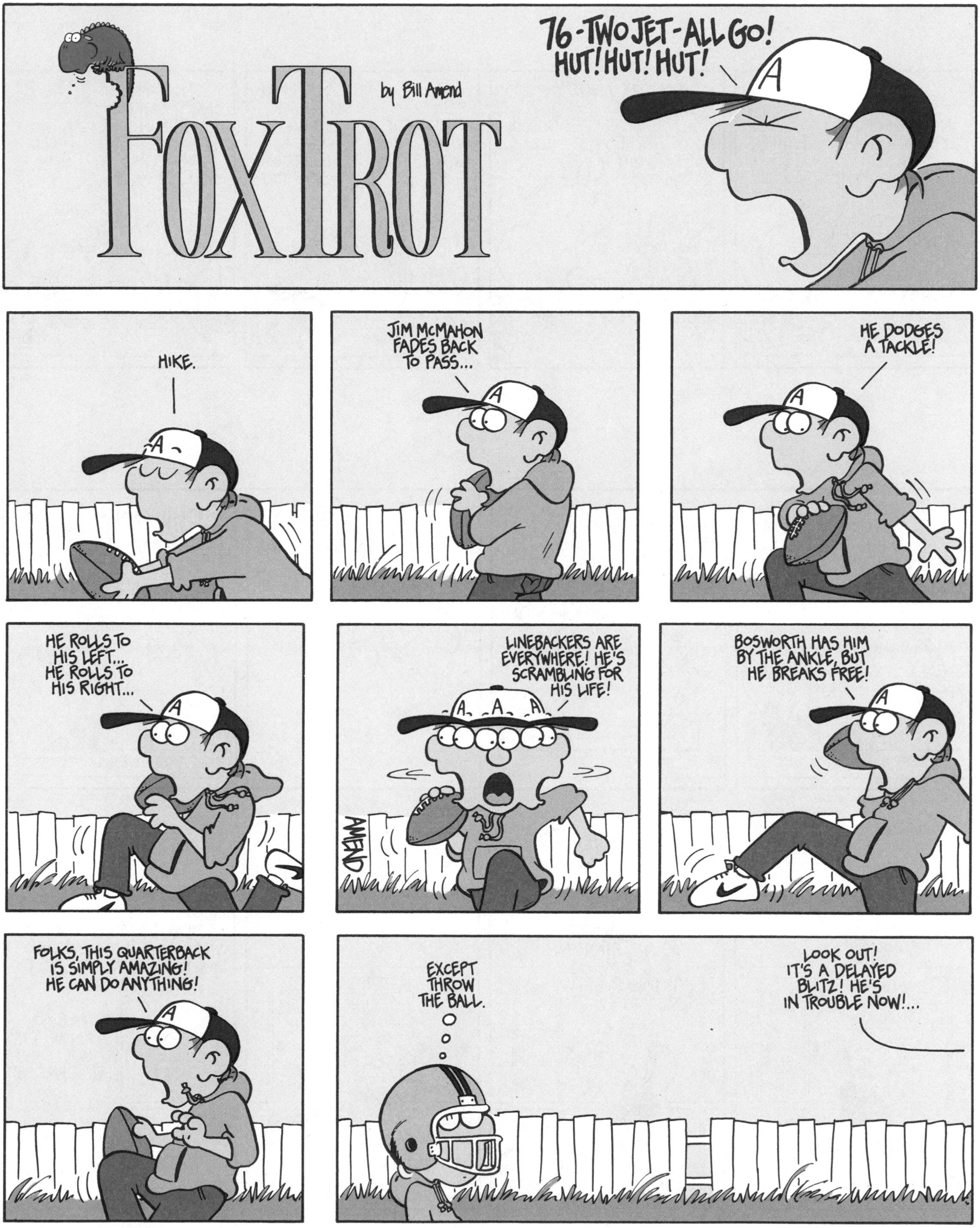
FoxTrot
by Bill Amend
76-TWO JET-ALL GO! HUT! HUT! HUT!
HIKE.
JIM McMAHON FADES BACK TO PASS...
HE DODGES A TACKLE!
HE ROLLS TO HIS LEFT... HE ROLLS TO HIS RIGHT...
LINEBACKERS ARE EVERYWHERE! HE'S SCRAMBLING FOR HIS LIFE!
AMEND
BOSWORTH HAS HIM BY THE ANKLE, BUT HE BREAKS FREE!
FOLKS, THIS QUARTERBACK IS SIMPLY AMAZING! HE CAN DO ANYTHING!
EXCEPT THROW THE BALL.
LOOK OUT! IT'S A DELAYED BLITZ! HE'S IN TROUBLE NOW!...

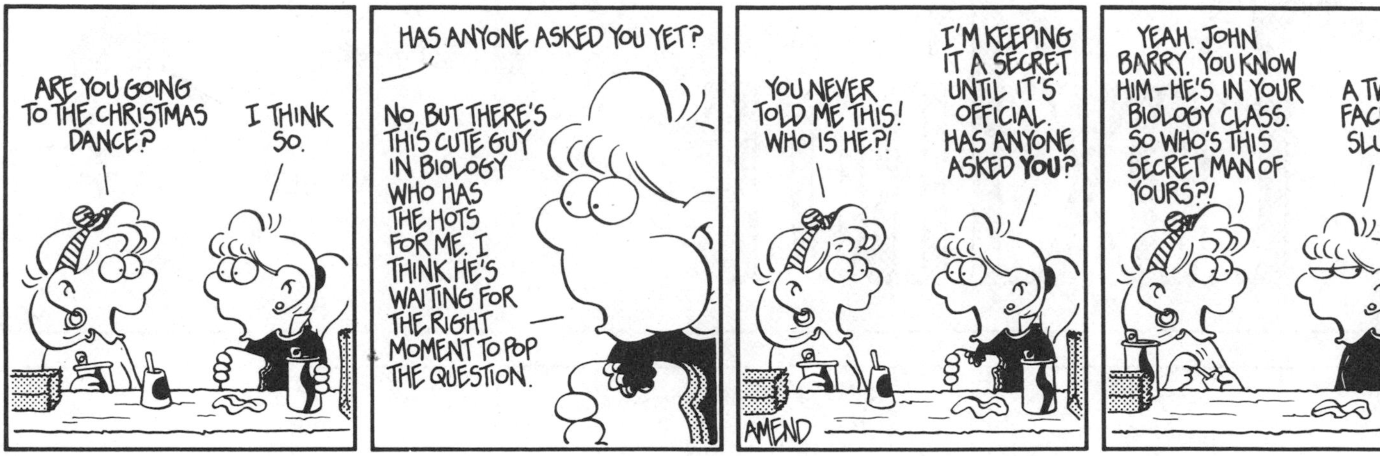
ARE YOU GOING TO THE CHRISTMAS DANCE?
I THINK SO.
HAS ANYONE ASKED YOU YET?
NO, BUT THERE'S THIS CUTE GUY IN BIOLOGY WHO HAS THE HOTS FOR ME. I THINK HE'S WAITING FOR THE RIGHT MOMENT TO POP THE QUESTION.
YOU NEVER TOLD ME THIS! WHO IS HE?!
I'M KEEPING IT A SECRET UNTIL IT'S OFFICIAL. HAS ANYONE ASKED **YOU**?
AMEND
YEAH. JOHN BARRY. YOU KNOW HIM—HE'S IN YOUR BIOLOGY CLASS. SO WHO'S THIS SECRET MAN OF YOURS?!
A TWO-FACED SLUG.

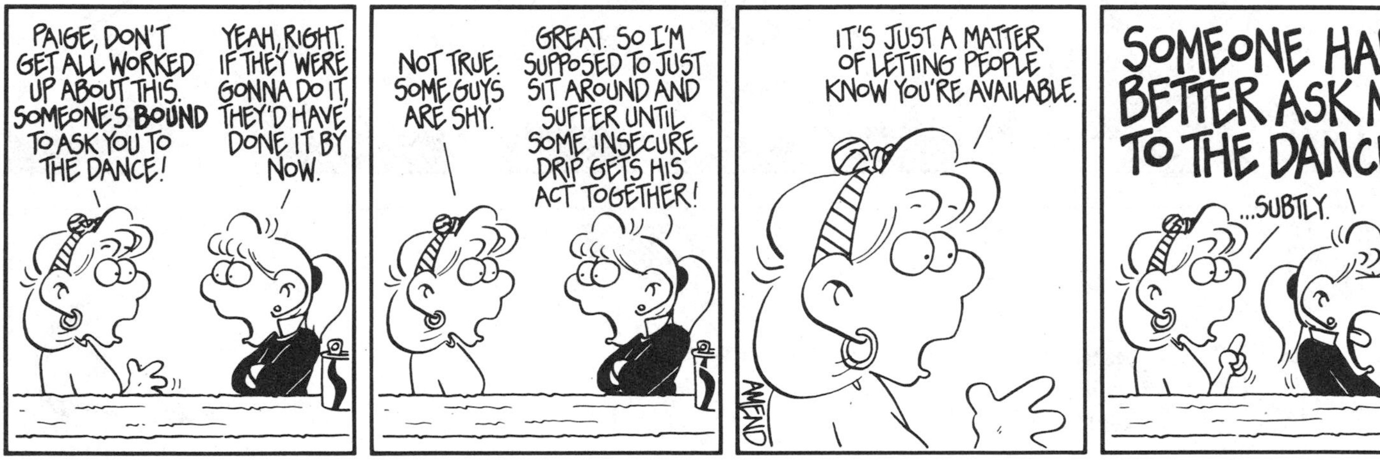
PAIGE, DON'T GET ALL WORKED UP ABOUT THIS. SOMEONE'S **BOUND** TO ASK YOU TO THE DANCE!
YEAH, RIGHT. IF THEY WERE GONNA DO IT, THEY'D HAVE DONE IT BY NOW.
NOT TRUE. SOME GUYS ARE SHY.
GREAT. SO I'M SUPPOSED TO JUST SIT AROUND AND SUFFER UNTIL SOME INSECURE DRIP GETS HIS ACT TOGETHER!
IT'S JUST A MATTER OF LETTING PEOPLE KNOW YOU'RE AVAILABLE.
AMEND
SOMEONE HAD BETTER ASK ME TO THE DANCE!
...SUBTLY.

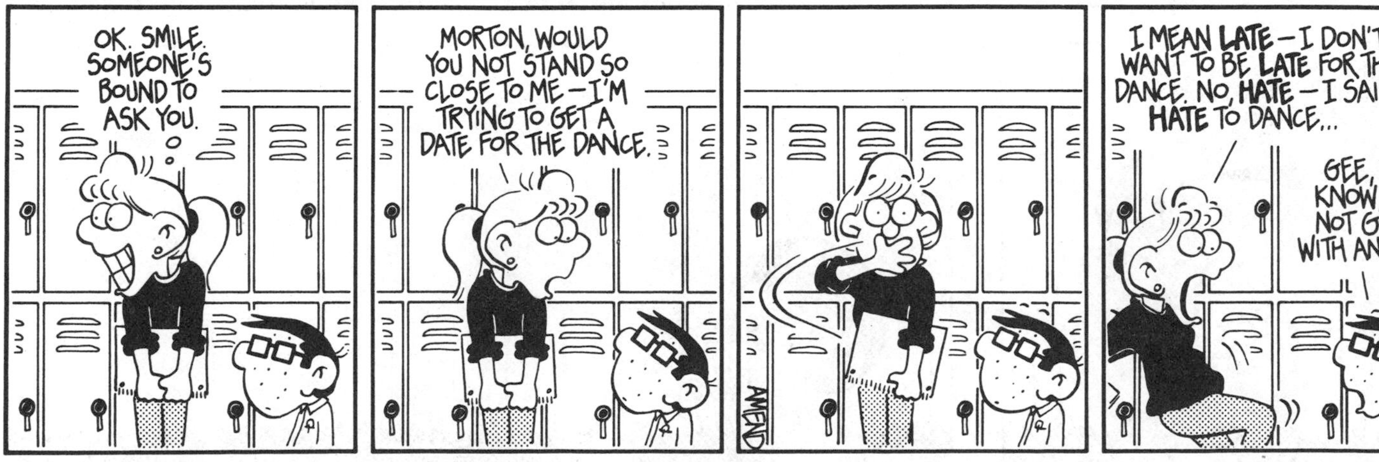
OK. SMILE. SOMEONE'S BOUND TO ASK YOU.
MORTON, WOULD YOU NOT STAND SO CLOSE TO ME—I'M TRYING TO GET A DATE FOR THE DANCE.
AMEND
I MEAN **LATE**—I DON'T WANT TO BE **LATE** FOR THE DANCE. NO, **HATE**—I SAID I **HATE** TO DANCE...
GEE, YOU KNOW, **I'M** NOT GOING WITH ANYONE...

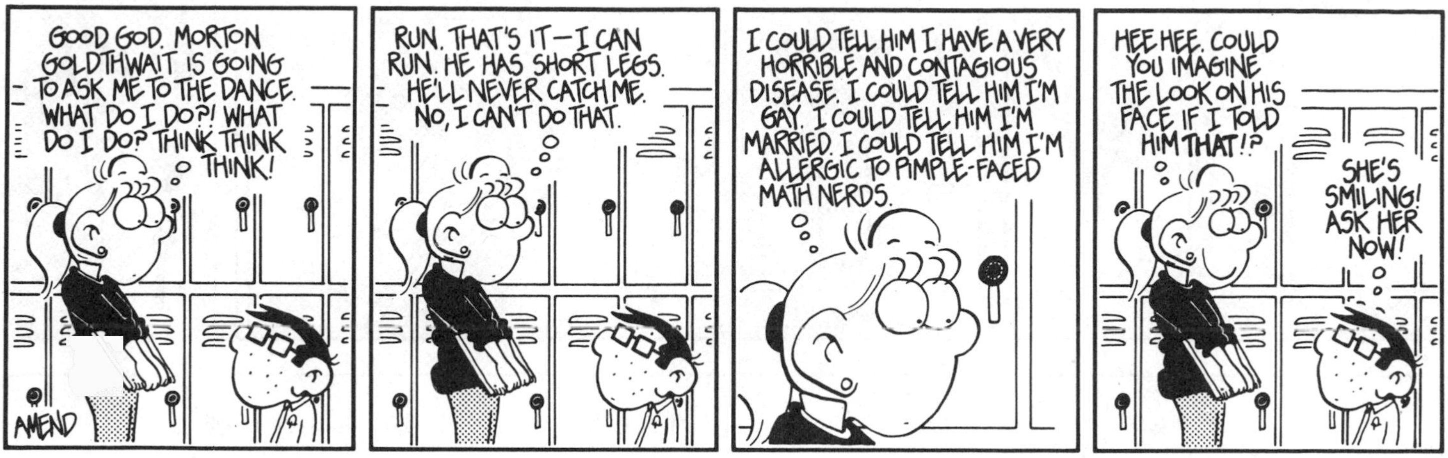
GOOD GOD. MORTON GOLDTHWAIT IS GOING TO ASK ME TO THE DANCE. WHAT DO I DO?! WHAT DO I DO? THINK THINK THINK!
AMEND
RUN. THAT'S IT—I CAN RUN. HE HAS SHORT LEGS. HE'LL NEVER CATCH ME. NO, I CAN'T DO THAT.
I COULD TELL HIM I HAVE A VERY HORRIBLE AND CONTAGIOUS DISEASE. I COULD TELL HIM I'M GAY. I COULD TELL HIM I'M MARRIED. I COULD TELL HIM I'M ALLERGIC TO PIMPLE-FACED MATH NERDS.
HEE HEE. COULD YOU IMAGINE THE LOOK ON HIS FACE IF I TOLD HIM THAT!?
SHE'S SMILING! ASK HER NOW!

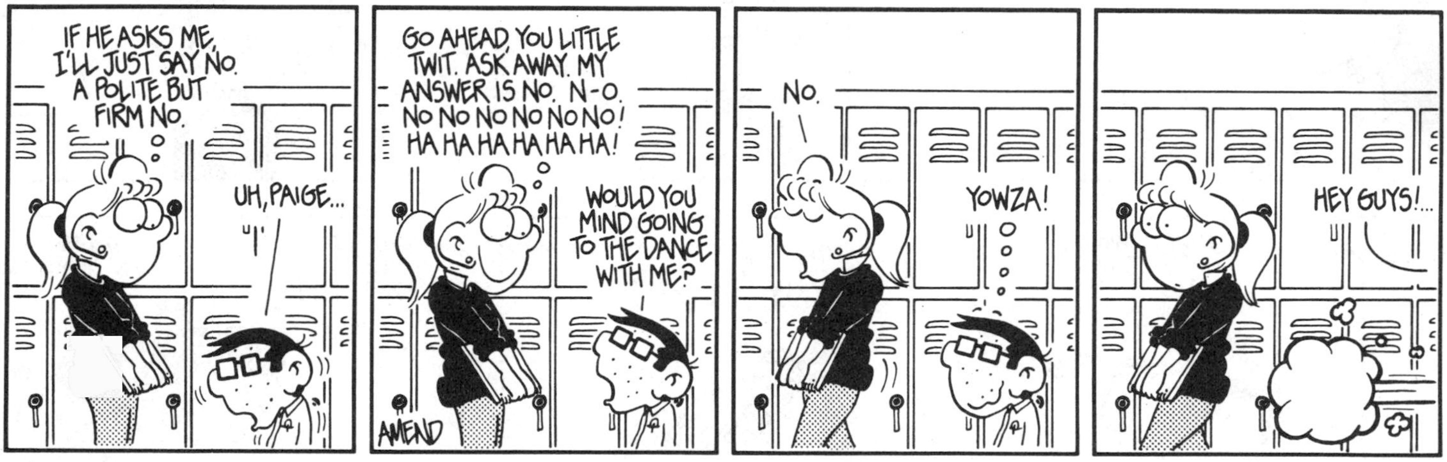
IF HE ASKS ME, I'LL JUST SAY NO. A POLITE BUT FIRM NO.
UH, PAIGE...
GO AHEAD, YOU LITTLE TWIT. ASK AWAY. MY ANSWER IS NO. N-O. NO NO NO NO NO NO! HA HA HA HA HA HA HA!
WOULD YOU MIND GOING TO THE DANCE WITH ME?
AMEND
NO.
YOWZA!
HEY GUYS!...

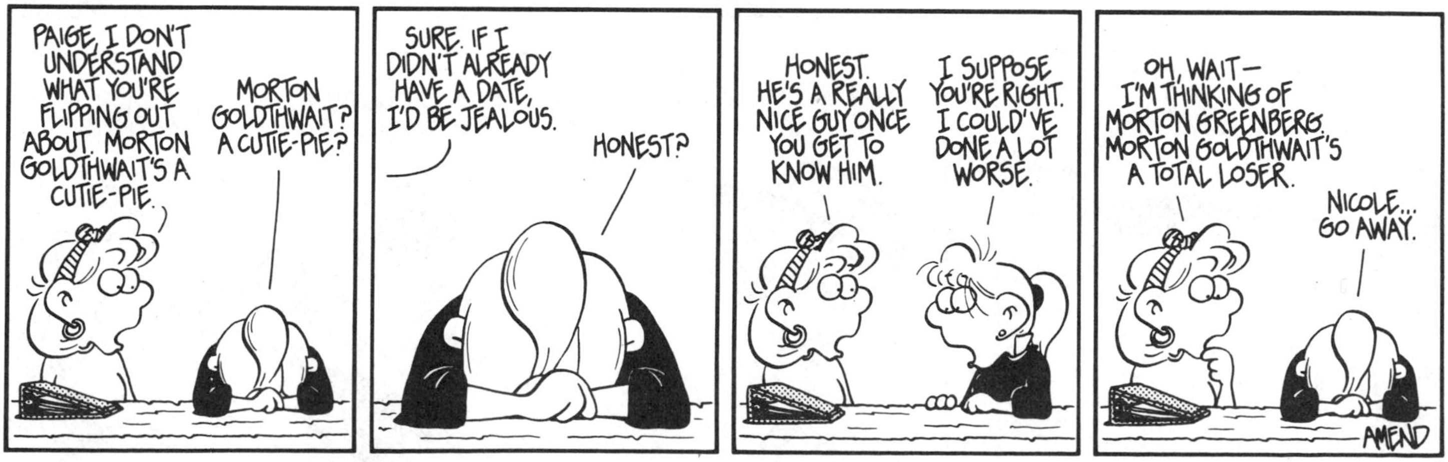
PAIGE, I DON'T UNDERSTAND WHAT YOU'RE FLIPPING OUT ABOUT. MORTON GOLDTHWAIT'S A CUTIE-PIE.
MORTON GOLDTHWAIT? A CUTIE-PIE?
SURE. IF I DIDN'T ALREADY HAVE A DATE, I'D BE JEALOUS.
HONEST?
HONEST. HE'S A REALLY NICE GUY ONCE YOU GET TO KNOW HIM.
I SUPPOSE YOU'RE RIGHT. I COULD'VE DONE A LOT WORSE.
OH, WAIT— I'M THINKING OF MORTON GREENBERG. MORTON GOLDTHWAIT'S A TOTAL LOSER.
NICOLE... GO AWAY.
AMEND

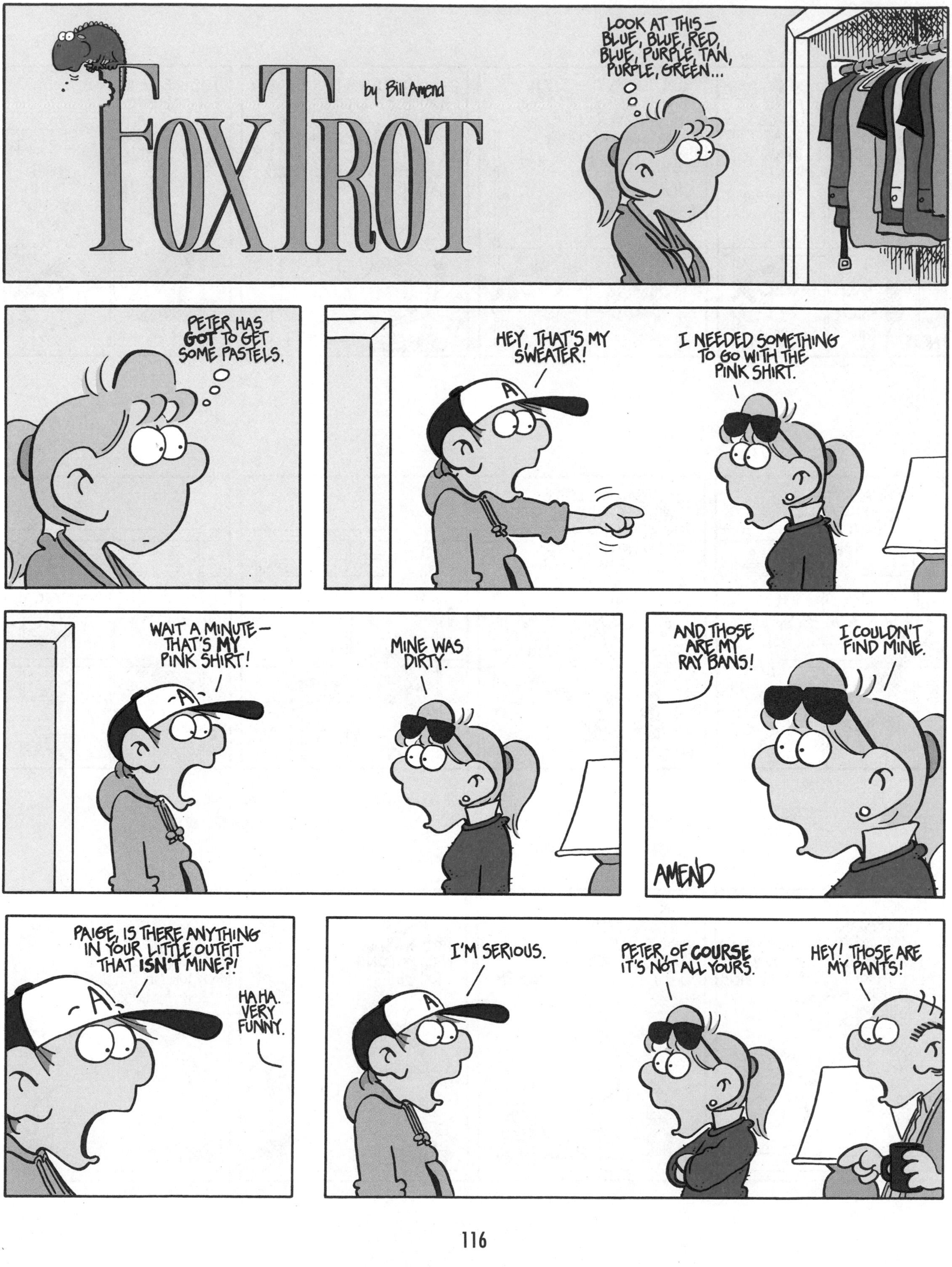
FoxTrot
by Bill Amend
LOOK AT THIS— BLUE, BLUE, RED, BLUE, PURPLE, TAN, PURPLE, GREEN...
PETER HAS GOT TO GET SOME PASTELS.
HEY, THAT'S MY SWEATER!
I NEEDED SOMETHING TO GO WITH THE PINK SHIRT.
WAIT A MINUTE— THAT'S MY PINK SHIRT!
MINE WAS DIRTY.
AND THOSE ARE MY RAY BANS!
I COULDN'T FIND MINE.
AMEND
PAIGE, IS THERE ANYTHING IN YOUR LITTLE OUTFIT THAT ISN'T MINE?!
HA HA. VERY FUNNY.
I'M SERIOUS.
PETER, OF COURSE IT'S NOT ALL YOURS.
HEY! THOSE ARE MY PANTS!

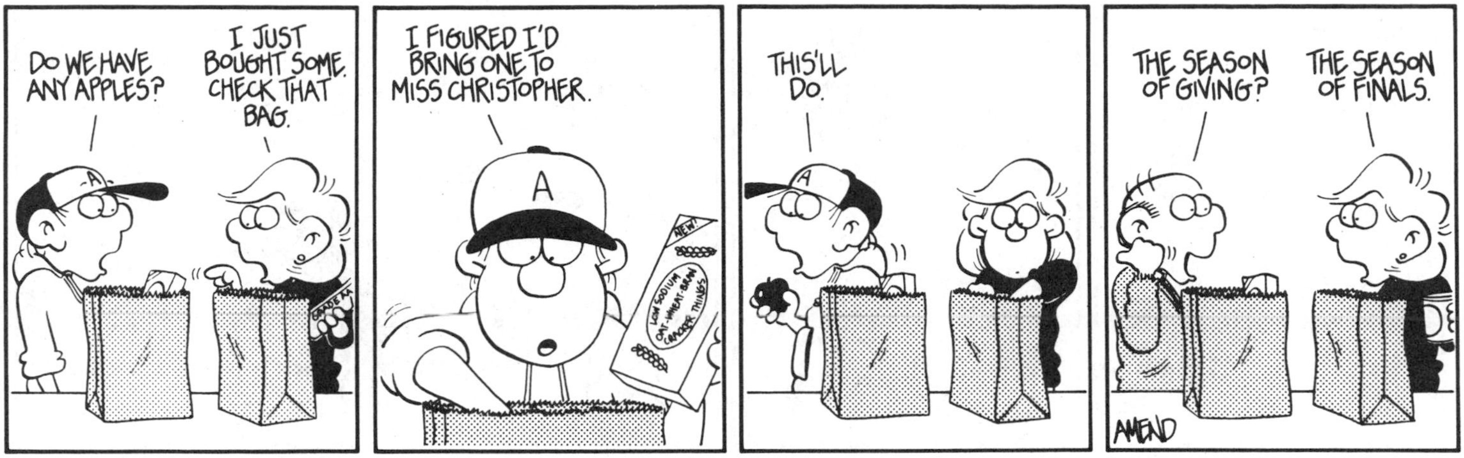
DO WE HAVE ANY APPLES?
I JUST BOUGHT SOME. CHECK THAT BAG.
I FIGURED I'D BRING ONE TO MISS CHRISTOPHER.
NEW!
LOW SODIUM OAT-WHEAT-BRAN CRACKER THINGS
THIS'LL DO.
THE SEASON OF GIVING?
THE SEASON OF FINALS.
AMEND

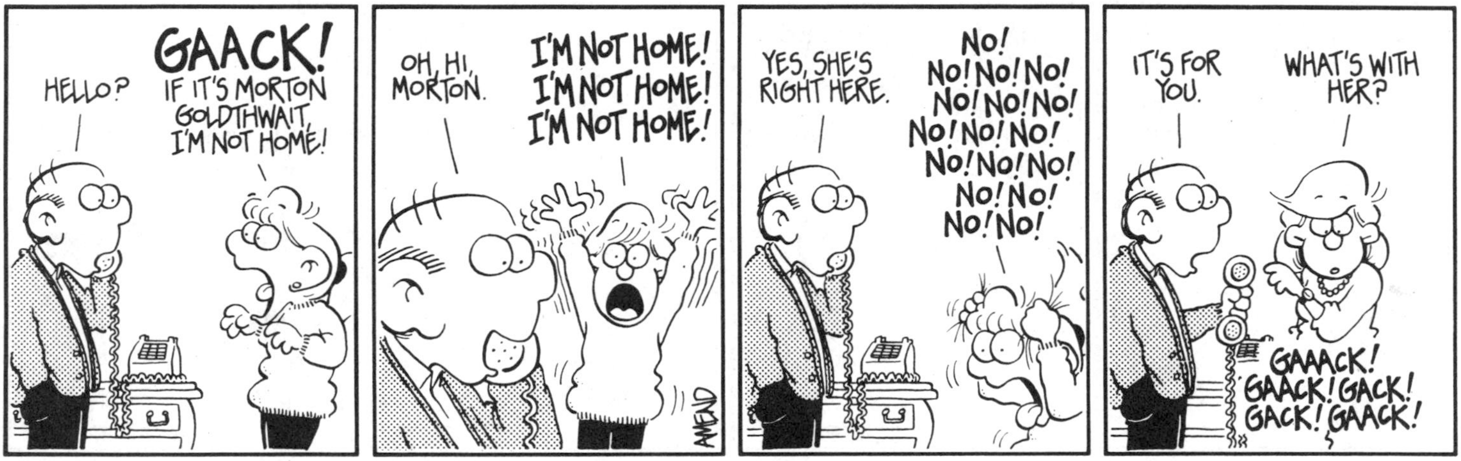
HELLO?
GAACK! IF IT'S MORTON GOLDTHWAIT, I'M NOT HOME!
OH, HI, MORTON.
I'M NOT HOME! I'M NOT HOME! I'M NOT HOME!
AMEND
YES, SHE'S RIGHT HERE.
NO! NO! NO! NO! NO! NO! NO! NO! NO! NO! NO! NO! NO! NO! NO! NO!
IT'S FOR YOU.
WHAT'S WITH HER?
GAAACK! GAACK! GACK! GACK! GAACK!

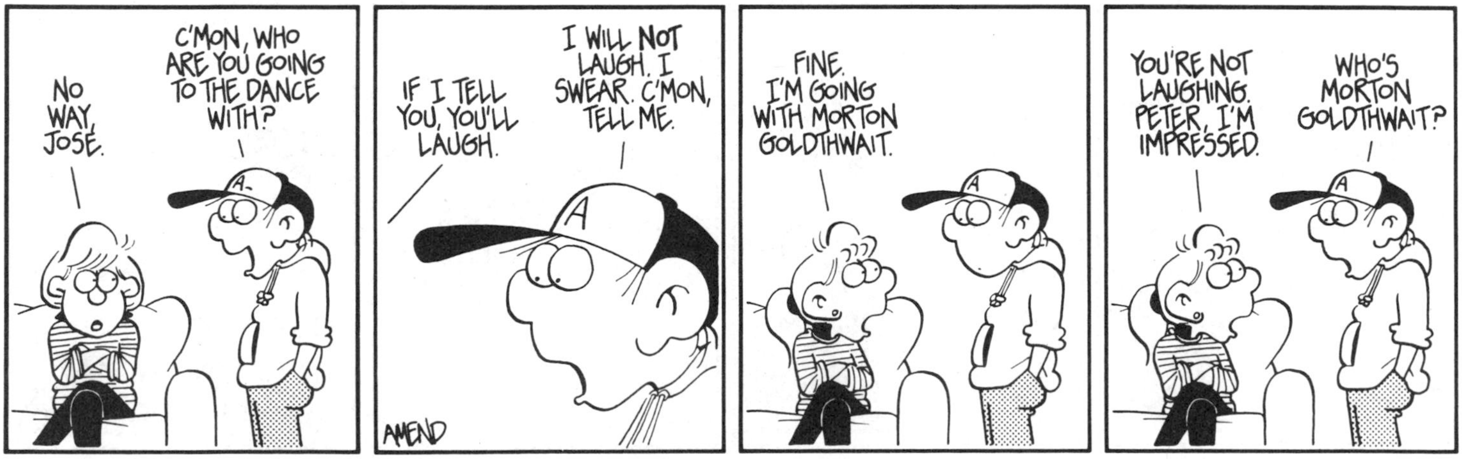
NO WAY, JOSÉ.
C'MON, WHO ARE YOU GOING TO THE DANCE WITH?
IF I TELL YOU, YOU'LL LAUGH.
I WILL NOT LAUGH. I SWEAR. C'MON, TELL ME.
AMEND
FINE. I'M GOING WITH MORTON GOLDTHWAIT.
YOU'RE NOT LAUGHING. PETER, I'M IMPRESSED.
WHO'S MORTON GOLDTHWAIT?

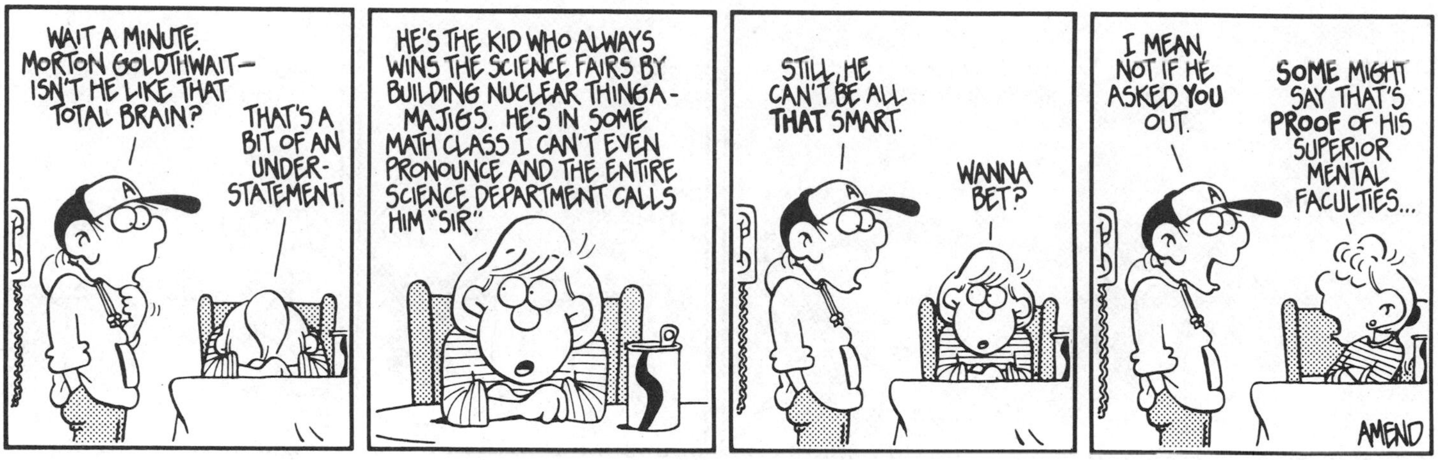

WAIT A MINUTE. MORTON GOLDTHWAIT— ISN'T HE LIKE THAT TOTAL BRAIN?
THAT'S A BIT OF AN UNDER-STATEMENT.
HE'S THE KID WHO ALWAYS WINS THE SCIENCE FAIRS BY BUILDING NUCLEAR THINGA-MAJIGS. HE'S IN SOME MATH CLASS I CAN'T EVEN PRONOUNCE AND THE ENTIRE SCIENCE DEPARTMENT CALLS HIM "SIR."
STILL, HE CAN'T BE ALL **THAT** SMART.
WANNA BET?
I MEAN, NOT IF HE ASKED **YOU** OUT.
SOME MIGHT SAY THAT'S **PROOF** OF HIS SUPERIOR MENTAL FACULTIES...
AMEND

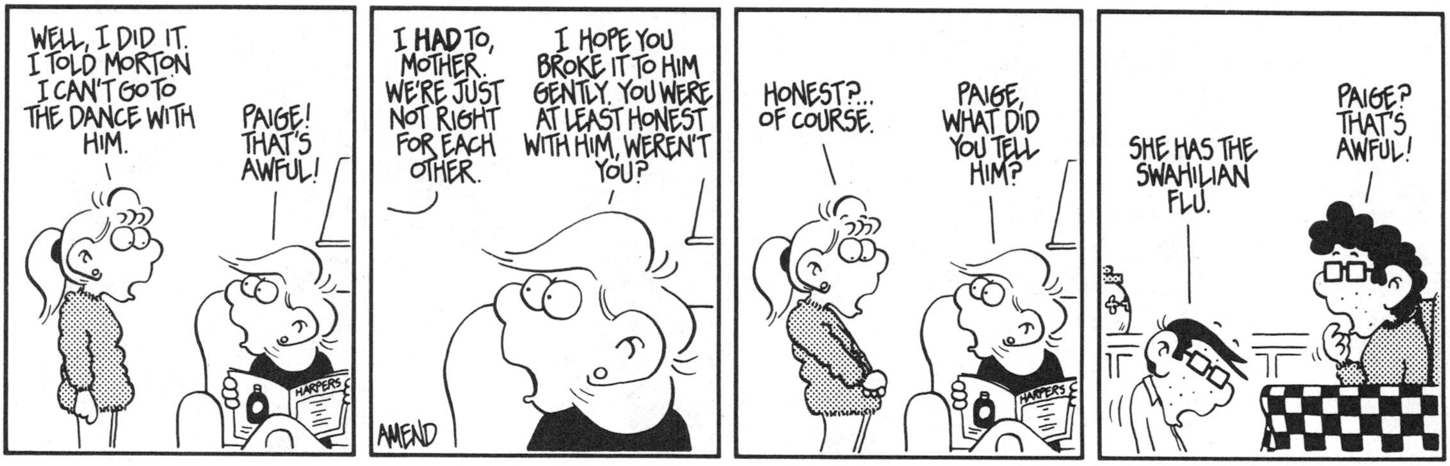

WELL, I DID IT. I TOLD MORTON I CAN'T GO TO THE DANCE WITH HIM.
PAIGE! THAT'S AWFUL!
I **HAD** TO, MOTHER. WE'RE JUST NOT RIGHT FOR EACH OTHER.
I HOPE YOU BROKE IT TO HIM GENTLY. YOU WERE AT LEAST HONEST WITH HIM, WEREN'T YOU?
AMEND
HONEST?... OF COURSE.
PAIGE, WHAT DID YOU TELL HIM?
SHE HAS THE SWAHILIAN FLU.
PAIGE? THAT'S AWFUL!

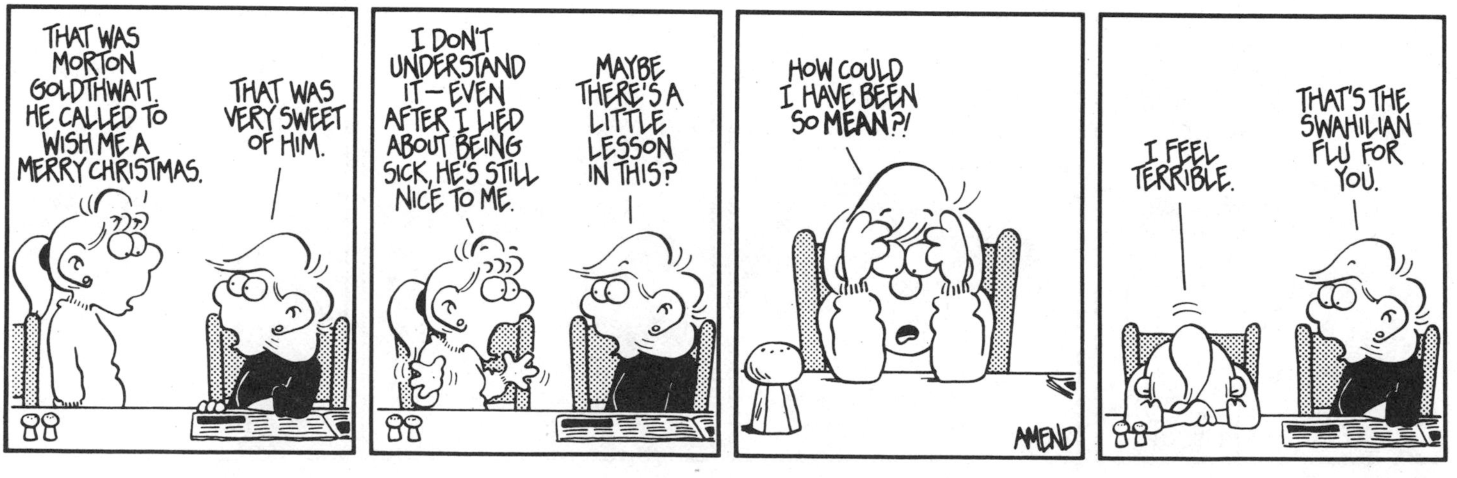

THAT WAS MORTON GOLDTHWAIT. HE CALLED TO WISH ME A MERRY CHRISTMAS.
THAT WAS VERY SWEET OF HIM.
I DON'T UNDERSTAND IT— EVEN AFTER I LIED ABOUT BEING SICK, HE'S STILL NICE TO ME.
MAYBE THERE'S A LITTLE LESSON IN THIS?
HOW COULD I HAVE BEEN SO **MEAN**?!
AMEND
I FEEL TERRIBLE.
THAT'S THE SWAHILIAN FLU FOR YOU.

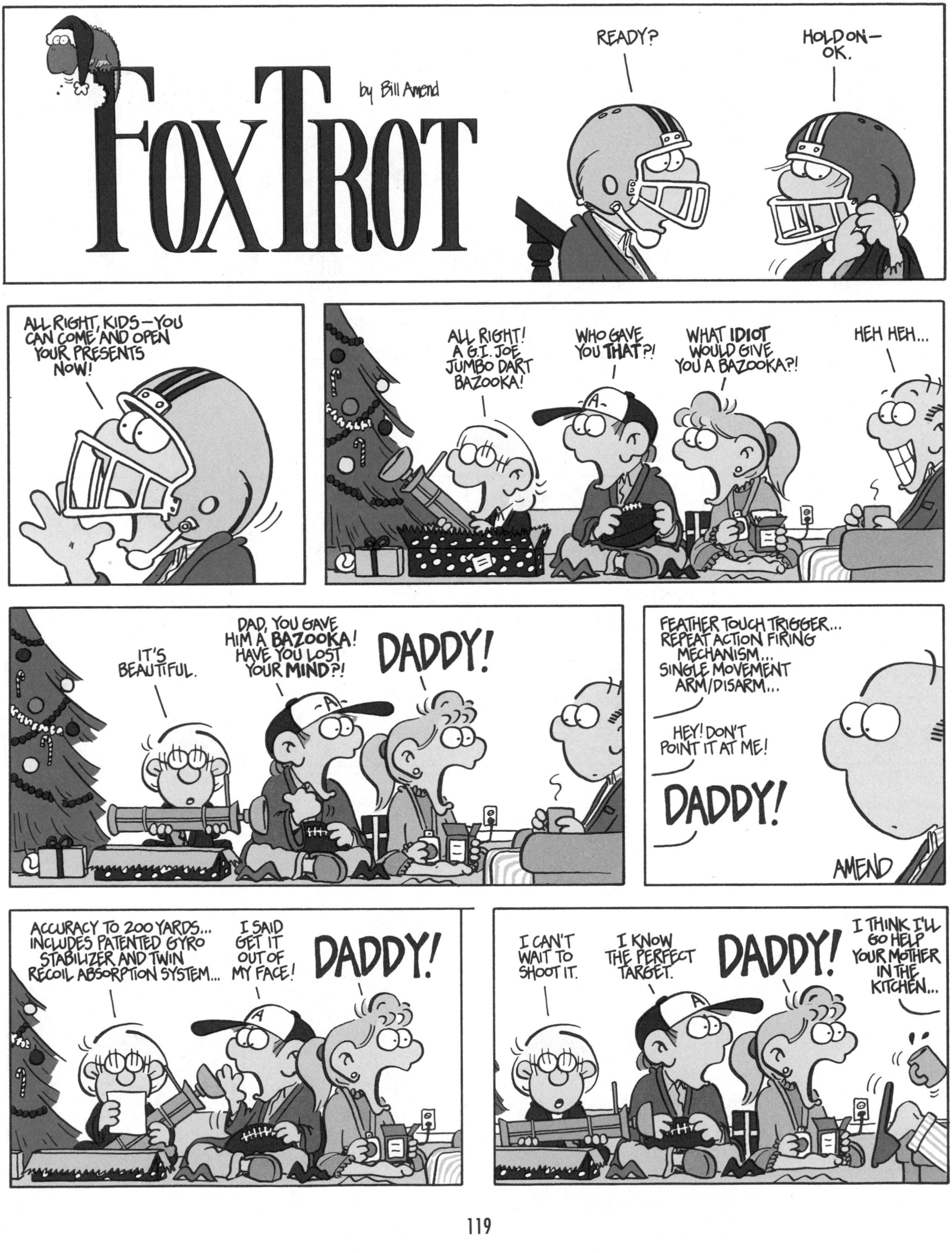

FoxTrot
by Bill Amend
READY?
HOLD ON— OK.
ALL RIGHT, KIDS—YOU CAN COME AND OPEN YOUR PRESENTS NOW!
ALL RIGHT! A G.I. JOE JUMBO DART BAZOOKA!
WHO GAVE YOU THAT?!
WHAT IDIOT WOULD GIVE YOU A BAZOOKA?!
HEH HEH...
IT'S BEAUTIFUL.
DAD, YOU GAVE HIM A BAZOOKA! HAVE YOU LOST YOUR MIND?!
DADDY!
FEATHER TOUCH TRIGGER... REPEAT ACTION FIRING MECHANISM... SINGLE MOVEMENT ARM/DISARM...
HEY! DON'T POINT IT AT ME!
DADDY!
AMEND
ACCURACY TO 200 YARDS... INCLUDES PATENTED GYRO STABILIZER AND TWIN RECOIL ABSORPTION SYSTEM...
I SAID GET IT OUT OF MY FACE!
DADDY!
I CAN'T WAIT TO SHOOT IT.
I KNOW THE PERFECT TARGET.
DADDY!
I THINK I'LL GO HELP YOUR MOTHER IN THE KITCHEN...

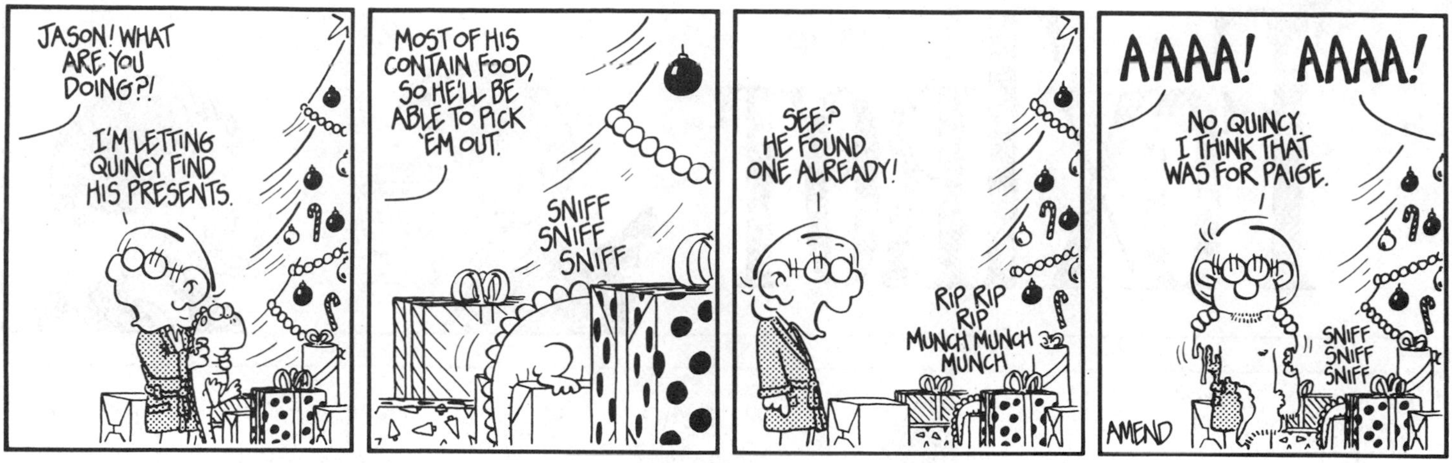
JASON! WHAT ARE YOU DOING?!
I'M LETTING QUINCY FIND HIS PRESENTS.
MOST OF HIS CONTAIN FOOD, SO HE'LL BE ABLE TO PICK 'EM OUT.
SNIFF SNIFF SNIFF
SEE? HE FOUND ONE ALREADY!
RIP RIP RIP MUNCH MUNCH MUNCH
AAAA! AAAA!
NO, QUINCY. I THINK THAT WAS FOR PAIGE.
SNIFF SNIFF SNIFF
AMEND

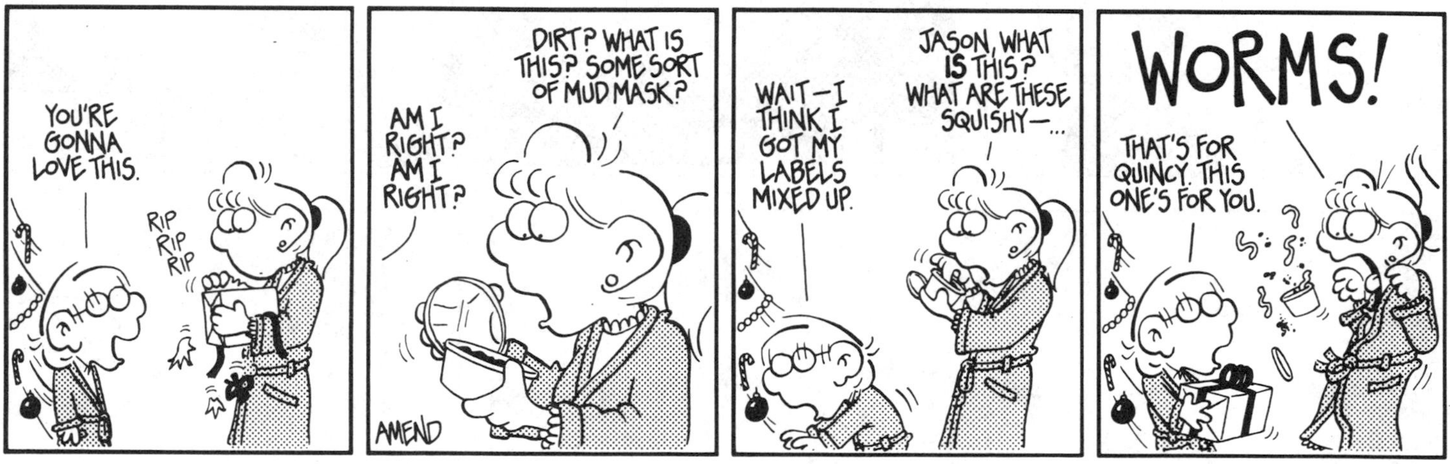
YOU'RE GONNA LOVE THIS.
RIP RIP RIP
AM I RIGHT? AM I RIGHT?
DIRT? WHAT IS THIS? SOME SORT OF MUD MASK?
AMEND
WAIT—I THINK I GOT MY LABELS MIXED UP.
JASON, WHAT IS THIS? WHAT ARE THESE SQUISHY—...
WORMS!
THAT'S FOR QUINCY. THIS ONE'S FOR YOU.

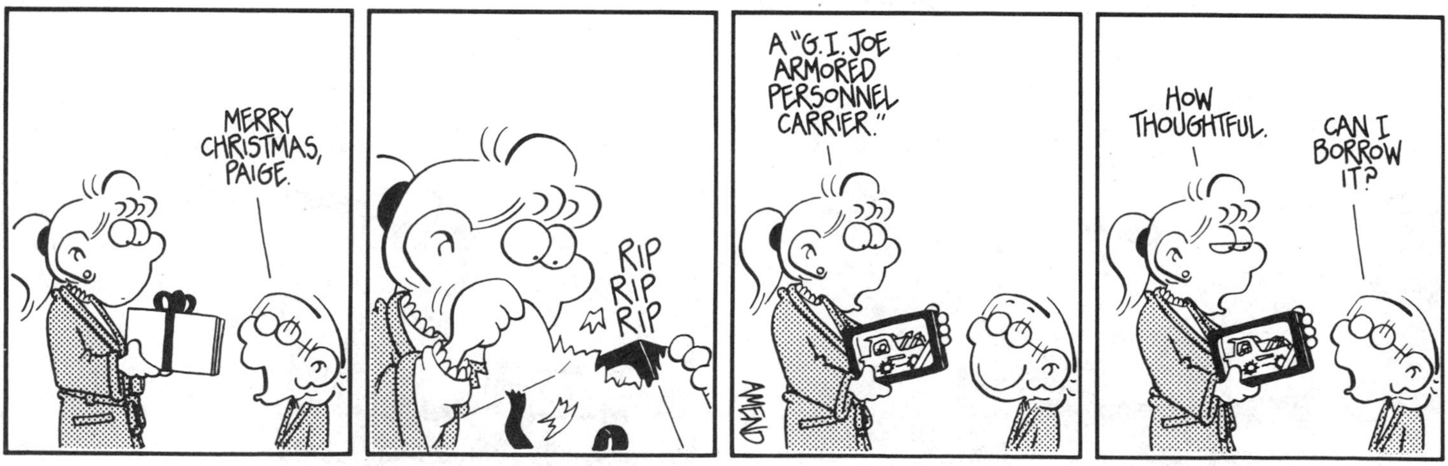
MERRY CHRISTMAS, PAIGE.
RIP RIP RIP
A "G.I. JOE ARMORED PERSONNEL CARRIER."
AMEND
HOW THOUGHTFUL.
CAN I BORROW IT?

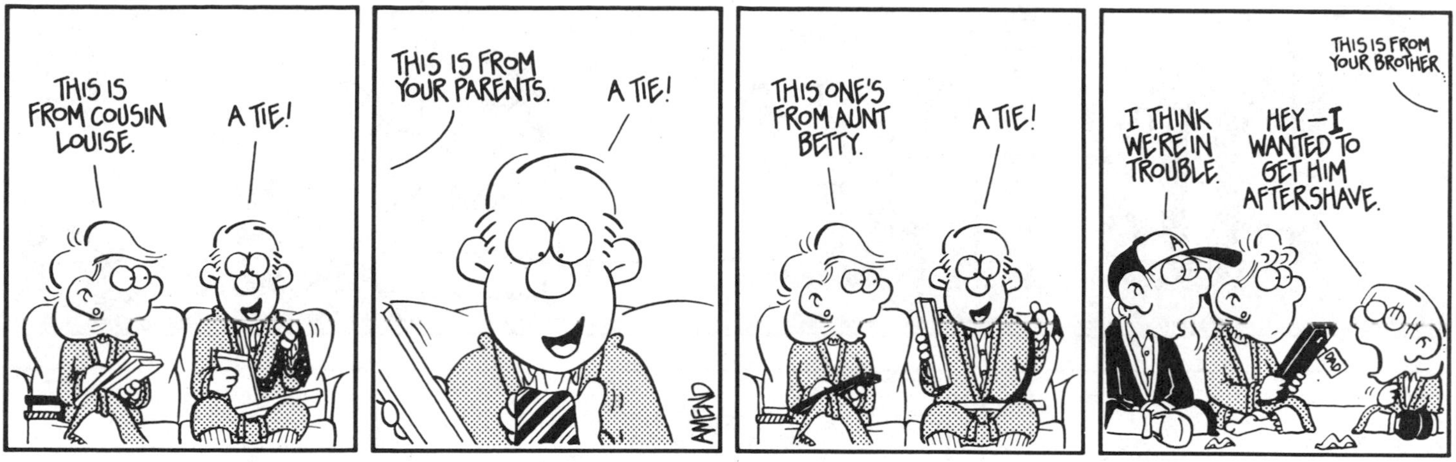

THIS IS FROM COUSIN LOUISE.
A TIE!
THIS IS FROM YOUR PARENTS.
A TIE!
AMEND
THIS ONE'S FROM AUNT BETTY.
A TIE!
THIS IS FROM YOUR BROTHER.
I THINK WE'RE IN TROUBLE.
HEY—I WANTED TO GET HIM AFTERSHAVE.

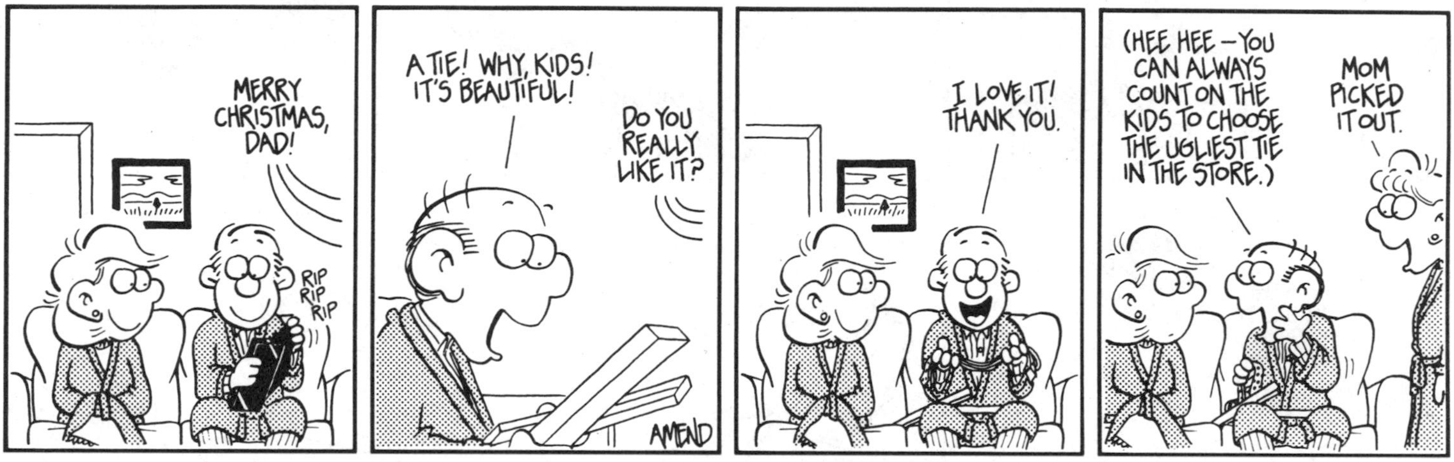

MERRY CHRISTMAS, DAD!
RIP RIP RIP
A TIE! WHY, KIDS! IT'S BEAUTIFUL!
DO YOU REALLY LIKE IT?
AMEND
I LOVE IT! THANK YOU.
(HEE HEE—YOU CAN ALWAYS COUNT ON THE KIDS TO CHOOSE THE UGLIEST TIE IN THE STORE.)
MOM PICKED IT OUT.

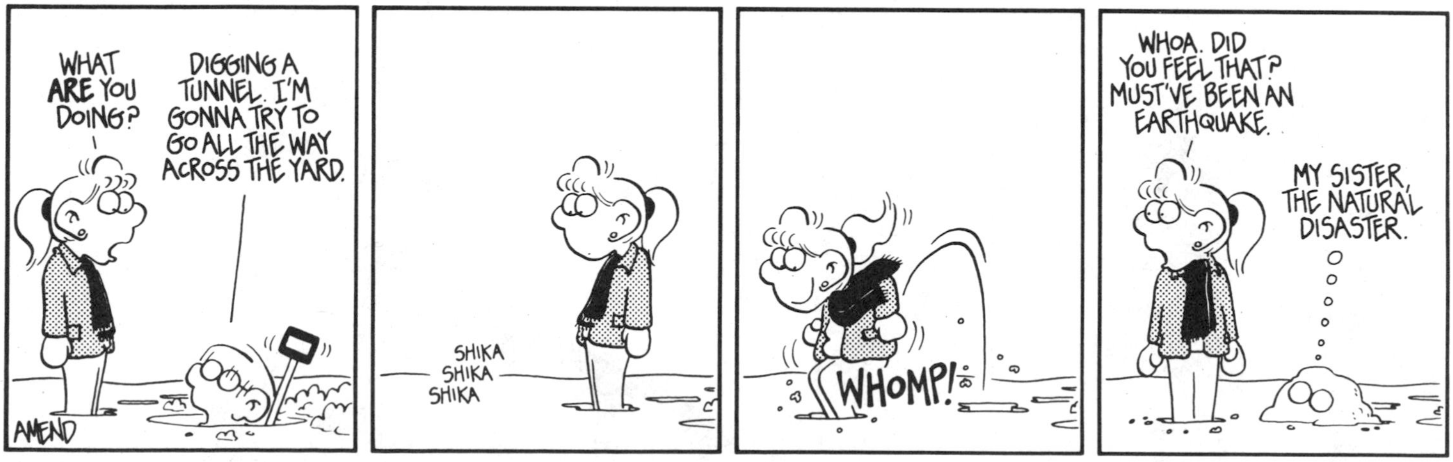

WHAT ARE YOU DOING?
DIGGING A TUNNEL. I'M GONNA TRY TO GO ALL THE WAY ACROSS THE YARD.
AMEND
SHIKA SHIKA SHIKA
WHOMP!
WHOA. DID YOU FEEL THAT? MUST'VE BEEN AN EARTHQUAKE.
MY SISTER, THE NATURAL DISASTER.

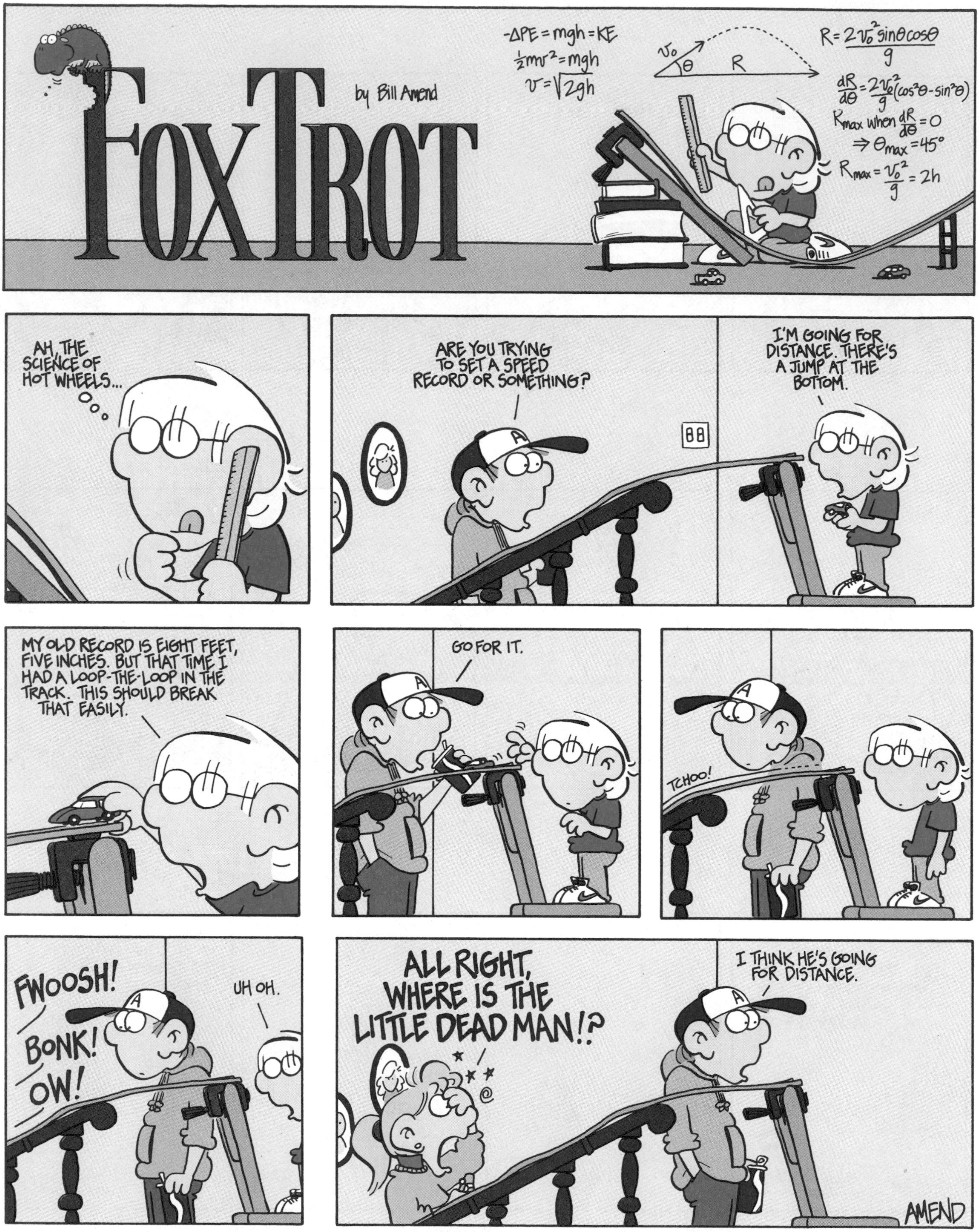
FoxTrot
by Bill Amend
$-\Delta PE = mgh = KE$
$\frac{1}{2}mv^2 = mgh$
$v = \sqrt{2gh}$
v_0 θ R
$R = \frac{2v_0^2 \sin\theta\cos\theta}{g}$
$\frac{dR}{d\theta} = \frac{2v_0^2}{g}(\cos^2\theta - \sin^2\theta)$
R_{max} when $\frac{dR}{d\theta} = 0$
$\Rightarrow \theta_{max} = 45°$
$R_{max} = \frac{v_0^2}{g} = 2h$
AH, THE SCIENCE OF HOT WHEELS...
ARE YOU TRYING TO SET A SPEED RECORD OR SOMETHING?
I'M GOING FOR DISTANCE. THERE'S A JUMP AT THE BOTTOM.
MY OLD RECORD IS EIGHT FEET, FIVE INCHES. BUT THAT TIME I HAD A LOOP-THE-LOOP IN THE TRACK. THIS SHOULD BREAK THAT EASILY.
GO FOR IT.
TCHOO!
FWOOSH!
BONK!
OW!
UH OH.
ALL RIGHT, WHERE IS THE LITTLE DEAD MAN!?
I THINK HE'S GOING FOR DISTANCE.
AMEND

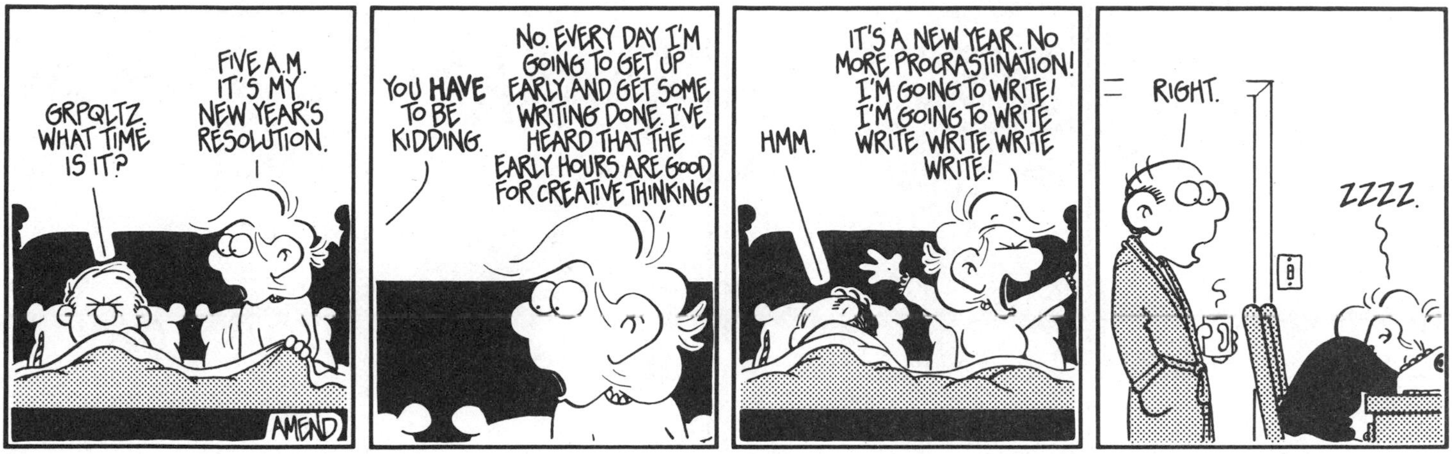
GRPQLTZ. WHAT TIME IS IT?
FIVE A.M. IT'S MY NEW YEAR'S RESOLUTION.
YOU **HAVE** TO BE KIDDING.
NO. EVERY DAY I'M GOING TO GET UP EARLY AND GET SOME WRITING DONE. I'VE HEARD THAT THE EARLY HOURS ARE GOOD FOR CREATIVE THINKING.
HMM.
IT'S A NEW YEAR. NO MORE PROCRASTINATION! I'M GOING TO WRITE! I'M GOING TO WRITE WRITE WRITE WRITE WRITE!
RIGHT.
ZZZZ.
AMEND

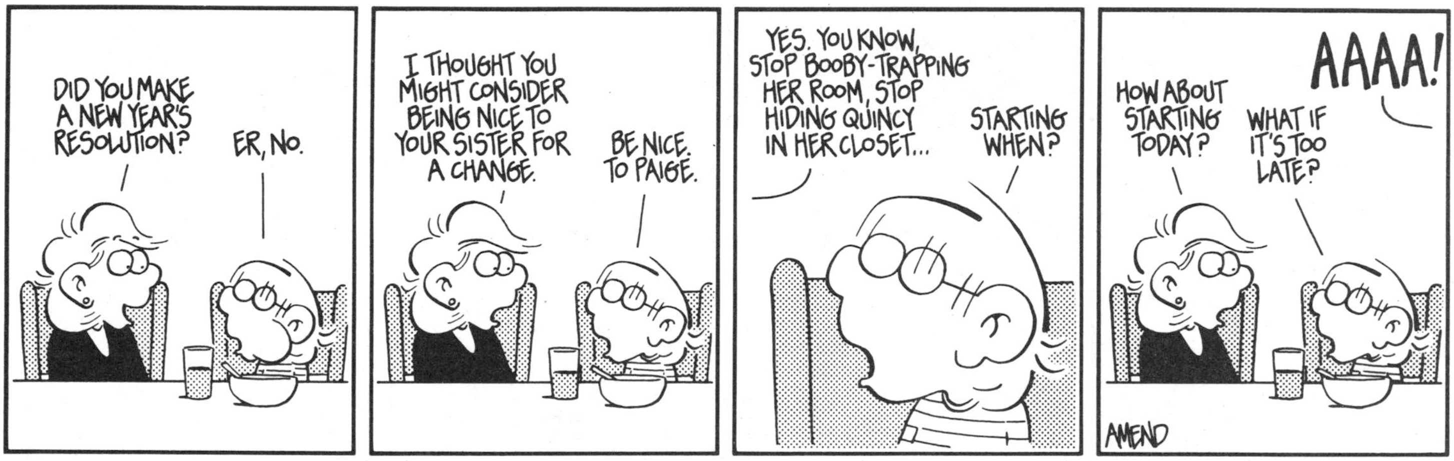
DID YOU MAKE A NEW YEAR'S RESOLUTION?
ER, NO.
I THOUGHT YOU MIGHT CONSIDER BEING NICE TO YOUR SISTER FOR A CHANGE.
BE NICE. TO PAIGE.
YES. YOU KNOW, STOP BOOBY-TRAPPING HER ROOM, STOP HIDING QUINCY IN HER CLOSET...
STARTING WHEN?
HOW ABOUT STARTING TODAY?
WHAT IF IT'S TOO LATE?
AAAA!
AMEND

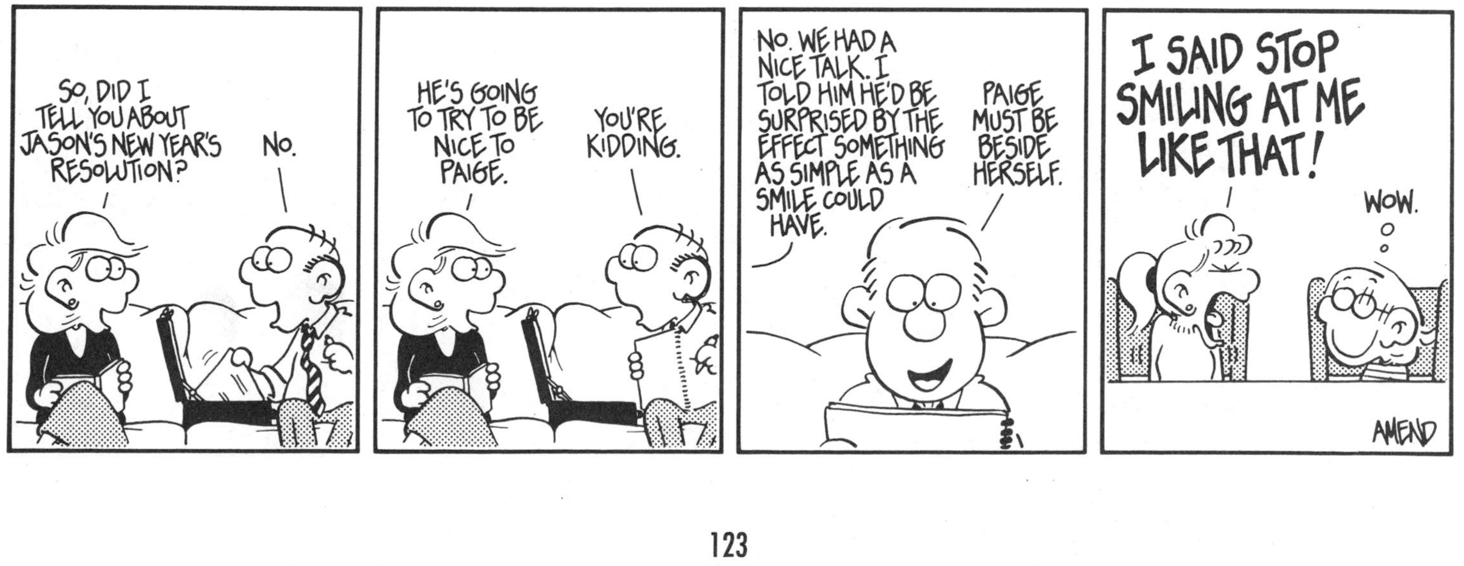
SO, DID I TELL YOU ABOUT JASON'S NEW YEAR'S RESOLUTION?
NO.
HE'S GOING TO TRY TO BE NICE TO PAIGE.
YOU'RE KIDDING.
NO. WE HAD A NICE TALK. I TOLD HIM HE'D BE SURPRISED BY THE EFFECT SOMETHING AS SIMPLE AS A SMILE COULD HAVE.
PAIGE MUST BE BESIDE HERSELF.
I SAID STOP SMILING AT ME LIKE THAT!
WOW.
AMEND

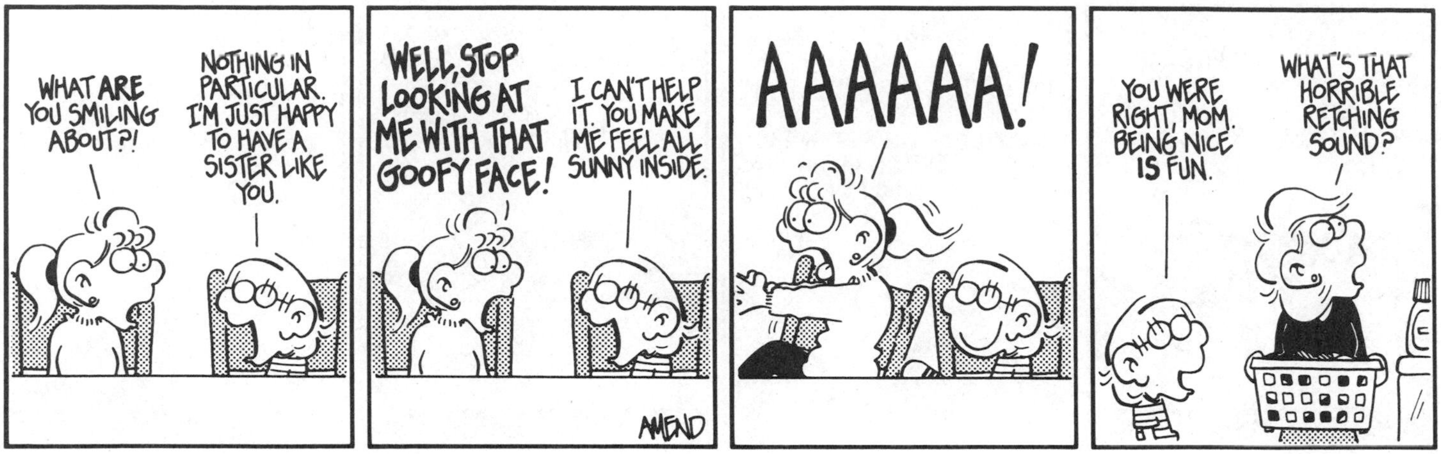
WHAT ARE YOU SMILING ABOUT?!
NOTHING IN PARTICULAR. I'M JUST HAPPY TO HAVE A SISTER LIKE YOU.
WELL, STOP LOOKING AT ME WITH THAT GOOFY FACE!
I CAN'T HELP IT. YOU MAKE ME FEEL ALL SUNNY INSIDE.
AMEND
AAAAAA!
YOU WERE RIGHT, MOM. BEING NICE IS FUN.
WHAT'S THAT HORRIBLE RETCHING SOUND?

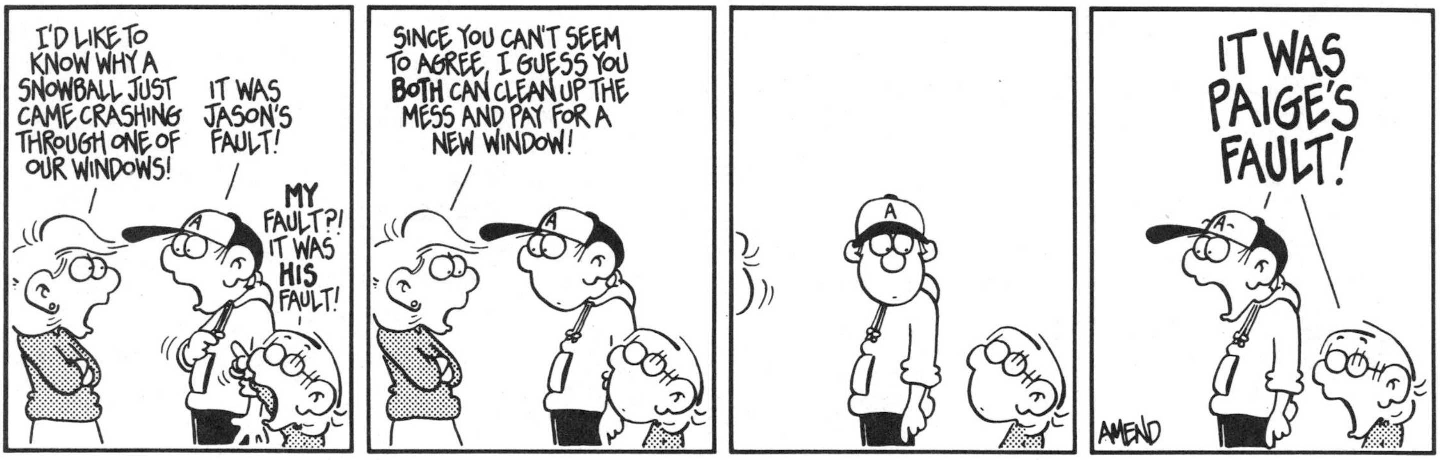
I'D LIKE TO KNOW WHY A SNOWBALL JUST CAME CRASHING THROUGH ONE OF OUR WINDOWS!
IT WAS JASON'S FAULT!
MY FAULT?! IT WAS HIS FAULT!
SINCE YOU CAN'T SEEM TO AGREE, I GUESS YOU BOTH CAN CLEAN UP THE MESS AND PAY FOR A NEW WINDOW!
IT WAS PAIGE'S FAULT!
AMEND

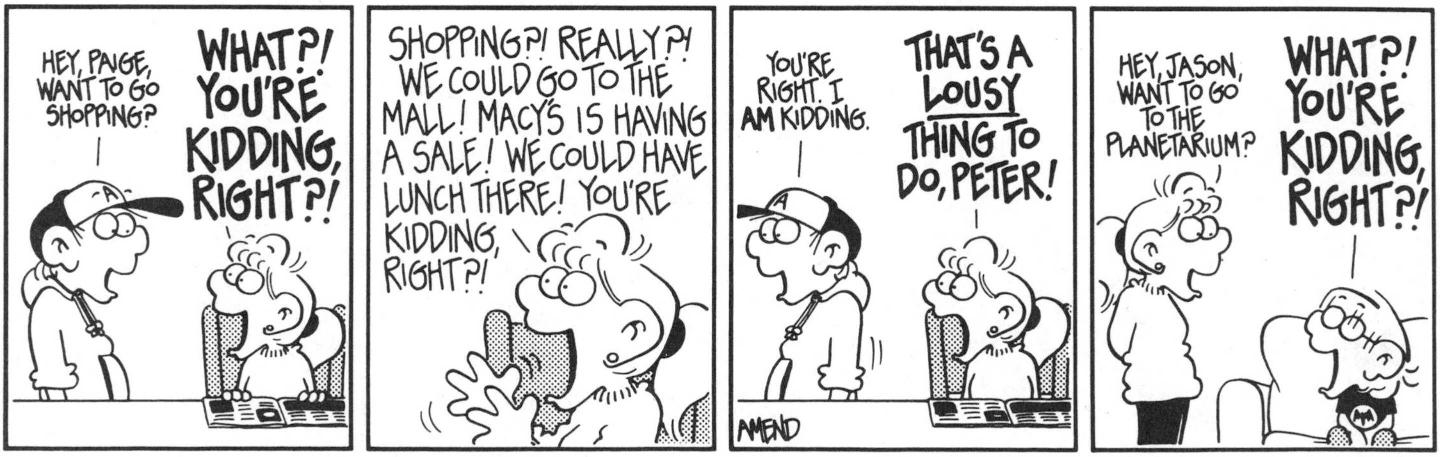
HEY, PAIGE, WANT TO GO SHOPPING?
WHAT?! YOU'RE KIDDING, RIGHT?!
SHOPPING?! REALLY?! WE COULD GO TO THE MALL! MACY'S IS HAVING A SALE! WE COULD HAVE LUNCH THERE! YOU'RE KIDDING, RIGHT?!
YOU'RE RIGHT. I AM KIDDING.
THAT'S A LOUSY THING TO DO, PETER!
AMEND
HEY, JASON, WANT TO GO TO THE PLANETARIUM?
WHAT?! YOU'RE KIDDING, RIGHT?!

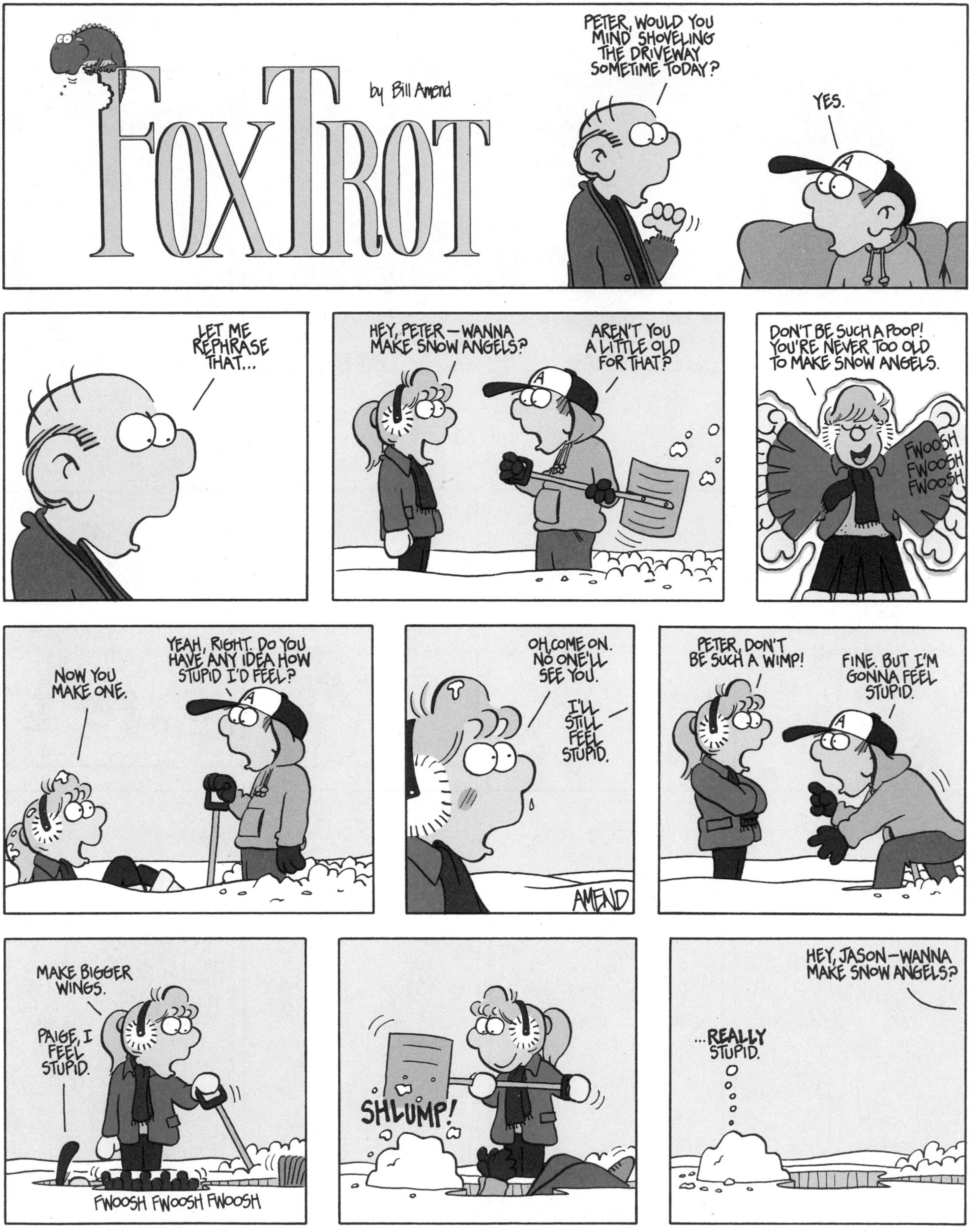
FoxTrot
by Bill Amend
PETER, WOULD YOU MIND SHOVELING THE DRIVEWAY SOMETIME TODAY?
YES.
LET ME REPHRASE THAT...
HEY, PETER—WANNA MAKE SNOW ANGELS?
AREN'T YOU A LITTLE OLD FOR THAT?
DON'T BE SUCH A POOP! YOU'RE NEVER TOO OLD TO MAKE SNOW ANGELS.
FWOOSH FWOOSH FWOOSH
NOW YOU MAKE ONE.
YEAH, RIGHT. DO YOU HAVE ANY IDEA HOW STUPID I'D FEEL?
OH, COME ON. NO ONE'LL SEE YOU.
I'LL STILL FEEL STUPID.
AMEND
PETER, DON'T BE SUCH A WIMP!
FINE. BUT I'M GONNA FEEL STUPID.
MAKE BIGGER WINGS.
PAIGE, I FEEL STUPID.
FWOOSH FWOOSH FWOOSH
SHLUMP!
HEY, JASON—WANNA MAKE SNOW ANGELS?
...REALLY STUPID.

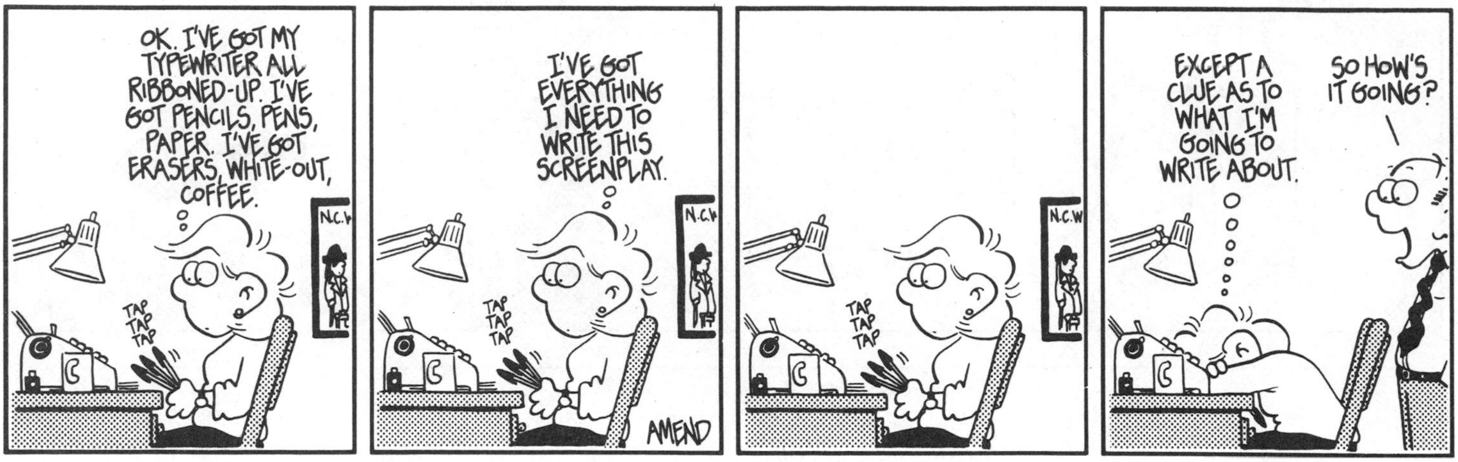
OK. I'VE GOT MY TYPEWRITER ALL RIBBONED-UP. I'VE GOT PENCILS, PENS, PAPER. I'VE GOT ERASERS, WHITE-OUT, COFFEE.
TAP TAP TAP
N.C.W
I'VE GOT EVERYTHING I NEED TO WRITE THIS SCREENPLAY.
TAP TAP TAP
AMEND
TAP TAP TAP
EXCEPT A CLUE AS TO WHAT I'M GOING TO WRITE ABOUT.
SO HOW'S IT GOING?

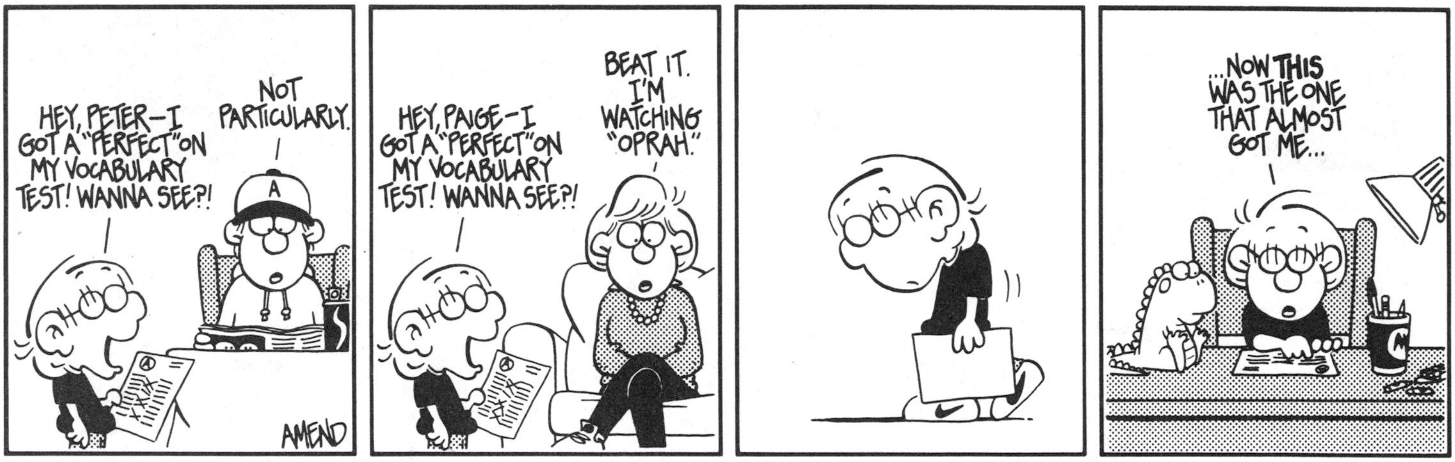
HEY, PETER—I GOT A "PERFECT" ON MY VOCABULARY TEST! WANNA SEE?!
NOT PARTICULARLY.
AMEND
HEY, PAIGE—I GOT A "PERFECT" ON MY VOCABULARY TEST! WANNA SEE?!
BEAT IT. I'M WATCHING "OPRAH."
...NOW THIS WAS THE ONE THAT ALMOST GOT ME...

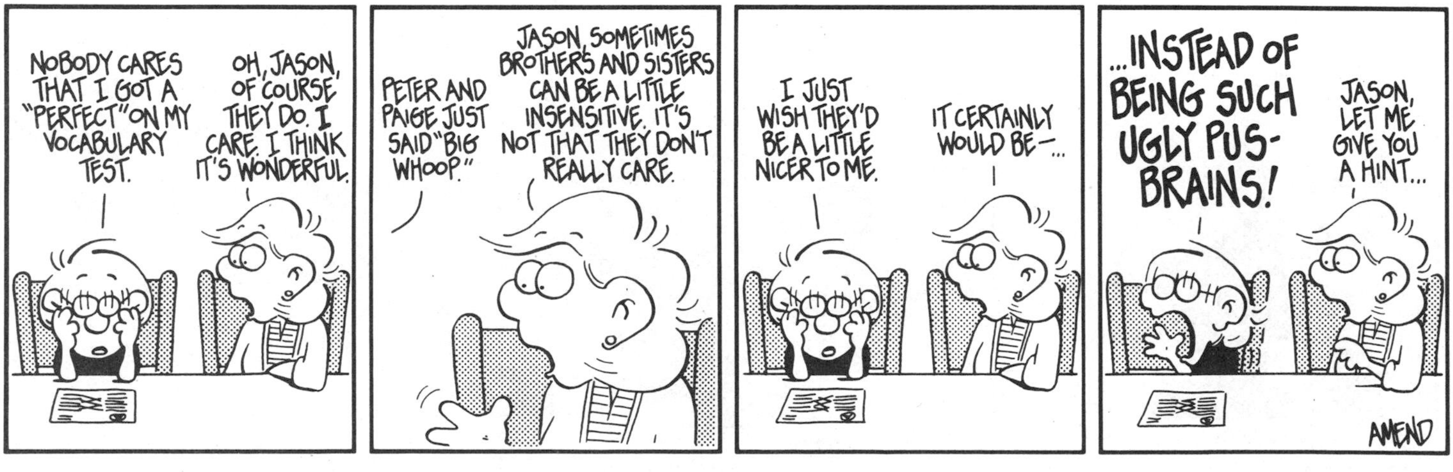
NOBODY CARES THAT I GOT A "PERFECT" ON MY VOCABULARY TEST.
OH, JASON, OF COURSE THEY DO. I CARE. I THINK IT'S WONDERFUL.
PETER AND PAIGE JUST SAID "BIG WHOOP."
JASON, SOMETIMES BROTHERS AND SISTERS CAN BE A LITTLE INSENSITIVE. IT'S NOT THAT THEY DON'T REALLY CARE.
I JUST WISH THEY'D BE A LITTLE NICER TO ME.
IT CERTAINLY WOULD BE—...
...INSTEAD OF BEING SUCH UGLY PUS-BRAINS!
JASON, LET ME GIVE YOU A HINT...
AMEND

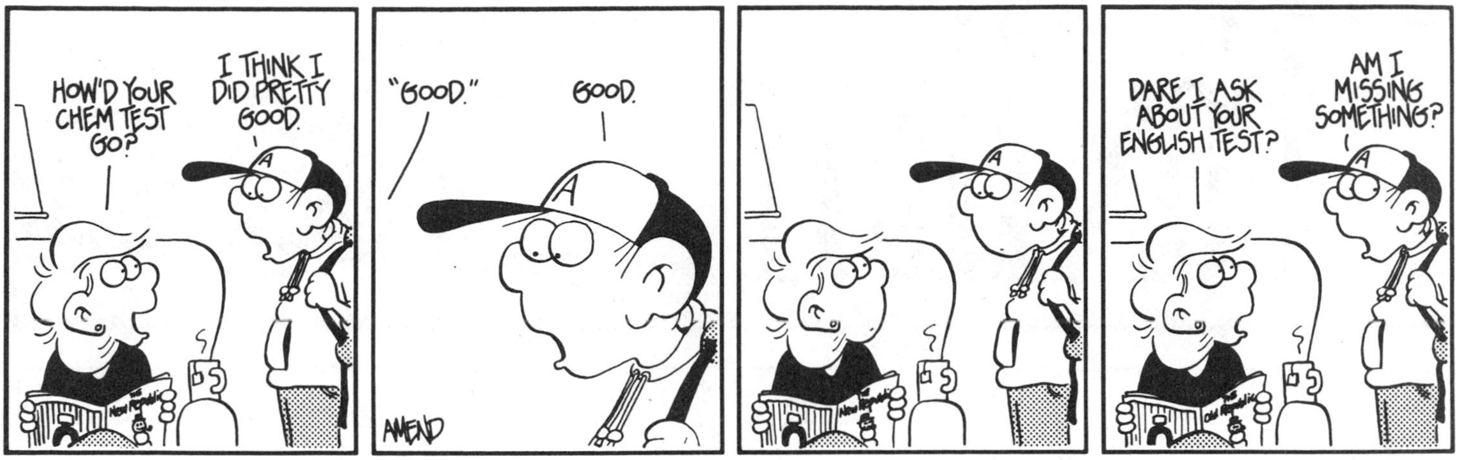
HOW'D YOUR CHEM TEST GO?
I THINK I DID PRETTY GOOD.
"GOOD."
GOOD.
AMEND
DARE I ASK ABOUT YOUR ENGLISH TEST?
AM I MISSING SOMETHING?

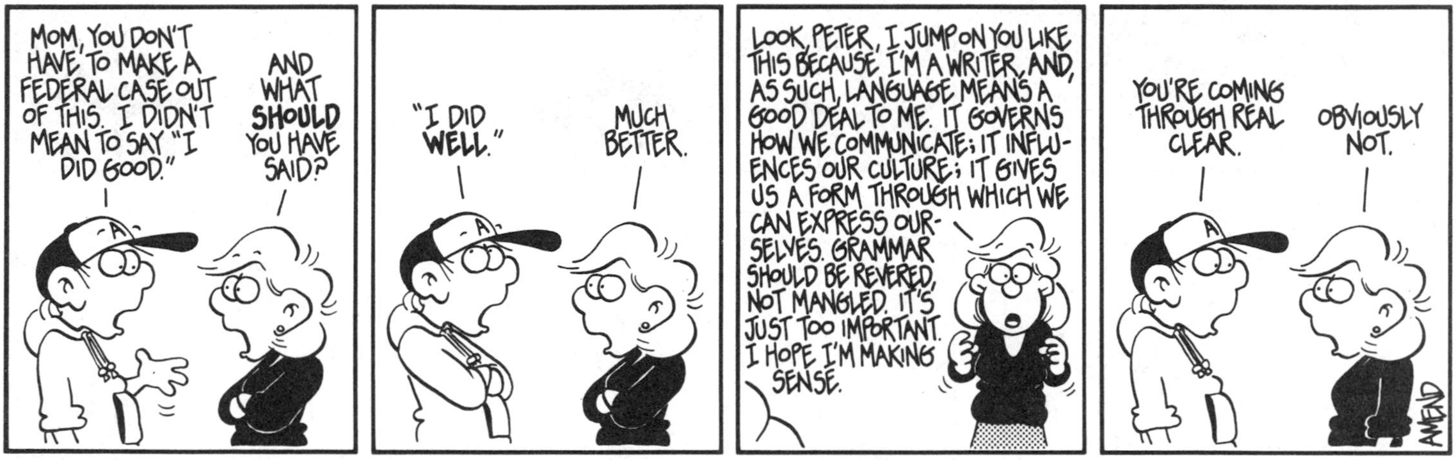
MOM, YOU DON'T HAVE TO MAKE A FEDERAL CASE OUT OF THIS. I DIDN'T MEAN TO SAY "I DID GOOD."
AND WHAT **SHOULD** YOU HAVE SAID?
"I DID **WELL**."
MUCH BETTER.
LOOK, PETER, I JUMP ON YOU LIKE THIS BECAUSE I'M A WRITER, AND, AS SUCH, LANGUAGE MEANS A GOOD DEAL TO ME. IT GOVERNS HOW WE COMMUNICATE; IT INFLUENCES OUR CULTURE; IT GIVES US A FORM THROUGH WHICH WE CAN EXPRESS OURSELVES. GRAMMAR SHOULD BE REVERED, NOT MANGLED. IT'S JUST TOO IMPORTANT. I HOPE I'M MAKING SENSE.
YOU'RE COMING THROUGH REAL CLEAR.
OBVIOUSLY NOT.
AMEND

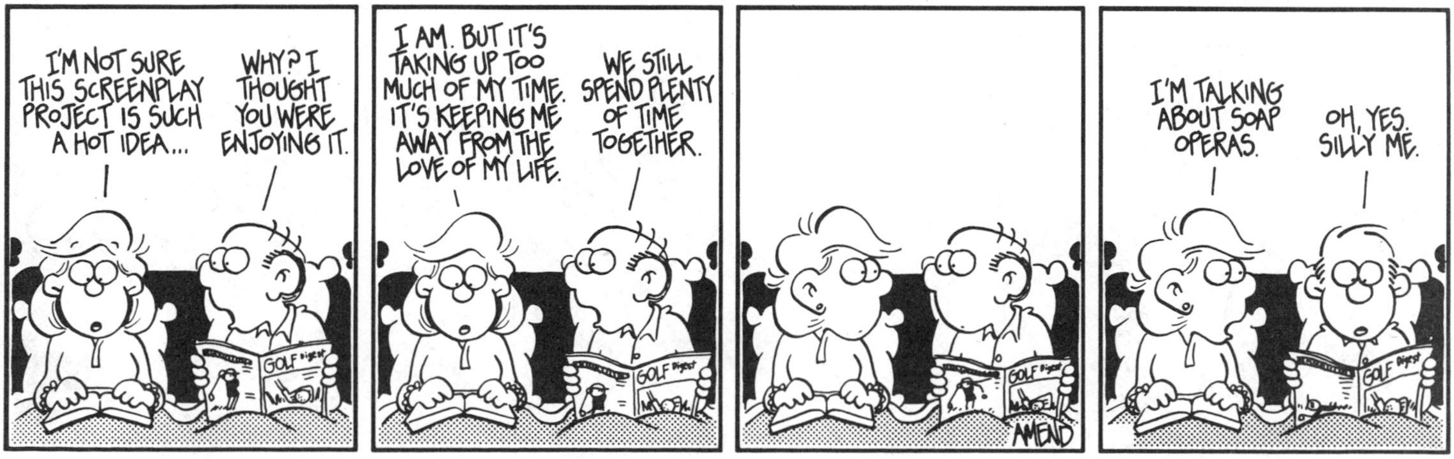
I'M NOT SURE THIS SCREENPLAY PROJECT IS SUCH A HOT IDEA...
WHY? I THOUGHT YOU WERE ENJOYING IT.
I AM. BUT IT'S TAKING UP TOO MUCH OF MY TIME. IT'S KEEPING ME AWAY FROM THE LOVE OF MY LIFE.
WE STILL SPEND PLENTY OF TIME TOGETHER.
AMEND
I'M TALKING ABOUT SOAP OPERAS.
OH, YES. SILLY ME.

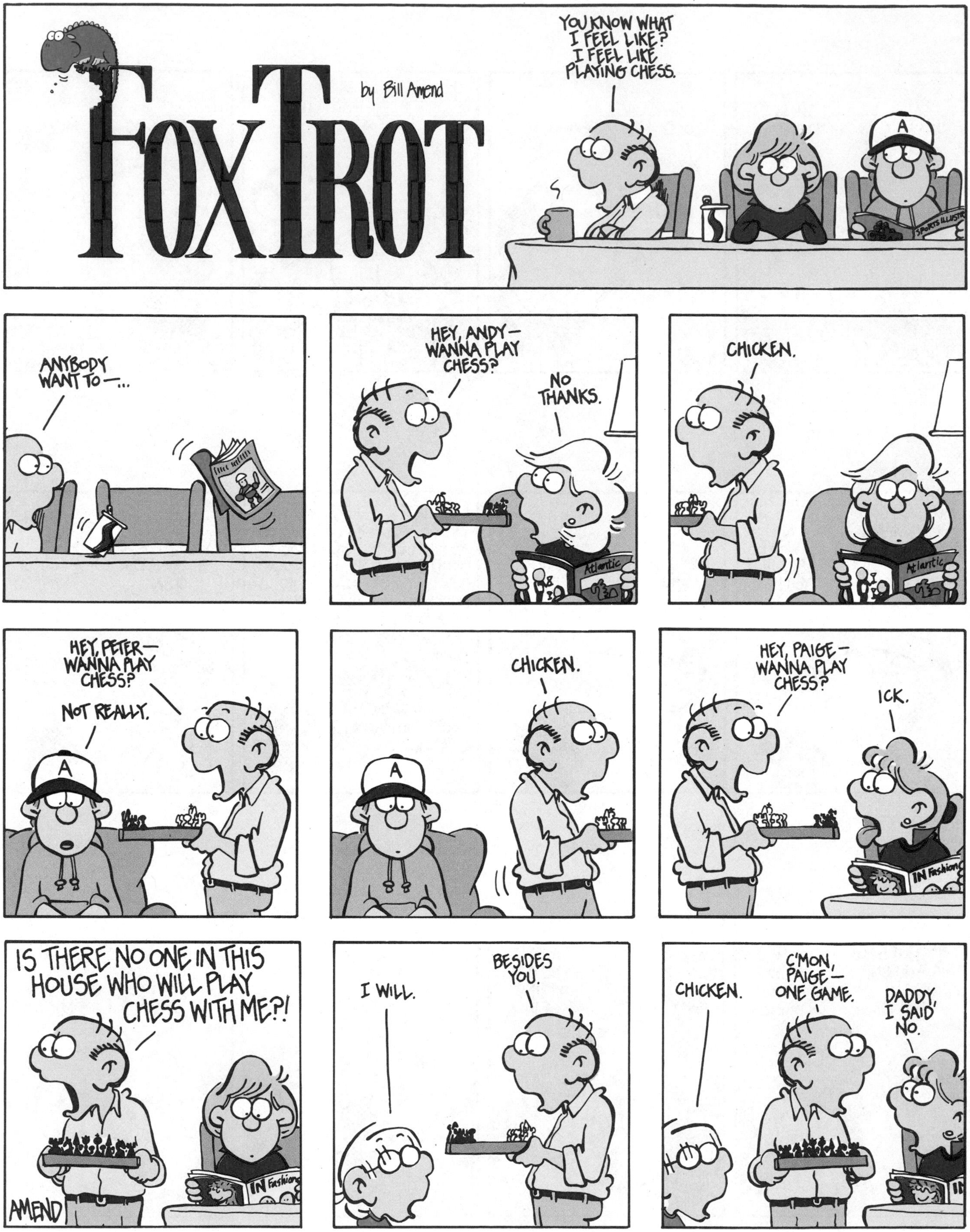
FoxTrot
by Bill Amend
YOU KNOW WHAT I FEEL LIKE? I FEEL LIKE PLAYING CHESS.
SPORTS ILLUSTR
ANYBODY WANT TO—...
HEY, ANDY— WANNA PLAY CHESS?
NO THANKS.
Atlantic
CHICKEN.
Atlantic
HEY, PETER— WANNA PLAY CHESS?
NOT REALLY.
A
CHICKEN.
A
HEY, PAIGE— WANNA PLAY CHESS?
ICK.
IN Fashion
IS THERE NO ONE IN THIS HOUSE WHO WILL PLAY CHESS WITH ME?!
IN Fashion
AMEND
I WILL.
BESIDES YOU.
CHICKEN.
C'MON, PAIGE— ONE GAME.
DADDY, I SAID NO.
IN

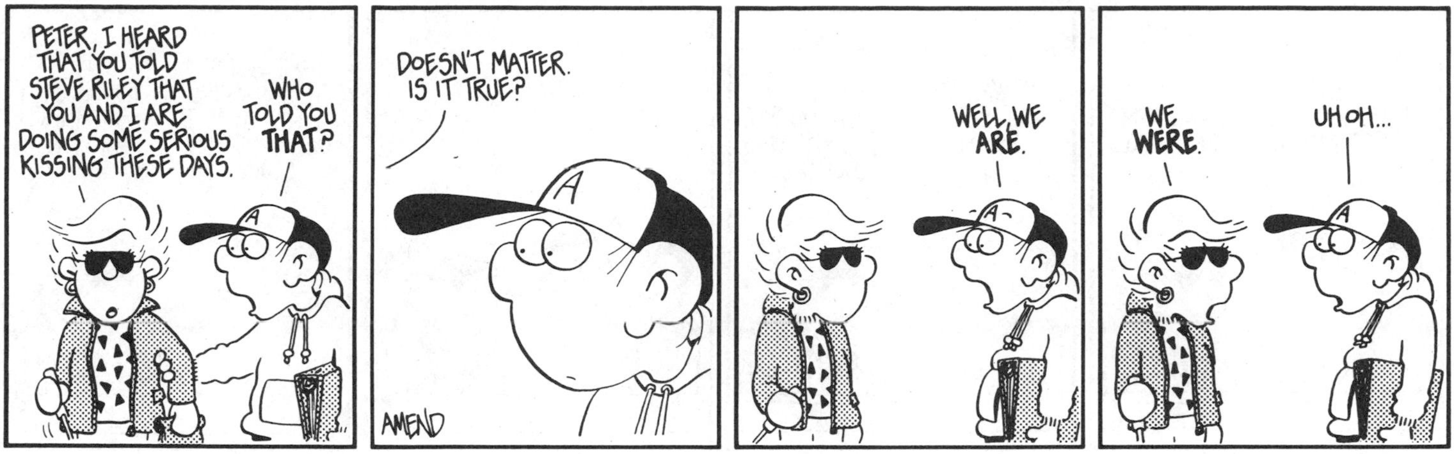
PETER, I HEARD THAT YOU TOLD STEVE RILEY THAT YOU AND I ARE DOING SOME SERIOUS KISSING THESE DAYS.
WHO TOLD YOU **THAT**?
DOESN'T MATTER. IS IT TRUE?
AMEND
WELL, WE **ARE**.
WE **WERE**.
UH OH...

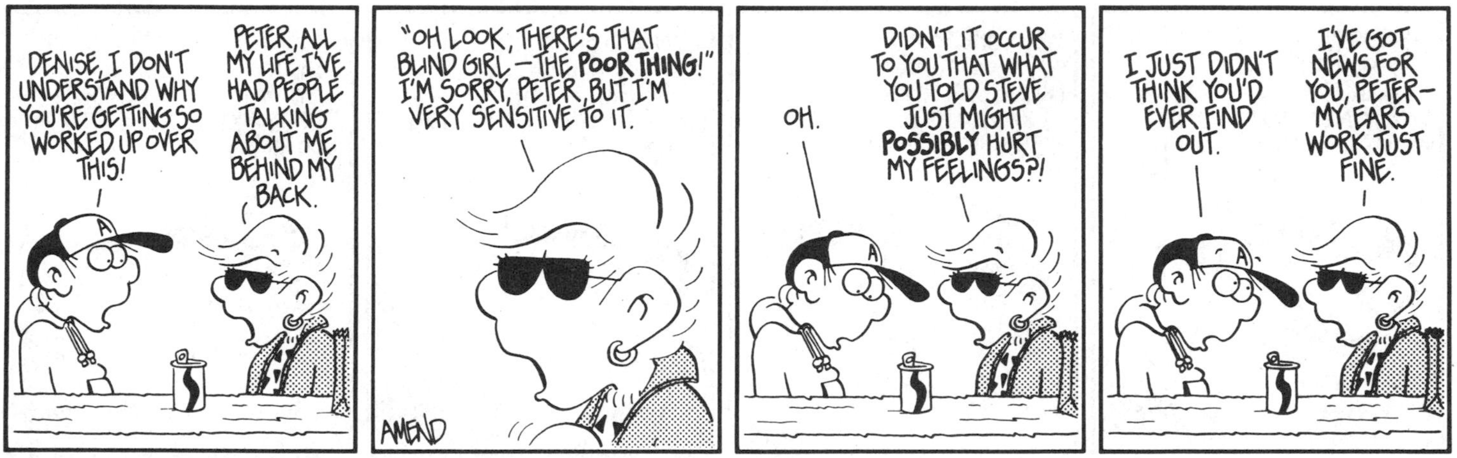
DENISE, I DON'T UNDERSTAND WHY YOU'RE GETTING SO WORKED UP OVER THIS!
PETER, ALL MY LIFE I'VE HAD PEOPLE TALKING ABOUT ME BEHIND MY BACK.
"OH LOOK, THERE'S THAT BLIND GIRL — THE **POOR THING**!" I'M SORRY, PETER, BUT I'M VERY SENSITIVE TO IT.
AMEND
OH.
DIDN'T IT OCCUR TO YOU THAT WHAT YOU TOLD STEVE JUST MIGHT **POSSIBLY** HURT MY FEELINGS?!
I JUST DIDN'T THINK YOU'D EVER FIND OUT.
I'VE GOT NEWS FOR YOU, PETER- MY EARS WORK JUST FINE.

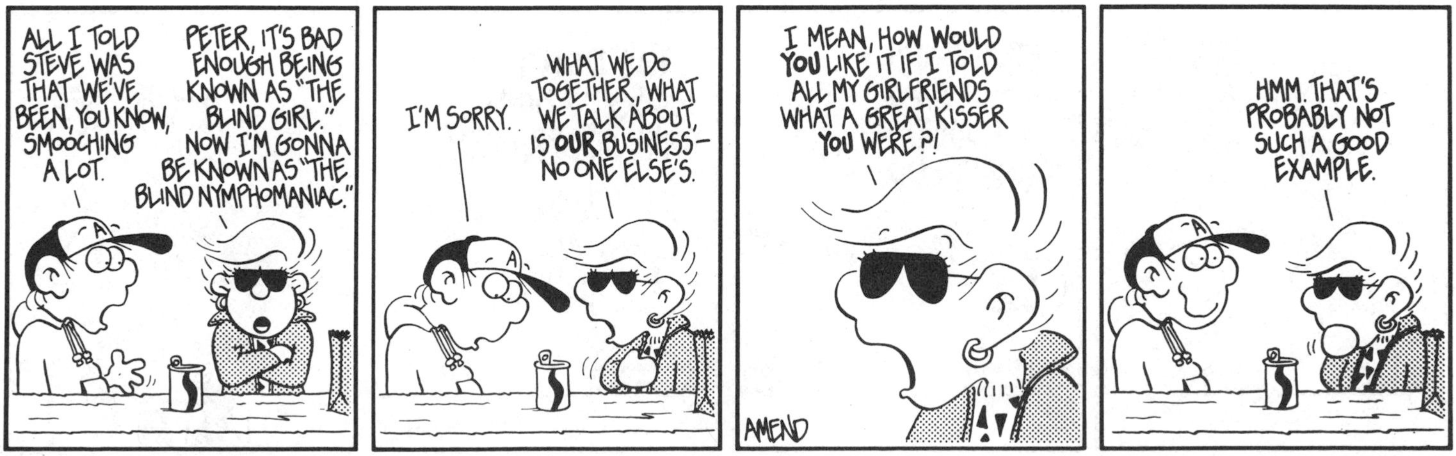
ALL I TOLD STEVE WAS THAT WE'VE BEEN, YOU KNOW, SMOOCHING A LOT.
PETER, IT'S BAD ENOUGH BEING KNOWN AS "THE BLIND GIRL." NOW I'M GONNA BE KNOWN AS "THE BLIND NYMPHOMANIAC."
I'M SORRY.
WHAT WE DO TOGETHER, WHAT WE TALK ABOUT, IS **OUR** BUSINESS- NO ONE ELSE'S.
I MEAN, HOW WOULD **YOU** LIKE IT IF I TOLD ALL MY GIRLFRIENDS WHAT A GREAT KISSER **YOU** WERE?!
AMEND
HMM. THAT'S PROBABLY NOT SUCH A GOOD EXAMPLE.

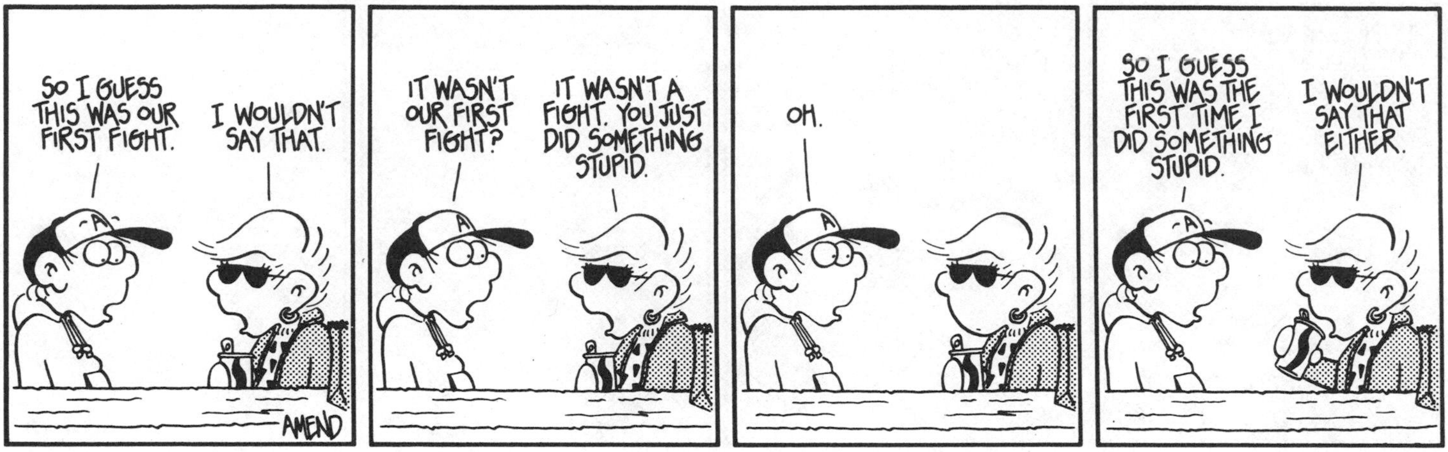
SO I GUESS THIS WAS OUR FIRST FIGHT.
I WOULDN'T SAY THAT.
AMEND
IT WASN'T OUR FIRST FIGHT?
IT WASN'T A FIGHT. YOU JUST DID SOMETHING STUPID.
OH.
SO I GUESS THIS WAS THE FIRST TIME I DID SOMETHING STUPID.
I WOULDN'T SAY THAT EITHER.

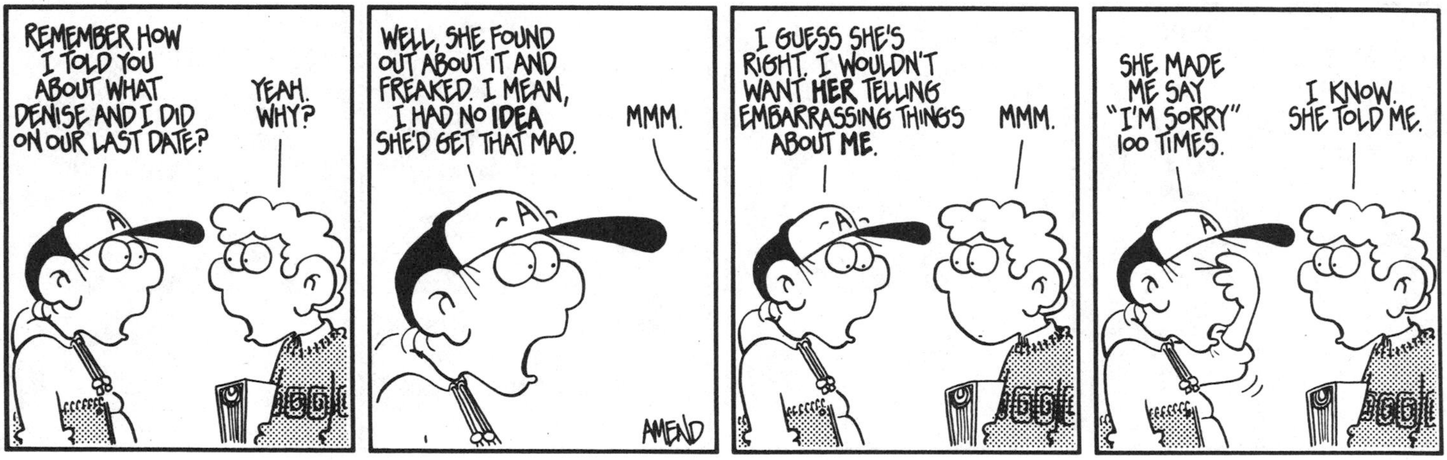
REMEMBER HOW I TOLD YOU ABOUT WHAT DENISE AND I DID ON OUR LAST DATE?
YEAH. WHY?
WELL, SHE FOUND OUT ABOUT IT AND FREAKED. I MEAN, I HAD NO IDEA SHE'D GET THAT MAD.
MMM.
AMEND
I GUESS SHE'S RIGHT. I WOULDN'T WANT HER TELLING EMBARRASSING THINGS ABOUT ME.
MMM.
SHE MADE ME SAY "I'M SORRY" 100 TIMES.
I KNOW. SHE TOLD ME.

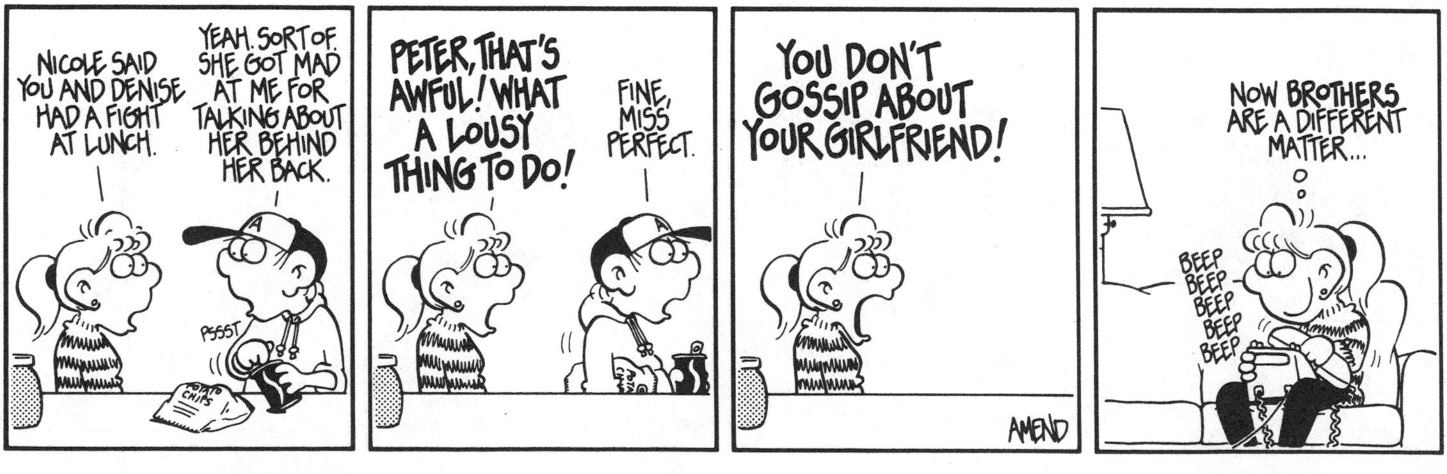
NICOLE SAID YOU AND DENISE HAD A FIGHT AT LUNCH.
YEAH. SORT OF. SHE GOT MAD AT ME FOR TALKING ABOUT HER BEHIND HER BACK.
PSSST
PETER, THAT'S AWFUL! WHAT A LOUSY THING TO DO!
FINE, MISS PERFECT.
YOU DON'T GOSSIP ABOUT YOUR GIRLFRIEND!
AMEND
NOW BROTHERS ARE A DIFFERENT MATTER...
BEEP BEEP BEEP BEEP BEEP

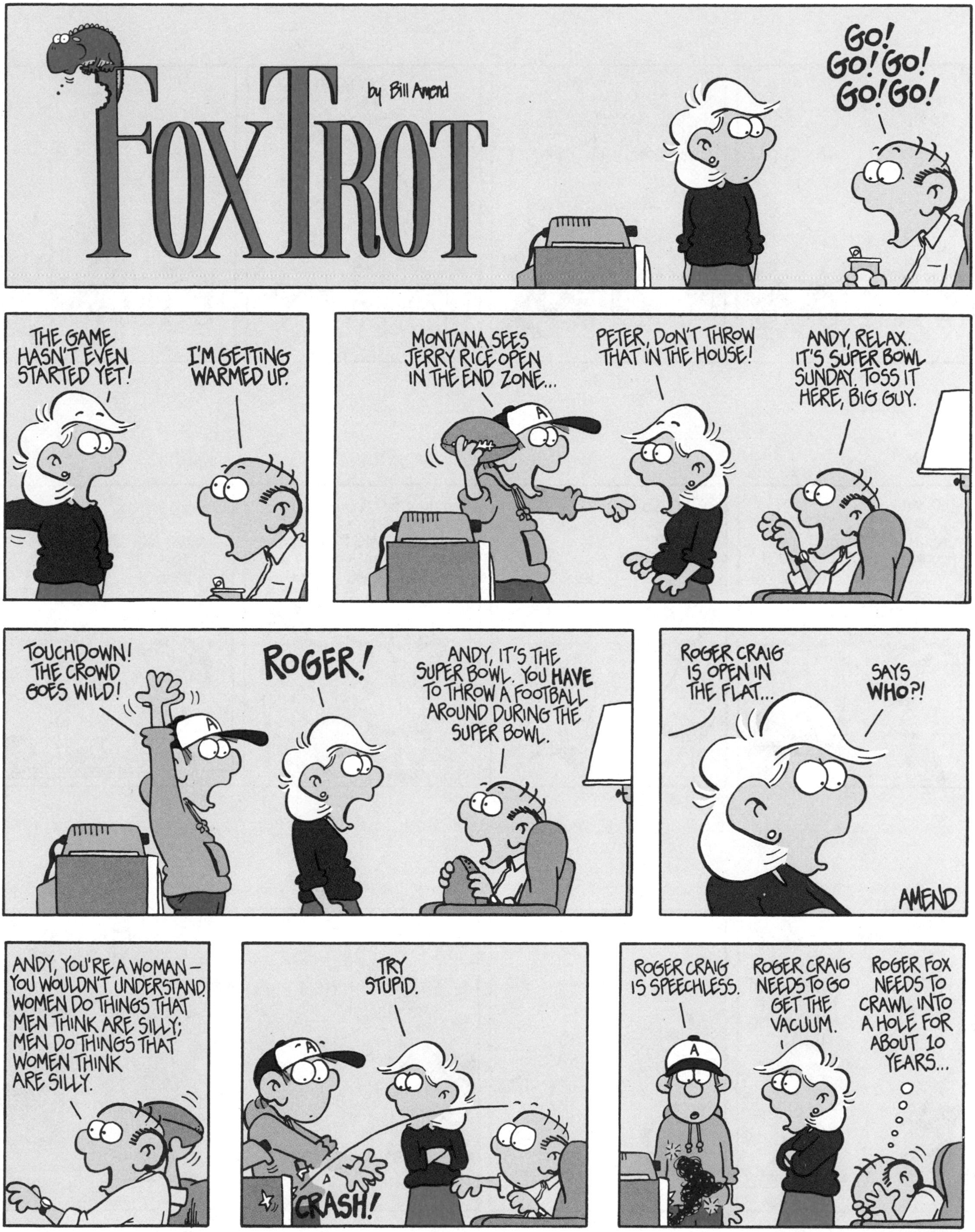
FoxTrot
by Bill Amend
GO! GO! GO! GO! GO! GO!
THE GAME HASN'T EVEN STARTED YET!
I'M GETTING WARMED UP.
MONTANA SEES JERRY RICE OPEN IN THE END ZONE...
PETER, DON'T THROW THAT IN THE HOUSE!
ANDY, RELAX. IT'S SUPER BOWL SUNDAY. TOSS IT HERE, BIG GUY.
TOUCHDOWN! THE CROWD GOES WILD!
ROGER!
ANDY, IT'S THE SUPER BOWL. YOU HAVE TO THROW A FOOTBALL AROUND DURING THE SUPER BOWL.
ROGER CRAIG IS OPEN IN THE FLAT...
SAYS WHO?!
AMEND
ANDY, YOU'RE A WOMAN – YOU WOULDN'T UNDERSTAND. WOMEN DO THINGS THAT MEN THINK ARE SILLY; MEN DO THINGS THAT WOMEN THINK ARE SILLY.
TRY STUPID.
CRASH!
ROGER CRAIG IS SPEECHLESS.
ROGER CRAIG NEEDS TO GO GET THE VACUUM.
ROGER FOX NEEDS TO CRAWL INTO A HOLE FOR ABOUT 10 YEARS...

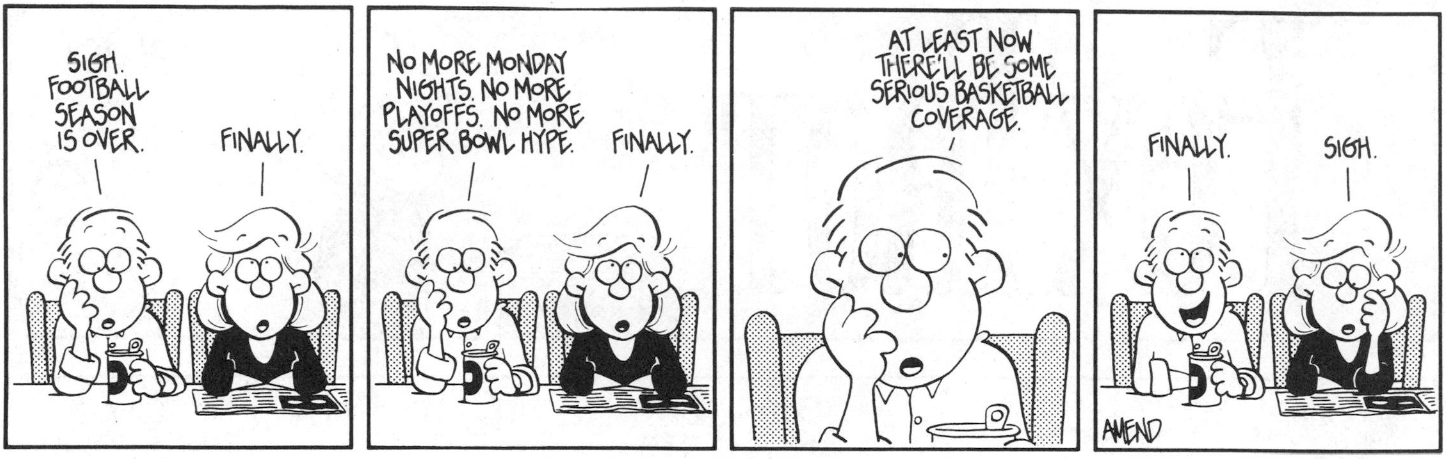
SIGH. FOOTBALL SEASON IS OVER.
FINALLY.
NO MORE MONDAY NIGHTS. NO MORE PLAYOFFS. NO MORE SUPER BOWL HYPE.
FINALLY.
AT LEAST NOW THERE'LL BE SOME SERIOUS BASKETBALL COVERAGE.
FINALLY.
SIGH.
AMEND

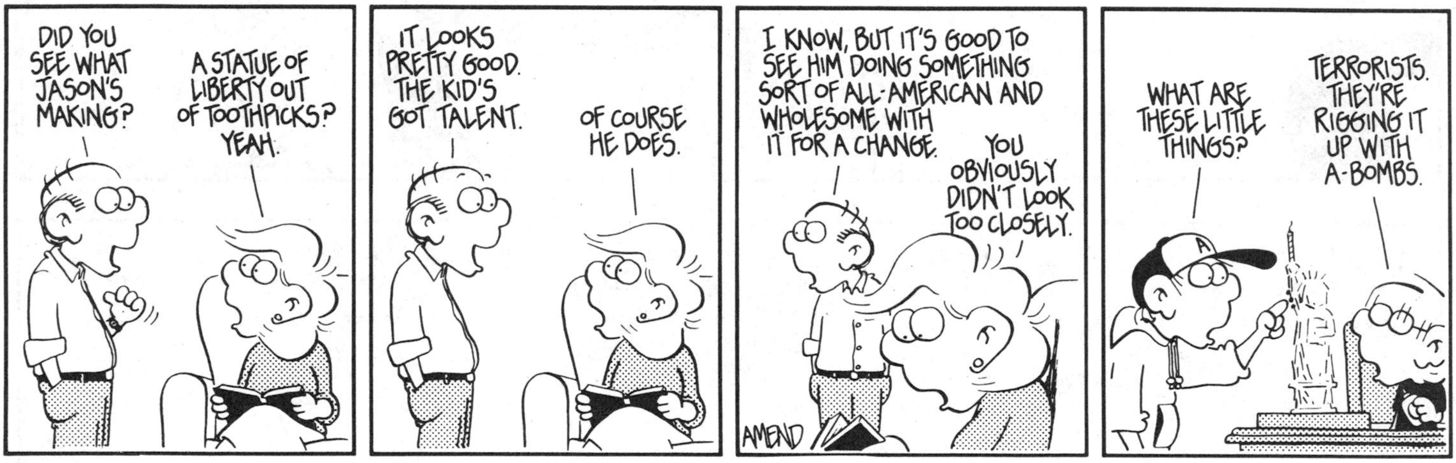
DID YOU SEE WHAT JASON'S MAKING?
A STATUE OF LIBERTY OUT OF TOOTHPICKS? YEAH.
IT LOOKS PRETTY GOOD. THE KID'S GOT TALENT.
OF COURSE HE DOES.
I KNOW, BUT IT'S GOOD TO SEE HIM DOING SOMETHING SORT OF ALL-AMERICAN AND WHOLESOME WITH IT FOR A CHANGE.
YOU OBVIOUSLY DIDN'T LOOK TOO CLOSELY.
AMEND
WHAT ARE THESE LITTLE THINGS?
TERRORISTS. THEY'RE RIGGING IT UP WITH A-BOMBS.

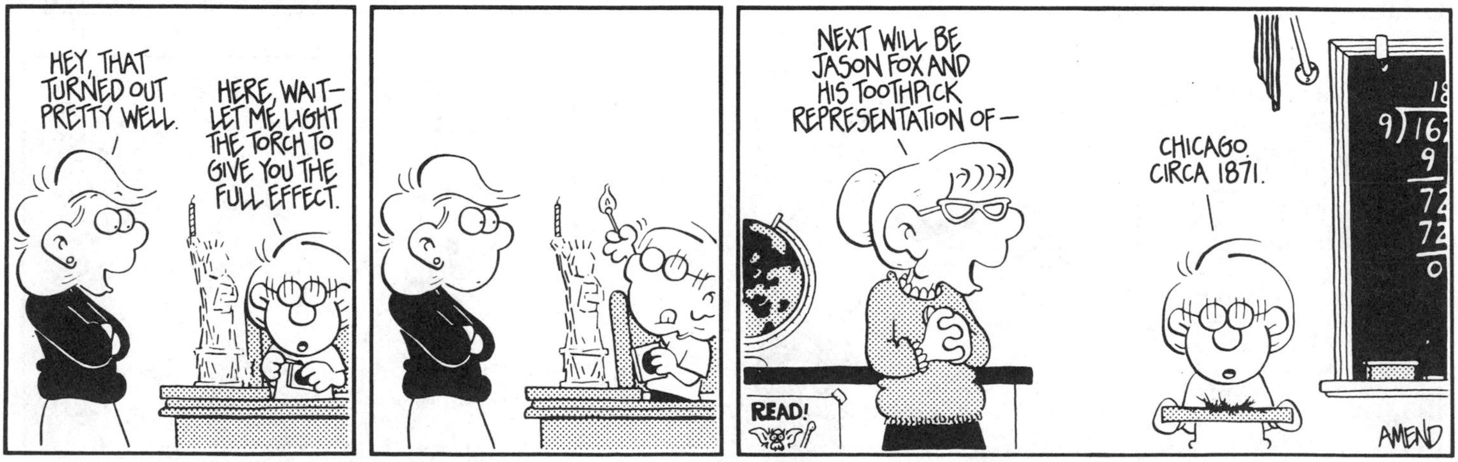
HEY, THAT TURNED OUT PRETTY WELL.
HERE, WAIT-LET ME LIGHT THE TORCH TO GIVE YOU THE FULL EFFECT.
NEXT WILL BE JASON FOX AND HIS TOOTHPICK REPRESENTATION OF—
READ!
CHICAGO CIRCA 1871.
AMEND

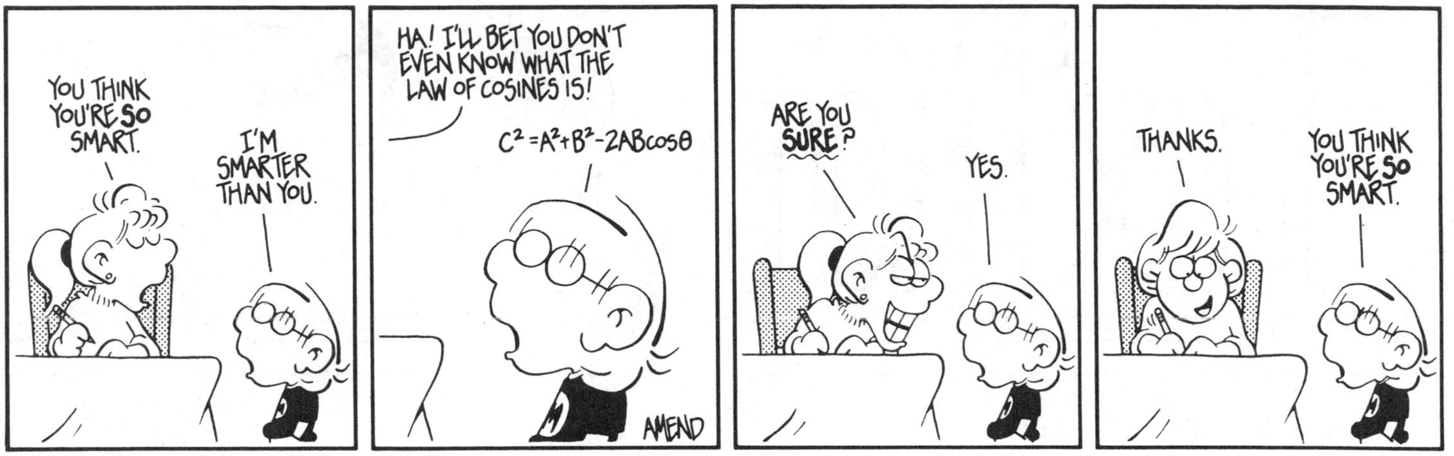
YOU THINK YOU'RE **SO** SMART.
I'M SMARTER THAN YOU.
HA! I'LL BET YOU DON'T EVEN KNOW WHAT THE LAW OF COSINES IS!
$C^2 = A^2 + B^2 - 2AB\cos\theta$
ARE YOU **SURE**?
YES.
THANKS.
YOU THINK YOU'RE **SO** SMART.
AMEND

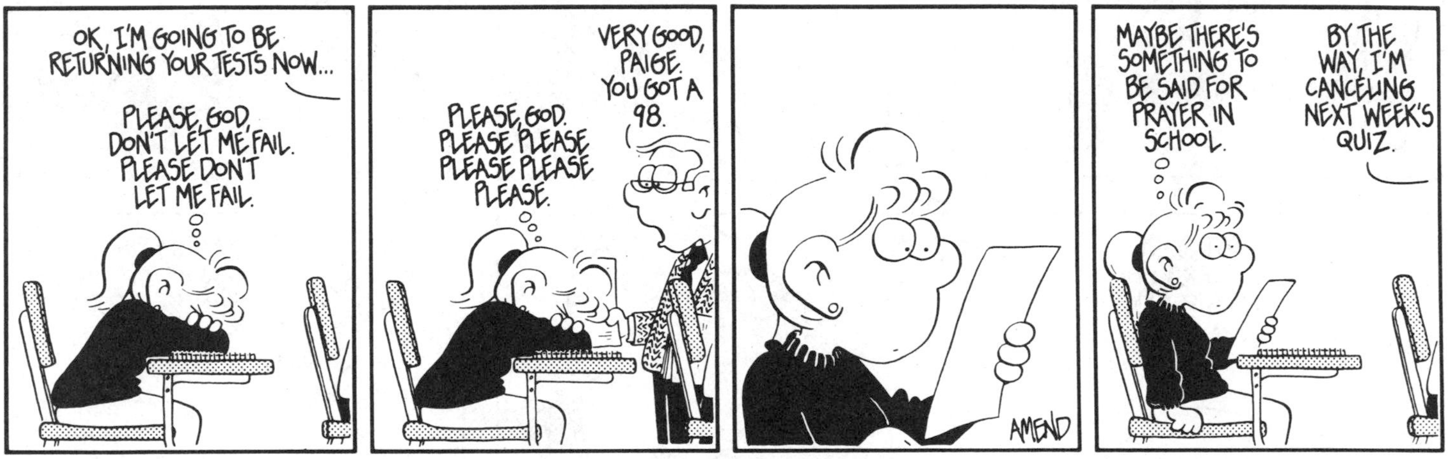
OK, I'M GOING TO BE RETURNING YOUR TESTS NOW...
PLEASE, GOD, DON'T LET ME FAIL. PLEASE DON'T LET ME FAIL.
PLEASE, GOD. PLEASE PLEASE PLEASE PLEASE PLEASE.
VERY GOOD, PAIGE. YOU GOT A 98.
MAYBE THERE'S SOMETHING TO BE SAID FOR PRAYER IN SCHOOL.
BY THE WAY, I'M CANCELING NEXT WEEK'S QUIZ.
AMEND

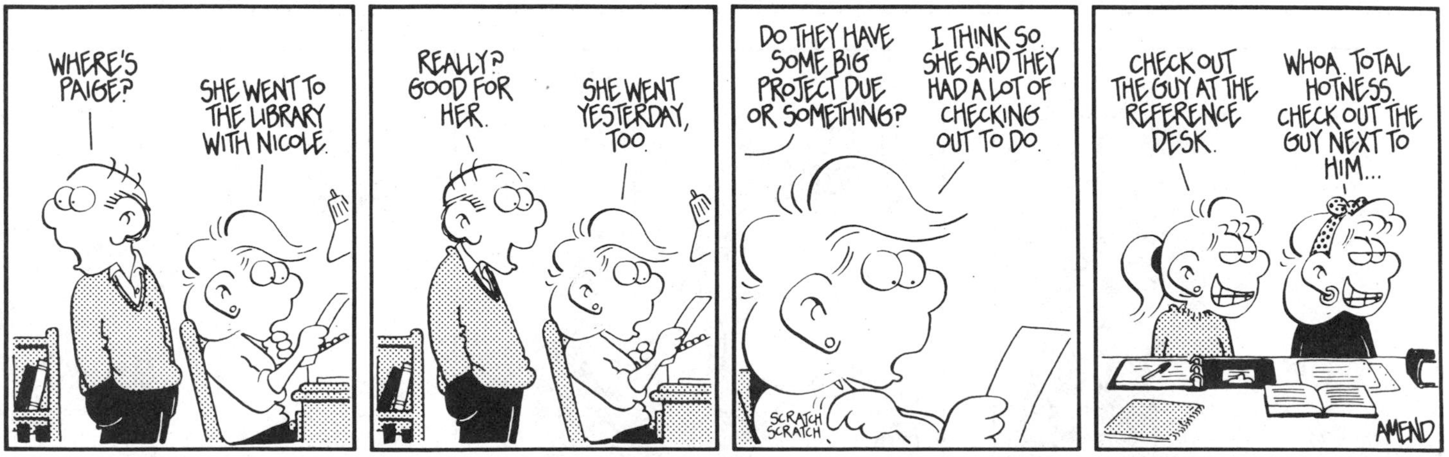
WHERE'S PAIGE?
SHE WENT TO THE LIBRARY WITH NICOLE.
REALLY? GOOD FOR HER.
SHE WENT YESTERDAY, TOO.
DO THEY HAVE SOME BIG PROJECT DUE OR SOMETHING?
I THINK SO. SHE SAID THEY HAD A LOT OF CHECKING OUT TO DO.
SCRATCH SCRATCH
CHECK OUT THE GUY AT THE REFERENCE DESK.
WHOA. TOTAL HOTNESS. CHECK OUT THE GUY NEXT TO HIM...
AMEND

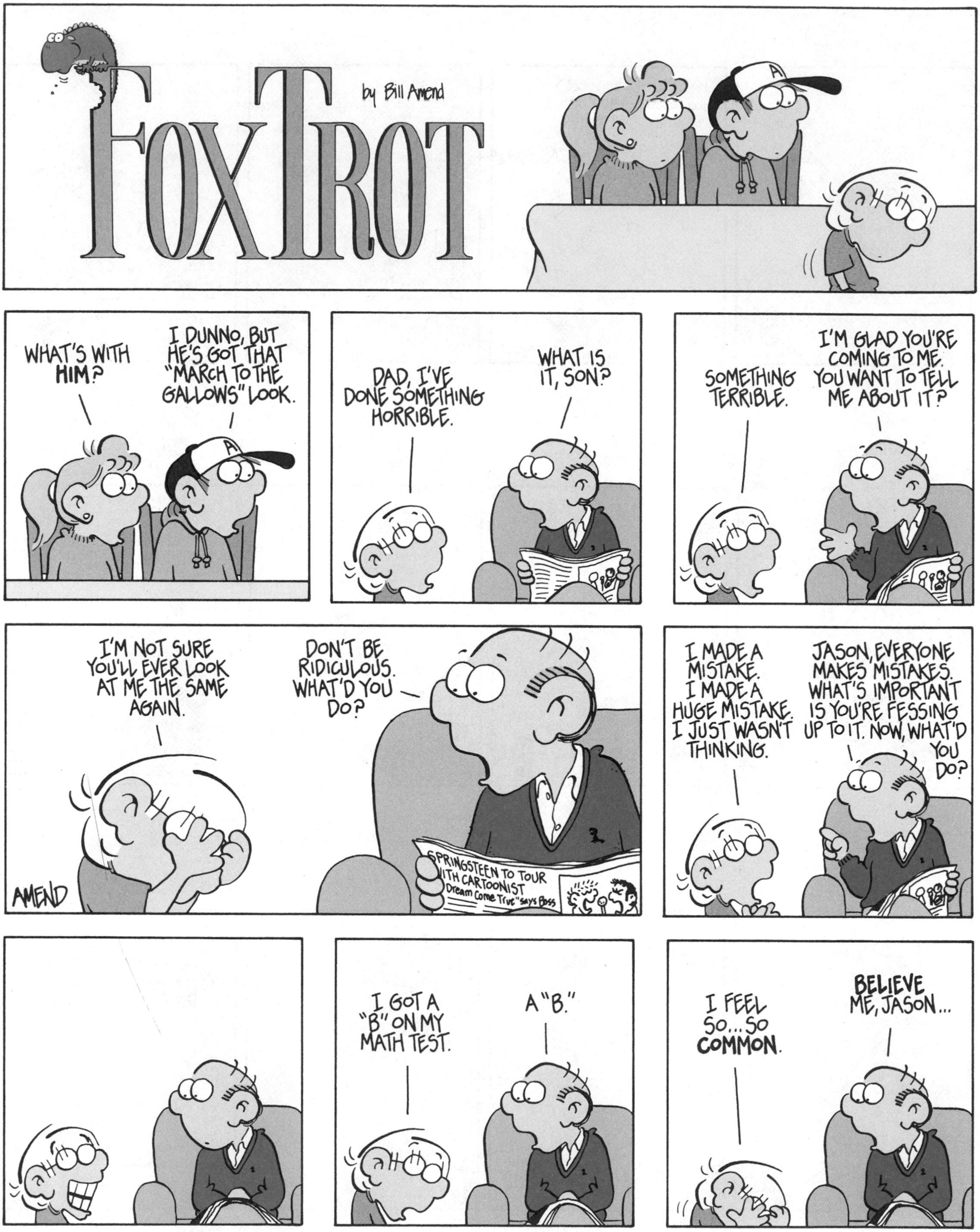
FoxTrot
by Bill Amend
WHAT'S WITH HIM?
I DUNNO, BUT HE'S GOT THAT "MARCH TO THE GALLOWS" LOOK.
DAD, I'VE DONE SOMETHING HORRIBLE.
WHAT IS IT, SON?
SOMETHING TERRIBLE.
I'M GLAD YOU'RE COMING TO ME. YOU WANT TO TELL ME ABOUT IT?
I'M NOT SURE YOU'LL EVER LOOK AT ME THE SAME AGAIN.
DON'T BE RIDICULOUS. WHAT'D YOU DO?
SPRINGSTEEN TO TOUR WITH CARTOONIST
"Dream Come True" says Boss
AMEND
I MADE A MISTAKE. I MADE A HUGE MISTAKE. I JUST WASN'T THINKING.
JASON, EVERYONE MAKES MISTAKES. WHAT'S IMPORTANT IS YOU'RE FESSING UP TO IT. NOW, WHAT'D YOU DO?
I GOT A "B" ON MY MATH TEST.
A "B."
I FEEL SO... SO COMMON.
BELIEVE ME, JASON...

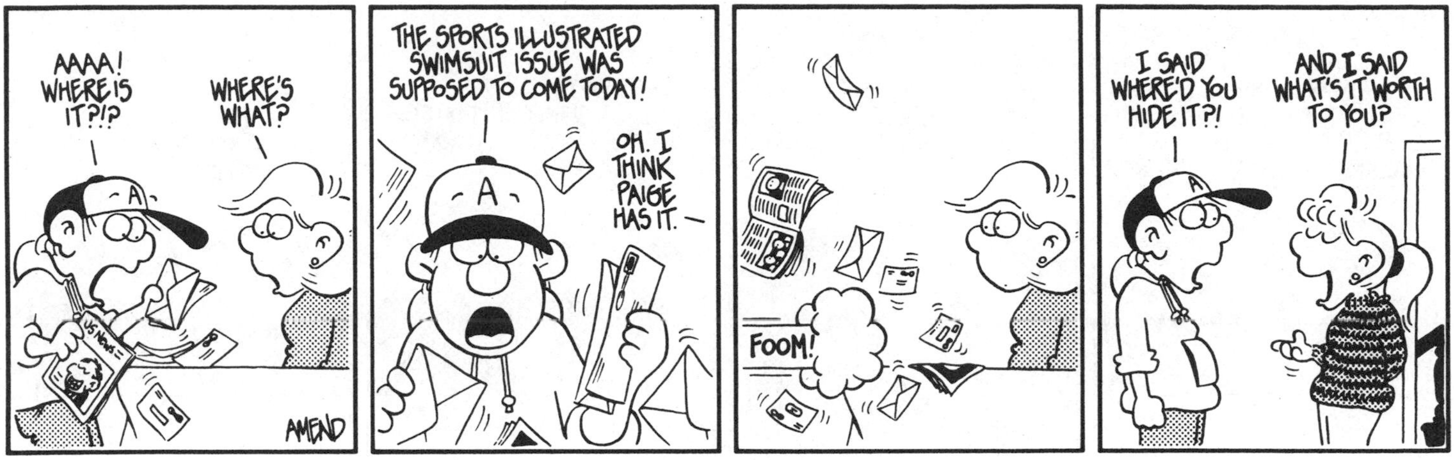
AAAA! WHERE IS IT?!?
WHERE'S WHAT?
US News
AMEND
THE SPORTS ILLUSTRATED SWIMSUIT ISSUE WAS SUPPOSED TO COME TODAY!
OH. I THINK PAIGE HAS IT.
FOOM!
I SAID WHERE'D YOU HIDE IT?!
AND I SAID WHAT'S IT WORTH TO YOU?

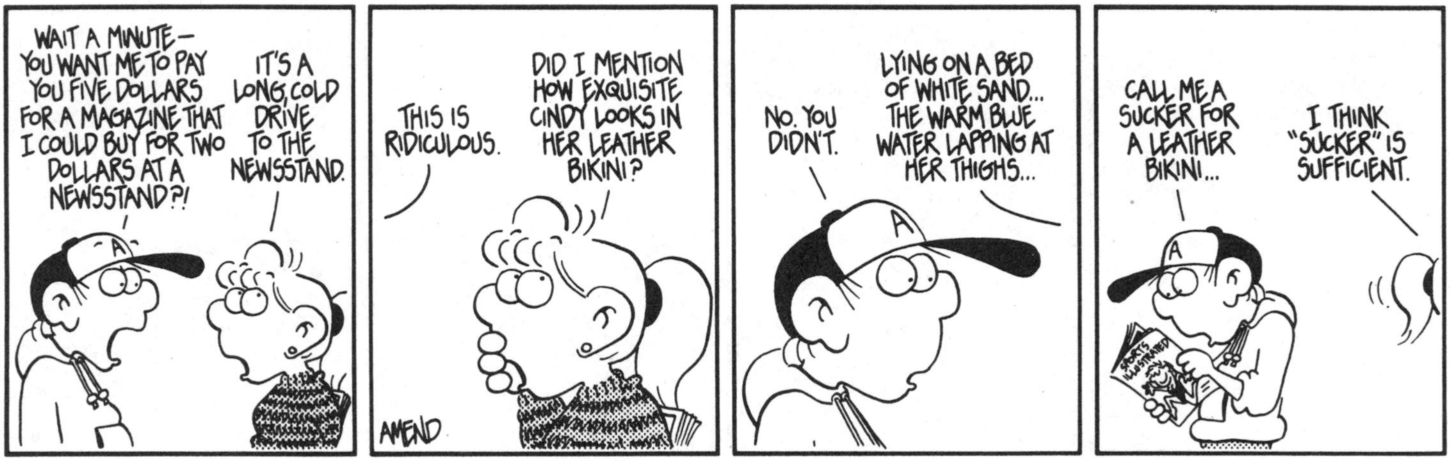
WAIT A MINUTE— YOU WANT ME TO PAY YOU FIVE DOLLARS FOR A MAGAZINE THAT I COULD BUY FOR TWO DOLLARS AT A NEWSSTAND?!
IT'S A LONG, COLD DRIVE TO THE NEWSSTAND.
THIS IS RIDICULOUS.
DID I MENTION HOW EXQUISITE CINDY LOOKS IN HER LEATHER BIKINI?
AMEND
NO. YOU DIDN'T.
LYING ON A BED OF WHITE SAND... THE WARM BLUE WATER LAPPING AT HER THIGHS...
CALL ME A SUCKER FOR A LEATHER BIKINI...
I THINK "SUCKER" IS SUFFICIENT.
SPORTS ILLUSTRATED

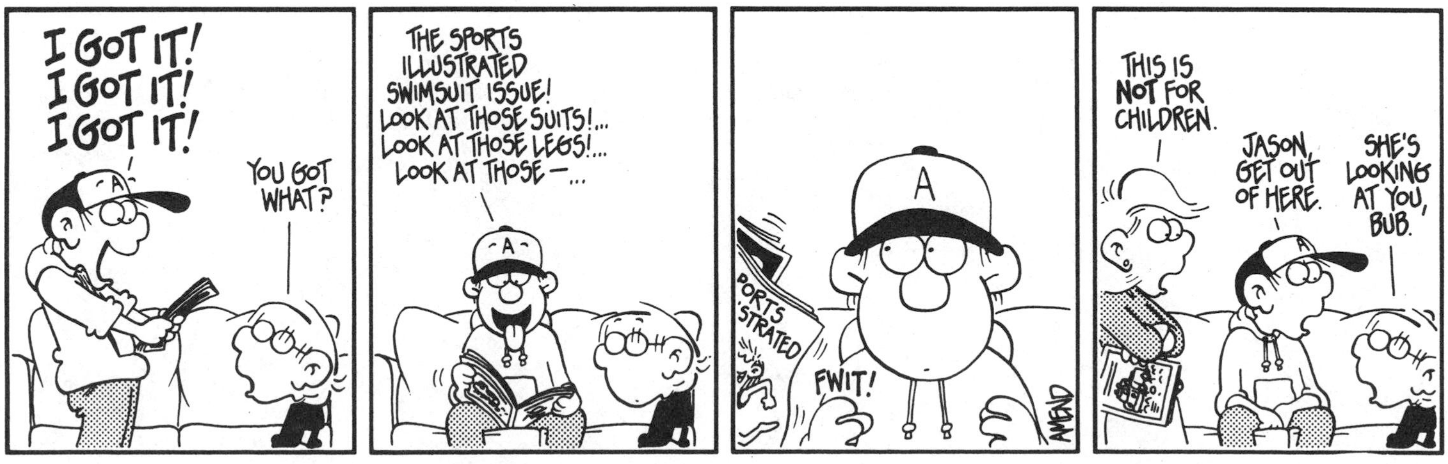
I GOT IT! I GOT IT! I GOT IT!
YOU GOT WHAT?
THE SPORTS ILLUSTRATED SWIMSUIT ISSUE! LOOK AT THOSE SUITS!... LOOK AT THOSE LEGS!... LOOK AT THOSE —...
PORTS STRATED
FWIT!
AMEND
THIS IS NOT FOR CHILDREN.
JASON, GET OUT OF HERE.
SHE'S LOOKING AT YOU, BUB.

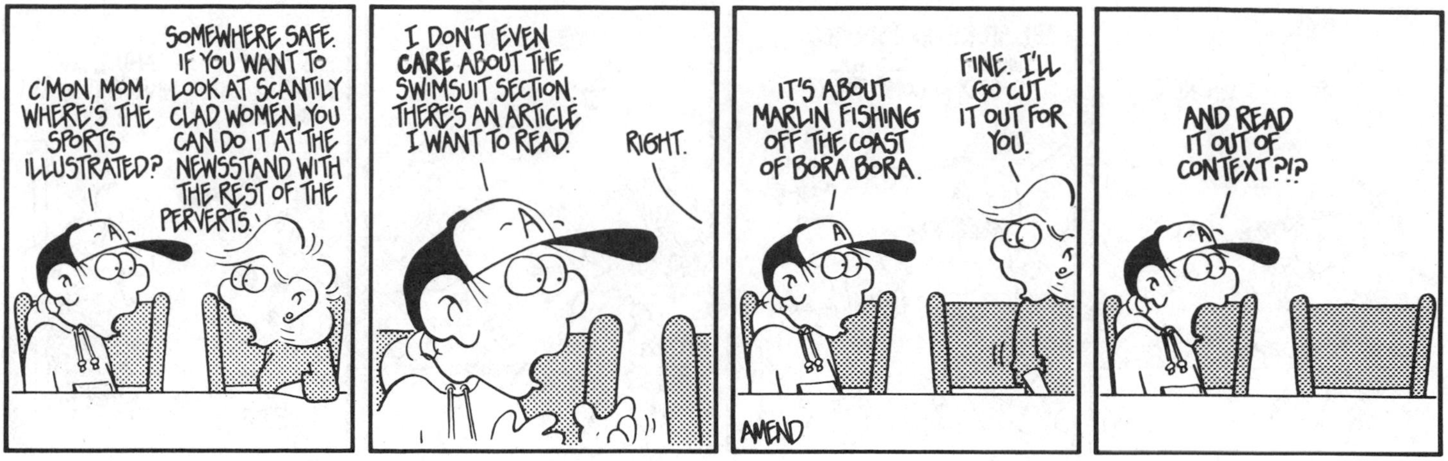
C'MON, MOM, WHERE'S THE SPORTS ILLUSTRATED?
SOMEWHERE SAFE. IF YOU WANT TO LOOK AT SCANTILY CLAD WOMEN, YOU CAN DO IT AT THE NEWSSTAND WITH THE REST OF THE PERVERTS.
I DON'T EVEN **CARE** ABOUT THE SWIMSUIT SECTION. THERE'S AN ARTICLE I WANT TO READ.
RIGHT.
IT'S ABOUT MARLIN FISHING OFF THE COAST OF BORA BORA.
FINE. I'LL GO CUT IT OUT FOR YOU.
AMEND
AND READ IT OUT OF CONTEXT?!?

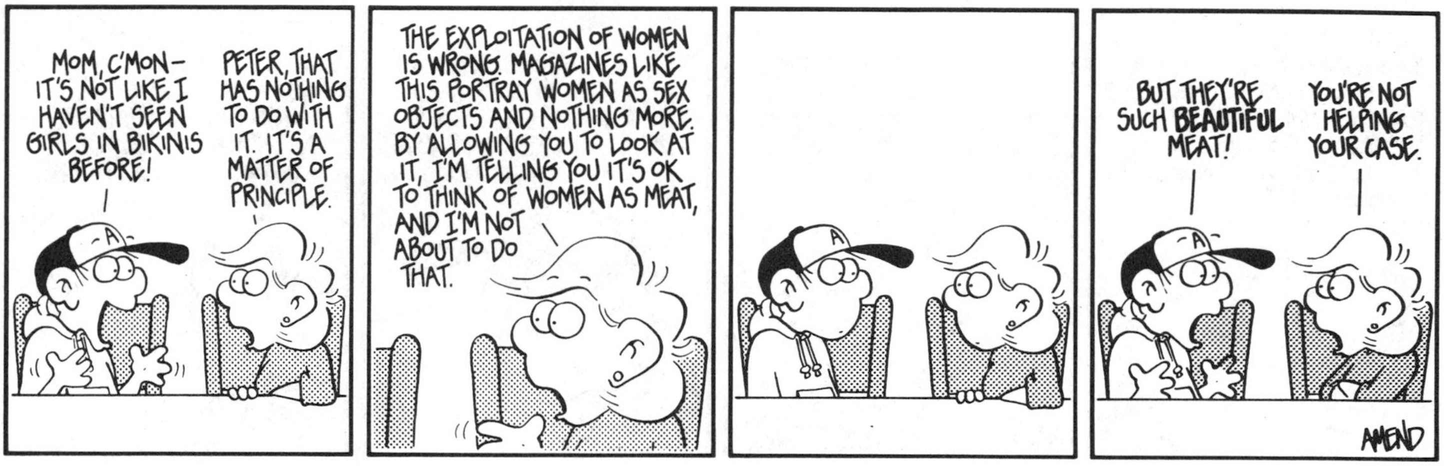
MOM, C'MON– IT'S NOT LIKE I HAVEN'T SEEN GIRLS IN BIKINIS BEFORE!
PETER, THAT HAS NOTHING TO DO WITH IT. IT'S A MATTER OF PRINCIPLE.
THE EXPLOITATION OF WOMEN IS **WRONG**. MAGAZINES LIKE THIS PORTRAY WOMEN AS SEX OBJECTS AND NOTHING MORE. BY ALLOWING YOU TO LOOK AT IT, I'M TELLING YOU IT'S OK TO THINK OF WOMEN AS MEAT, AND I'M NOT ABOUT TO DO THAT.
BUT THEY'RE SUCH **BEAUTIFUL** MEAT!
YOU'RE NOT HELPING YOUR CASE.
AMEND

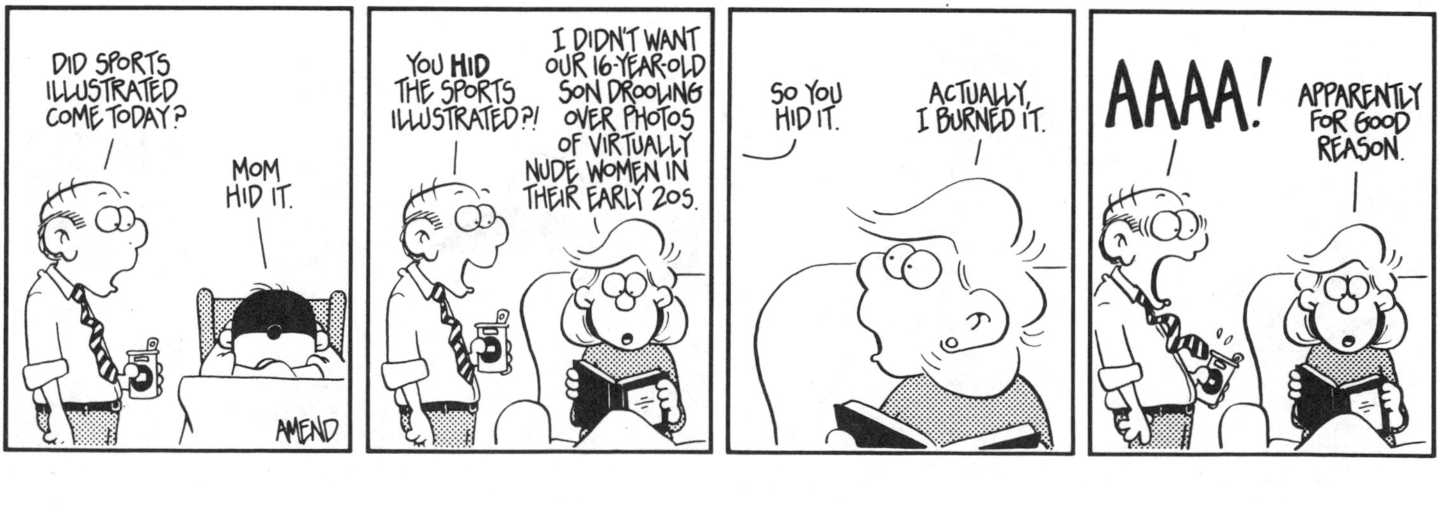
DID SPORTS ILLUSTRATED COME TODAY?
MOM HID IT.
AMEND
YOU **HID** THE SPORTS ILLUSTRATED?!
I DIDN'T WANT OUR 16-YEAR-OLD SON DROOLING OVER PHOTOS OF VIRTUALLY NUDE WOMEN IN THEIR EARLY 20S.
SO YOU HID IT.
ACTUALLY, I BURNED IT.
AAAA!
APPARENTLY FOR GOOD REASON.

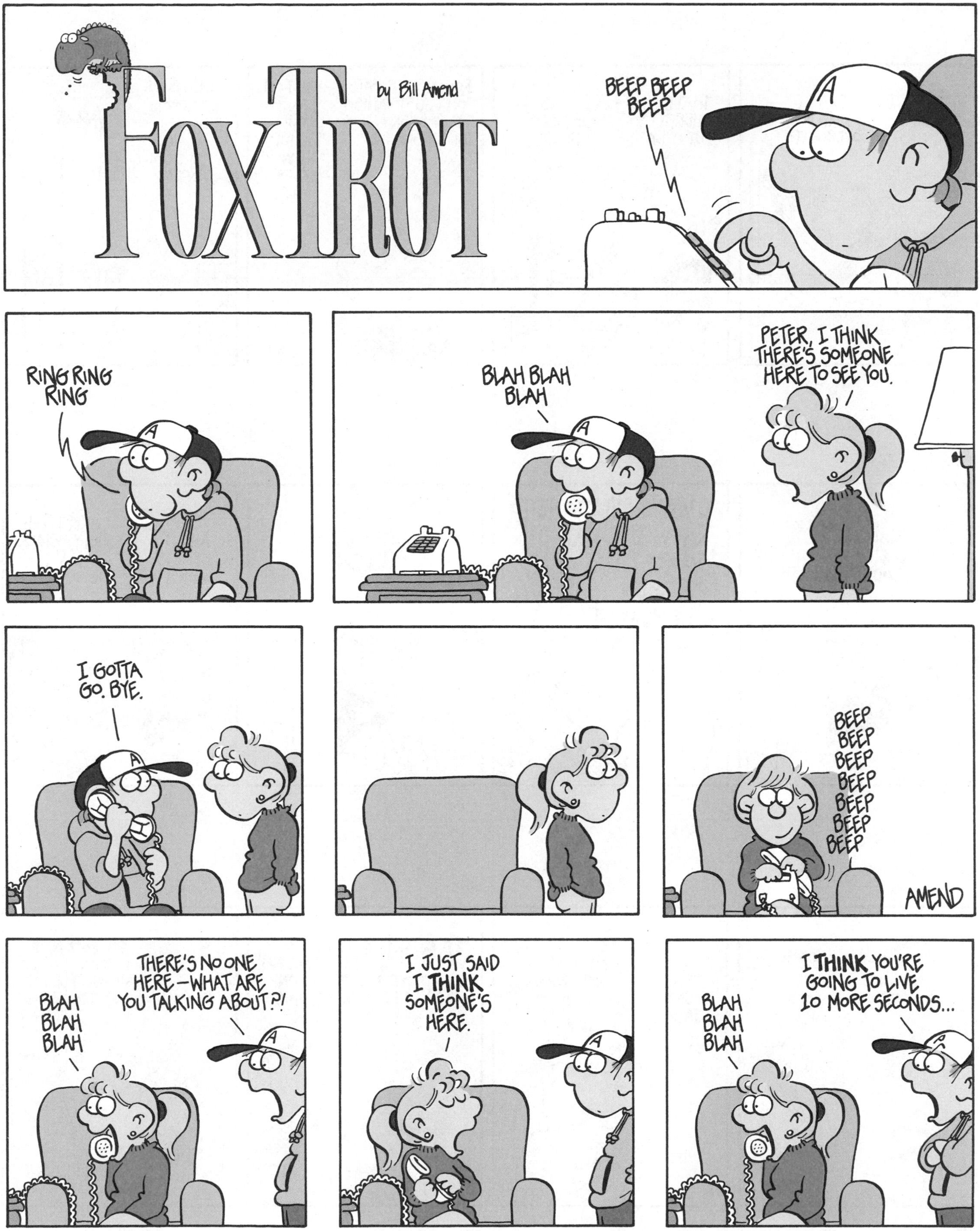
FoxTrot
by Bill Amend
BEEP BEEP BEEP
RING RING RING
BLAH BLAH BLAH
PETER, I THINK THERE'S SOMEONE HERE TO SEE YOU.
I GOTTA GO. BYE.
BEEP BEEP BEEP BEEP BEEP BEEP BEEP
AMEND
BLAH BLAH BLAH
THERE'S NO ONE HERE—WHAT ARE YOU TALKING ABOUT?!
I JUST SAID I **THINK** SOMEONE'S HERE.
BLAH BLAH BLAH
I **THINK** YOU'RE GOING TO LIVE 10 MORE SECONDS...

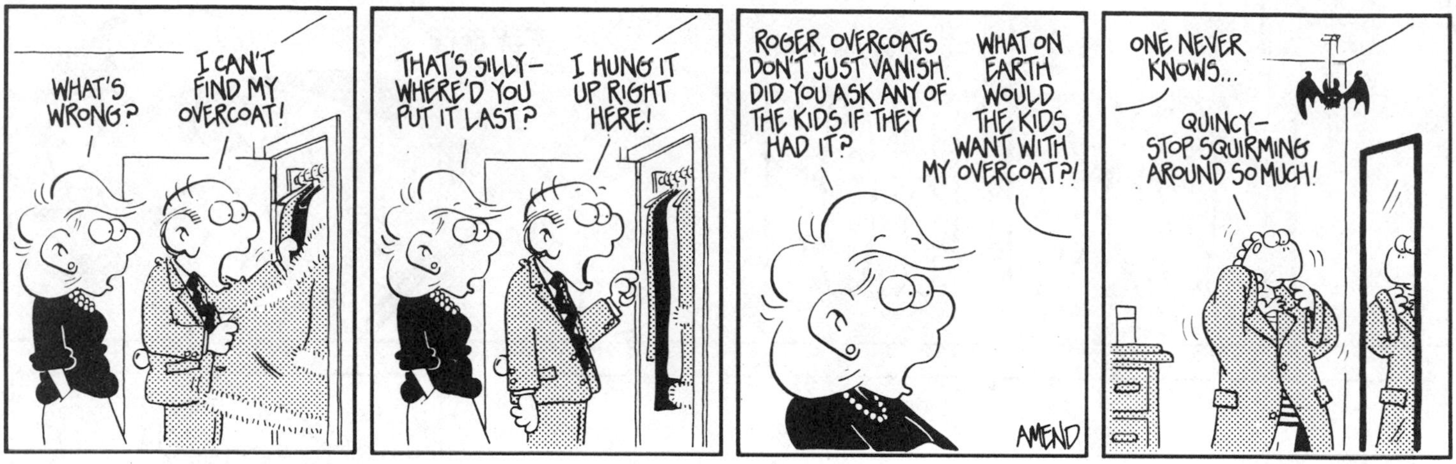
WHAT'S WRONG?
I CAN'T FIND MY OVERCOAT!
THAT'S SILLY— WHERE'D YOU PUT IT LAST?
I HUNG IT UP RIGHT HERE!
ROGER, OVERCOATS DON'T JUST VANISH. DID YOU ASK ANY OF THE KIDS IF THEY HAD IT?
WHAT ON EARTH WOULD THE KIDS WANT WITH MY OVERCOAT?!
AMEND
ONE NEVER KNOWS...
QUINCY— STOP SQUIRMING AROUND SO MUCH!

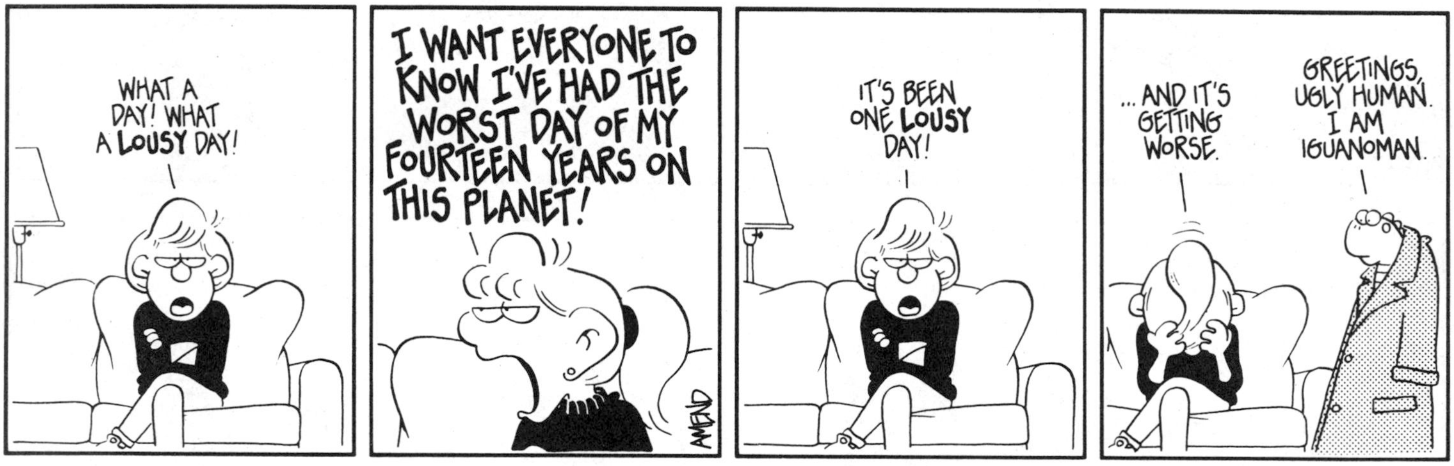
WHAT A DAY! WHAT A LOUSY DAY!
I WANT EVERYONE TO KNOW I'VE HAD THE WORST DAY OF MY FOURTEEN YEARS ON THIS PLANET!
AMEND
IT'S BEEN ONE LOUSY DAY!
... AND IT'S GETTING WORSE.
GREETINGS, UGLY HUMAN. I AM IGUANOMAN.

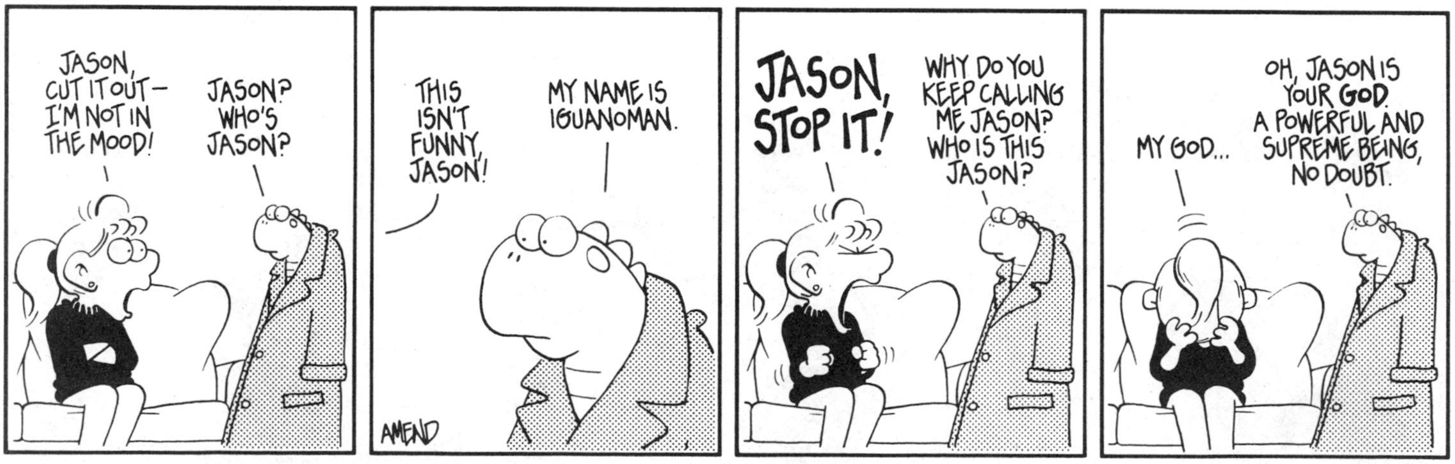
JASON, CUT IT OUT— I'M NOT IN THE MOOD!
JASON? WHO'S JASON?
THIS ISN'T FUNNY, JASON!
MY NAME IS IGUANOMAN.
AMEND
JASON, STOP IT!
WHY DO YOU KEEP CALLING ME JASON? WHO IS THIS JASON?
MY GOD...
OH, JASON IS YOUR GOD. A POWERFUL AND SUPREME BEING, NO DOUBT.

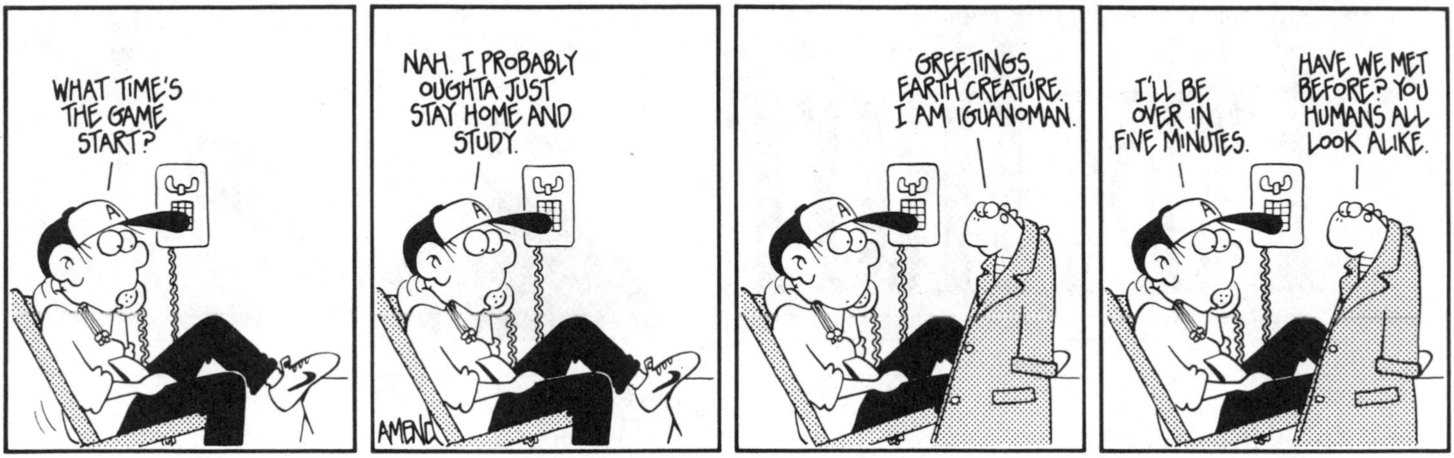
WHAT TIME'S THE GAME START?
NAH. I PROBABLY OUGHTA JUST STAY HOME AND STUDY.
AMEND
GREETINGS, EARTH CREATURE. I AM IGUANOMAN.
I'LL BE OVER IN FIVE MINUTES.
HAVE WE MET BEFORE? YOU HUMANS ALL LOOK ALIKE.

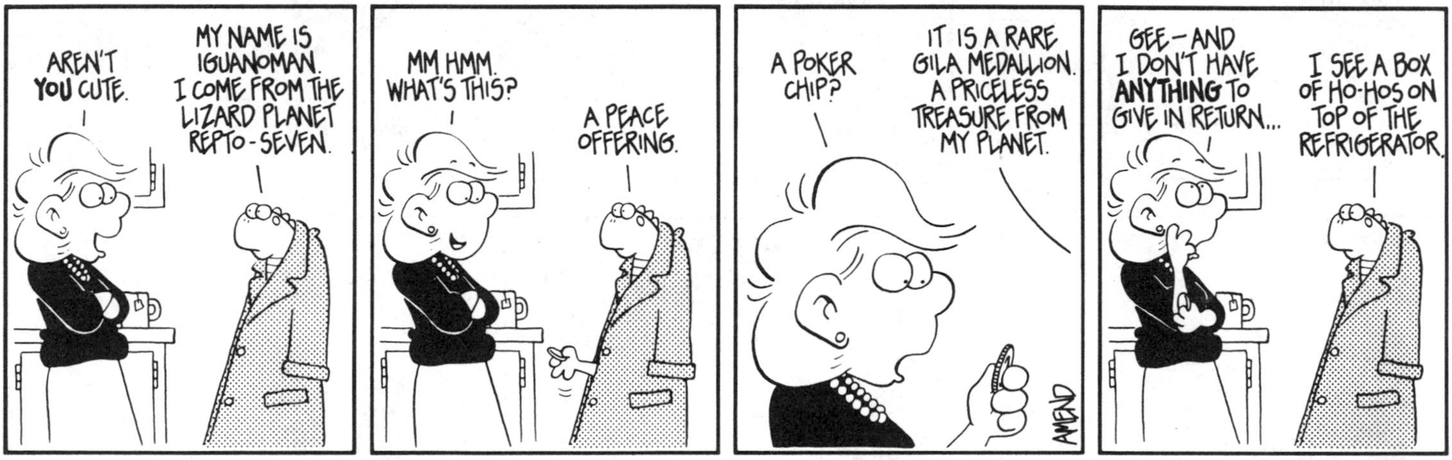
AREN'T **YOU** CUTE.
MY NAME IS IGUANOMAN. I COME FROM THE LIZARD PLANET REPTO-SEVEN.
MM HMM. WHAT'S THIS?
A PEACE OFFERING.
A POKER CHIP?
IT IS A RARE GILA MEDALLION. A PRICELESS TREASURE FROM MY PLANET.
AMEND
GEE—AND I DON'T HAVE **ANYTHING** TO GIVE IN RETURN...
I SEE A BOX OF HO-HOS ON TOP OF THE REFRIGERATOR.

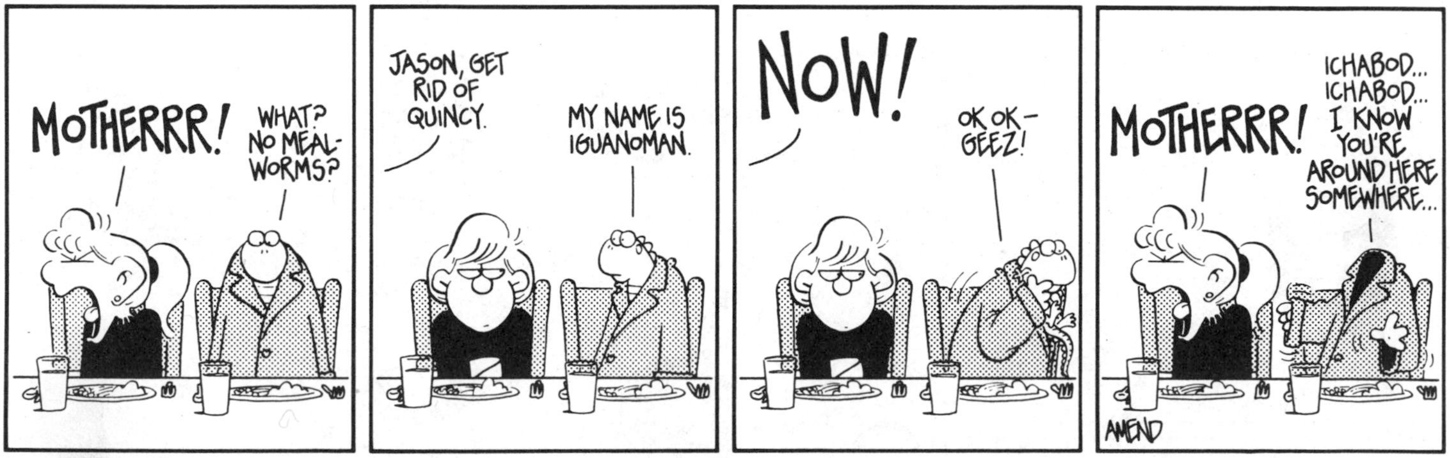
MOTHERRR!
WHAT? NO MEAL-WORMS?
JASON, GET RID OF QUINCY.
MY NAME IS IGUANOMAN.
NOW!
OK OK-GEEZ!
MOTHERRR!
ICHABOD... ICHABOD... I KNOW YOU'RE AROUND HERE SOMEWHERE...
AMEND

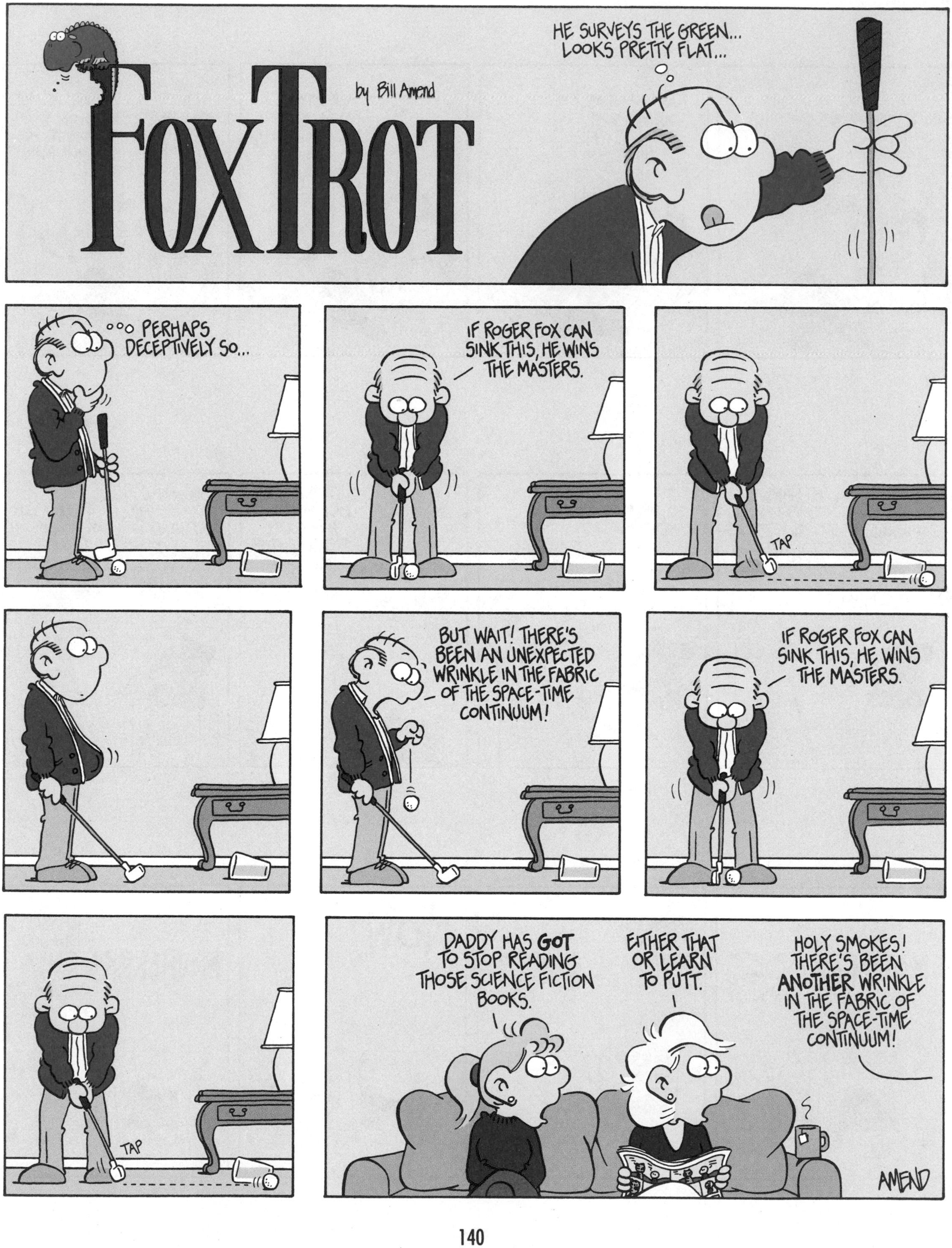

FoxTrot
by Bill Amend
HE SURVEYS THE GREEN... LOOKS PRETTY FLAT...
PERHAPS DECEPTIVELY SO...
IF ROGER FOX CAN SINK THIS, HE WINS THE MASTERS.
TAP
BUT WAIT! THERE'S BEEN AN UNEXPECTED WRINKLE IN THE FABRIC OF THE SPACE-TIME CONTINUUM!
IF ROGER FOX CAN SINK THIS, HE WINS THE MASTERS.
TAP
DADDY HAS GOT TO STOP READING THOSE SCIENCE FICTION BOOKS.
EITHER THAT OR LEARN TO PUTT.
HOLY SMOKES! THERE'S BEEN ANOTHER WRINKLE IN THE FABRIC OF THE SPACE-TIME CONTINUUM!
AMEND

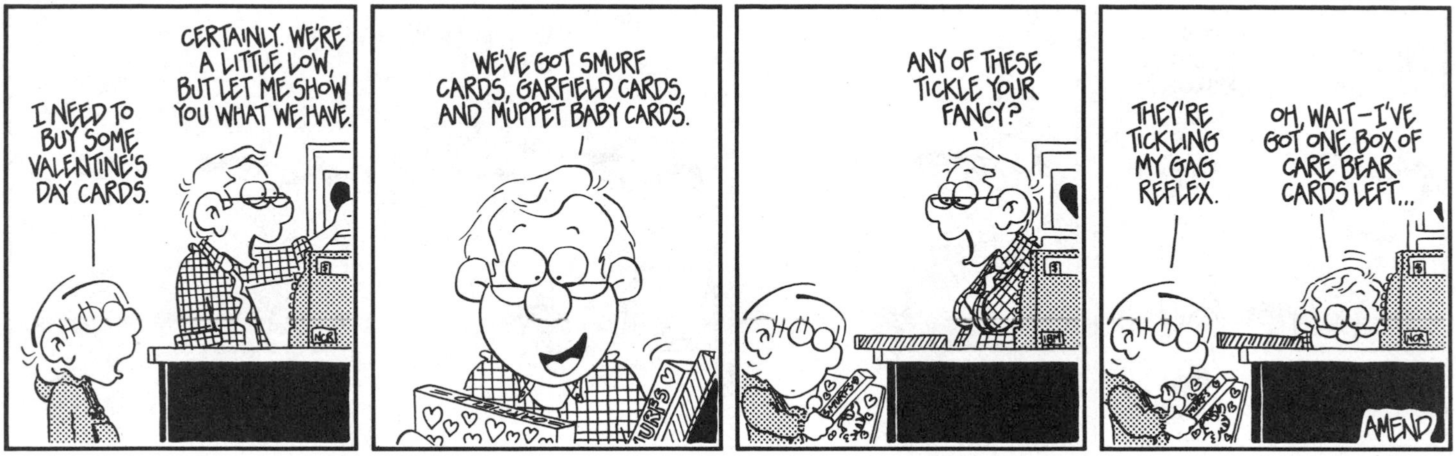
I NEED TO BUY SOME VALENTINE'S DAY CARDS.
CERTAINLY. WE'RE A LITTLE LOW, BUT LET ME SHOW YOU WHAT WE HAVE.
WE'VE GOT SMURF CARDS, GARFIELD CARDS, AND MUPPET BABY CARDS.
ANY OF THESE TICKLE YOUR FANCY?
THEY'RE TICKLING MY GAG REFLEX.
OH, WAIT—I'VE GOT ONE BOX OF CARE BEAR CARDS LEFT...
AMEND

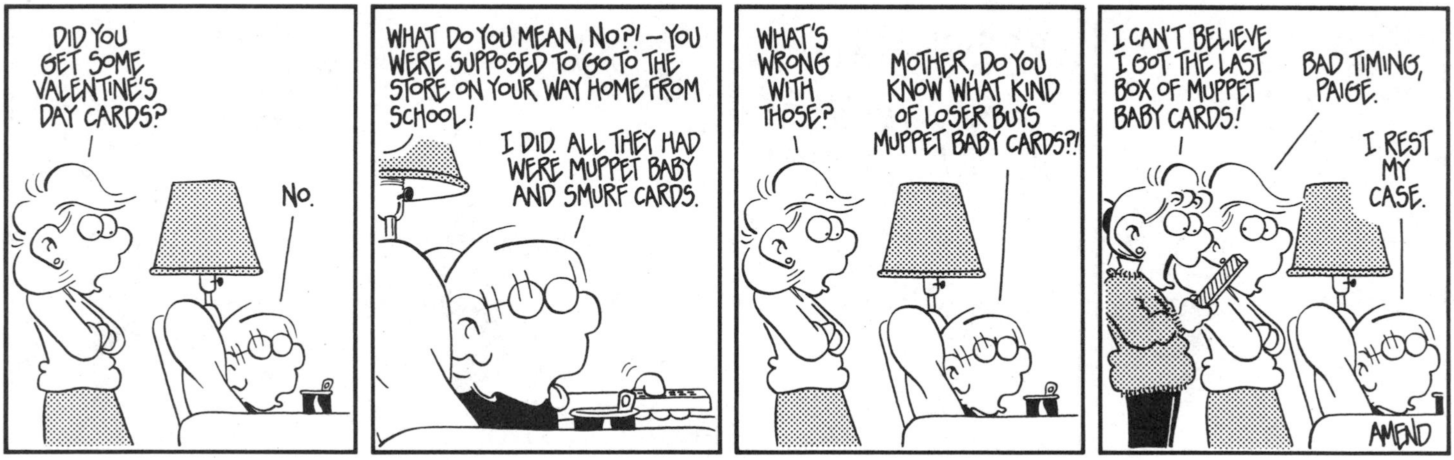
DID YOU GET SOME VALENTINE'S DAY CARDS?
NO.
WHAT DO YOU MEAN, NO?! —YOU WERE SUPPOSED TO GO TO THE STORE ON YOUR WAY HOME FROM SCHOOL!
I DID. ALL THEY HAD WERE MUPPET BABY AND SMURF CARDS.
WHAT'S WRONG WITH THOSE?
MOTHER, DO YOU KNOW WHAT KIND OF LOSER BUYS MUPPET BABY CARDS?!
I CAN'T BELIEVE I GOT THE LAST BOX OF MUPPET BABY CARDS!
BAD TIMING, PAIGE.
I REST MY CASE.
AMEND

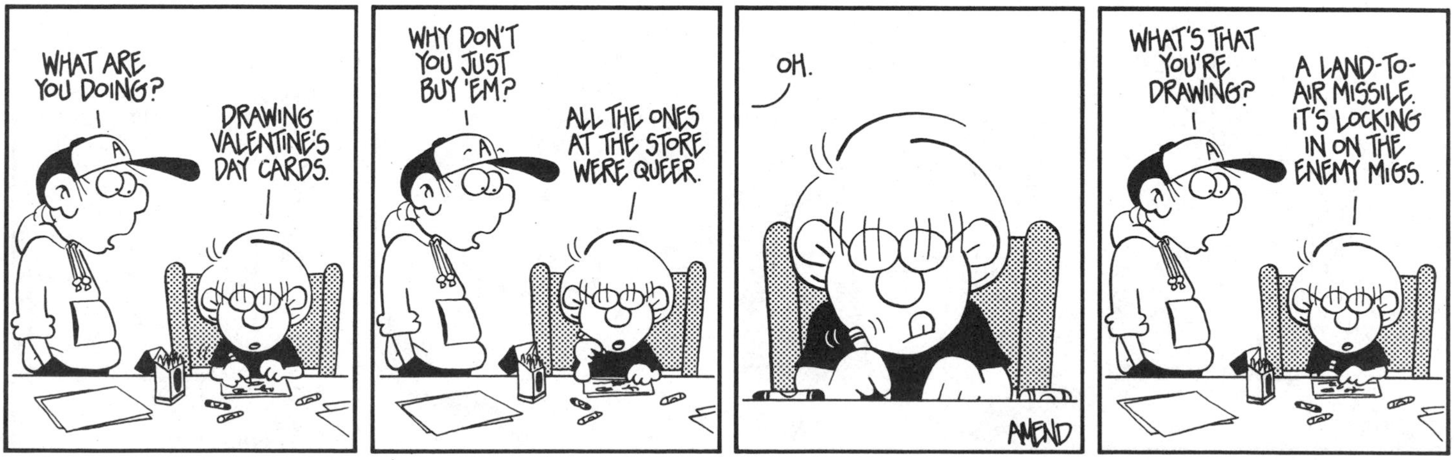
WHAT ARE YOU DOING?
DRAWING VALENTINE'S DAY CARDS.
WHY DON'T YOU JUST BUY 'EM?
ALL THE ONES AT THE STORE WERE QUEER.
OH.
AMEND
WHAT'S THAT YOU'RE DRAWING?
A LAND-TO-AIR MISSILE. IT'S LOCKING IN ON THE ENEMY MIGS.

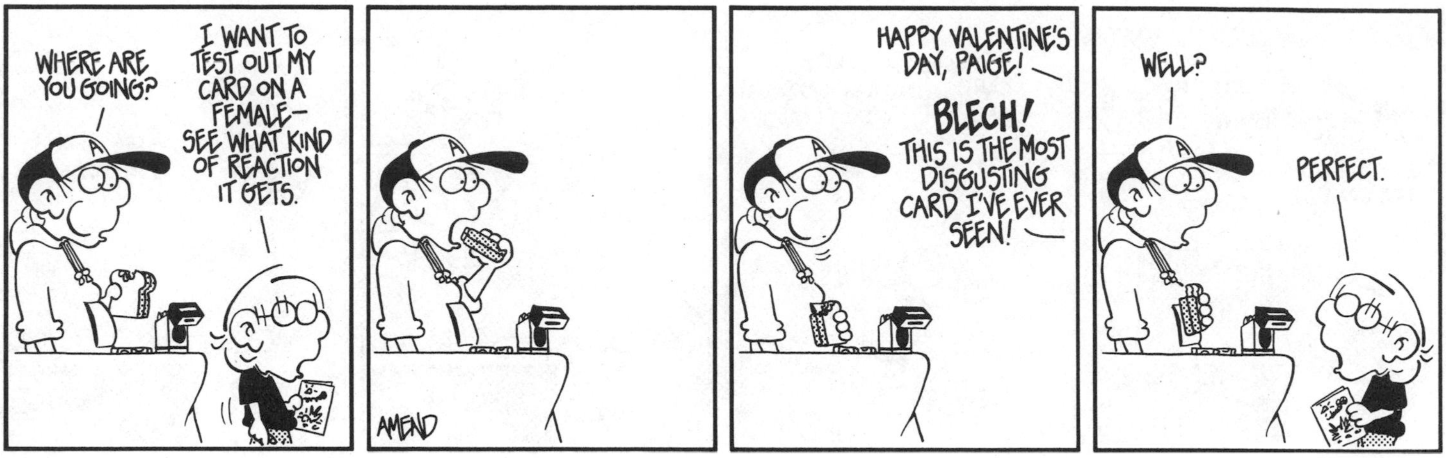
WHERE ARE YOU GOING?
I WANT TO TEST OUT MY CARD ON A FEMALE—SEE WHAT KIND OF REACTION IT GETS.
AMEND
HAPPY VALENTINE'S DAY, PAIGE!
BLECH! THIS IS THE MOST DISGUSTING CARD I'VE EVER SEEN!
WELL?
PERFECT.

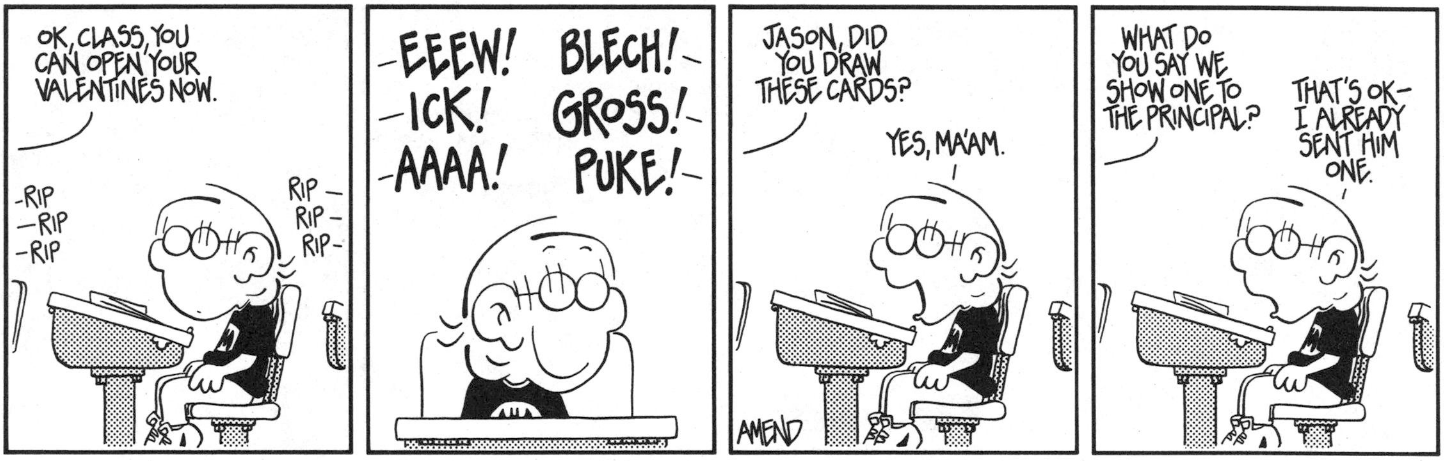
OK, CLASS, YOU CAN OPEN YOUR VALENTINES NOW.
-RIP -RIP -RIP
RIP- RIP- RIP-
EEEW! ICK! AAAA!
BLECH! GROSS! PUKE!
JASON, DID YOU DRAW THESE CARDS?
YES, MA'AM.
AMEND
WHAT DO YOU SAY WE SHOW ONE TO THE PRINCIPAL?
THAT'S OK—I ALREADY SENT HIM ONE.

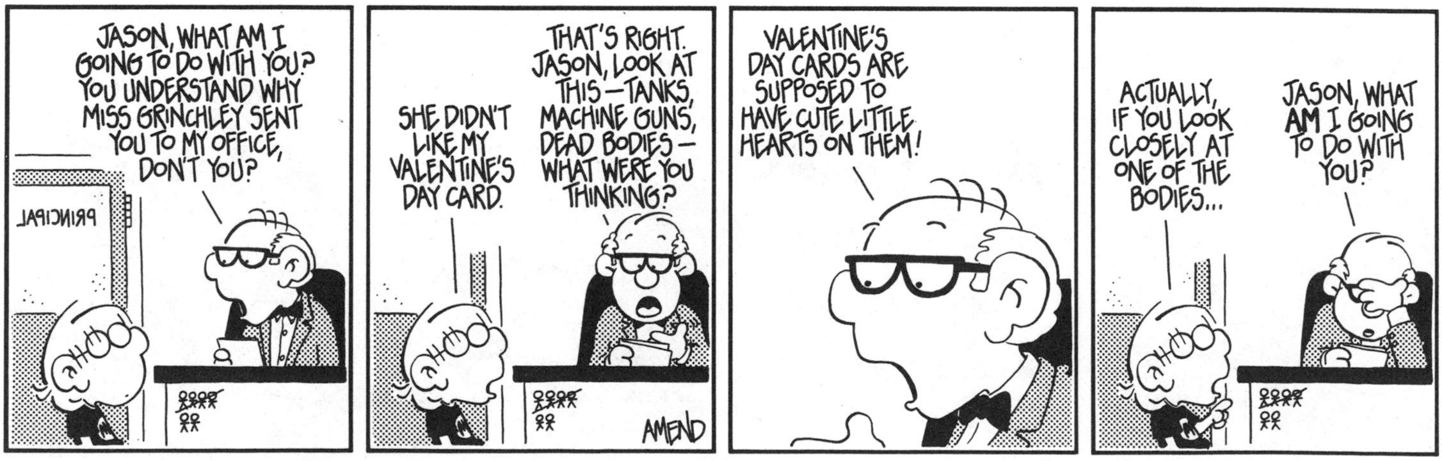
JASON, WHAT AM I GOING TO DO WITH YOU? YOU UNDERSTAND WHY MISS GRINCHLEY SENT YOU TO MY OFFICE, DON'T YOU?
SHE DIDN'T LIKE MY VALENTINE'S DAY CARD.
THAT'S RIGHT. JASON, LOOK AT THIS—TANKS, MACHINE GUNS, DEAD BODIES—WHAT WERE YOU THINKING?
AMEND
VALENTINE'S DAY CARDS ARE SUPPOSED TO HAVE CUTE LITTLE HEARTS ON THEM!
ACTUALLY, IF YOU LOOK CLOSELY AT ONE OF THE BODIES...
JASON, WHAT AM I GOING TO DO WITH YOU?

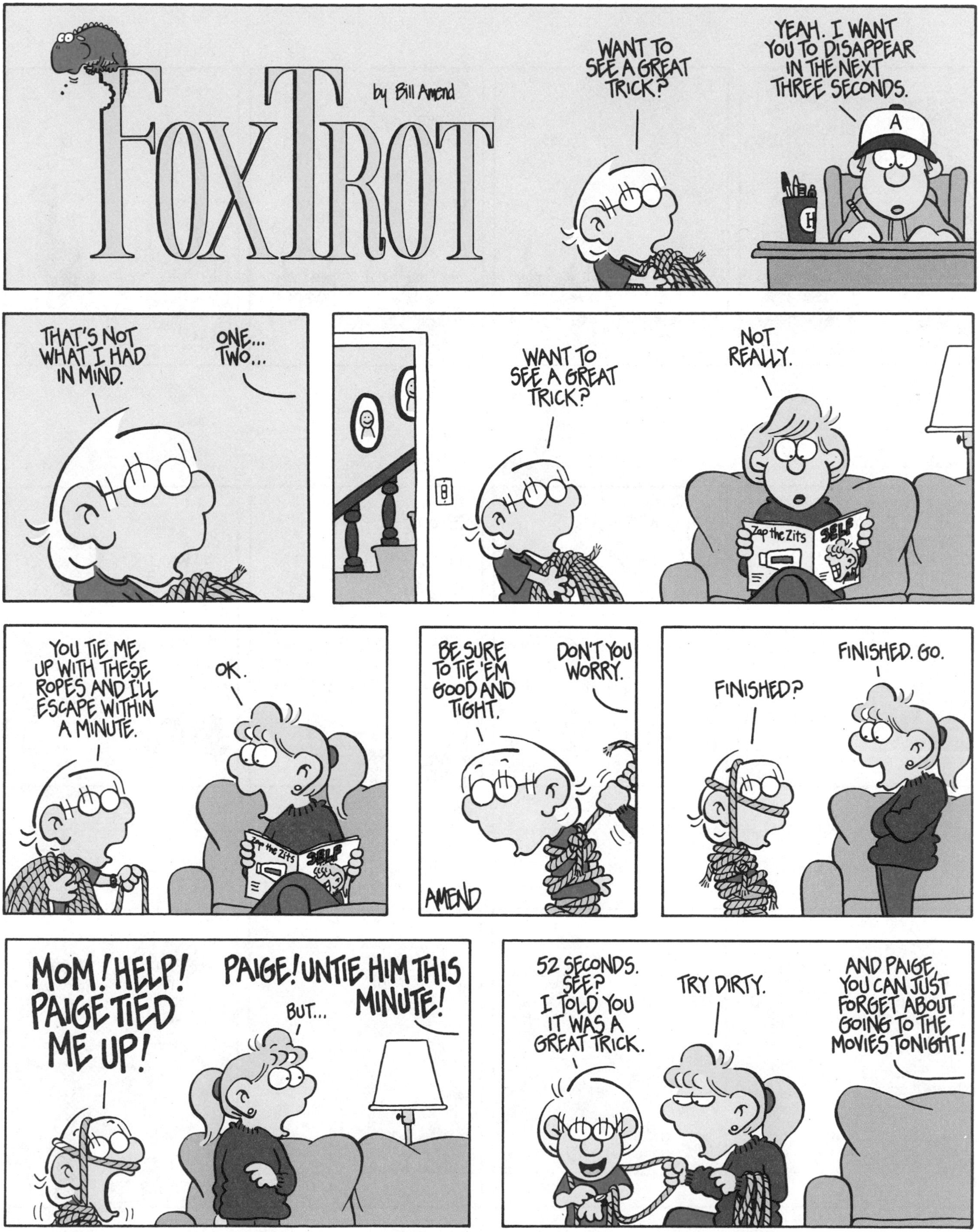
FoxTrot
by Bill Amend
WANT TO SEE A GREAT TRICK?
YEAH. I WANT YOU TO DISAPPEAR IN THE NEXT THREE SECONDS.
THAT'S NOT WHAT I HAD IN MIND.
ONE... TWO...
WANT TO SEE A GREAT TRICK?
NOT REALLY.
Zap the Zits
SELF
YOU TIE ME UP WITH THESE ROPES AND I'LL ESCAPE WITHIN A MINUTE.
OK.
BE SURE TO TIE 'EM GOOD AND TIGHT.
DON'T YOU WORRY.
AMEND
FINISHED?
FINISHED. GO.
MOM! HELP! PAIGE TIED ME UP!
PAIGE! UNTIE HIM THIS MINUTE!
BUT...
52 SECONDS. SEE? I TOLD YOU IT WAS A GREAT TRICK.
TRY DIRTY.
AND PAIGE, YOU CAN JUST FORGET ABOUT GOING TO THE MOVIES TONIGHT!

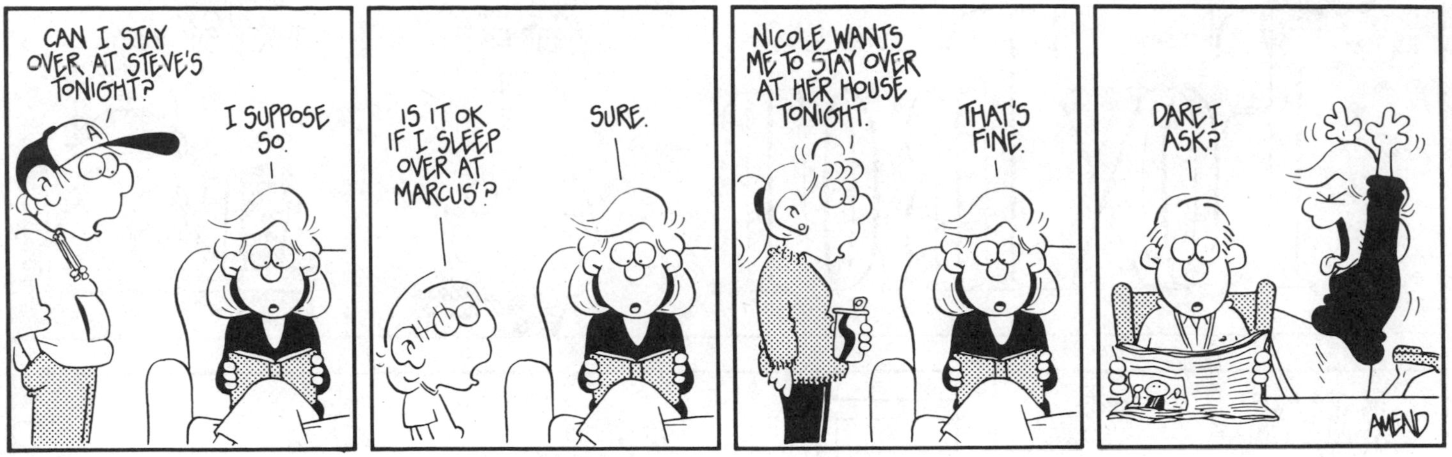
CAN I STAY OVER AT STEVE'S TONIGHT?
I SUPPOSE SO.
IS IT OK IF I SLEEP OVER AT MARCUS'?
SURE.
NICOLE WANTS ME TO STAY OVER AT HER HOUSE TONIGHT.
THAT'S FINE.
DARE I ASK?
AMEND

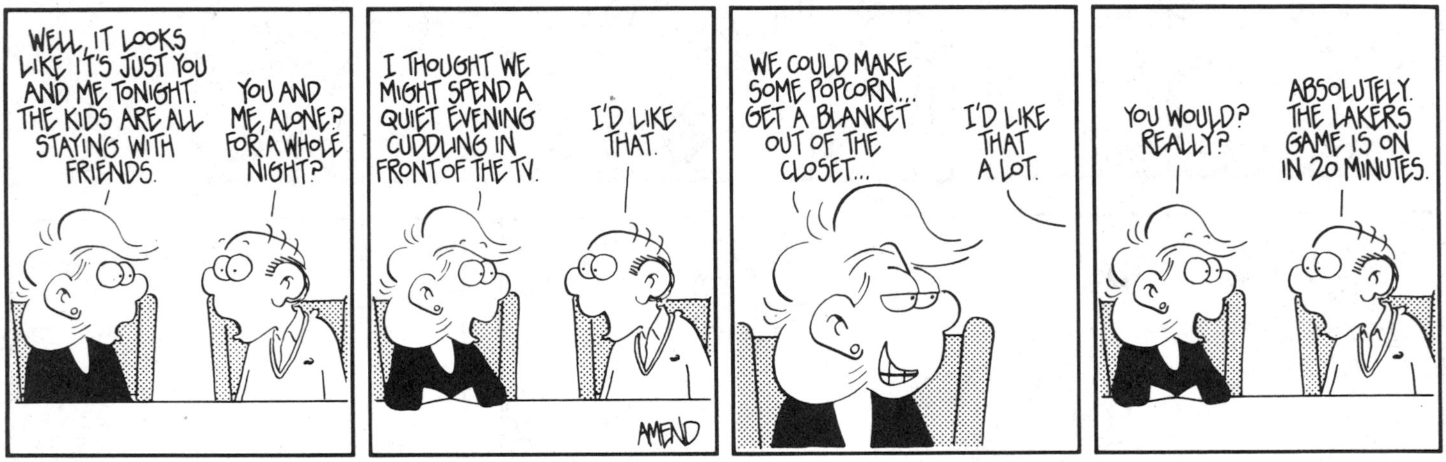
WELL, IT LOOKS LIKE IT'S JUST YOU AND ME TONIGHT. THE KIDS ARE ALL STAYING WITH FRIENDS.
YOU AND ME, ALONE? FOR A WHOLE NIGHT?
I THOUGHT WE MIGHT SPEND A QUIET EVENING CUDDLING IN FRONT OF THE TV.
I'D LIKE THAT.
AMEND
WE COULD MAKE SOME POPCORN... GET A BLANKET OUT OF THE CLOSET...
I'D LIKE THAT A LOT.
YOU WOULD? REALLY?
ABSOLUTELY. THE LAKERS GAME IS ON IN 20 MINUTES.

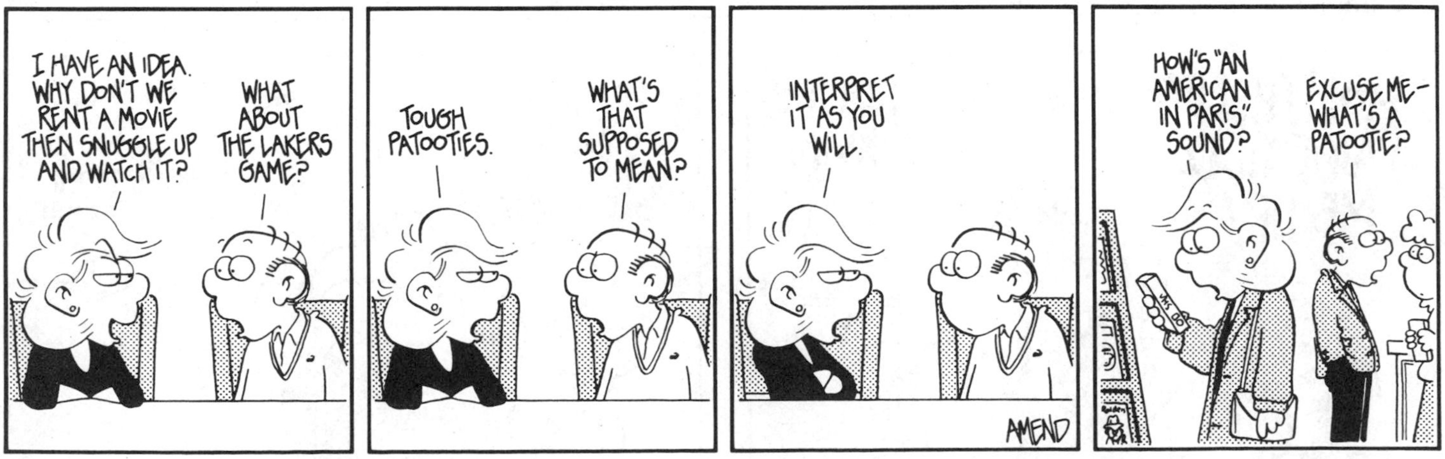
I HAVE AN IDEA. WHY DON'T WE RENT A MOVIE THEN SNUGGLE UP AND WATCH IT?
WHAT ABOUT THE LAKERS GAME?
TOUGH PATOOTIES.
WHAT'S THAT SUPPOSED TO MEAN?
INTERPRET IT AS YOU WILL.
AMEND
HOW'S "AN AMERICAN IN PARIS" SOUND?
EXCUSE ME-WHAT'S A PATOOTIE?

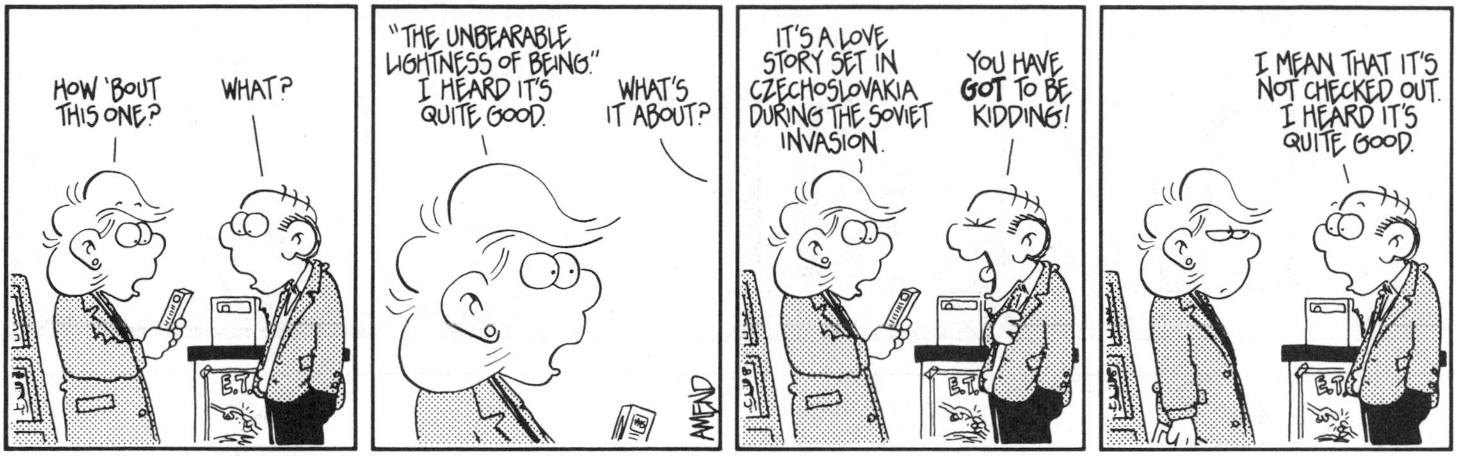
HOW 'BOUT THIS ONE?
WHAT?
"THE UNBEARABLE LIGHTNESS OF BEING." I HEARD IT'S QUITE GOOD.
WHAT'S IT ABOUT?
IT'S A LOVE STORY SET IN CZECHOSLOVAKIA DURING THE SOVIET INVASION.
YOU HAVE **GOT** TO BE KIDDING!
I MEAN THAT IT'S NOT CHECKED OUT. I HEARD IT'S QUITE GOOD.
E.T.
AMEND

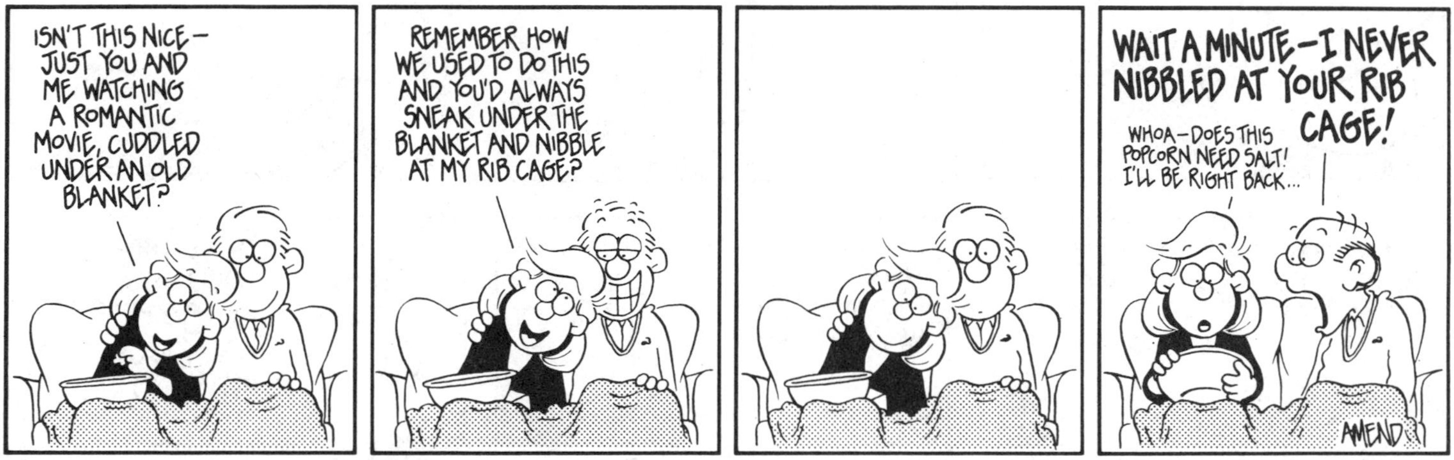
ISN'T THIS NICE— JUST YOU AND ME WATCHING A ROMANTIC MOVIE, CUDDLED UNDER AN OLD BLANKET?
REMEMBER HOW WE USED TO DO THIS AND YOU'D ALWAYS SNEAK UNDER THE BLANKET AND NIBBLE AT MY RIB CAGE?
WAIT A MINUTE—I NEVER NIBBLED AT YOUR RIB CAGE!
WHOA—DOES THIS POPCORN NEED SALT! I'LL BE RIGHT BACK...
AMEND

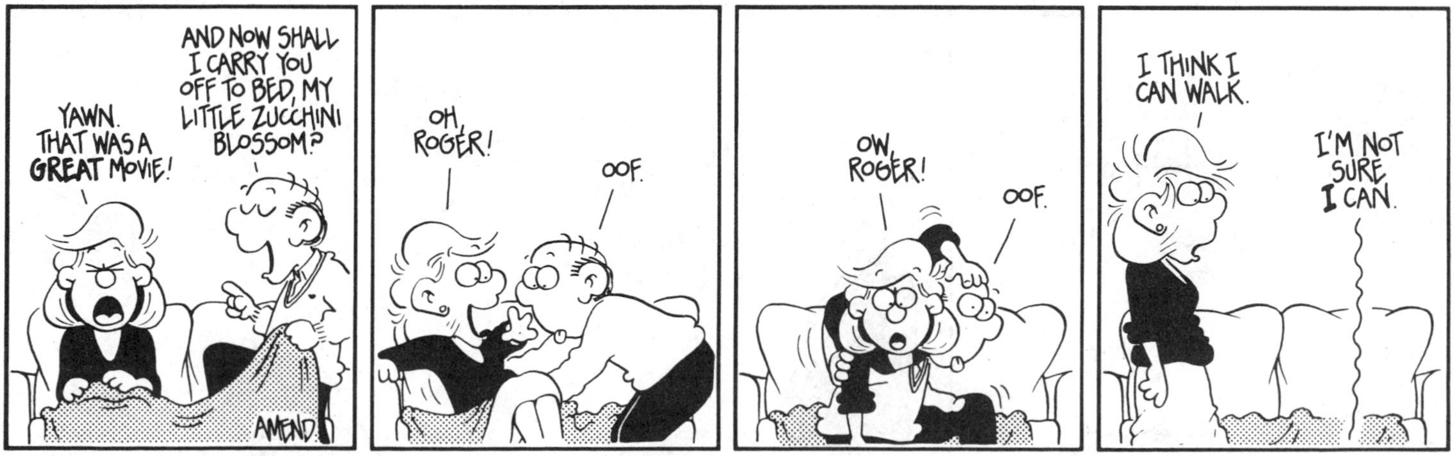
YAWN. THAT WAS A **GREAT** MOVIE!
AND NOW SHALL I CARRY YOU OFF TO BED, MY LITTLE ZUCCHINI BLOSSOM?
AMEND
OH, ROGER!
OOF.
OW, ROGER!
OOF.
I THINK I CAN WALK.
I'M NOT SURE **I** CAN.

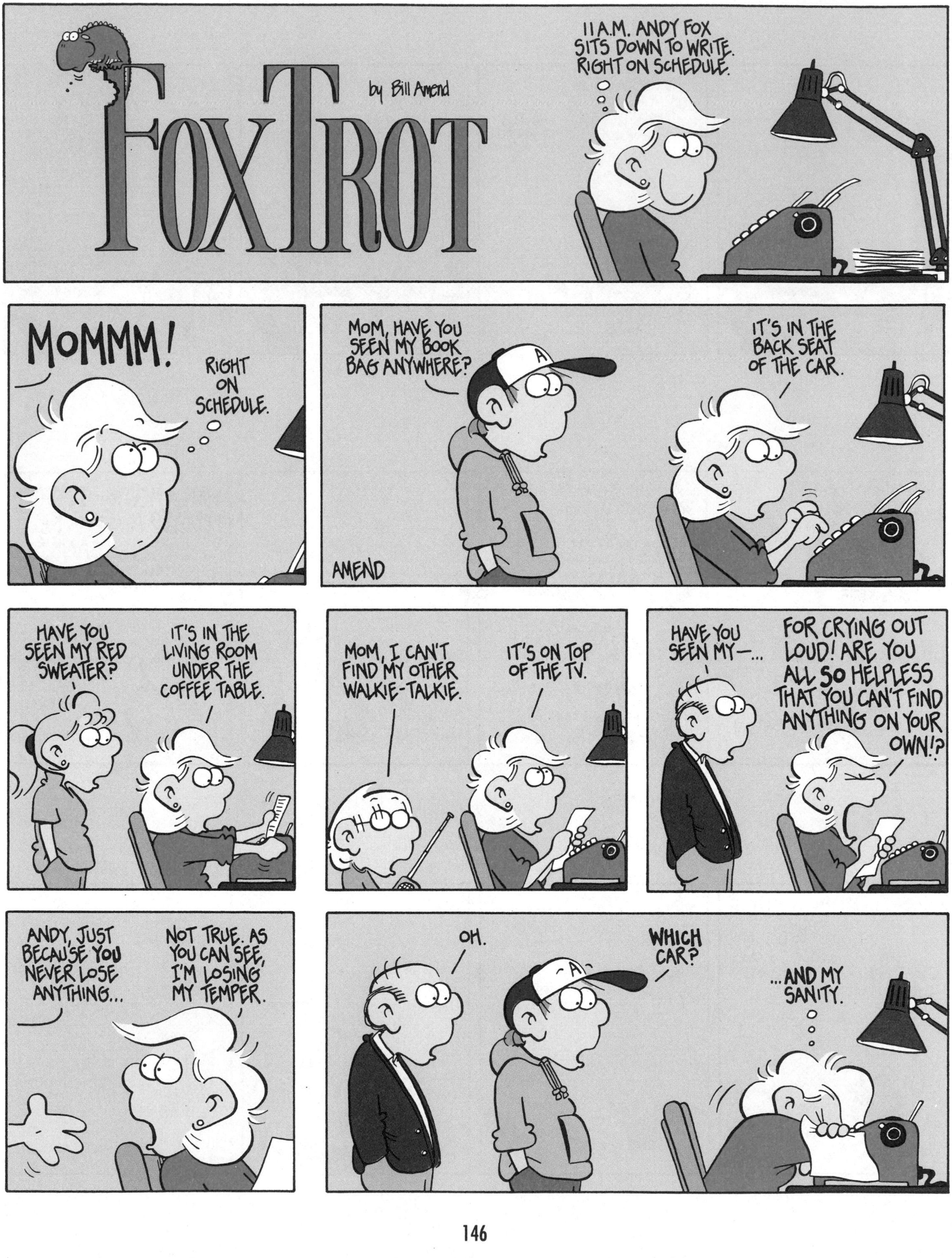
FoxTrot
by Bill Amend
11 A.M. ANDY FOX SITS DOWN TO WRITE. RIGHT ON SCHEDULE.
MOMMM!
RIGHT ON SCHEDULE.
MOM, HAVE YOU SEEN MY BOOK BAG ANYWHERE?
IT'S IN THE BACK SEAT OF THE CAR.
AMEND
HAVE YOU SEEN MY RED SWEATER?
IT'S IN THE LIVING ROOM UNDER THE COFFEE TABLE.
MOM, I CAN'T FIND MY OTHER WALKIE-TALKIE.
IT'S ON TOP OF THE TV.
HAVE YOU SEEN MY—...
FOR CRYING OUT LOUD! ARE YOU ALL SO HELPLESS THAT YOU CAN'T FIND ANYTHING ON YOUR OWN!?
ANDY, JUST BECAUSE YOU NEVER LOSE ANYTHING...
NOT TRUE. AS YOU CAN SEE, I'M LOSING MY TEMPER.
OH.
WHICH CAR?
...AND MY SANITY.

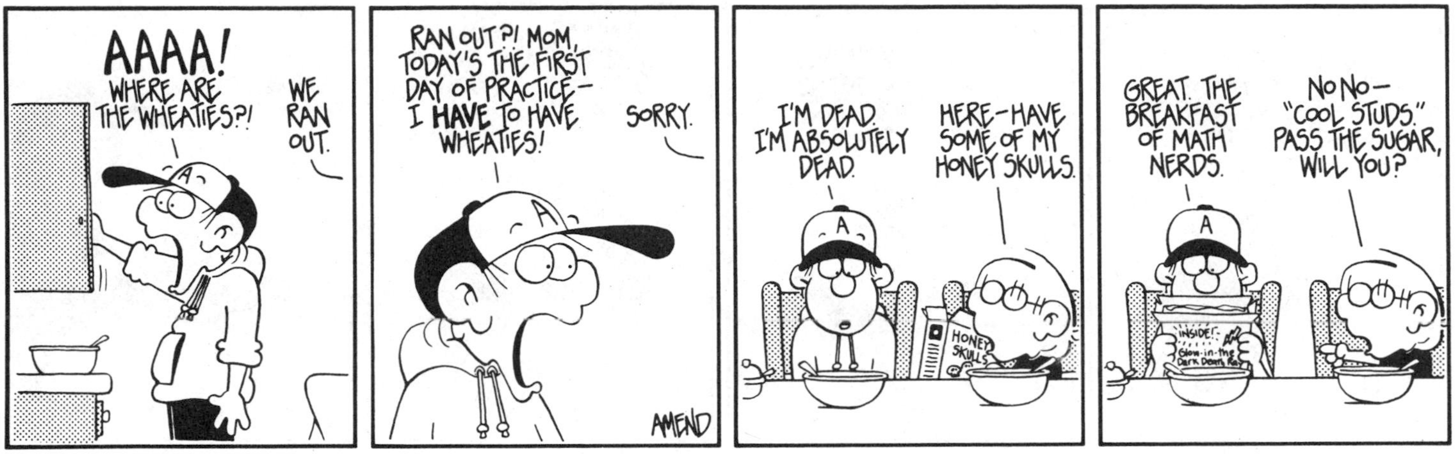
AAAA! WHERE ARE THE WHEATIES?!
WE RAN OUT.
RAN OUT?! MOM, TODAY'S THE FIRST DAY OF PRACTICE– I **HAVE** TO HAVE WHEATIES!
SORRY.
AMEND
I'M DEAD. I'M ABSOLUTELY DEAD.
HERE–HAVE SOME OF MY HONEY SKULLS.
HONEY SKULLS
GREAT. THE BREAKFAST OF MATH NERDS.
No No– "COOL STUDS." PASS THE SUGAR, WILL YOU?
INSIDE! Glow-in-the-Dark Death Ray

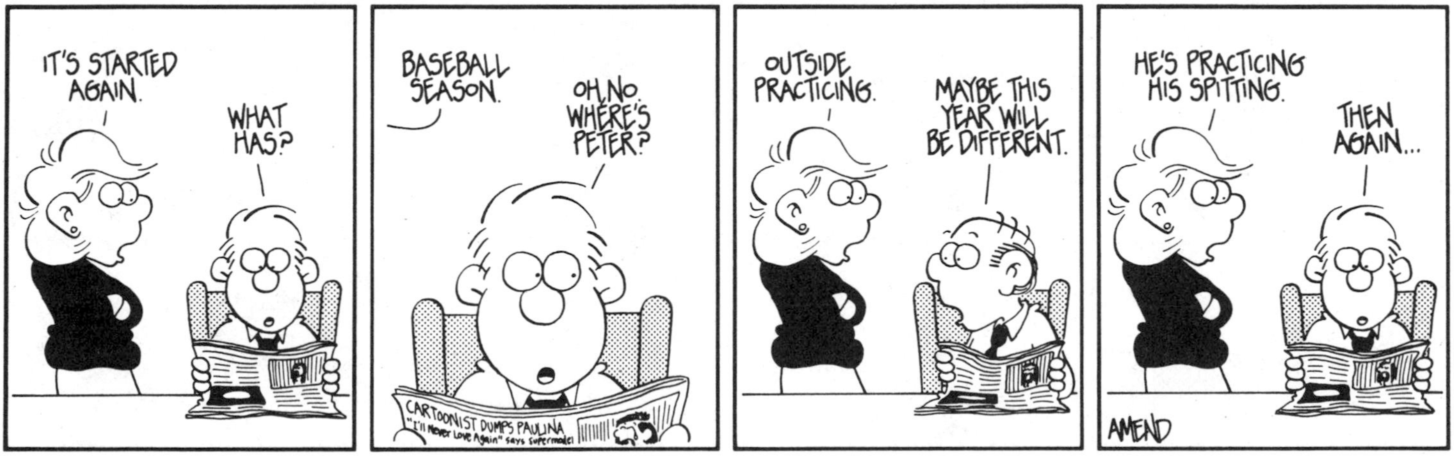
IT'S STARTED AGAIN.
WHAT HAS?
BASEBALL SEASON.
OH NO. WHERE'S PETER?
CARTOONIST DUMPS PAULINA
"I'll Never Love Again" says supermodel
OUTSIDE PRACTICING.
MAYBE THIS YEAR WILL BE DIFFERENT.
HE'S PRACTICING HIS SPITTING.
THEN AGAIN...
AMEND

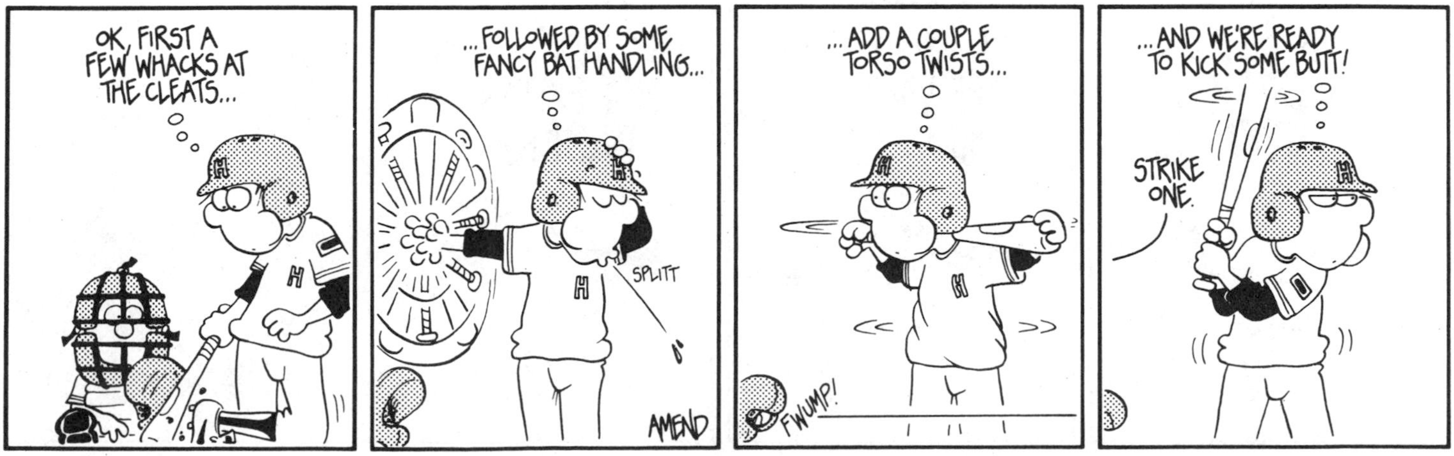
OK, FIRST A FEW WHACKS AT THE CLEATS...
...FOLLOWED BY SOME FANCY BAT HANDLING...
SPLITT
AMEND
...ADD A COUPLE TORSO TWISTS...
FWUMP!
...AND WE'RE READY TO KICK SOME BUTT!
STRIKE ONE.

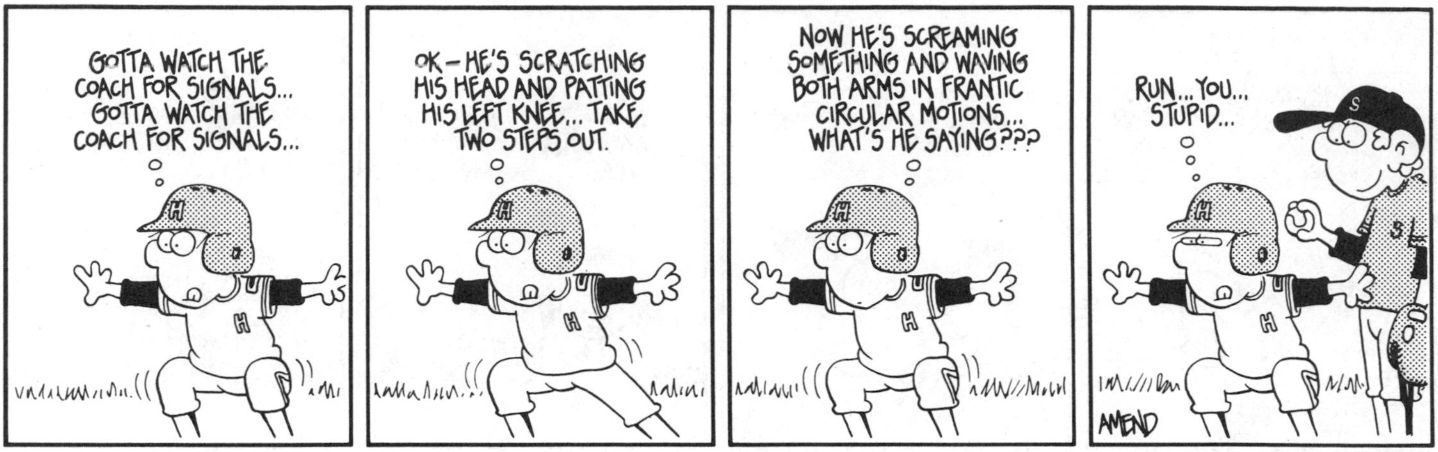
GOTTA WATCH THE COACH FOR SIGNALS... GOTTA WATCH THE COACH FOR SIGNALS...
OK – HE'S SCRATCHING HIS HEAD AND PATTING HIS LEFT KNEE... TAKE TWO STEPS OUT.
NOW HE'S SCREAMING SOMETHING AND WAVING BOTH ARMS IN FRANTIC CIRCULAR MOTIONS... WHAT'S HE SAYING???
RUN... YOU... STUPID...
AMEND

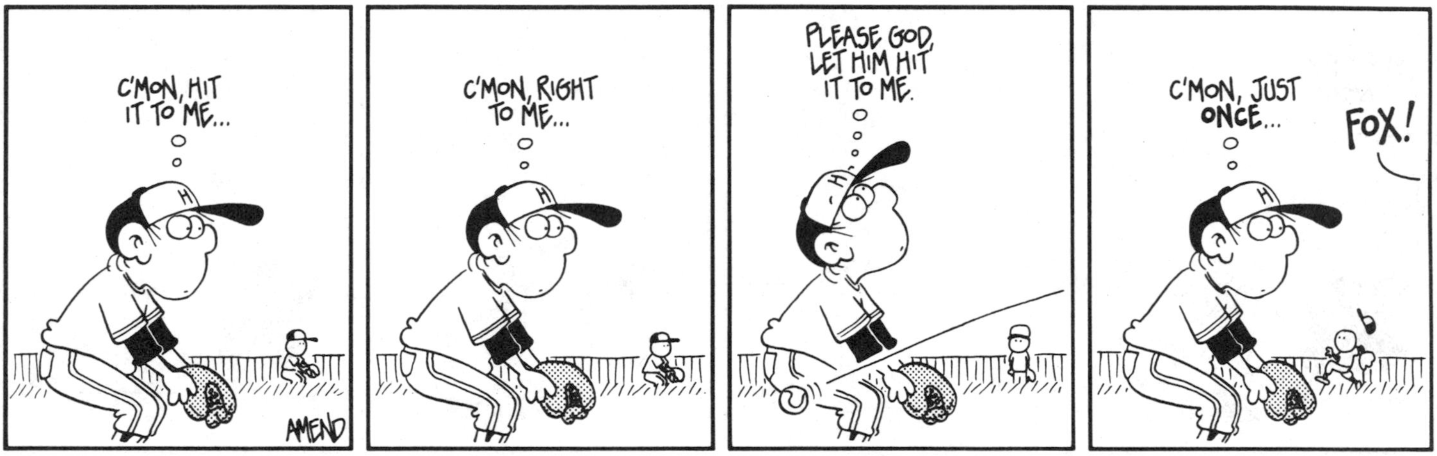
C'MON, HIT IT TO ME...
AMEND
C'MON, RIGHT TO ME...
PLEASE GOD LET HIM HIT IT TO ME.
C'MON, JUST ONCE...
FOX!

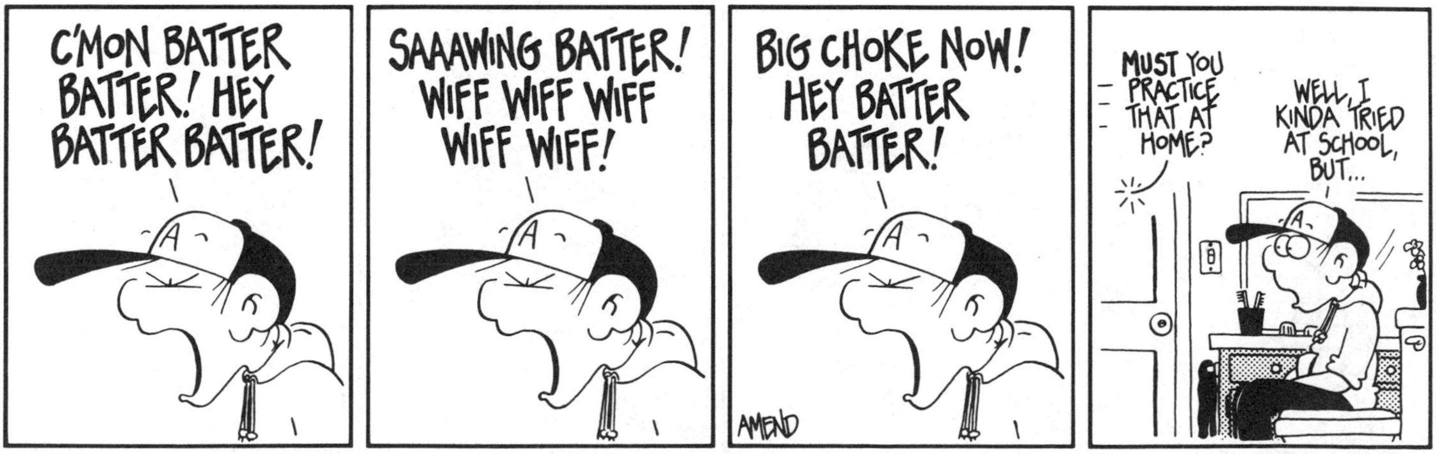
C'MON BATTER BATTER! HEY BATTER BATTER!
SAAAWING BATTER! WIFF WIFF WIFF WIFF WIFF!
BIG CHOKE NOW! HEY BATTER BATTER!
AMEND
MUST YOU PRACTICE THAT AT HOME?
WELL, I KINDA TRIED AT SCHOOL, BUT...

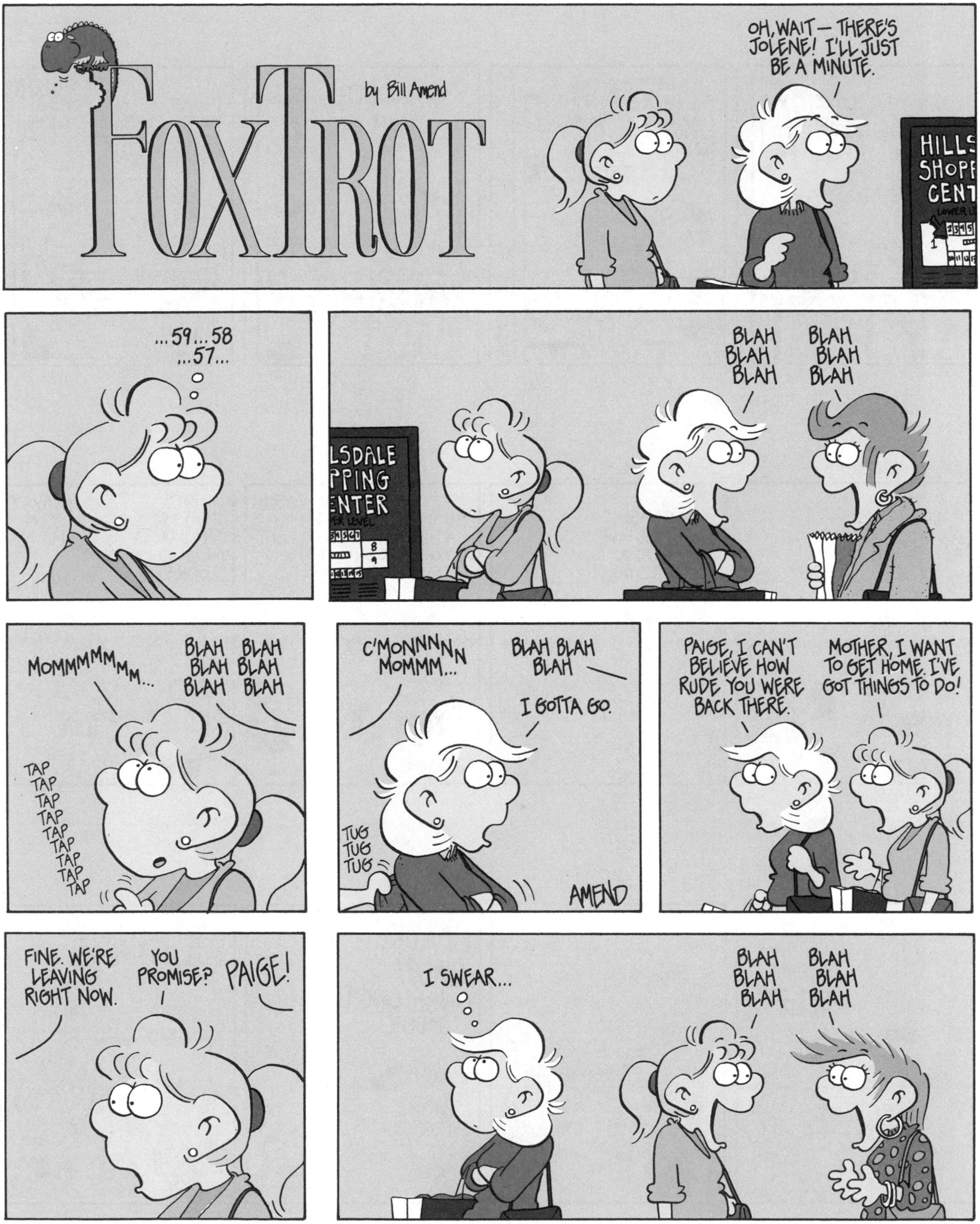
FoxTrot
by Bill Amend
OH, WAIT — THERE'S JOLENE! I'LL JUST BE A MINUTE.
HILLS SHOPP CENT
...59...58 ...57...
LSDALE PPING ENTER
BLAH BLAH BLAH
BLAH BLAH BLAH
MOMMMMMMM...
BLAH BLAH BLAH BLAH BLAH BLAH
TAP TAP TAP TAP TAP TAP TAP TAP TAP
C'MONNNNN MOMMM...
BLAH BLAH BLAH
I GOTTA GO.
TUG TUG TUG
AMEND
PAIGE, I CAN'T BELIEVE HOW RUDE YOU WERE BACK THERE.
MOTHER, I WANT TO GET HOME. I'VE GOT THINGS TO DO!
FINE. WE'RE LEAVING RIGHT NOW.
YOU PROMISE?
PAIGE!
I SWEAR...
BLAH BLAH BLAH
BLAH BLAH BLAH

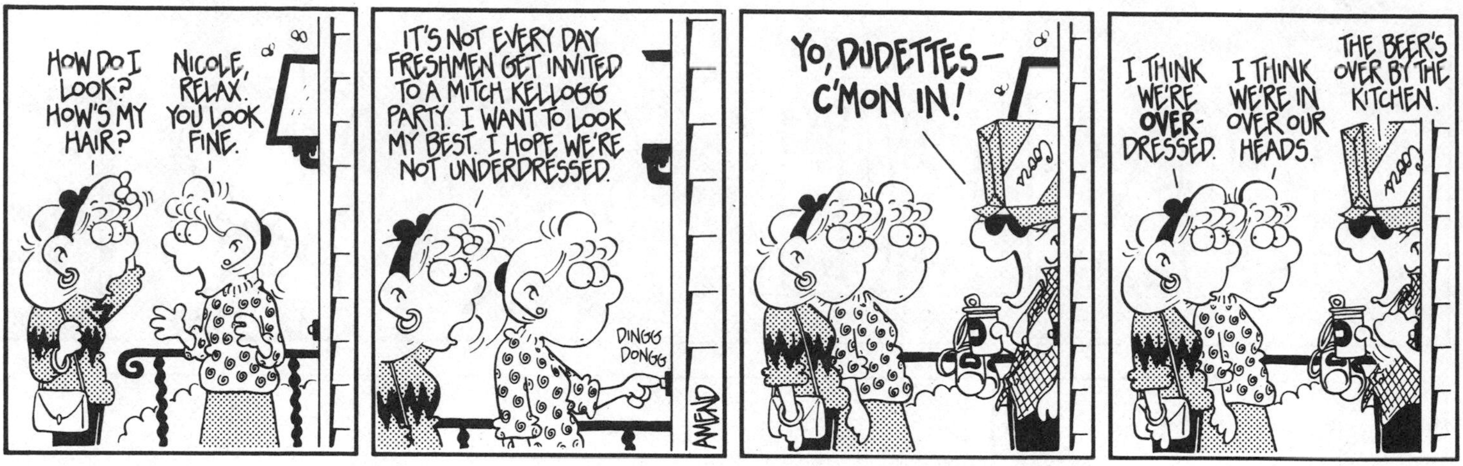
HOW DO I LOOK? HOW'S MY HAIR?
NICOLE, RELAX. YOU LOOK FINE.
IT'S NOT EVERY DAY FRESHMEN GET INVITED TO A MITCH KELLOGG PARTY. I WANT TO LOOK MY BEST. I HOPE WE'RE NOT UNDERDRESSED.
DINGG DONGG
AMEND
YO, DUDETTES–C'MON IN!
I THINK WE'RE **OVER**-DRESSED.
I THINK WE'RE IN OVER OUR HEADS.
THE BEER'S OVER BY THE KITCHEN.

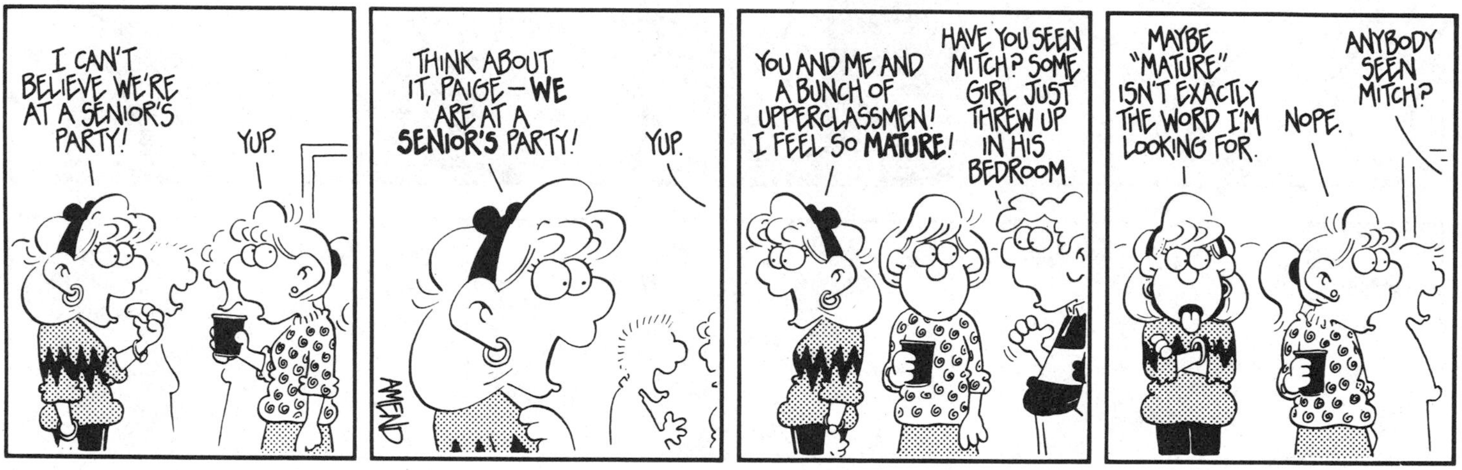
I CAN'T BELIEVE WE'RE AT A SENIOR'S PARTY!
YUP.
THINK ABOUT IT, PAIGE–**WE** ARE AT A **SENIOR'S** PARTY!
YUP.
AMEND
YOU AND ME AND A BUNCH OF UPPERCLASSMEN! I FEEL SO **MATURE**!
HAVE YOU SEEN MITCH? SOME GIRL JUST THREW UP IN HIS BEDROOM.
MAYBE "MATURE" ISN'T EXACTLY THE WORD I'M LOOKING FOR.
NOPE.
ANYBODY SEEN MITCH?

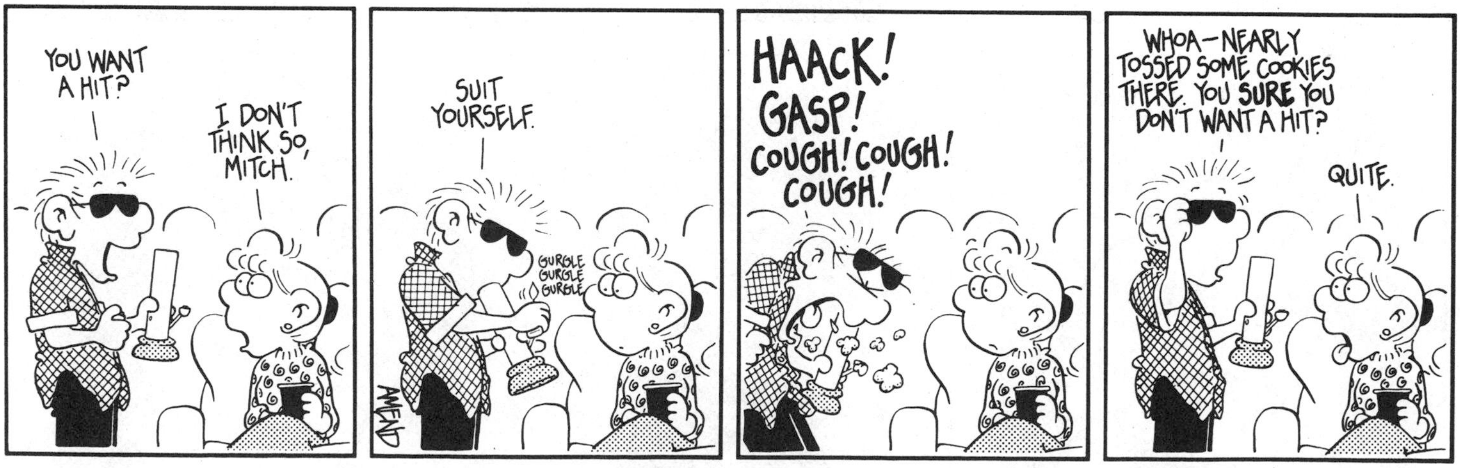
YOU WANT A HIT?
I DON'T THINK SO, MITCH.
SUIT YOURSELF.
GURGLE GURGLE GURGLE
AMEND
HAACK! GASP! COUGH! COUGH! COUGH!
WHOA–NEARLY TOSSED SOME COOKIES THERE. YOU **SURE** YOU DON'T WANT A HIT?
QUITE.

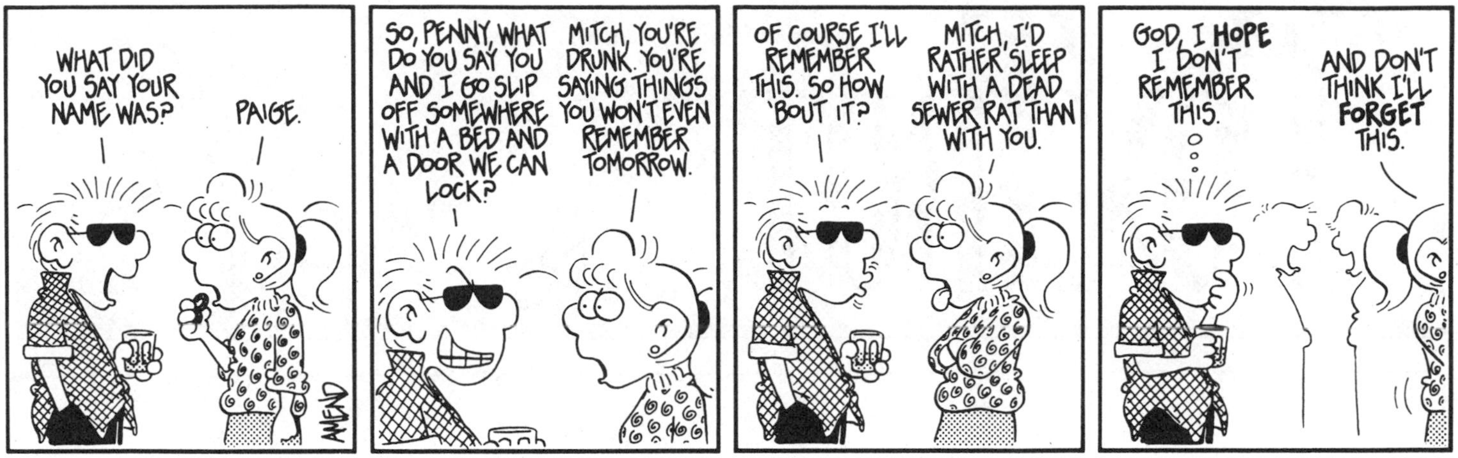
WHAT DID YOU SAY YOUR NAME WAS?
PAIGE.
AMEND
SO, PENNY, WHAT DO YOU SAY YOU AND I GO SLIP OFF SOMEWHERE WITH A BED AND A DOOR WE CAN LOCK?
MITCH, YOU'RE DRUNK. YOU'RE SAYING THINGS YOU WON'T EVEN REMEMBER TOMORROW.
OF COURSE I'LL REMEMBER THIS. SO HOW 'BOUT IT?
MITCH, I'D RATHER SLEEP WITH A DEAD SEWER RAT THAN WITH YOU.
GOD, I **HOPE** I DON'T REMEMBER THIS.
AND DON'T THINK I'LL **FORGET** THIS.

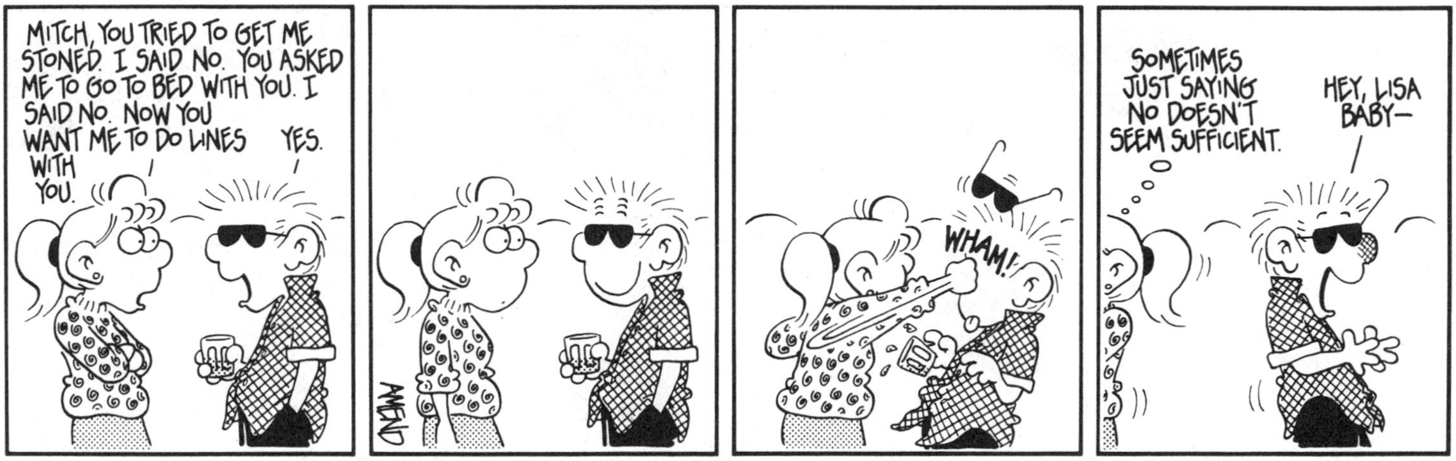
MITCH, YOU TRIED TO GET ME STONED. I SAID NO. YOU ASKED ME TO GO TO BED WITH YOU. I SAID NO. NOW YOU WANT ME TO DO LINES WITH YOU.
YES.
AMEND
WHAM!
SOMETIMES JUST SAYING NO DOESN'T SEEM SUFFICIENT.
HEY, LISA BABY—

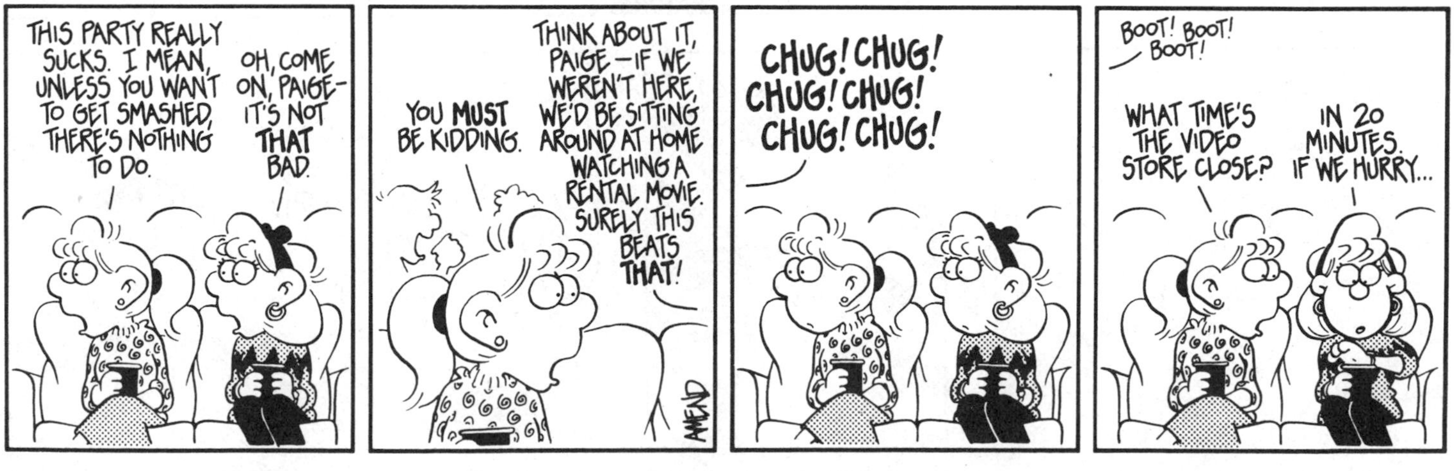
THIS PARTY REALLY SUCKS. I MEAN, UNLESS YOU WANT TO GET SMASHED, THERE'S NOTHING TO DO.
OH, COME ON, PAIGE- IT'S NOT **THAT** BAD.
YOU **MUST** BE KIDDING.
THINK ABOUT IT, PAIGE—IF WE WEREN'T HERE, WE'D BE SITTING AROUND AT HOME WATCHING A RENTAL MOVIE. SURELY THIS BEATS **THAT**!
AMEND
CHUG! CHUG! CHUG! CHUG! CHUG! CHUG!
BOOT! BOOT! BOOT!
WHAT TIME'S THE VIDEO STORE CLOSE?
IN 20 MINUTES. IF WE HURRY...

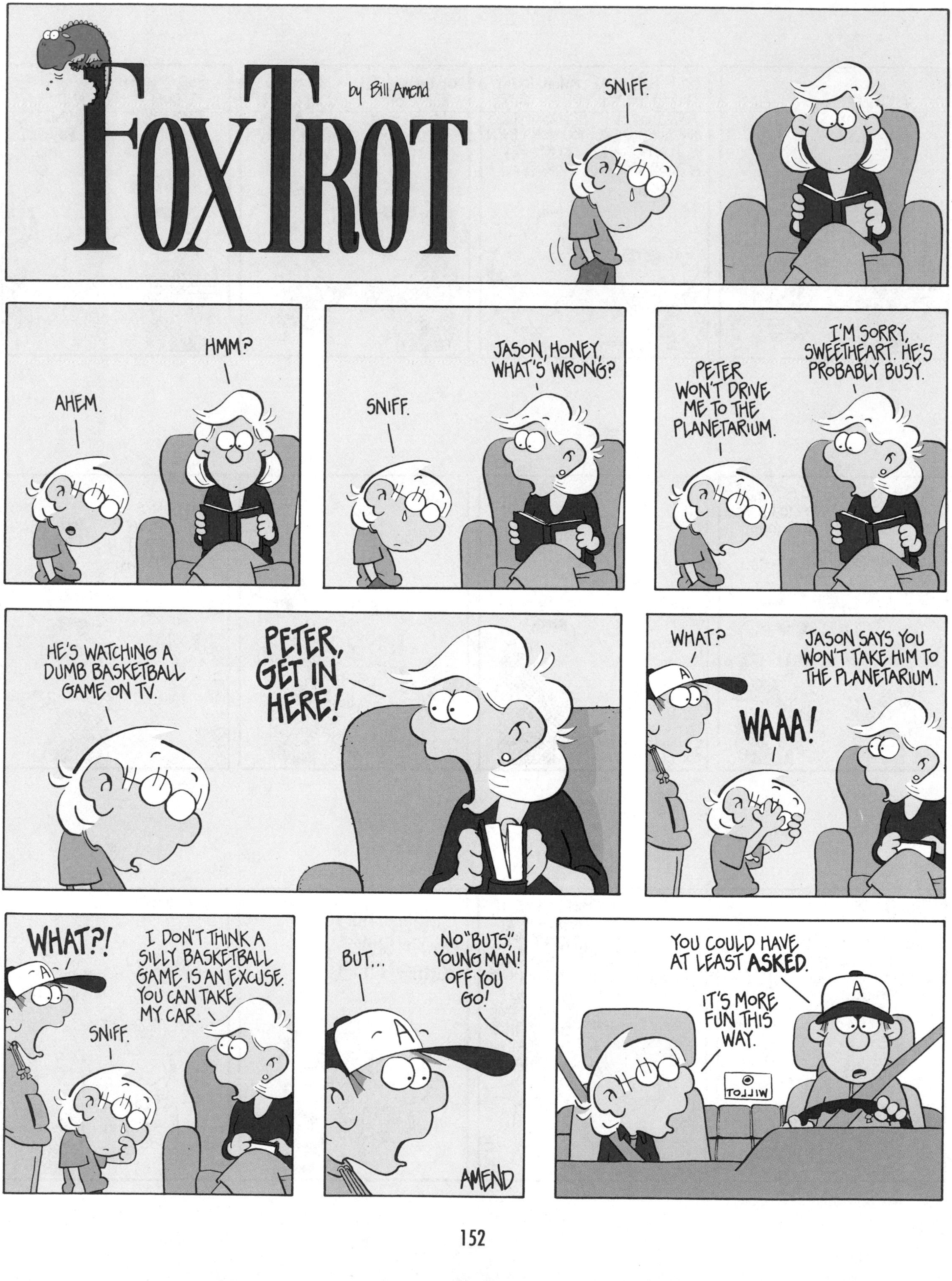

FOXTROT
by Bill Amend
SNIFF.
AHEM.
HMM?
SNIFF.
JASON, HONEY, WHAT'S WRONG?
PETER WON'T DRIVE ME TO THE PLANETARIUM.
I'M SORRY, SWEETHEART. HE'S PROBABLY BUSY.
HE'S WATCHING A DUMB BASKETBALL GAME ON TV.
PETER, GET IN HERE!
WHAT?
JASON SAYS YOU WON'T TAKE HIM TO THE PLANETARIUM.
WAAA!
WHAT?!
I DON'T THINK A SILLY BASKETBALL GAME IS AN EXCUSE. YOU CAN TAKE MY CAR.
SNIFF.
BUT...
NO "BUTS," YOUNG MAN! OFF YOU GO!
AMEND
YOU COULD HAVE AT LEAST **ASKED**.
IT'S MORE FUN THIS WAY.

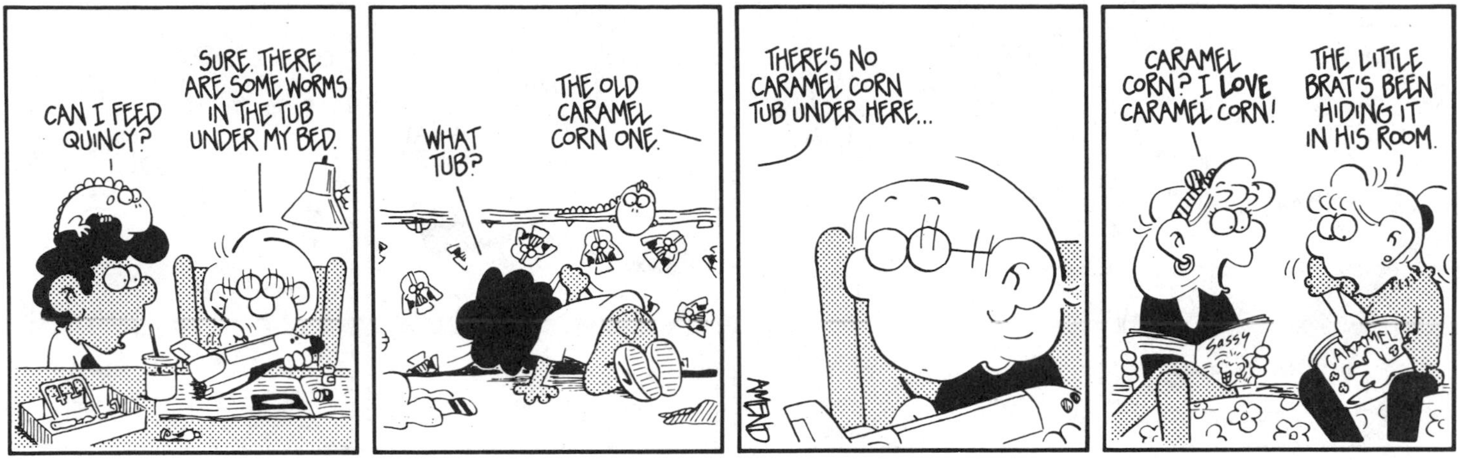
CAN I FEED QUINCY?
SURE. THERE ARE SOME WORMS IN THE TUB UNDER MY BED.
WHAT TUB?
THE OLD CARAMEL CORN ONE.
THERE'S NO CARAMEL CORN TUB UNDER HERE...
AMEND
CARAMEL CORN? I LOVE CARAMEL CORN!
THE LITTLE BRAT'S BEEN HIDING IT IN HIS ROOM.
SASSY
CARAMEL

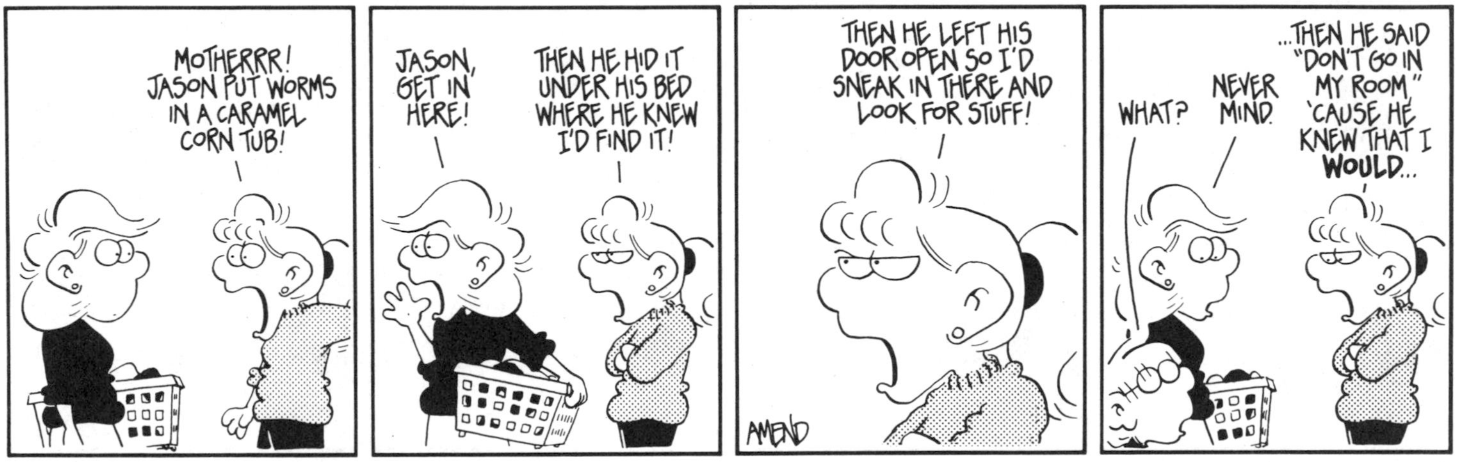
MOTHERRR! JASON PUT WORMS IN A CARAMEL CORN TUB!
JASON, GET IN HERE!
THEN HE HID IT UNDER HIS BED WHERE HE KNEW I'D FIND IT!
THEN HE LEFT HIS DOOR OPEN SO I'D SNEAK IN THERE AND LOOK FOR STUFF!
AMEND
WHAT?
NEVER MIND.
...THEN HE SAID "DON'T GO IN MY ROOM," 'CAUSE HE KNEW THAT I WOULD...

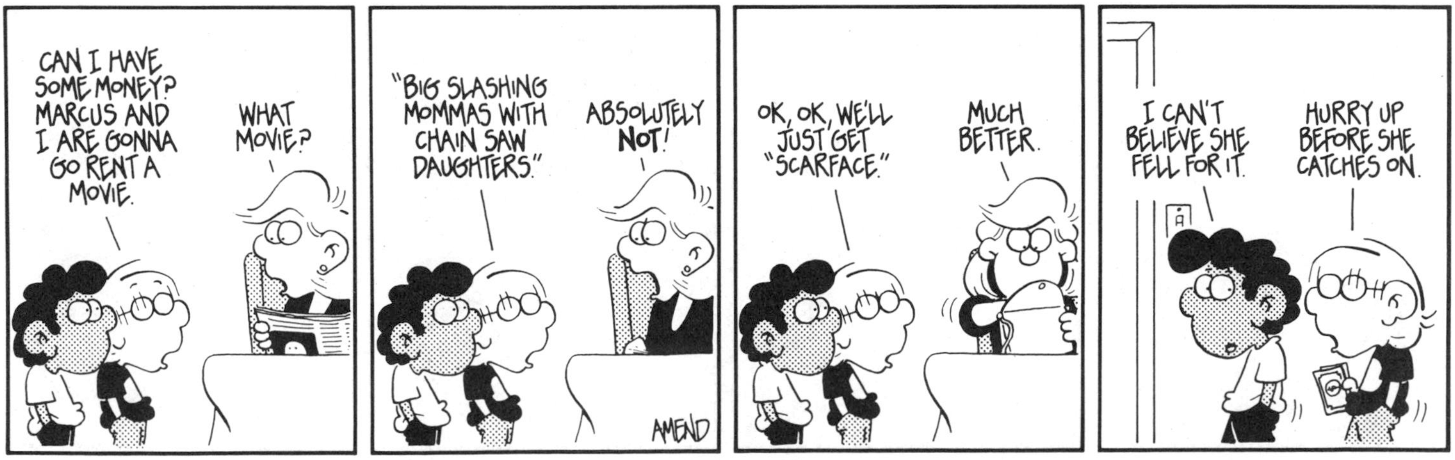
CAN I HAVE SOME MONEY? MARCUS AND I ARE GONNA GO RENT A MOVIE.
WHAT MOVIE?
"BIG SLASHING MOMMAS WITH CHAIN SAW DAUGHTERS."
ABSOLUTELY NOT!
AMEND
OK, OK, WE'LL JUST GET "SCARFACE."
MUCH BETTER.
I CAN'T BELIEVE SHE FELL FOR IT.
HURRY UP BEFORE SHE CATCHES ON.

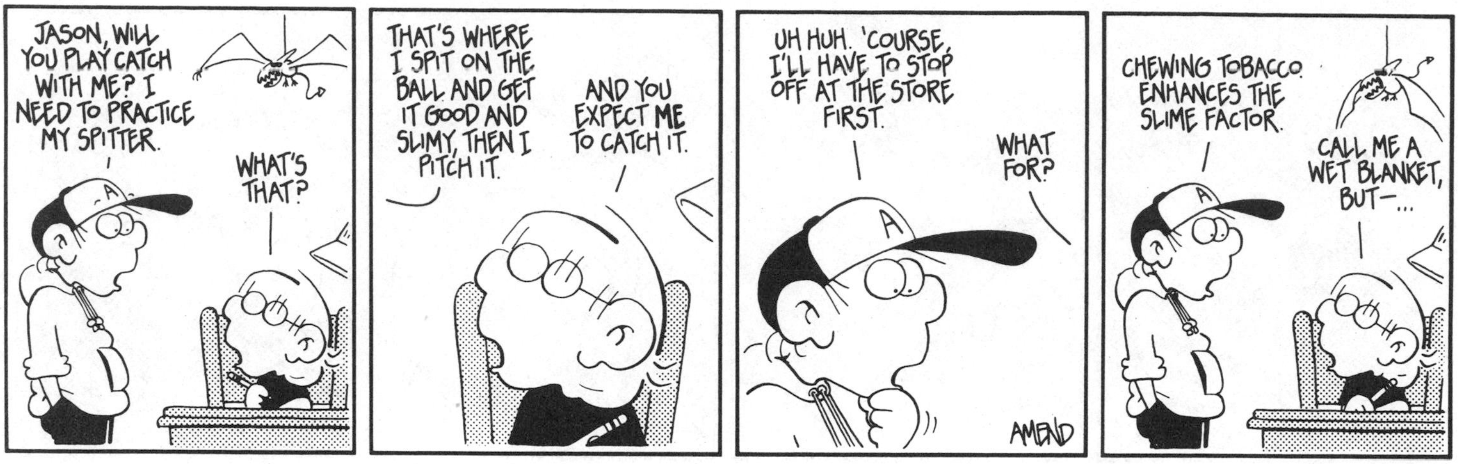
JASON, WILL YOU PLAY CATCH WITH ME? I NEED TO PRACTICE MY SPITTER.
WHAT'S THAT?
THAT'S WHERE I SPIT ON THE BALL AND GET IT GOOD AND SLIMY, THEN I PITCH IT.
AND YOU EXPECT ME TO CATCH IT.
UH HUH. 'COURSE, I'LL HAVE TO STOP OFF AT THE STORE FIRST.
WHAT FOR?
AMEND
CHEWING TOBACCO ENHANCES THE SLIME FACTOR.
CALL ME A WET BLANKET, BUT—...

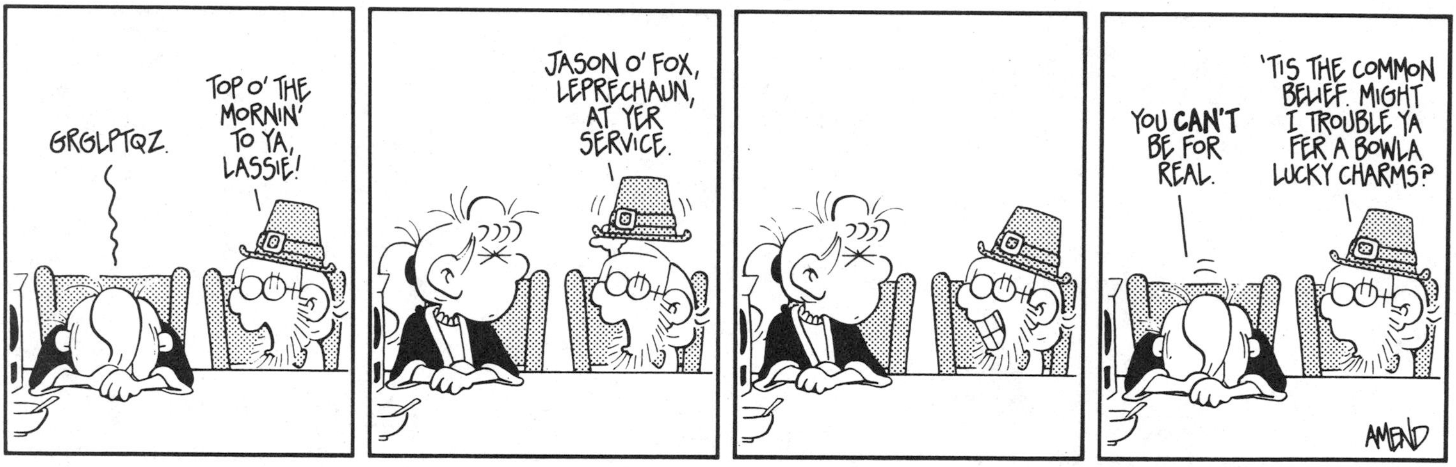
GRGLPTQZ.
TOP O' THE MORNIN' TO YA, LASSIE!
JASON O' FOX, LEPRECHAUN, AT YER SERVICE.
YOU CAN'T BE FOR REAL.
'TIS THE COMMON BELIEF. MIGHT I TROUBLE YA FER A BOWLA LUCKY CHARMS?
AMEND

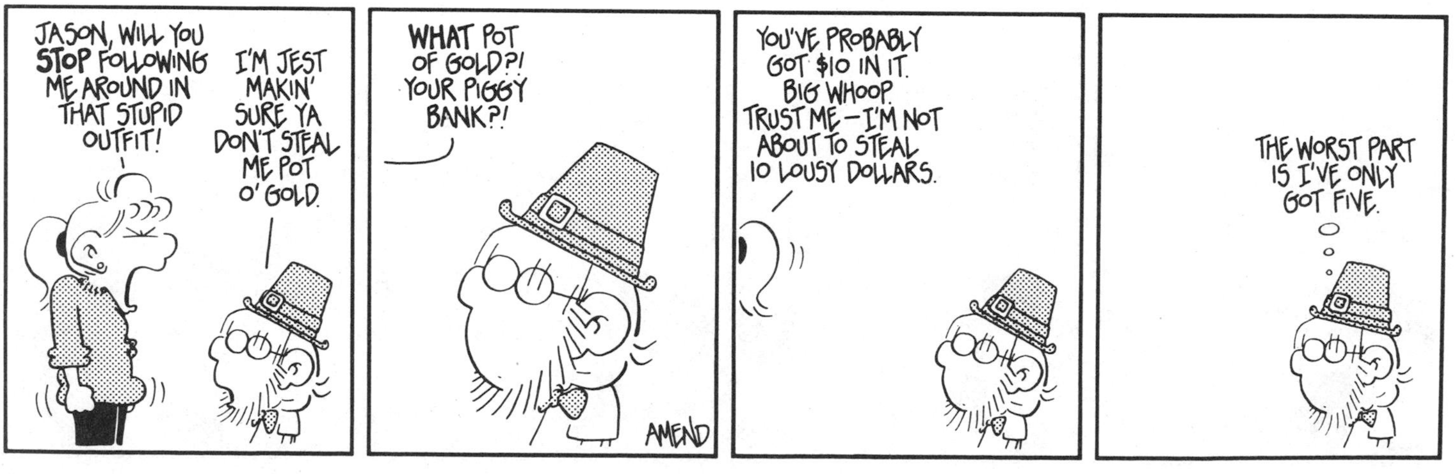
JASON, WILL YOU STOP FOLLOWING ME AROUND IN THAT STUPID OUTFIT!
I'M JEST MAKIN' SURE YA DON'T STEAL ME POT O' GOLD.
WHAT POT OF GOLD?! YOUR PIGGY BANK?!
AMEND
YOU'VE PROBABLY GOT $10 IN IT. BIG WHOOP. TRUST ME—I'M NOT ABOUT TO STEAL 10 LOUSY DOLLARS.
THE WORST PART IS I'VE ONLY GOT FIVE.

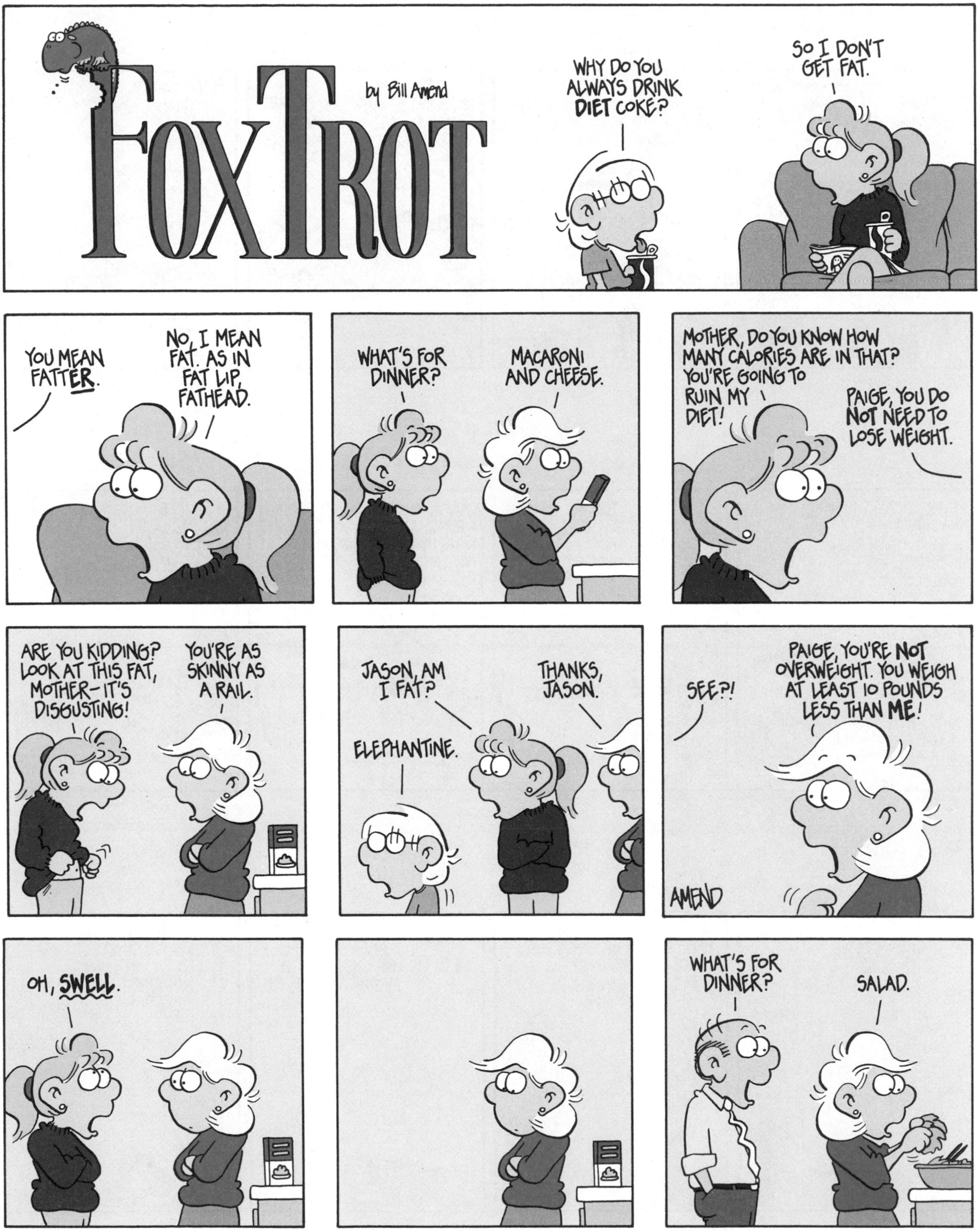
FoxTrot
by Bill Amend
WHY DO YOU ALWAYS DRINK DIET COKE?
SO I DON'T GET FAT.
YOU MEAN FATTER.
NO, I MEAN FAT. AS IN FAT LIP, FATHEAD.
WHAT'S FOR DINNER?
MACARONI AND CHEESE.
MOTHER, DO YOU KNOW HOW MANY CALORIES ARE IN THAT? YOU'RE GOING TO RUIN MY DIET!
PAIGE, YOU DO NOT NEED TO LOSE WEIGHT.
ARE YOU KIDDING? LOOK AT THIS FAT, MOTHER– IT'S DISGUSTING!
YOU'RE AS SKINNY AS A RAIL.
JASON, AM I FAT?
ELEPHANTINE.
THANKS, JASON.
SEE?!
PAIGE, YOU'RE NOT OVERWEIGHT. YOU WEIGH AT LEAST 10 POUNDS LESS THAN ME!
AMEND
OH, SWELL.
WHAT'S FOR DINNER?
SALAD.

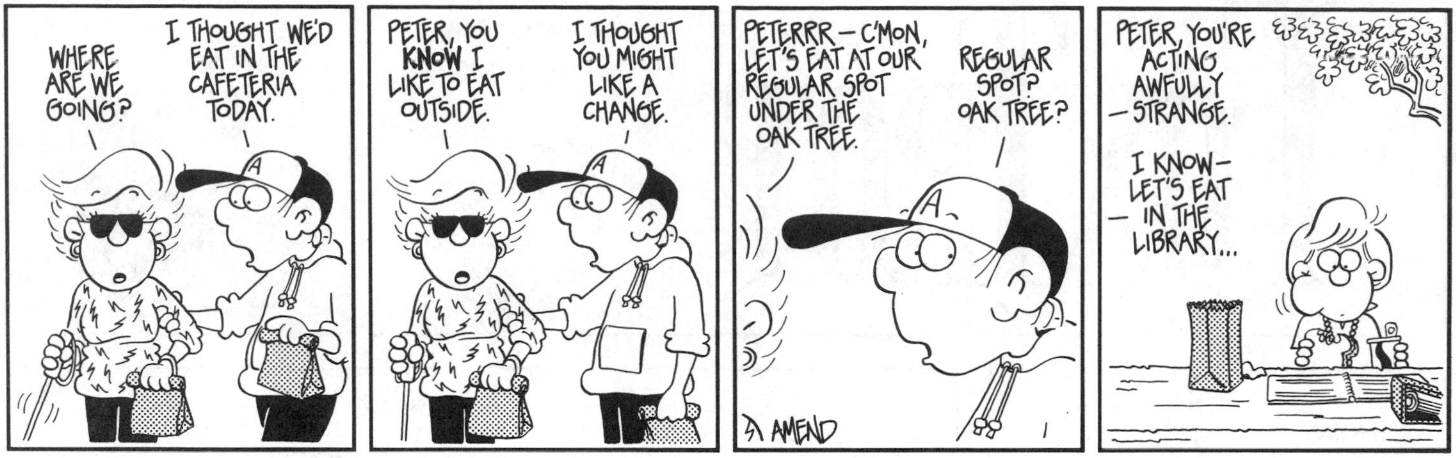
WHERE ARE WE GOING?
I THOUGHT WE'D EAT IN THE CAFETERIA TODAY.
PETER, YOU **KNOW** I LIKE TO EAT OUTSIDE.
I THOUGHT YOU MIGHT LIKE A CHANGE.
PETERRR — C'MON, LET'S EAT AT OUR REGULAR SPOT UNDER THE OAK TREE.
REGULAR SPOT? OAK TREE?
AMEND
PETER, YOU'RE ACTING AWFULLY — STRANGE.
I KNOW— LET'S EAT — IN THE LIBRARY...

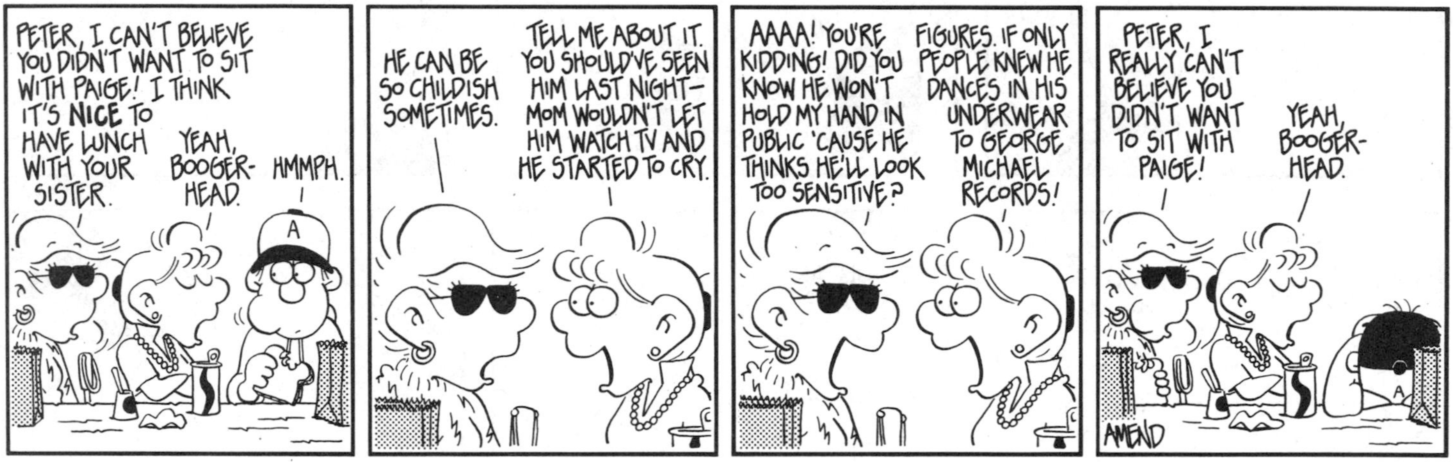
PETER, I CAN'T BELIEVE YOU DIDN'T WANT TO SIT WITH PAIGE! I THINK IT'S **NICE** TO HAVE LUNCH WITH YOUR SISTER.
YEAH, BOOGER-HEAD.
HMMPH.
HE CAN BE SO CHILDISH SOMETIMES.
TELL ME ABOUT IT. YOU SHOULD'VE SEEN HIM LAST NIGHT— MOM WOULDN'T LET HIM WATCH TV AND HE STARTED TO CRY.
AAAA! YOU'RE KIDDING! DID YOU KNOW HE WON'T HOLD MY HAND IN PUBLIC 'CAUSE HE THINKS HE'LL LOOK TOO SENSITIVE?
FIGURES. IF ONLY PEOPLE KNEW HE DANCES IN HIS UNDERWEAR TO GEORGE MICHAEL RECORDS!
PETER, I REALLY CAN'T BELIEVE YOU DIDN'T WANT TO SIT WITH PAIGE!
YEAH, BOOGER-HEAD.
AMEND

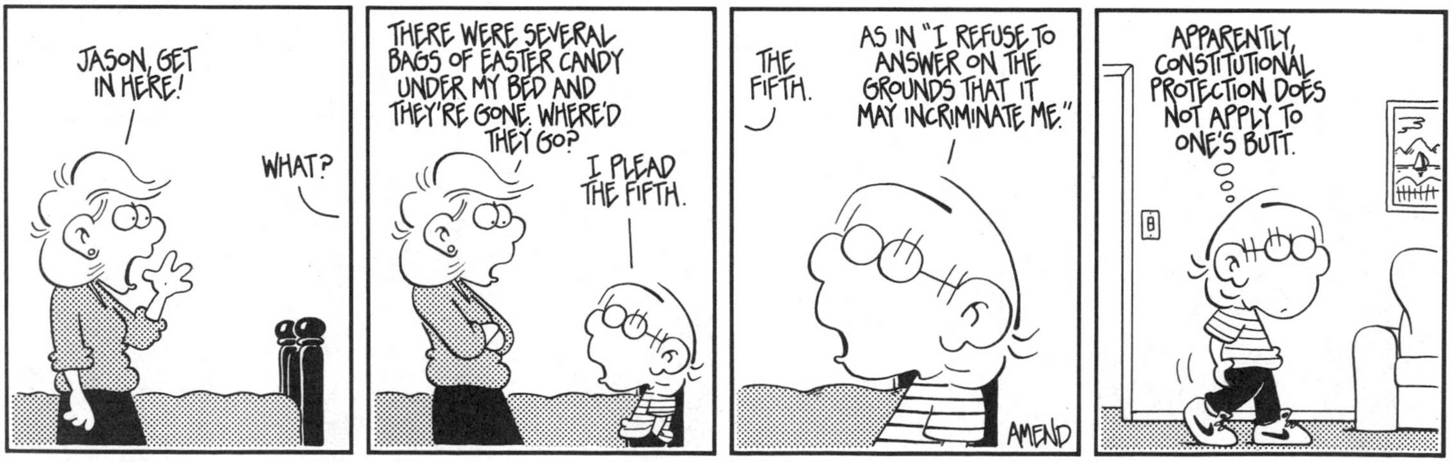
JASON, GET IN HERE!
WHAT?
THERE WERE SEVERAL BAGS OF EASTER CANDY UNDER MY BED AND THEY'RE GONE. WHERE'D THEY GO?
I PLEAD THE FIFTH.
THE FIFTH.
AS IN "I REFUSE TO ANSWER ON THE GROUNDS THAT IT MAY INCRIMINATE ME."
AMEND
APPARENTLY, CONSTITUTIONAL PROTECTION DOES NOT APPLY TO ONE'S BUTT.

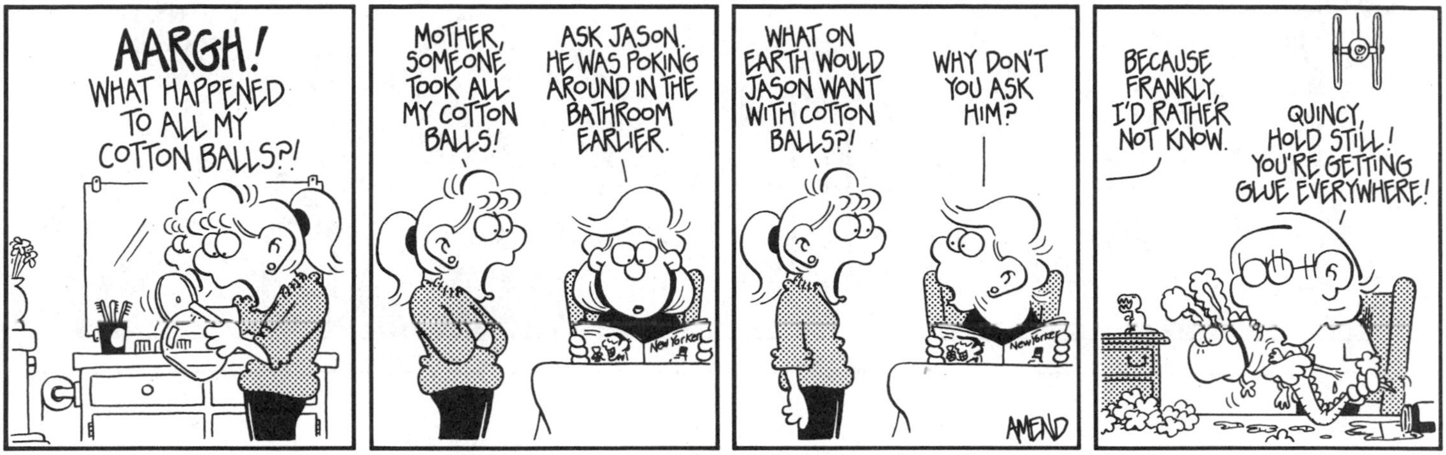
AARGH! WHAT HAPPENED TO ALL MY COTTON BALLS?!
MOTHER, SOMEONE TOOK ALL MY COTTON BALLS!
ASK JASON. HE WAS POKING AROUND IN THE BATHROOM EARLIER.
WHAT ON EARTH WOULD JASON WANT WITH COTTON BALLS?!
WHY DON'T YOU ASK HIM?
BECAUSE FRANKLY, I'D RATHER NOT KNOW.
QUINCY, HOLD STILL! YOU'RE GETTING GLUE EVERYWHERE!

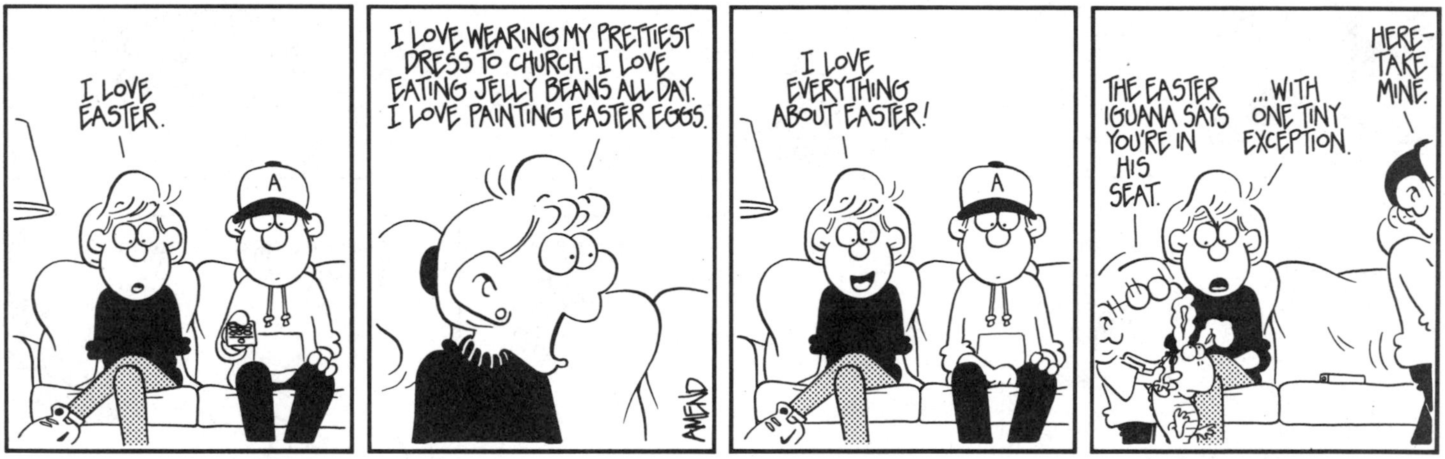
I LOVE EASTER.
I LOVE WEARING MY PRETTIEST DRESS TO CHURCH. I LOVE EATING JELLY BEANS ALL DAY. I LOVE PAINTING EASTER EGGS.
I LOVE EVERYTHING ABOUT EASTER!
THE EASTER IGUANA SAYS YOU'RE IN HIS SEAT.
...WITH ONE TINY EXCEPTION.
HERE-TAKE MINE.

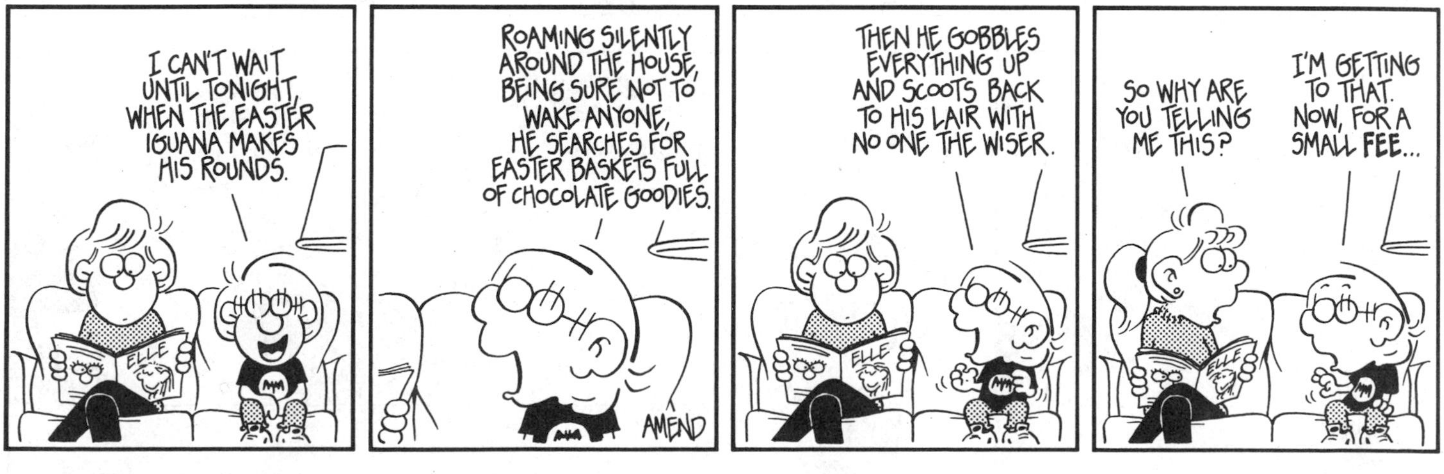
I CAN'T WAIT UNTIL TONIGHT, WHEN THE EASTER IGUANA MAKES HIS ROUNDS.
ROAMING SILENTLY AROUND THE HOUSE, BEING SURE NOT TO WAKE ANYONE, HE SEARCHES FOR EASTER BASKETS FULL OF CHOCOLATE GOODIES.
THEN HE GOBBLES EVERYTHING UP AND SCOOTS BACK TO HIS LAIR WITH NO ONE THE WISER.
SO WHY ARE YOU TELLING ME THIS?
I'M GETTING TO THAT. NOW, FOR A SMALL FEE...

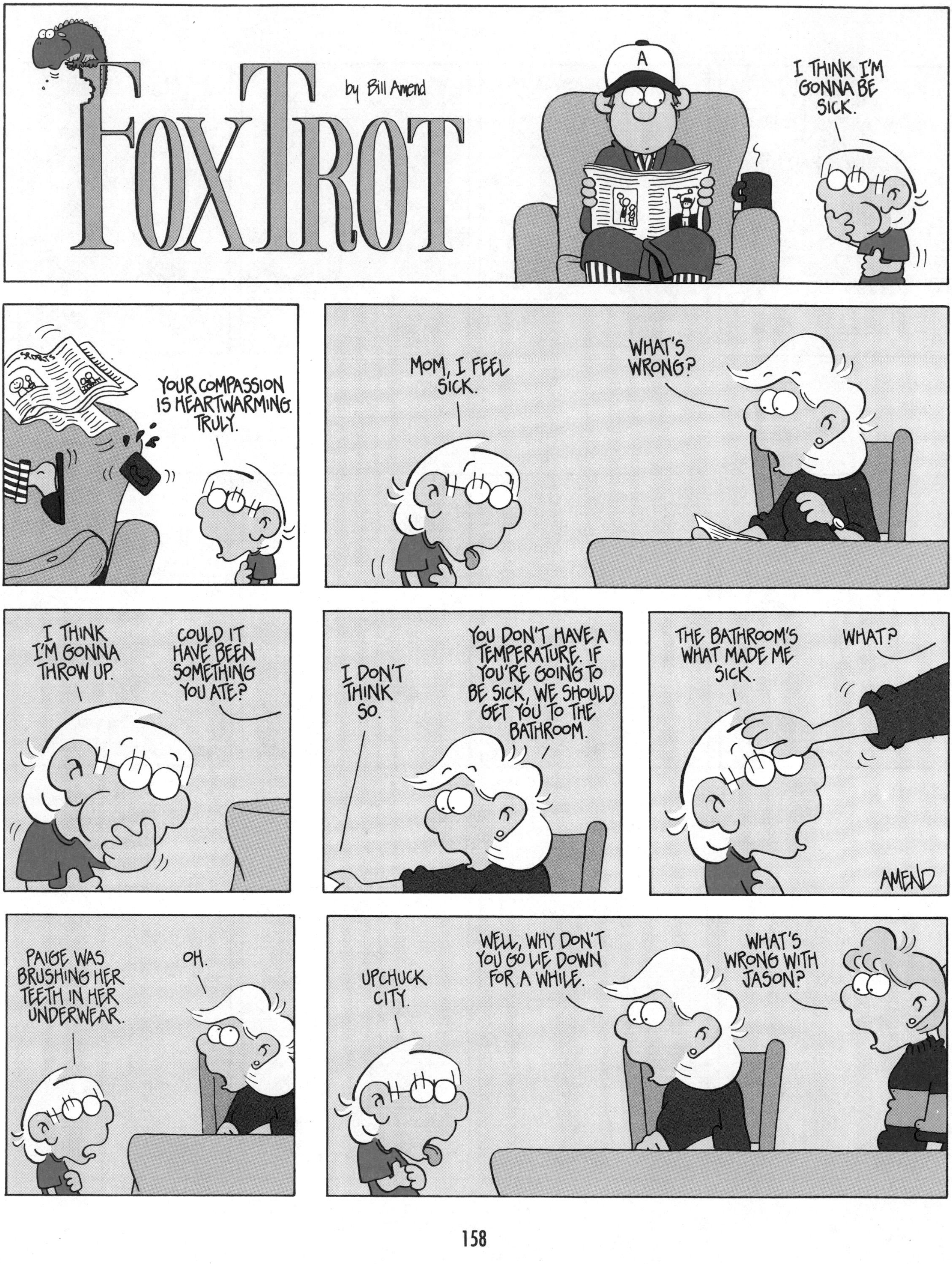
FoxTrot
by Bill Amend
I THINK I'M GONNA BE SICK.
YOUR COMPASSION IS HEARTWARMING. TRULY.
MOM, I FEEL SICK.
WHAT'S WRONG?
I THINK I'M GONNA THROW UP.
COULD IT HAVE BEEN SOMETHING YOU ATE?
I DON'T THINK SO.
YOU DON'T HAVE A TEMPERATURE. IF YOU'RE GOING TO BE SICK, WE SHOULD GET YOU TO THE BATHROOM.
THE BATHROOM'S WHAT MADE ME SICK.
WHAT?
AMEND
PAIGE WAS BRUSHING HER TEETH IN HER UNDERWEAR.
OH.
UPCHUCK CITY.
WELL, WHY DON'T YOU GO LIE DOWN FOR A WHILE.
WHAT'S WRONG WITH JASON?

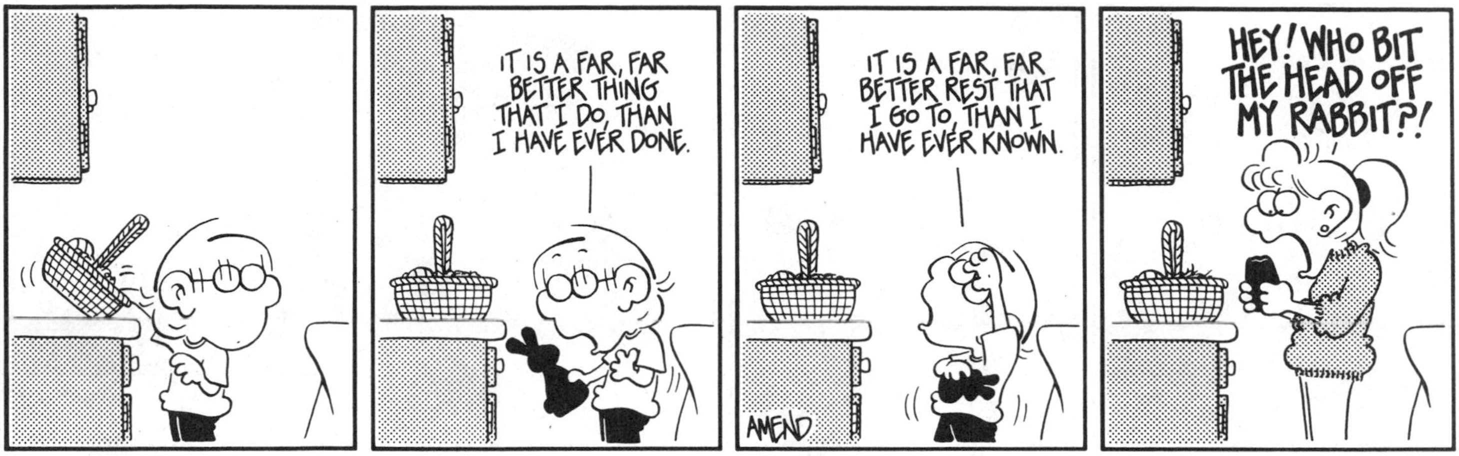

IT IS A FAR, FAR BETTER THING THAT I DO, THAN I HAVE EVER DONE.
IT IS A FAR, FAR BETTER REST THAT I GO TO, THAN I HAVE EVER KNOWN.
AMEND
HEY! WHO BIT THE HEAD OFF MY RABBIT?!

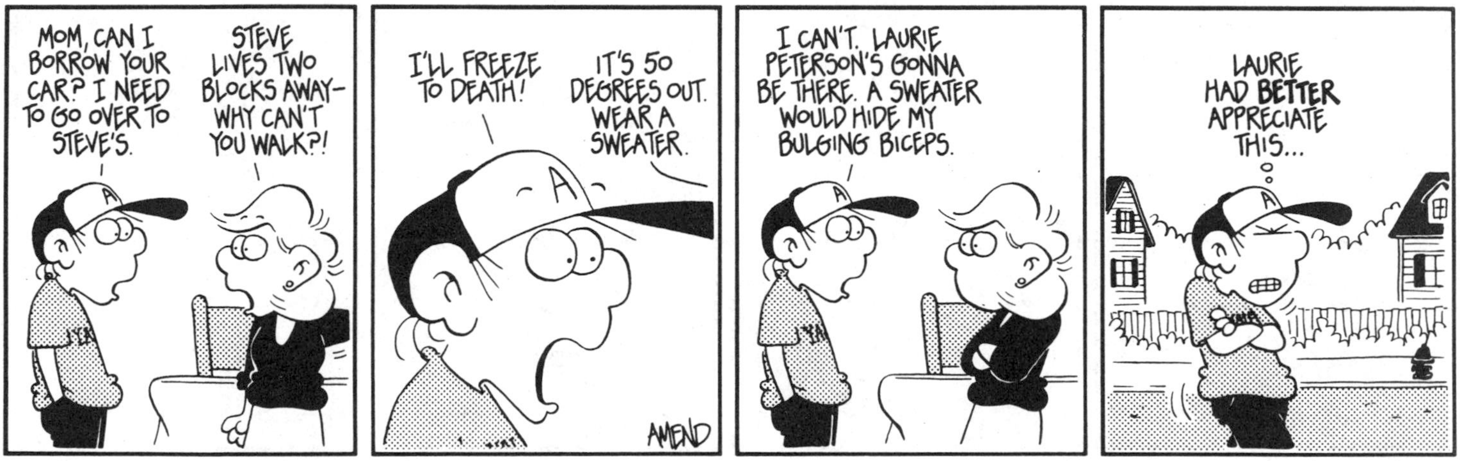

MOM, CAN I BORROW YOUR CAR? I NEED TO GO OVER TO STEVE'S.
STEVE LIVES TWO BLOCKS AWAY– WHY CAN'T YOU WALK?!
I'LL FREEZE TO DEATH!
IT'S 50 DEGREES OUT. WEAR A SWEATER.
AMEND
I CAN'T. LAURIE PETERSON'S GONNA BE THERE. A SWEATER WOULD HIDE MY BULGING BICEPS.
LAURIE HAD **BETTER** APPRECIATE THIS...

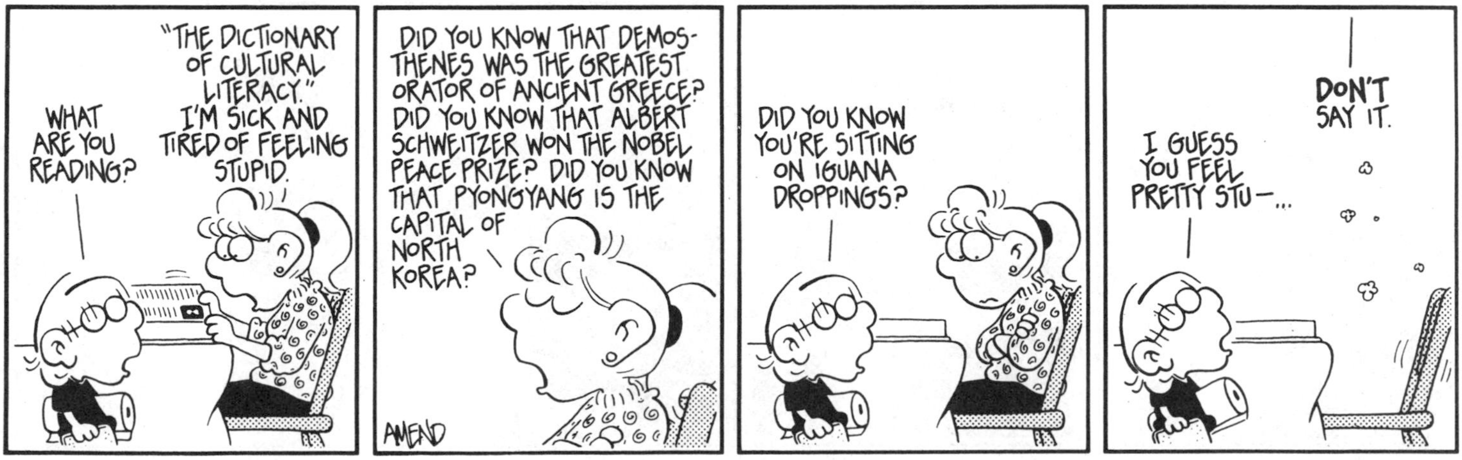

WHAT ARE YOU READING?
"THE DICTIONARY OF CULTURAL LITERACY." I'M SICK AND TIRED OF FEELING STUPID.
DID YOU KNOW THAT DEMOSTHENES WAS THE GREATEST ORATOR OF ANCIENT GREECE? DID YOU KNOW THAT ALBERT SCHWEITZER WON THE NOBEL PEACE PRIZE? DID YOU KNOW THAT PYONGYANG IS THE CAPITAL OF NORTH KOREA?
AMEND
DID YOU KNOW YOU'RE SITTING ON IGUANA DROPPINGS?
I GUESS YOU FEEL PRETTY STU–...
DON'T SAY IT.

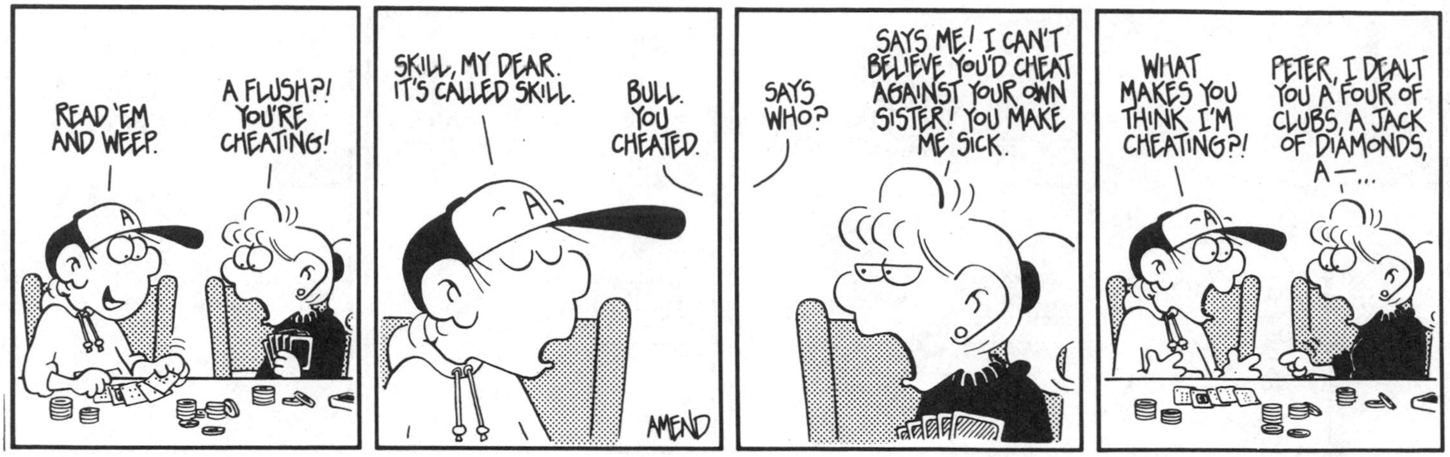
READ 'EM AND WEEP.
A FLUSH?! YOU'RE CHEATING!
SKILL, MY DEAR. IT'S CALLED SKILL.
BULL. YOU CHEATED.
AMEND
SAYS WHO?
SAYS ME! I CAN'T BELIEVE YOU'D CHEAT AGAINST YOUR OWN SISTER! YOU MAKE ME SICK.
WHAT MAKES YOU THINK I'M CHEATING?!
PETER, I DEALT YOU A FOUR OF CLUBS, A JACK OF DIAMONDS, A—...

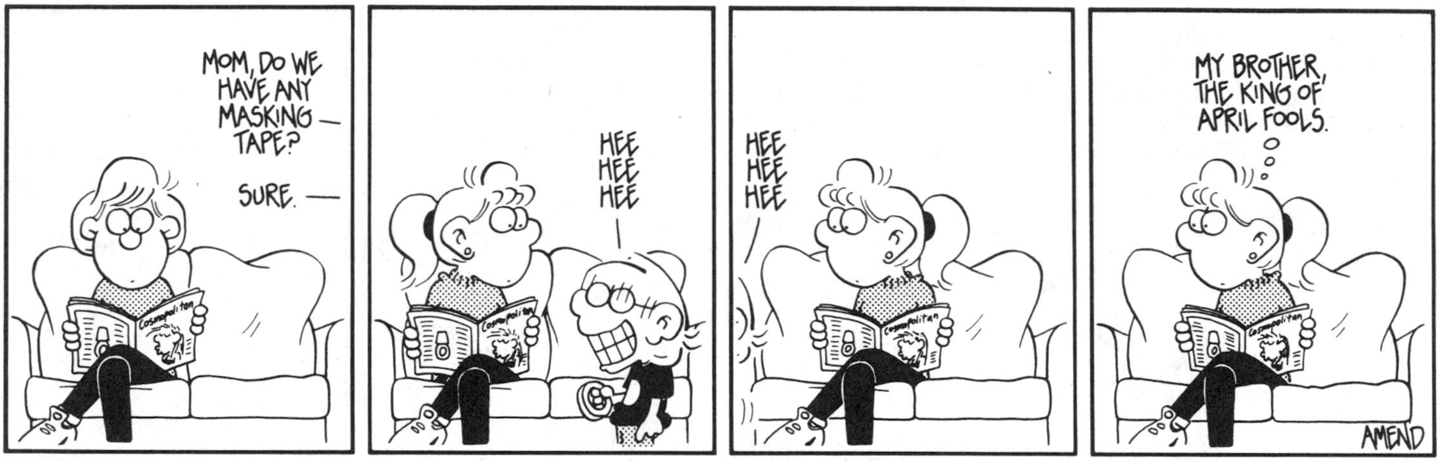
MOM, DO WE HAVE ANY MASKING TAPE?
SURE.
HEE HEE HEE
HEE HEE HEE
MY BROTHER, THE KING OF APRIL FOOLS.
AMEND

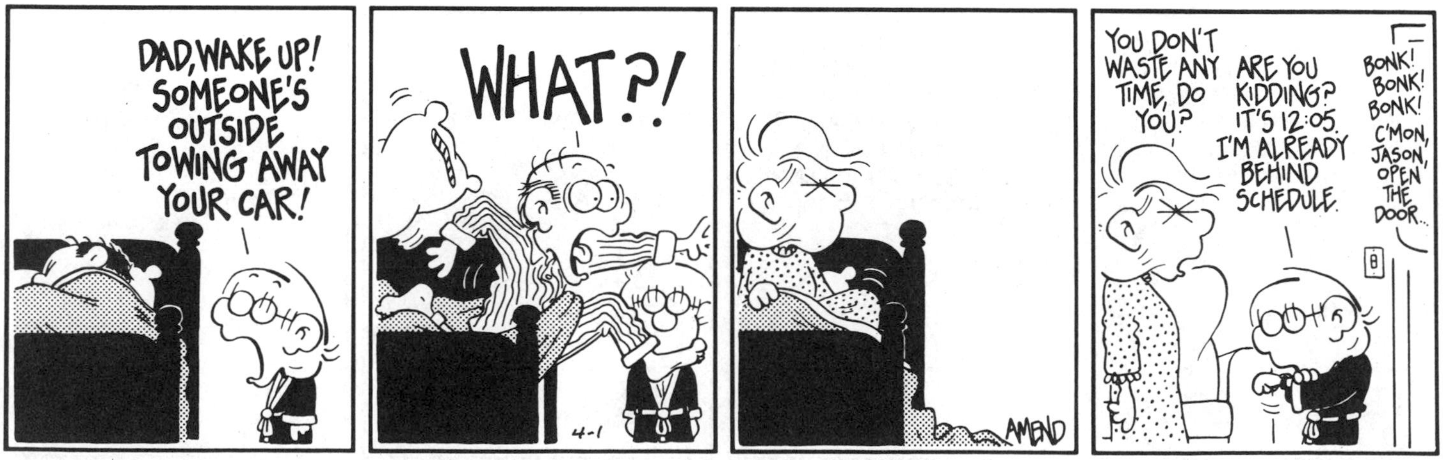
DAD, WAKE UP! SOMEONE'S OUTSIDE TOWING AWAY YOUR CAR!
WHAT?!
4-1
AMEND
YOU DON'T WASTE ANY TIME, DO YOU?
ARE YOU KIDDING? IT'S 12:05. I'M ALREADY BEHIND SCHEDULE.
BONK! BONK! BONK! C'MON, JASON, OPEN THE DOOR...

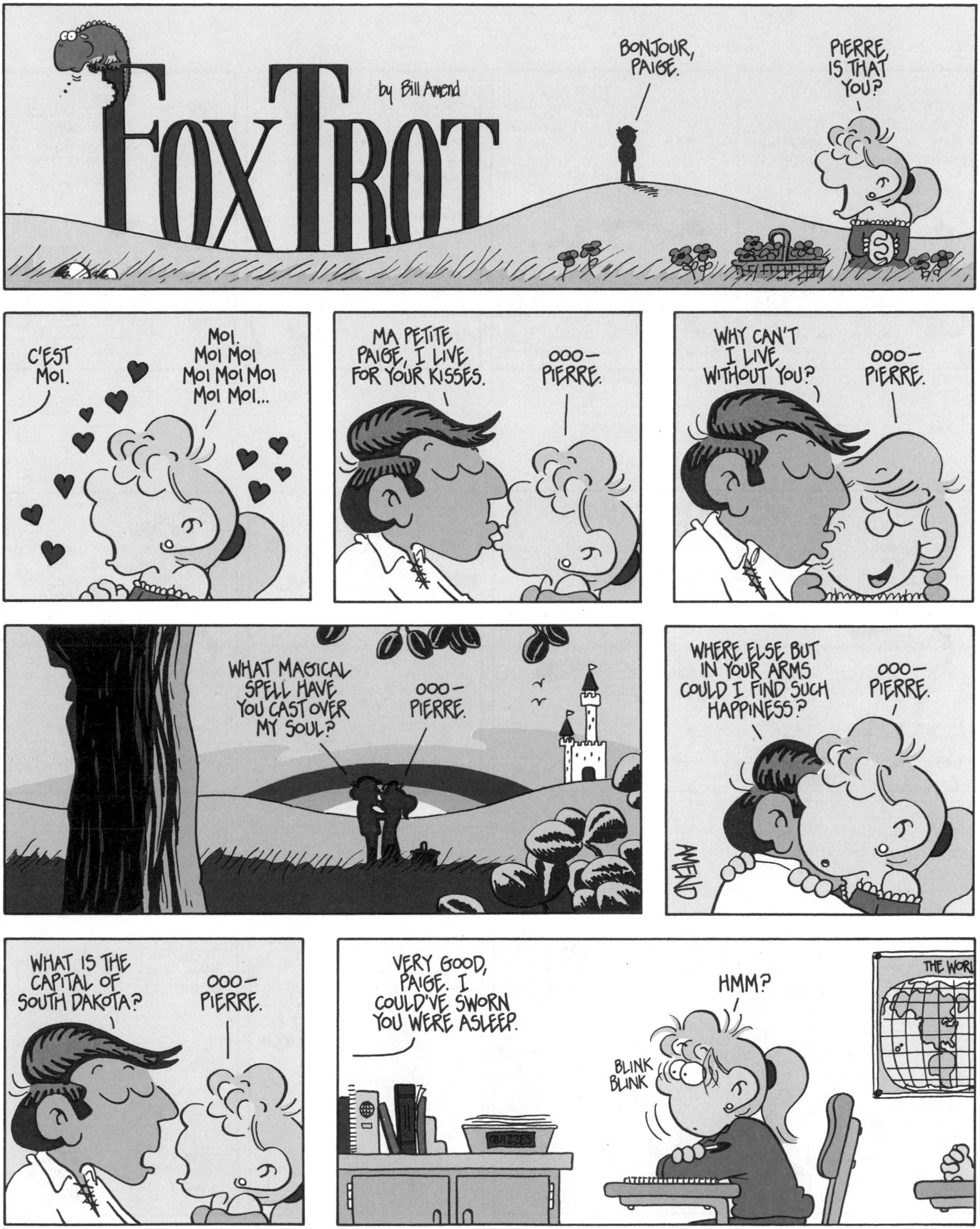

FoxTrot
by Bill Amend
BONJOUR, PAIGE.
PIERRE, IS THAT YOU?
C'EST MOI.
MOI. MOI MOI MOI MOI MOI MOI MOI...
MA PETITE PAIGE, I LIVE FOR YOUR KISSES.
OOO-PIERRE.
WHY CAN'T I LIVE WITHOUT YOU?
OOO-PIERRE.
WHAT MAGICAL SPELL HAVE YOU CAST OVER MY SOUL?
OOO-PIERRE.
WHERE ELSE BUT IN YOUR ARMS COULD I FIND SUCH HAPPINESS?
OOO-PIERRE.
AMEND
WHAT IS THE CAPITAL OF SOUTH DAKOTA?
OOO-PIERRE.
VERY GOOD, PAIGE. I COULD'VE SWORN YOU WERE ASLEEP.
HMM?
BLINK BLINK
THE WORL
QUIZZES

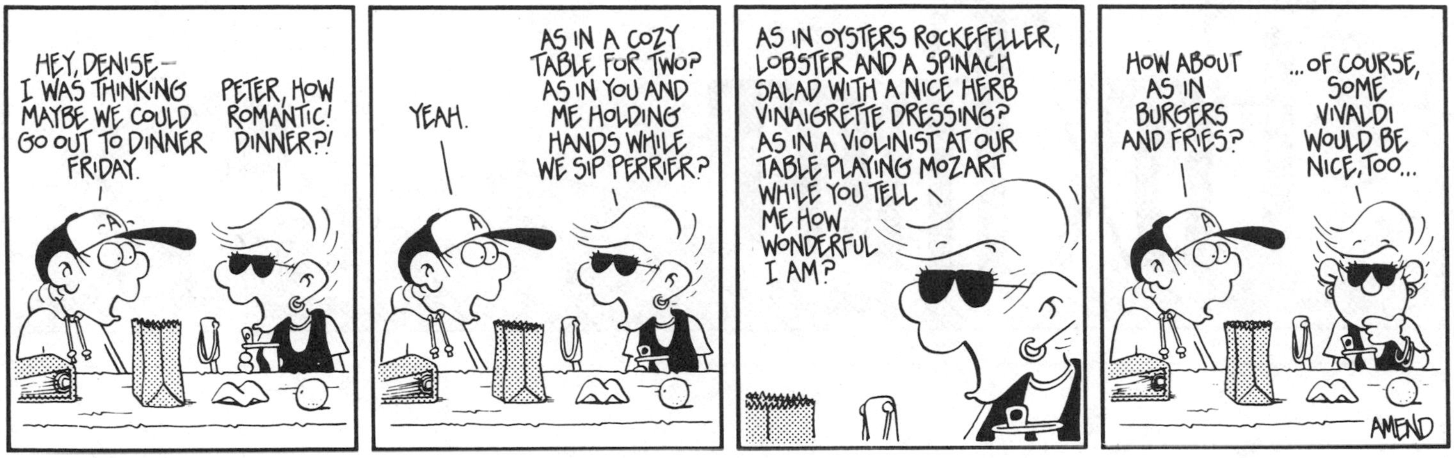
HEY, DENISE—
I WAS THINKING MAYBE WE COULD GO OUT TO DINNER FRIDAY.
PETER, HOW ROMANTIC! DINNER?!
YEAH.
AS IN A COZY TABLE FOR TWO? AS IN YOU AND ME HOLDING HANDS WHILE WE SIP PERRIER?
AS IN OYSTERS ROCKEFELLER, LOBSTER AND A SPINACH SALAD WITH A NICE HERB VINAIGRETTE DRESSING? AS IN A VIOLINIST AT OUR TABLE PLAYING MOZART WHILE YOU TELL ME HOW WONDERFUL I AM?
HOW ABOUT AS IN BURGERS AND FRIES?
...OF COURSE, SOME VIVALDI WOULD BE NICE, TOO...
AMEND

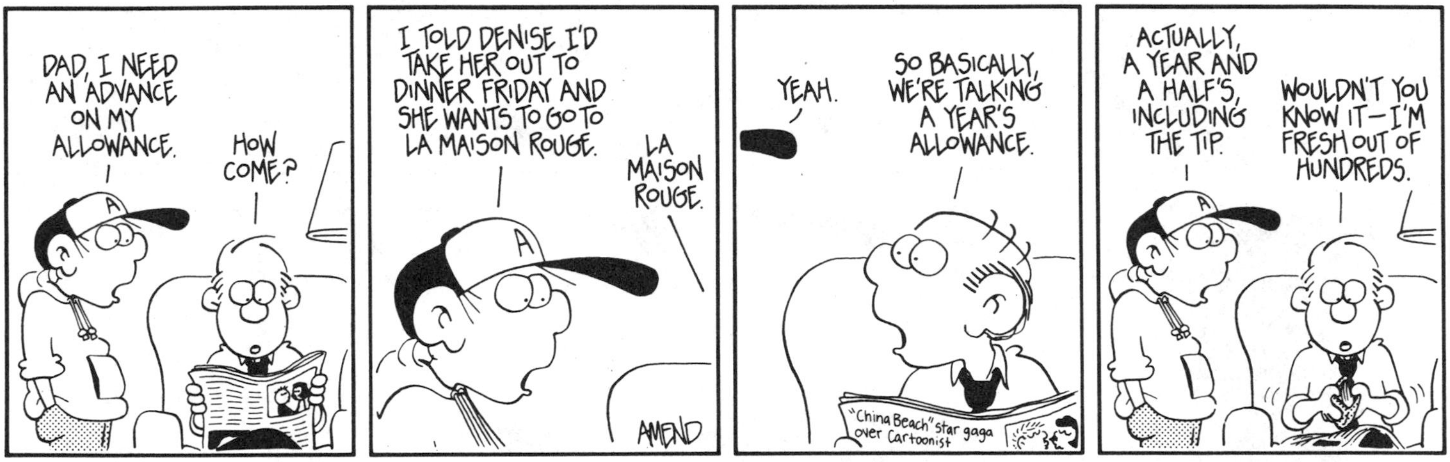
DAD, I NEED AN ADVANCE ON MY ALLOWANCE.
HOW COME?
I TOLD DENISE I'D TAKE HER OUT TO DINNER FRIDAY AND SHE WANTS TO GO TO LA MAISON ROUGE.
LA MAISON ROUGE.
AMEND
YEAH.
SO BASICALLY, WE'RE TALKING A YEAR'S ALLOWANCE.
"China Beach" star gaga over Cartoonist
ACTUALLY, A YEAR AND A HALF'S, INCLUDING THE TIP.
WOULDN'T YOU KNOW IT—I'M FRESH OUT OF HUNDREDS.

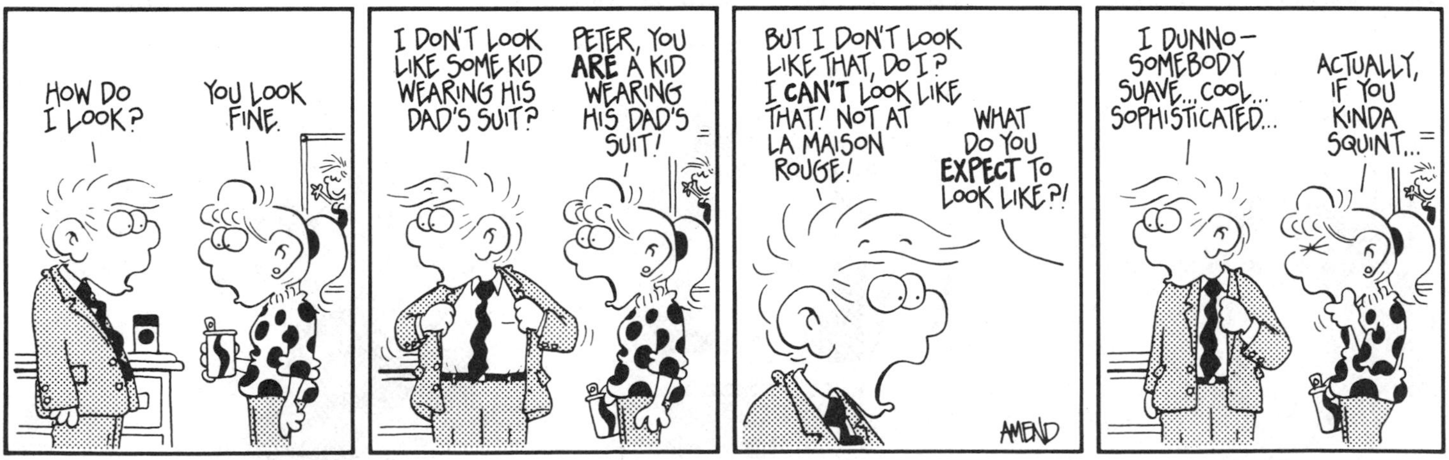
HOW DO I LOOK?
YOU LOOK FINE.
I DON'T LOOK LIKE SOME KID WEARING HIS DAD'S SUIT?
PETER, YOU **ARE** A KID WEARING HIS DAD'S SUIT!
BUT I DON'T LOOK LIKE THAT, DO I? I **CAN'T** LOOK LIKE THAT! NOT AT LA MAISON ROUGE!
WHAT DO YOU **EXPECT** TO LOOK LIKE?!
AMEND
I DUNNO—SOMEBODY SUAVE... COOL... SOPHISTICATED...
ACTUALLY, IF YOU KINDA SQUINT...

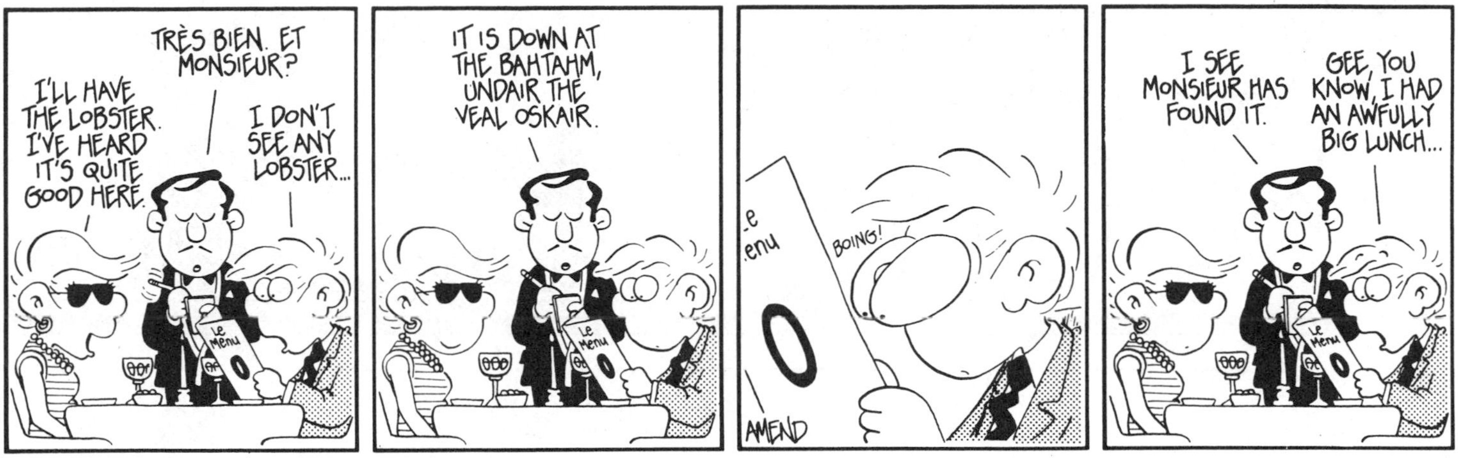
I'LL HAVE THE LOBSTER. I'VE HEARD IT'S QUITE GOOD HERE.
TRÈS BIEN. ET MONSIEUR?
I DON'T SEE ANY LOBSTER...
Le Menu
IT IS DOWN AT THE BAHTAHM, UNDAIR THE VEAL OSKAIR.
BOING!
AMEND
I SEE MONSIEUR HAS FOUND IT.
GEE, YOU KNOW, I HAD AN AWFULLY BIG LUNCH...

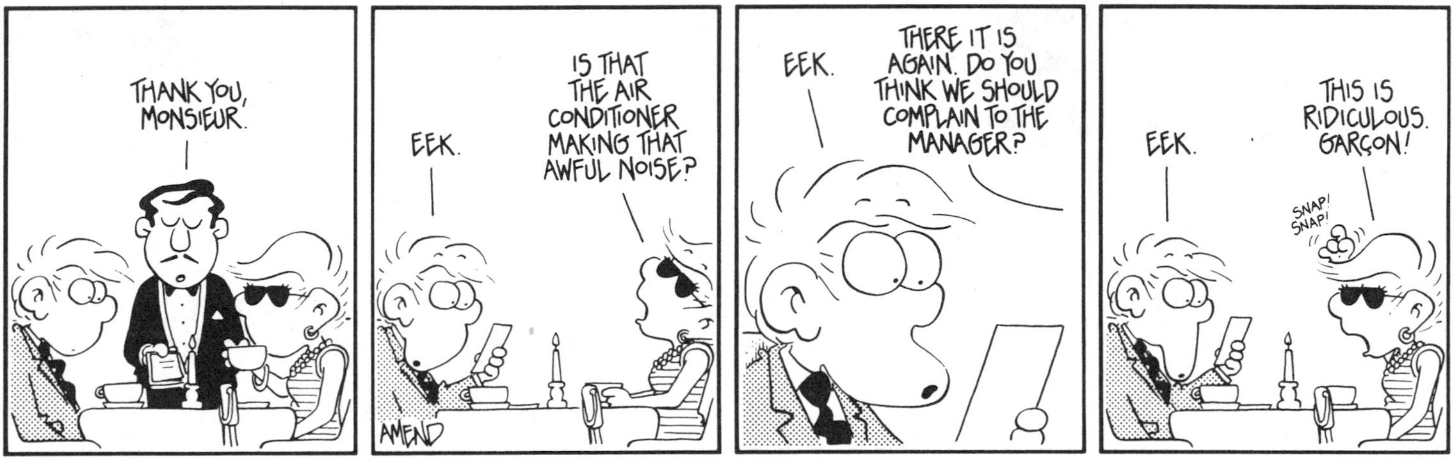
THANK YOU, MONSIEUR.
EEK.
IS THAT THE AIR CONDITIONER MAKING THAT AWFUL NOISE?
AMEND
EEK.
THERE IT IS AGAIN. DO YOU THINK WE SHOULD COMPLAIN TO THE MANAGER?
EEK.
THIS IS RIDICULOUS. GARÇON!
SNAP! SNAP!

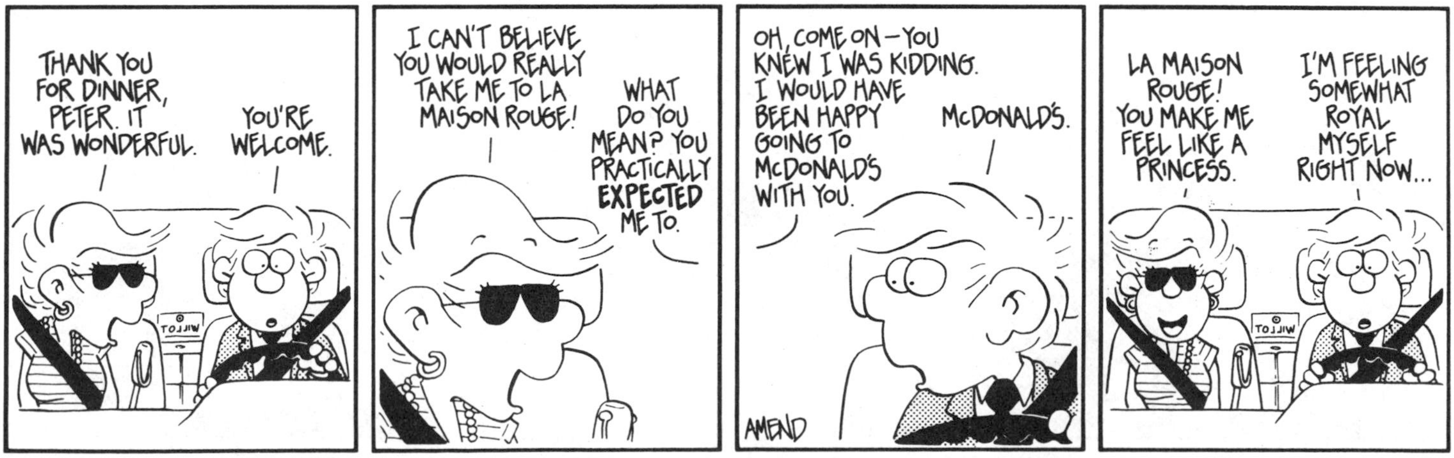
THANK YOU FOR DINNER, PETER. IT WAS WONDERFUL.
YOU'RE WELCOME.
I CAN'T BELIEVE YOU WOULD REALLY TAKE ME TO LA MAISON ROUGE!
WHAT DO YOU MEAN? YOU PRACTICALLY **EXPECTED** ME TO.
OH, COME ON—YOU KNEW I WAS KIDDING. I WOULD HAVE BEEN HAPPY GOING TO McDONALD'S WITH YOU.
McDONALD'S.
AMEND
LA MAISON ROUGE! YOU MAKE ME FEEL LIKE A PRINCESS.
I'M FEELING SOMEWHAT ROYAL MYSELF RIGHT NOW...

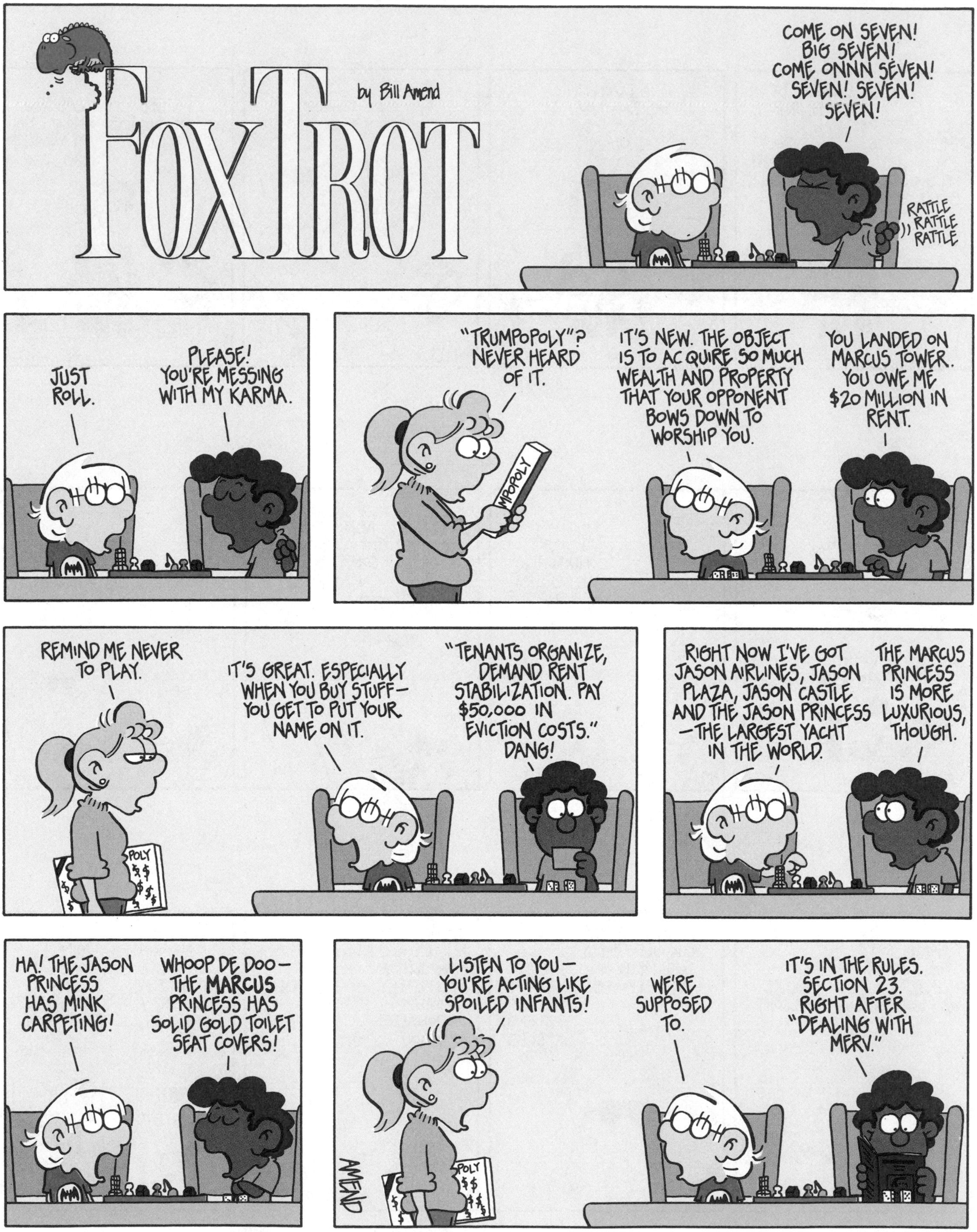
FOXTROT
by Bill Amend
COME ON SEVEN! BIG SEVEN! COME ONNN SEVEN! SEVEN! SEVEN! SEVEN!
RATTLE RATTLE RATTLE
JUST ROLL.
PLEASE! YOU'RE MESSING WITH MY KARMA.
"TRUMPOPOLY"? NEVER HEARD OF IT.
MPOPOLY
IT'S NEW. THE OBJECT IS TO ACQUIRE SO MUCH WEALTH AND PROPERTY THAT YOUR OPPONENT BOWS DOWN TO WORSHIP YOU.
YOU LANDED ON MARCUS TOWER. YOU OWE ME $20 MILLION IN RENT.
REMIND ME NEVER TO PLAY.
IT'S GREAT. ESPECIALLY WHEN YOU BUY STUFF— YOU GET TO PUT YOUR NAME ON IT.
"TENANTS ORGANIZE, DEMAND RENT STABILIZATION. PAY $50,000 IN EVICTION COSTS." DANG!
POLY
RIGHT NOW I'VE GOT JASON AIRLINES, JASON PLAZA, JASON CASTLE AND THE JASON PRINCESS —THE LARGEST YACHT IN THE WORLD.
THE MARCUS PRINCESS IS MORE LUXURIOUS, THOUGH.
HA! THE JASON PRINCESS HAS MINK CARPETING!
WHOOP DE DOO— THE MARCUS PRINCESS HAS SOLID GOLD TOILET SEAT COVERS!
LISTEN TO YOU— YOU'RE ACTING LIKE SPOILED INFANTS!
WE'RE SUPPOSED TO.
IT'S IN THE RULES. SECTION 23. RIGHT AFTER "DEALING WITH MERV."
AMEND

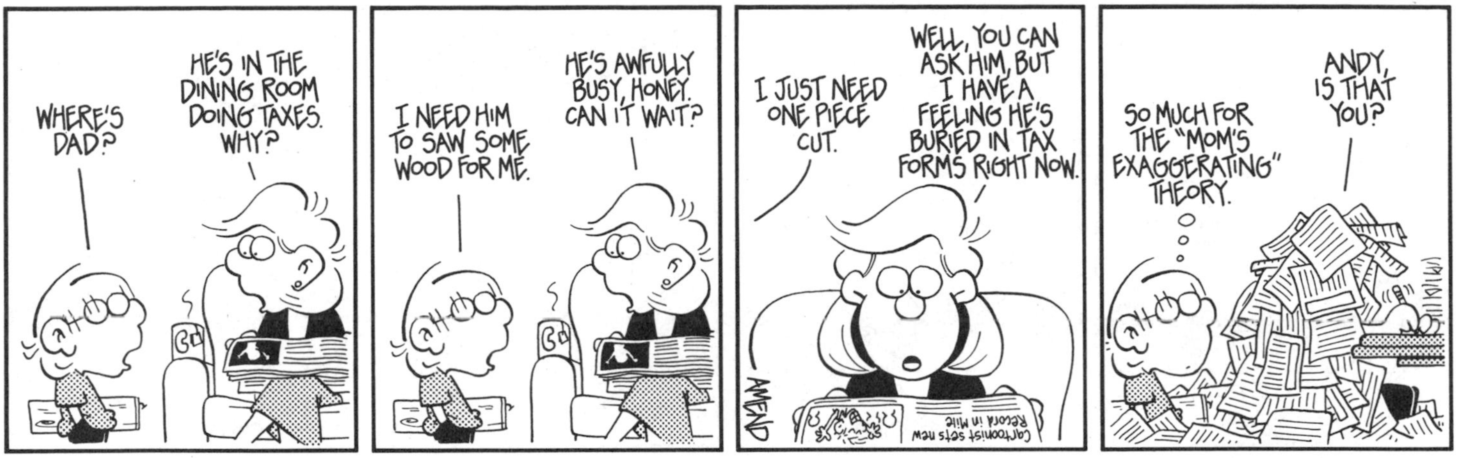
WHERE'S DAD?
HE'S IN THE DINING ROOM DOING TAXES. WHY?
I NEED HIM TO SAW SOME WOOD FOR ME.
HE'S AWFULLY BUSY, HONEY. CAN IT WAIT?
I JUST NEED ONE PIECE CUT.
WELL, YOU CAN ASK HIM, BUT I HAVE A FEELING HE'S BURIED IN TAX FORMS RIGHT NOW.
Cartoonist sets new Record in Mile
AMEND
SO MUCH FOR THE "MOM'S EXAGGERATING" THEORY.
ANDY, IS THAT YOU?

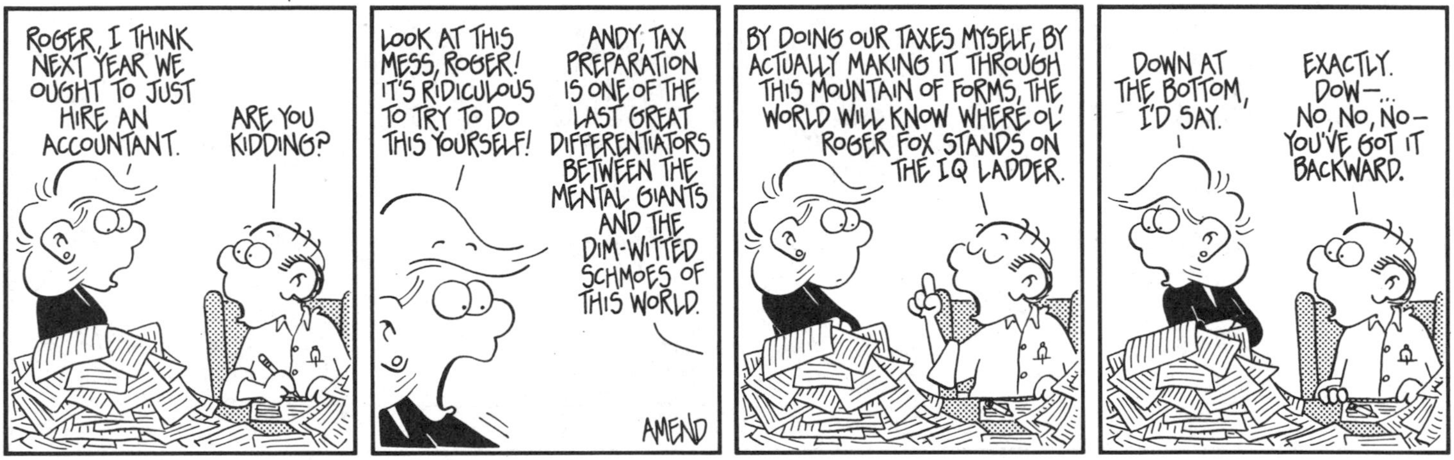
ROGER, I THINK NEXT YEAR WE OUGHT TO JUST HIRE AN ACCOUNTANT.
ARE YOU KIDDING?
LOOK AT THIS MESS, ROGER! IT'S RIDICULOUS TO TRY TO DO THIS YOURSELF!
ANDY, TAX PREPARATION IS ONE OF THE LAST GREAT DIFFERENTIATORS BETWEEN THE MENTAL GIANTS AND THE DIM-WITTED SCHMOES OF THIS WORLD.
AMEND
BY DOING OUR TAXES MYSELF, BY ACTUALLY MAKING IT THROUGH THIS MOUNTAIN OF FORMS, THE WORLD WILL KNOW WHERE OL' ROGER FOX STANDS ON THE IQ LADDER.
DOWN AT THE BOTTOM, I'D SAY.
EXACTLY. DOW—... NO, NO, NO— YOU'VE GOT IT BACKWARD.

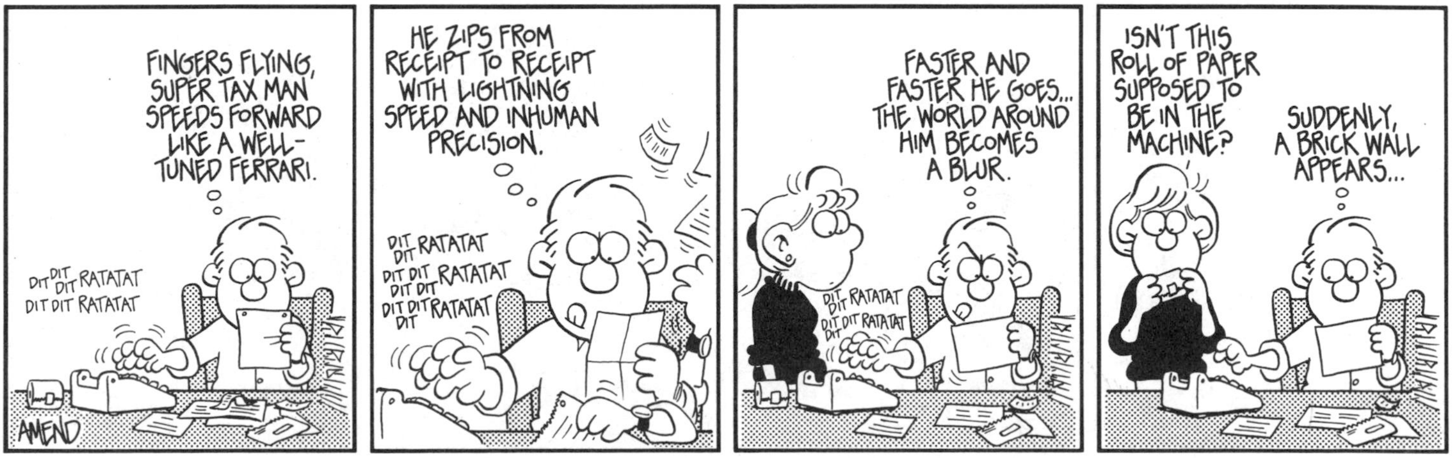
FINGERS FLYING, SUPER TAX MAN SPEEDS FORWARD LIKE A WELL-TUNED FERRARI.
DIT DIT DIT RATATAT DIT DIT RATATAT
AMEND
HE ZIPS FROM RECEIPT TO RECEIPT WITH LIGHTNING SPEED AND INHUMAN PRECISION.
DIT DIT RATATAT DIT DIT DIT DIT RATATAT DIT DIT DIT RATATAT
FASTER AND FASTER HE GOES... THE WORLD AROUND HIM BECOMES A BLUR.
DIT DIT RATATAT DIT DIT RATATAT
ISN'T THIS ROLL OF PAPER SUPPOSED TO BE IN THE MACHINE?
SUDDENLY, A BRICK WALL APPEARS...

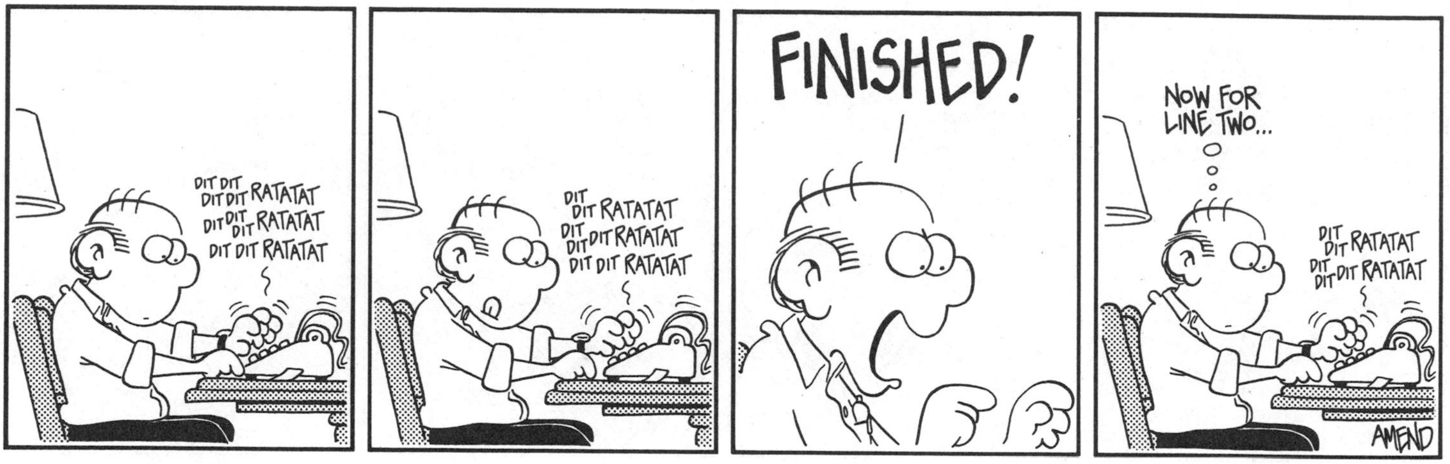
DIT DIT DIT DIT RATATAT DIT DIT DIT RATATAT DIT DIT RATATAT
DIT DIT RATATAT DIT DIT DIT RATATAT DIT DIT RATATAT
FINISHED!
NOW FOR LINE TWO...
DIT DIT RATATAT DIT DIT DIT RATATAT
AMEND

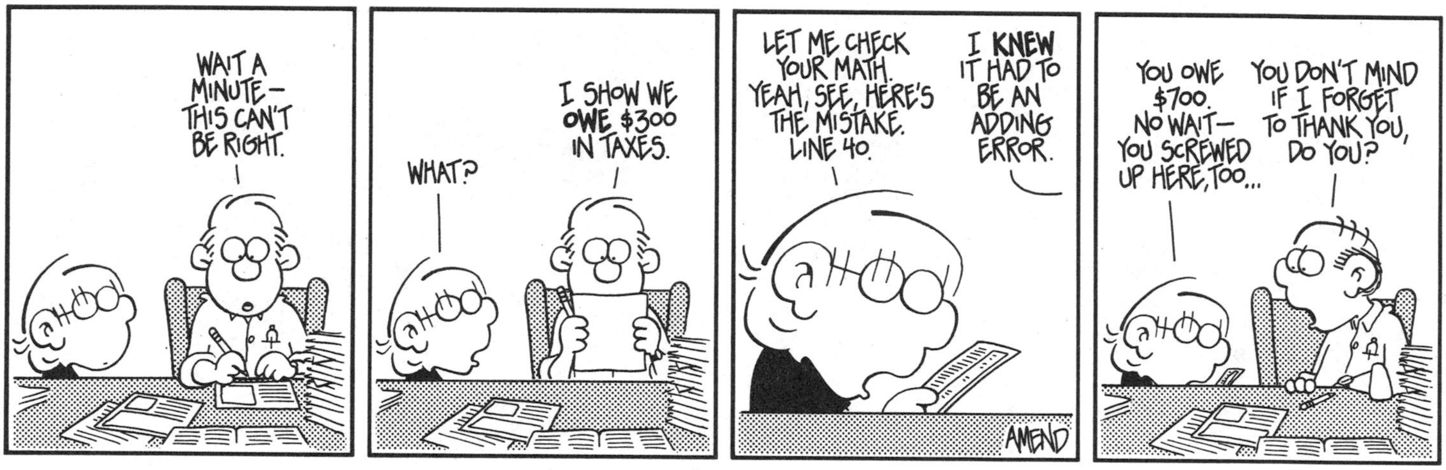
WAIT A MINUTE— THIS CAN'T BE RIGHT.
WHAT?
I SHOW WE **OWE** $300 IN TAXES.
LET ME CHECK YOUR MATH. YEAH, SEE, HERE'S THE MISTAKE. LINE 40.
I **KNEW** IT HAD TO BE AN ADDING ERROR.
AMEND
YOU OWE $700. NO WAIT— YOU SCREWED UP HERE, TOO...
YOU DON'T MIND IF I FORGET TO THANK YOU, DO YOU?

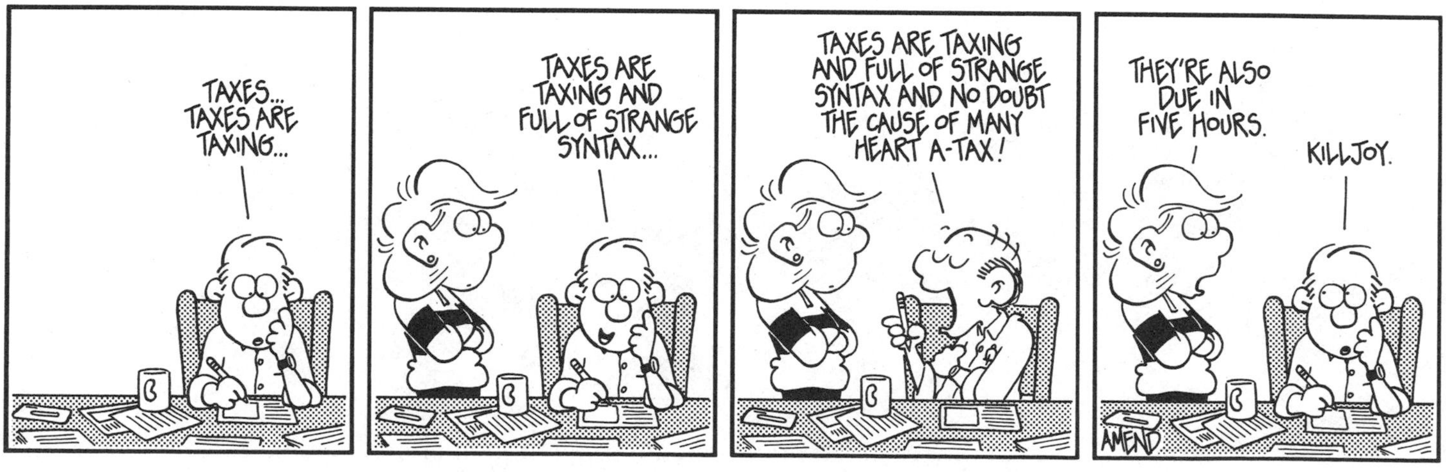
TAXES... TAXES ARE TAXING...
TAXES ARE TAXING AND FULL OF STRANGE SYNTAX...
TAXES ARE TAXING AND FULL OF STRANGE SYNTAX AND NO DOUBT THE CAUSE OF MANY HEART A-TAX!
THEY'RE ALSO DUE IN FIVE HOURS.
KILLJOY.
AMEND

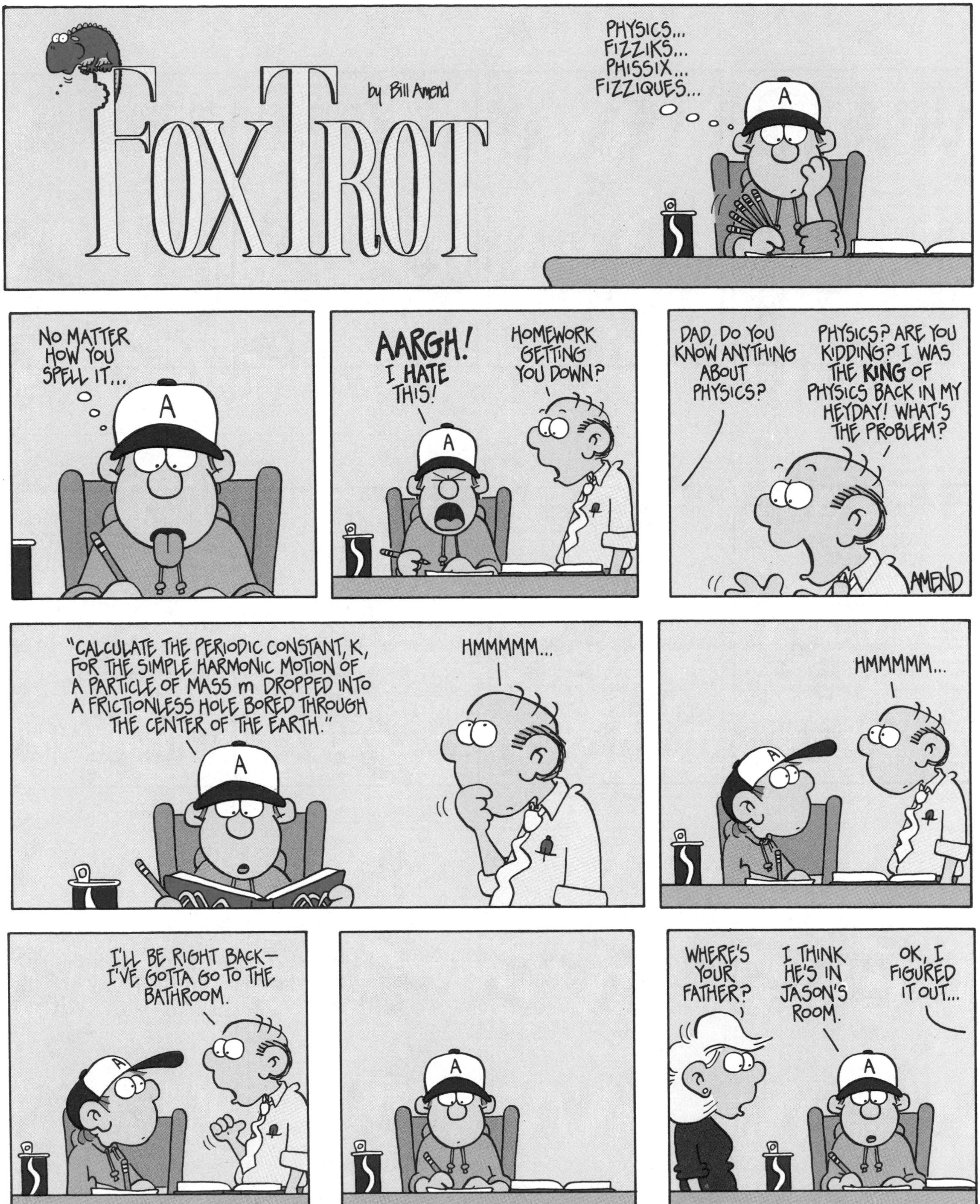
FoxTrot
by Bill Amend
PHYSICS... FIZZIKS... PHISSIX... FIZZIQUES...
NO MATTER HOW YOU SPELL IT...
AARGH! I HATE THIS!
HOMEWORK GETTING YOU DOWN?
DAD, DO YOU KNOW ANYTHING ABOUT PHYSICS?
PHYSICS? ARE YOU KIDDING? I WAS THE KING OF PHYSICS BACK IN MY HEYDAY! WHAT'S THE PROBLEM?
AMEND
"CALCULATE THE PERIODIC CONSTANT, K, FOR THE SIMPLE HARMONIC MOTION OF A PARTICLE OF MASS m DROPPED INTO A FRICTIONLESS HOLE BORED THROUGH THE CENTER OF THE EARTH."
HMMMMM...
HMMMMM...
I'LL BE RIGHT BACK— I'VE GOTTA GO TO THE BATHROOM.
WHERE'S YOUR FATHER?
I THINK HE'S IN JASON'S ROOM.
OK, I FIGURED IT OUT...

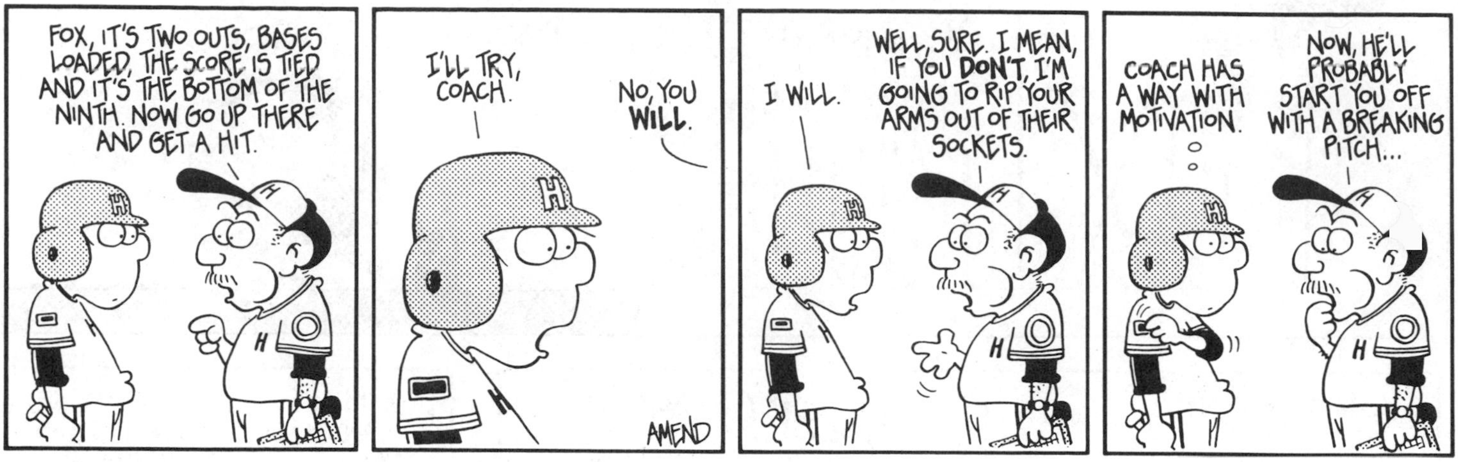
FOX, IT'S TWO OUTS, BASES LOADED, THE SCORE IS TIED AND IT'S THE BOTTOM OF THE NINTH. NOW GO UP THERE AND GET A HIT.
I'LL TRY, COACH.
NO, YOU WILL.
AMEND
I WILL.
WELL, SURE. I MEAN, IF YOU DON'T, I'M GOING TO RIP YOUR ARMS OUT OF THEIR SOCKETS.
COACH HAS A WAY WITH MOTIVATION.
NOW, HE'LL PROBABLY START YOU OFF WITH A BREAKING PITCH...

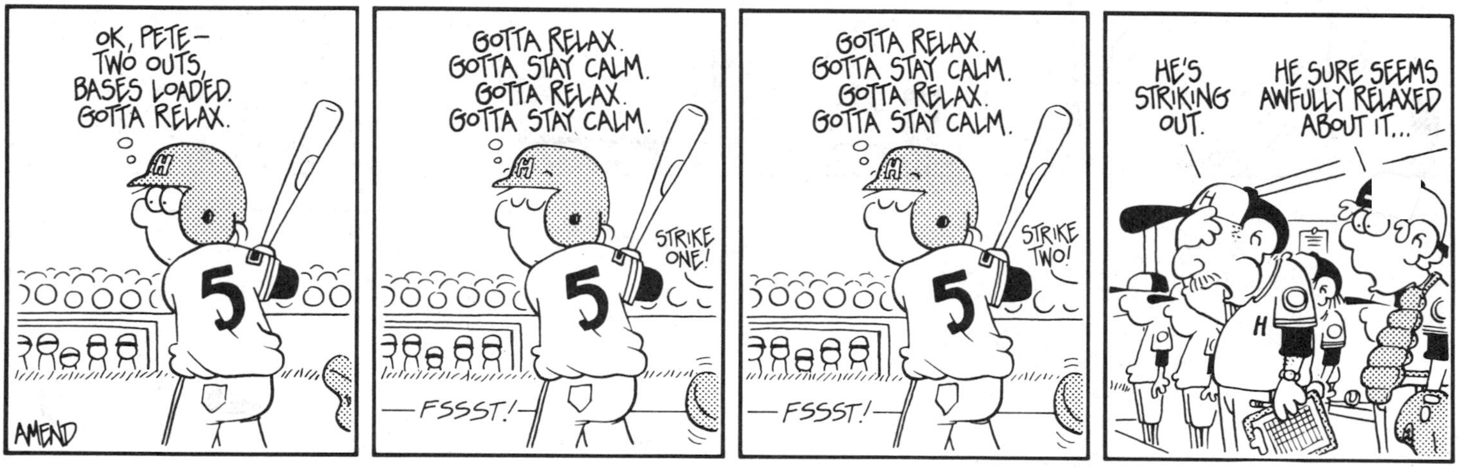
OK, PETE— TWO OUTS, BASES LOADED. GOTTA RELAX.
AMEND
GOTTA RELAX. GOTTA STAY CALM. GOTTA RELAX. GOTTA STAY CALM.
STRIKE ONE!
—FSSST!—
GOTTA RELAX. GOTTA STAY CALM. GOTTA RELAX. GOTTA STAY CALM.
STRIKE TWO!
—FSSST!—
HE'S STRIKING OUT.
HE SURE SEEMS AWFULLY RELAXED ABOUT IT...

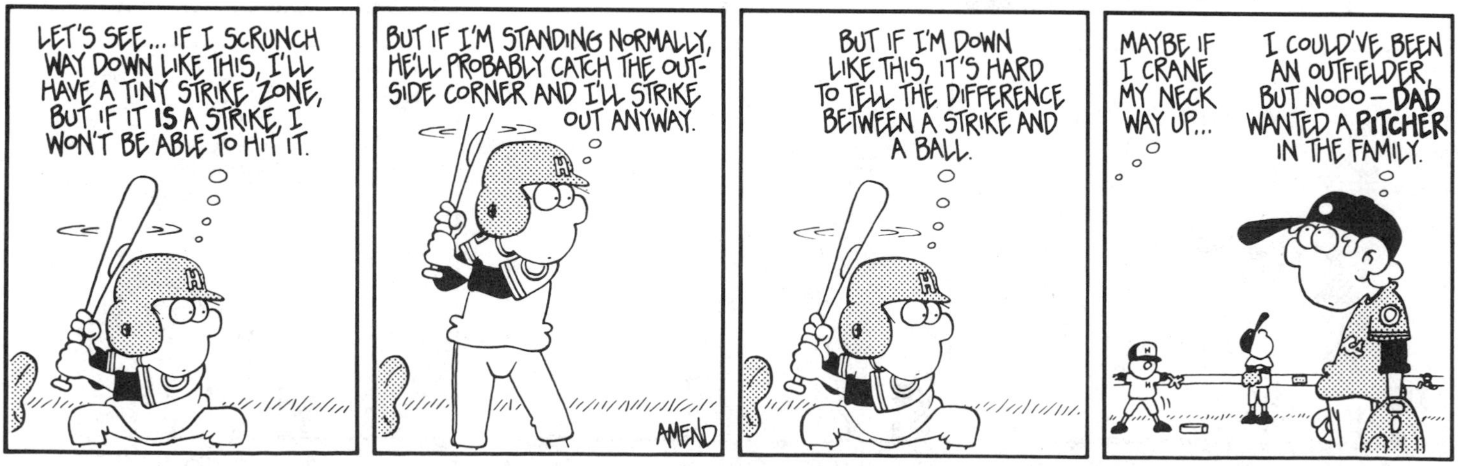
LET'S SEE... IF I SCRUNCH WAY DOWN LIKE THIS, I'LL HAVE A TINY STRIKE ZONE, BUT IF IT IS A STRIKE, I WON'T BE ABLE TO HIT IT.
BUT IF I'M STANDING NORMALLY, HE'LL PROBABLY CATCH THE OUTSIDE CORNER AND I'LL STRIKE OUT ANYWAY.
AMEND
BUT IF I'M DOWN LIKE THIS, IT'S HARD TO TELL THE DIFFERENCE BETWEEN A STRIKE AND A BALL.
MAYBE IF I CRANE MY NECK WAY UP...
I COULD'VE BEEN AN OUTFIELDER, BUT NOOO— DAD WANTED A PITCHER IN THE FAMILY.

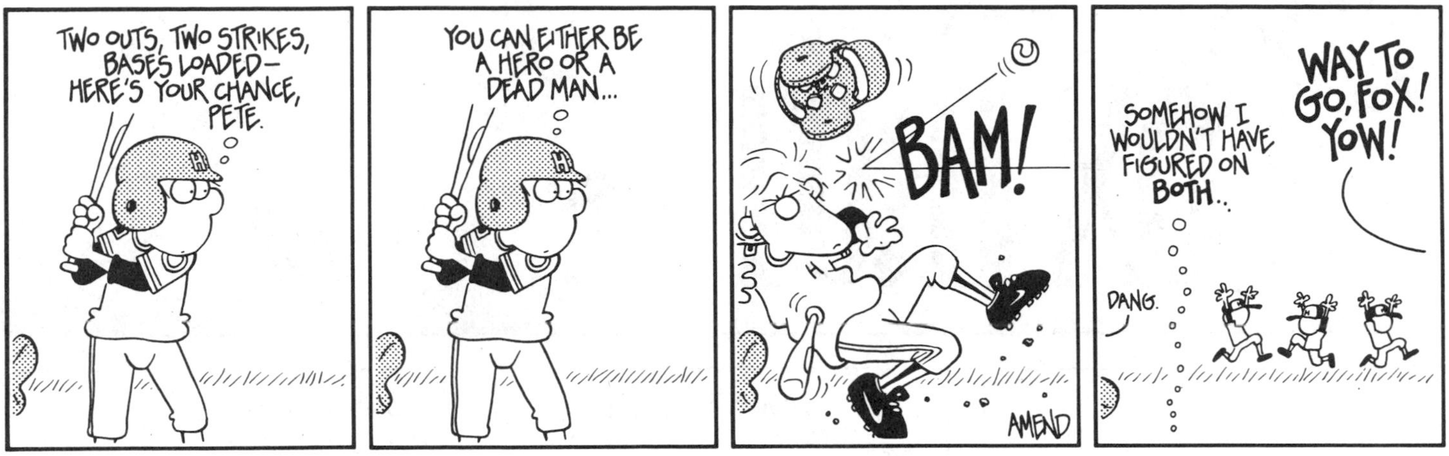

TWO OUTS, TWO STRIKES, BASES LOADED— HERE'S YOUR CHANCE, PETE.
YOU CAN EITHER BE A HERO OR A DEAD MAN...
BAM!
AMEND
SOMEHOW I WOULDN'T HAVE FIGURED ON BOTH...
WAY TO GO, FOX! YOW!
DANG.

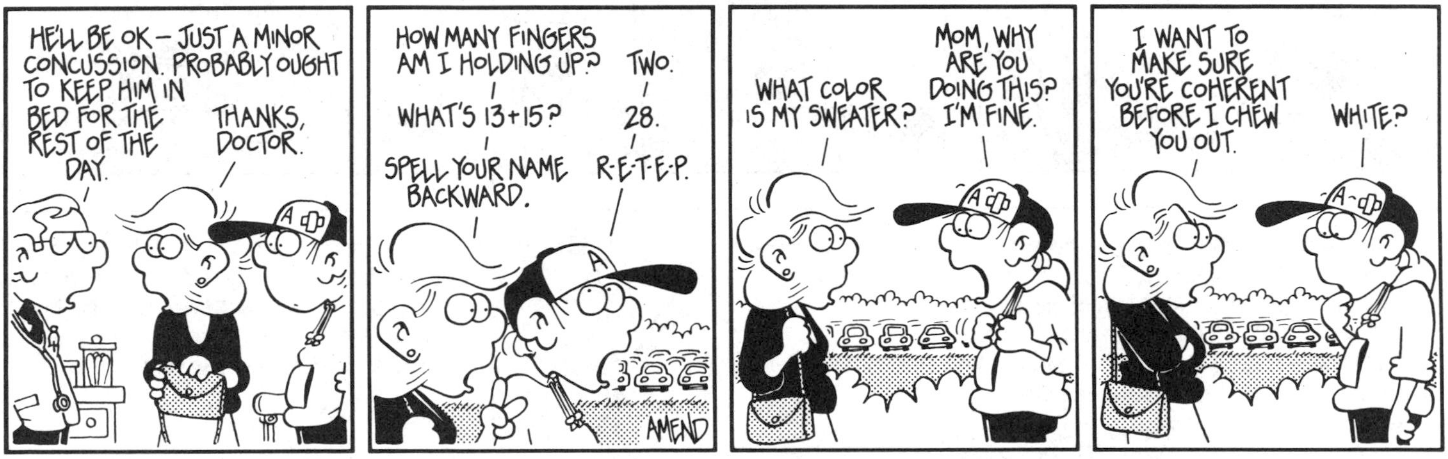

HE'LL BE OK — JUST A MINOR CONCUSSION. PROBABLY OUGHT TO KEEP HIM IN BED FOR THE REST OF THE DAY.
THANKS, DOCTOR.
HOW MANY FINGERS AM I HOLDING UP?
TWO.
WHAT'S 13+15?
28.
SPELL YOUR NAME BACKWARD.
R-E-T-E-P.
AMEND
WHAT COLOR IS MY SWEATER?
MOM, WHY ARE YOU DOING THIS? I'M FINE.
I WANT TO MAKE SURE YOU'RE COHERENT BEFORE I CHEW YOU OUT.
WHITE?

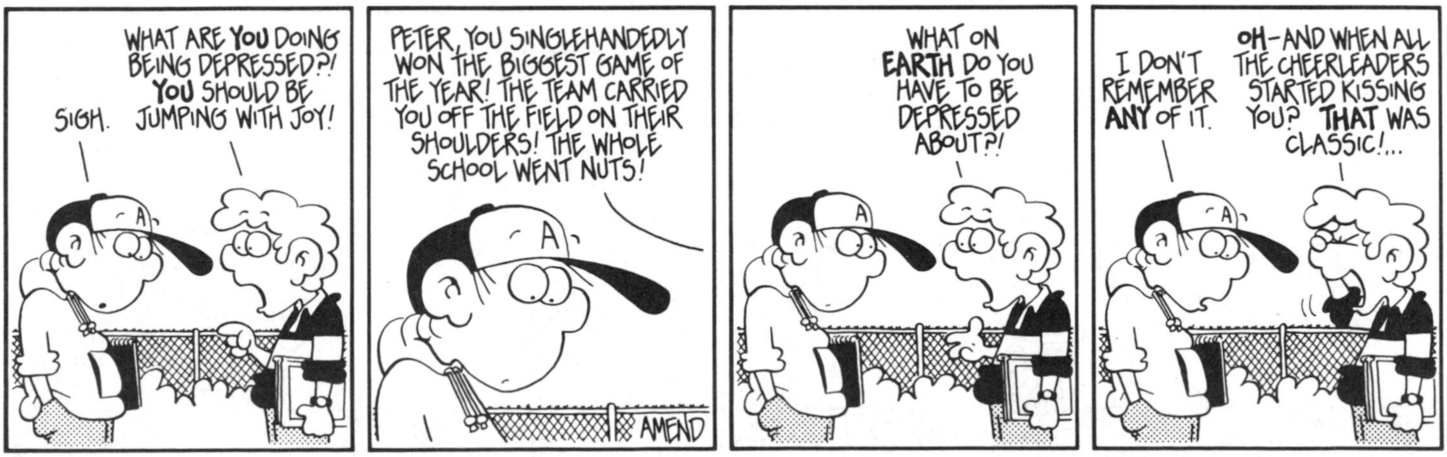

SIGH.
WHAT ARE YOU DOING BEING DEPRESSED?! YOU SHOULD BE JUMPING WITH JOY!
PETER, YOU SINGLEHANDEDLY WON THE BIGGEST GAME OF THE YEAR! THE TEAM CARRIED YOU OFF THE FIELD ON THEIR SHOULDERS! THE WHOLE SCHOOL WENT NUTS!
AMEND
WHAT ON EARTH DO YOU HAVE TO BE DEPRESSED ABOUT?!
I DON'T REMEMBER ANY OF IT.
OH—AND WHEN ALL THE CHEERLEADERS STARTED KISSING YOU? THAT WAS CLASSIC!...

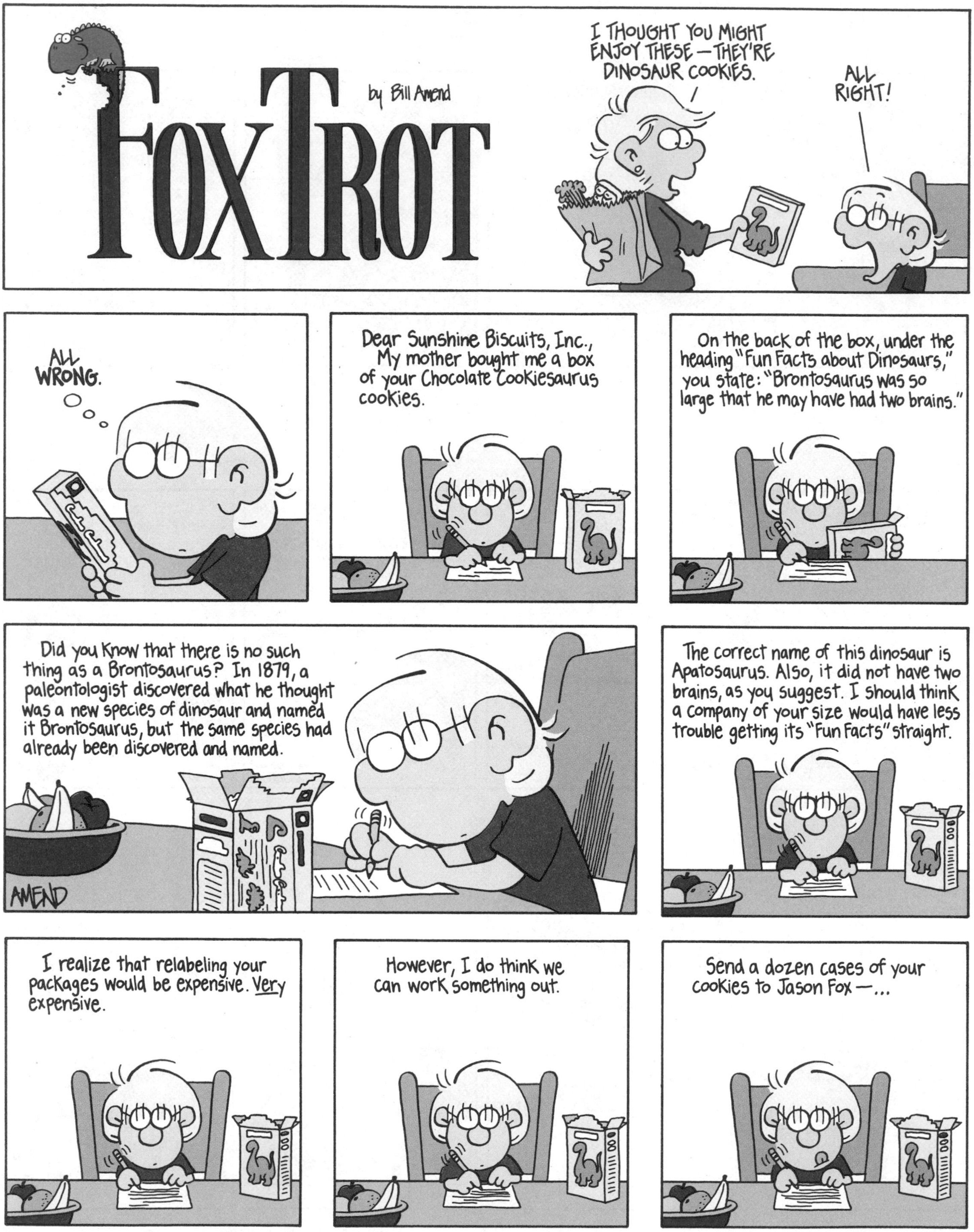
FoxTrot
by Bill Amend
I THOUGHT YOU MIGHT ENJOY THESE — THEY'RE DINOSAUR COOKIES.
ALL RIGHT!
ALL WRONG.
Dear Sunshine Biscuits, Inc.,
My mother bought me a box of your Chocolate Cookiesaurus cookies.
On the back of the box, under the heading "Fun Facts about Dinosaurs," you state: "Brontosaurus was so large that he may have had two brains."
Did you know that there is no such thing as a Brontosaurus? In 1879, a paleontologist discovered what he thought was a new species of dinosaur and named it Brontosaurus, but the same species had already been discovered and named.
AMEND
The correct name of this dinosaur is Apatosaurus. Also, it did not have two brains, as you suggest. I should think a company of your size would have less trouble getting its "Fun Facts" straight.
I realize that relabeling your packages would be expensive. Very expensive.
However, I do think we can work something out.
Send a dozen cases of your cookies to Jason Fox —...

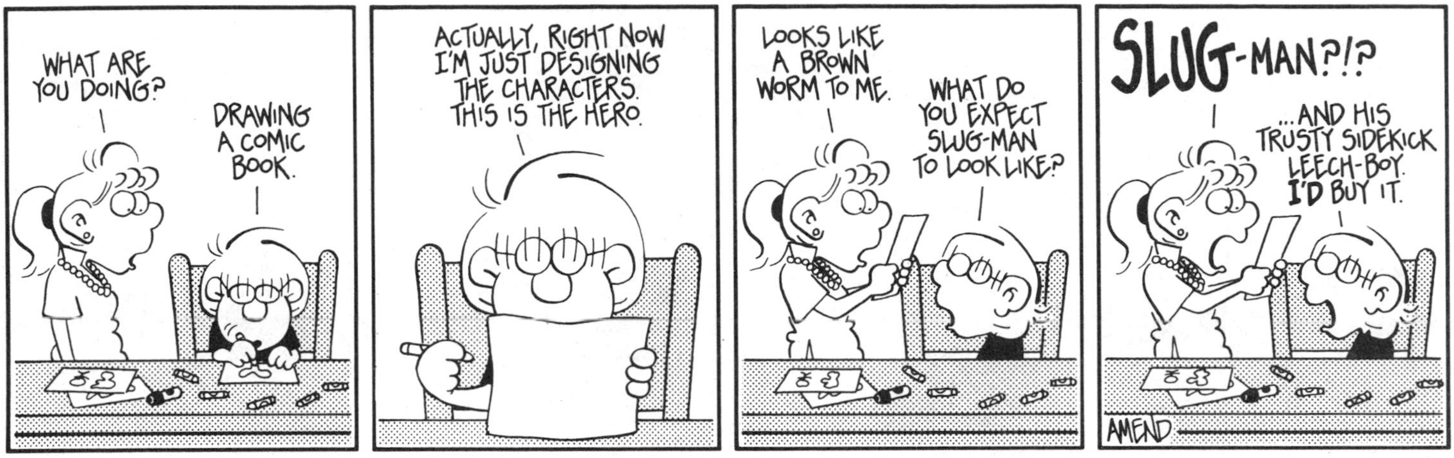
WHAT ARE YOU DOING?
DRAWING A COMIC BOOK.
ACTUALLY, RIGHT NOW I'M JUST DESIGNING THE CHARACTERS. THIS IS THE HERO.
LOOKS LIKE A BROWN WORM TO ME.
WHAT DO YOU EXPECT SLUG-MAN TO LOOK LIKE?
SLUG-MAN?!?
...AND HIS TRUSTY SIDEKICK LEECH-BOY. I'D BUY IT.
AMEND

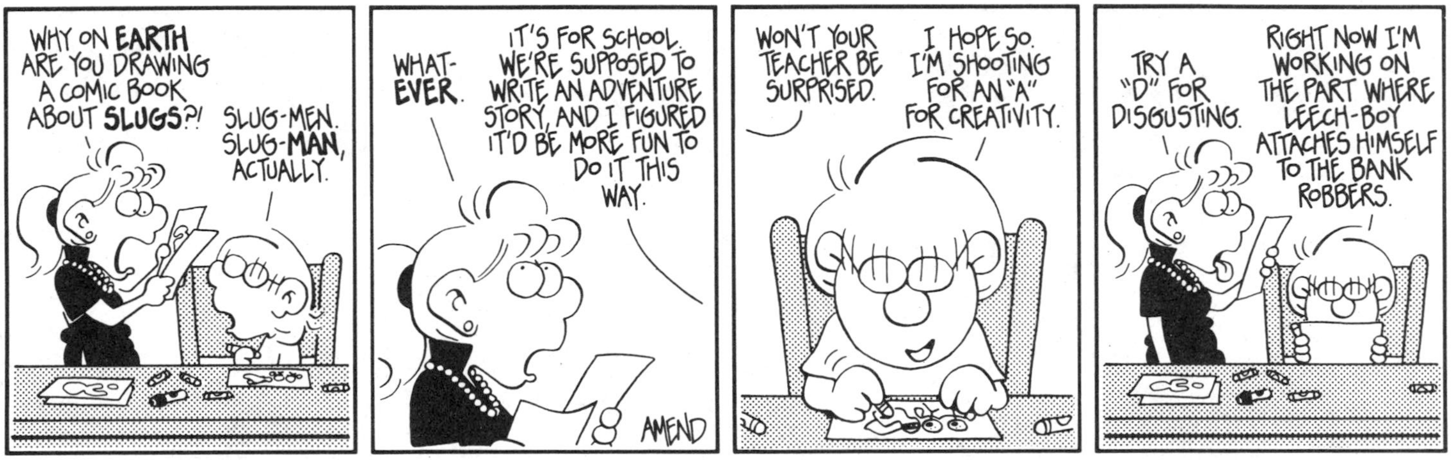
WHY ON EARTH ARE YOU DRAWING A COMIC BOOK ABOUT SLUGS?!
SLUG-MEN. SLUG-MAN, ACTUALLY.
IT'S FOR SCHOOL. WE'RE SUPPOSED TO WRITE AN ADVENTURE STORY, AND I FIGURED IT'D BE MORE FUN TO DO IT THIS WAY.
WHAT-EVER.
AMEND
WON'T YOUR TEACHER BE SURPRISED.
I HOPE SO. I'M SHOOTING FOR AN "A" FOR CREATIVITY.
TRY A "D" FOR DISGUSTING.
RIGHT NOW I'M WORKING ON THE PART WHERE LEECH-BOY ATTACHES HIMSELF TO THE BANK ROBBERS.

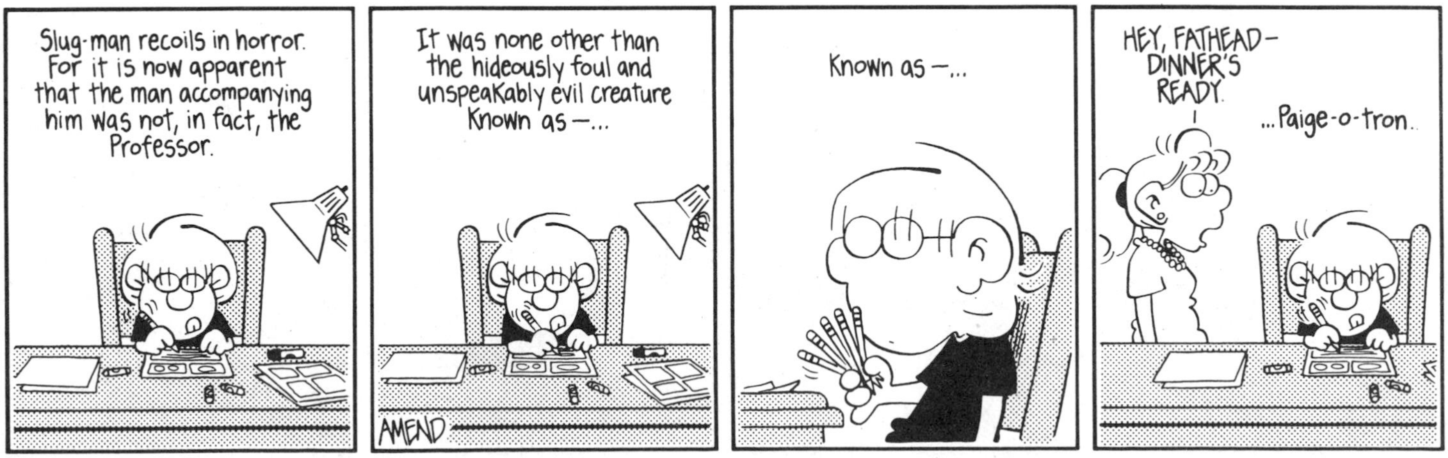
Slug-man recoils in horror. For it is now apparent that the man accompanying him was not, in fact, the Professor.
It was none other than the hideously foul and unspeakably evil creature known as —...
AMEND
Known as —...
HEY, FATHEAD-DINNER'S READY.
...Paige-o-tron.

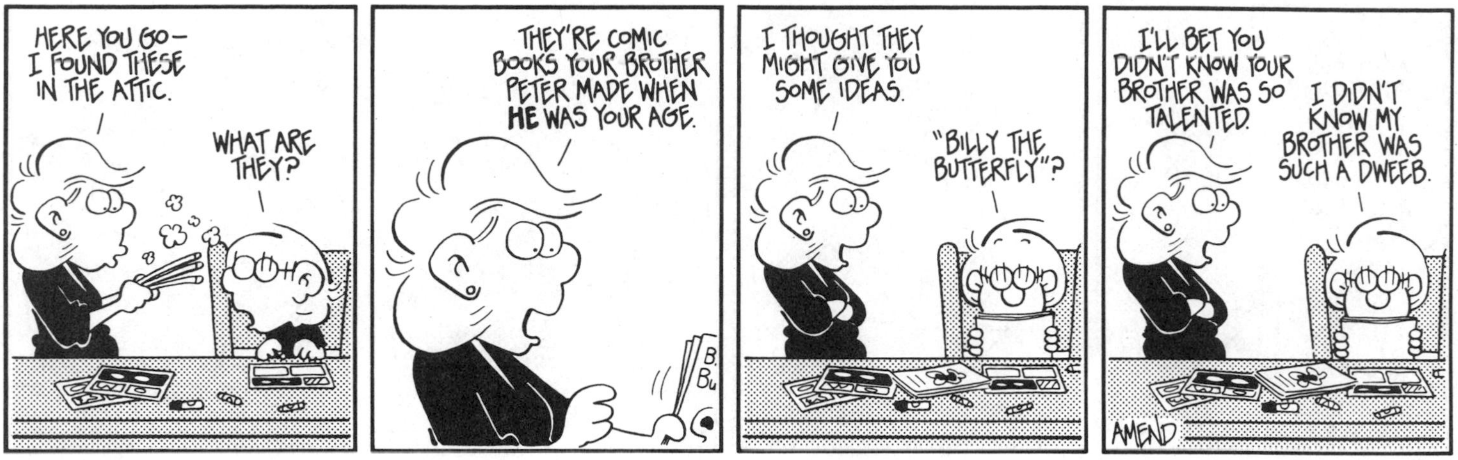
HERE YOU GO— I FOUND THESE IN THE ATTIC.
WHAT ARE THEY?
THEY'RE COMIC BOOKS YOUR BROTHER PETER MADE WHEN HE WAS YOUR AGE.
I THOUGHT THEY MIGHT GIVE YOU SOME IDEAS.
"BILLY THE BUTTERFLY"?
I'LL BET YOU DIDN'T KNOW YOUR BROTHER WAS SO TALENTED.
I DIDN'T KNOW MY BROTHER WAS SUCH A DWEEB.
AMEND

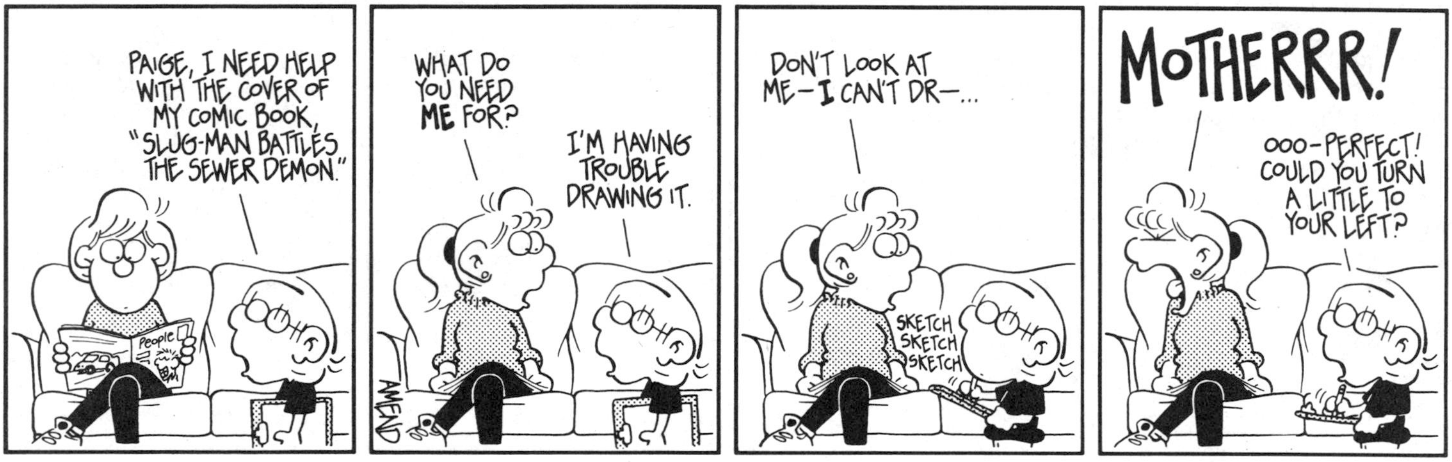
PAIGE, I NEED HELP WITH THE COVER OF MY COMIC BOOK, "SLUG-MAN BATTLES THE SEWER DEMON."
People
WHAT DO YOU NEED ME FOR?
I'M HAVING TROUBLE DRAWING IT.
AMEND
DON'T LOOK AT ME—I CAN'T DR—...
SKETCH SKETCH SKETCH
MOTHERRR!
OOO-PERFECT! COULD YOU TURN A LITTLE TO YOUR LEFT?

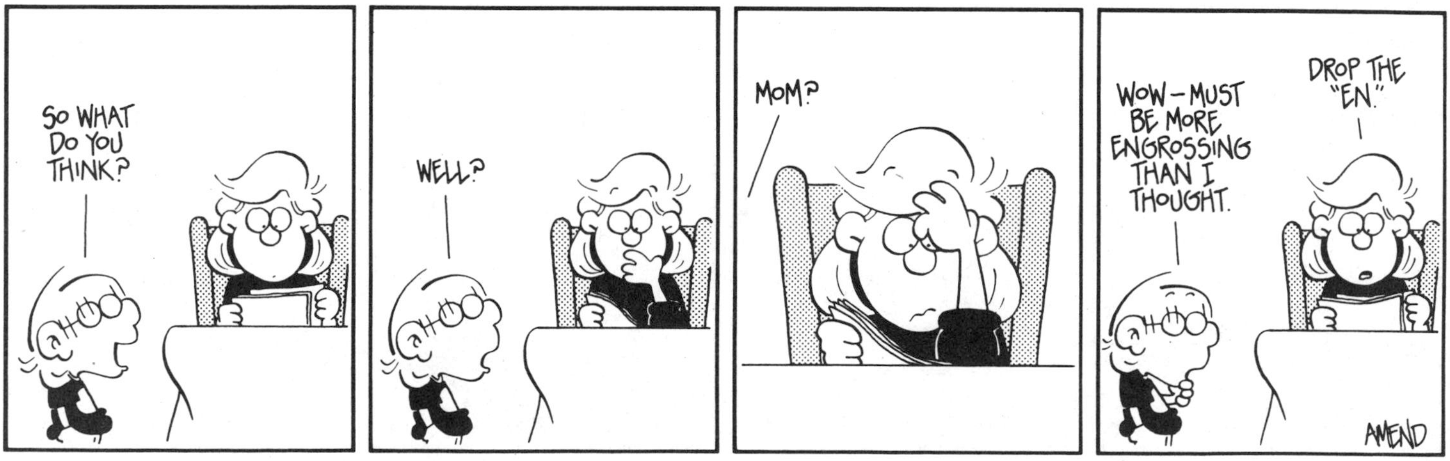
SO WHAT DO YOU THINK?
WELL?
MOM?
WOW—MUST BE MORE ENGROSSING THAN I THOUGHT.
DROP THE "EN."
AMEND

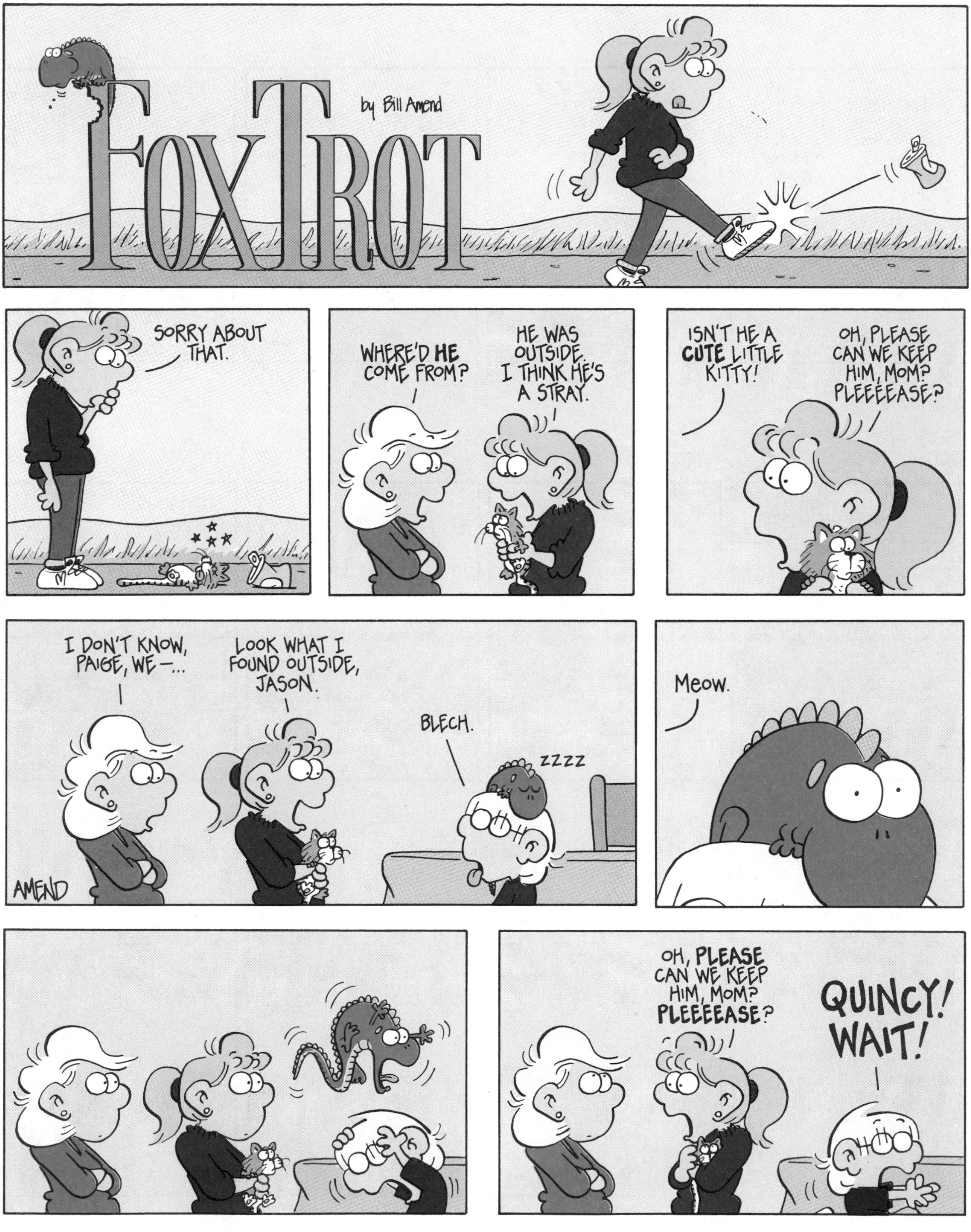
FoxTrot
by Bill Amend
SORRY ABOUT THAT.
WHERE'D HE COME FROM?
HE WAS OUTSIDE. I THINK HE'S A STRAY.
ISN'T HE A CUTE LITTLE KITTY!
OH, PLEASE CAN WE KEEP HIM, MOM? PLEEEEASE?
I DON'T KNOW, PAIGE, WE—...
LOOK WHAT I FOUND OUTSIDE, JASON.
BLECH.
ZZZZ
AMEND
Meow.
OH, PLEASE CAN WE KEEP HIM, MOM? PLEEEEASE?
QUINCY! WAIT!

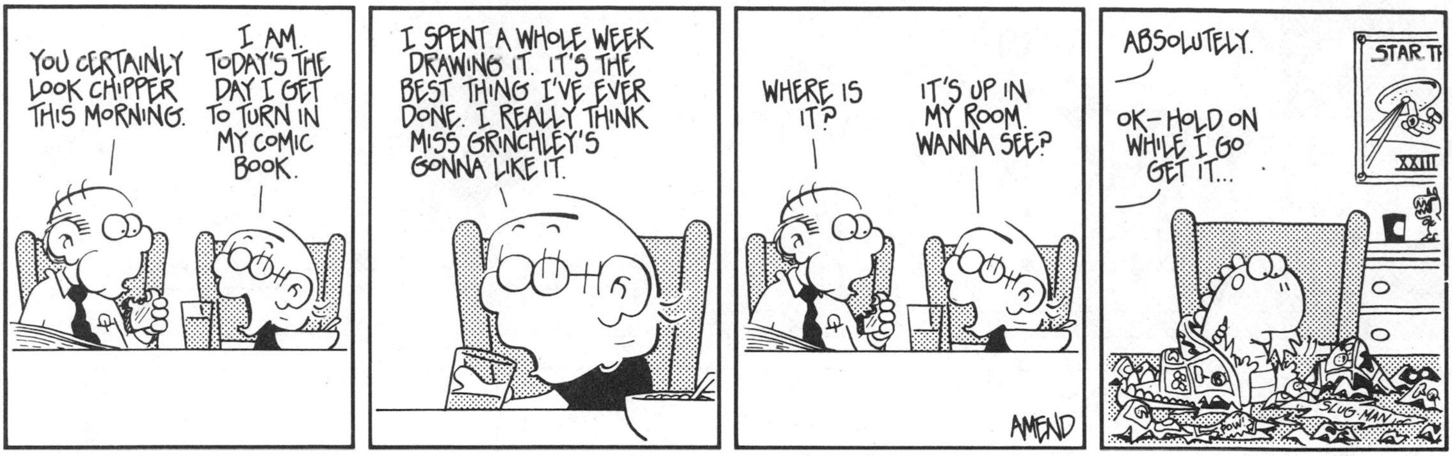
YOU CERTAINLY LOOK CHIPPER THIS MORNING.
I AM. TODAY'S THE DAY I GET TO TURN IN MY COMIC BOOK.
I SPENT A WHOLE WEEK DRAWING IT. IT'S THE BEST THING I'VE EVER DONE. I REALLY THINK MISS GRINCHLEY'S GONNA LIKE IT.
WHERE IS IT?
IT'S UP IN MY ROOM. WANNA SEE?
AMEND
ABSOLUTELY.
OK–HOLD ON WHILE I GO GET IT...
XXIII
SLUG-MAN
POW!

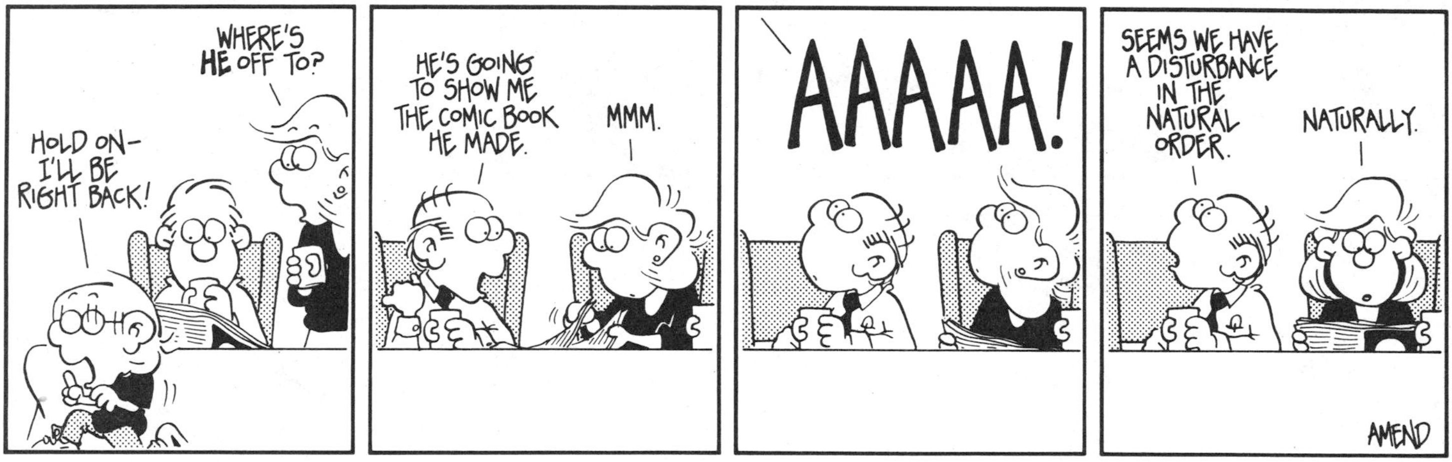
WHERE'S **HE** OFF TO?
HOLD ON– I'LL BE RIGHT BACK!
HE'S GOING TO SHOW ME THE COMIC BOOK HE MADE.
MMM.
AAAAA!
SEEMS WE HAVE A DISTURBANCE IN THE NATURAL ORDER.
NATURALLY.
AMEND

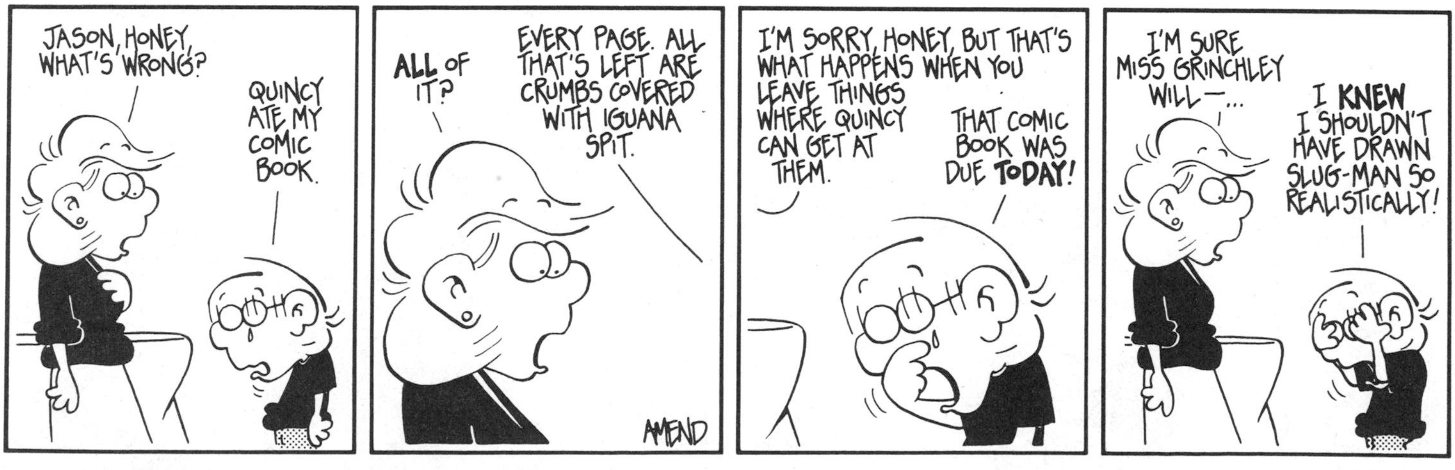
JASON, HONEY, WHAT'S WRONG?
QUINCY ATE MY COMIC BOOK.
ALL OF IT?
EVERY PAGE. ALL THAT'S LEFT ARE CRUMBS COVERED WITH IGUANA SPIT.
AMEND
I'M SORRY, HONEY, BUT THAT'S WHAT HAPPENS WHEN YOU LEAVE THINGS WHERE QUINCY CAN GET AT THEM.
THAT COMIC BOOK WAS DUE **TODAY**!
I'M SURE MISS GRINCHLEY WILL–...
I **KNEW** I SHOULDN'T HAVE DRAWN SLUG-MAN SO REALISTICALLY!

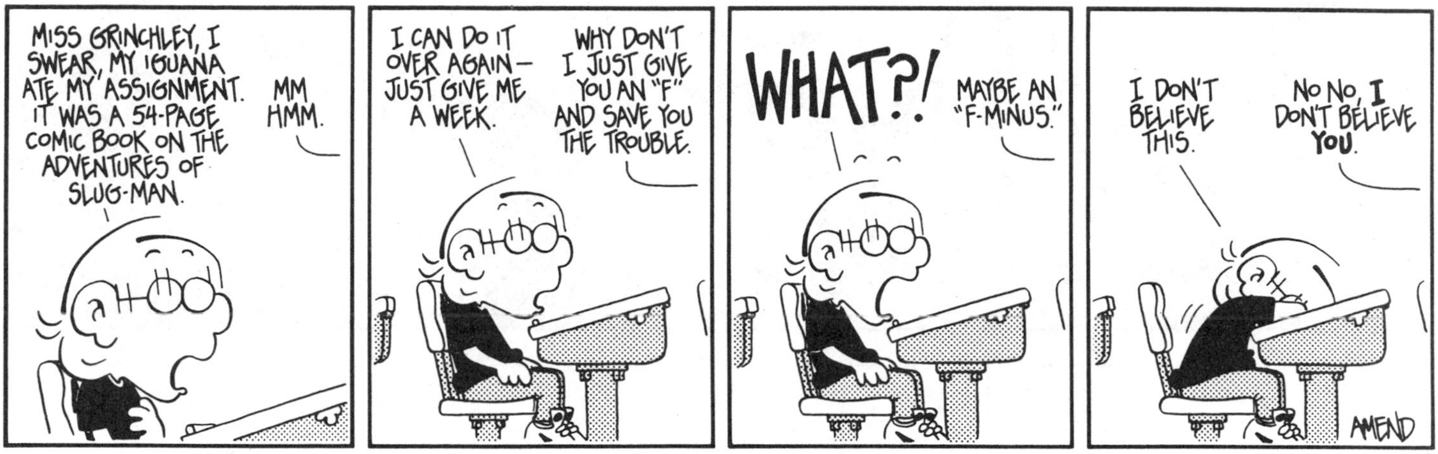
MISS GRINCHLEY, I SWEAR, MY IGUANA ATE MY ASSIGNMENT. IT WAS A 54-PAGE COMIC BOOK ON THE ADVENTURES OF SLUG-MAN.
MM HMM.
I CAN DO IT OVER AGAIN— JUST GIVE ME A WEEK.
WHY DON'T I JUST GIVE YOU AN "F" AND SAVE YOU THE TROUBLE.
WHAT?!
MAYBE AN "F-MINUS."
I DON'T BELIEVE THIS.
NO NO, I DON'T BELIEVE YOU.
AMEND

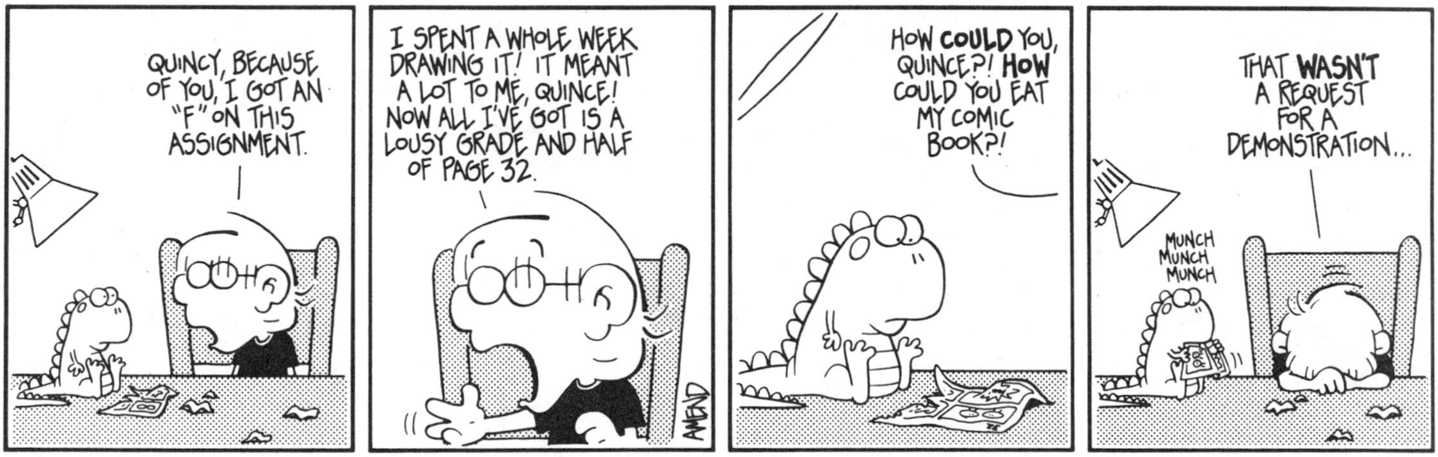
QUINCY, BECAUSE OF YOU, I GOT AN "F" ON THIS ASSIGNMENT.
I SPENT A WHOLE WEEK DRAWING IT! IT MEANT A LOT TO ME, QUINCE! NOW ALL I'VE GOT IS A LOUSY GRADE AND HALF OF PAGE 32.
AMEND
HOW COULD YOU, QUINCE?! HOW COULD YOU EAT MY COMIC BOOK?!
MUNCH MUNCH MUNCH
THAT WASN'T A REQUEST FOR A DEMONSTRATION...

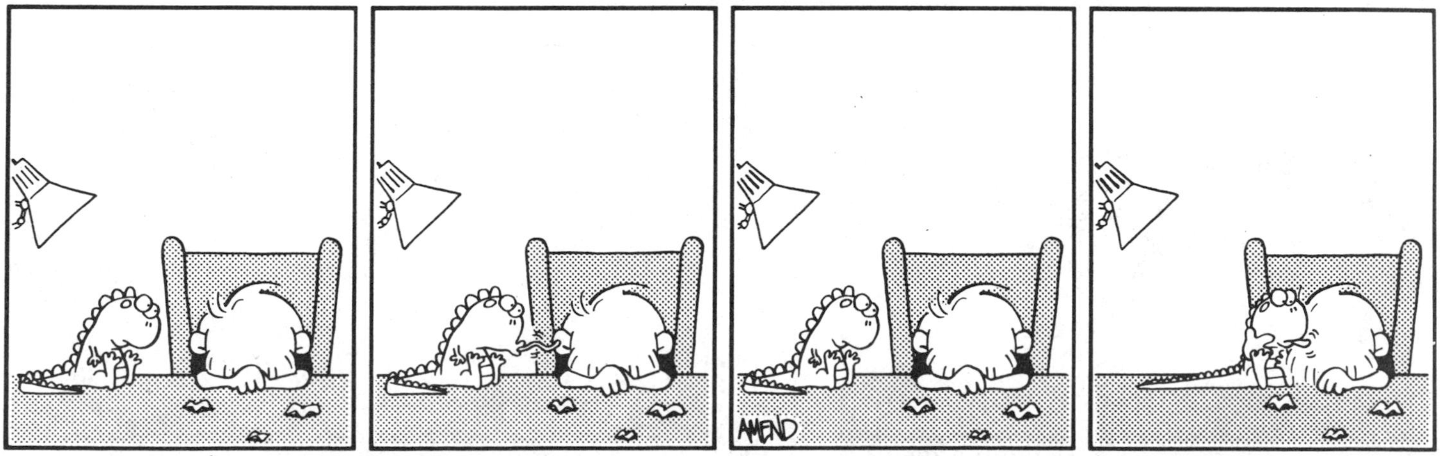
AMEND

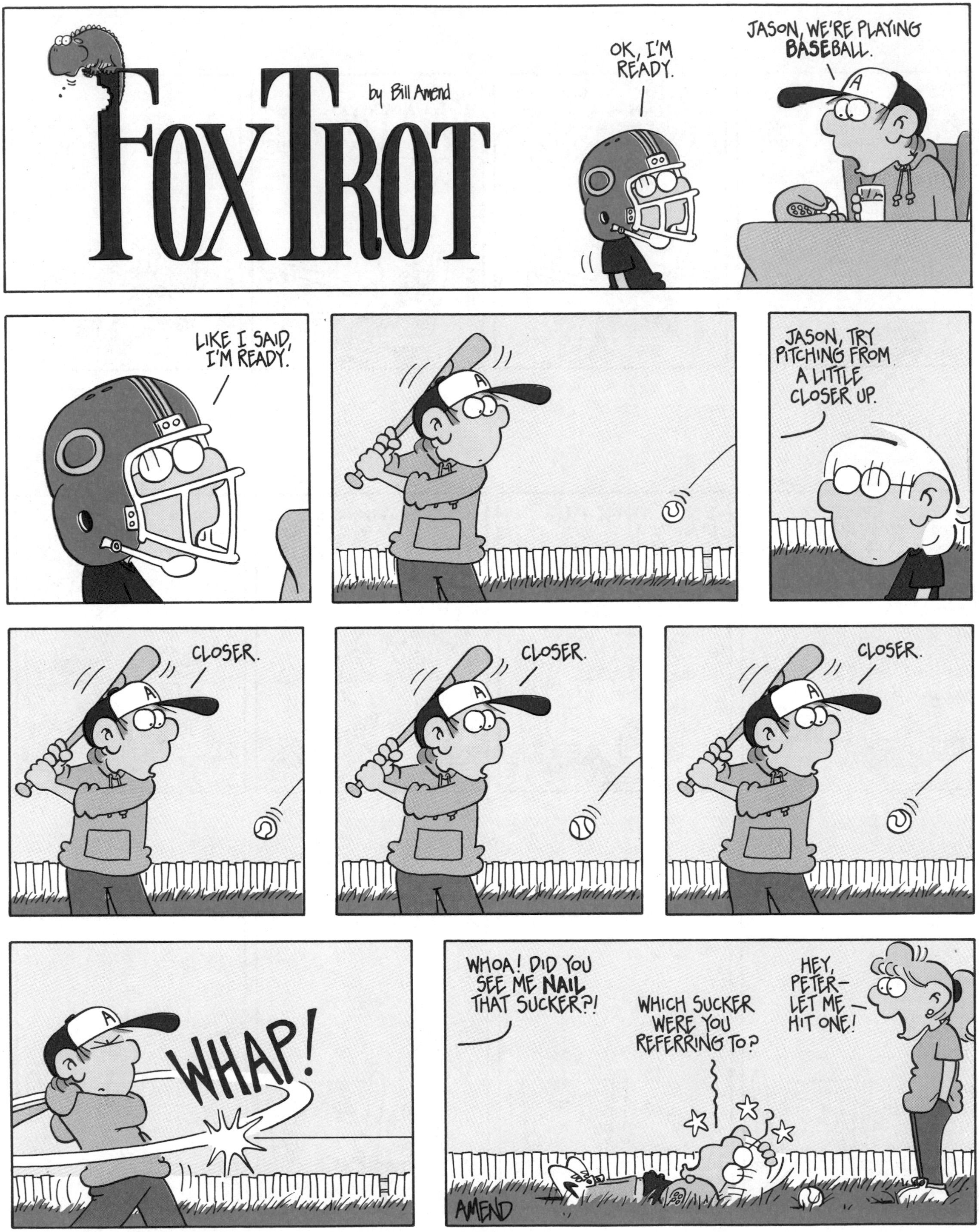

FoxTrot
by Bill Amend
OK, I'M READY.
JASON, WE'RE PLAYING **BASE**BALL.
LIKE I SAID, I'M READY.
JASON, TRY PITCHING FROM A LITTLE CLOSER UP.
CLOSER.
CLOSER.
CLOSER.
WHAP!
WHOA! DID YOU SEE ME **NAIL** THAT SUCKER?!
WHICH SUCKER WERE YOU REFERRING TO?
HEY, PETER–LET ME HIT ONE!
AMEND

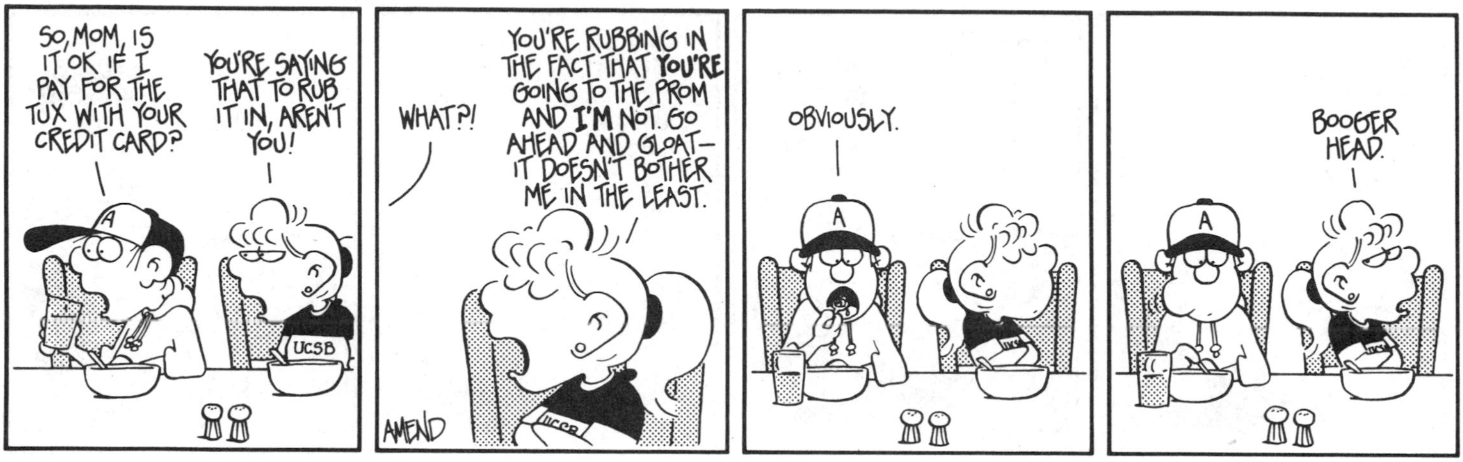
SO, MOM, IS IT OK IF I PAY FOR THE TUX WITH YOUR CREDIT CARD?
YOU'RE SAYING THAT TO RUB IT IN, AREN'T YOU!
UCSB
WHAT?!
YOU'RE RUBBING IN THE FACT THAT **YOU'RE** GOING TO THE PROM AND **I'M** NOT. GO AHEAD AND GLOAT— IT DOESN'T BOTHER ME IN THE LEAST.
AMEND
OBVIOUSLY.
BOOGER HEAD.

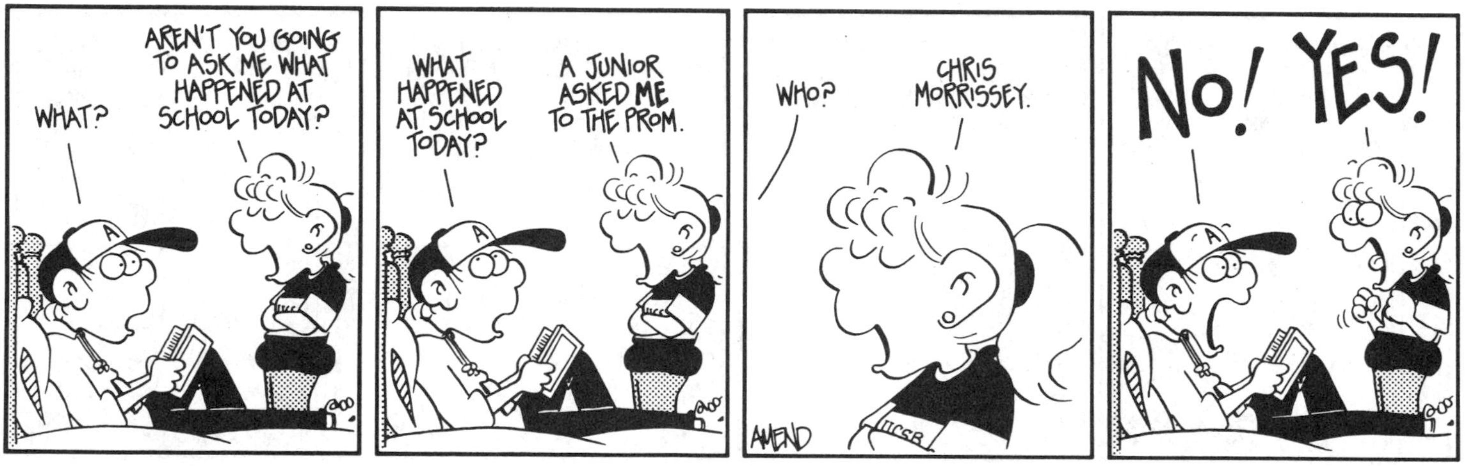
WHAT?
AREN'T YOU GOING TO ASK ME WHAT HAPPENED AT SCHOOL TODAY?
WHAT HAPPENED AT SCHOOL TODAY?
A JUNIOR ASKED **ME** TO THE PROM.
WHO?
CHRIS MORRISSEY.
AMEND
NO!
YES!

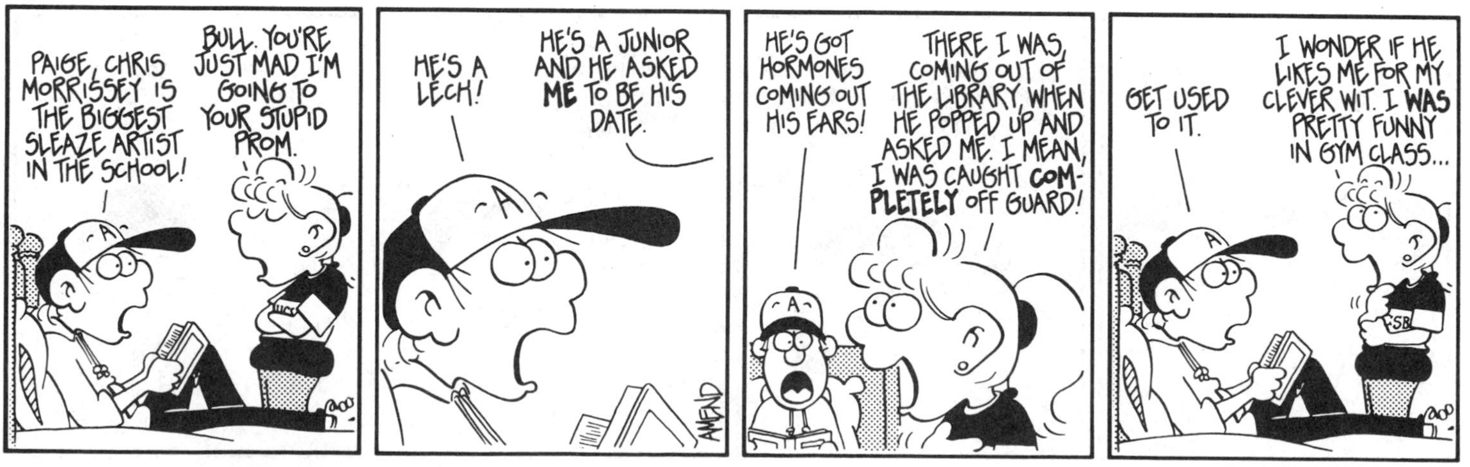
PAIGE, CHRIS MORRISSEY IS THE BIGGEST SLEAZE ARTIST IN THE SCHOOL!
BULL. YOU'RE JUST MAD I'M GOING TO YOUR STUPID PROM.
HE'S A LECH!
HE'S A JUNIOR AND HE ASKED **ME** TO BE HIS DATE.
AMEND
HE'S GOT HORMONES COMING OUT HIS EARS!
THERE I WAS, COMING OUT OF THE LIBRARY, WHEN HE POPPED UP AND ASKED ME. I MEAN, I WAS CAUGHT **COMPLETELY** OFF GUARD!
GET USED TO IT.
I WONDER IF HE LIKES ME FOR MY CLEVER WIT. I **WAS** PRETTY FUNNY IN GYM CLASS...

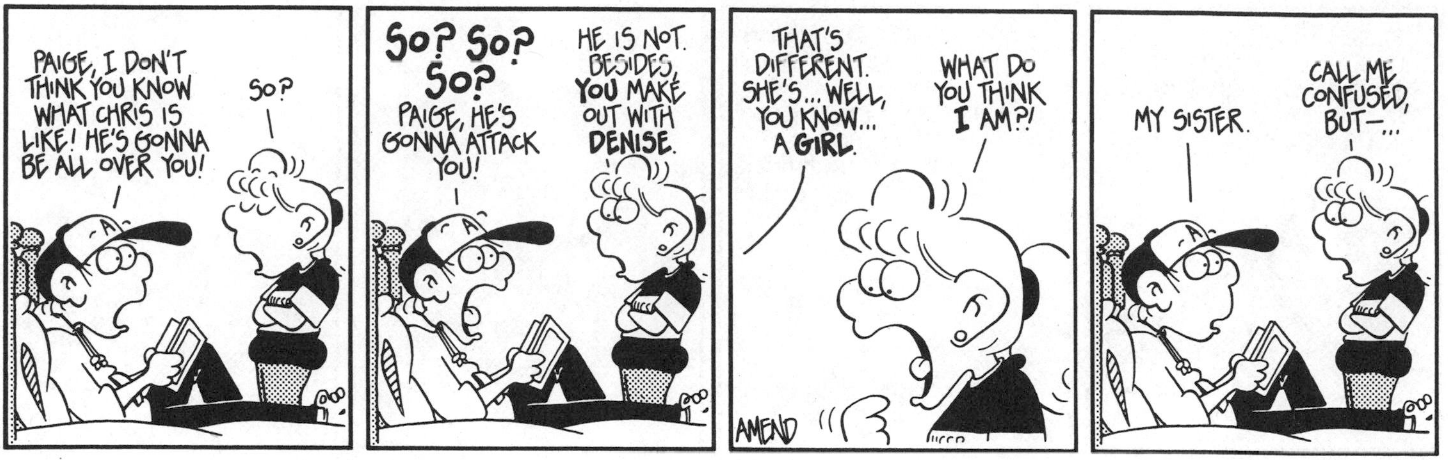
PAIGE, I DON'T THINK YOU KNOW WHAT CHRIS IS LIKE! HE'S GONNA BE ALL OVER YOU!
SO?
SO? SO? SO? PAIGE, HE'S GONNA ATTACK YOU!
HE IS NOT. BESIDES, **YOU** MAKE OUT WITH **DENISE**.
THAT'S DIFFERENT. SHE'S... WELL, YOU KNOW... A **GIRL**.
WHAT DO YOU THINK **I** AM?!
AMEND
MY SISTER.
CALL ME CONFUSED, BUT—...

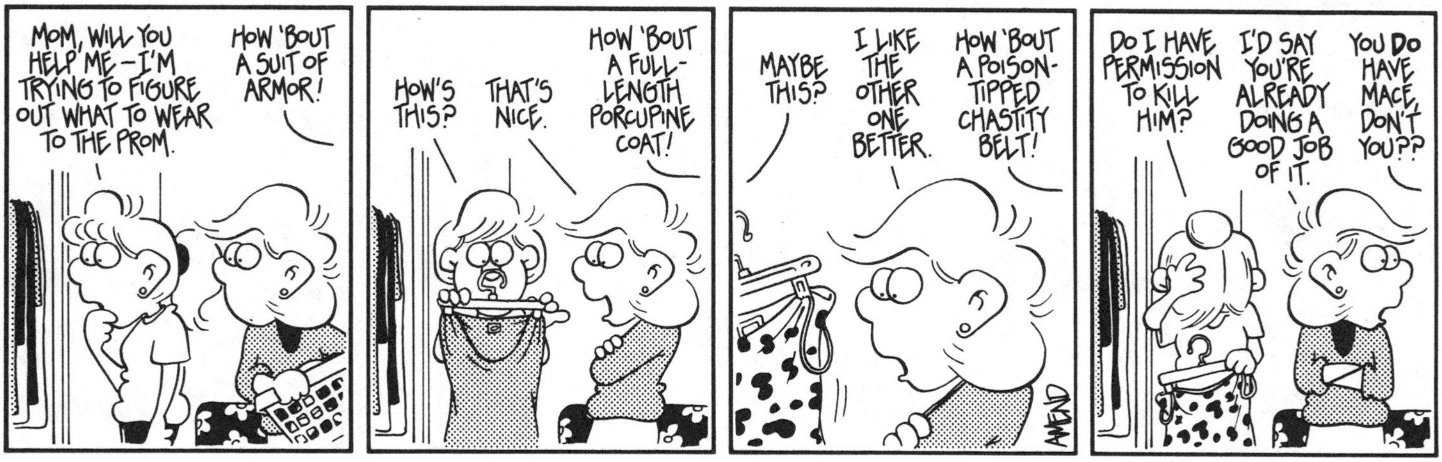
MOM, WILL YOU HELP ME—I'M TRYING TO FIGURE OUT WHAT TO WEAR TO THE PROM.
HOW 'BOUT A SUIT OF ARMOR!
HOW'S THIS?
THAT'S NICE.
HOW 'BOUT A FULL-LENGTH PORCUPINE COAT!
MAYBE THIS?
I LIKE THE OTHER ONE BETTER.
HOW 'BOUT A POISON-TIPPED CHASTITY BELT!
AMEND
DO I HAVE PERMISSION TO KILL HIM?
I'D SAY YOU'RE ALREADY DOING A GOOD JOB OF IT.
YOU **DO** HAVE MACE, DON'T YOU??

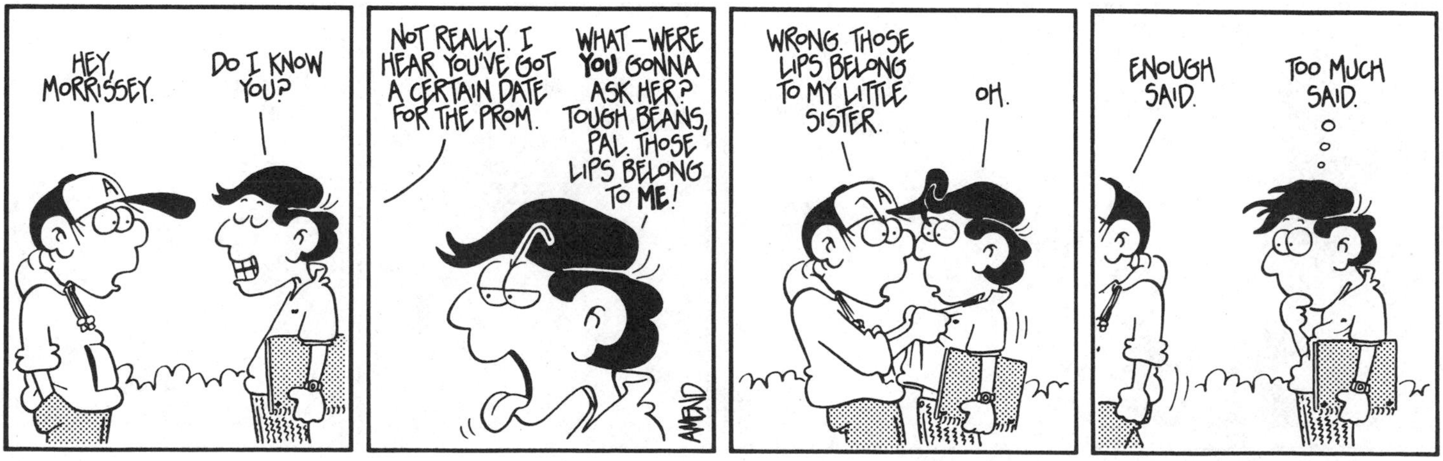
HEY, MORRISSEY.
DO I KNOW YOU?
NOT REALLY. I HEAR YOU'VE GOT A CERTAIN DATE FOR THE PROM.
WHAT—WERE **YOU** GONNA ASK HER? TOUGH BEANS, PAL. THOSE LIPS BELONG TO **ME**!
AMEND
WRONG. THOSE LIPS BELONG TO MY LITTLE SISTER.
OH.
ENOUGH SAID.
TOO MUCH SAID.

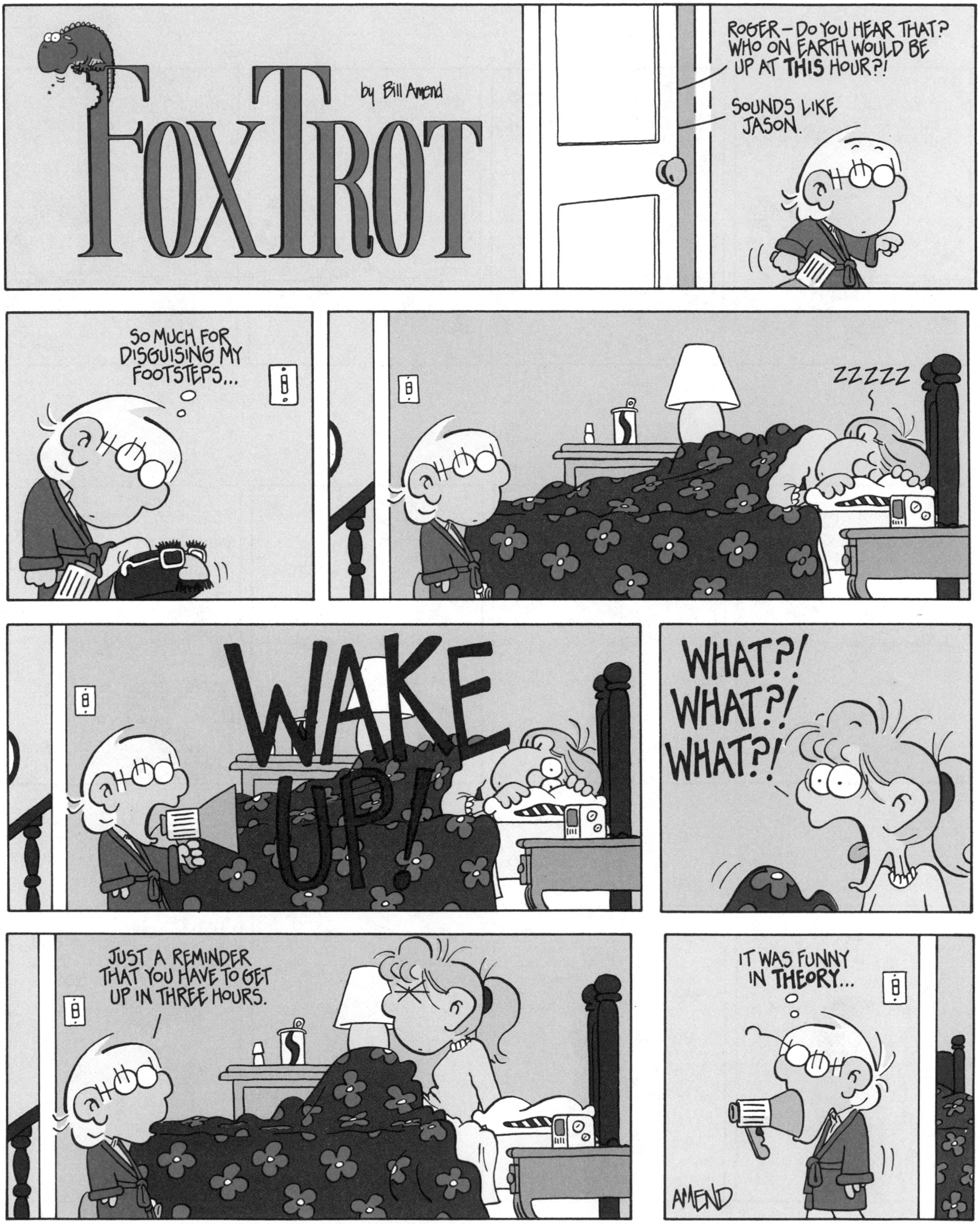
FoxTrot
by Bill Amend
ROGER – DO YOU HEAR THAT? WHO ON EARTH WOULD BE UP AT THIS HOUR?!
SOUNDS LIKE JASON.
SO MUCH FOR DISGUISING MY FOOTSTEPS...
ZZZZZ
WAKE UP!
WHAT?! WHAT?! WHAT?!
JUST A REMINDER THAT YOU HAVE TO GET UP IN THREE HOURS.
IT WAS FUNNY IN THEORY...
AMEND

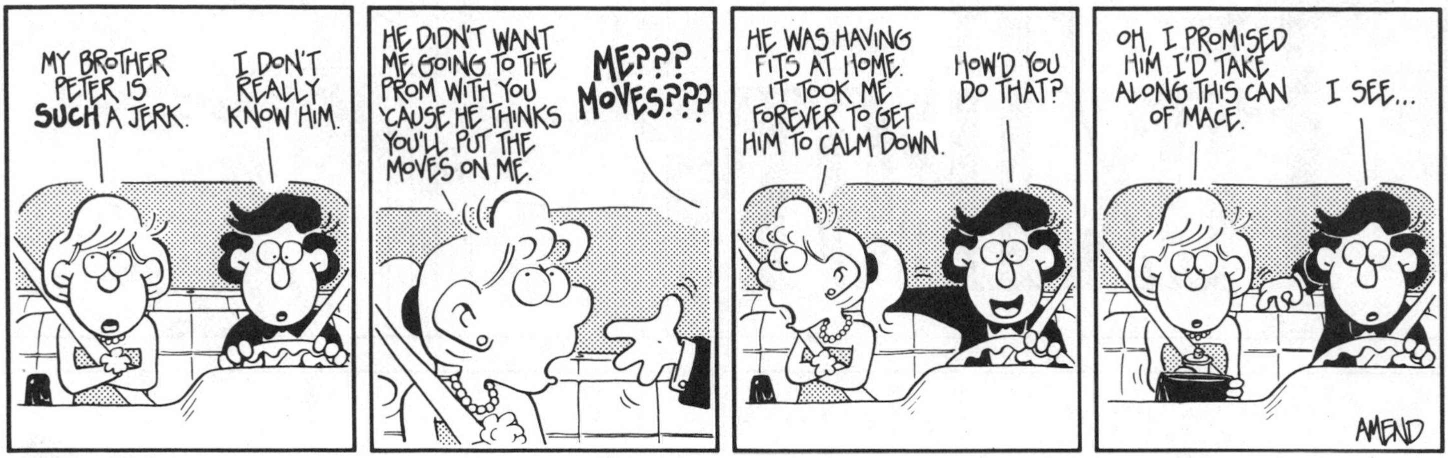
MY BROTHER PETER IS **SUCH** A JERK.
I DON'T REALLY KNOW HIM.
HE DIDN'T WANT ME GOING TO THE PROM WITH YOU 'CAUSE HE THINKS YOU'LL PUT THE MOVES ON ME.
ME??? MOVES???
HE WAS HAVING FITS AT HOME. IT TOOK ME FOREVER TO GET HIM TO CALM DOWN.
HOW'D YOU DO THAT?
OH, I PROMISED HIM I'D TAKE ALONG THIS CAN OF MACE.
I SEE...
AMEND

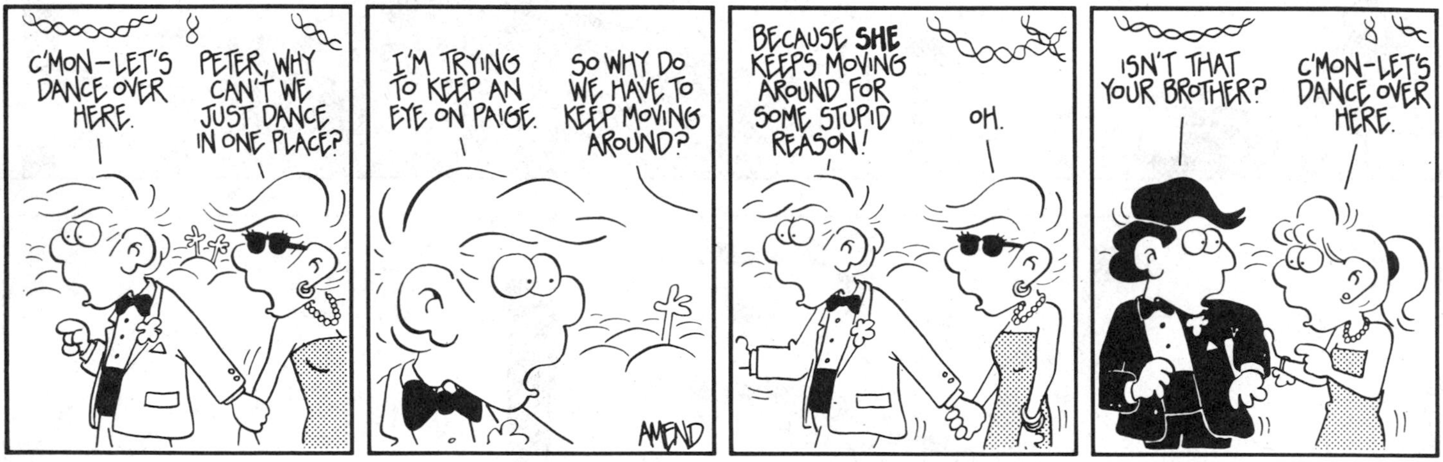
C'MON—LET'S DANCE OVER HERE.
PETER, WHY CAN'T WE JUST DANCE IN ONE PLACE?
I'M TRYING TO KEEP AN EYE ON PAIGE.
SO WHY DO WE HAVE TO KEEP MOVING AROUND?
AMEND
BECAUSE **SHE** KEEPS MOVING AROUND FOR SOME STUPID REASON!
OH.
ISN'T THAT YOUR BROTHER?
C'MON—LET'S DANCE OVER HERE.

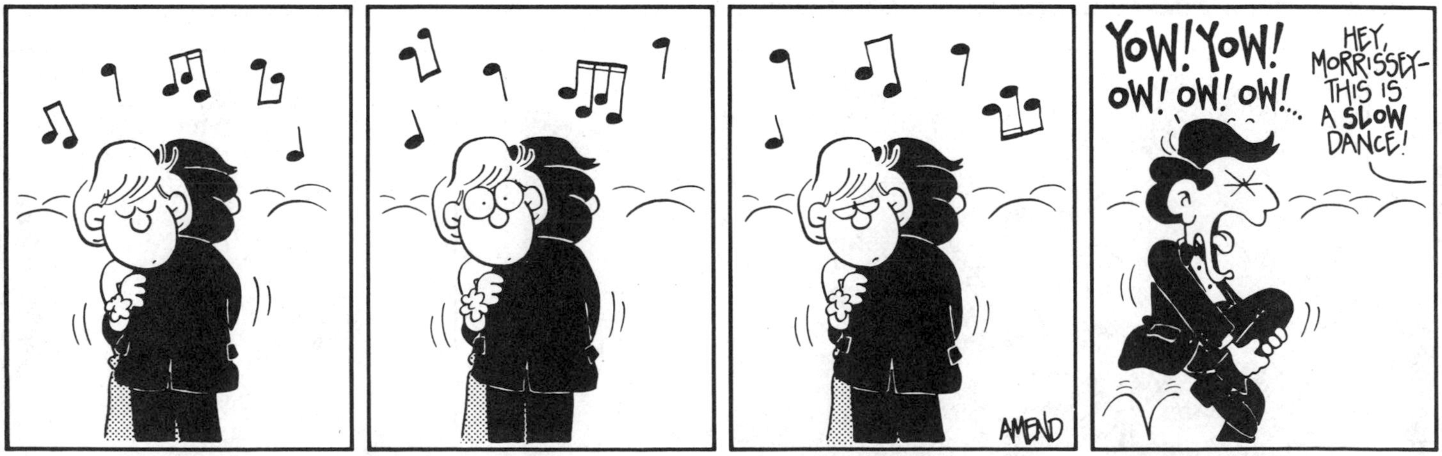
AMEND
YOW! YOW! OW! OW! OW!...
HEY, MORRISSEY—THIS IS A **SLOW** DANCE!

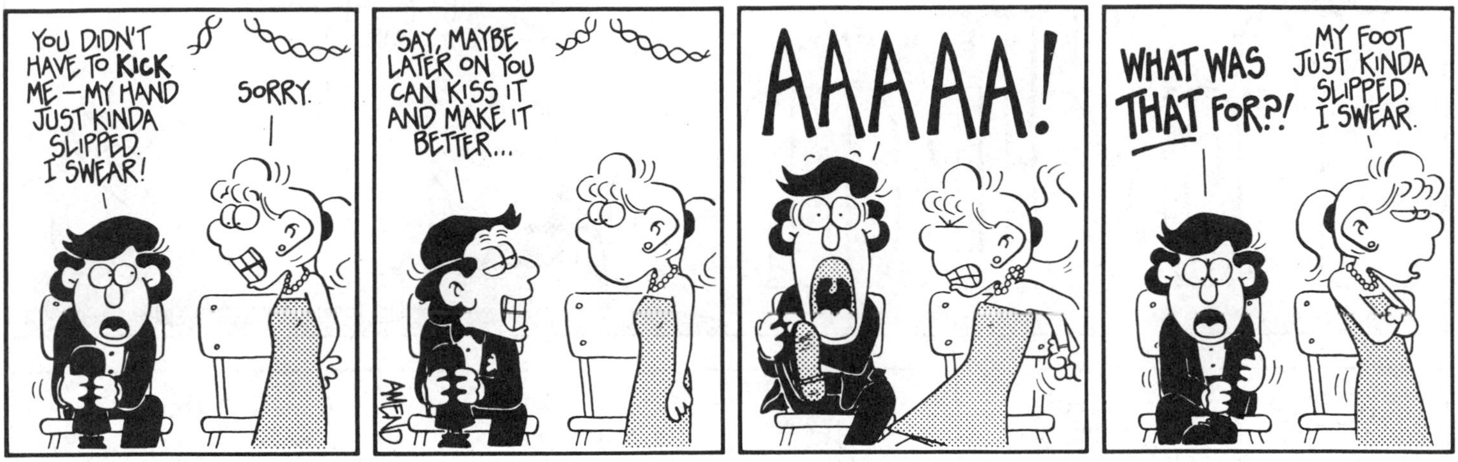
YOU DIDN'T HAVE TO **KICK** ME — MY HAND JUST KINDA SLIPPED. I SWEAR!
SORRY.
SAY, MAYBE LATER ON YOU CAN KISS IT AND MAKE IT BETTER...
AMEND
AAAAA!
WHAT WAS THAT FOR?!
MY FOOT JUST KINDA SLIPPED. I SWEAR.

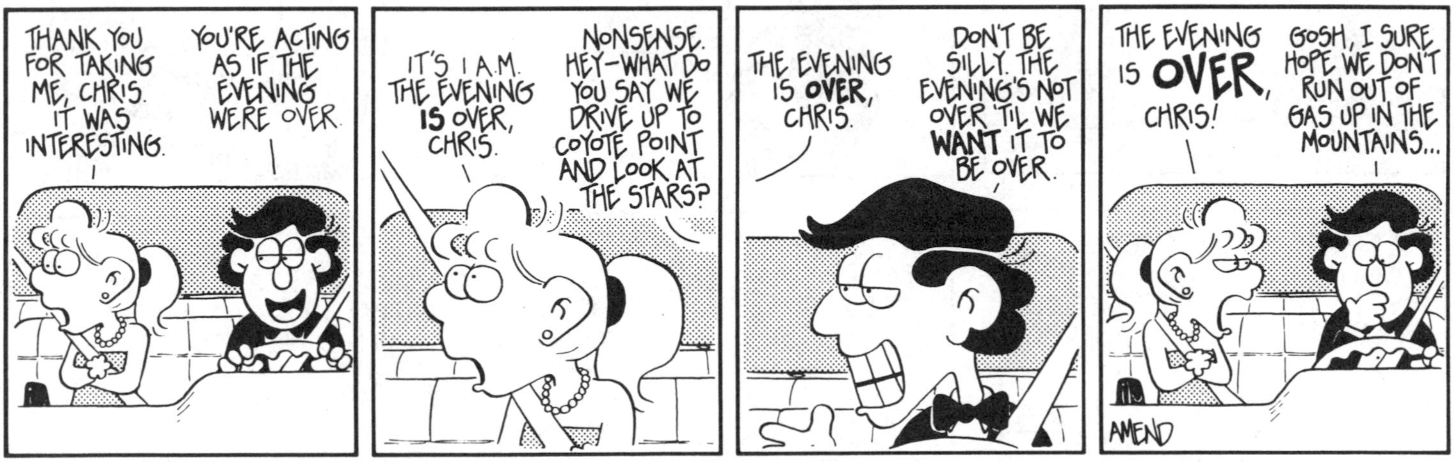
THANK YOU FOR TAKING ME, CHRIS. IT WAS INTERESTING.
YOU'RE ACTING AS IF THE EVENING WERE OVER.
IT'S 1 A.M. THE EVENING **IS** OVER, CHRIS.
NONSENSE. HEY—WHAT DO YOU SAY WE DRIVE UP TO COYOTE POINT AND LOOK AT THE STARS?
THE EVENING IS **OVER**, CHRIS.
DON'T BE SILLY. THE EVENING'S NOT OVER 'TIL WE **WANT** IT TO BE OVER.
THE EVENING IS **OVER**, CHRIS!
GOSH, I SURE HOPE WE DON'T RUN OUT OF GAS UP IN THE MOUNTAINS...
AMEND

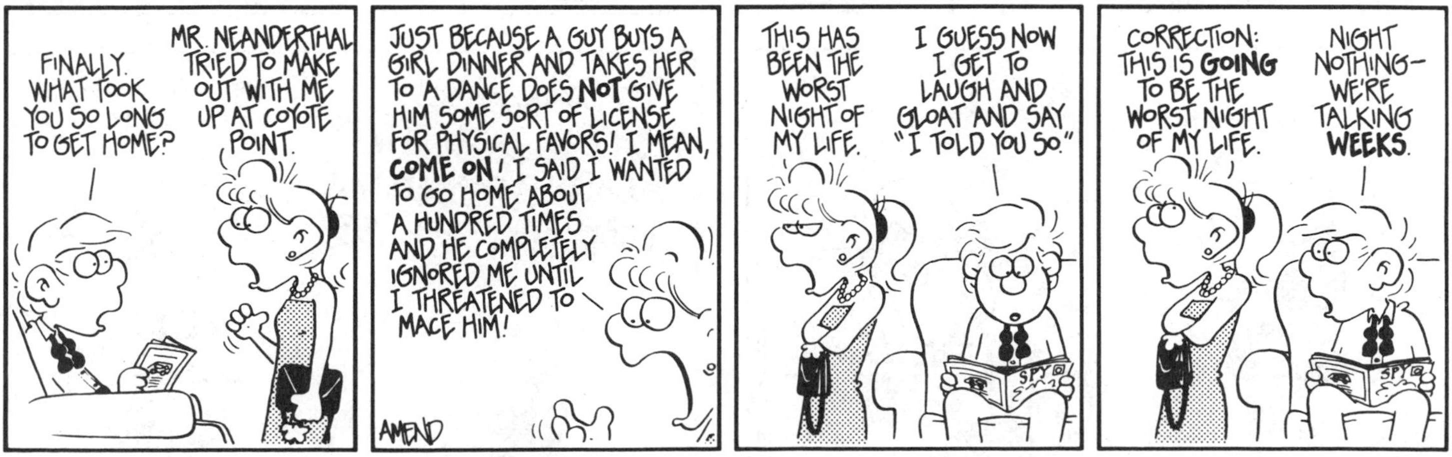
FINALLY. WHAT TOOK YOU SO LONG TO GET HOME?
MR. NEANDERTHAL TRIED TO MAKE OUT WITH ME UP AT COYOTE POINT.
JUST BECAUSE A GUY BUYS A GIRL DINNER AND TAKES HER TO A DANCE DOES **NOT** GIVE HIM SOME SORT OF LICENSE FOR PHYSICAL FAVORS! I MEAN, **COME ON**! I SAID I WANTED TO GO HOME ABOUT A HUNDRED TIMES AND HE COMPLETELY IGNORED ME UNTIL I THREATENED TO MACE HIM!
AMEND
THIS HAS BEEN THE WORST NIGHT OF MY LIFE.
I GUESS NOW I GET TO LAUGH AND GLOAT AND SAY "I TOLD YOU SO."
CORRECTION: THIS IS **GOING** TO BE THE WORST NIGHT OF MY LIFE.
NIGHT NOTHING— WE'RE TALKING **WEEKS**.

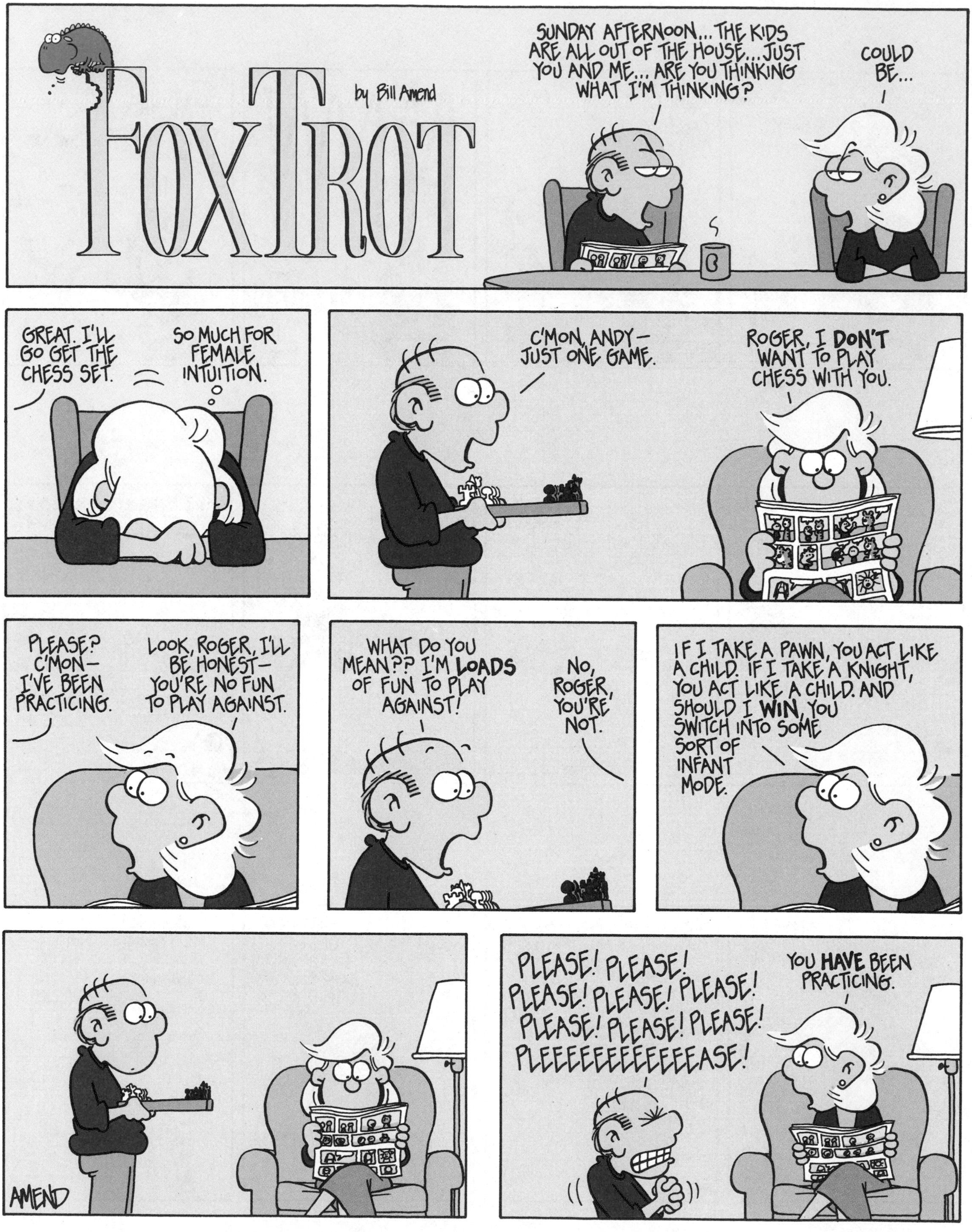

FoxTrot
by Bill Amend
SUNDAY AFTERNOON... THE KIDS ARE ALL OUT OF THE HOUSE... JUST YOU AND ME... ARE YOU THINKING WHAT I'M THINKING?
COULD BE...
GREAT. I'LL GO GET THE CHESS SET.
SO MUCH FOR FEMALE INTUITION.
C'MON, ANDY— JUST ONE GAME.
ROGER, I **DON'T** WANT TO PLAY CHESS WITH YOU.
PLEASE? C'MON— I'VE BEEN PRACTICING.
LOOK, ROGER, I'LL BE HONEST— YOU'RE NO FUN TO PLAY AGAINST.
WHAT DO YOU MEAN?? I'M **LOADS** OF FUN TO PLAY AGAINST!
NO, ROGER, YOU'RE NOT.
IF I TAKE A PAWN, YOU ACT LIKE A CHILD. IF I TAKE A KNIGHT, YOU ACT LIKE A CHILD. AND SHOULD I **WIN**, YOU SWITCH INTO SOME SORT OF INFANT MODE.
AMEND
PLEASE! PLEASE! PLEASE! PLEASE! PLEASE! PLEASE! PLEASE! PLEASE! PLEEEEEEEEEEEEEASE!
YOU **HAVE** BEEN PRACTICING.

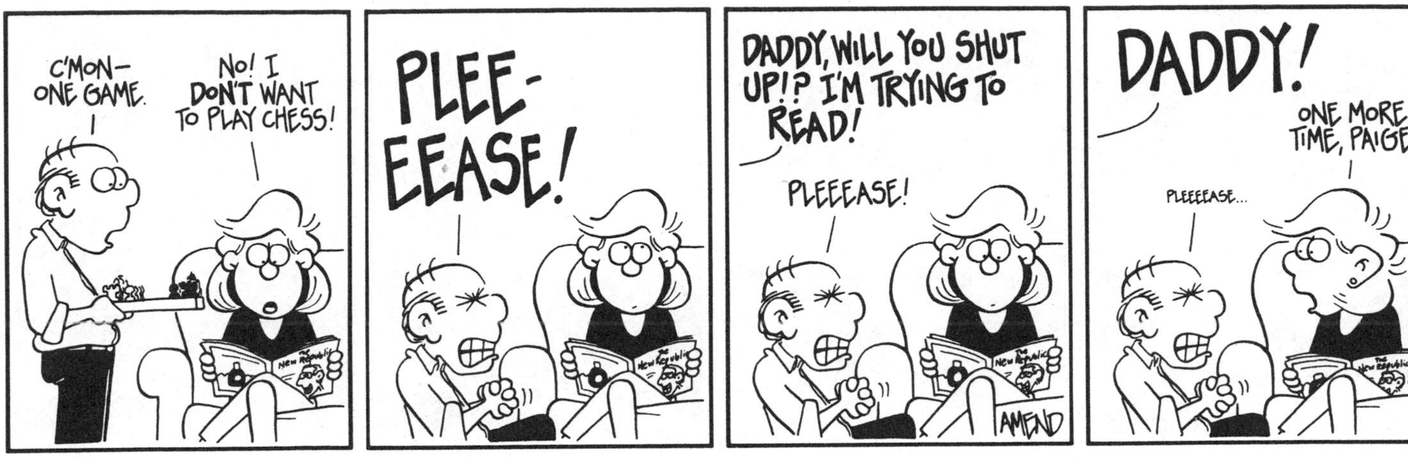
C'MON— ONE GAME.
NO! I DON'T WANT TO PLAY CHESS!
PLEE-EEASE!
DADDY, WILL YOU SHUT UP!? I'M TRYING TO READ!
PLEEEASE!
AMEND
DADDY!
ONE MORE TIME, PAIGE.
PLEEEEASE...

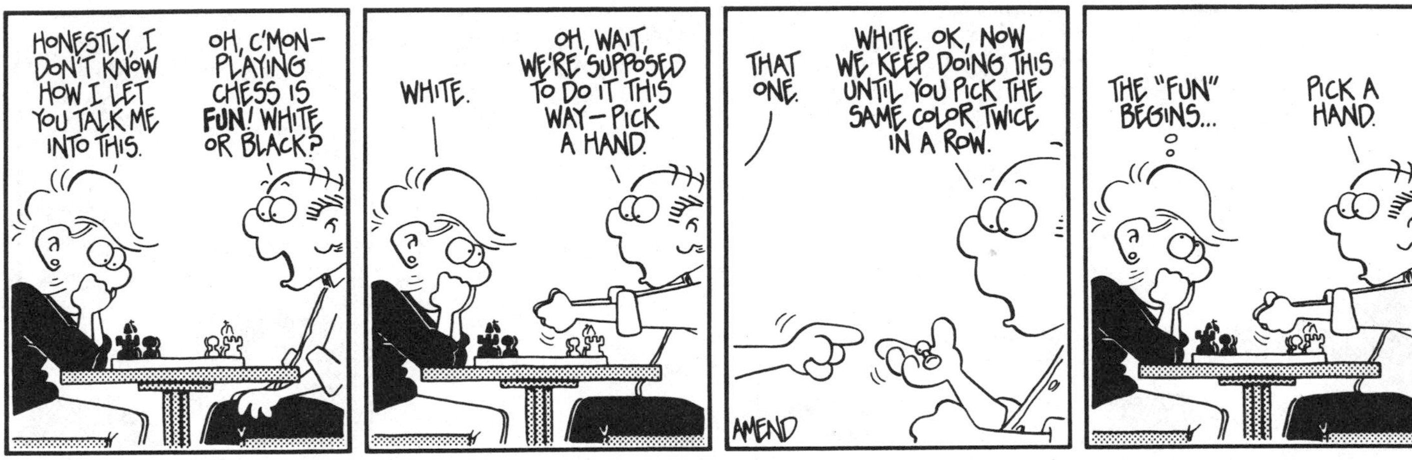
HONESTLY, I DON'T KNOW HOW I LET YOU TALK ME INTO THIS.
OH, C'MON— PLAYING CHESS IS FUN! WHITE OR BLACK?
WHITE.
OH, WAIT, WE'RE SUPPOSED TO DO IT THIS WAY— PICK A HAND.
THAT ONE.
WHITE. OK, NOW WE KEEP DOING THIS UNTIL YOU PICK THE SAME COLOR TWICE IN A ROW.
AMEND
THE "FUN" BEGINS...
PICK A HAND.

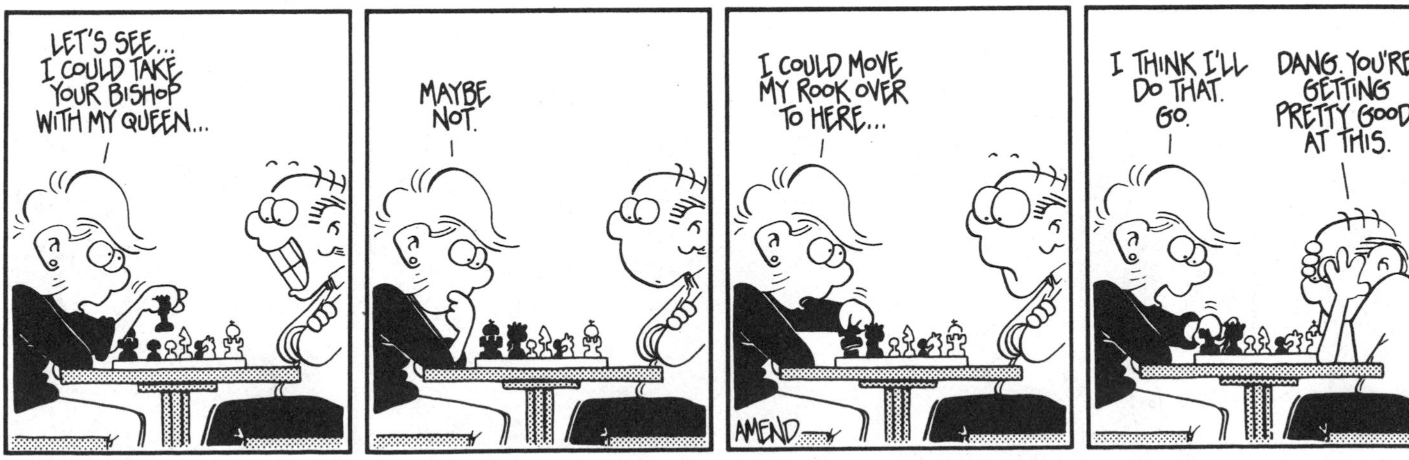
LET'S SEE... I COULD TAKE YOUR BISHOP WITH MY QUEEN...
MAYBE NOT.
I COULD MOVE MY ROOK OVER TO HERE...
AMEND
I THINK I'LL DO THAT. GO.
DANG. YOU'RE GETTING PRETTY GOOD AT THIS.

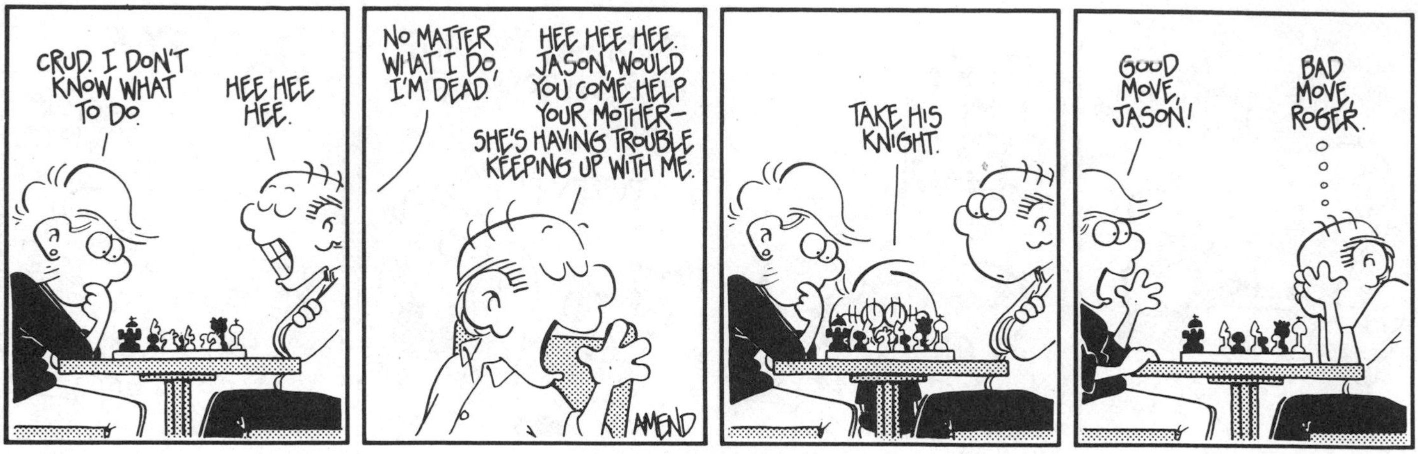
CRUD. I DON'T KNOW WHAT TO DO.
HEE HEE HEE.
NO MATTER WHAT I DO, I'M DEAD.
HEE HEE HEE. JASON, WOULD YOU COME HELP YOUR MOTHER– SHE'S HAVING TROUBLE KEEPING UP WITH ME.
AMEND
TAKE HIS KNIGHT.
GOOD MOVE, JASON!
BAD MOVE, ROGER.

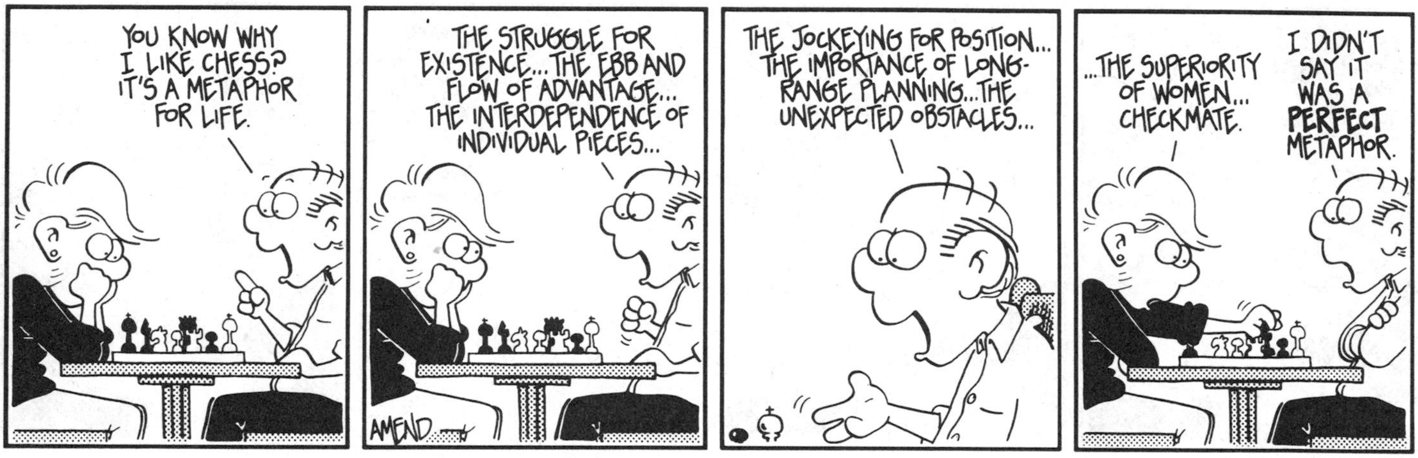
YOU KNOW WHY I LIKE CHESS? IT'S A METAPHOR FOR LIFE.
THE STRUGGLE FOR EXISTENCE... THE EBB AND FLOW OF ADVANTAGE... THE INTERDEPENDENCE OF INDIVIDUAL PIECES...
AMEND
THE JOCKEYING FOR POSITION... THE IMPORTANCE OF LONG-RANGE PLANNING... THE UNEXPECTED OBSTACLES...
...THE SUPERIORITY OF WOMEN... CHECKMATE.
I DIDN'T SAY IT WAS A **PERFECT** METAPHOR.

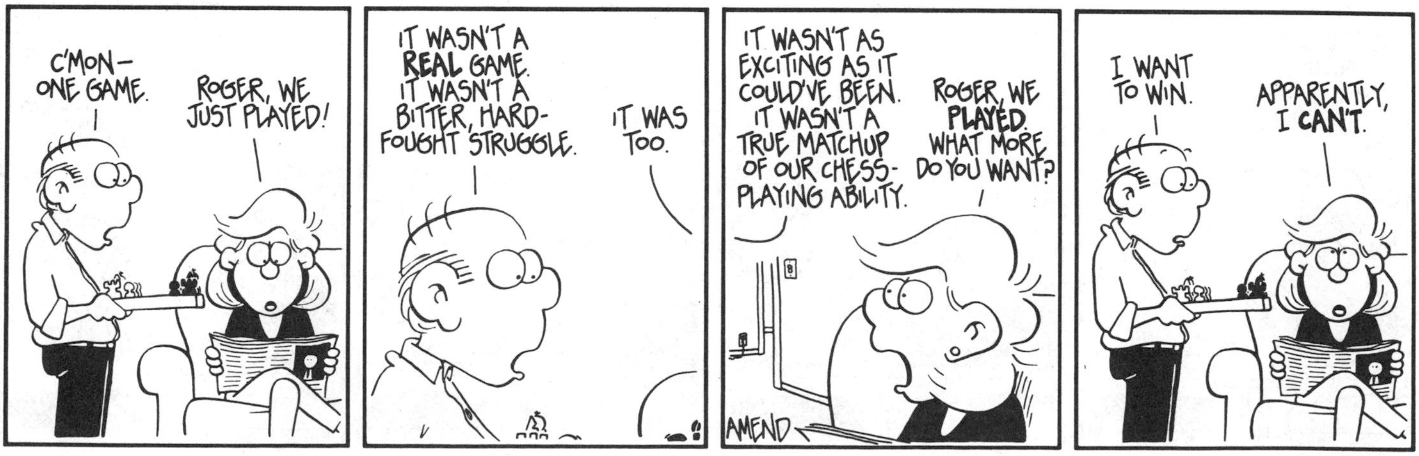
C'MON– ONE GAME.
ROGER, WE JUST PLAYED!
IT WASN'T A **REAL** GAME. IT WASN'T A BITTER, HARD-FOUGHT STRUGGLE.
IT WAS TOO.
IT WASN'T AS EXCITING AS IT COULD'VE BEEN. IT WASN'T A TRUE MATCHUP OF OUR CHESS-PLAYING ABILITY.
ROGER, WE **PLAYED**. WHAT MORE DO YOU WANT?
AMEND
I WANT TO WIN.
APPARENTLY, I **CAN'T**.

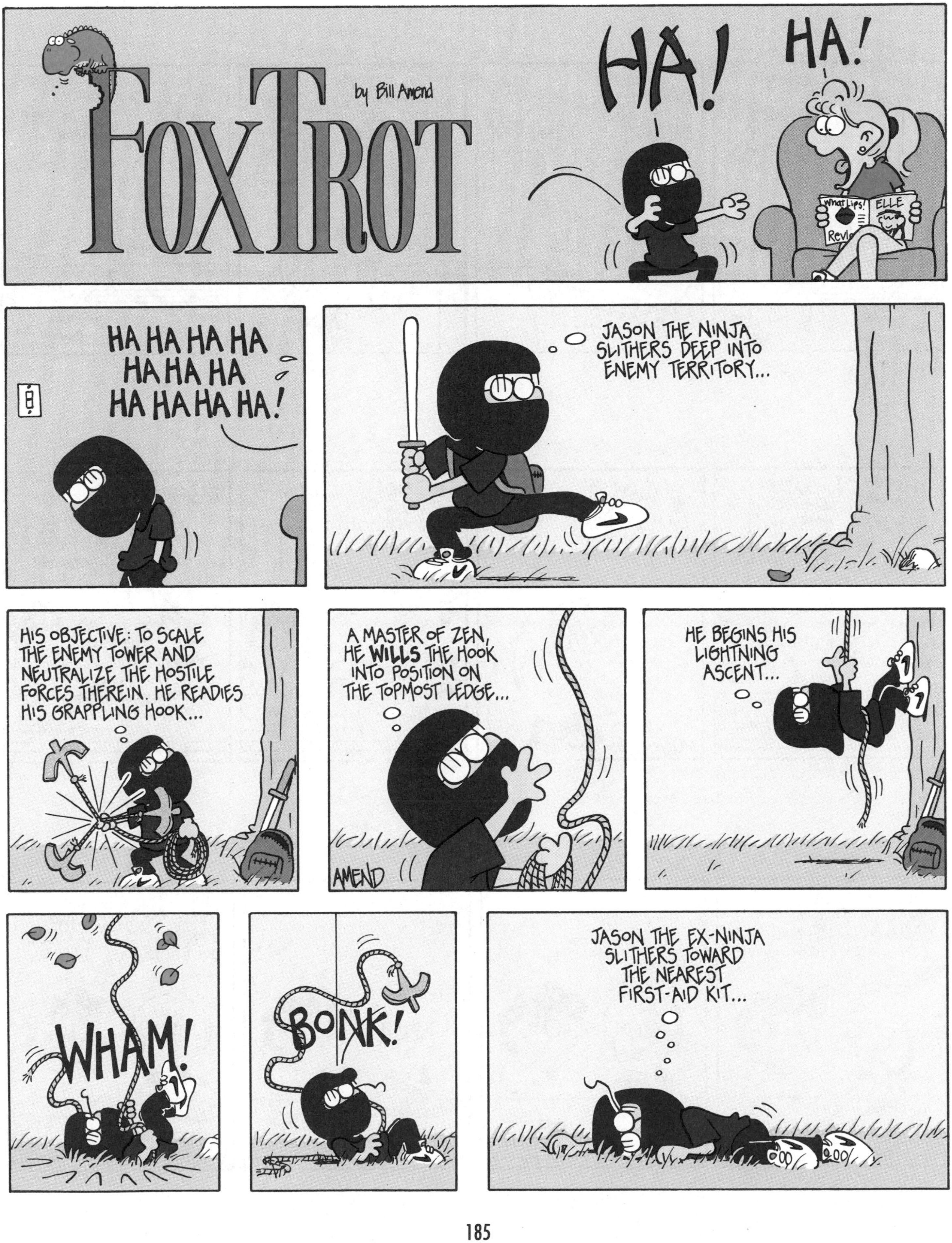
FoxTrot
by Bill Amend
HA!
HA!
HA HA HA HA HA HA HA HA HA HA HA HA!
JASON THE NINJA SLITHERS DEEP INTO ENEMY TERRITORY...
HIS OBJECTIVE: TO SCALE THE ENEMY TOWER AND NEUTRALIZE THE HOSTILE FORCES THEREIN. HE READIES HIS GRAPPLING HOOK...
A MASTER OF ZEN, HE **WILLS** THE HOOK INTO POSITION ON THE TOPMOST LEDGE...
AMEND
HE BEGINS HIS LIGHTNING ASCENT...
WHAM!
BONK!
JASON THE EX-NINJA SLITHERS TOWARD THE NEAREST FIRST-AID KIT...

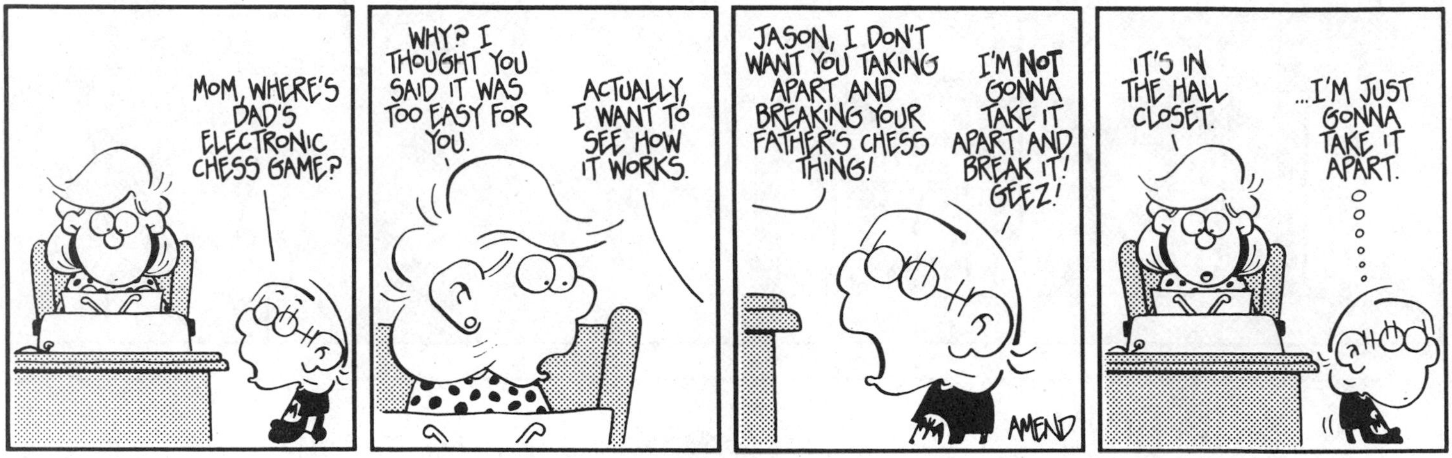
MOM, WHERE'S DAD'S ELECTRONIC CHESS GAME?
WHY? I THOUGHT YOU SAID IT WAS TOO EASY FOR YOU.
ACTUALLY, I WANT TO SEE HOW IT WORKS.
JASON, I DON'T WANT YOU TAKING APART AND BREAKING YOUR FATHER'S CHESS THING!
I'M NOT GONNA TAKE IT APART AND BREAK IT! GEEZ!
AMEND
IT'S IN THE HALL CLOSET.
...I'M JUST GONNA TAKE IT APART.

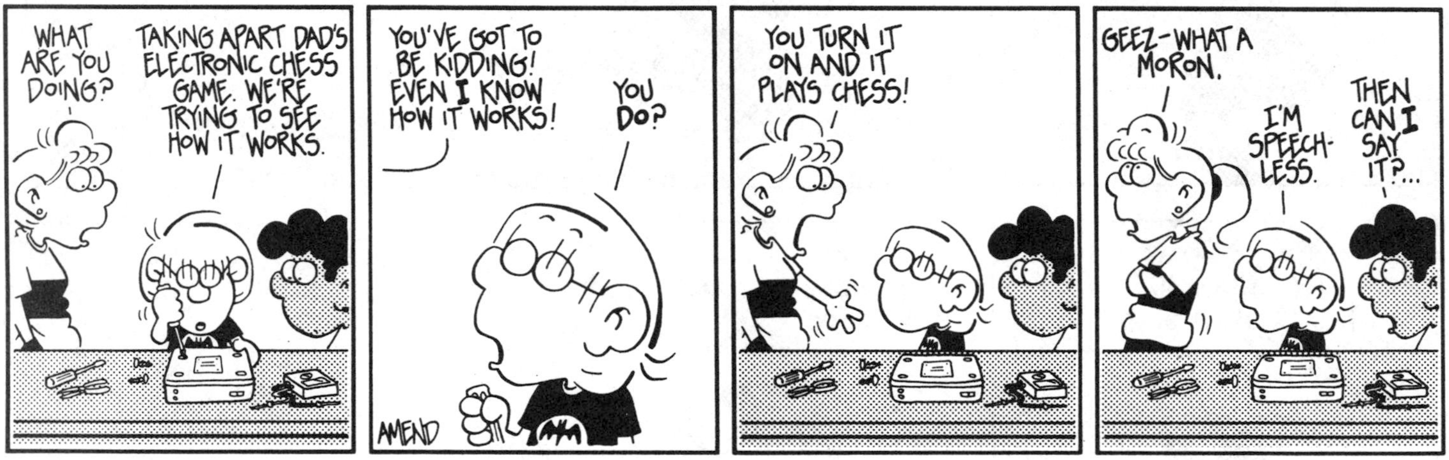
WHAT ARE YOU DOING?
TAKING APART DAD'S ELECTRONIC CHESS GAME. WE'RE TRYING TO SEE HOW IT WORKS.
YOU'VE GOT TO BE KIDDING! EVEN I KNOW HOW IT WORKS!
YOU DO?
AMEND
YOU TURN IT ON AND IT PLAYS CHESS!
GEEZ-WHAT A MORON.
I'M SPEECHLESS.
THEN CAN I SAY IT?...

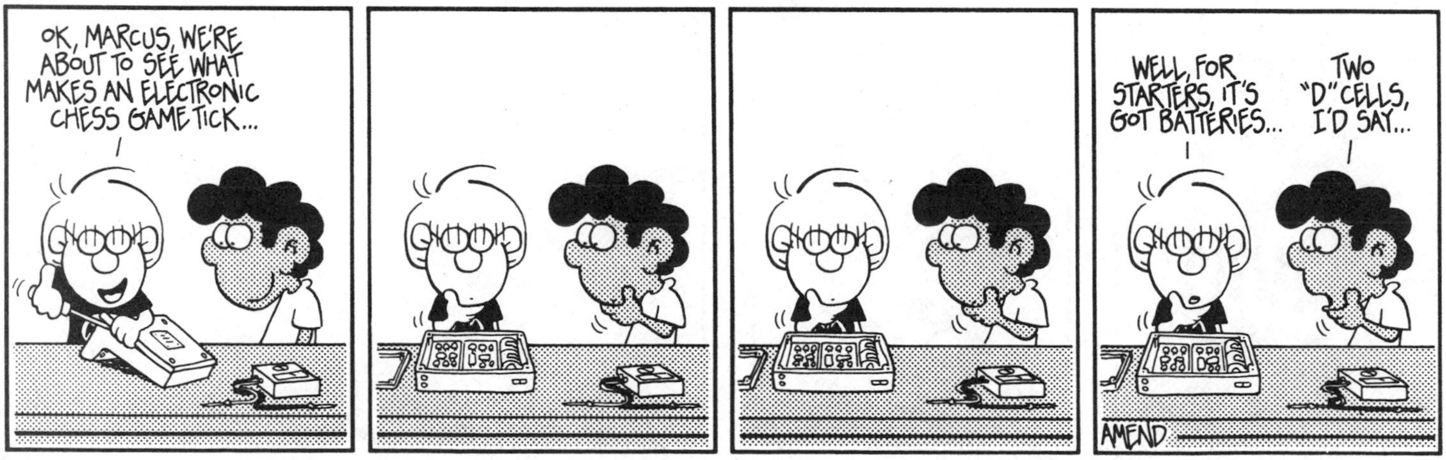
OK, MARCUS, WE'RE ABOUT TO SEE WHAT MAKES AN ELECTRONIC CHESS GAME TICK...
WELL, FOR STARTERS, IT'S GOT BATTERIES...
TWO "D" CELLS, I'D SAY...
AMEND

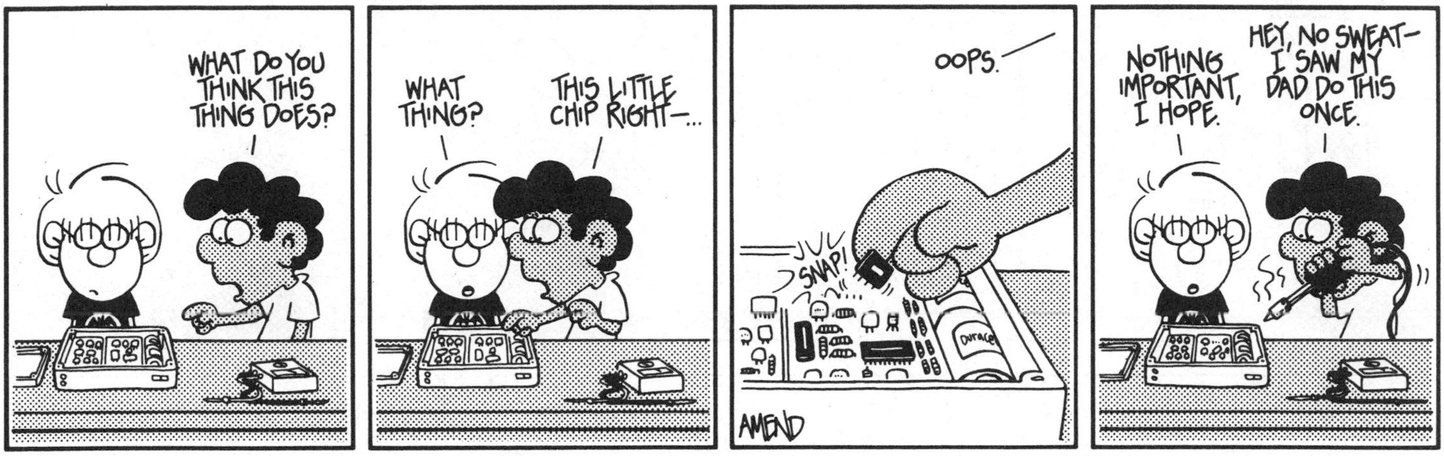
WHAT DO YOU THINK THIS THING DOES?
WHAT THING?
THIS LITTLE CHIP RIGHT—...
SNAP!
OOPS.
AMEND
NOTHING IMPORTANT, I HOPE.
HEY, NO SWEAT— I SAW MY DAD DO THIS ONCE.

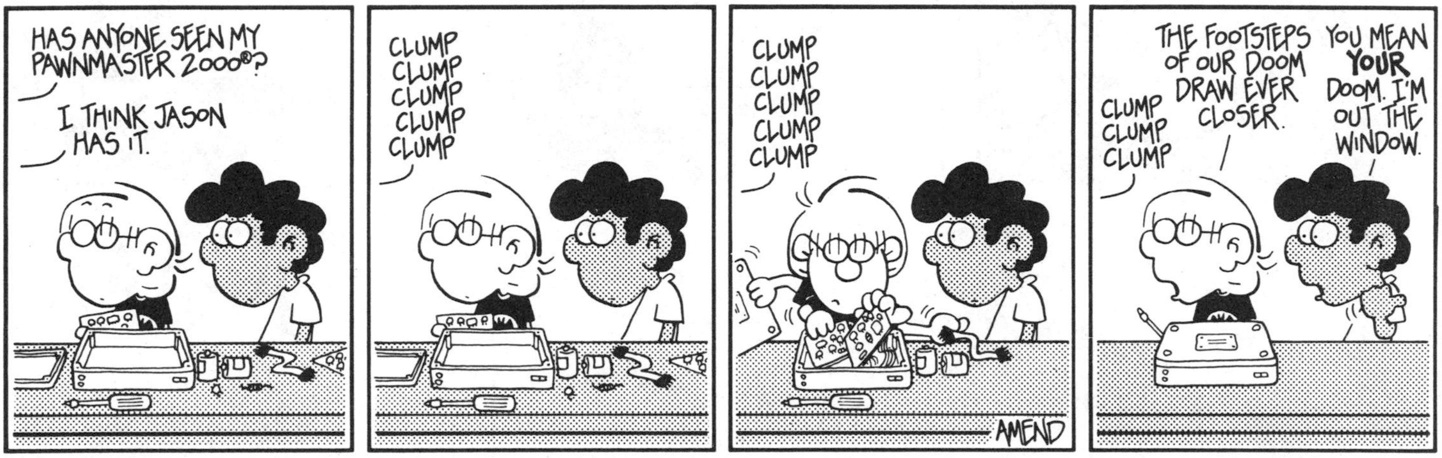
HAS ANYONE SEEN MY PAWNMASTER 2000®?
I THINK JASON HAS IT.
CLUMP CLUMP CLUMP CLUMP CLUMP
CLUMP CLUMP CLUMP CLUMP CLUMP
AMEND
CLUMP CLUMP CLUMP
THE FOOTSTEPS OF OUR DOOM DRAW EVER CLOSER.
YOU MEAN **YOUR** DOOM. I'M OUT THE WINDOW.

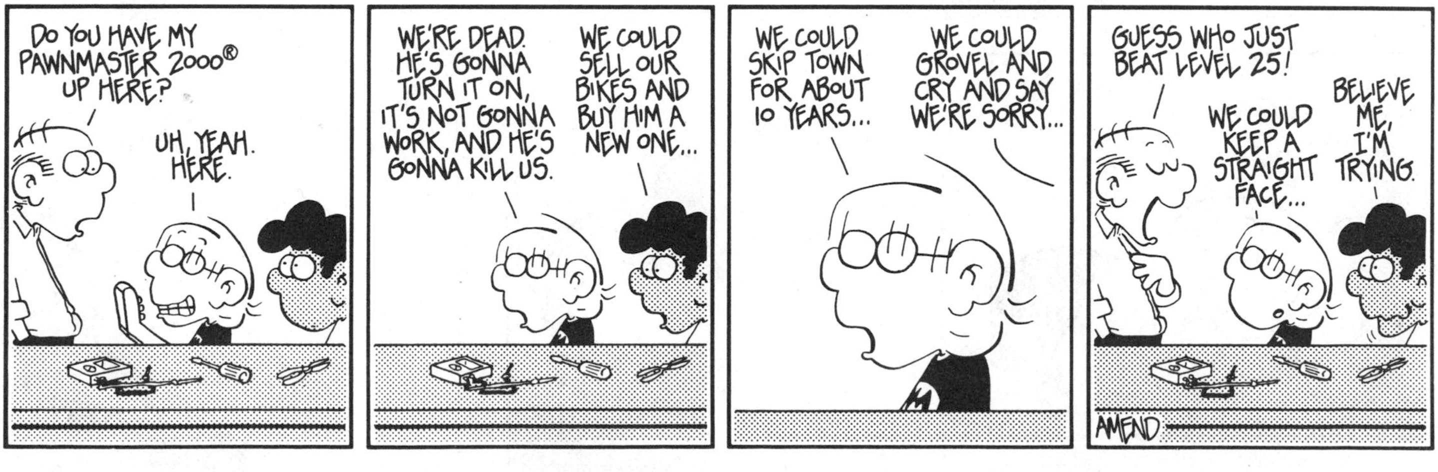
DO YOU HAVE MY PAWNMASTER 2000® UP HERE?
UH, YEAH. HERE.
WE'RE DEAD. HE'S GONNA TURN IT ON, IT'S NOT GONNA WORK, AND HE'S GONNA KILL US.
WE COULD SELL OUR BIKES AND BUY HIM A NEW ONE...
WE COULD SKIP TOWN FOR ABOUT 10 YEARS...
WE COULD GROVEL AND CRY AND SAY WE'RE SORRY...
GUESS WHO JUST BEAT LEVEL 25!
WE COULD KEEP A STRAIGHT FACE...
BELIEVE ME, I'M TRYING.
AMEND

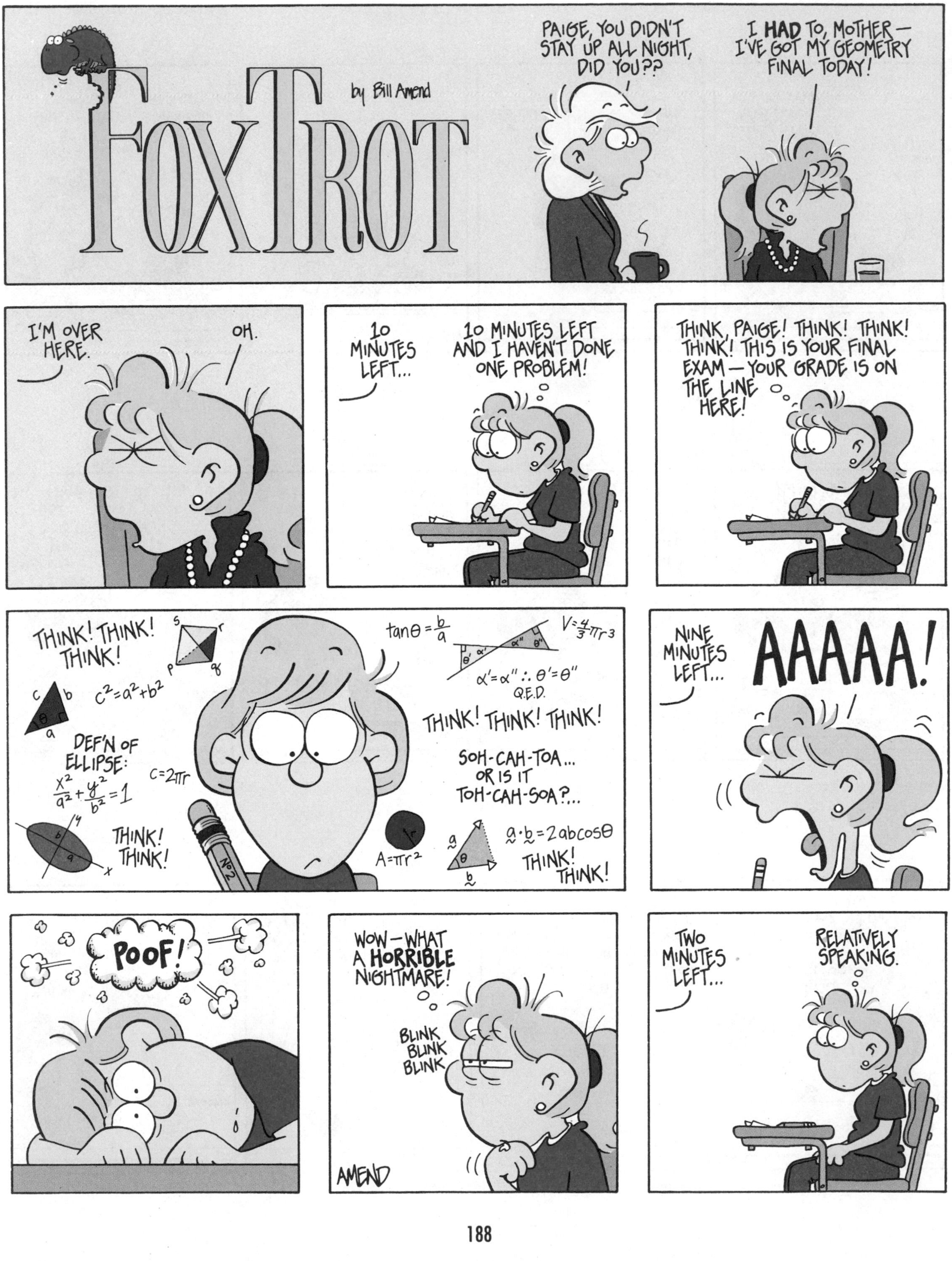
FOXTROT
by Bill Amend
PAIGE, YOU DIDN'T STAY UP ALL NIGHT, DID YOU??
I **HAD** TO, MOTHER — I'VE GOT MY GEOMETRY FINAL TODAY!
I'M OVER HERE.
OH.
10 MINUTES LEFT...
10 MINUTES LEFT AND I HAVEN'T DONE ONE PROBLEM!
THINK, PAIGE! THINK! THINK! THINK! THIS IS YOUR FINAL EXAM — YOUR GRADE IS ON THE LINE HERE!
THINK! THINK! THINK!
c b a θ
c²=a²+b²
s r p q
tanθ = b/a
V=4/3πr³
α'=α" ∴ θ'=θ"
Q.E.D.
DEF'N OF ELLIPSE:
x²/a² + y²/b² = 1
C=2πr
THINK! THINK! THINK!
SOH-CAH-TOA... OR IS IT TOH-CAH-SOA?...
THINK! THINK!
A=πr²
a·b=2abcosθ
THINK! THINK!
No. 2
NINE MINUTES LEFT...
AAAAA!
POOF!
WOW — WHAT A **HORRIBLE** NIGHTMARE!
BLINK BLINK BLINK
AMEND
TWO MINUTES LEFT...
RELATIVELY SPEAKING.

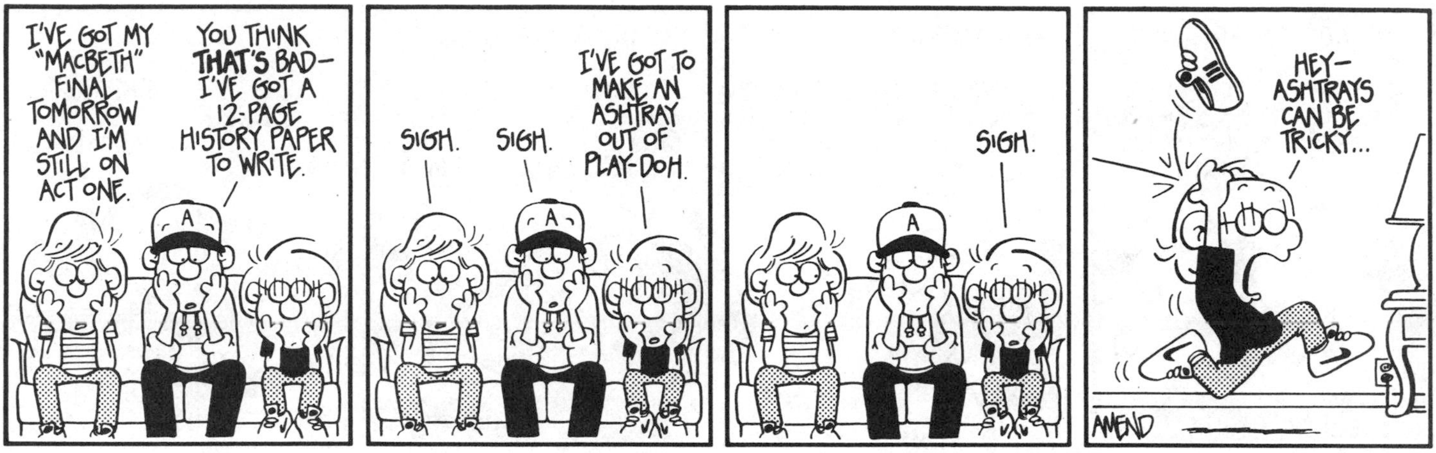
I'VE GOT MY "MACBETH" FINAL TOMORROW AND I'M STILL ON ACT ONE.
YOU THINK **THAT'S** BAD– I'VE GOT A 12-PAGE HISTORY PAPER TO WRITE.
SIGH.
SIGH.
I'VE GOT TO MAKE AN ASHTRAY OUT OF PLAY-DOH.
SIGH.
HEY– ASHTRAYS CAN BE TRICKY...
AMEND

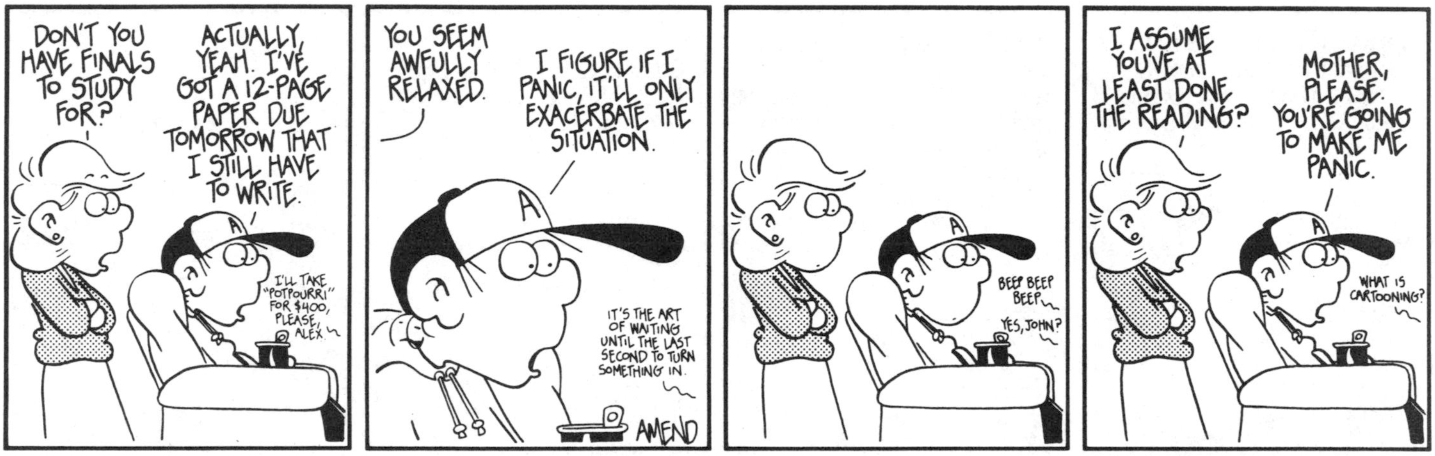
DON'T YOU HAVE FINALS TO STUDY FOR?
ACTUALLY, YEAH. I'VE GOT A 12-PAGE PAPER DUE TOMORROW THAT I STILL HAVE TO WRITE.
I'LL TAKE "POTPOURRI" FOR $400, PLEASE, ALEX.
YOU SEEM AWFULLY RELAXED.
I FIGURE IF I PANIC, IT'LL ONLY EXACERBATE THE SITUATION.
IT'S THE ART OF WAITING UNTIL THE LAST SECOND TO TURN SOMETHING IN.
AMEND
BEEP BEEP BEEP
YES, JOHN?
I ASSUME YOU'VE AT LEAST DONE THE READING?
MOTHER, PLEASE. YOU'RE GOING TO MAKE ME PANIC.
WHAT IS CARTOONING?

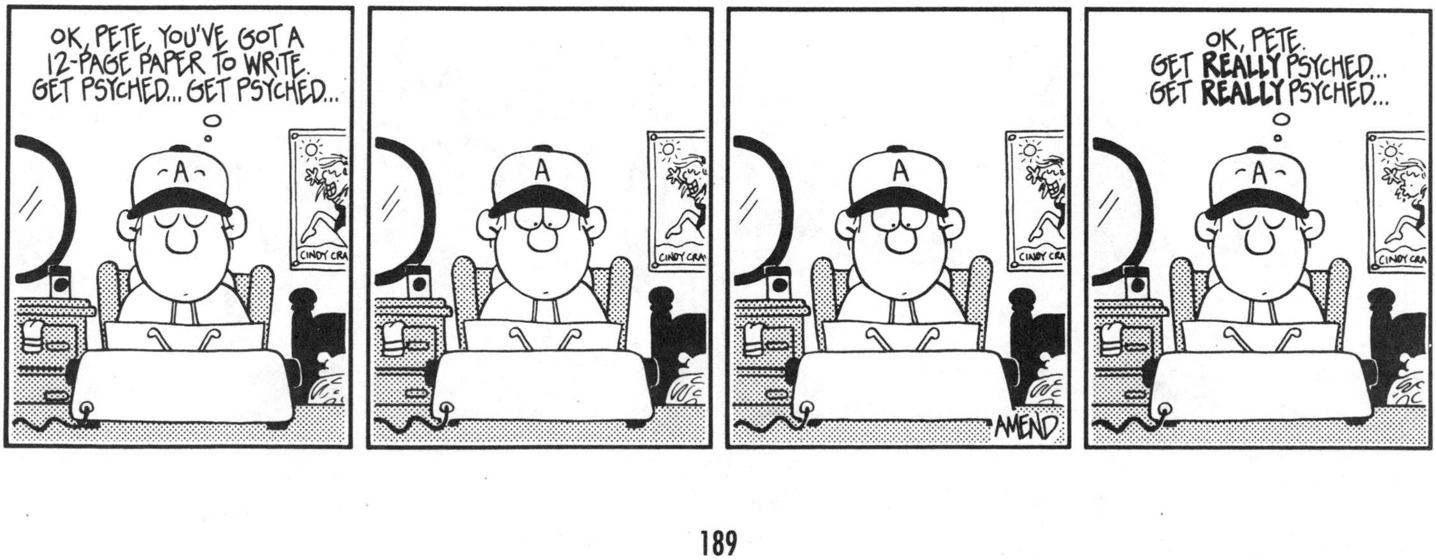
OK, PETE, YOU'VE GOT A 12-PAGE PAPER TO WRITE. GET PSYCHED... GET PSYCHED...
AMEND
OK, PETE. GET **REALLY** PSYCHED... GET **REALLY** PSYCHED...

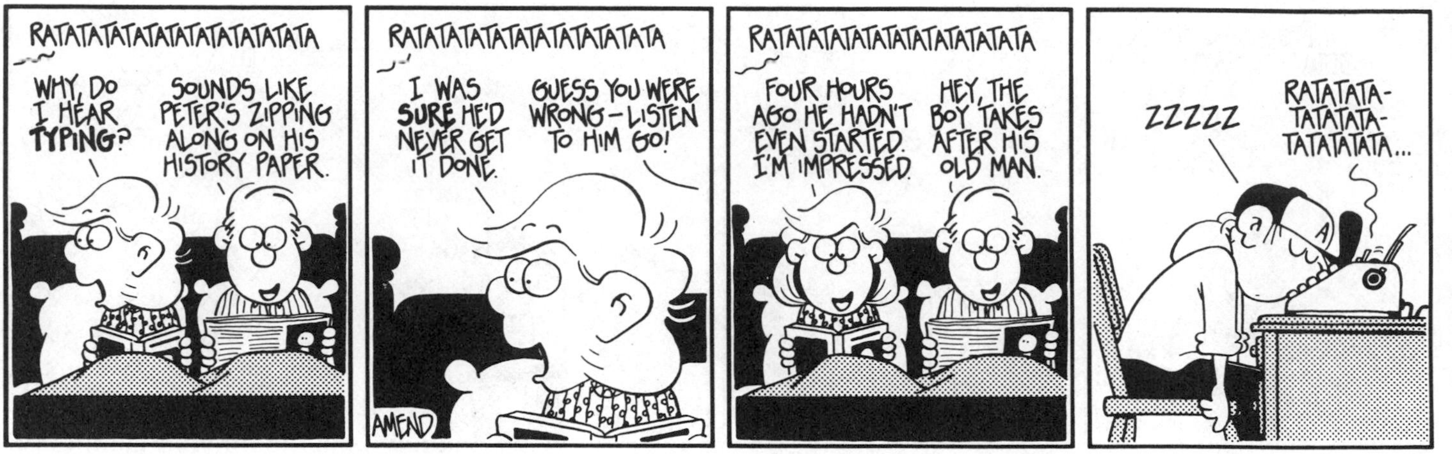
RATATATATATATATATATATATATA
WHY, DO I HEAR **TYPING**?
SOUNDS LIKE PETER'S ZIPPING ALONG ON HIS HISTORY PAPER.
RATATATATATATATATATATATATA
I WAS **SURE** HE'D NEVER GET IT DONE.
GUESS YOU WERE WRONG – LISTEN TO HIM GO!
AMEND
RATATATATATATATATATATATATA
FOUR HOURS AGO HE HADN'T EVEN STARTED. I'M IMPRESSED.
HEY, THE BOY TAKES AFTER HIS OLD MAN.
ZZZZZ
RATATATA-TATATATA-TATATATATA...

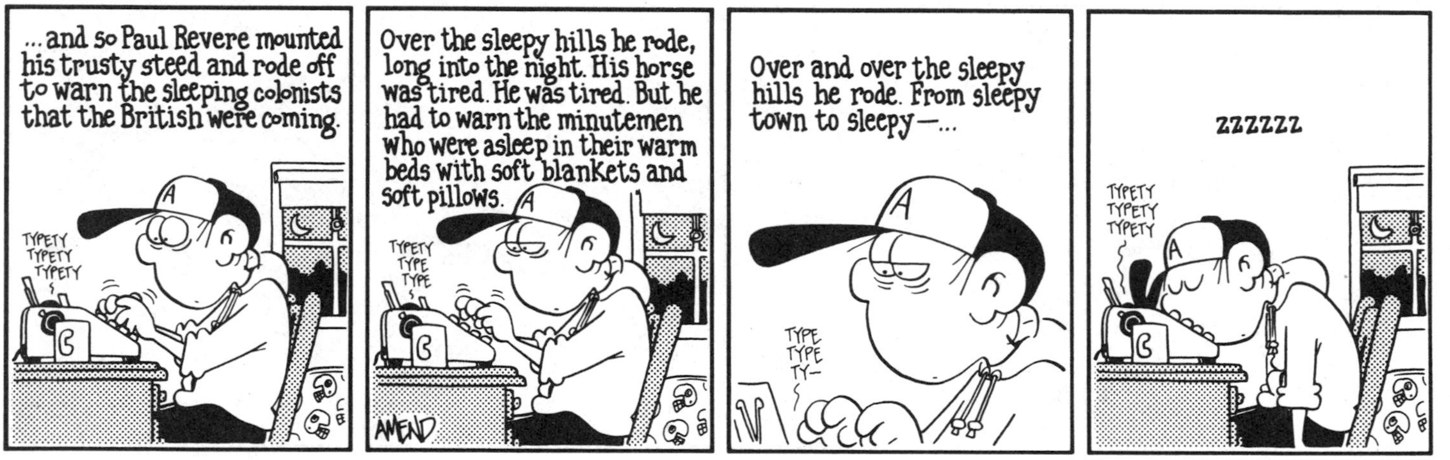
...and so Paul Revere mounted his trusty steed and rode off to warn the sleeping colonists that the British were coming.
TYPETY TYPETY TYPETY
Over the sleepy hills he rode, long into the night. His horse was tired. He was tired. But he had to warn the minutemen who were asleep in their warm beds with soft blankets and soft pillows.
TYPETY TYPE TYPE
AMEND
Over and over the sleepy hills he rode. From sleepy town to sleepy—...
TYPE TYPE TY—
ZZZZZZ
TYPETY TYPETY TYPETY

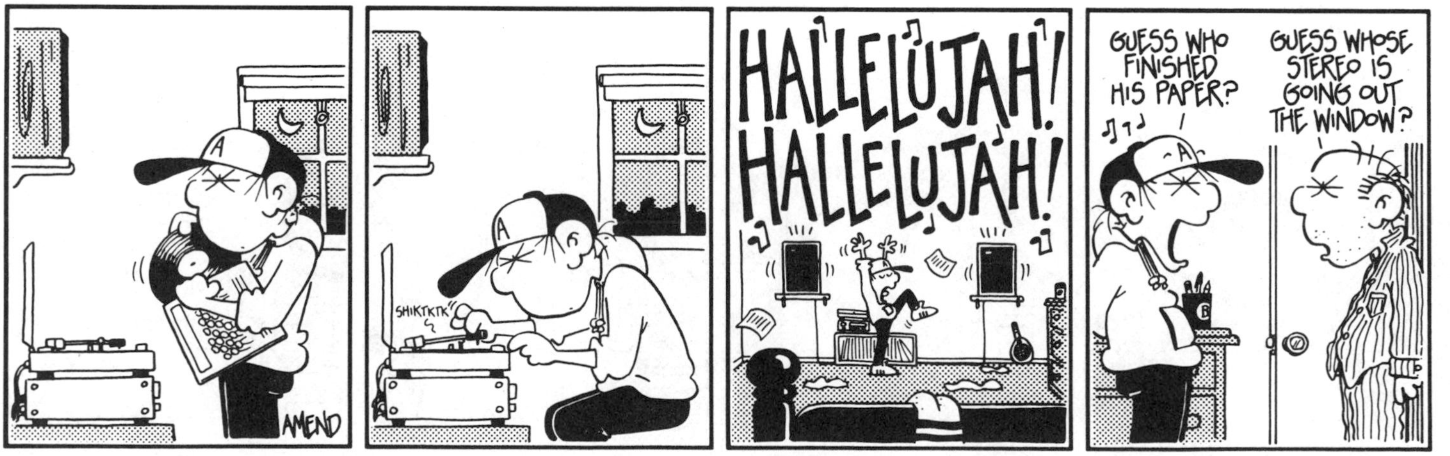
AMEND
SHIKTKTK
HALLELUJAH! HALLELUJAH!
GUESS WHO FINISHED HIS PAPER?
GUESS WHOSE STEREO IS GOING OUT THE WINDOW?

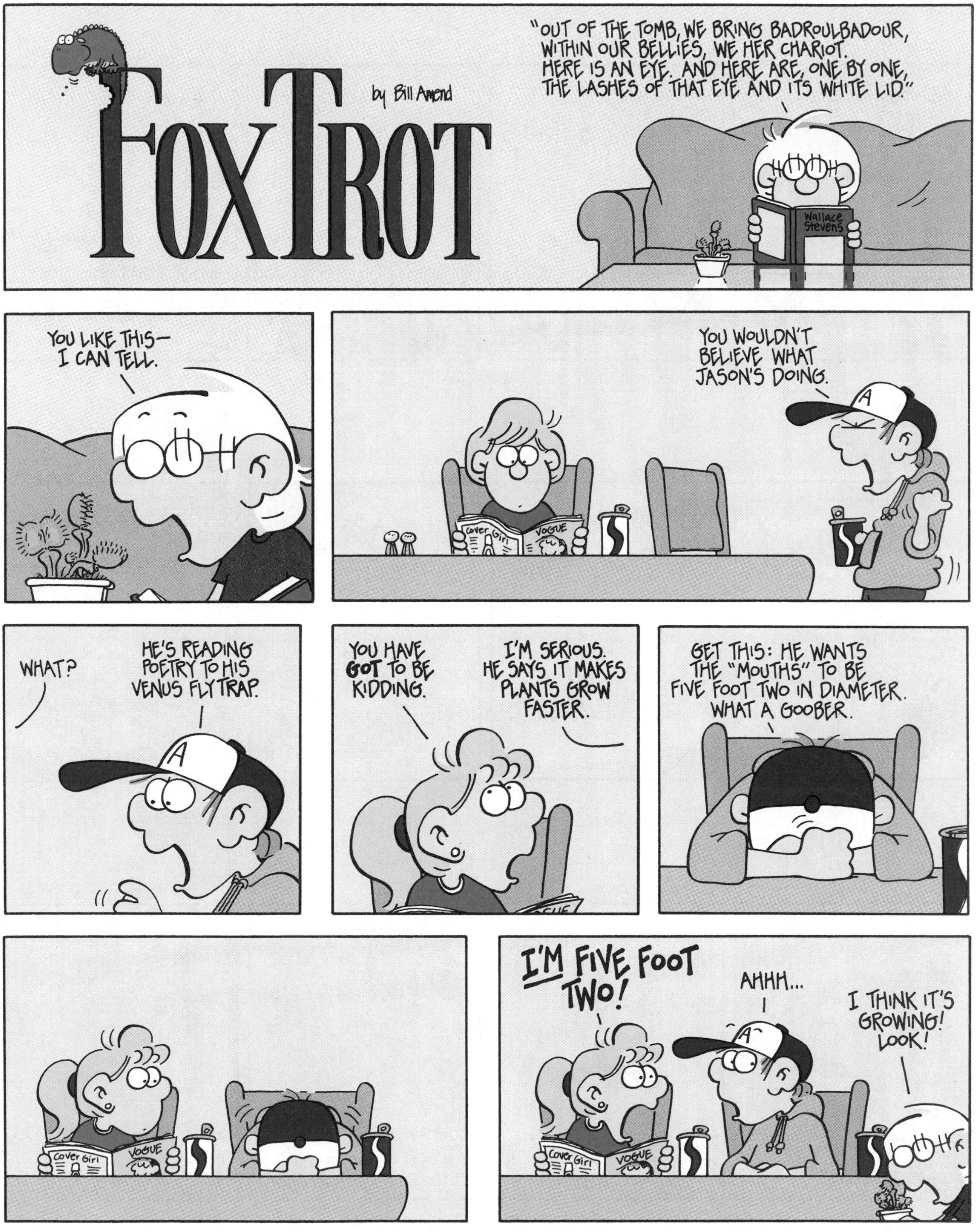
FoxTrot
by Bill Amend
"OUT OF THE TOMB, WE BRING BADROULBADOUR, WITHIN OUR BELLIES, WE HER CHARIOT. HERE IS AN EYE. AND HERE ARE, ONE BY ONE, THE LASHES OF THAT EYE AND ITS WHITE LID."
Wallace Stevens
YOU LIKE THIS— I CAN TELL.
YOU WOULDN'T BELIEVE WHAT JASON'S DOING.
Cover Girl
VOGUE
WHAT?
HE'S READING POETRY TO HIS VENUS FLYTRAP.
YOU HAVE GOT TO BE KIDDING.
I'M SERIOUS. HE SAYS IT MAKES PLANTS GROW FASTER.
GET THIS: HE WANTS THE "MOUTHS" TO BE FIVE FOOT TWO IN DIAMETER. WHAT A GOOBER.
I'M FIVE FOOT TWO!
AHHH...
I THINK IT'S GROWING! LOOK!

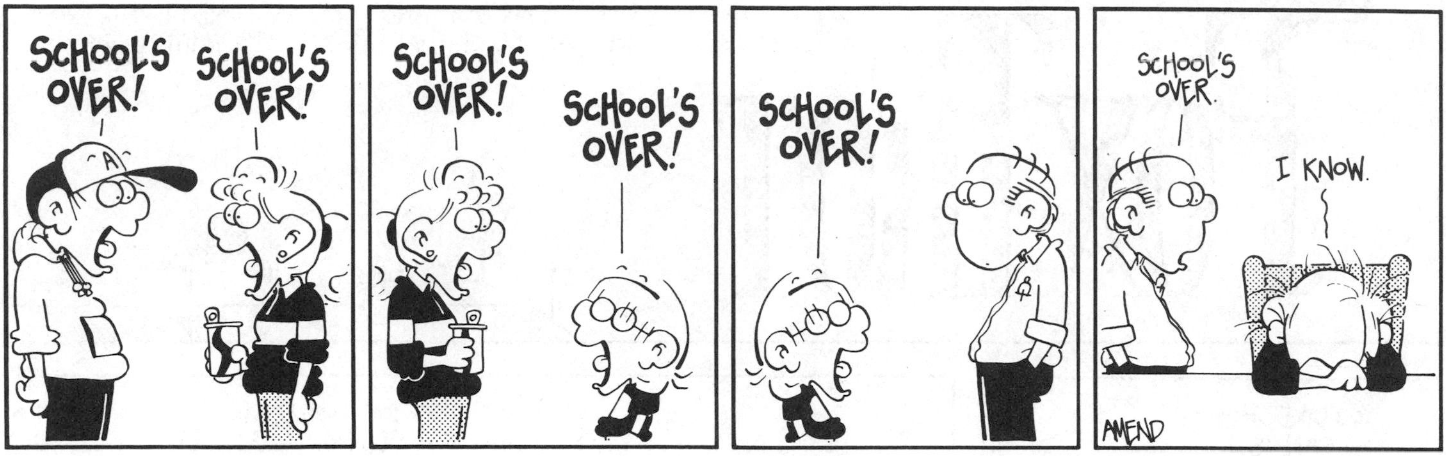
SCHOOL'S OVER!
SCHOOL'S OVER!
SCHOOL'S OVER!
SCHOOL'S OVER!
SCHOOL'S OVER!
SCHOOL'S OVER.
I KNOW.
AMEND

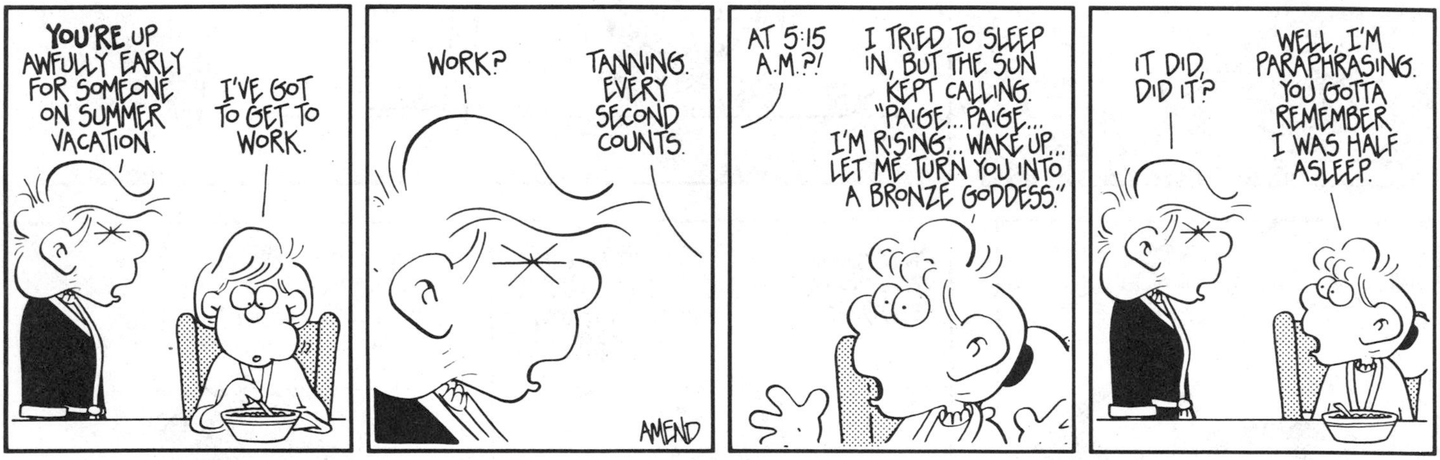
YOU'RE UP AWFULLY EARLY FOR SOMEONE ON SUMMER VACATION.
I'VE GOT TO GET TO WORK.
WORK?
TANNING. EVERY SECOND COUNTS.
AMEND
AT 5:15 A.M.?!
I TRIED TO SLEEP IN, BUT THE SUN KEPT CALLING. "PAIGE... PAIGE... I'M RISING... WAKE UP... LET ME TURN YOU INTO A BRONZE GODDESS."
IT DID, DID IT?
WELL, I'M PARAPHRASING. YOU GOTTA REMEMBER I WAS HALF ASLEEP.

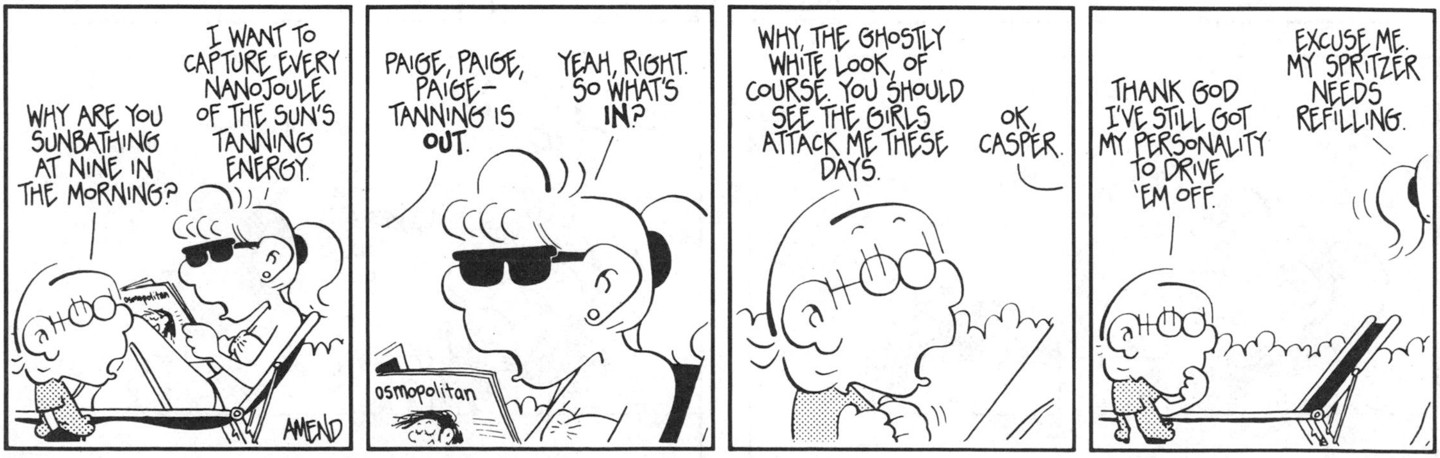
WHY ARE YOU SUNBATHING AT NINE IN THE MORNING?
I WANT TO CAPTURE EVERY NANOJOULE OF THE SUN'S TANNING ENERGY.
osmopolitan
AMEND
PAIGE, PAIGE, PAIGE— TANNING IS **OUT**.
YEAH, RIGHT. SO WHAT'S **IN**?
osmopolitan
WHY, THE GHOSTLY WHITE LOOK, OF COURSE. YOU SHOULD SEE THE GIRLS ATTACK ME THESE DAYS.
OK, CASPER.
THANK GOD I'VE STILL GOT MY PERSONALITY TO DRIVE 'EM OFF.
EXCUSE ME. MY SPRITZER NEEDS REFILLING.

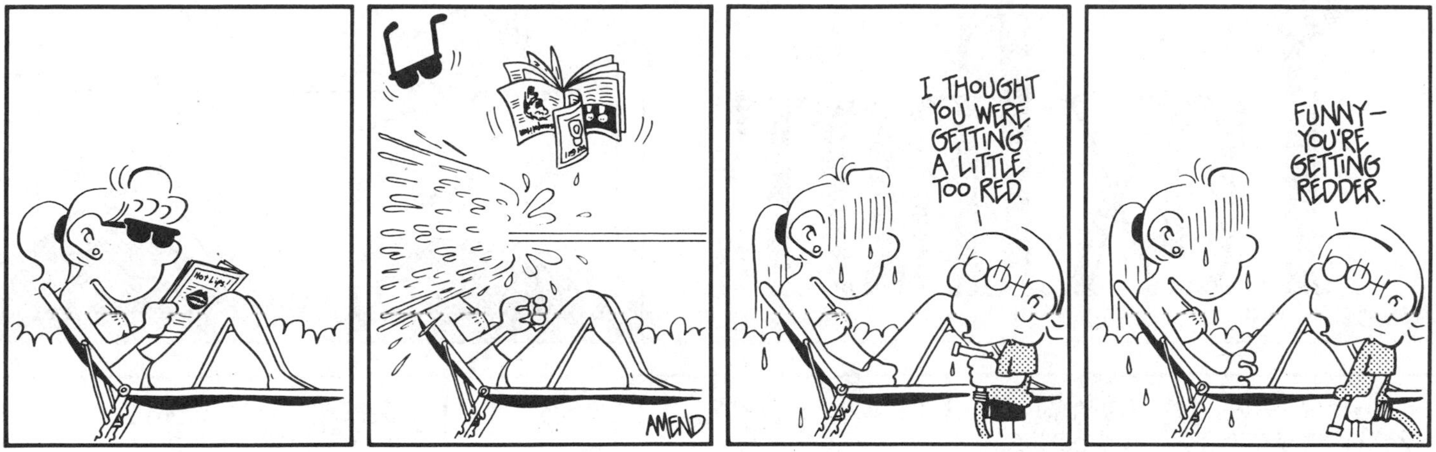
I THOUGHT YOU WERE GETTING A LITTLE TOO RED.
FUNNY— YOU'RE GETTING REDDER.

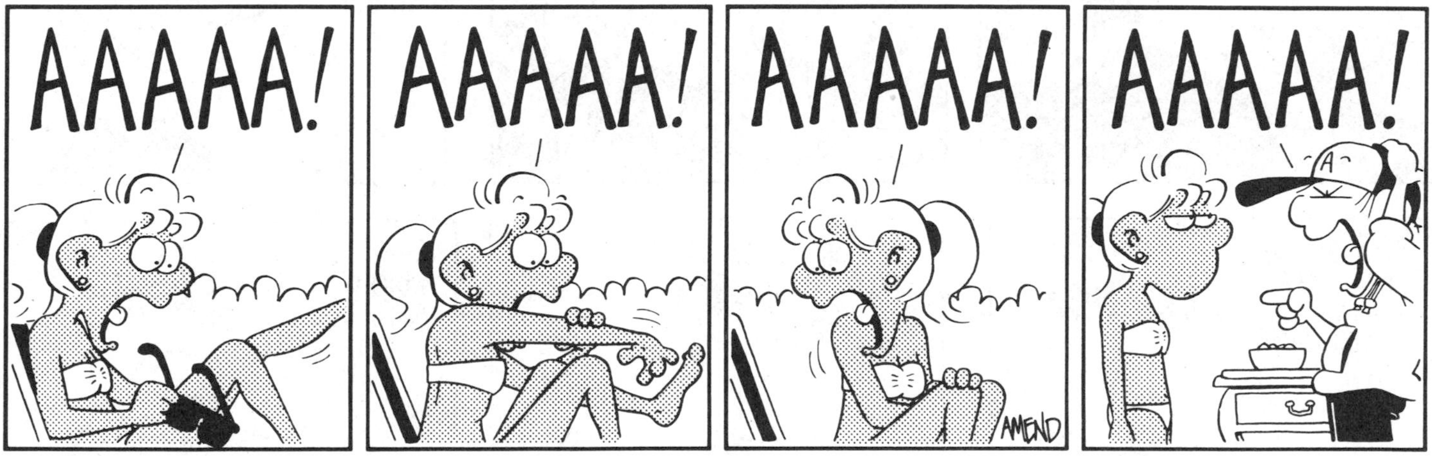
AAAAA!
AAAAA!
AAAAA!
AAAAA!

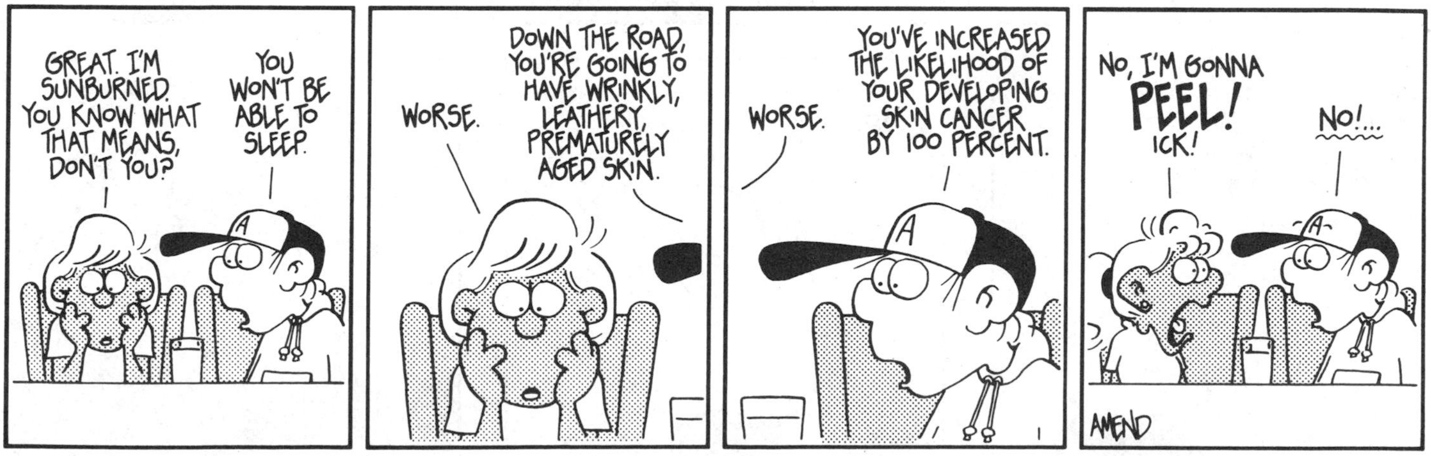
GREAT. I'M SUNBURNED. YOU KNOW WHAT THAT MEANS, DON'T YOU?
YOU WON'T BE ABLE TO SLEEP.
WORSE.
DOWN THE ROAD, YOU'RE GOING TO HAVE WRINKLY, LEATHERY, PREMATURELY AGED SKIN.
WORSE.
YOU'VE INCREASED THE LIKELIHOOD OF YOUR DEVELOPING SKIN CANCER BY 100 PERCENT.
NO, I'M GONNA PEEL! ICK!
NO!...

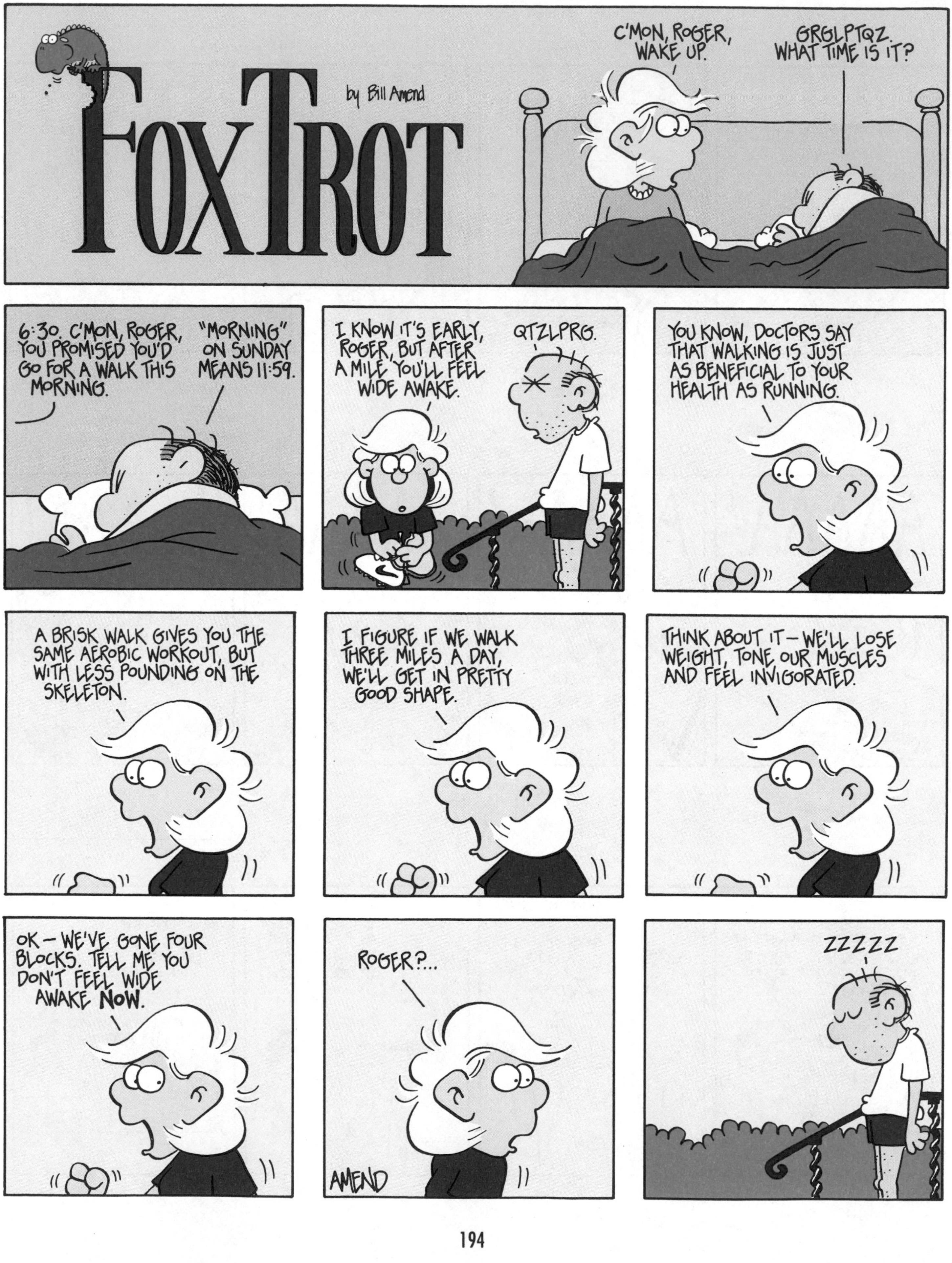
FoxTrot
by Bill Amend
C'MON, ROGER, WAKE UP.
GRGLPTQZ. WHAT TIME IS IT?
6:30. C'MON, ROGER, YOU PROMISED YOU'D GO FOR A WALK THIS MORNING.
"MORNING" ON SUNDAY MEANS 11:59.
I KNOW IT'S EARLY, ROGER, BUT AFTER A MILE YOU'LL FEEL WIDE AWAKE.
QTZLPRG.
YOU KNOW, DOCTORS SAY THAT WALKING IS JUST AS BENEFICIAL TO YOUR HEALTH AS RUNNING.
A BRISK WALK GIVES YOU THE SAME AEROBIC WORKOUT, BUT WITH LESS POUNDING ON THE SKELETON.
I FIGURE IF WE WALK THREE MILES A DAY, WE'LL GET IN PRETTY GOOD SHAPE.
THINK ABOUT IT— WE'LL LOSE WEIGHT, TONE OUR MUSCLES AND FEEL INVIGORATED.
OK— WE'VE GONE FOUR BLOCKS. TELL ME YOU DON'T FEEL WIDE AWAKE NOW.
ROGER?...
AMEND
ZZZZZ

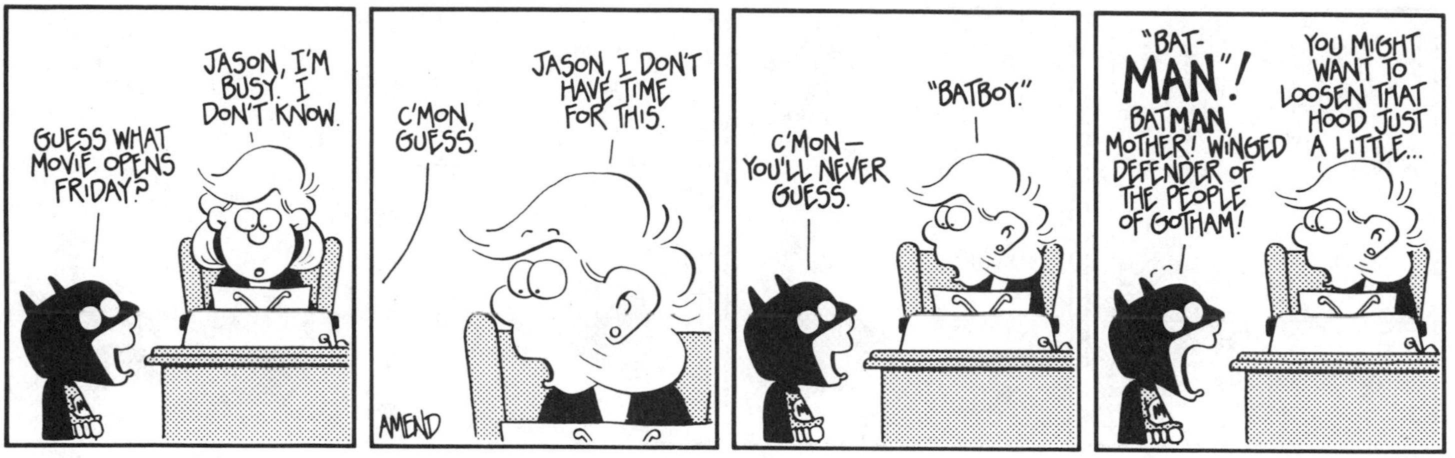
GUESS WHAT MOVIE OPENS FRIDAY?
JASON, I'M BUSY. I DON'T KNOW.
C'MON, GUESS.
JASON, I DON'T HAVE TIME FOR THIS.
AMEND
C'MON— YOU'LL NEVER GUESS.
"BATBOY."
"BAT-MAN"! BATMAN, MOTHER! WINGED DEFENDER OF THE PEOPLE OF GOTHAM!
YOU MIGHT WANT TO LOOSEN THAT HOOD JUST A LITTLE...

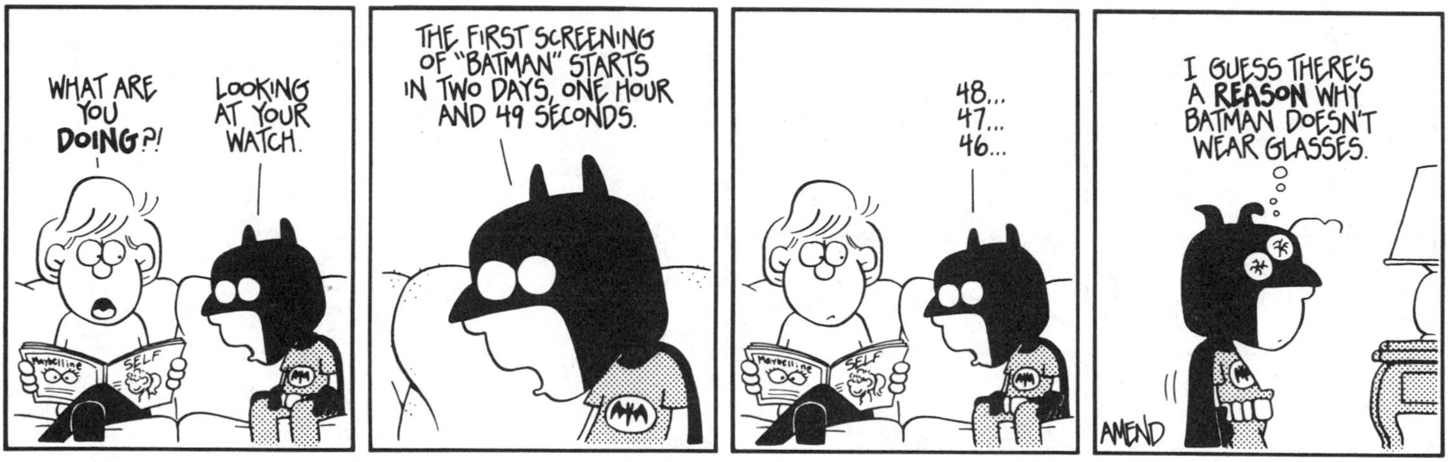
WHAT ARE YOU DOING?!
LOOKING AT YOUR WATCH.
THE FIRST SCREENING OF "BATMAN" STARTS IN TWO DAYS, ONE HOUR AND 49 SECONDS.
48... 47... 46...
I GUESS THERE'S A REASON WHY BATMAN DOESN'T WEAR GLASSES.
AMEND

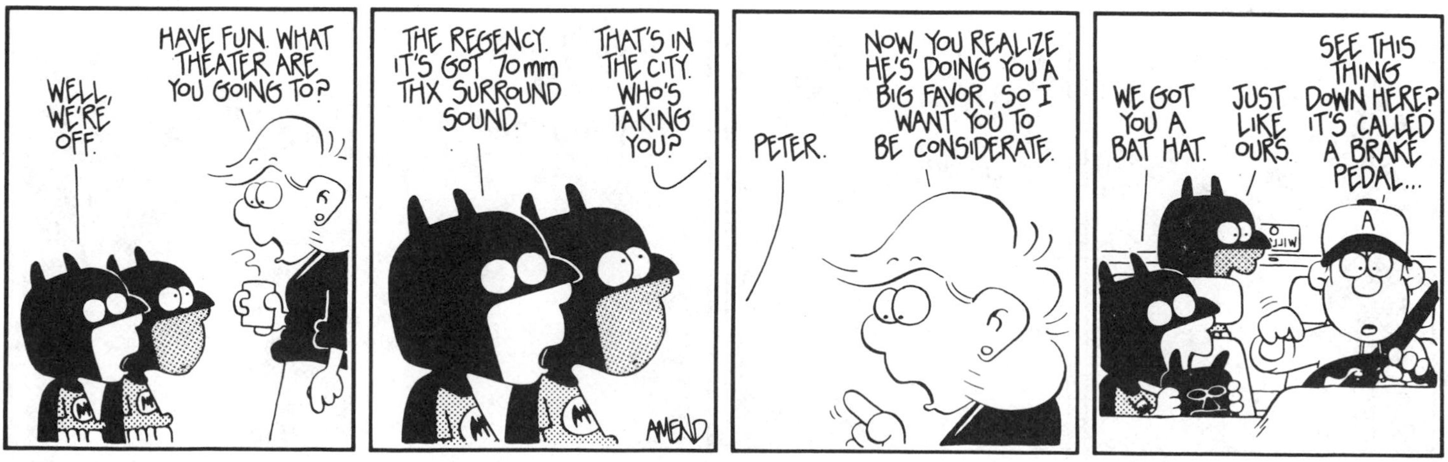
WELL, WE'RE OFF.
HAVE FUN. WHAT THEATER ARE YOU GOING TO?
THE REGENCY. IT'S GOT 70mm THX SURROUND SOUND.
THAT'S IN THE CITY. WHO'S TAKING YOU?
AMEND
PETER.
NOW, YOU REALIZE HE'S DOING YOU A BIG FAVOR, SO I WANT YOU TO BE CONSIDERATE.
WE GOT YOU A BAT HAT.
JUST LIKE OURS.
SEE THIS THING DOWN HERE? IT'S CALLED A BRAKE PEDAL...

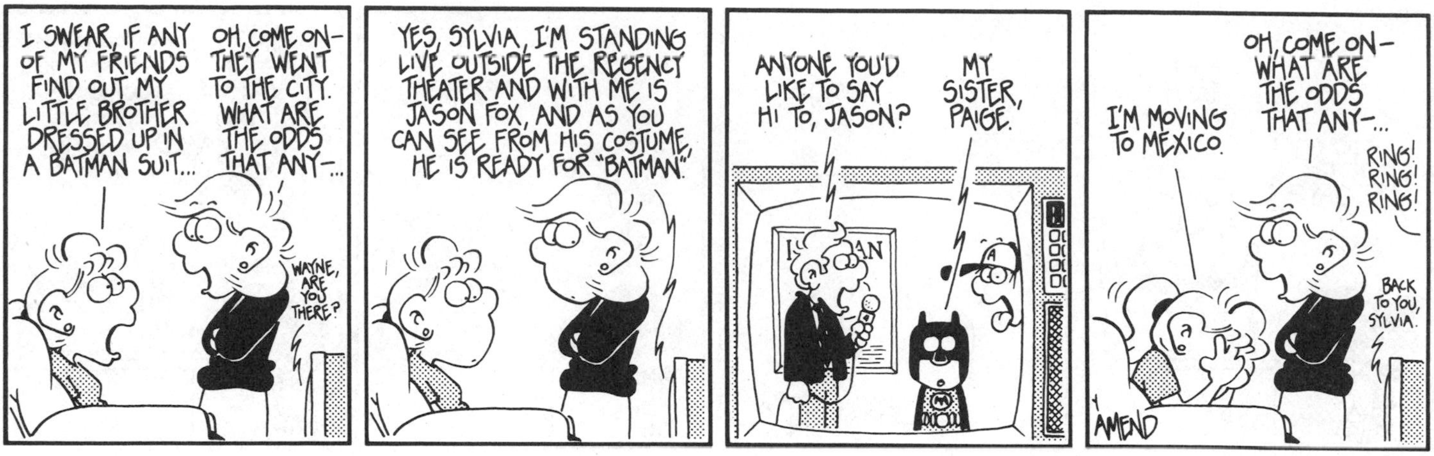
I SWEAR, IF ANY OF MY FRIENDS FIND OUT MY LITTLE BROTHER DRESSED UP IN A BATMAN SUIT...
OH, COME ON– THEY WENT TO THE CITY. WHAT ARE THE ODDS THAT ANY–...
WAYNE, ARE YOU THERE?
YES, SYLVIA, I'M STANDING LIVE OUTSIDE THE REGENCY THEATER AND WITH ME IS JASON FOX, AND AS YOU CAN SEE FROM HIS COSTUME, HE IS READY FOR "BATMAN."
ANYONE YOU'D LIKE TO SAY HI TO, JASON?
MY SISTER, PAIGE.
I'M MOVING TO MEXICO.
OH, COME ON– WHAT ARE THE ODDS THAT ANY–...
RING! RING! RING!
BACK TO YOU, SYLVIA.
AMEND

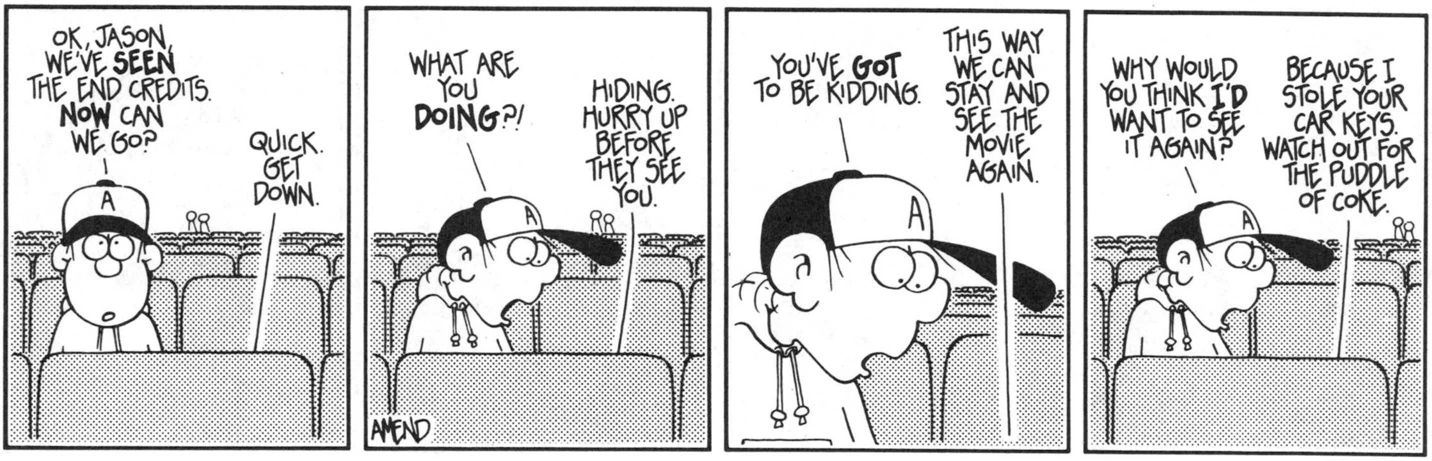
OK, JASON, WE'VE SEEN THE END CREDITS. NOW CAN WE GO?
QUICK. GET DOWN.
WHAT ARE YOU DOING?!
HIDING. HURRY UP BEFORE THEY SEE YOU.
AMEND
YOU'VE GOT TO BE KIDDING.
THIS WAY WE CAN STAY AND SEE THE MOVIE AGAIN.
WHY WOULD YOU THINK I'D WANT TO SEE IT AGAIN?
BECAUSE I STOLE YOUR CAR KEYS. WATCH OUT FOR THE PUDDLE OF COKE.

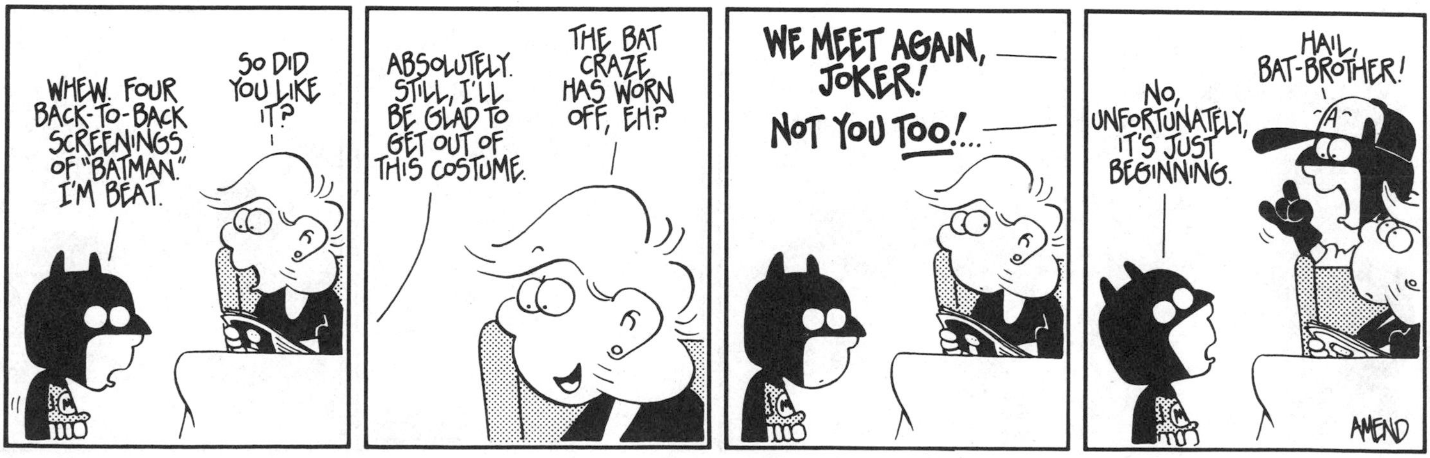
WHEW. FOUR BACK-TO-BACK SCREENINGS OF "BATMAN." I'M BEAT.
SO DID YOU LIKE IT?
ABSOLUTELY. STILL, I'LL BE GLAD TO GET OUT OF THIS COSTUME.
THE BAT CRAZE HAS WORN OFF, EH?
WE MEET AGAIN, JOKER!
NOT YOU TOO!...
NO, UNFORTUNATELY, IT'S JUST BEGINNING.
HAIL, BAT-BROTHER!
AMEND

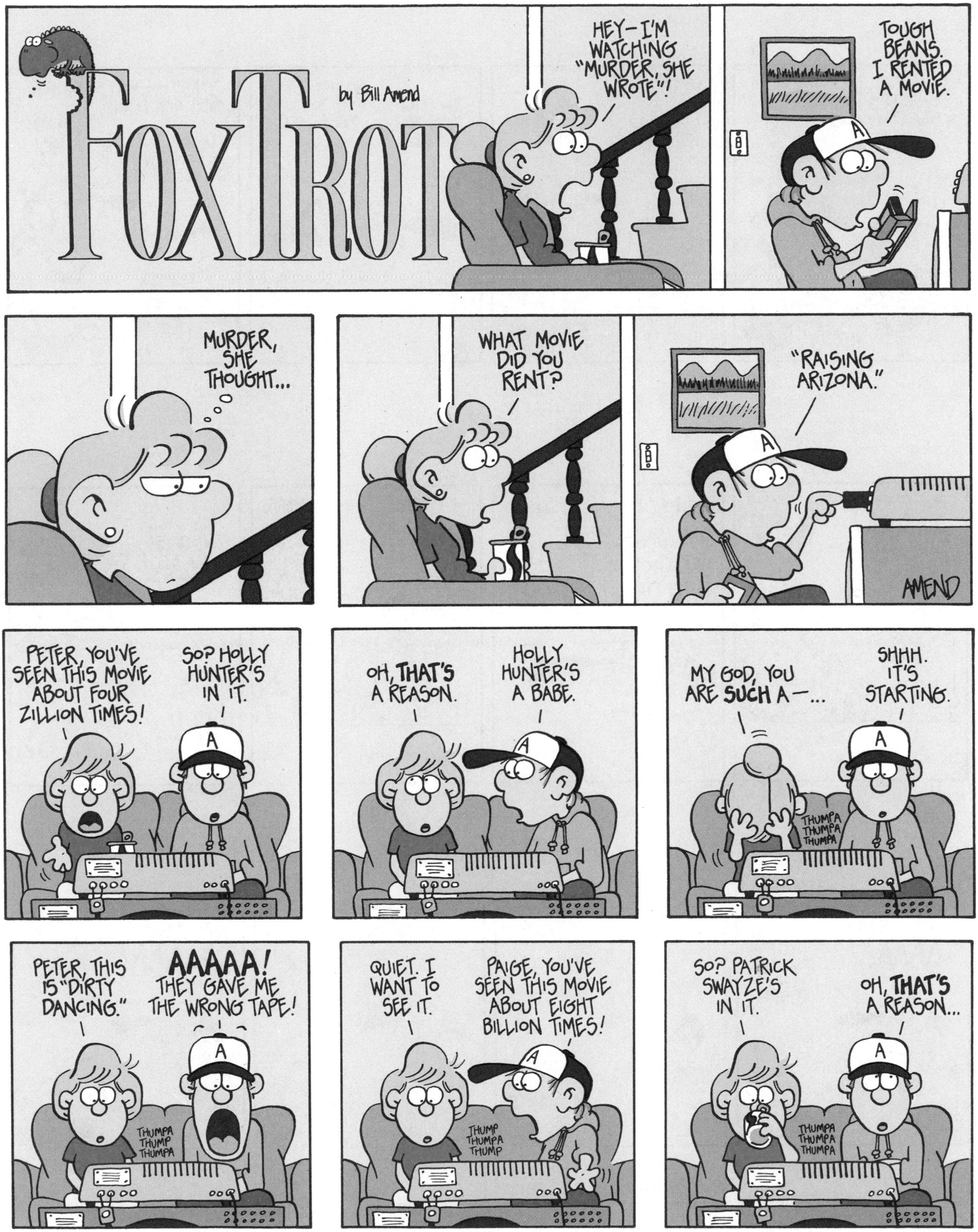
FoxTrot
by Bill Amend
HEY— I'M WATCHING "MURDER, SHE WROTE"!
TOUGH BEANS. I RENTED A MOVIE.
MURDER, SHE THOUGHT...
WHAT MOVIE DID YOU RENT?
"RAISING ARIZONA."
AMEND
PETER, YOU'VE SEEN THIS MOVIE ABOUT FOUR ZILLION TIMES!
SO? HOLLY HUNTER'S IN IT.
OH, THAT'S A REASON.
HOLLY HUNTER'S A BABE.
MY GOD, YOU ARE SUCH A—...
SHHH. IT'S STARTING.
THUMPA THUMPA THUMPA
PETER, THIS IS "DIRTY DANCING."
AAAAA! THEY GAVE ME THE WRONG TAPE!
THUMPA THUMP THUMPA
QUIET. I WANT TO SEE IT.
PAIGE, YOU'VE SEEN THIS MOVIE ABOUT EIGHT BILLION TIMES!
THUMP THUMPA THUMP
SO? PATRICK SWAYZE'S IN IT.
OH, THAT'S A REASON...
THUMPA THUMPA THUMPA

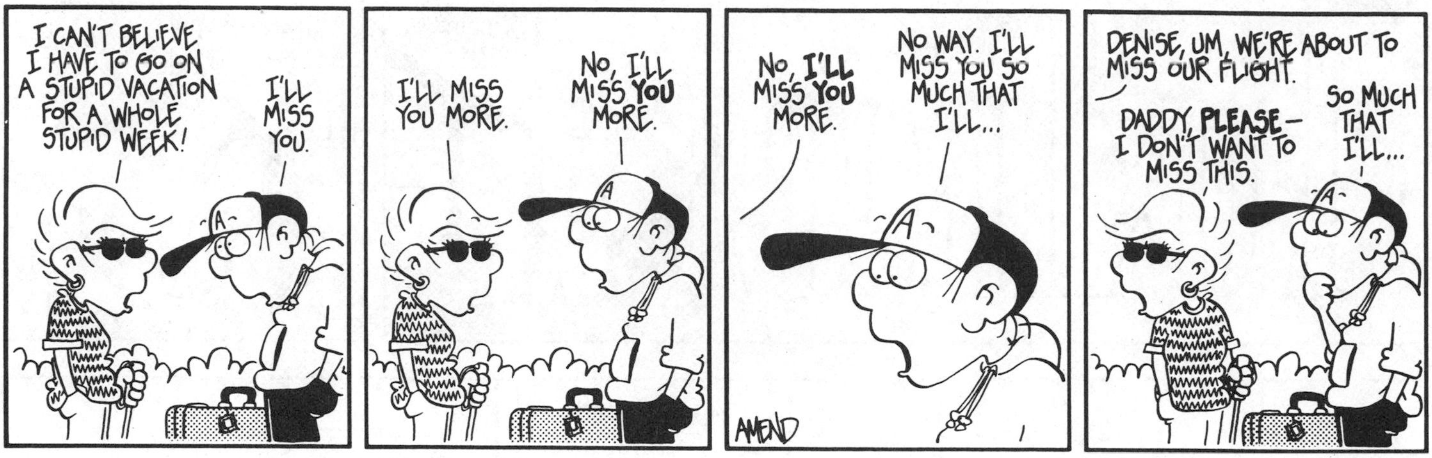
I CAN'T BELIEVE I HAVE TO GO ON A STUPID VACATION FOR A WHOLE STUPID WEEK!
I'LL MISS YOU.
I'LL MISS YOU MORE.
NO, I'LL MISS **YOU** MORE.
NO, **I'LL** MISS **YOU** MORE.
NO WAY. I'LL MISS YOU SO MUCH THAT I'LL...
DENISE, UM, WE'RE ABOUT TO MISS OUR FLIGHT.
DADDY, **PLEASE**– I DON'T WANT TO MISS THIS.
SO MUCH THAT I'LL...
AMEND

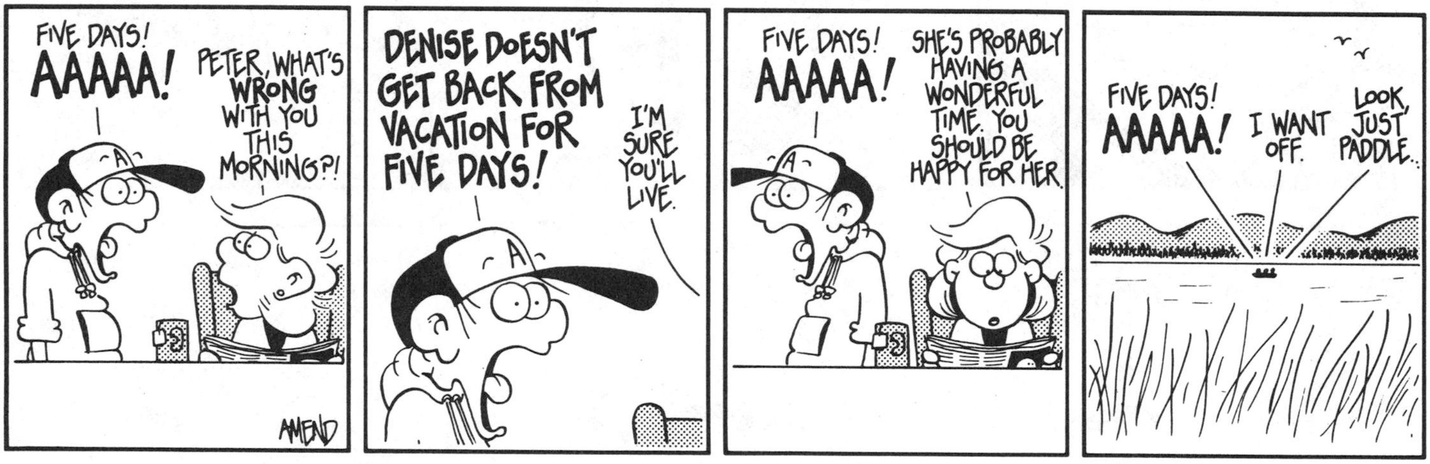
FIVE DAYS! AAAAA!
PETER, WHAT'S **WRONG** WITH YOU THIS MORNING?!
AMEND
DENISE DOESN'T GET BACK FROM VACATION FOR FIVE DAYS!
I'M SURE YOU'LL LIVE.
FIVE DAYS! AAAAA!
SHE'S PROBABLY HAVING A WONDERFUL TIME. YOU SHOULD BE HAPPY FOR HER.
FIVE DAYS! AAAAA!
I WANT OFF.
LOOK, JUST PADDLE...

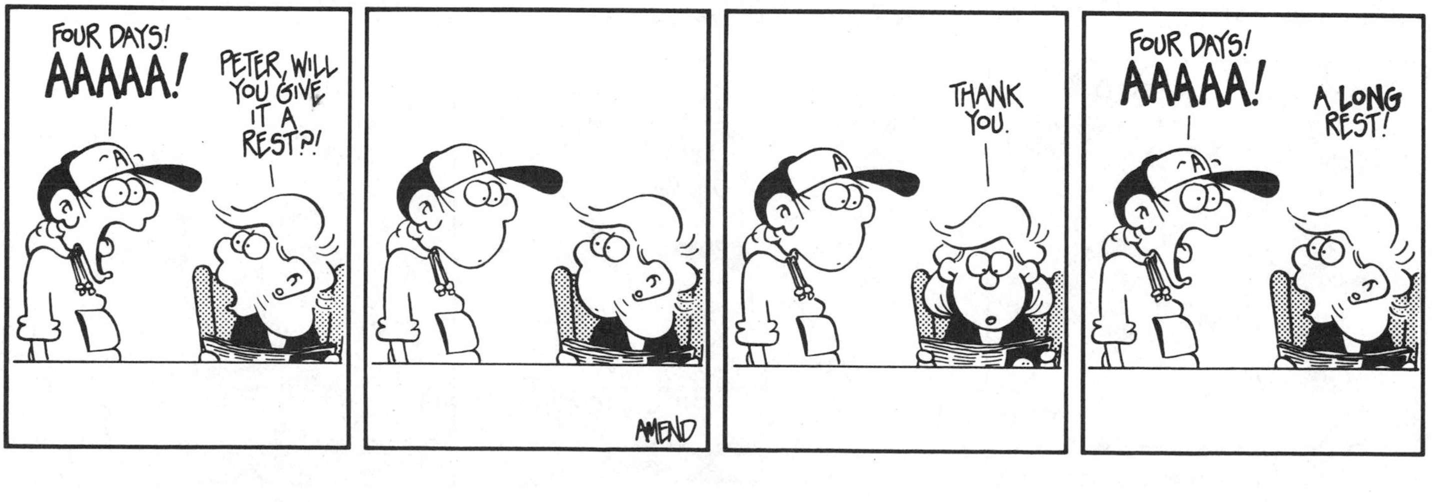
FOUR DAYS! AAAAA!
PETER, WILL YOU GIVE IT A REST?!
AMEND
THANK YOU.
FOUR DAYS! AAAAA!
A **LONG** REST!

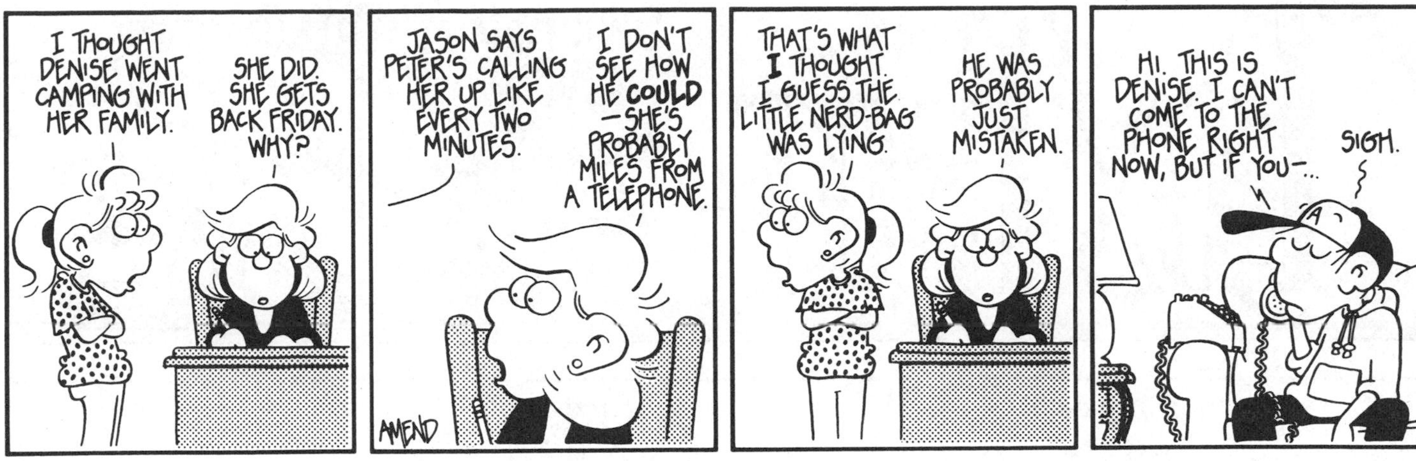
I THOUGHT DENISE WENT CAMPING WITH HER FAMILY.
SHE DID. SHE GETS BACK FRIDAY. WHY?
JASON SAYS PETER'S CALLING HER UP LIKE EVERY TWO MINUTES.
I DON'T SEE HOW HE COULD — SHE'S PROBABLY MILES FROM A TELEPHONE.
AMEND
THAT'S WHAT I THOUGHT. I GUESS THE LITTLE NERD-BAG WAS LYING.
HE WAS PROBABLY JUST MISTAKEN.
HI. THIS IS DENISE. I CAN'T COME TO THE PHONE RIGHT NOW, BUT IF YOU—...
SIGH.

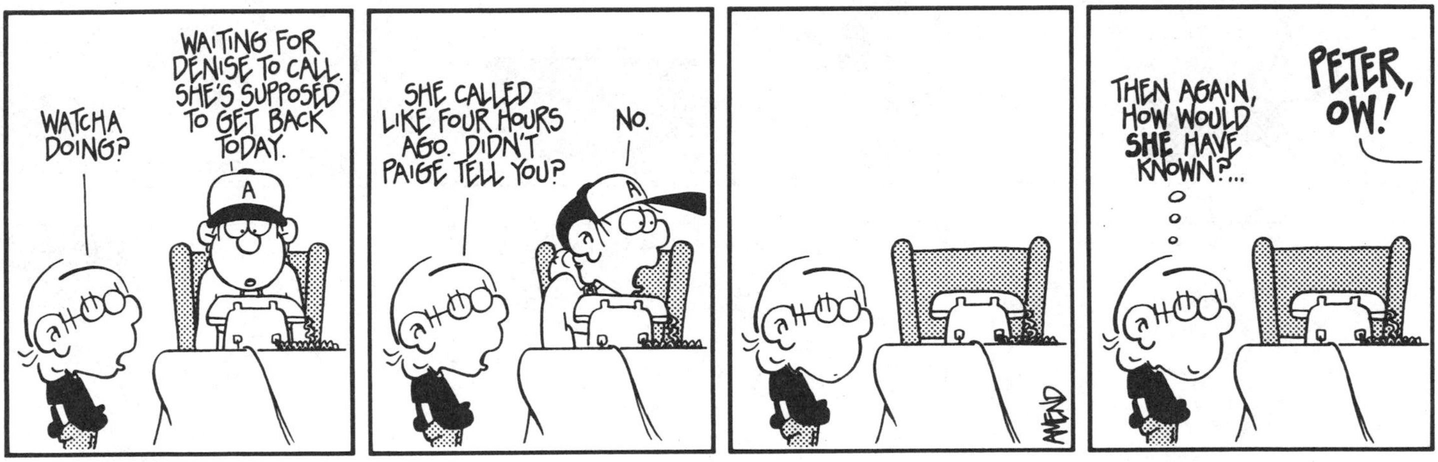
WATCHA DOING?
WAITING FOR DENISE TO CALL. SHE'S SUPPOSED TO GET BACK TODAY.
SHE CALLED LIKE FOUR HOURS AGO. DIDN'T PAIGE TELL YOU?
NO.
AMEND
THEN AGAIN, HOW WOULD SHE HAVE KNOWN?...
PETER, OW!

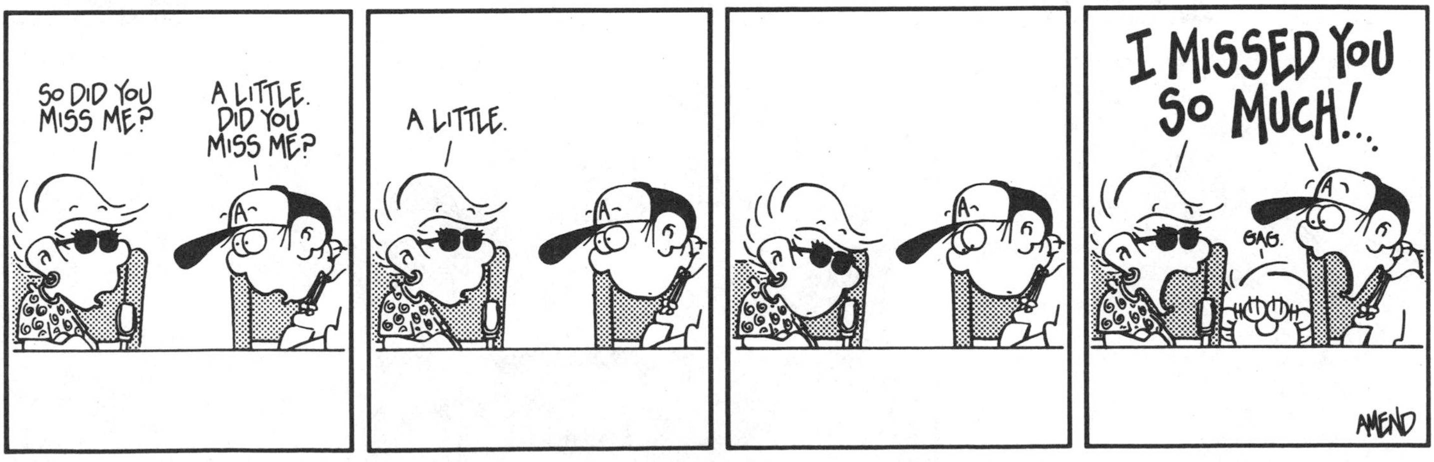
SO DID YOU MISS ME?
A LITTLE. DID YOU MISS ME?
A LITTLE.
I MISSED YOU SO MUCH!...
GAG.
AMEND

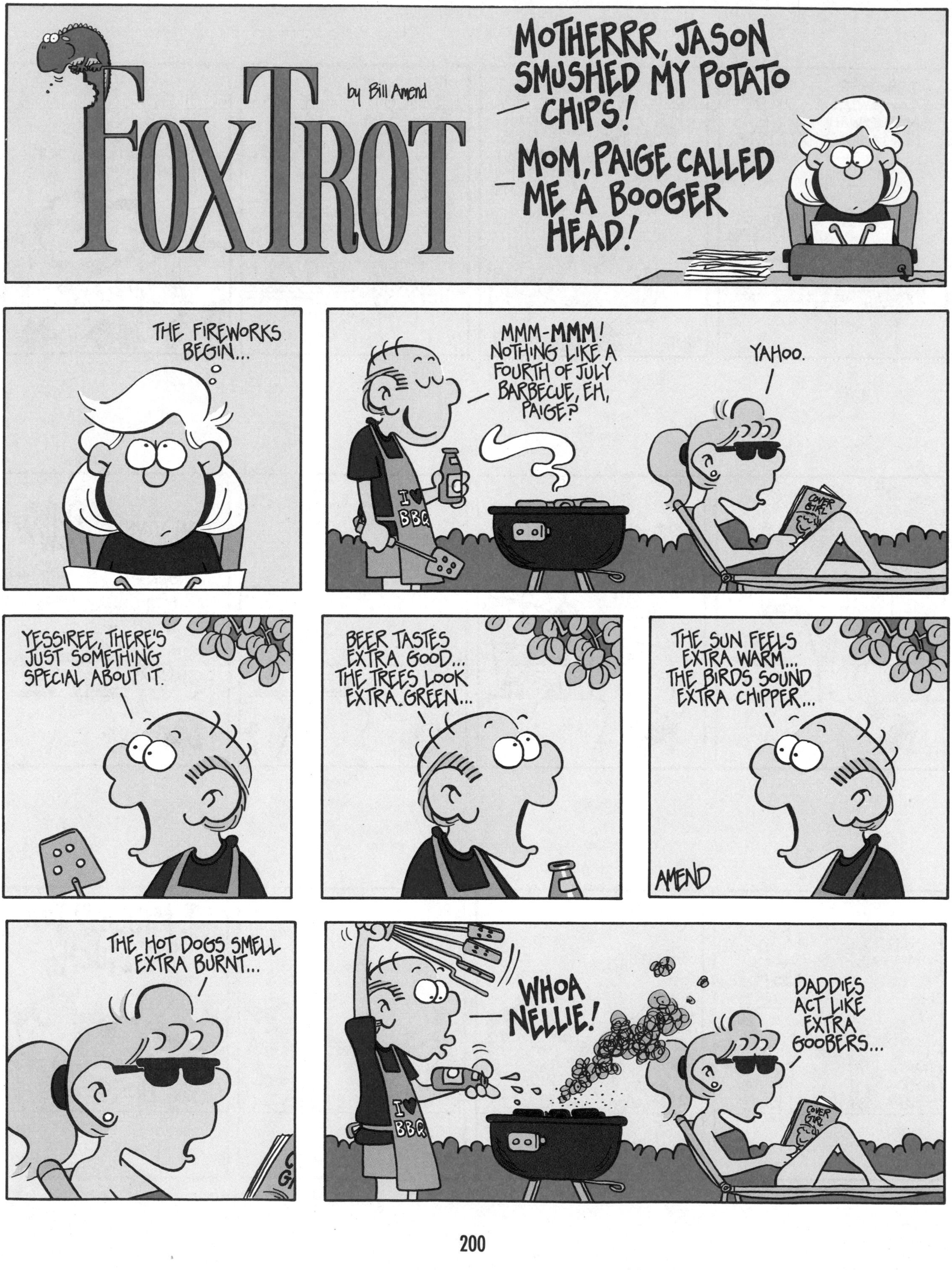
FoxTrot
by Bill Amend
MOTHERRR, JASON SMUSHED MY POTATO CHIPS!
MOM, PAIGE CALLED ME A BOOGER HEAD!
THE FIREWORKS BEGIN...
MMM-MMM! NOTHING LIKE A FOURTH OF JULY BARBECUE, EH, PAIGE?
YAHOO.
COVER GIRL
I ♥ BBQ
YESSIREE, THERE'S JUST SOMETHING SPECIAL ABOUT IT.
BEER TASTES EXTRA GOOD... THE TREES LOOK EXTRA GREEN...
THE SUN FEELS EXTRA WARM... THE BIRDS SOUND EXTRA CHIPPER...
AMEND
THE HOT DOGS SMELL EXTRA BURNT...
WHOA NELLIE!
DADDIES ACT LIKE EXTRA GOOBERS...
I ♥ BBQ
COVER GIRL

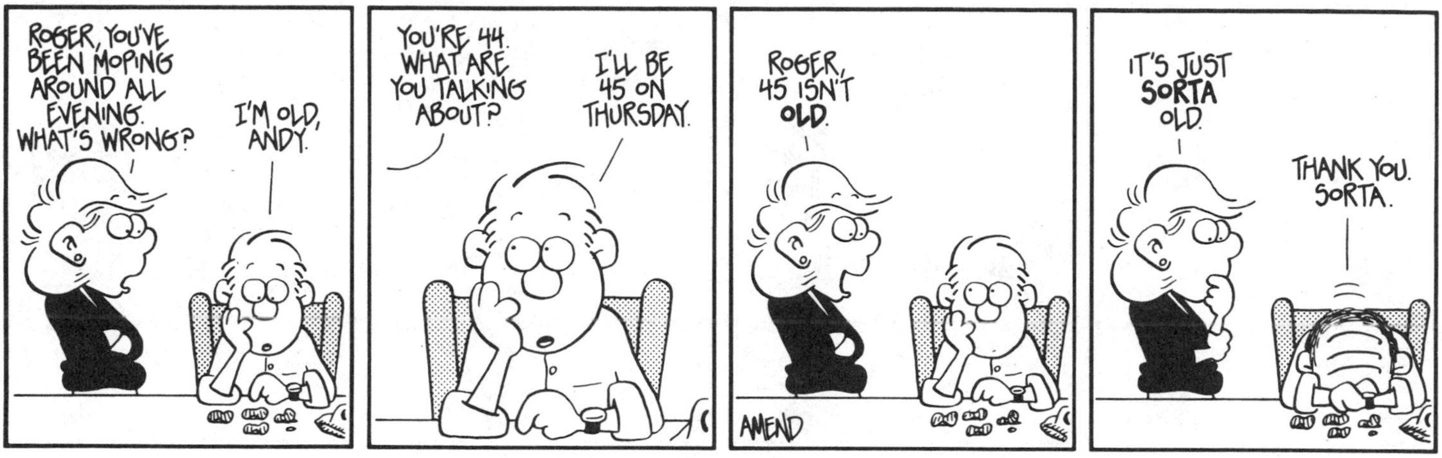
ROGER, YOU'VE BEEN MOPING AROUND ALL EVENING. WHAT'S WRONG?
I'M OLD, ANDY.
YOU'RE 44. WHAT ARE YOU TALKING ABOUT?
I'LL BE 45 ON THURSDAY.
ROGER, 45 ISN'T OLD.
AMEND
IT'S JUST SORTA OLD.
THANK YOU. SORTA.

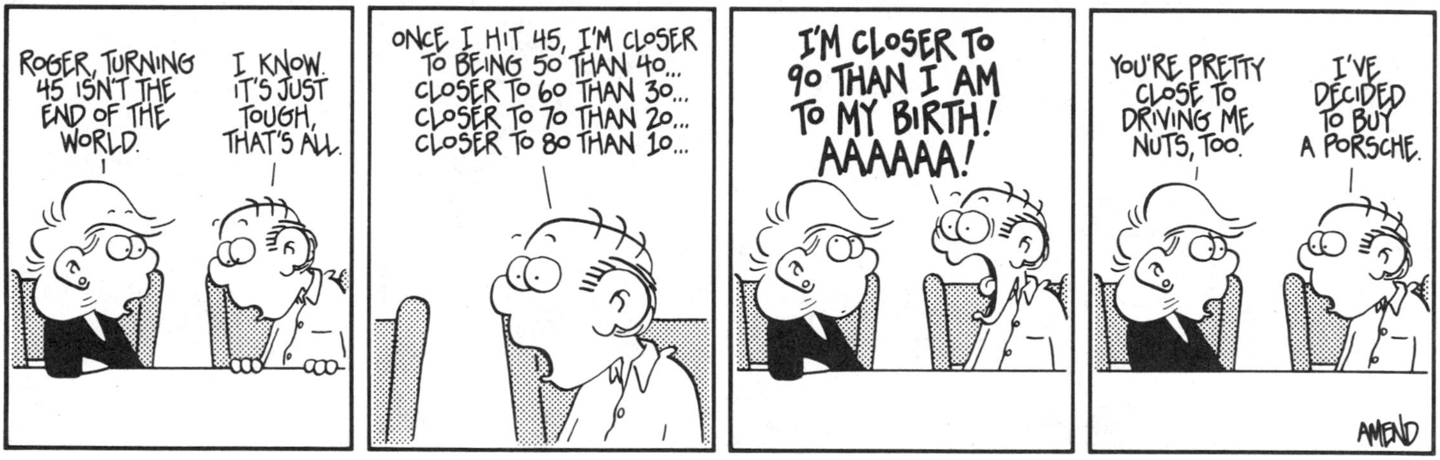
ROGER, TURNING 45 ISN'T THE END OF THE WORLD.
I KNOW. IT'S JUST TOUGH, THAT'S ALL.
ONCE I HIT 45, I'M CLOSER TO BEING 50 THAN 40... CLOSER TO 60 THAN 30... CLOSER TO 70 THAN 20... CLOSER TO 80 THAN 10...
I'M CLOSER TO 90 THAN I AM TO MY BIRTH! AAAAAA!
YOU'RE PRETTY CLOSE TO DRIVING ME NUTS, TOO.
I'VE DECIDED TO BUY A PORSCHE.
AMEND

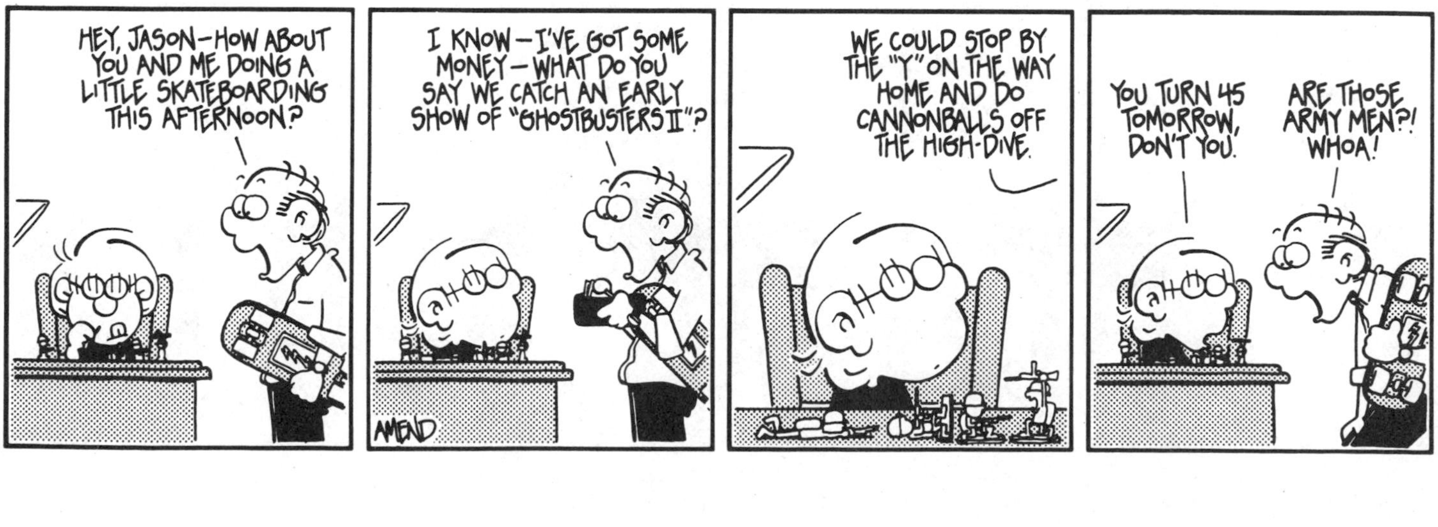
HEY, JASON—HOW ABOUT YOU AND ME DOING A LITTLE SKATEBOARDING THIS AFTERNOON?
I KNOW—I'VE GOT SOME MONEY—WHAT DO YOU SAY WE CATCH AN EARLY SHOW OF "GHOSTBUSTERS II"?
AMEND
WE COULD STOP BY THE "Y" ON THE WAY HOME AND DO CANNONBALLS OFF THE HIGH-DIVE.
YOU TURN 45 TOMORROW, DON'T YOU.
ARE THOSE ARMY MEN?! WHOA!

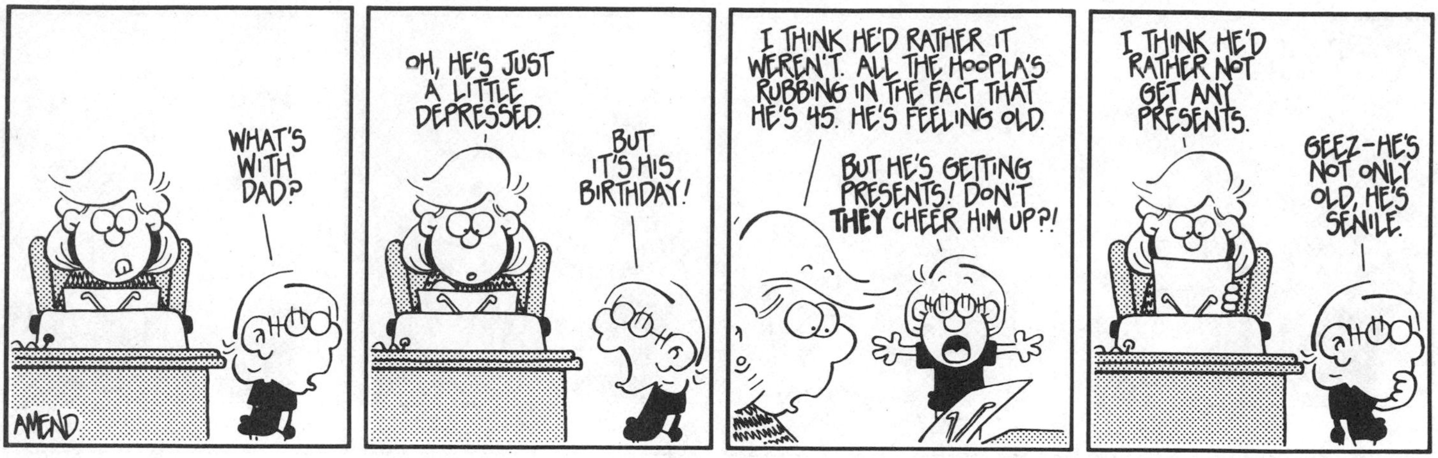
WHAT'S WITH DAD?
AMEND
OH, HE'S JUST A LITTLE DEPRESSED.
BUT IT'S HIS BIRTHDAY!
I THINK HE'D RATHER IT WEREN'T. ALL THE HOOPLA'S RUBBING IN THE FACT THAT HE'S 45. HE'S FEELING OLD.
BUT HE'S GETTING PRESENTS! DON'T **THEY** CHEER HIM UP?!
I THINK HE'D RATHER NOT GET ANY PRESENTS.
GEEZ–HE'S NOT ONLY OLD, HE'S SENILE.

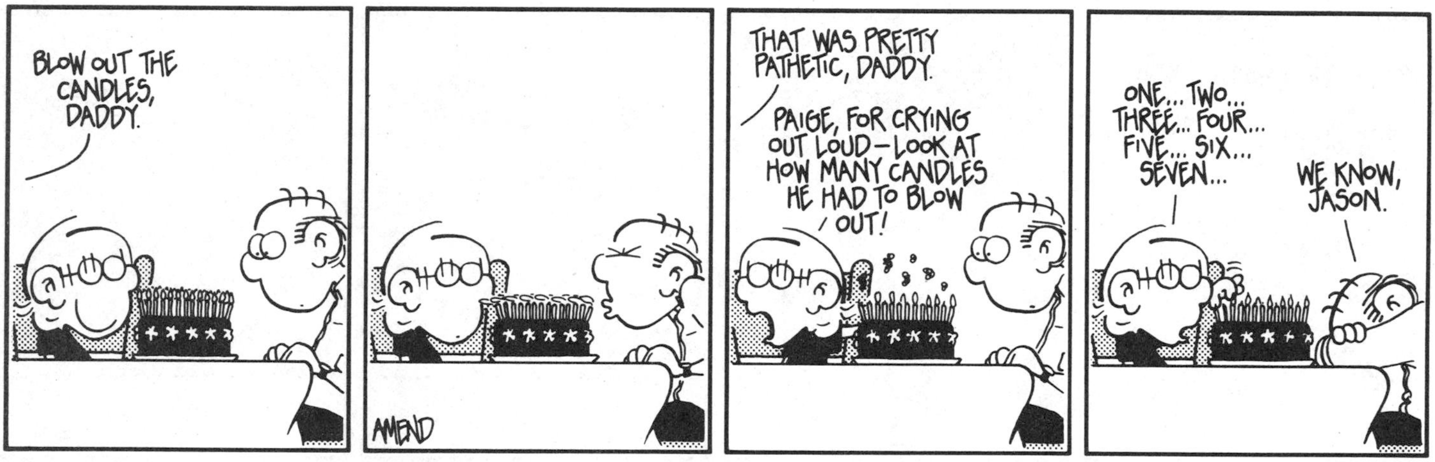
BLOW OUT THE CANDLES, DADDY.
AMEND
THAT WAS PRETTY PATHETIC, DADDY.
PAIGE, FOR CRYING OUT LOUD–LOOK AT HOW MANY CANDLES HE HAD TO BLOW OUT!
ONE... TWO... THREE... FOUR... FIVE... SIX... SEVEN...
WE KNOW, JASON.

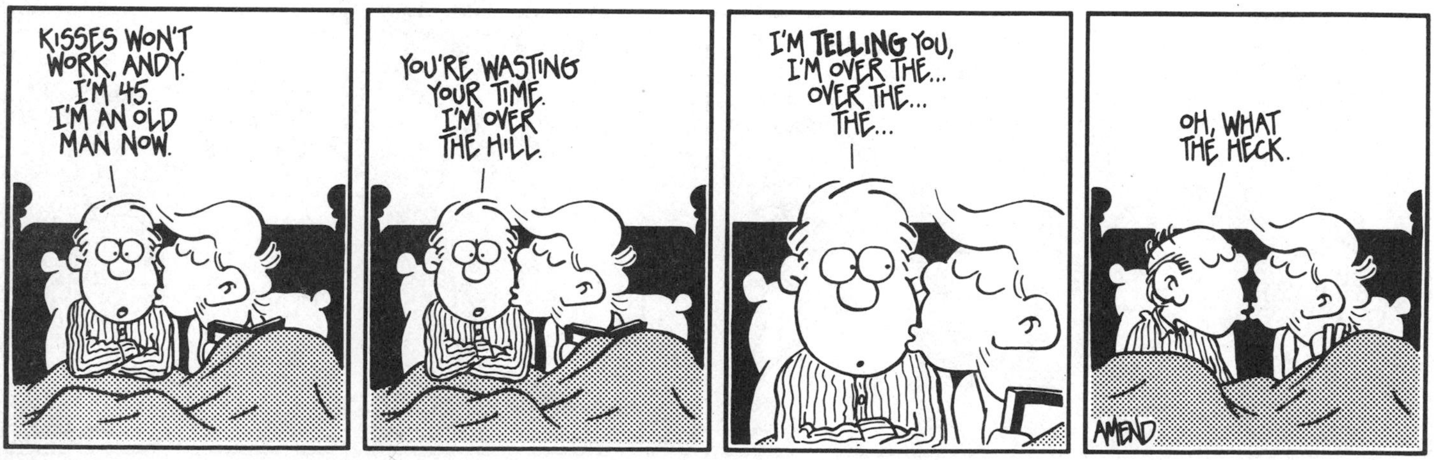
KISSES WON'T WORK, ANDY. I'M 45. I'M AN OLD MAN NOW.
YOU'RE WASTING YOUR TIME. I'M OVER THE HILL.
I'M **TELLING** YOU, I'M OVER THE... OVER THE... THE...
OH, WHAT THE HECK.
AMEND

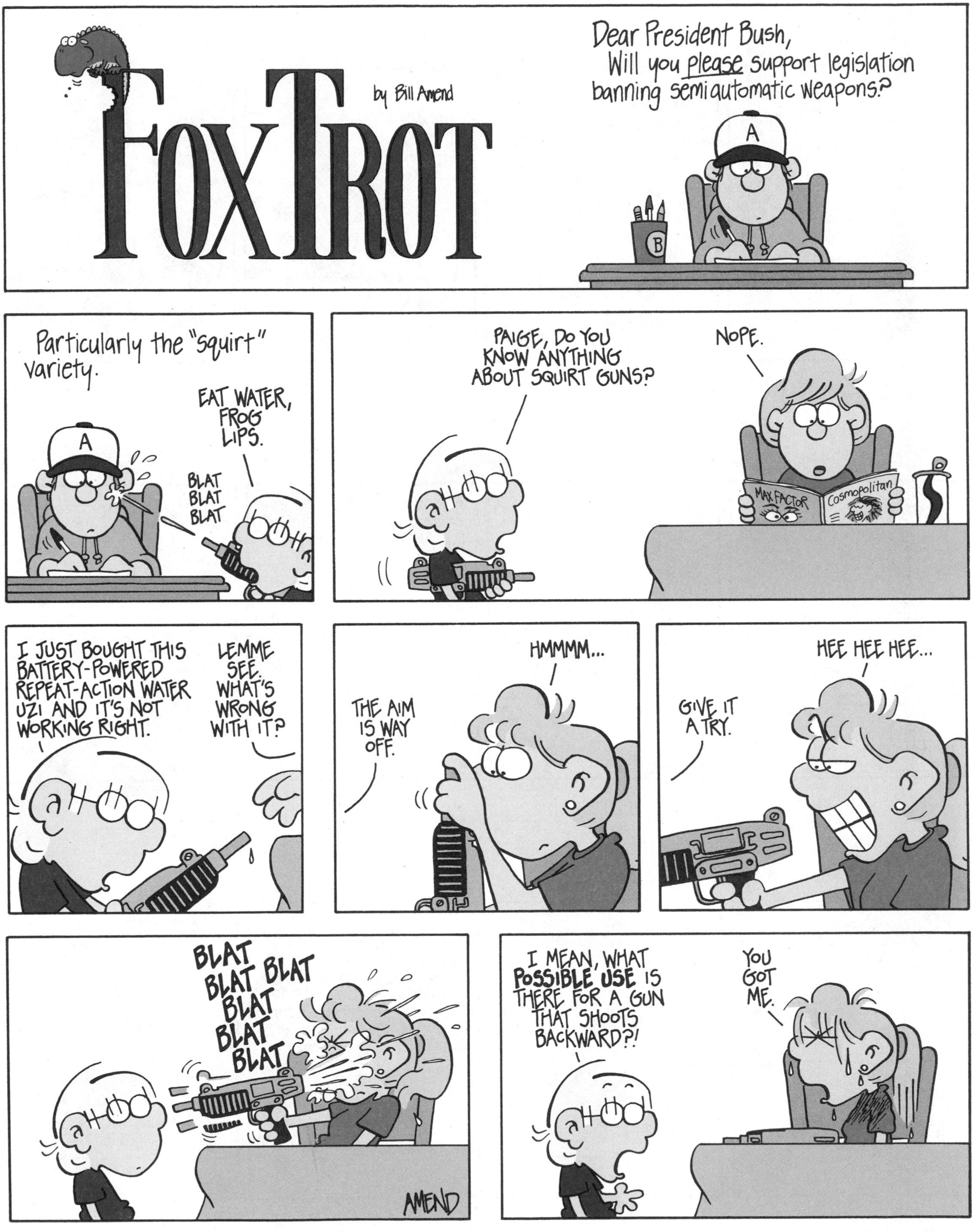

FoxTrot
by Bill Amend
Dear President Bush,
Will you please support legislation banning semiautomatic weapons?
Particularly the "squirt" variety.
EAT WATER, FROG LIPS.
BLAT BLAT BLAT
PAIGE, DO YOU KNOW ANYTHING ABOUT SQUIRT GUNS?
NOPE.
MAX FACTOR
Cosmopolitan
I JUST BOUGHT THIS BATTERY-POWERED REPEAT-ACTION WATER UZI AND IT'S NOT WORKING RIGHT.
LEMME SEE. WHAT'S WRONG WITH IT?
THE AIM IS WAY OFF.
HMMMM...
GIVE IT A TRY.
HEE HEE HEE...
BLAT BLAT BLAT BLAT BLAT BLAT
AMEND
I MEAN, WHAT **POSSIBLE USE** IS THERE FOR A GUN THAT SHOOTS BACKWARD?!
YOU GOT ME.

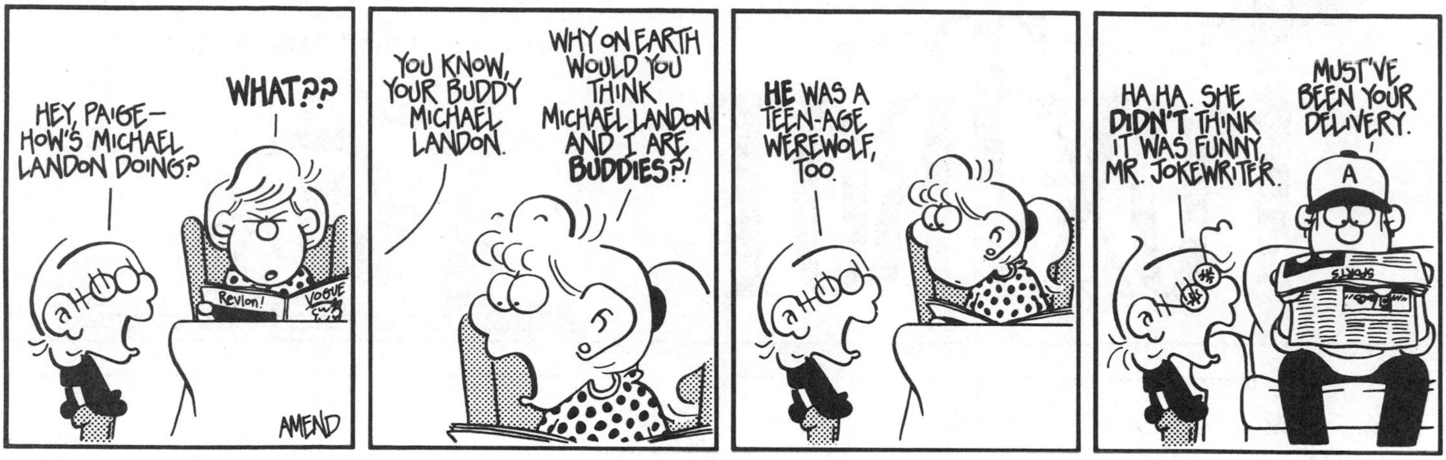
HEY, PAIGE— HOW'S MICHAEL LANDON DOING?
WHAT??
Revlon!
VOGUE
AMEND
YOU KNOW, YOUR BUDDY MICHAEL LANDON.
WHY ON EARTH WOULD YOU THINK MICHAEL LANDON AND I ARE BUDDIES?!
HE WAS A TEEN-AGE WEREWOLF, TOO.
HA HA. SHE DIDN'T THINK IT WAS FUNNY, MR. JOKEWRITER.
MUST'VE BEEN YOUR DELIVERY.
A
SPORTS

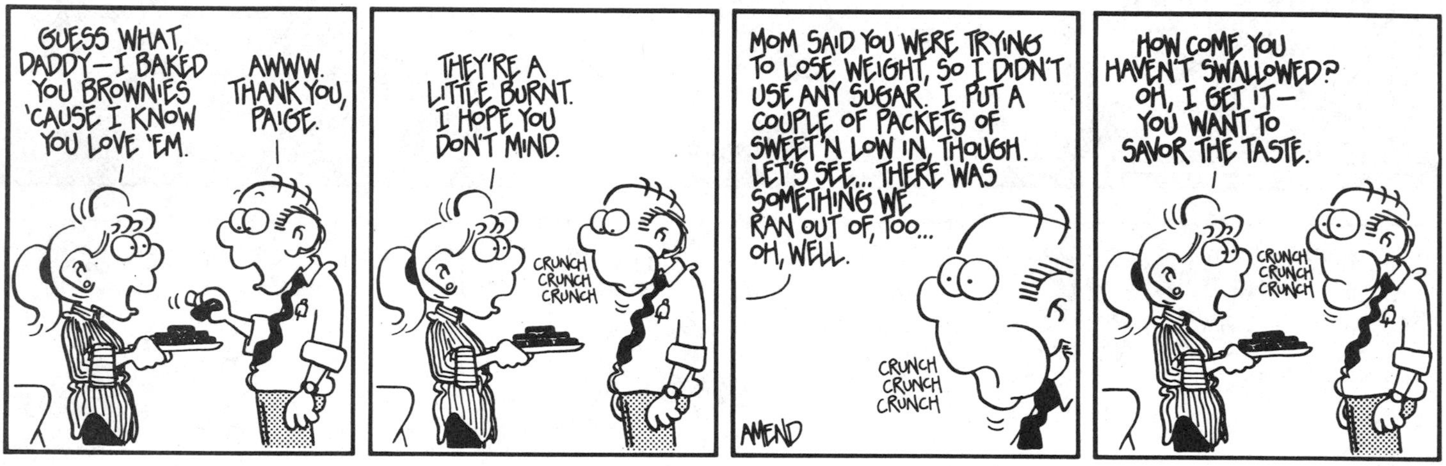
GUESS WHAT, DADDY—I BAKED YOU BROWNIES 'CAUSE I KNOW YOU LOVE 'EM.
AWWW. THANK YOU, PAIGE.
THEY'RE A LITTLE BURNT. I HOPE YOU DON'T MIND.
CRUNCH CRUNCH CRUNCH
MOM SAID YOU WERE TRYING TO LOSE WEIGHT, SO I DIDN'T USE ANY SUGAR. I PUT A COUPLE OF PACKETS OF SWEET'N LOW IN, THOUGH. LET'S SEE... THERE WAS SOMETHING WE RAN OUT OF, TOO... OH, WELL.
CRUNCH CRUNCH CRUNCH
AMEND
HOW COME YOU HAVEN'T SWALLOWED? OH, I GET IT— YOU WANT TO SAVOR THE TASTE.
CRUNCH CRUNCH CRUNCH

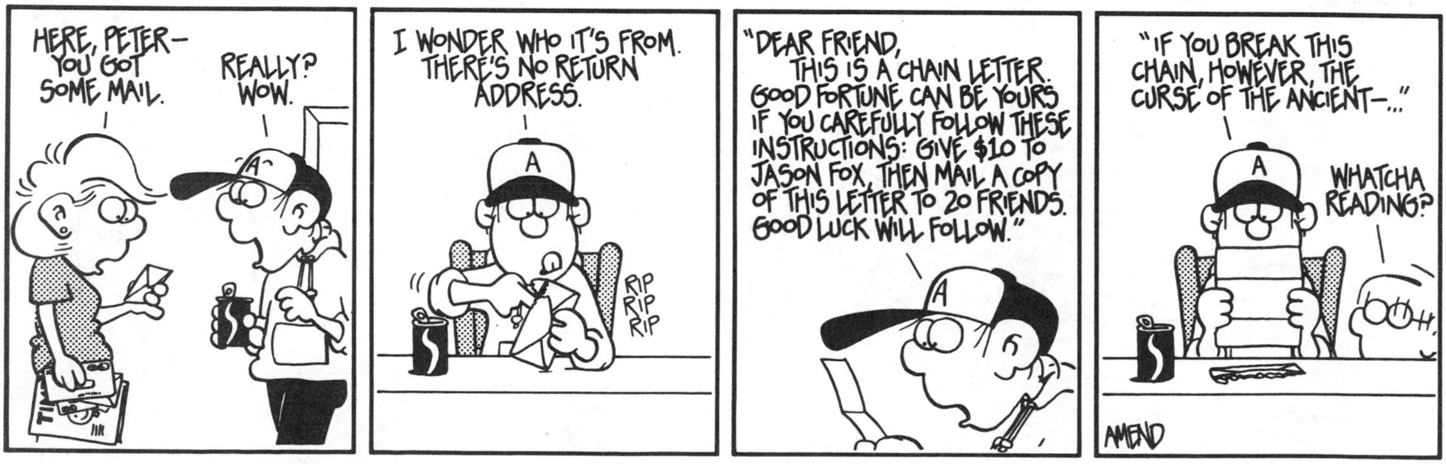
HERE, PETER— YOU GOT SOME MAIL.
REALLY? WOW.
A
I WONDER WHO IT'S FROM. THERE'S NO RETURN ADDRESS.
A
RIP RIP RIP
"DEAR FRIEND, THIS IS A CHAIN LETTER. GOOD FORTUNE CAN BE YOURS IF YOU CAREFULLY FOLLOW THESE INSTRUCTIONS: GIVE $10 TO JASON FOX, THEN MAIL A COPY OF THIS LETTER TO 20 FRIENDS. GOOD LUCK WILL FOLLOW."
A
"IF YOU BREAK THIS CHAIN, HOWEVER, THE CURSE OF THE ANCIENT—..."
A
WHATCHA READING?
AMEND

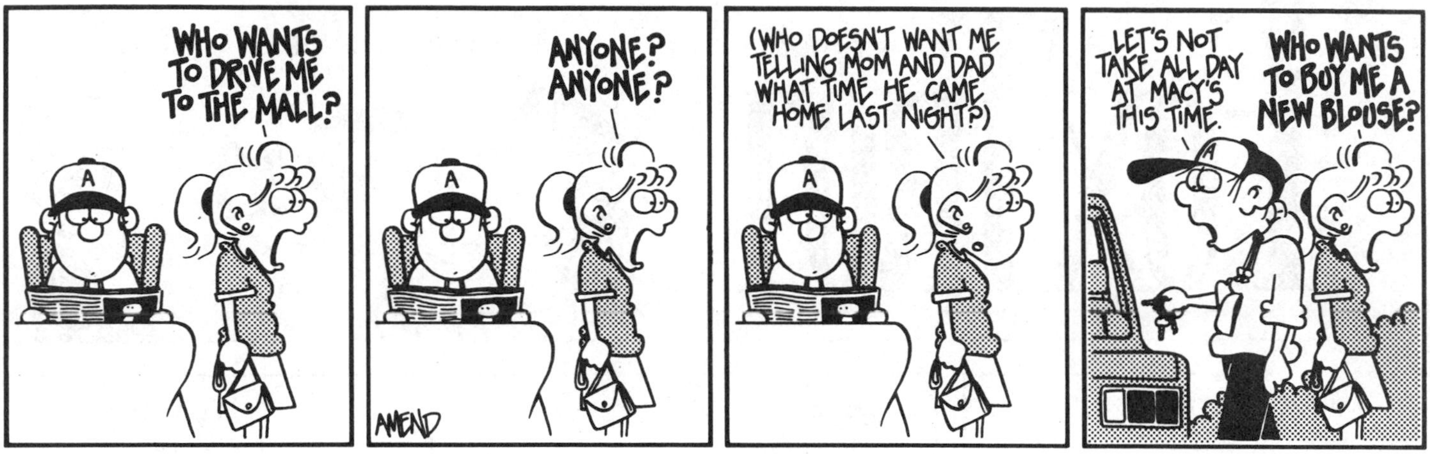
WHO WANTS TO DRIVE ME TO THE MALL?
ANYONE? ANYONE?
AMEND
(WHO DOESN'T WANT ME TELLING MOM AND DAD WHAT TIME HE CAME HOME LAST NIGHT?)
LET'S NOT TAKE ALL DAY AT MACY'S THIS TIME.
WHO WANTS TO BUY ME A NEW BLOUSE?

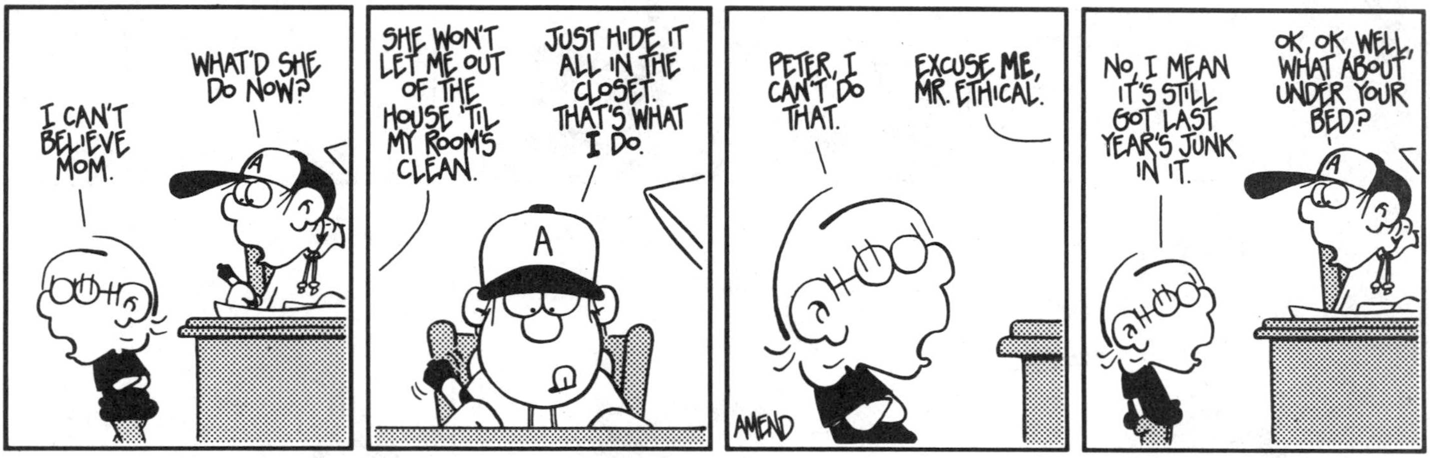
I CAN'T BELIEVE MOM.
WHAT'D SHE DO NOW?
SHE WON'T LET ME OUT OF THE HOUSE 'TIL MY ROOM'S CLEAN.
JUST HIDE IT ALL IN THE CLOSET. THAT'S WHAT I DO.
PETER, I CAN'T DO THAT.
EXCUSE ME, MR. ETHICAL.
AMEND
NO, I MEAN IT'S STILL GOT LAST YEAR'S JUNK IN IT.
OK, OK, WELL, WHAT ABOUT UNDER YOUR BED?

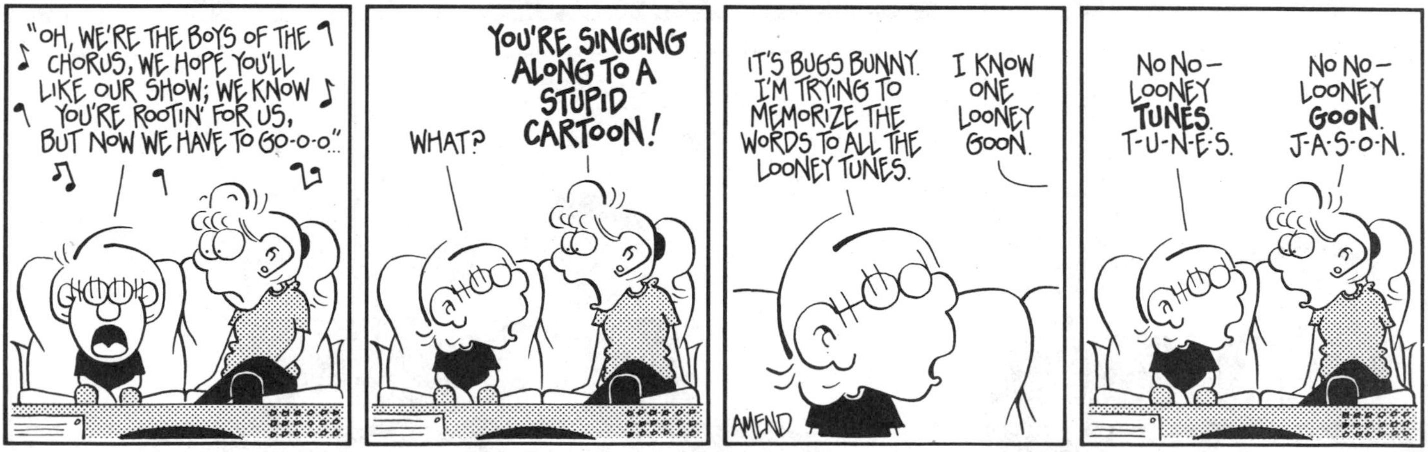
"OH, WE'RE THE BOYS OF THE CHORUS, WE HOPE YOU'LL LIKE OUR SHOW; WE KNOW YOU'RE ROOTIN' FOR US, BUT NOW WE HAVE TO GO-O-O."
WHAT?
YOU'RE SINGING ALONG TO A STUPID CARTOON!
IT'S BUGS BUNNY. I'M TRYING TO MEMORIZE THE WORDS TO ALL THE LOONEY TUNES.
I KNOW ONE LOONEY GOON.
AMEND
NO NO— LOONEY TUNES. T-U-N-E-S.
NO NO— LOONEY GOON. J-A-S-O-N.

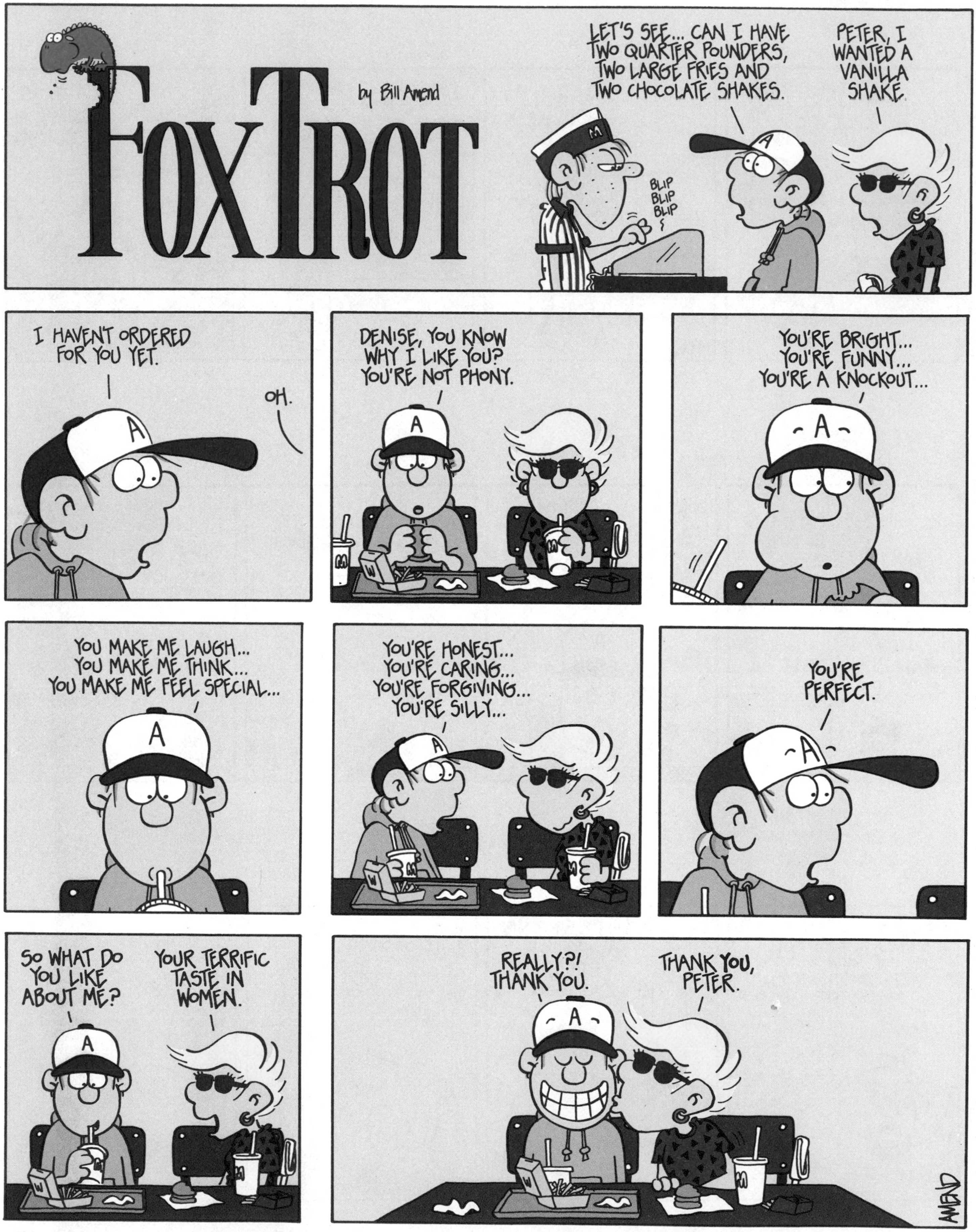
FoxTrot
by Bill Amend
LET'S SEE... CAN I HAVE TWO QUARTER POUNDERS, TWO LARGE FRIES AND TWO CHOCOLATE SHAKES.
PETER, I WANTED A VANILLA SHAKE.
BLIP BLIP BLIP
I HAVEN'T ORDERED FOR YOU YET.
OH.
DENISE, YOU KNOW WHY I LIKE YOU? YOU'RE NOT PHONY.
YOU'RE BRIGHT... YOU'RE FUNNY... YOU'RE A KNOCKOUT...
YOU MAKE ME LAUGH... YOU MAKE ME THINK... YOU MAKE ME FEEL SPECIAL...
YOU'RE HONEST... YOU'RE CARING... YOU'RE FORGIVING... YOU'RE SILLY...
YOU'RE PERFECT.
SO WHAT DO YOU LIKE ABOUT ME?
YOUR TERRIFIC TASTE IN WOMEN.
REALLY?! THANK YOU.
THANK YOU, PETER.
AMEND

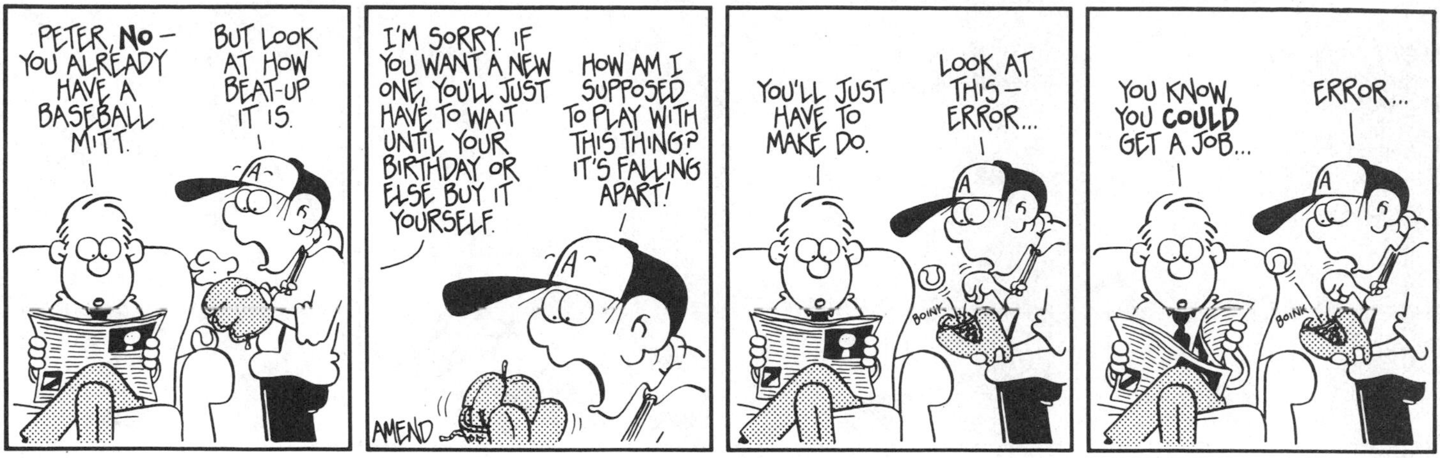
PETER, NO — YOU ALREADY HAVE A BASEBALL MITT.
BUT LOOK AT HOW BEAT-UP IT IS.
I'M SORRY. IF YOU WANT A NEW ONE, YOU'LL JUST HAVE TO WAIT UNTIL YOUR BIRTHDAY OR ELSE BUY IT YOURSELF.
HOW AM I SUPPOSED TO PLAY WITH THIS THING? IT'S FALLING APART!
AMEND
YOU'LL JUST HAVE TO MAKE DO.
LOOK AT THIS — ERROR...
BOINK
YOU KNOW, YOU COULD GET A JOB...
ERROR...
BOINK

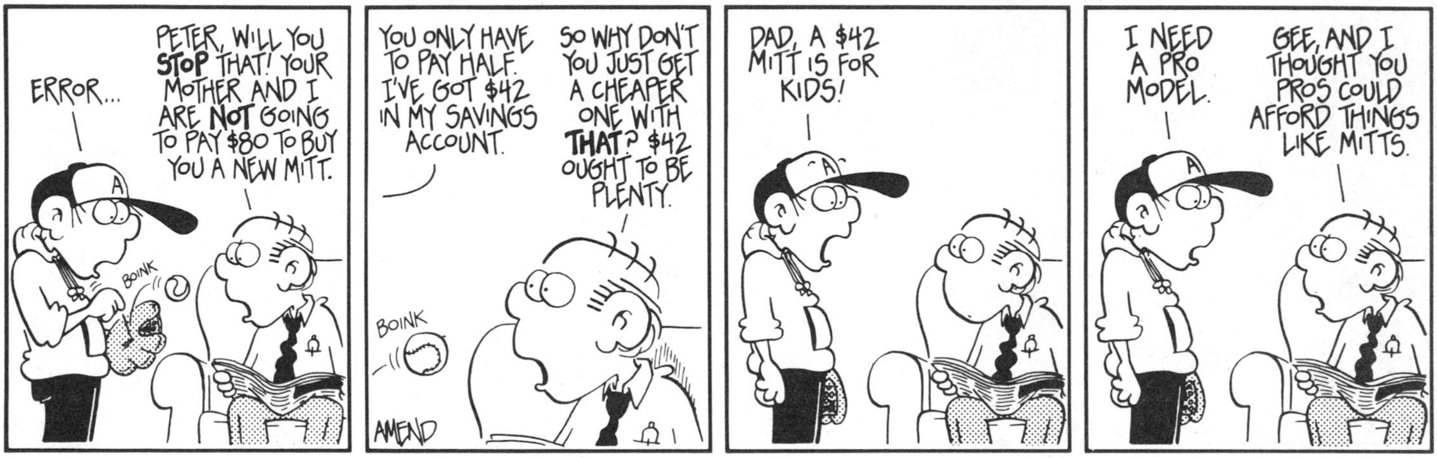
ERROR...
PETER, WILL YOU STOP THAT! YOUR MOTHER AND I ARE NOT GOING TO PAY $80 TO BUY YOU A NEW MITT.
BOINK
YOU ONLY HAVE TO PAY HALF. I'VE GOT $42 IN MY SAVINGS ACCOUNT.
SO WHY DON'T YOU JUST GET A CHEAPER ONE WITH THAT? $42 OUGHT TO BE PLENTY.
BOINK
AMEND
DAD, A $42 MITT IS FOR KIDS!
I NEED A PRO MODEL.
GEE, AND I THOUGHT YOU PROS COULD AFFORD THINGS LIKE MITTS.

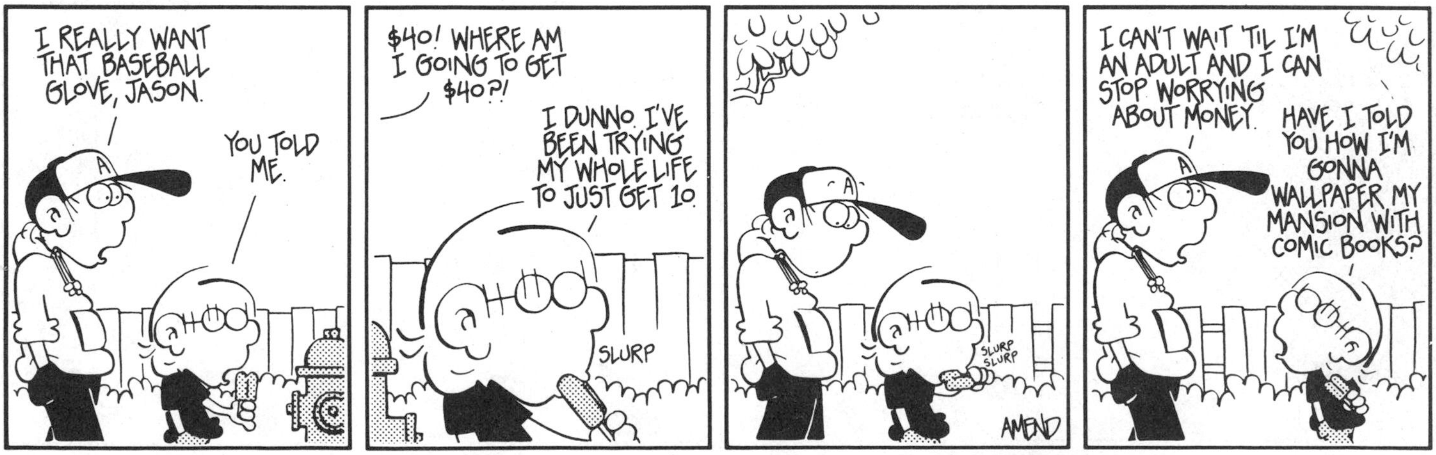
I REALLY WANT THAT BASEBALL GLOVE, JASON.
YOU TOLD ME.
$40! WHERE AM I GOING TO GET $40?!
I DUNNO. I'VE BEEN TRYING MY WHOLE LIFE TO JUST GET 10.
SLURP
SLURP SLURP
AMEND
I CAN'T WAIT 'TIL I'M AN ADULT AND I CAN STOP WORRYING ABOUT MONEY.
HAVE I TOLD YOU HOW I'M GONNA WALLPAPER MY MANSION WITH COMIC BOOKS?

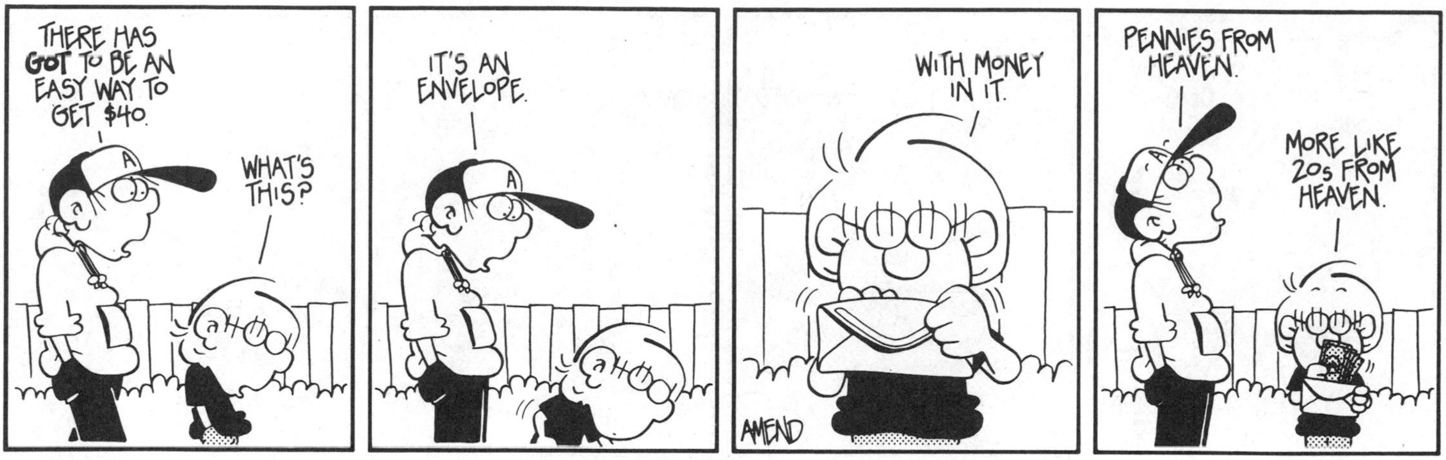
THERE HAS GOT TO BE AN EASY WAY TO GET $40.
WHAT'S THIS?
IT'S AN ENVELOPE.
WITH MONEY IN IT.
AMEND
PENNIES FROM HEAVEN.
MORE LIKE 20s FROM HEAVEN.

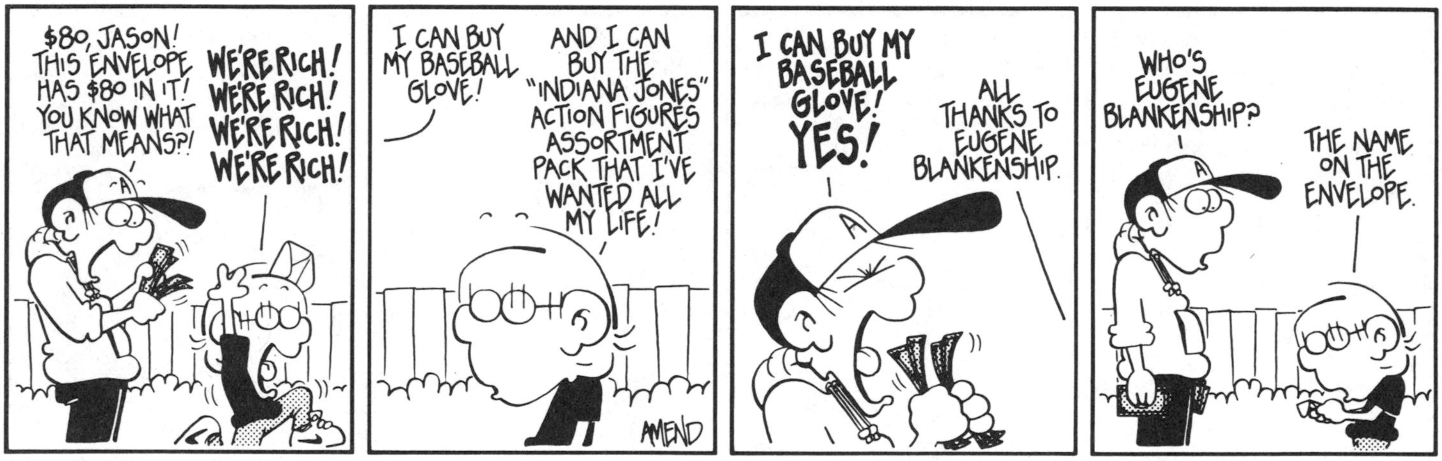
$80, JASON! THIS ENVELOPE HAS $80 IN IT! YOU KNOW WHAT THAT MEANS?!
WE'RE RICH! WE'RE RICH! WE'RE RICH! WE'RE RICH!
I CAN BUY MY BASEBALL GLOVE!
AND I CAN BUY THE "INDIANA JONES" ACTION FIGURES ASSORTMENT PACK THAT I'VE WANTED ALL MY LIFE!
AMEND
I CAN BUY MY BASEBALL GLOVE! YES!
ALL THANKS TO EUGENE BLANKENSHIP.
WHO'S EUGENE BLANKENSHIP?
THE NAME ON THE ENVELOPE.

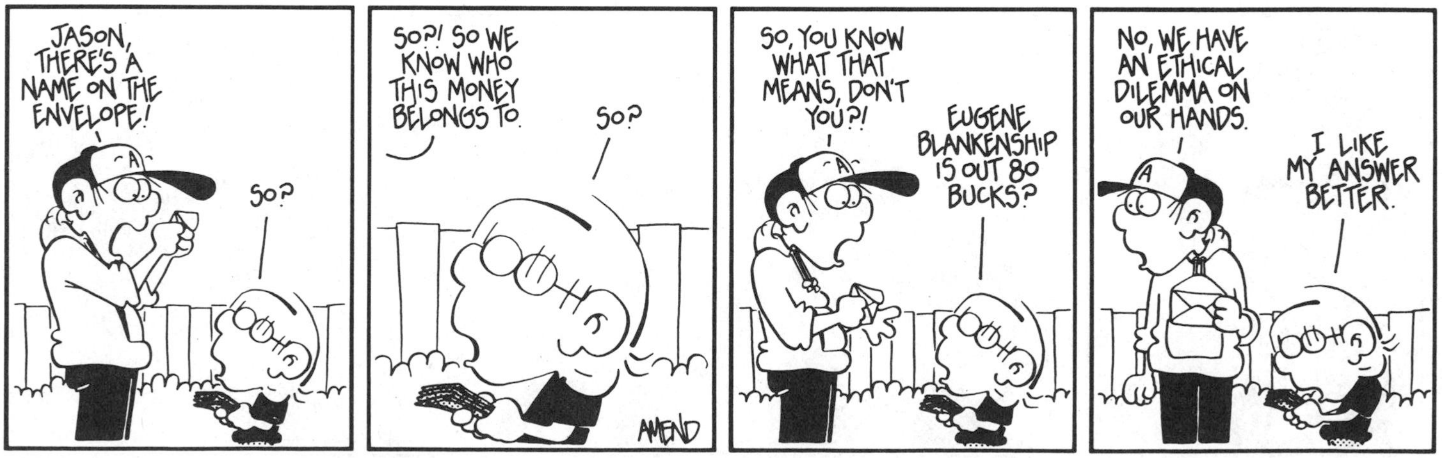
JASON, THERE'S A NAME ON THE ENVELOPE!
SO?
SO?! SO WE KNOW WHO THIS MONEY BELONGS TO.
SO?
AMEND
SO, YOU KNOW WHAT THAT MEANS, DON'T YOU?!
EUGENE BLANKENSHIP IS OUT 80 BUCKS?
NO, WE HAVE AN ETHICAL DILEMMA ON OUR HANDS.
I LIKE MY ANSWER BETTER.

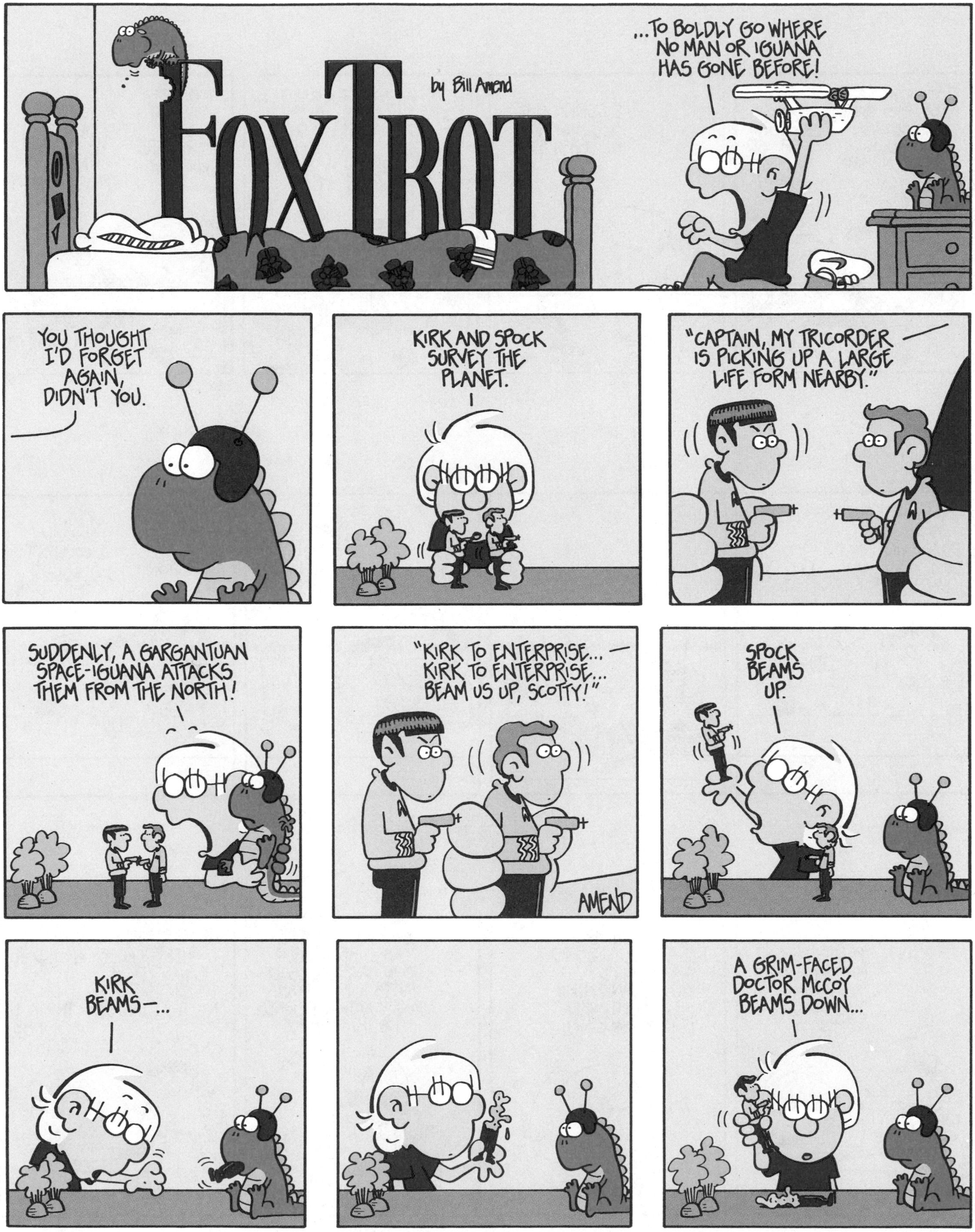
FoxTrot
by Bill Amend
...TO BOLDLY GO WHERE NO MAN OR IGUANA HAS GONE BEFORE!
YOU THOUGHT I'D FORGET AGAIN, DIDN'T YOU.
KIRK AND SPOCK SURVEY THE PLANET.
"CAPTAIN, MY TRICORDER IS PICKING UP A LARGE LIFE FORM NEARBY."
SUDDENLY, A GARGANTUAN SPACE-IGUANA ATTACKS THEM FROM THE NORTH!
"KIRK TO ENTERPRISE... KIRK TO ENTERPRISE... BEAM US UP, SCOTTY!"
AMEND
SPOCK BEAMS UP.
KIRK BEAMS—...
A GRIM-FACED DOCTOR McCOY BEAMS DOWN...

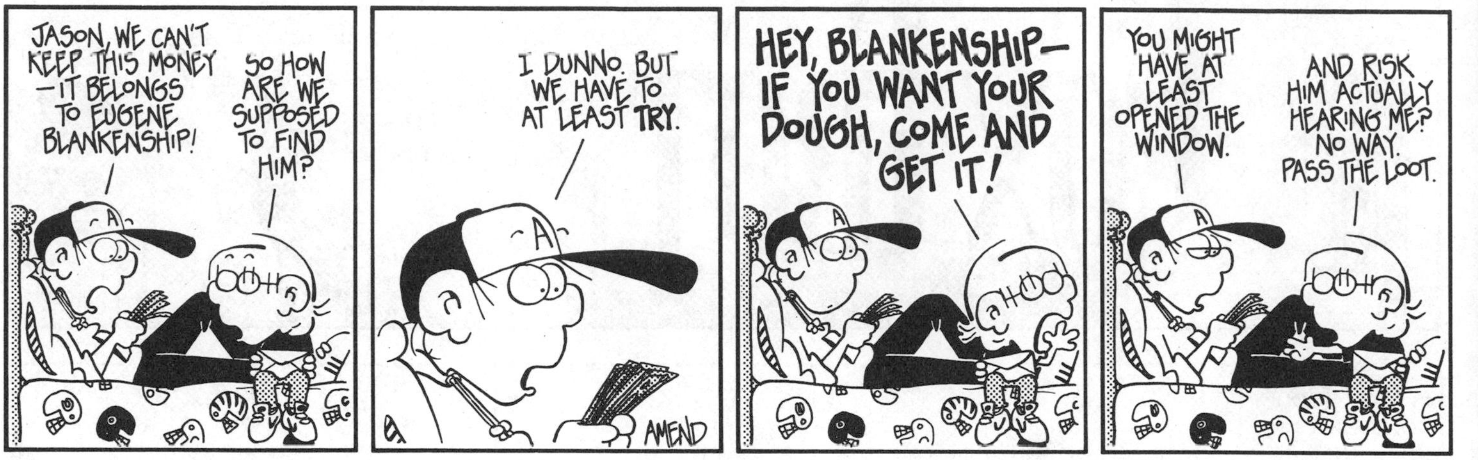
JASON, WE CAN'T KEEP THIS MONEY — IT BELONGS TO EUGENE BLANKENSHIP!
SO HOW ARE WE SUPPOSED TO FIND HIM?
I DUNNO. BUT WE HAVE TO AT LEAST **TRY**.
AMEND
HEY, BLANKENSHIP— IF YOU WANT YOUR DOUGH, COME AND GET IT!
YOU MIGHT HAVE AT LEAST OPENED THE WINDOW.
AND RISK HIM ACTUALLY HEARING ME? NO WAY. PASS THE LOOT.

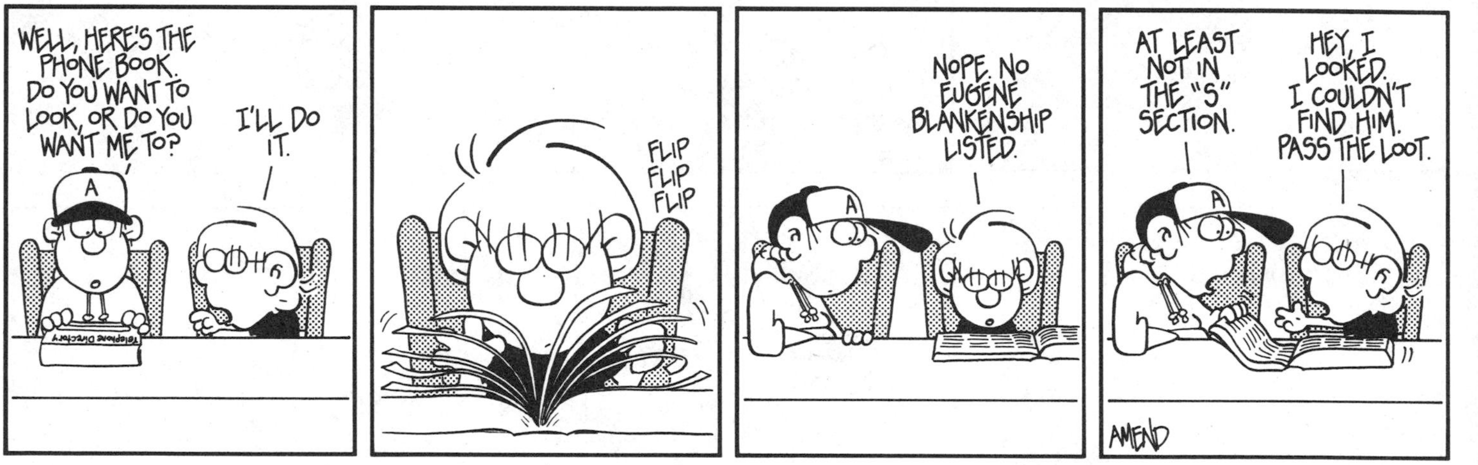
WELL, HERE'S THE PHONE BOOK. DO YOU WANT TO LOOK, OR DO YOU WANT ME TO?
I'LL DO IT.
FLIP FLIP FLIP
NOPE. NO EUGENE BLANKENSHIP LISTED.
AT LEAST NOT IN THE "S" SECTION.
HEY, I LOOKED. I COULDN'T FIND HIM. PASS THE LOOT.
AMEND

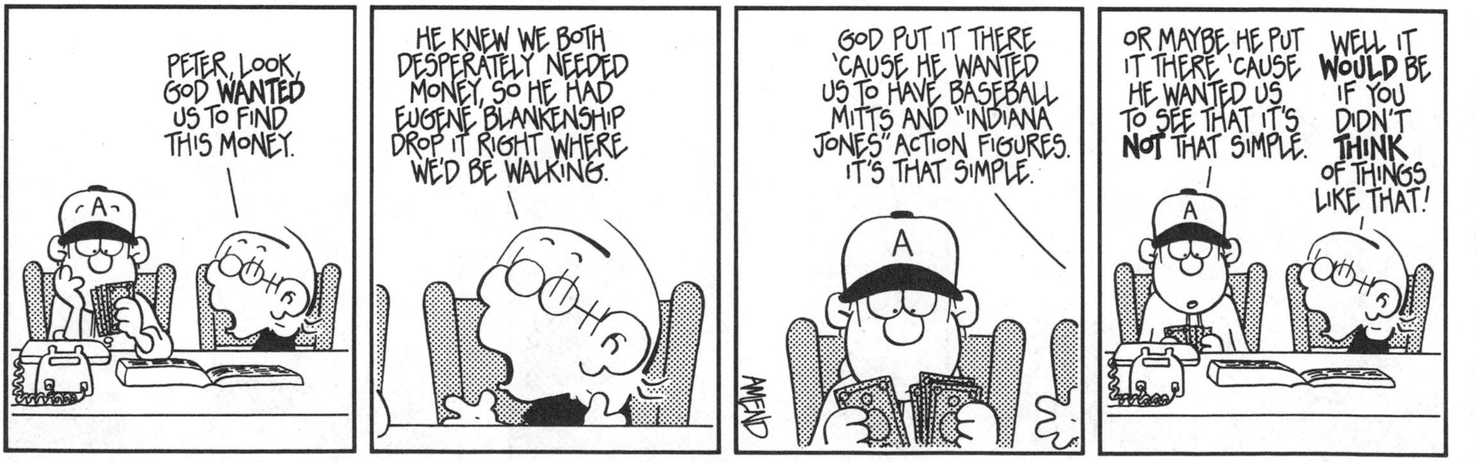
PETER, LOOK, GOD **WANTED** US TO FIND THIS MONEY.
HE KNEW WE BOTH DESPERATELY NEEDED MONEY, SO HE HAD EUGENE BLANKENSHIP DROP IT RIGHT WHERE WE'D BE WALKING.
AMEND
GOD PUT IT THERE 'CAUSE HE WANTED US TO HAVE BASEBALL MITTS AND "INDIANA JONES" ACTION FIGURES. IT'S THAT SIMPLE.
OR MAYBE HE PUT IT THERE 'CAUSE HE WANTED US TO SEE THAT IT'S **NOT** THAT SIMPLE.
WELL IT **WOULD** BE IF YOU DIDN'T **THINK** OF THINGS LIKE THAT!

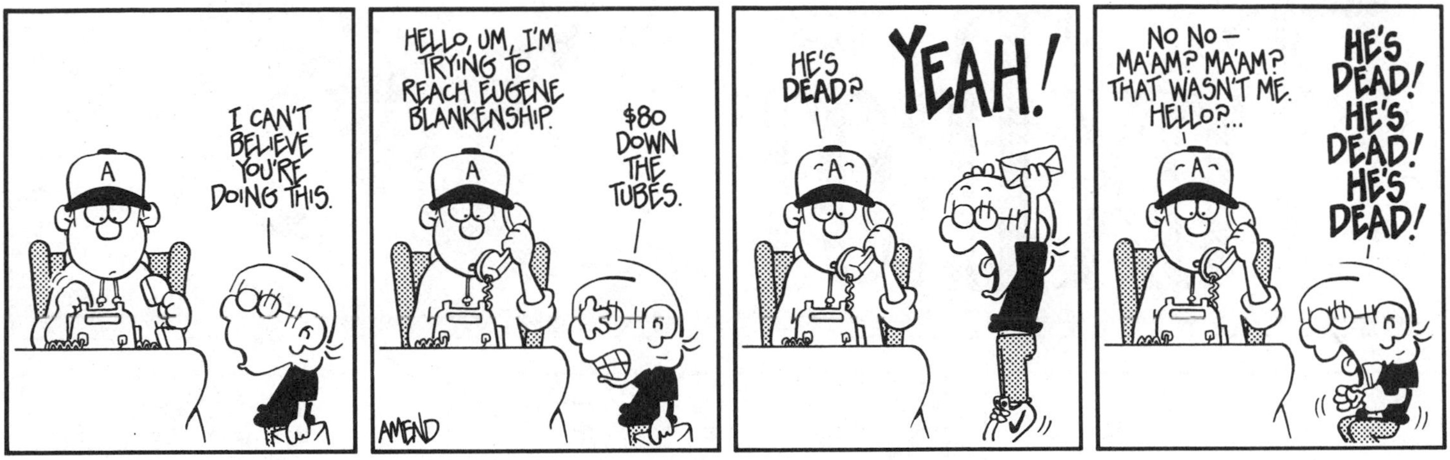
I CAN'T BELIEVE YOU'RE DOING THIS.
HELLO, UM, I'M TRYING TO REACH EUGENE BLANKENSHIP.
$80 DOWN THE TUBES.
AMEND
HE'S **DEAD**?
YEAH!
NO NO – MA'AM? MA'AM? THAT WASN'T ME. HELLO?...
HE'S DEAD! HE'S DEAD! HE'S DEAD!

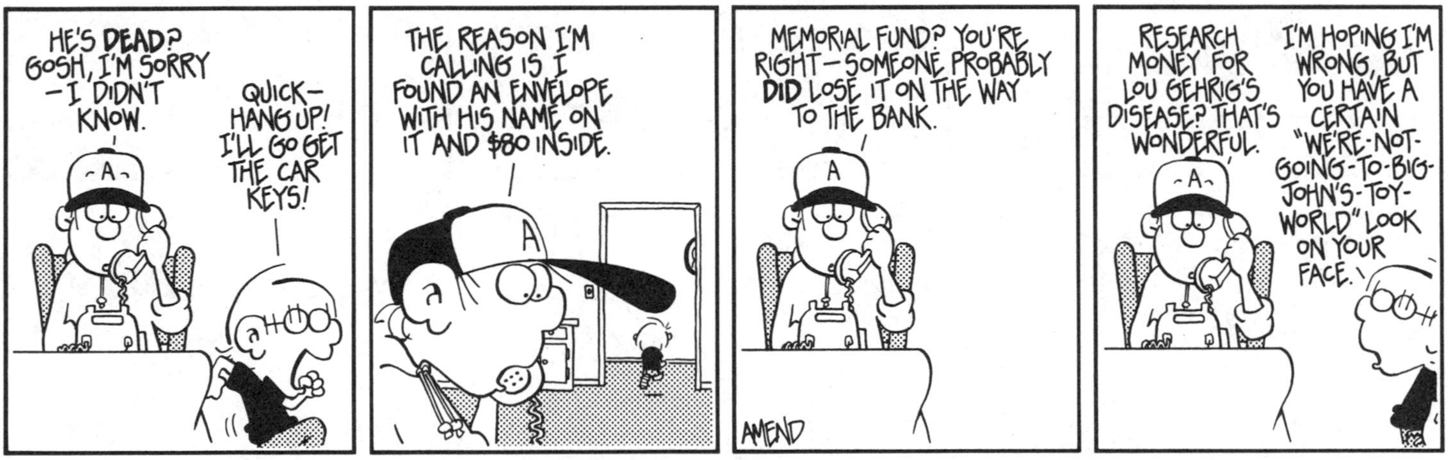
HE'S **DEAD**? GOSH, I'M SORRY – I DIDN'T KNOW.
QUICK– HANG UP! I'LL GO GET THE CAR KEYS!
THE REASON I'M CALLING IS I FOUND AN ENVELOPE WITH HIS NAME ON IT AND $80 INSIDE.
MEMORIAL FUND? YOU'RE RIGHT – SOMEONE PROBABLY **DID** LOSE IT ON THE WAY TO THE BANK.
AMEND
RESEARCH MONEY FOR LOU GEHRIG'S DISEASE? THAT'S WONDERFUL.
I'M HOPING I'M WRONG, BUT YOU HAVE A CERTAIN "WE'RE-NOT-GOING-TO-BIG-JOHN'S-TOY-WORLD" LOOK ON YOUR FACE.

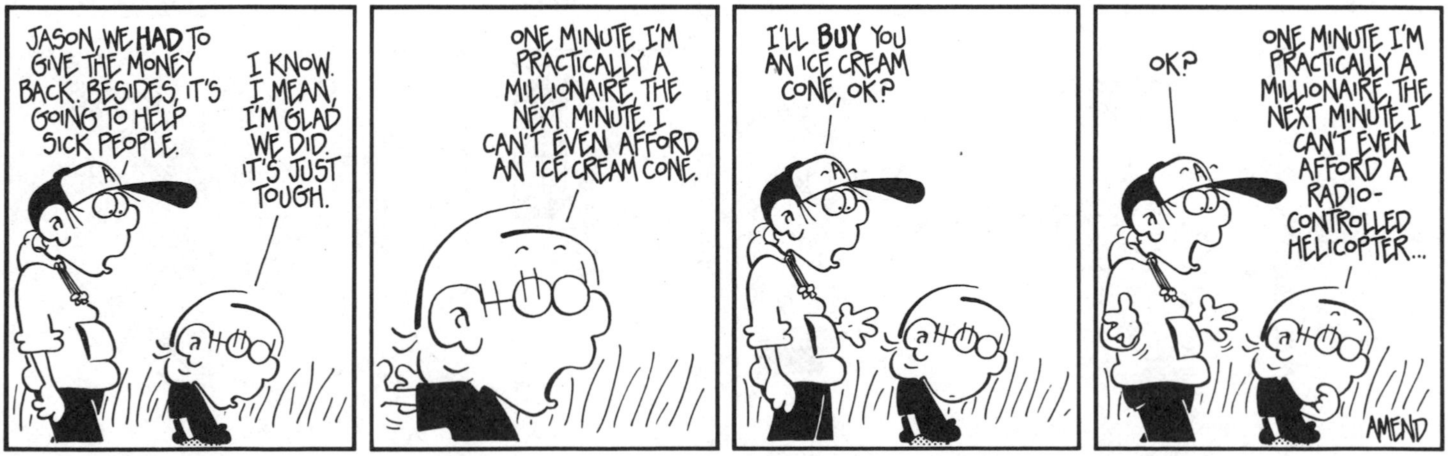
JASON, WE **HAD** TO GIVE THE MONEY BACK. BESIDES, IT'S GOING TO HELP SICK PEOPLE.
I KNOW. I MEAN, I'M GLAD WE DID. IT'S JUST TOUGH.
ONE MINUTE I'M PRACTICALLY A MILLIONAIRE, THE NEXT MINUTE I CAN'T EVEN AFFORD AN ICE CREAM CONE.
I'LL **BUY** YOU AN ICE CREAM CONE, OK?
OK?
ONE MINUTE I'M PRACTICALLY A MILLIONAIRE, THE NEXT MINUTE I CAN'T EVEN AFFORD A RADIO-CONTROLLED HELICOPTER...
AMEND

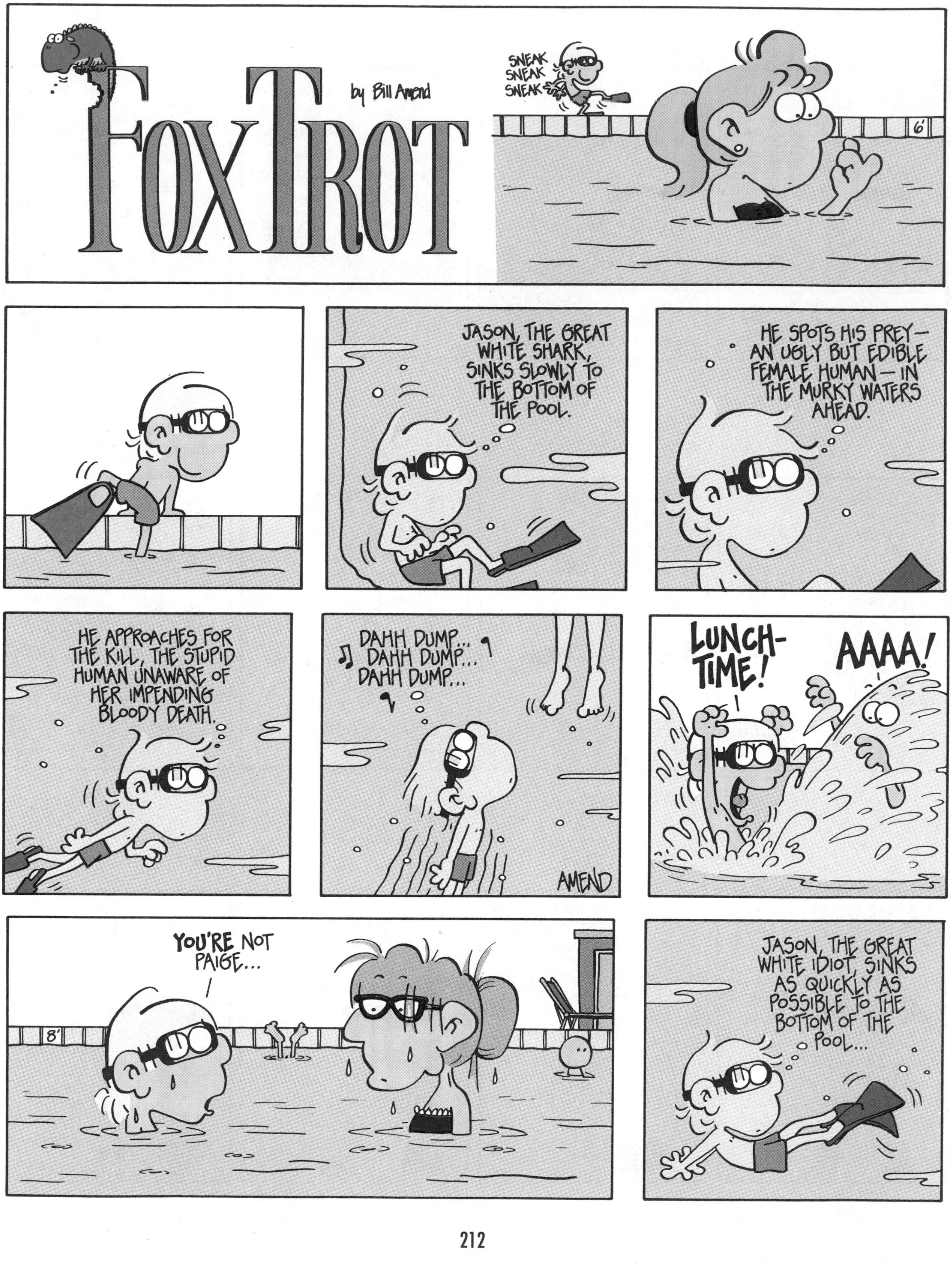
FoxTrot
by Bill Amend
SNEAK SNEAK SNEAK
6'
JASON, THE GREAT WHITE SHARK, SINKS SLOWLY TO THE BOTTOM OF THE POOL.
HE SPOTS HIS PREY— AN UGLY BUT EDIBLE FEMALE HUMAN— IN THE MURKY WATERS AHEAD.
HE APPROACHES FOR THE KILL, THE STUPID HUMAN UNAWARE OF HER IMPENDING BLOODY DEATH.
DAHH DUMP... DAHH DUMP... DAHH DUMP...
AMEND
LUNCH-TIME!
AAAA!
YOU'RE NOT PAIGE...
8'
JASON, THE GREAT WHITE IDIOT, SINKS AS QUICKLY AS POSSIBLE TO THE BOTTOM OF THE POOL...

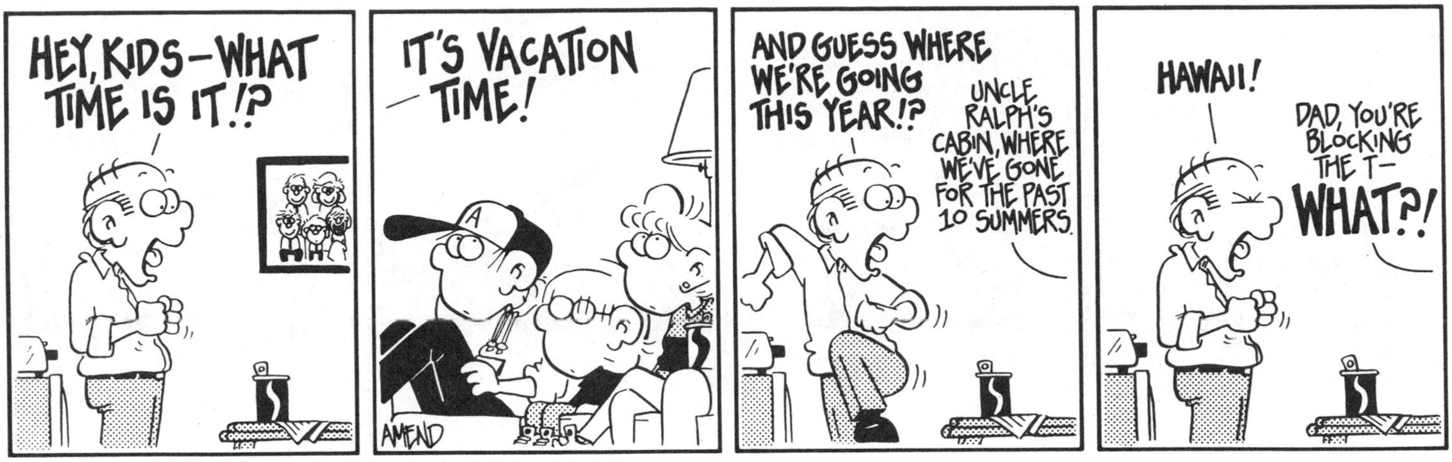
HEY, KIDS—WHAT TIME IS IT!?
IT'S VACATION — TIME!
AMEND
AND GUESS WHERE WE'RE GOING THIS YEAR!?
UNCLE RALPH'S CABIN, WHERE WE'VE GONE FOR THE PAST 10 SUMMERS.
HAWAII!
DAD, YOU'RE BLOCKING THE T— WHAT?!

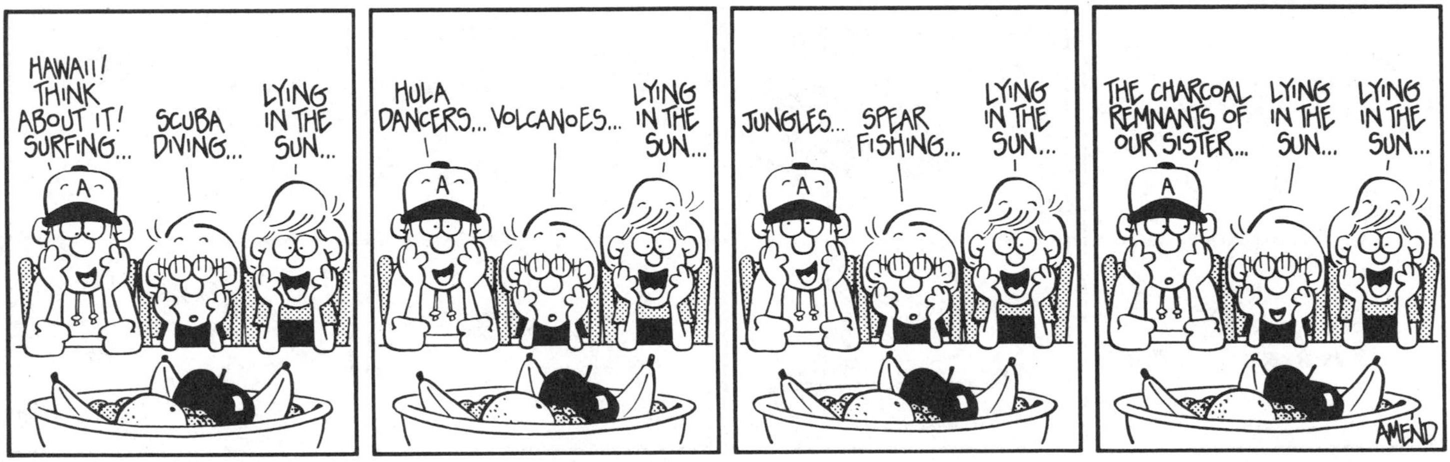
HAWAII! THINK ABOUT IT! SURFING...
SCUBA DIVING...
LYING IN THE SUN...
HULA DANCERS...
VOLCANOES...
LYING IN THE SUN...
JUNGLES...
SPEAR FISHING...
LYING IN THE SUN...
THE CHARCOAL REMNANTS OF OUR SISTER...
LYING IN THE SUN...
LYING IN THE SUN...
AMEND

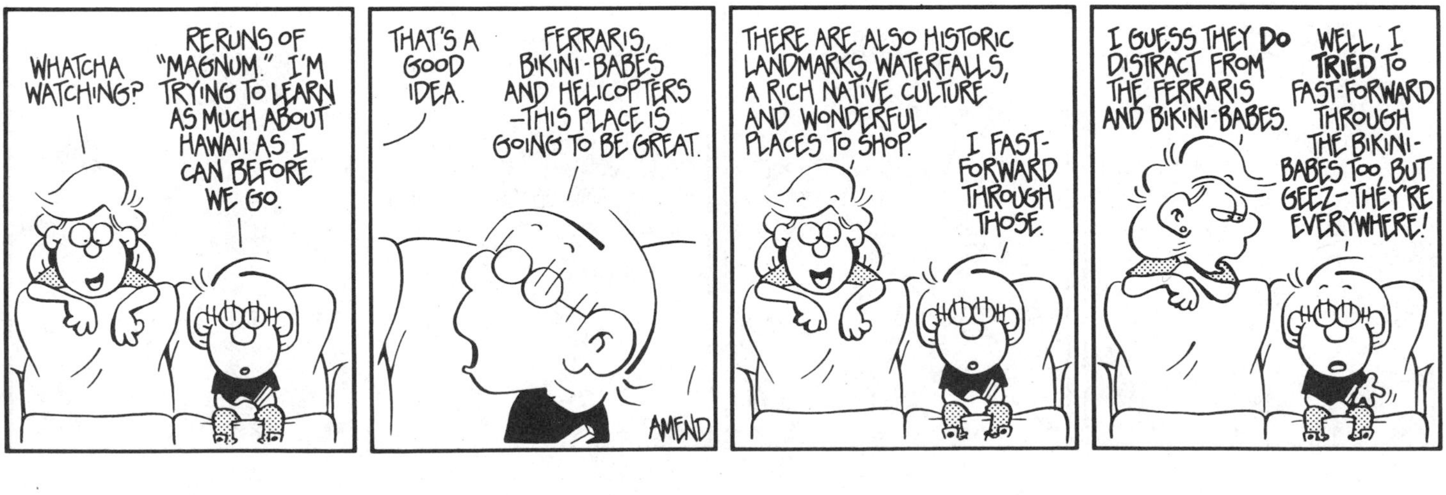
WHATCHA WATCHING?
RERUNS OF "MAGNUM." I'M TRYING TO LEARN AS MUCH ABOUT HAWAII AS I CAN BEFORE WE GO.
THAT'S A GOOD IDEA.
FERRARIS, BIKINI-BABES AND HELICOPTERS —THIS PLACE IS GOING TO BE GREAT.
AMEND
THERE ARE ALSO HISTORIC LANDMARKS, WATERFALLS, A RICH NATIVE CULTURE AND WONDERFUL PLACES TO SHOP.
I FAST-FORWARD THROUGH THOSE.
I GUESS THEY DO DISTRACT FROM THE FERRARIS AND BIKINI-BABES.
WELL, I TRIED TO FAST-FORWARD THROUGH THE BIKINI-BABES TOO, BUT GEEZ—THEY'RE EVERYWHERE!

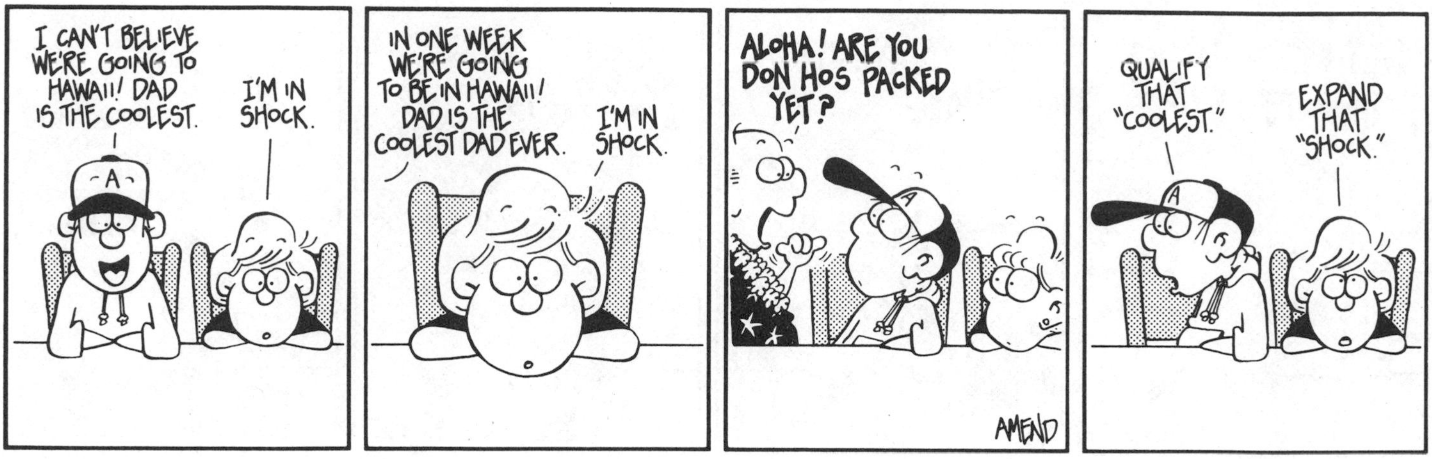
I CAN'T BELIEVE WE'RE GOING TO HAWAII! DAD IS THE COOLEST.
I'M IN SHOCK.
IN ONE WEEK WE'RE GOING TO BE IN HAWAII! DAD IS THE COOLEST DAD EVER.
I'M IN SHOCK.
ALOHA! ARE YOU DON HOS PACKED YET?
QUALIFY THAT "COOLEST."
EXPAND THAT "SHOCK."
AMEND

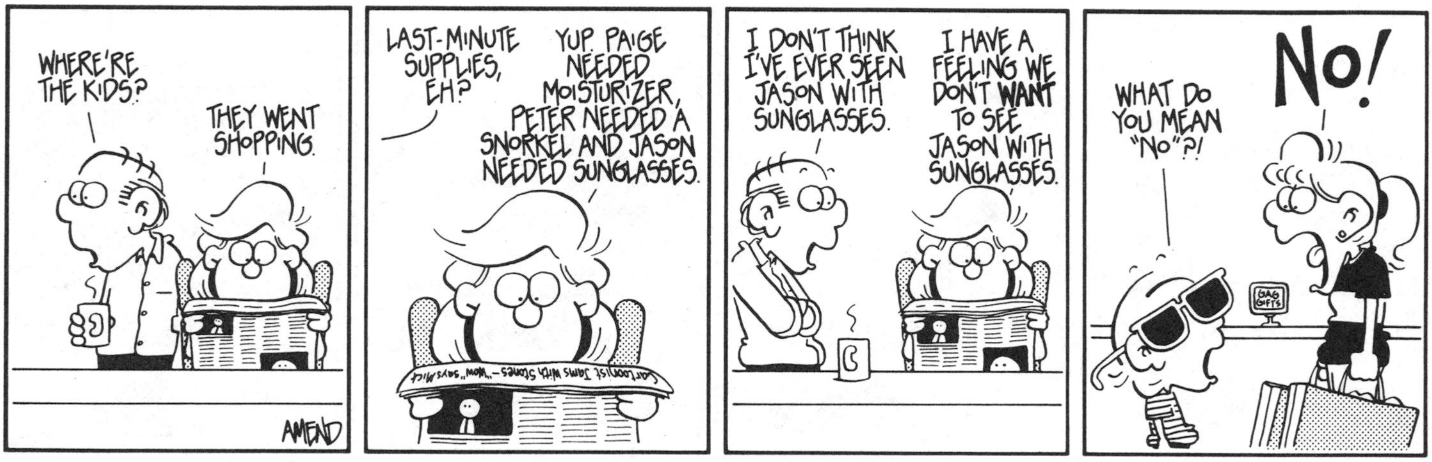
WHERE'RE THE KIDS?
THEY WENT SHOPPING.
AMEND
LAST-MINUTE SUPPLIES, EH?
YUP. PAIGE NEEDED MOISTURIZER, PETER NEEDED A SNORKEL AND JASON NEEDED SUNGLASSES.
I DON'T THINK I'VE EVER SEEN JASON WITH SUNGLASSES.
I HAVE A FEELING WE DON'T WANT TO SEE JASON WITH SUNGLASSES.
WHAT DO YOU MEAN "NO"?!
No!

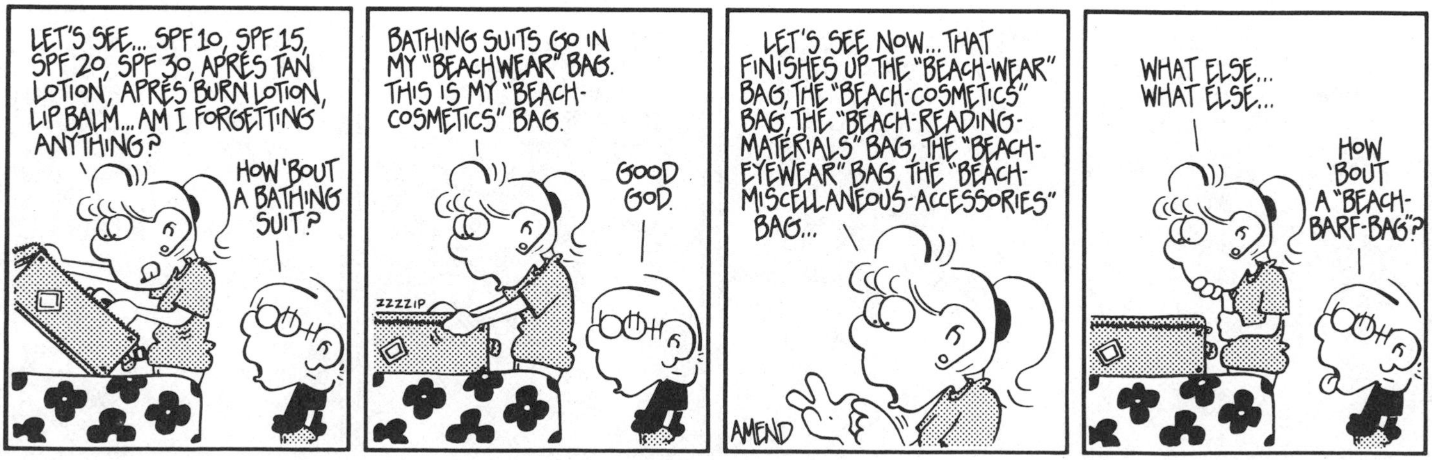
LET'S SEE... SPF 10, SPF 15, SPF 20, SPF 30, APRÈS TAN LOTION, APRÈS BURN LOTION, LIP BALM... AM I FORGETTING ANYTHING?
HOW 'BOUT A BATHING SUIT?
BATHING SUITS GO IN MY "BEACHWEAR" BAG. THIS IS MY "BEACH-COSMETICS" BAG.
ZZZZIP
GOOD GOD.
LET'S SEE NOW... THAT FINISHES UP THE "BEACH-WEAR" BAG, THE "BEACH-COSMETICS" BAG, THE "BEACH-READING-MATERIALS" BAG, THE "BEACH-EYEWEAR" BAG, THE "BEACH-MISCELLANEOUS-ACCESSORIES" BAG...
AMEND
WHAT ELSE... WHAT ELSE...
HOW 'BOUT A "BEACH-BARF-BAG"?

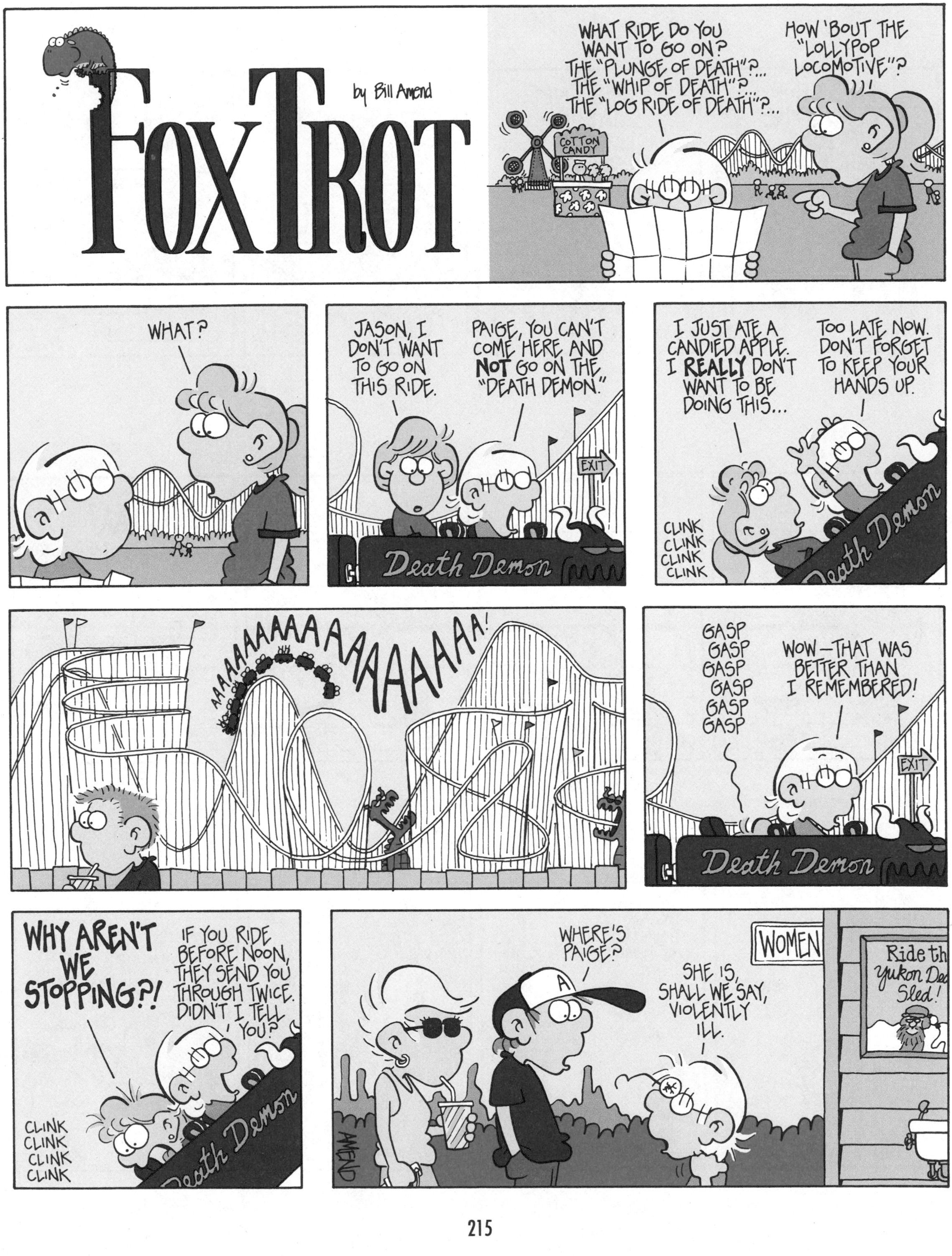
FoxTrot
by Bill Amend
WHAT RIDE DO YOU WANT TO GO ON? THE "PLUNGE OF DEATH"?... THE "WHIP OF DEATH"?... THE "LOG RIDE OF DEATH"?...
HOW 'BOUT THE "LOLLYPOP LOCOMOTIVE"?
COTTON CANDY
WHAT?
JASON, I DON'T WANT TO GO ON THIS RIDE.
PAIGE, YOU CAN'T COME HERE AND **NOT** GO ON THE "DEATH DEMON."
EXIT
Death Demon
I JUST ATE A CANDIED APPLE. I **REALLY** DON'T WANT TO BE DOING THIS...
TOO LATE NOW. DON'T FORGET TO KEEP YOUR HANDS UP.
CLINK CLINK CLINK CLINK
Death Demon
AAAAAAAAAAAAAAAAAAAAAAAA!
GASP GASP GASP GASP GASP GASP
WOW—THAT WAS BETTER THAN I REMEMBERED!
EXIT
Death Demon
WHY AREN'T WE STOPPING?!
IF YOU RIDE BEFORE NOON, THEY SEND YOU THROUGH TWICE. DIDN'T I TELL YOU?
CLINK CLINK CLINK CLINK
Death Demon
WHERE'S PAIGE?
SHE IS, SHALL WE SAY, VIOLENTLY ILL.
WOMEN
Ride the Yukon Dea Sled!
AMEND

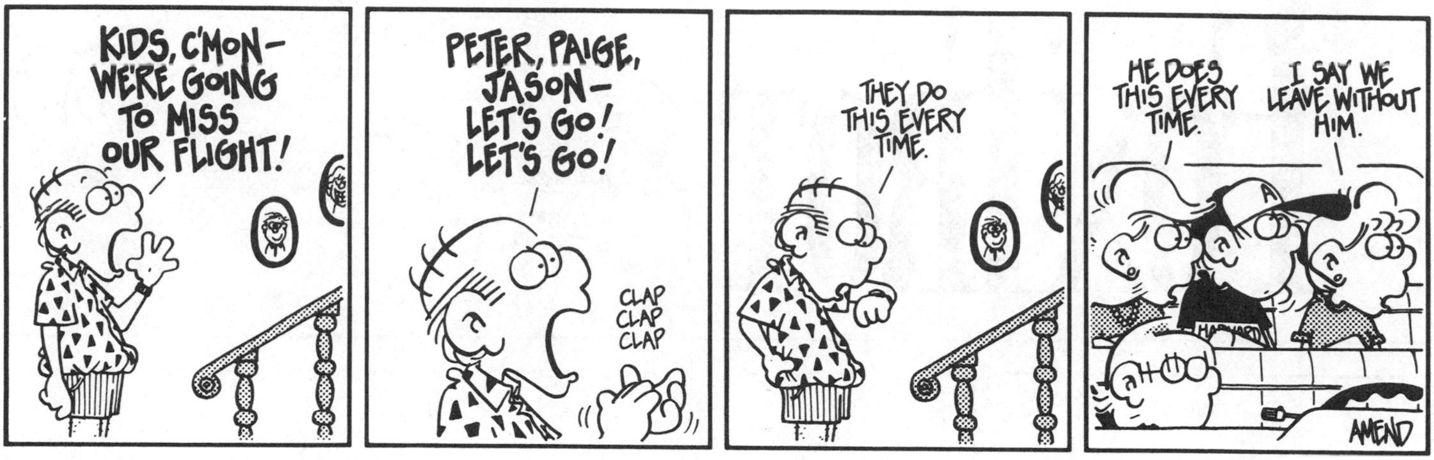

KIDS, C'MON-
WE'RE GOING TO MISS OUR FLIGHT!
PETER, PAIGE, JASON-
LET'S GO! LET'S GO!
CLAP CLAP CLAP
THEY DO THIS EVERY TIME.
HE DOES THIS EVERY TIME.
I SAY WE LEAVE WITHOUT HIM.
AMEND

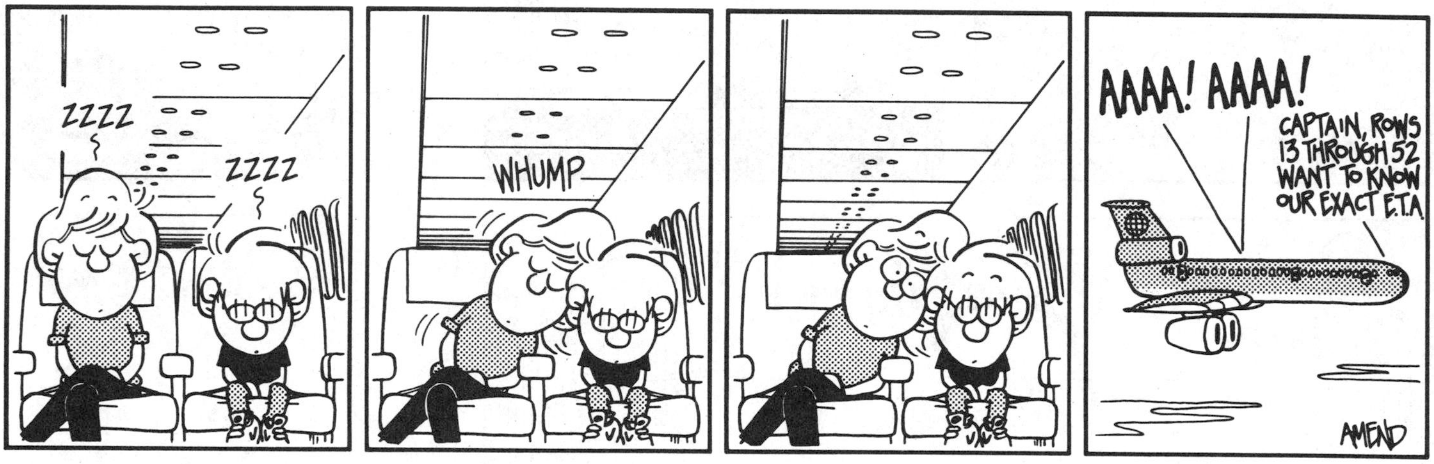

ZZZZ
ZZZZ
WHUMP
AAAA! AAAA!
CAPTAIN, ROWS 13 THROUGH 52 WANT TO KNOW OUR EXACT E.T.A.
AMEND

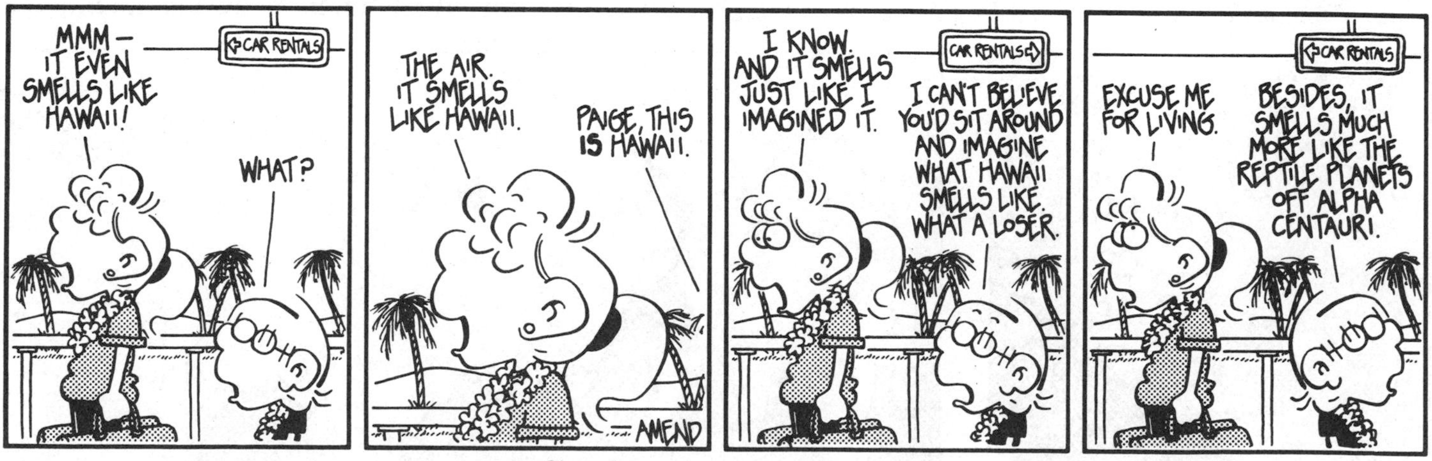

CAR RENTALS
MMM- IT EVEN SMELLS LIKE HAWAII!
WHAT?
THE AIR. IT SMELLS LIKE HAWAII.
PAIGE, THIS **IS** HAWAII.
AMEND
CAR RENTALS
I KNOW. AND IT SMELLS JUST LIKE I IMAGINED IT.
I CAN'T BELIEVE YOU'D SIT AROUND AND IMAGINE WHAT HAWAII SMELLS LIKE. WHAT A LOSER.
CAR RENTALS
EXCUSE ME FOR LIVING.
BESIDES, IT SMELLS MUCH MORE LIKE THE REPTILE PLANETS OFF ALPHA CENTAURI.

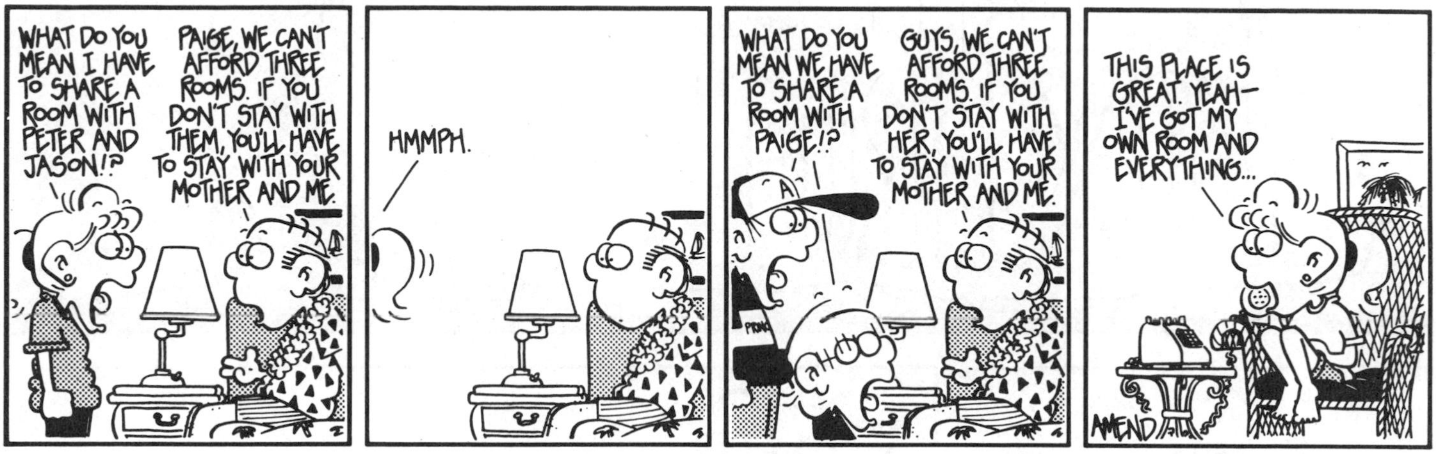
WHAT DO YOU MEAN I HAVE TO SHARE A ROOM WITH PETER AND JASON!?
PAIGE, WE CAN'T AFFORD THREE ROOMS. IF YOU DON'T STAY WITH THEM, YOU'LL HAVE TO STAY WITH YOUR MOTHER AND ME.
HMMPH.
WHAT DO YOU MEAN WE HAVE TO SHARE A ROOM WITH PAIGE!?
GUYS, WE CAN'T AFFORD THREE ROOMS. IF YOU DON'T STAY WITH HER, YOU'LL HAVE TO STAY WITH YOUR MOTHER AND ME.
THIS PLACE IS GREAT. YEAH—I'VE GOT MY OWN ROOM AND EVERYTHING...
AMEND

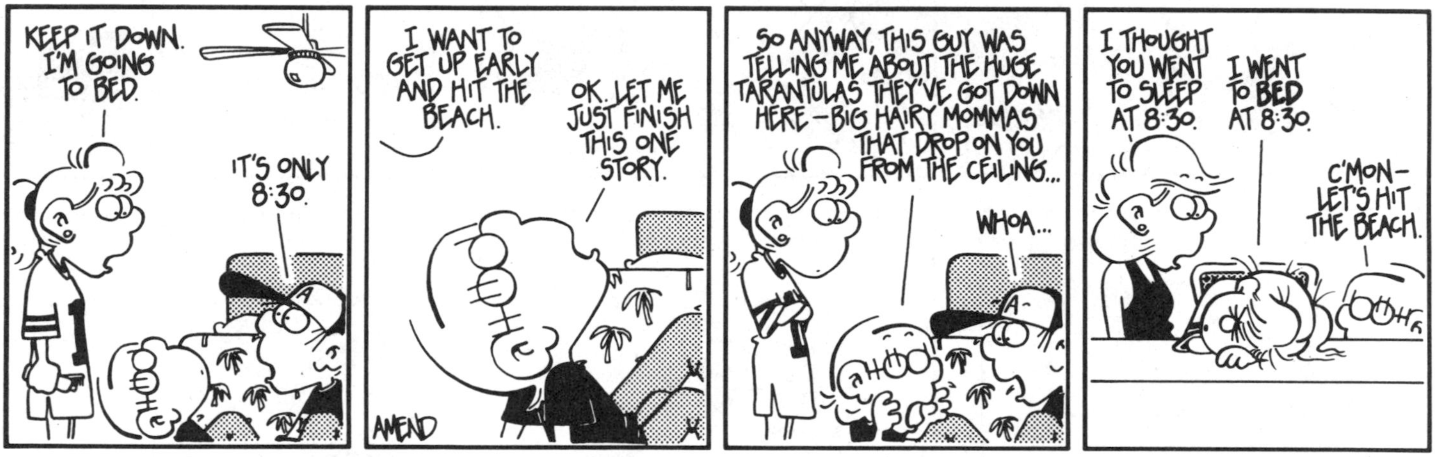
KEEP IT DOWN. I'M GOING TO BED.
IT'S ONLY 8:30.
I WANT TO GET UP EARLY AND HIT THE BEACH.
OK. LET ME JUST FINISH THIS ONE STORY.
AMEND
SO ANYWAY, THIS GUY WAS TELLING ME ABOUT THE HUGE TARANTULAS THEY'VE GOT DOWN HERE—BIG HAIRY MOMMAS THAT DROP ON YOU FROM THE CEILING...
WHOA...
I THOUGHT YOU WENT TO SLEEP AT 8:30.
I WENT TO BED AT 8:30.
C'MON—LET'S HIT THE BEACH.

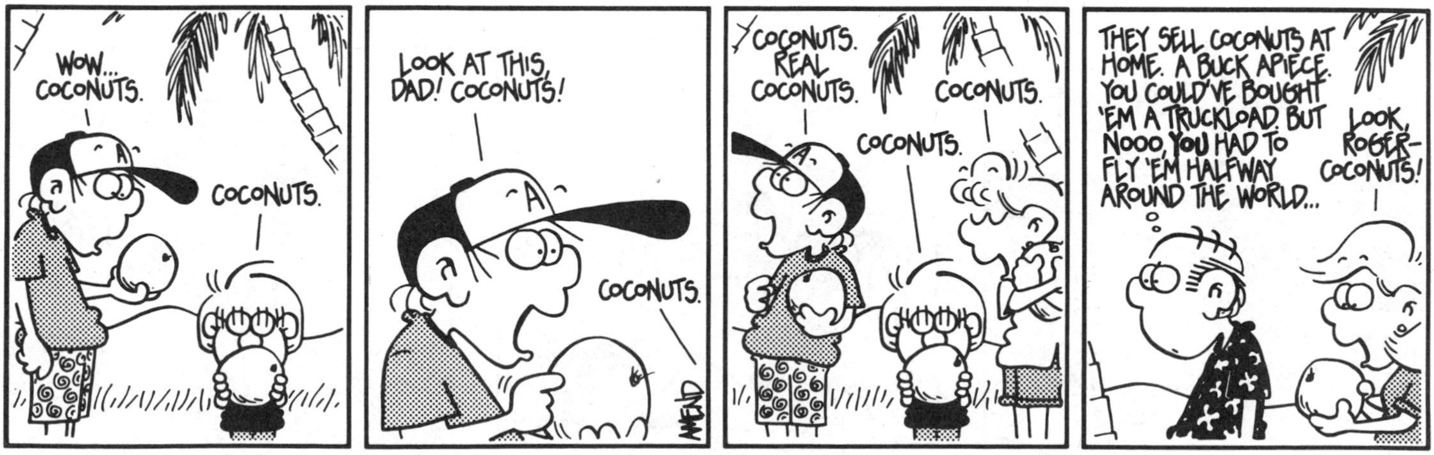
WOW... COCONUTS.
COCONUTS.
LOOK AT THIS, DAD! COCONUTS!
COCONUTS.
AMEND
COCONUTS. REAL COCONUTS.
COCONUTS.
COCONUTS.
THEY SELL COCONUTS AT HOME. A BUCK APIECE. YOU COULD'VE BOUGHT 'EM A TRUCKLOAD. BUT NOOO, YOU HAD TO FLY 'EM HALFWAY AROUND THE WORLD...
LOOK, ROGER—COCONUTS!

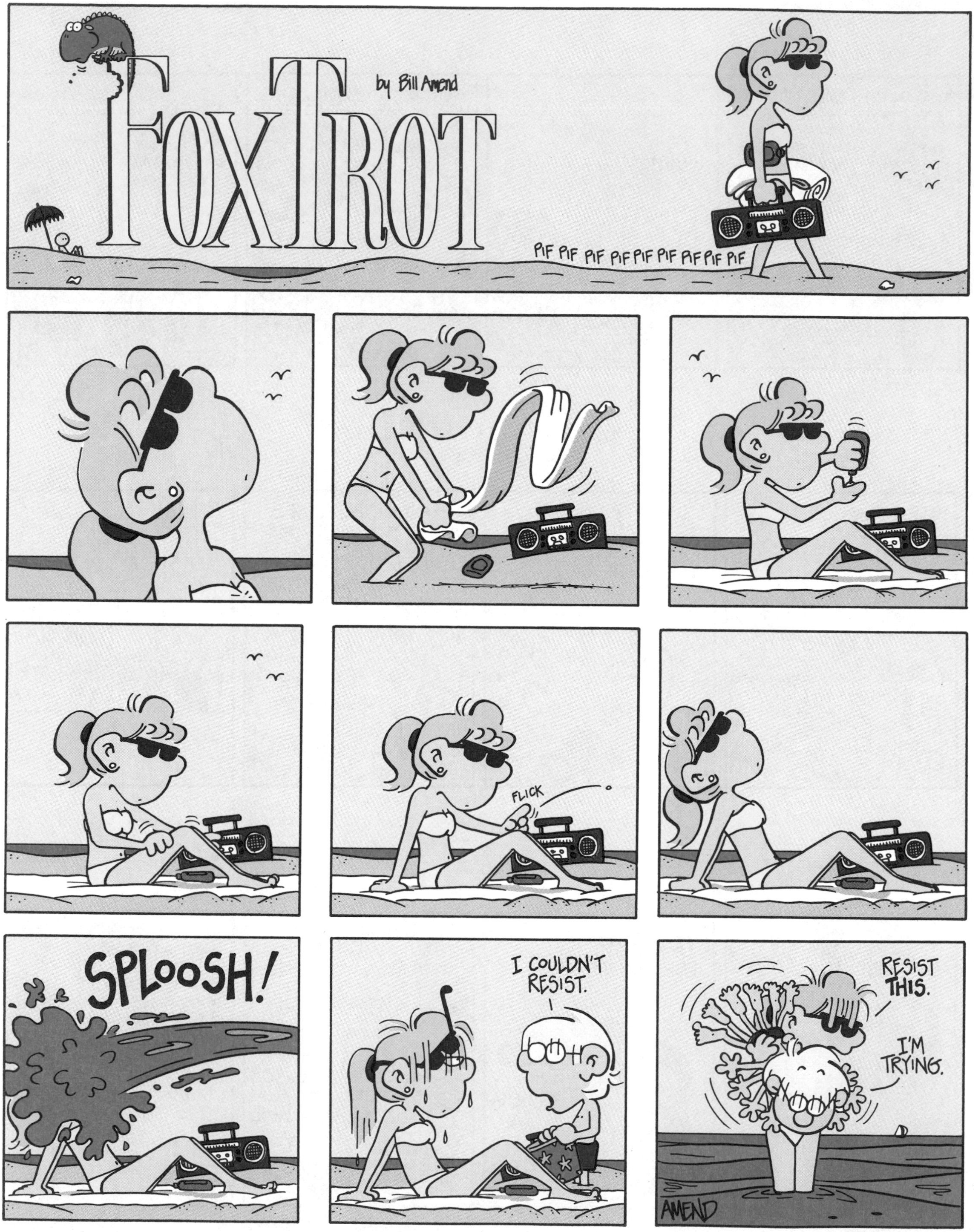
FoxTrot
by Bill Amend
PIF PIF PIF PIF PIF PIF PIF PIF PIF PIF PIF
FLICK
SPLOOSH!
I COULDN'T RESIST.
RESIST THIS.
I'M TRYING.
AMEND

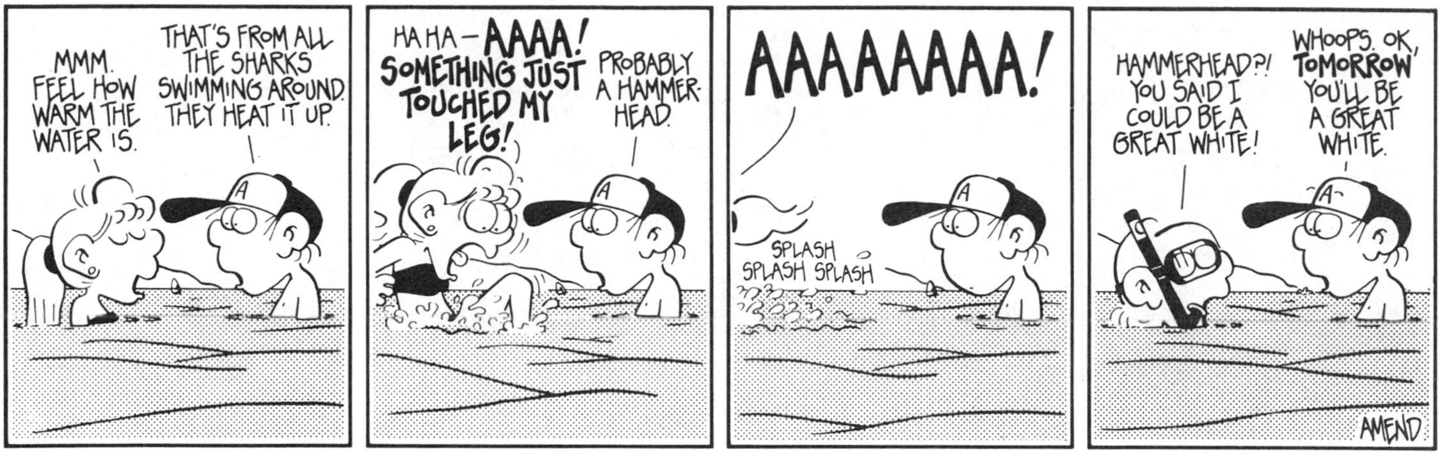
MMM. FEEL HOW WARM THE WATER IS.
THAT'S FROM ALL THE SHARKS SWIMMING AROUND. THEY HEAT IT UP.
HA HA — AAAA! SOMETHING JUST TOUCHED MY LEG!
PROBABLY A HAMMERHEAD.
AAAAAAAA!
SPLASH SPLASH SPLASH
HAMMERHEAD?! YOU SAID I COULD BE A GREAT WHITE!
WHOOPS. OK, TOMORROW YOU'LL BE A GREAT WHITE.
AMEND

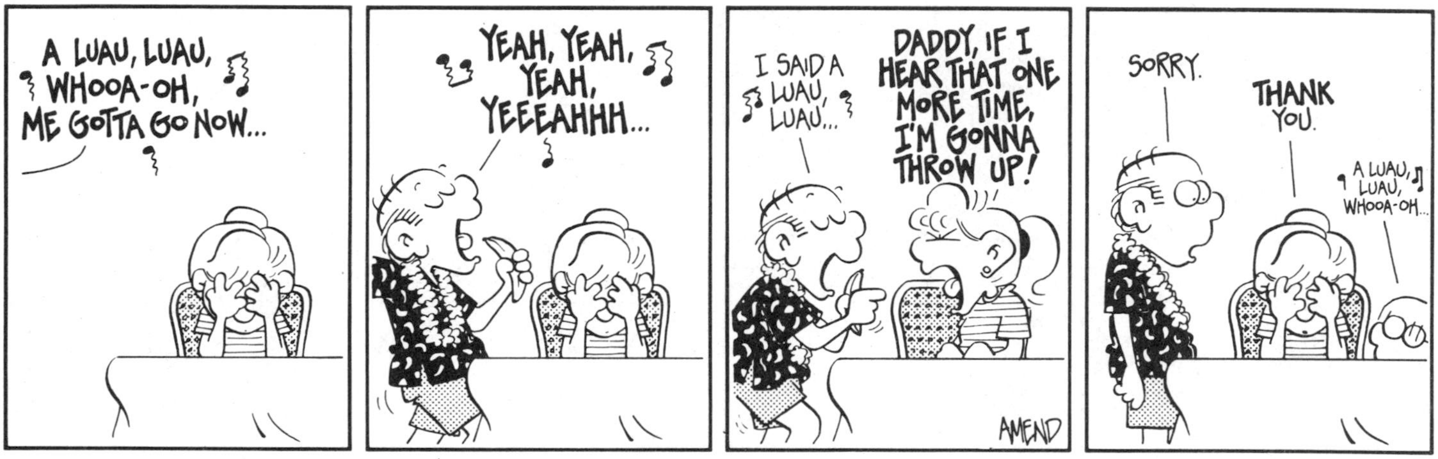
A LUAU, LUAU, WHOOA-OH, ME GOTTA GO NOW...
YEAH, YEAH, YEAH, YEEEAHHH...
I SAID A LUAU, LUAU...
DADDY, IF I HEAR THAT ONE MORE TIME, I'M GONNA THROW UP!
AMEND
SORRY.
THANK YOU.
A LUAU, LUAU, WHOOA-OH...

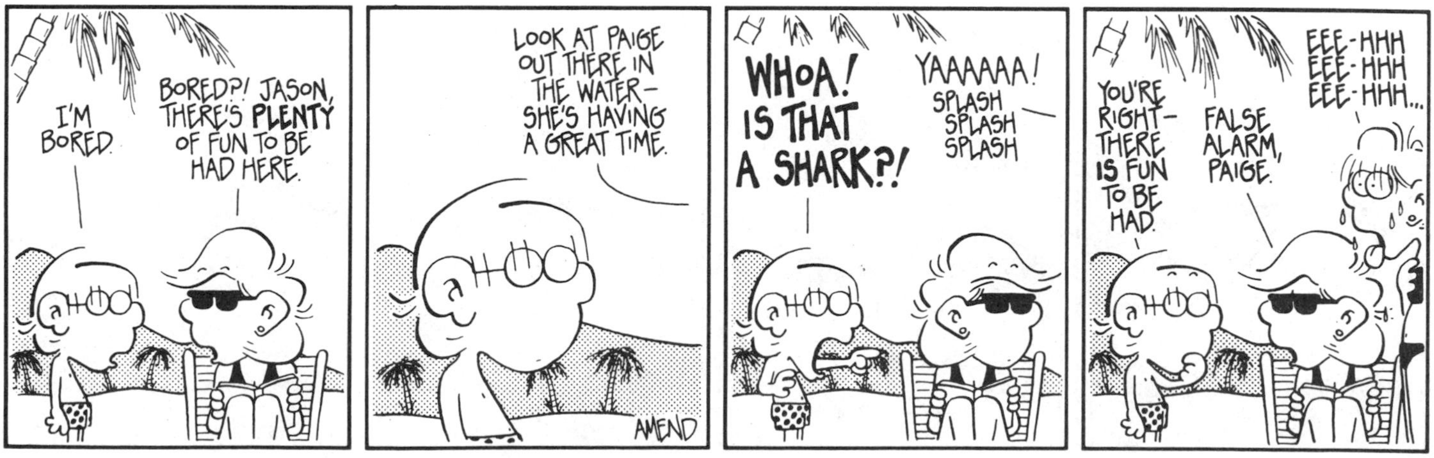
I'M BORED.
BORED?! JASON, THERE'S PLENTY OF FUN TO BE HAD HERE.
LOOK AT PAIGE OUT THERE IN THE WATER — SHE'S HAVING A GREAT TIME.
AMEND
WHOA! IS THAT A SHARK?!
YAAAAAA! SPLASH SPLASH SPLASH
YOU'RE RIGHT — THERE IS FUN TO BE HAD.
FALSE ALARM, PAIGE.
EEE-HHH EEE-HHH EEE-HHH...

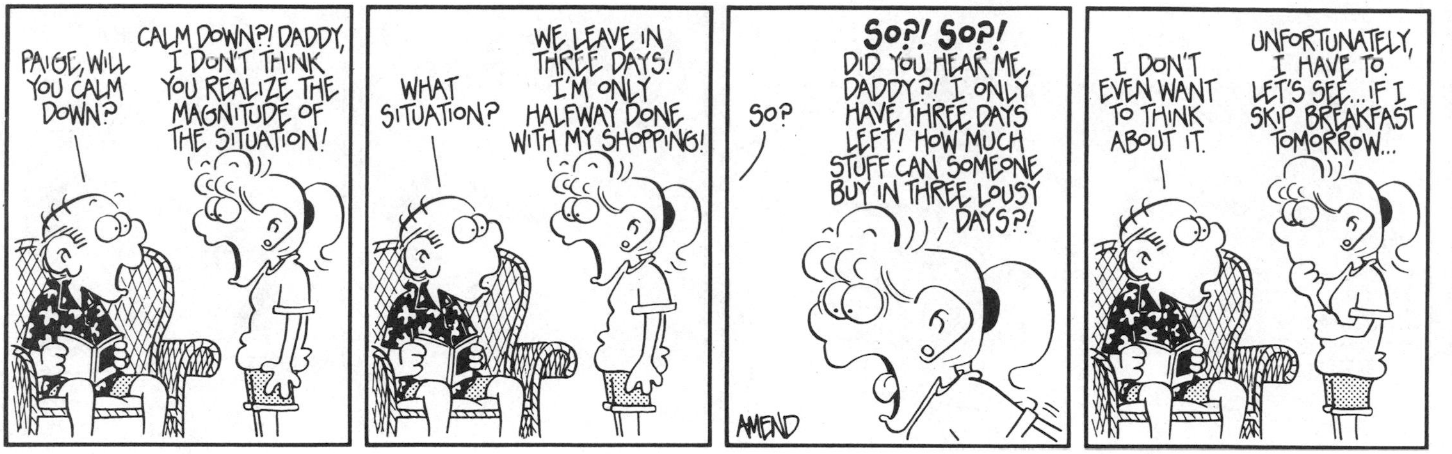
PAIGE, WILL YOU CALM DOWN?
CALM DOWN?! DADDY, I DON'T THINK YOU REALIZE THE MAGNITUDE OF THE SITUATION!
WHAT SITUATION?
WE LEAVE IN THREE DAYS! I'M ONLY HALFWAY DONE WITH MY SHOPPING!
SO?
SO?! SO?! DID YOU HEAR ME, DADDY?! I ONLY HAVE THREE DAYS LEFT! HOW MUCH STUFF CAN SOMEONE BUY IN THREE LOUSY DAYS?!
AMEND
I DON'T EVEN WANT TO THINK ABOUT IT.
UNFORTUNATELY, I HAVE TO. LET'S SEE... IF I SKIP BREAKFAST TOMORROW...

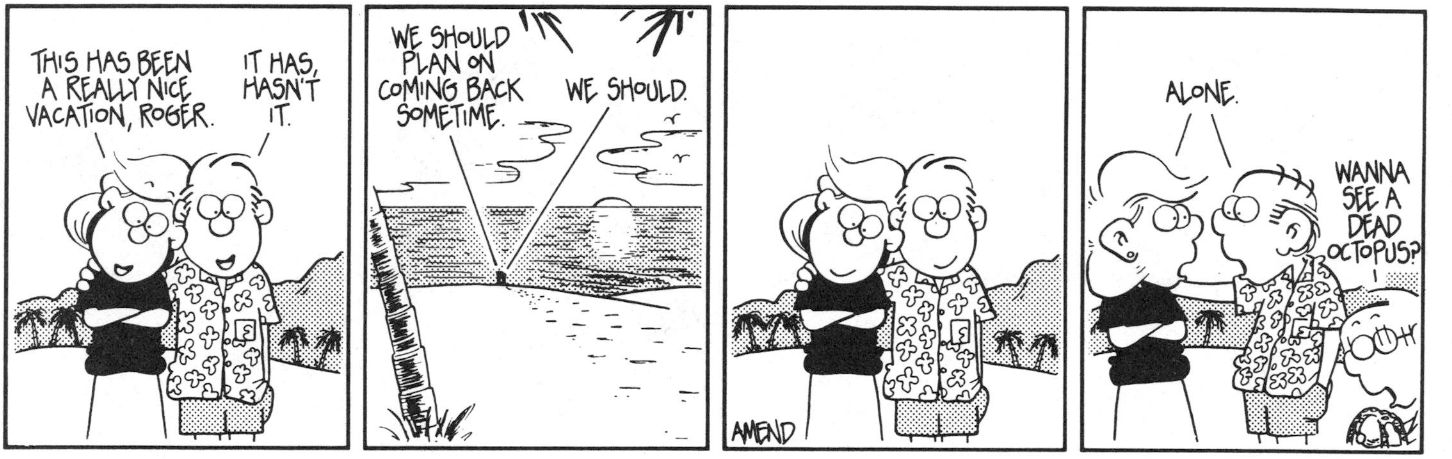
THIS HAS BEEN A REALLY NICE VACATION, ROGER.
IT HAS, HASN'T IT.
WE SHOULD PLAN ON COMING BACK SOMETIME.
WE SHOULD.
AMEND
ALONE.
WANNA SEE A DEAD OCTOPUS?

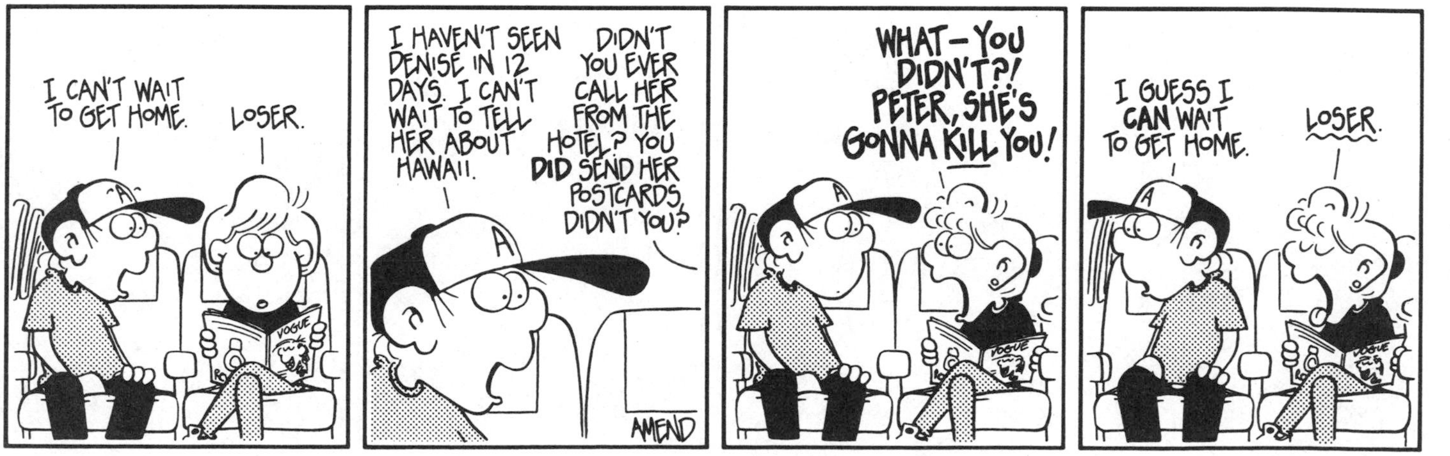
I CAN'T WAIT TO GET HOME.
LOSER.
I HAVEN'T SEEN DENISE IN 12 DAYS. I CAN'T WAIT TO TELL HER ABOUT HAWAII.
DIDN'T YOU EVER CALL HER FROM THE HOTEL? YOU DID SEND HER POSTCARDS, DIDN'T YOU?
AMEND
WHAT– YOU DIDN'T?! PETER, SHE'S GONNA KILL YOU!
I GUESS I CAN WAIT TO GET HOME.
LOSER.

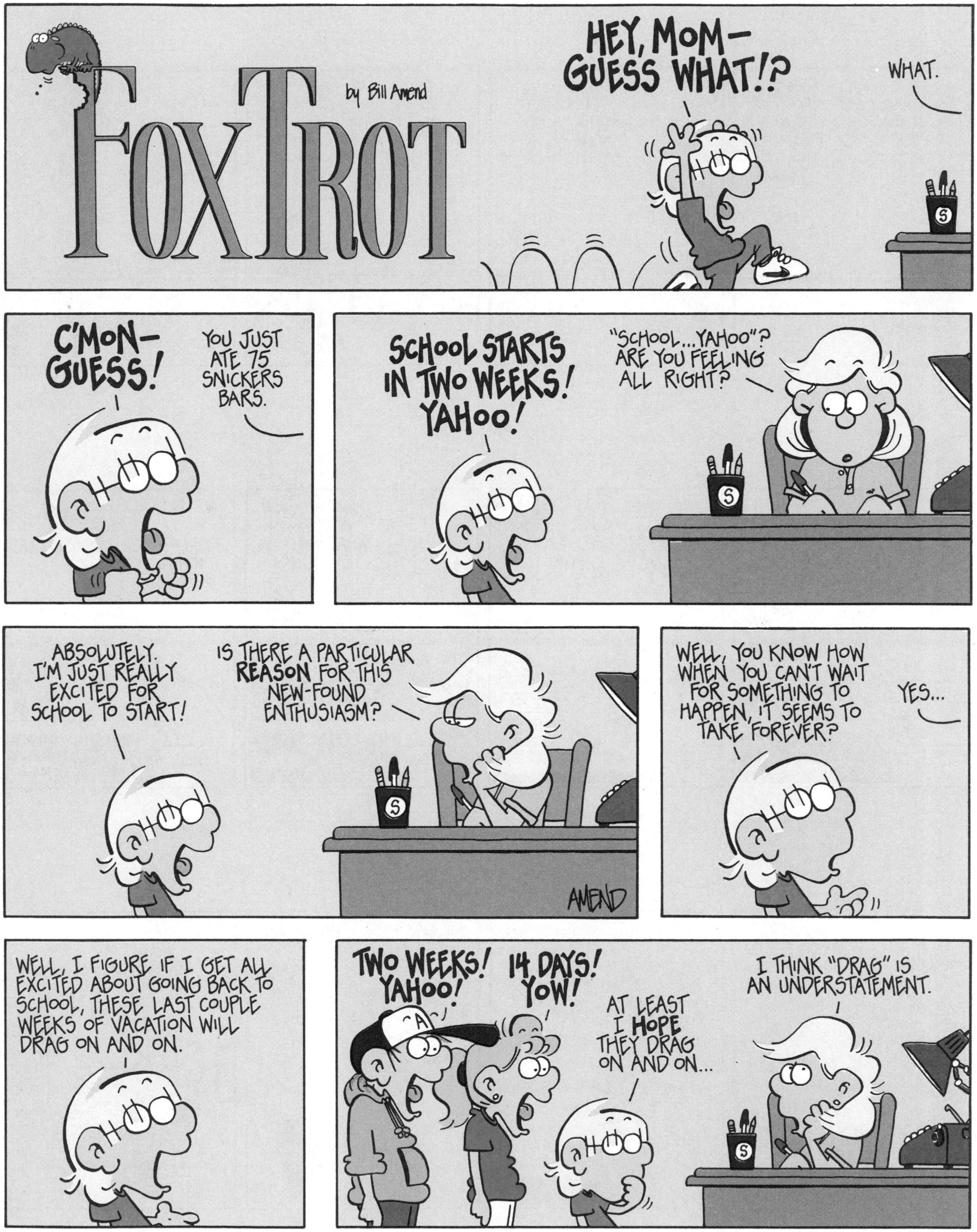
FoxTrot
by Bill Amend
HEY, MOM— GUESS WHAT!?
WHAT.
C'MON— GUESS!
YOU JUST ATE 75 SNICKERS BARS.
SCHOOL STARTS IN TWO WEEKS! YAHOO!
"SCHOOL...YAHOO"? ARE YOU FEELING ALL RIGHT?
ABSOLUTELY. I'M JUST REALLY EXCITED FOR SCHOOL TO START!
IS THERE A PARTICULAR REASON FOR THIS NEW-FOUND ENTHUSIASM?
AMEND
WELL, YOU KNOW HOW WHEN YOU CAN'T WAIT FOR SOMETHING TO HAPPEN, IT SEEMS TO TAKE FOREVER?
YES...
WELL, I FIGURE IF I GET ALL EXCITED ABOUT GOING BACK TO SCHOOL, THESE LAST COUPLE WEEKS OF VACATION WILL DRAG ON AND ON.
TWO WEEKS! YAHOO!
14 DAYS! YOW!
AT LEAST I HOPE THEY DRAG ON AND ON...
I THINK "DRAG" IS AN UNDERSTATEMENT.

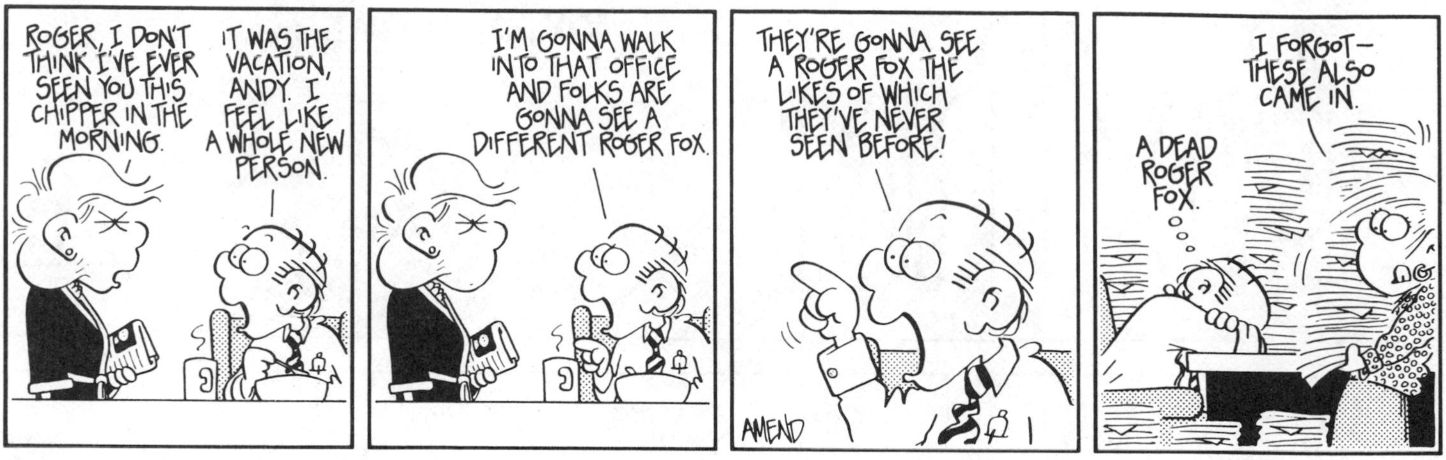
ROGER, I DON'T THINK I'VE EVER SEEN YOU THIS CHIPPER IN THE MORNING.
IT WAS THE VACATION, ANDY. I FEEL LIKE A WHOLE NEW PERSON.
I'M GONNA WALK INTO THAT OFFICE AND FOLKS ARE GONNA SEE A DIFFERENT ROGER FOX.
THEY'RE GONNA SEE A ROGER FOX THE LIKES OF WHICH THEY'VE NEVER SEEN BEFORE!
AMEND
I FORGOT— THESE ALSO CAME IN.
A DEAD ROGER FOX.

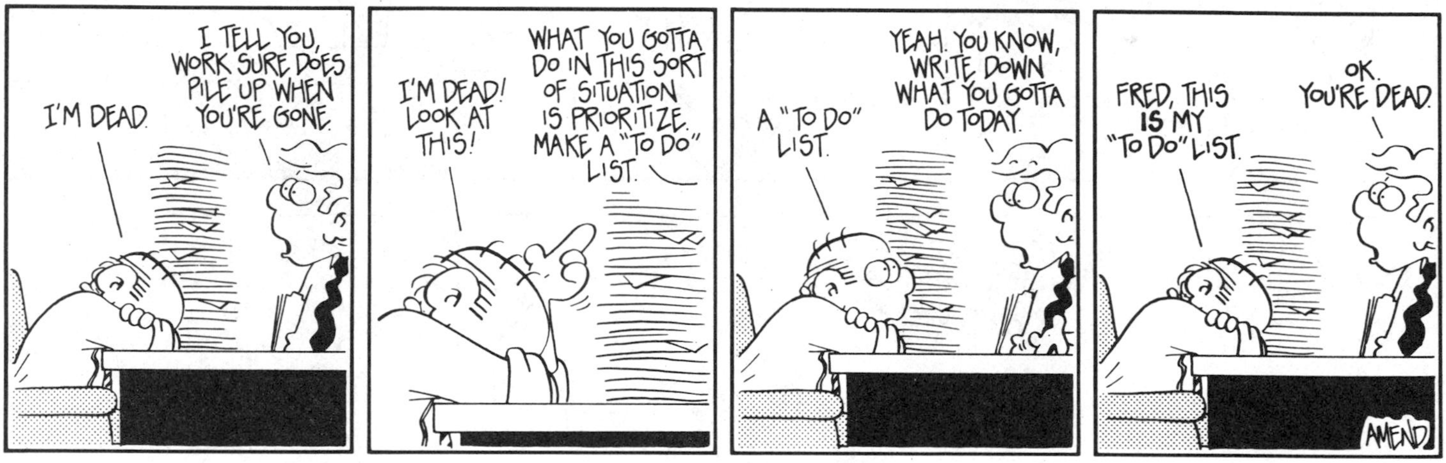
I'M DEAD.
I TELL YOU, WORK SURE DOES PILE UP WHEN YOU'RE GONE.
I'M DEAD! LOOK AT THIS!
WHAT YOU GOTTA DO IN THIS SORT OF SITUATION IS PRIORITIZE. MAKE A "TO DO" LIST.
A "TO DO" LIST.
YEAH. YOU KNOW, WRITE DOWN WHAT YOU GOTTA DO TODAY.
FRED, THIS **IS** MY "TO DO" LIST.
OK. YOU'RE DEAD.
AMEND

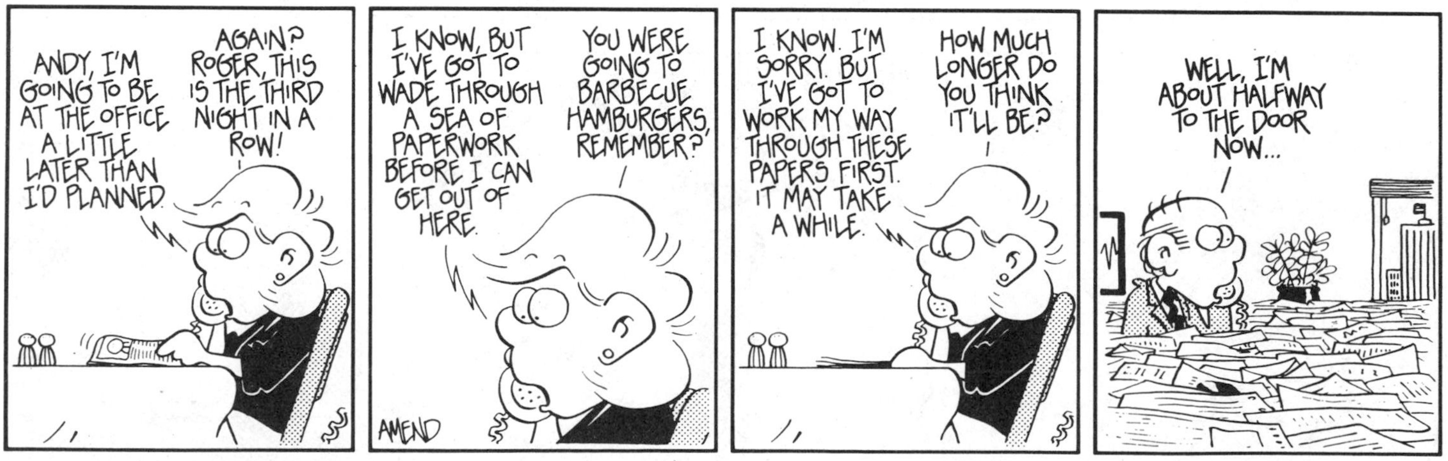
ANDY, I'M GOING TO BE AT THE OFFICE A LITTLE LATER THAN I'D PLANNED.
AGAIN? ROGER, THIS IS THE THIRD NIGHT IN A ROW!
I KNOW, BUT I'VE GOT TO WADE THROUGH A SEA OF PAPERWORK BEFORE I CAN GET OUT OF HERE.
YOU WERE GOING TO BARBECUE HAMBURGERS, REMEMBER?
AMEND
I KNOW. I'M SORRY. BUT I'VE GOT TO WORK MY WAY THROUGH THESE PAPERS FIRST. IT MAY TAKE A WHILE.
HOW MUCH LONGER DO YOU THINK IT'LL BE?
WELL, I'M ABOUT HALFWAY TO THE DOOR NOW...

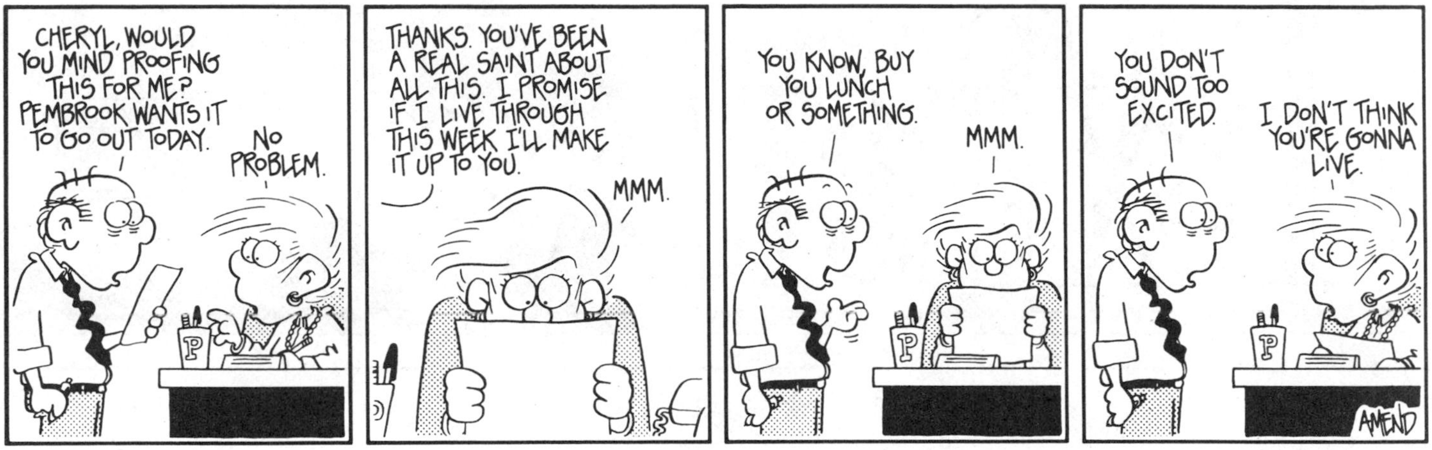
CHERYL, WOULD YOU MIND PROOFING THIS FOR ME? PEMBROOK WANTS IT TO GO OUT TODAY.
NO PROBLEM.
THANKS. YOU'VE BEEN A REAL SAINT ABOUT ALL THIS. I PROMISE IF I LIVE THROUGH THIS WEEK I'LL MAKE IT UP TO YOU.
MMM.
YOU KNOW, BUY YOU LUNCH OR SOMETHING.
MMM.
YOU DON'T SOUND TOO EXCITED.
I DON'T THINK YOU'RE GONNA LIVE.
AMEND

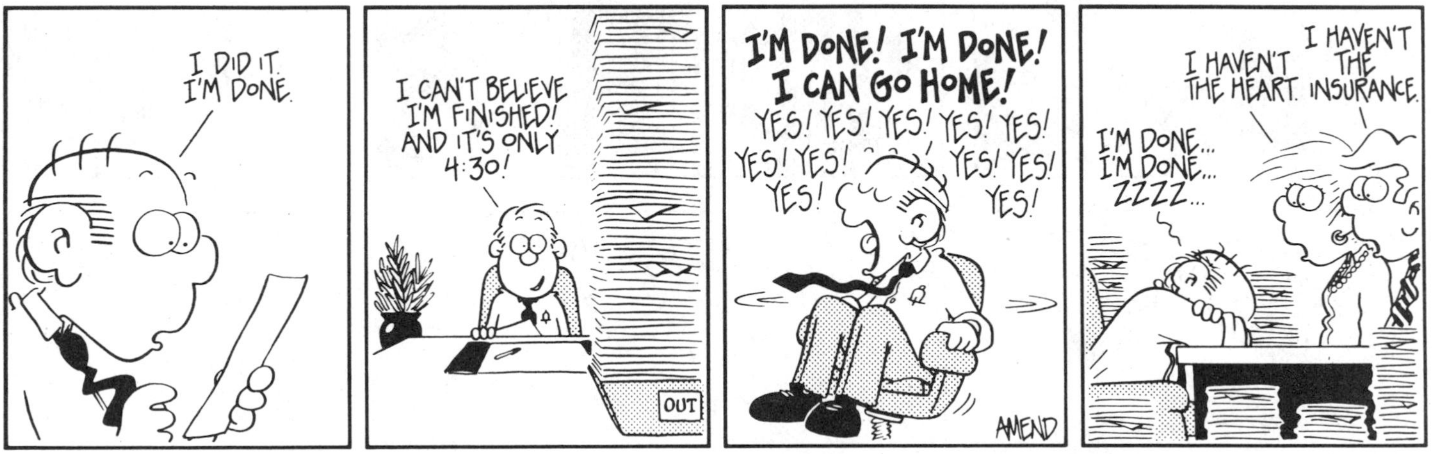
I DID IT. I'M DONE.
I CAN'T BELIEVE I'M FINISHED! AND IT'S ONLY 4:30!
OUT
I'M DONE! I'M DONE! I CAN GO HOME!
YES! YES! YES! YES! YES! YES! YES! YES! YES! YES! YES!
AMEND
I'M DONE... I'M DONE... ZZZZ...
I HAVEN'T THE HEART.
I HAVEN'T THE INSURANCE.

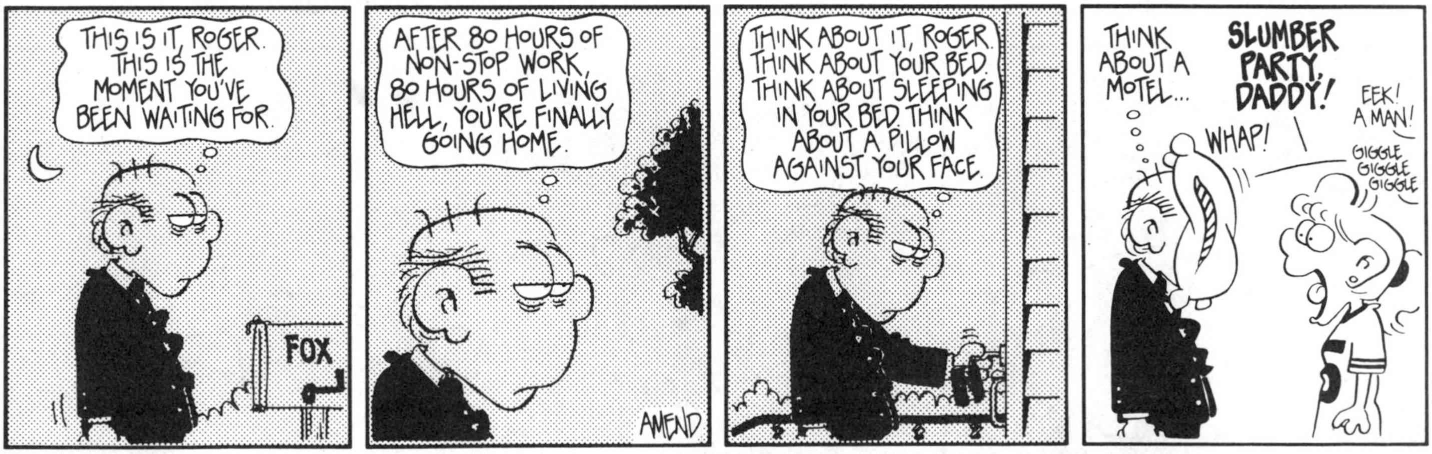
THIS IS IT, ROGER. THIS IS THE MOMENT YOU'VE BEEN WAITING FOR.
FOX
AFTER 80 HOURS OF NON-STOP WORK, 80 HOURS OF LIVING HELL, YOU'RE FINALLY GOING HOME.
AMEND
THINK ABOUT IT, ROGER. THINK ABOUT YOUR BED. THINK ABOUT SLEEPING IN YOUR BED. THINK ABOUT A PILLOW AGAINST YOUR FACE.
THINK ABOUT A MOTEL...
SLUMBER PARTY, DADDY!
WHAP!
EEK! A MAN!
GIGGLE GIGGLE GIGGLE

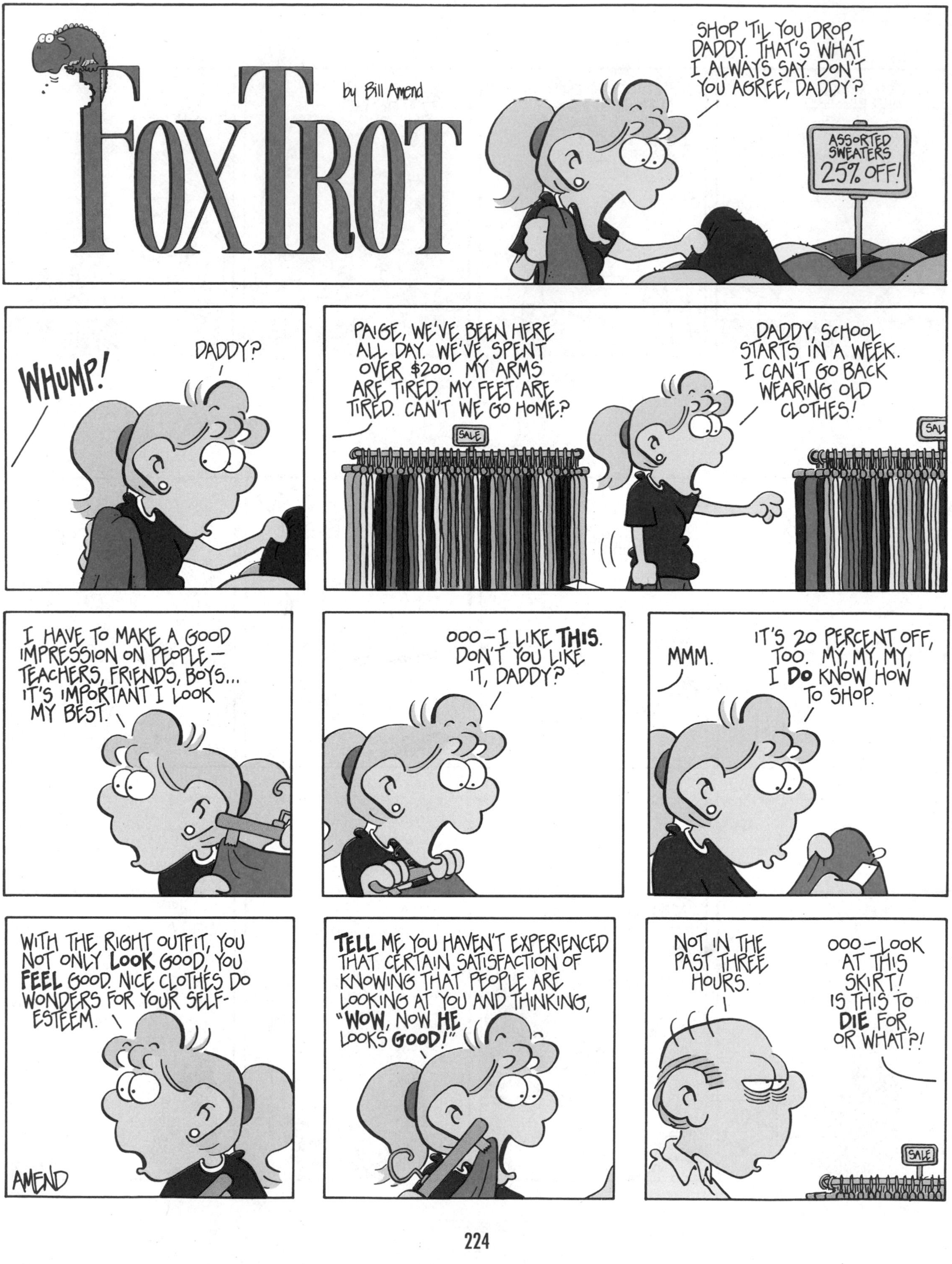
FoxTrot
by Bill Amend
SHOP 'TIL YOU DROP, DADDY. THAT'S WHAT I ALWAYS SAY. DON'T YOU AGREE, DADDY?
ASSORTED SWEATERS 25% OFF!
WHUMP!
DADDY?
PAIGE, WE'VE BEEN HERE ALL DAY. WE'VE SPENT OVER $200. MY ARMS ARE TIRED. MY FEET ARE TIRED. CAN'T WE GO HOME?
SALE
DADDY, SCHOOL STARTS IN A WEEK. I CAN'T GO BACK WEARING OLD CLOTHES!
I HAVE TO MAKE A GOOD IMPRESSION ON PEOPLE— TEACHERS, FRIENDS, BOYS... IT'S IMPORTANT I LOOK MY BEST.
OOO—I LIKE THIS. DON'T YOU LIKE IT, DADDY?
MMM.
IT'S 20 PERCENT OFF, TOO. MY, MY, MY, I DO KNOW HOW TO SHOP.
WITH THE RIGHT OUTFIT, YOU NOT ONLY LOOK GOOD, YOU FEEL GOOD. NICE CLOTHES DO WONDERS FOR YOUR SELF-ESTEEM.
AMEND
TELL ME YOU HAVEN'T EXPERIENCED THAT CERTAIN SATISFACTION OF KNOWING THAT PEOPLE ARE LOOKING AT YOU AND THINKING, "WOW, NOW HE LOOKS GOOD!"
NOT IN THE PAST THREE HOURS.
OOO—LOOK AT THIS SKIRT! IS THIS TO DIE FOR, OR WHAT?!
SALE

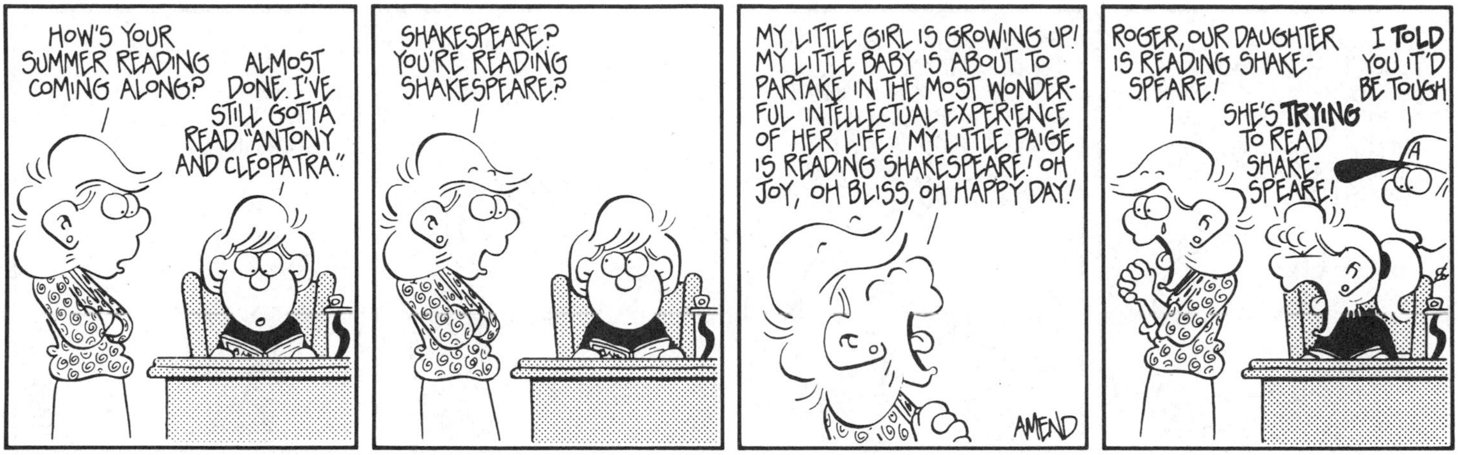
HOW'S YOUR SUMMER READING COMING ALONG?
ALMOST DONE. I'VE STILL GOTTA READ "ANTONY AND CLEOPATRA."
SHAKESPEARE? YOU'RE READING SHAKESPEARE?
MY LITTLE GIRL IS GROWING UP! MY LITTLE BABY IS ABOUT TO PARTAKE IN THE MOST WONDERFUL INTELLECTUAL EXPERIENCE OF HER LIFE! MY LITTLE PAIGE IS READING SHAKESPEARE! OH JOY, OH BLISS, OH HAPPY DAY!
AMEND
ROGER, OUR DAUGHTER IS READING SHAKESPEARE!
SHE'S TRYING TO READ SHAKESPEARE!
I TOLD YOU IT'D BE TOUGH.

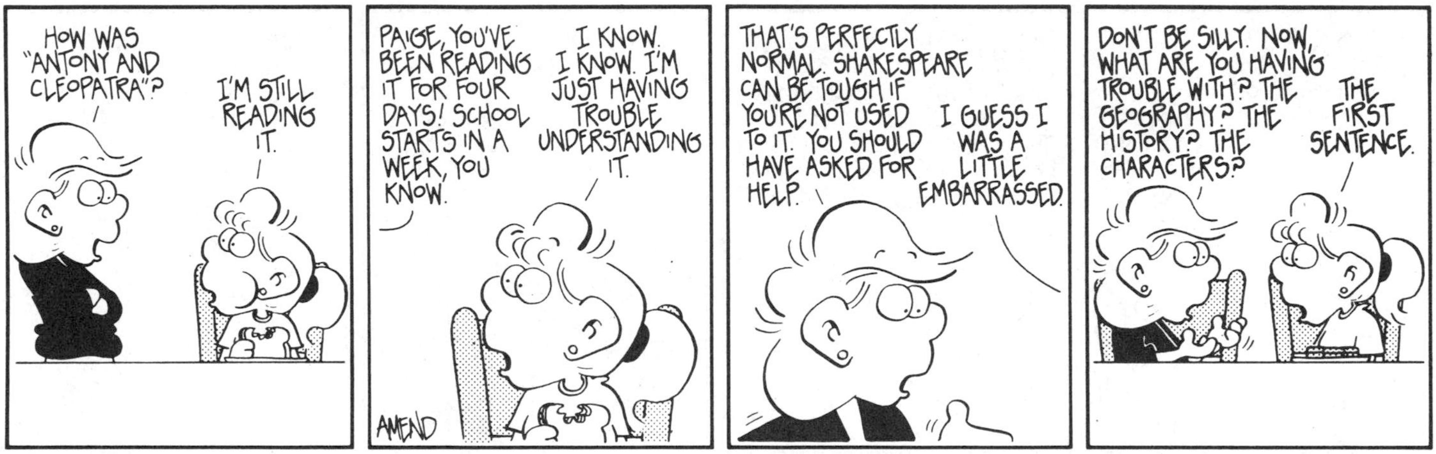
HOW WAS "ANTONY AND CLEOPATRA"?
I'M STILL READING IT.
PAIGE, YOU'VE BEEN READING IT FOR FOUR DAYS! SCHOOL STARTS IN A WEEK, YOU KNOW.
I KNOW. I KNOW. I'M JUST HAVING TROUBLE UNDERSTANDING IT.
AMEND
THAT'S PERFECTLY NORMAL. SHAKESPEARE CAN BE TOUGH IF YOU'RE NOT USED TO IT. YOU SHOULD HAVE ASKED FOR HELP.
I GUESS I WAS A LITTLE EMBARRASSED.
DON'T BE SILLY. NOW, WHAT ARE YOU HAVING TROUBLE WITH? THE GEOGRAPHY? THE HISTORY? THE CHARACTERS?
THE FIRST SENTENCE.

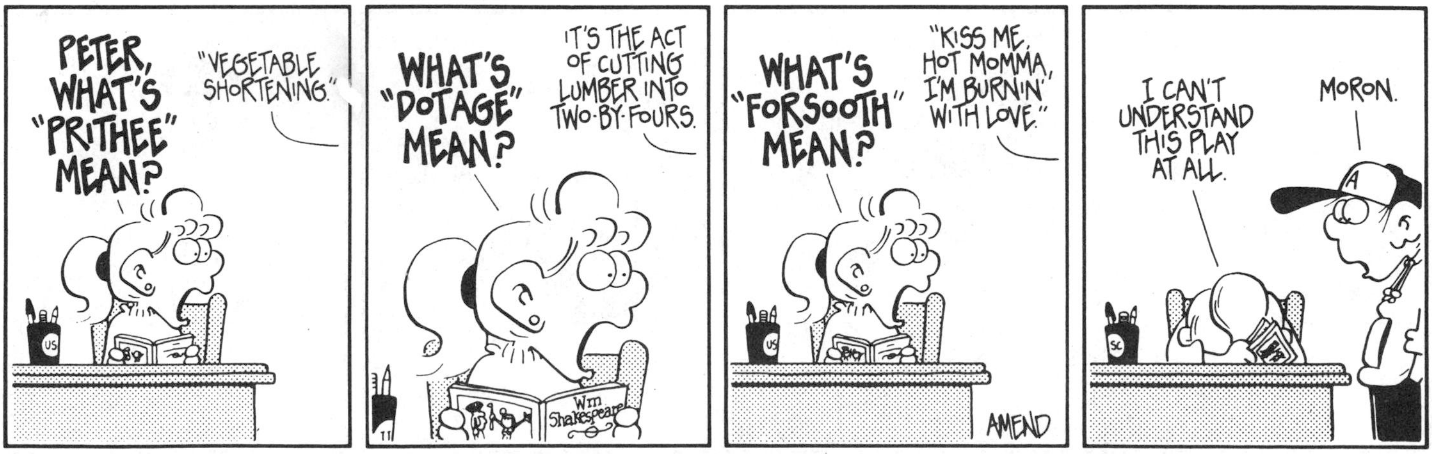
PETER, WHAT'S "PRITHEE" MEAN?
"VEGETABLE SHORTENING."
WHAT'S "DOTAGE" MEAN?
IT'S THE ACT OF CUTTING LUMBER INTO TWO-BY-FOURS.
WHAT'S "FORSOOTH" MEAN?
"KISS ME, HOT MOMMA, I'M BURNIN' WITH LOVE."
AMEND
I CAN'T UNDERSTAND THIS PLAY AT ALL.
MORON.

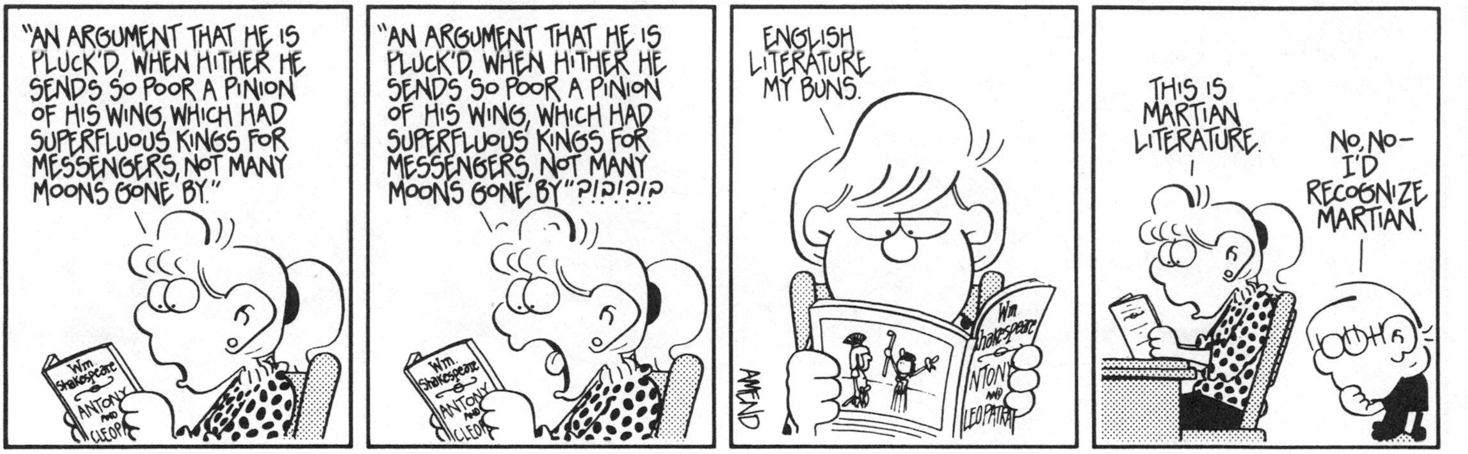
"AN ARGUMENT THAT HE IS PLUCK'D, WHEN HITHER HE SENDS SO POOR A PINION OF HIS WING, WHICH HAD SUPERFLUOUS KINGS FOR MESSENGERS, NOT MANY MOONS GONE BY."
"AN ARGUMENT THAT HE IS PLUCK'D, WHEN HITHER HE SENDS SO POOR A PINION OF HIS WING, WHICH HAD SUPERFLUOUS KINGS FOR MESSENGERS, NOT MANY MOONS GONE BY"?!?!?!?
ENGLISH LITERATURE MY BUNS.
THIS IS MARTIAN LITERATURE.
NO, NO– I'D RECOGNIZE MARTIAN.

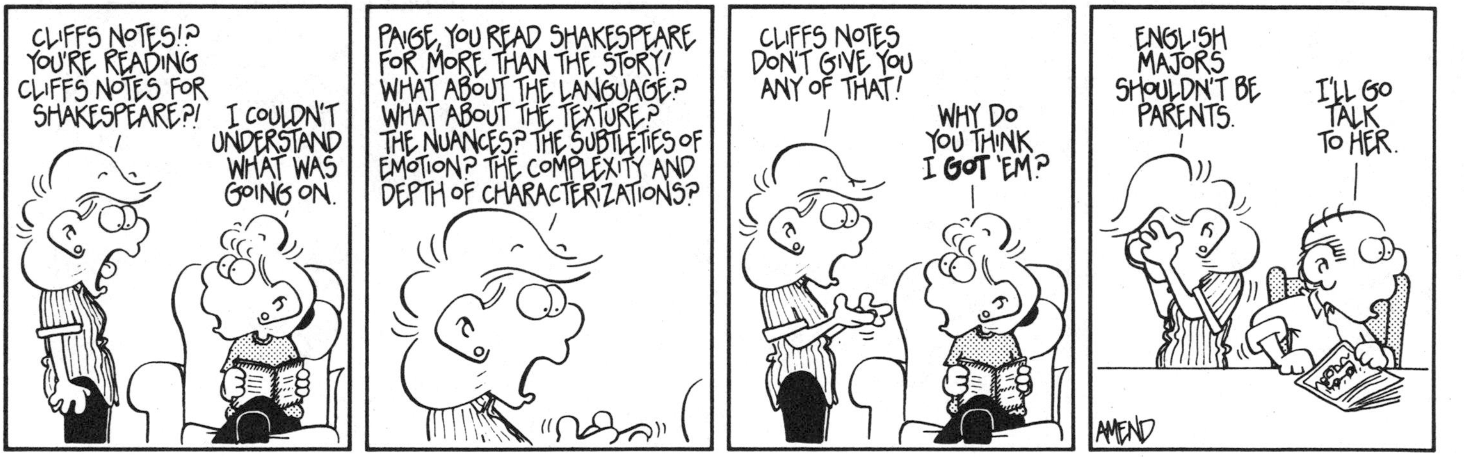
CLIFFS NOTES!? YOU'RE READING CLIFFS NOTES FOR SHAKESPEARE?!
I COULDN'T UNDERSTAND WHAT WAS GOING ON.
PAIGE, YOU READ SHAKESPEARE FOR MORE THAN THE STORY! WHAT ABOUT THE LANGUAGE? WHAT ABOUT THE TEXTURE? THE NUANCES? THE SUBTLETIES OF EMOTION? THE COMPLEXITY AND DEPTH OF CHARACTERIZATIONS?
CLIFFS NOTES DON'T GIVE YOU ANY OF THAT!
WHY DO YOU THINK I **GOT** 'EM?
ENGLISH MAJORS SHOULDN'T BE PARENTS.
I'LL GO TALK TO HER.

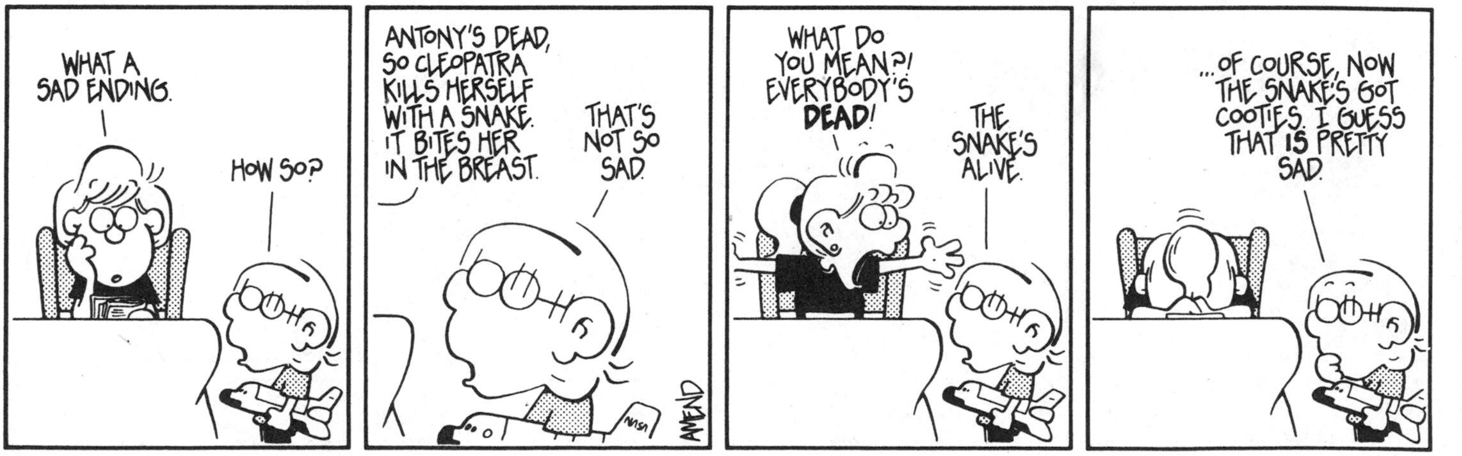
WHAT A SAD ENDING.
HOW SO?
ANTONY'S DEAD, SO CLEOPATRA KILLS HERSELF WITH A SNAKE. IT BITES HER IN THE BREAST.
THAT'S NOT SO SAD.
WHAT DO YOU MEAN?! EVERYBODY'S **DEAD**!
THE SNAKE'S ALIVE.
...OF COURSE, NOW THE SNAKE'S GOT COOTIES. I GUESS THAT **IS** PRETTY SAD.

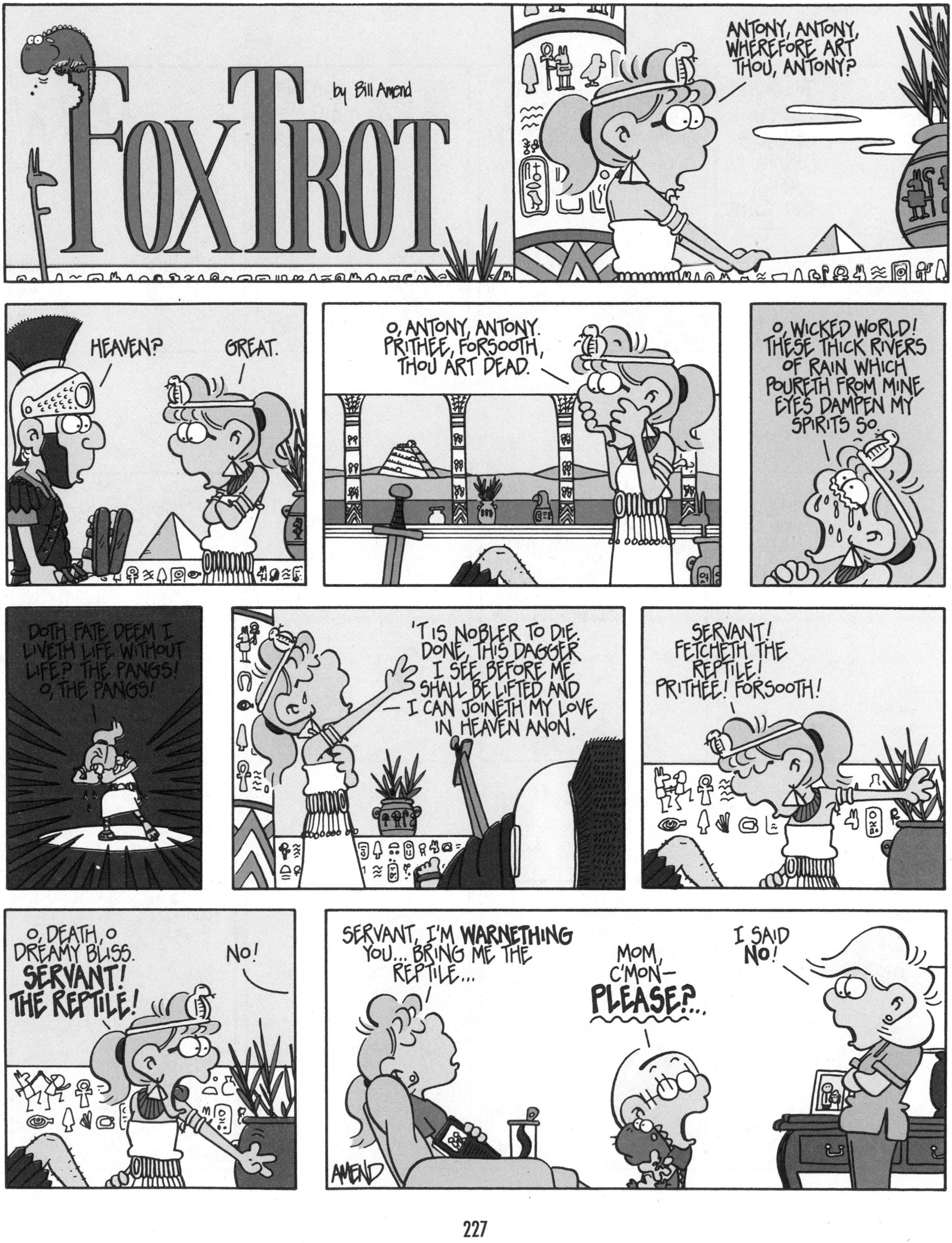
FOXTROT
by Bill Amend
ANTONY, ANTONY, WHEREFORE ART THOU, ANTONY?
HEAVEN?
GREAT.
O, ANTONY, ANTONY. PRITHEE, FORSOOTH, THOU ART DEAD.
O, WICKED WORLD! THESE THICK RIVERS OF RAIN WHICH POURETH FROM MINE EYES DAMPEN MY SPIRITS SO.
DOTH FATE DEEM I LIVETH LIFE WITHOUT LIFE? THE PANGS! O, THE PANGS!
'TIS NOBLER TO DIE. DONE, THIS DAGGER I SEE BEFORE ME SHALL BE LIFTED AND I CAN JOINETH MY LOVE IN HEAVEN ANON.
SERVANT! FETCHETH THE REPTILE! PRITHEE! FORSOOTH!
O, DEATH, O DREAMY BLISS. SERVANT! THE REPTILE!
NO!
SERVANT, I'M WARNETHING YOU... BRING ME THE REPTILE...
MOM, C'MON— PLEASE?...
I SAID NO!
AMEND

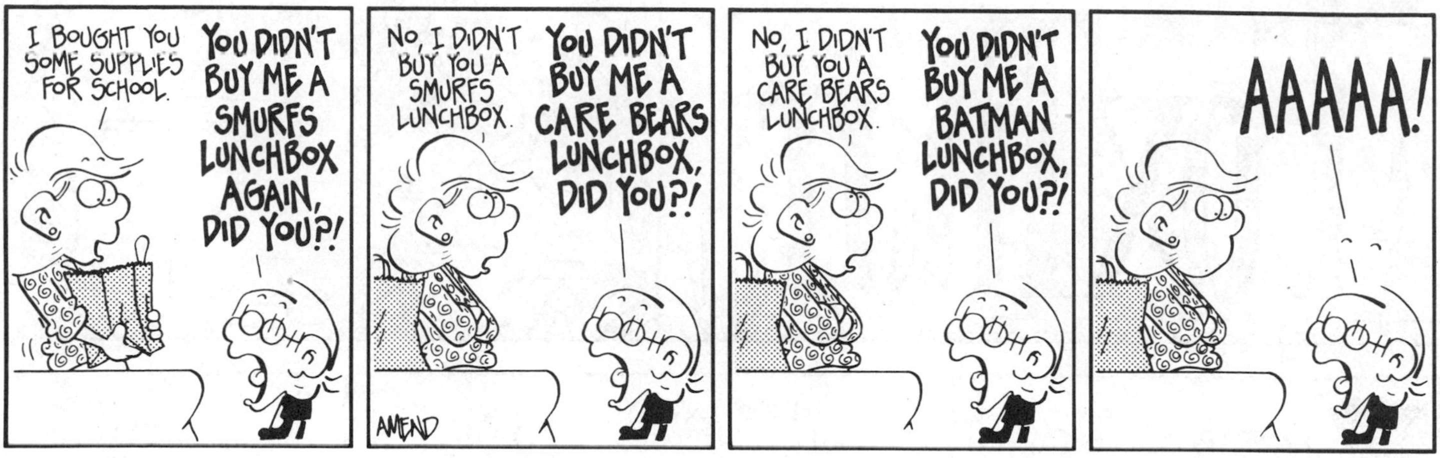
I BOUGHT YOU SOME SUPPLIES FOR SCHOOL.
YOU DIDN'T BUY ME A SMURFS LUNCHBOX AGAIN, DID YOU?!
NO, I DIDN'T BUY YOU A SMURFS LUNCHBOX.
YOU DIDN'T BUY ME A CARE BEARS LUNCHBOX, DID YOU?!
AMEND
NO, I DIDN'T BUY YOU A CARE BEARS LUNCHBOX.
YOU DIDN'T BUY ME A BATMAN LUNCHBOX, DID YOU?!
AAAAA!

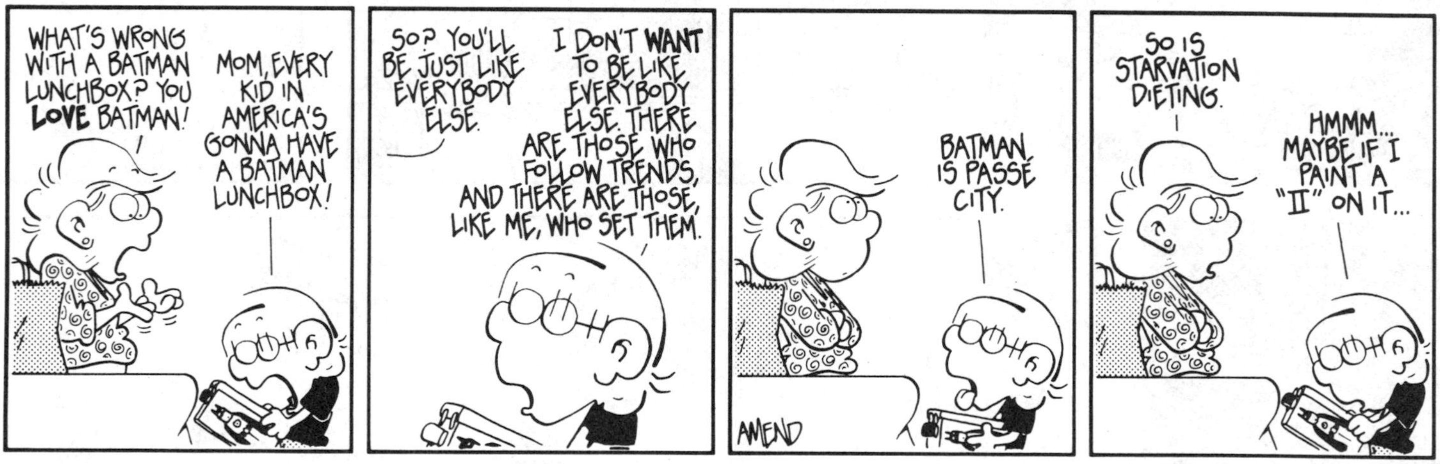
WHAT'S WRONG WITH A BATMAN LUNCHBOX? YOU LOVE BATMAN!
MOM, EVERY KID IN AMERICA'S GONNA HAVE A BATMAN LUNCHBOX!
SO? YOU'LL BE JUST LIKE EVERYBODY ELSE.
I DON'T WANT TO BE LIKE EVERYBODY ELSE. THERE ARE THOSE WHO FOLLOW TRENDS, AND THERE ARE THOSE, LIKE ME, WHO SET THEM.
BATMAN IS PASSÉ CITY.
AMEND
SO IS STARVATION DIETING.
HMMM... MAYBE IF I PAINT A "II" ON IT...

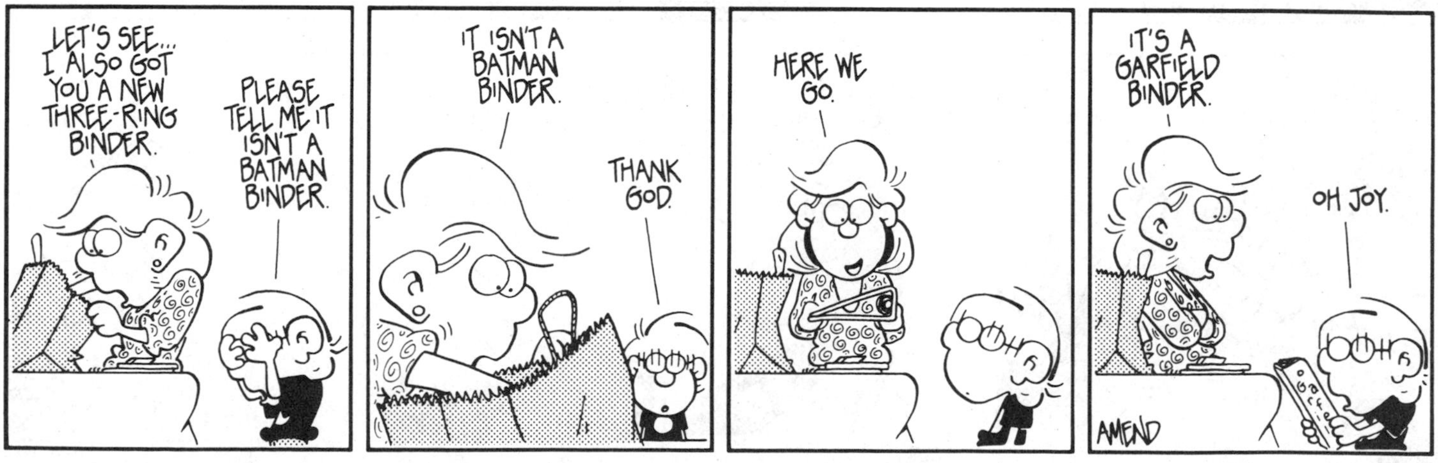
LET'S SEE... I ALSO GOT YOU A NEW THREE-RING BINDER.
PLEASE TELL ME IT ISN'T A BATMAN BINDER.
IT ISN'T A BATMAN BINDER.
THANK GOD.
HERE WE GO.
IT'S A GARFIELD BINDER.
OH JOY.
AMEND

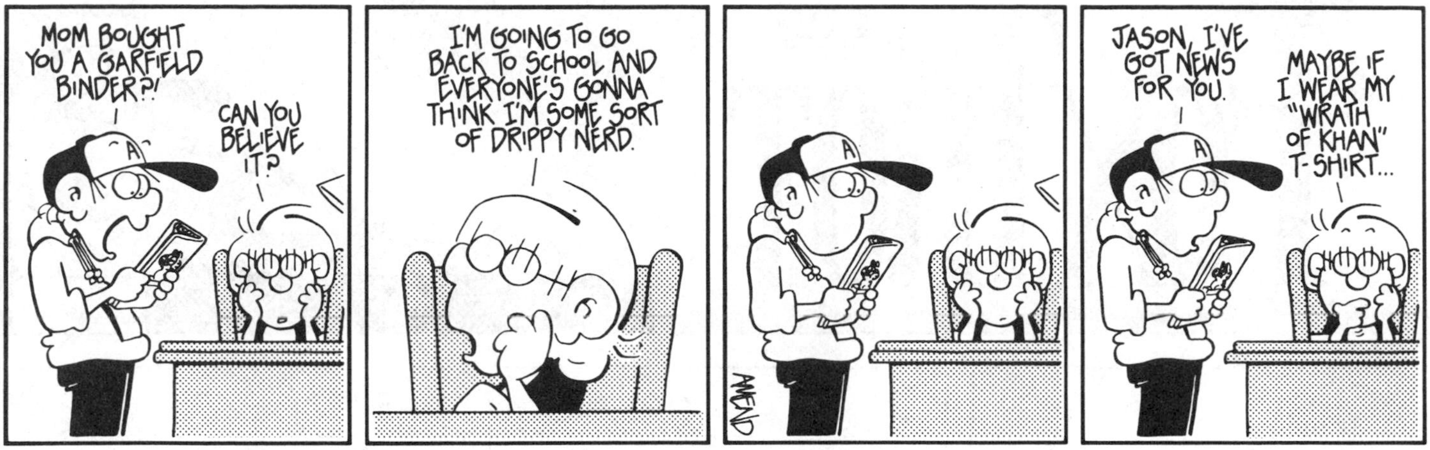
MOM BOUGHT YOU A GARFIELD BINDER?!
CAN YOU BELIEVE IT?
I'M GOING TO GO BACK TO SCHOOL AND EVERYONE'S GONNA THINK I'M SOME SORT OF DRIPPY NERD.
AMEND
JASON, I'VE GOT NEWS FOR YOU.
MAYBE IF I WEAR MY "WRATH OF KHAN" T-SHIRT...

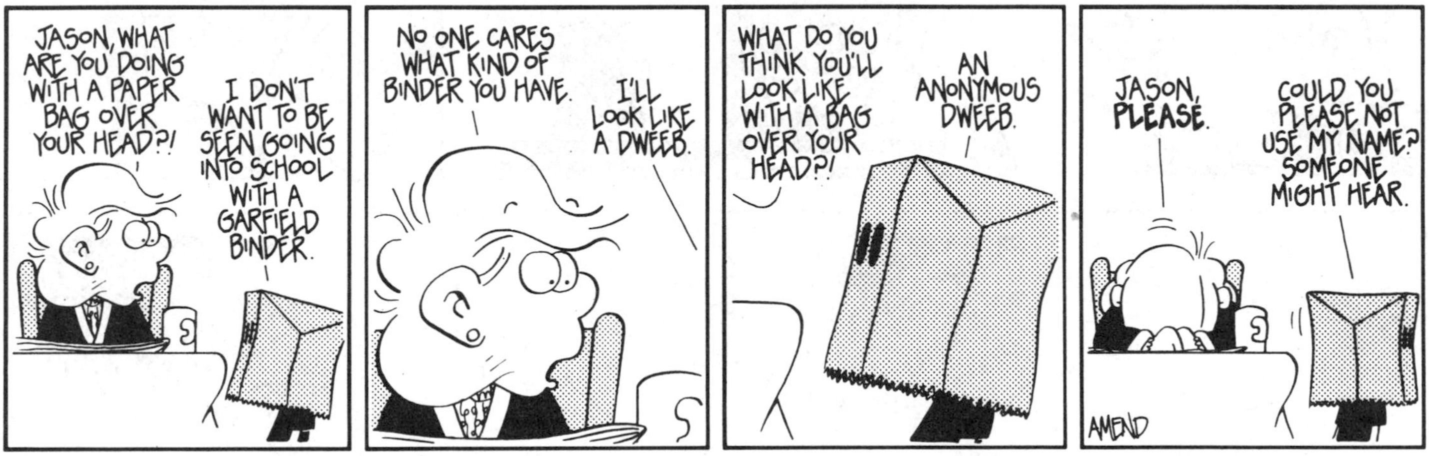
JASON, WHAT ARE YOU DOING WITH A PAPER BAG OVER YOUR HEAD?!
I DON'T WANT TO BE SEEN GOING INTO SCHOOL WITH A GARFIELD BINDER.
NO ONE CARES WHAT KIND OF BINDER YOU HAVE.
I'LL LOOK LIKE A DWEEB.
WHAT DO YOU THINK YOU'LL LOOK LIKE WITH A BAG OVER YOUR HEAD?!
AN ANONYMOUS DWEEB.
JASON, PLEASE.
COULD YOU PLEASE NOT USE MY NAME? SOMEONE MIGHT HEAR.
AMEND

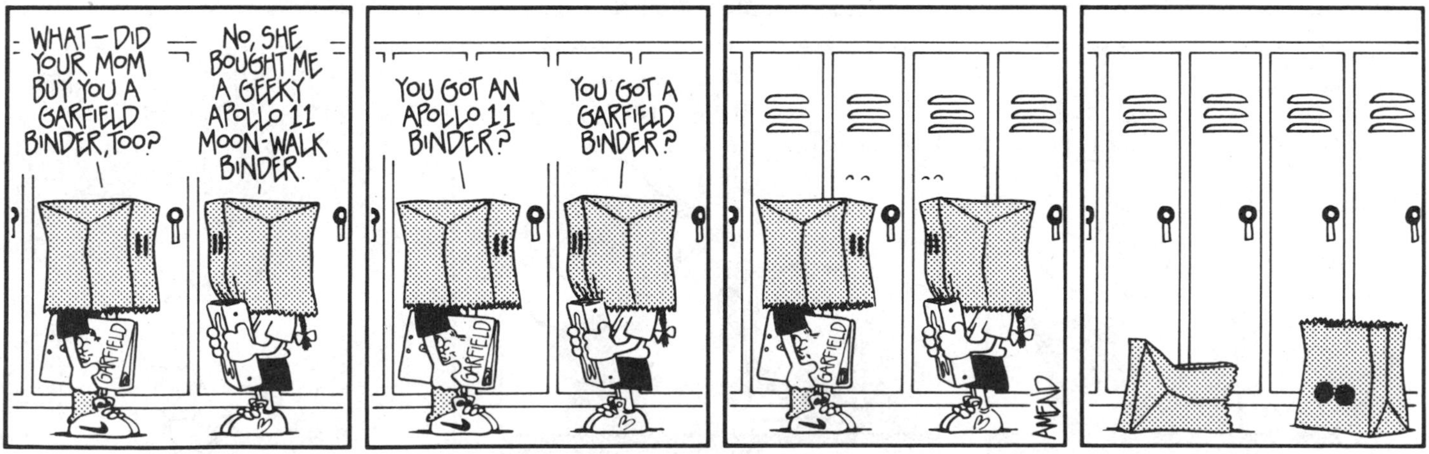
WHAT—DID YOUR MOM BUY YOU A GARFIELD BINDER, TOO?
NO, SHE BOUGHT ME A GEEKY APOLLO 11 MOON-WALK BINDER.
GARFIELD
YOU GOT AN APOLLO 11 BINDER?
YOU GOT A GARFIELD BINDER?
GARFIELD
AMEND

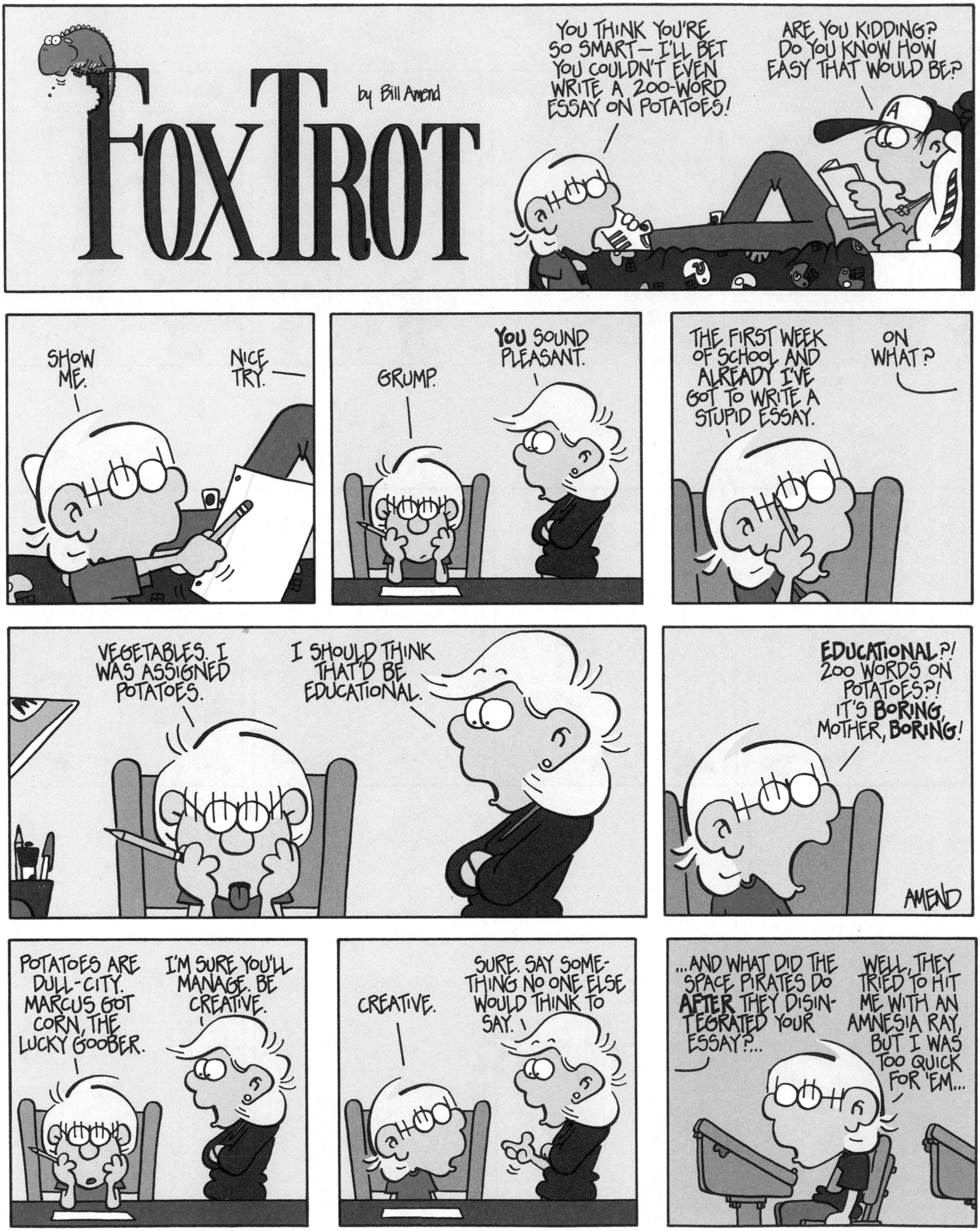
FoxTrot
by Bill Amend
YOU THINK YOU'RE SO SMART— I'LL BET YOU COULDN'T EVEN WRITE A 200-WORD ESSAY ON POTATOES!
ARE YOU KIDDING? DO YOU KNOW HOW EASY THAT WOULD BE?
SHOW ME.
NICE TRY.
GRUMP.
YOU SOUND PLEASANT.
THE FIRST WEEK OF SCHOOL AND ALREADY I'VE GOT TO WRITE A STUPID ESSAY.
ON WHAT?
VEGETABLES. I WAS ASSIGNED POTATOES.
I SHOULD THINK THAT'D BE EDUCATIONAL.
EDUCATIONAL?! 200 WORDS ON POTATOES?! IT'S BORING, MOTHER, BORING!
AMEND
POTATOES ARE DULL-CITY. MARCUS GOT CORN, THE LUCKY GOOBER.
I'M SURE YOU'LL MANAGE. BE CREATIVE.
CREATIVE.
SURE. SAY SOMETHING NO ONE ELSE WOULD THINK TO SAY.
...AND WHAT DID THE SPACE PIRATES DO AFTER THEY DISINTEGRATED YOUR ESSAY?...
WELL, THEY TRIED TO HIT ME WITH AN AMNESIA RAY, BUT I WAS TOO QUICK FOR 'EM...

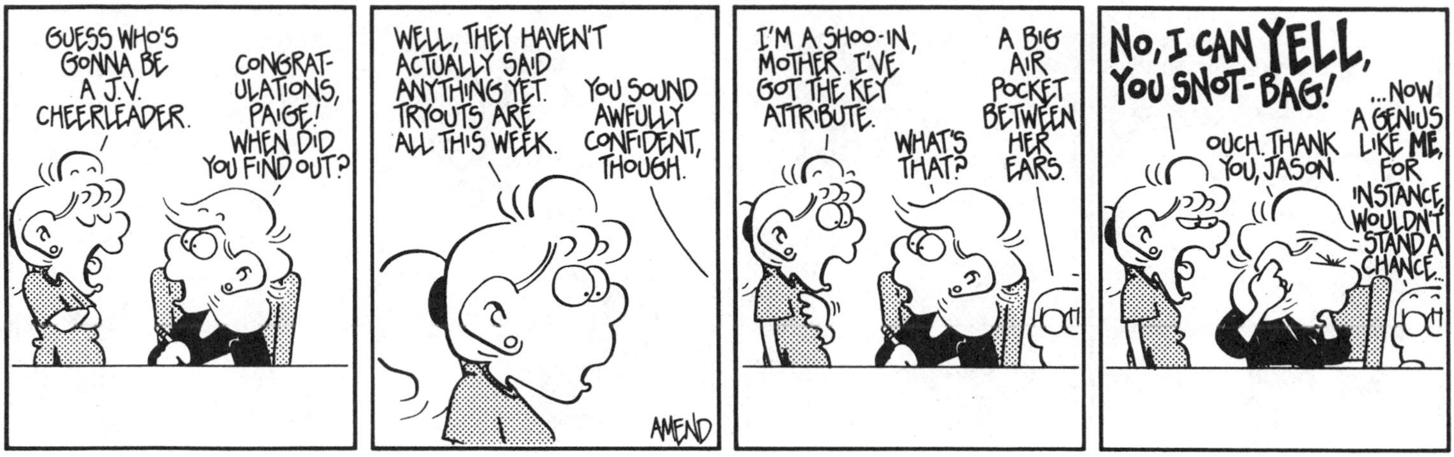
GUESS WHO'S GONNA BE A J.V. CHEERLEADER.
CONGRATULATIONS, PAIGE! WHEN DID YOU FIND OUT?
WELL, THEY HAVEN'T ACTUALLY SAID ANYTHING YET. TRYOUTS ARE ALL THIS WEEK.
YOU SOUND AWFULLY CONFIDENT, THOUGH.
AMEND
I'M A SHOO-IN, MOTHER. I'VE GOT THE KEY ATTRIBUTE.
WHAT'S THAT?
A BIG AIR POCKET BETWEEN HER EARS.
NO, I CAN YELL, YOU SNOT-BAG!
OUCH. THANK YOU, JASON.
...NOW A GENIUS LIKE ME, FOR INSTANCE, WOULDN'T STAND A CHANCE...

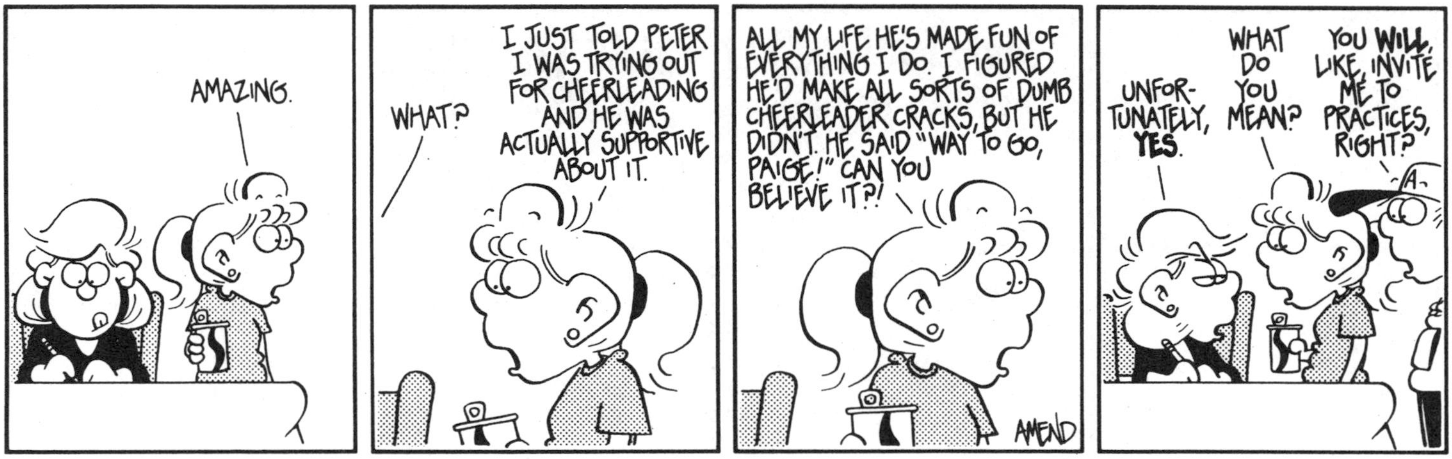
AMAZING.
WHAT?
I JUST TOLD PETER I WAS TRYING OUT FOR CHEERLEADING AND HE WAS ACTUALLY SUPPORTIVE ABOUT IT.
ALL MY LIFE HE'S MADE FUN OF EVERYTHING I DO. I FIGURED HE'D MAKE ALL SORTS OF DUMB CHEERLEADER CRACKS, BUT HE DIDN'T. HE SAID "WAY TO GO, PAIGE!" CAN YOU BELIEVE IT?!
AMEND
UNFORTUNATELY, YES.
WHAT DO YOU MEAN?
YOU WILL, LIKE, INVITE ME TO PRACTICES, RIGHT?

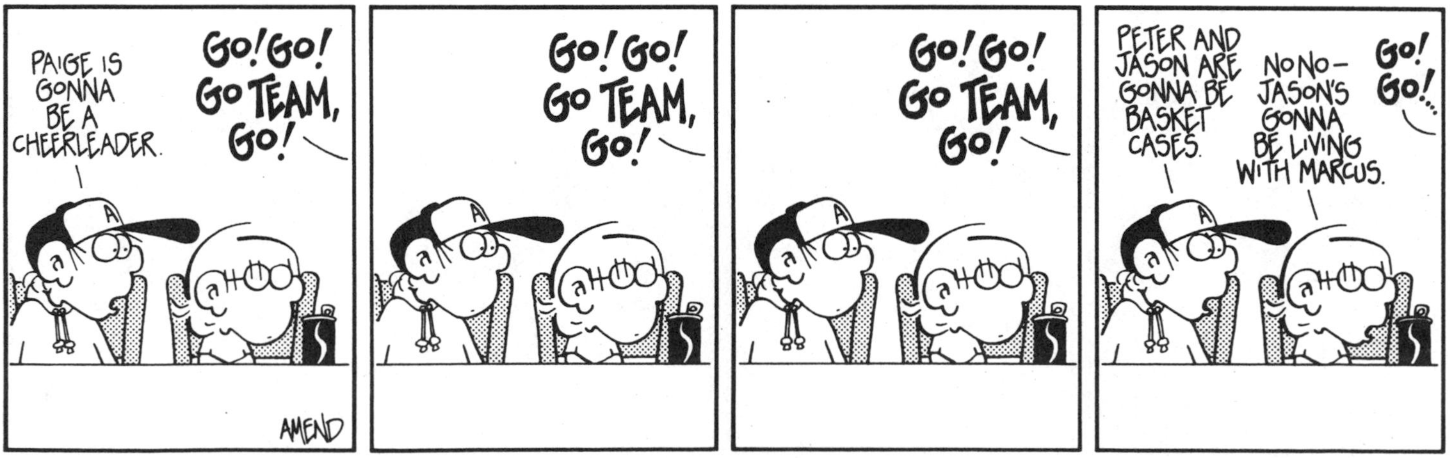
PAIGE IS GONNA BE A CHEERLEADER.
GO! GO! GO TEAM, GO!
AMEND
GO! GO! GO TEAM, GO!
GO! GO! GO TEAM, GO!
PETER AND JASON ARE GONNA BE BASKET CASES.
NO NO – JASON'S GONNA BE LIVING WITH MARCUS.
GO! GO!...

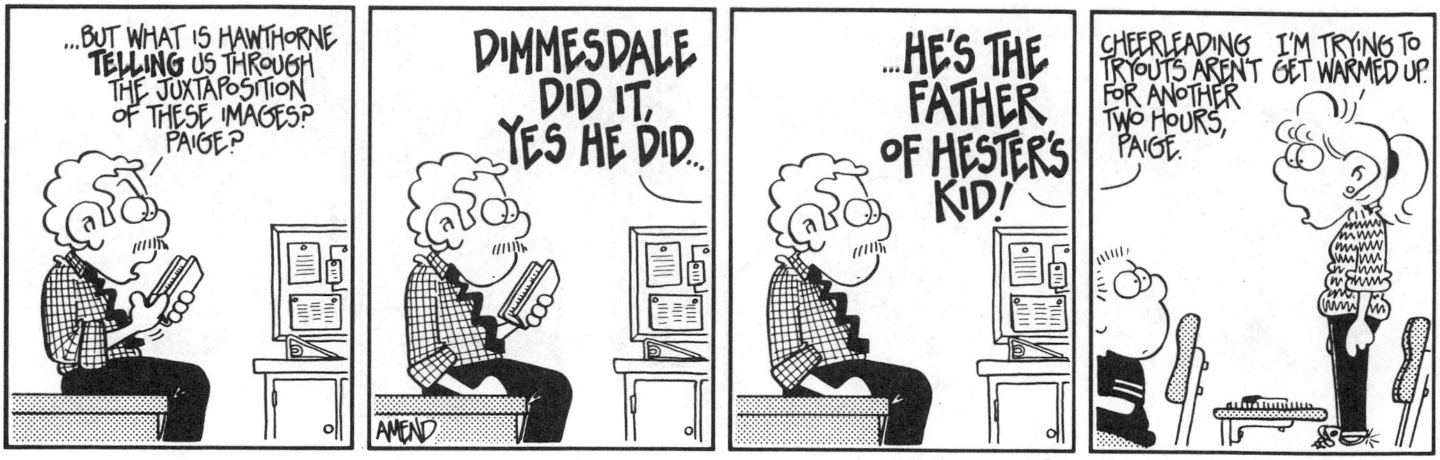
...BUT WHAT IS HAWTHORNE TELLING US THROUGH THE JUXTAPOSITION OF THESE IMAGES? PAIGE?
DIMMESDALE DID IT, YES HE DID...
...HE'S THE FATHER OF HESTER'S KID!
CHEERLEADING TRYOUTS AREN'T FOR ANOTHER TWO HOURS, PAIGE.
I'M TRYING TO GET WARMED UP.
AMEND

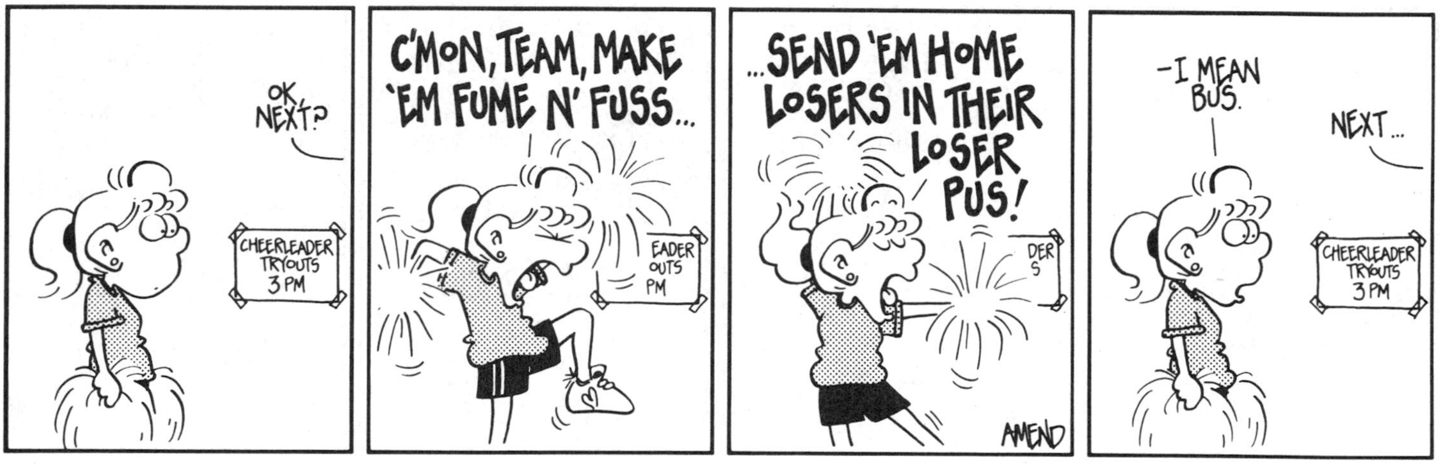
OK, NEXT?
CHEERLEADER TRYOUTS 3 PM
C'MON, TEAM, MAKE 'EM FUME N' FUSS...
...SEND 'EM HOME LOSERS IN THEIR LOSER PUS!
AMEND
-I MEAN BUS.
NEXT...
CHEERLEADER TRYOUTS 3 PM

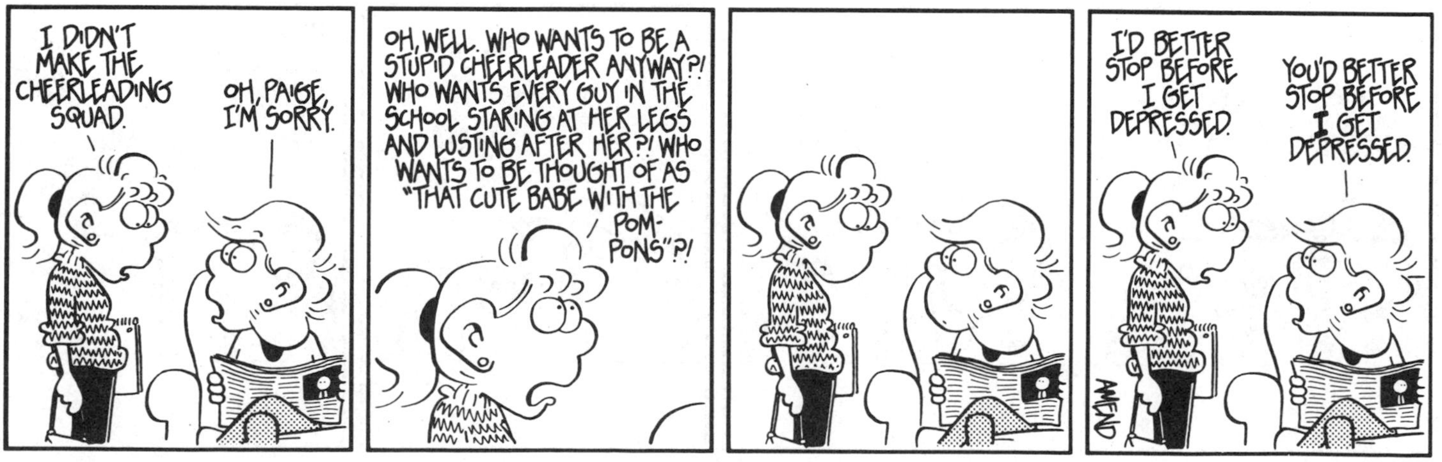
I DIDN'T MAKE THE CHEERLEADING SQUAD.
OH, PAIGE, I'M SORRY.
OH, WELL. WHO WANTS TO BE A STUPID CHEERLEADER ANYWAY?! WHO WANTS EVERY GUY IN THE SCHOOL STARING AT HER LEGS AND LUSTING AFTER HER?! WHO WANTS TO BE THOUGHT OF AS "THAT CUTE BABE WITH THE POM-PONS"?!
I'D BETTER STOP BEFORE I GET DEPRESSED.
YOU'D BETTER STOP BEFORE I GET DEPRESSED.
AMEND

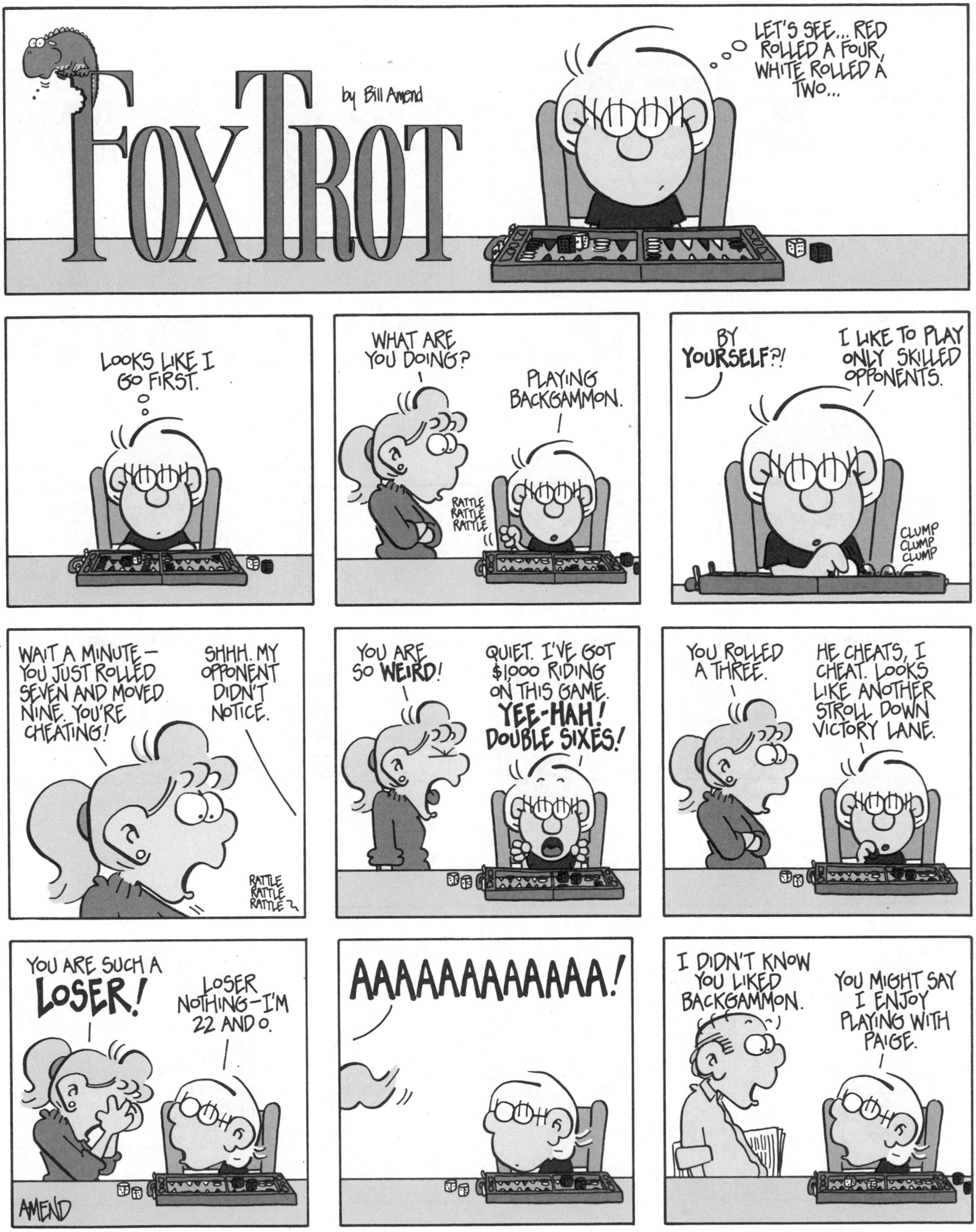
FoxTrot
by Bill Amend
LET'S SEE... RED ROLLED A FOUR, WHITE ROLLED A TWO...
LOOKS LIKE I GO FIRST.
WHAT ARE YOU DOING?
PLAYING BACKGAMMON.
RATTLE RATTLE RATTLE
BY YOURSELF?!
I LIKE TO PLAY ONLY SKILLED OPPONENTS.
CLUMP CLUMP CLUMP
WAIT A MINUTE— YOU JUST ROLLED SEVEN AND MOVED NINE. YOU'RE CHEATING!
SHHH. MY OPPONENT DIDN'T NOTICE.
RATTLE RATTLE RATTLE
YOU ARE SO WEIRD!
QUIET. I'VE GOT $1,000 RIDING ON THIS GAME. YEE-HAH! DOUBLE SIXES!
YOU ROLLED A THREE.
HE CHEATS, I CHEAT. LOOKS LIKE ANOTHER STROLL DOWN VICTORY LANE.
YOU ARE SUCH A LOSER!
LOSER NOTHING—I'M 22 AND 0.
AMEND
AAAAAAAAAAAA!
I DIDN'T KNOW YOU LIKED BACKGAMMON.
YOU MIGHT SAY I ENJOY PLAYING WITH PAIGE.

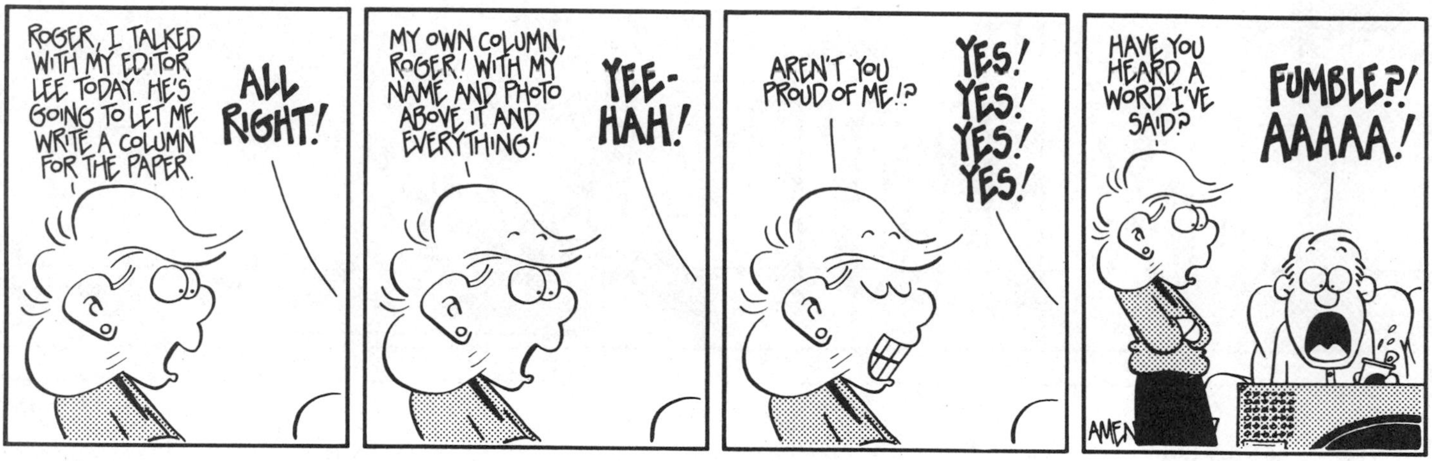
ROGER, I TALKED WITH MY EDITOR LEE TODAY. HE'S GOING TO LET ME WRITE A COLUMN FOR THE PAPER.
ALL RIGHT!
MY OWN COLUMN, ROGER! WITH MY NAME AND PHOTO ABOVE IT AND EVERYTHING!
YEE-HAH!
AREN'T YOU PROUD OF ME!?
YES! YES! YES! YES!
HAVE YOU HEARD A WORD I'VE SAID?
FUMBLE?! AAAAA!
AMEND

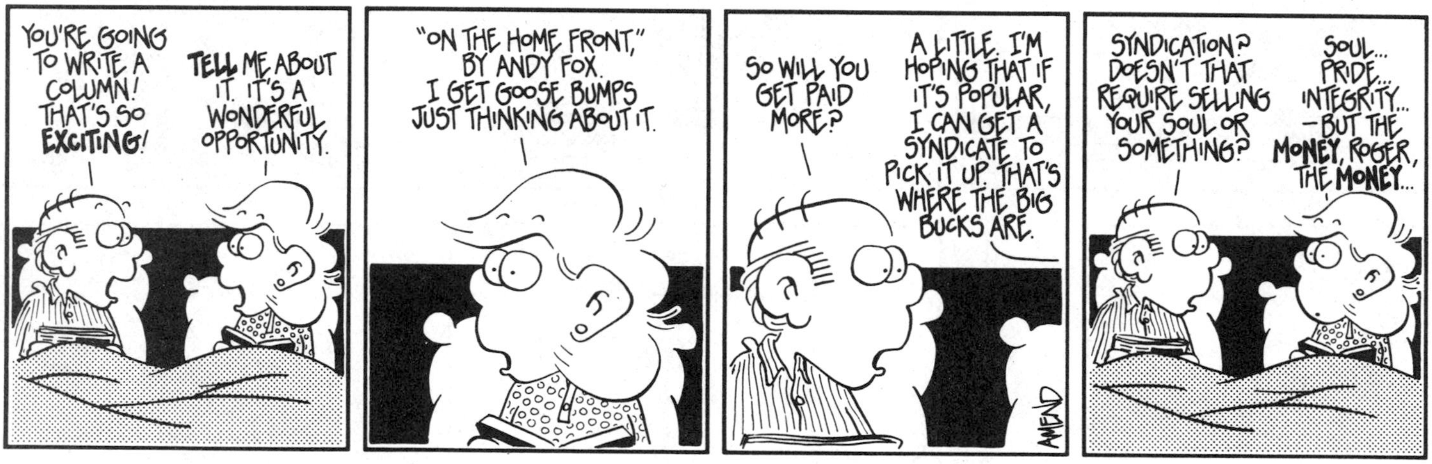
YOU'RE GOING TO WRITE A COLUMN! THAT'S SO EXCITING!
TELL ME ABOUT IT. IT'S A WONDERFUL OPPORTUNITY.
"ON THE HOME FRONT," BY ANDY FOX. I GET GOOSE BUMPS JUST THINKING ABOUT IT.
SO WILL YOU GET PAID MORE?
A LITTLE. I'M HOPING THAT IF IT'S POPULAR, I CAN GET A SYNDICATE TO PICK IT UP. THAT'S WHERE THE BIG BUCKS ARE.
AMEND
SYNDICATION? DOESN'T THAT REQUIRE SELLING YOUR SOUL OR SOMETHING?
SOUL... PRIDE... INTEGRITY... — BUT THE MONEY, ROGER, THE MONEY...

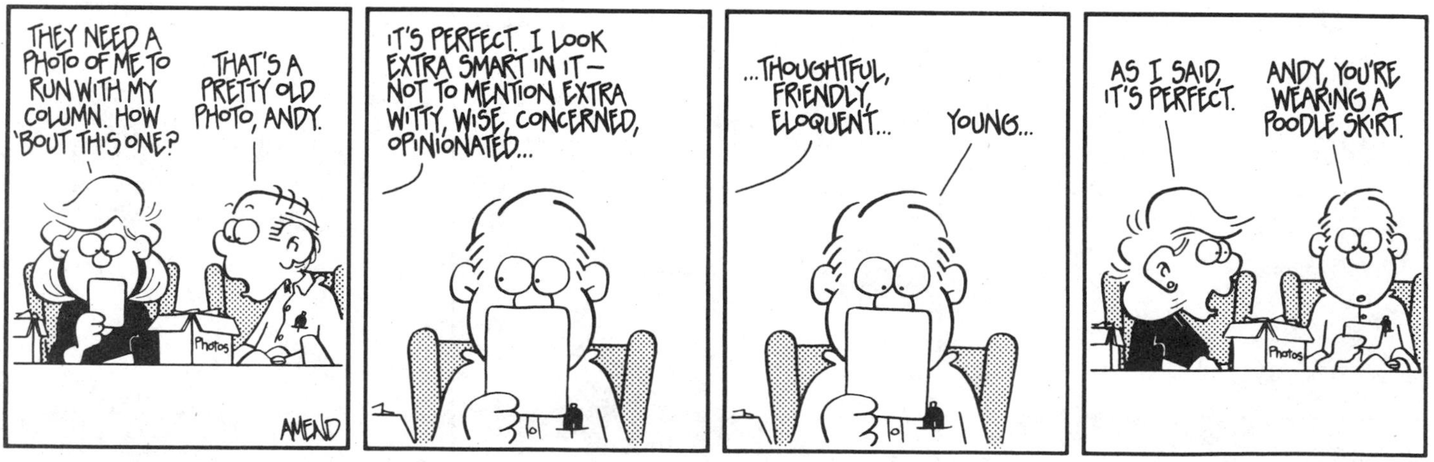
THEY NEED A PHOTO OF ME TO RUN WITH MY COLUMN. HOW 'BOUT THIS ONE?
THAT'S A PRETTY OLD PHOTO, ANDY.
Photos
AMEND
IT'S PERFECT. I LOOK EXTRA SMART IN IT — NOT TO MENTION EXTRA WITTY, WISE, CONCERNED, OPINIONATED...
...THOUGHTFUL, FRIENDLY, ELOQUENT...
YOUNG...
AS I SAID, IT'S PERFECT.
ANDY, YOU'RE WEARING A POODLE SKIRT.
Photos

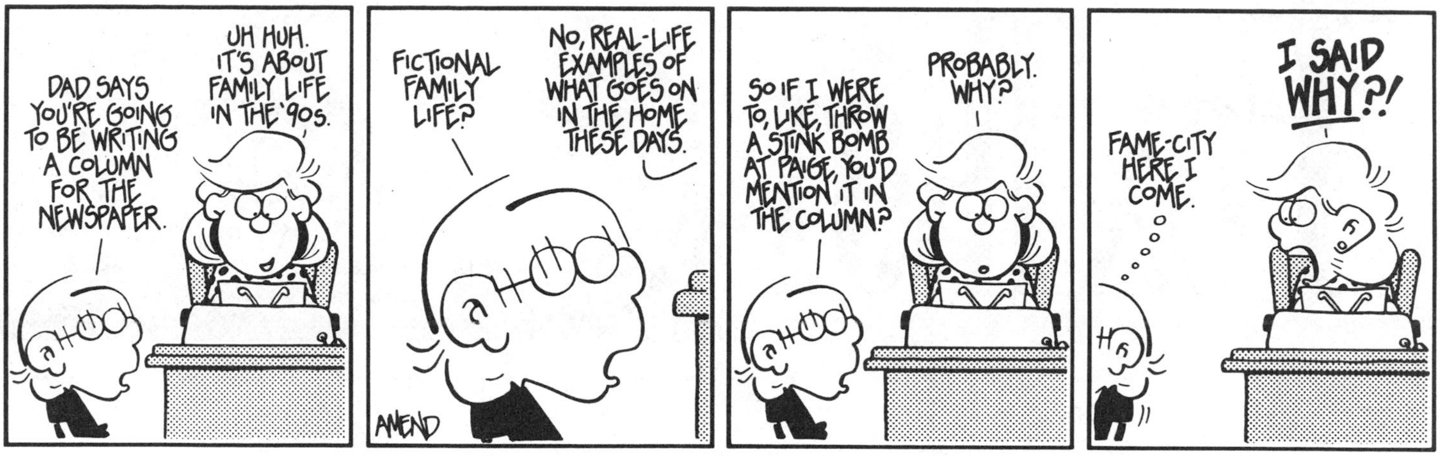
DAD SAYS YOU'RE GOING TO BE WRITING A COLUMN FOR THE NEWSPAPER.
UH HUH. IT'S ABOUT FAMILY LIFE IN THE '90S.
FICTIONAL FAMILY LIFE?
NO, REAL-LIFE EXAMPLES OF WHAT GOES ON IN THE HOME THESE DAYS.
AMEND
SO IF I WERE TO, LIKE, THROW A STINK BOMB AT PAIGE, YOU'D MENTION IT IN THE COLUMN?
PROBABLY. WHY?
FAME-CITY HERE I COME.
I SAID WHY?!

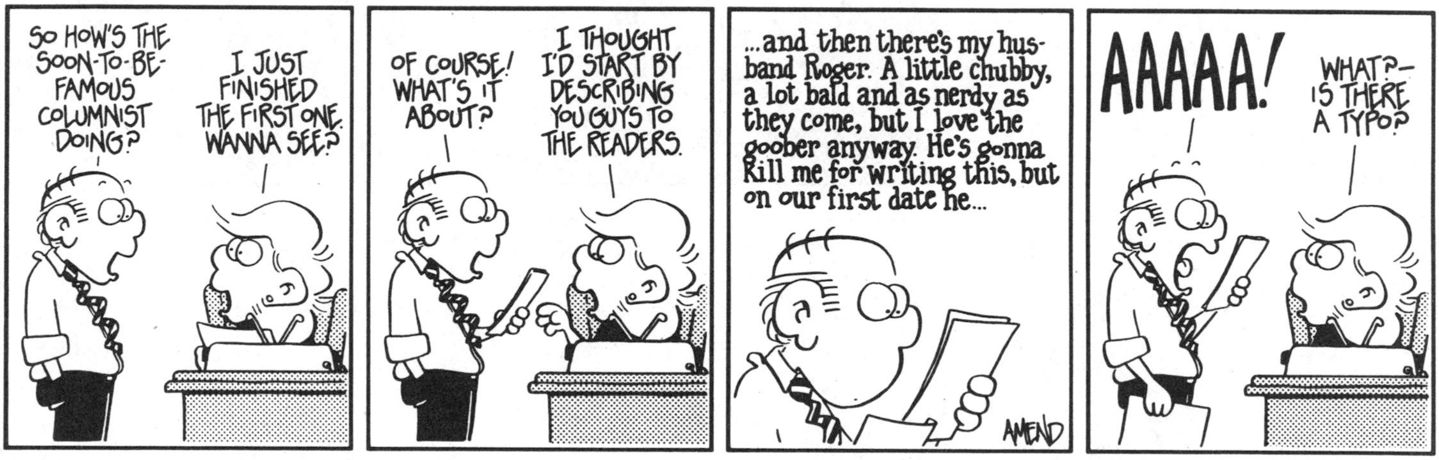
SO HOW'S THE SOON-TO-BE-FAMOUS COLUMNIST DOING?
I JUST FINISHED THE FIRST ONE. WANNA SEE?
OF COURSE! WHAT'S IT ABOUT?
I THOUGHT I'D START BY DESCRIBING YOU GUYS TO THE READERS.
...and then there's my husband Roger. A little chubby, a lot bald and as nerdy as they come, but I love the goober anyway. He's gonna kill me for writing this, but on our first date he...
AMEND
AAAAA!
WHAT?– IS THERE A TYPO?

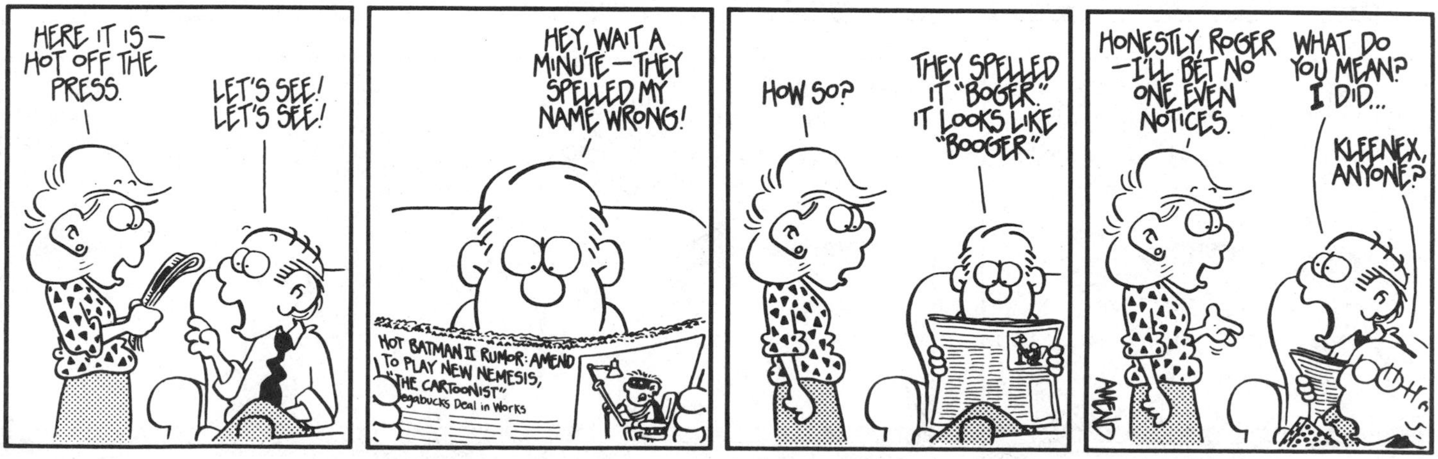
HERE IT IS– HOT OFF THE PRESS.
LET'S SEE! LET'S SEE!
HEY, WAIT A MINUTE–THEY SPELLED MY NAME WRONG!
HOT BATMAN II RUMOR: AMEND TO PLAY NEW NEMESIS, "THE CARTOONIST"
egabucks Deal in Works
HOW SO?
THEY SPELLED IT "BOGER." IT LOOKS LIKE "BOOGER."
AMEND
HONESTLY, ROGER –I'LL BET NO ONE EVEN NOTICES.
WHAT DO YOU MEAN? I DID...
KLEENEX, ANYONE?

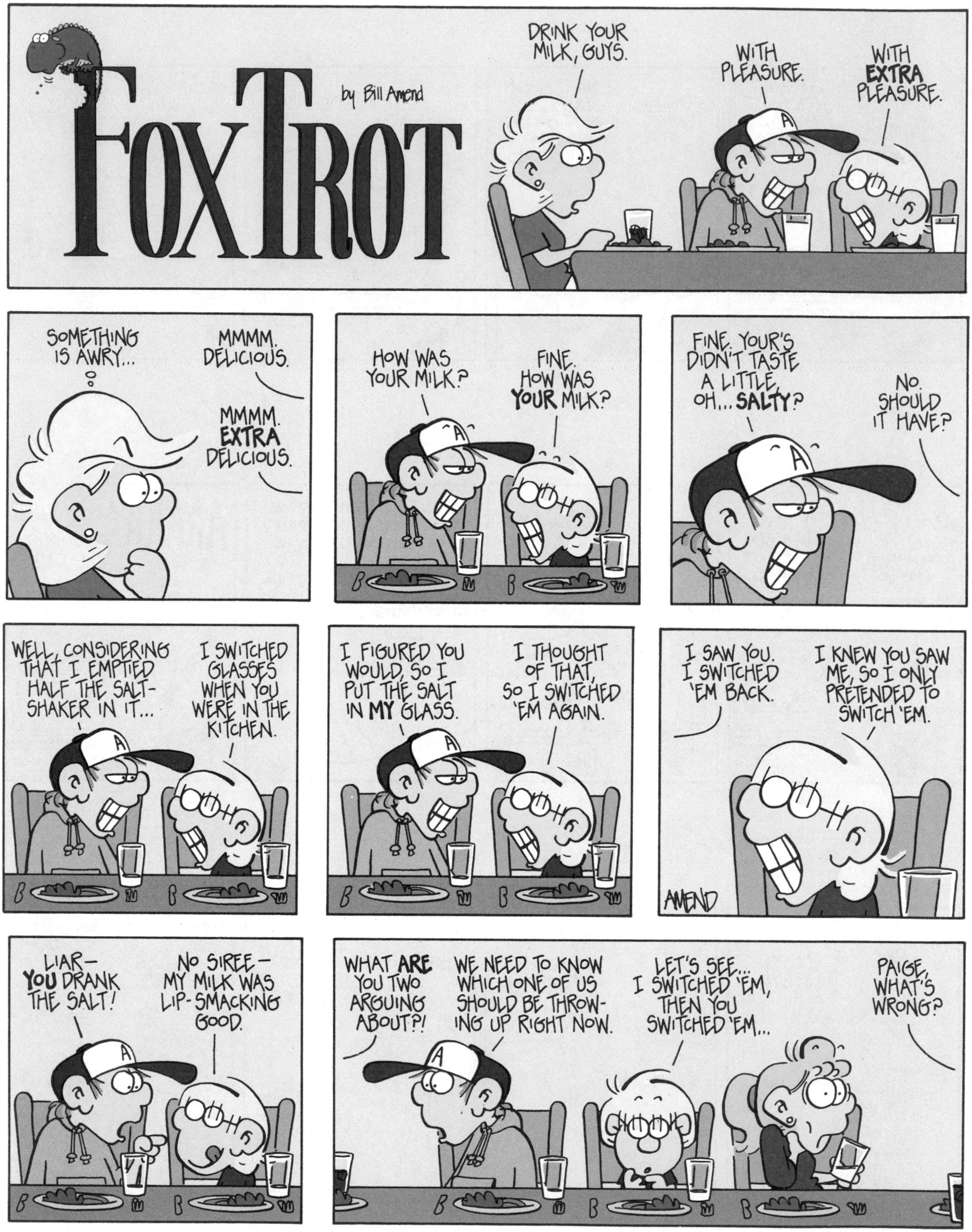
FoxTrot
by Bill Amend
DRINK YOUR MILK, GUYS.
WITH PLEASURE.
WITH EXTRA PLEASURE.
SOMETHING IS AWRY...
MMMM. DELICIOUS.
MMMM. EXTRA DELICIOUS.
HOW WAS YOUR MILK?
FINE. HOW WAS YOUR MILK?
FINE. YOUR'S DIDN'T TASTE A LITTLE, OH,... SALTY?
NO. SHOULD IT HAVE?
WELL, CONSIDERING THAT I EMPTIED HALF THE SALT-SHAKER IN IT...
I SWITCHED GLASSES WHEN YOU WERE IN THE KITCHEN.
I FIGURED YOU WOULD, SO I PUT THE SALT IN MY GLASS.
I THOUGHT OF THAT, SO I SWITCHED 'EM AGAIN.
I SAW YOU. I SWITCHED 'EM BACK.
I KNEW YOU SAW ME, SO I ONLY PRETENDED TO SWITCH 'EM.
AMEND
LIAR— YOU DRANK THE SALT!
NO SIREE— MY MILK WAS LIP-SMACKING GOOD.
WHAT ARE YOU TWO ARGUING ABOUT?!
WE NEED TO KNOW WHICH ONE OF US SHOULD BE THROWING UP RIGHT NOW.
LET'S SEE... I SWITCHED 'EM, THEN YOU SWITCHED 'EM...
PAIGE, WHAT'S WRONG?

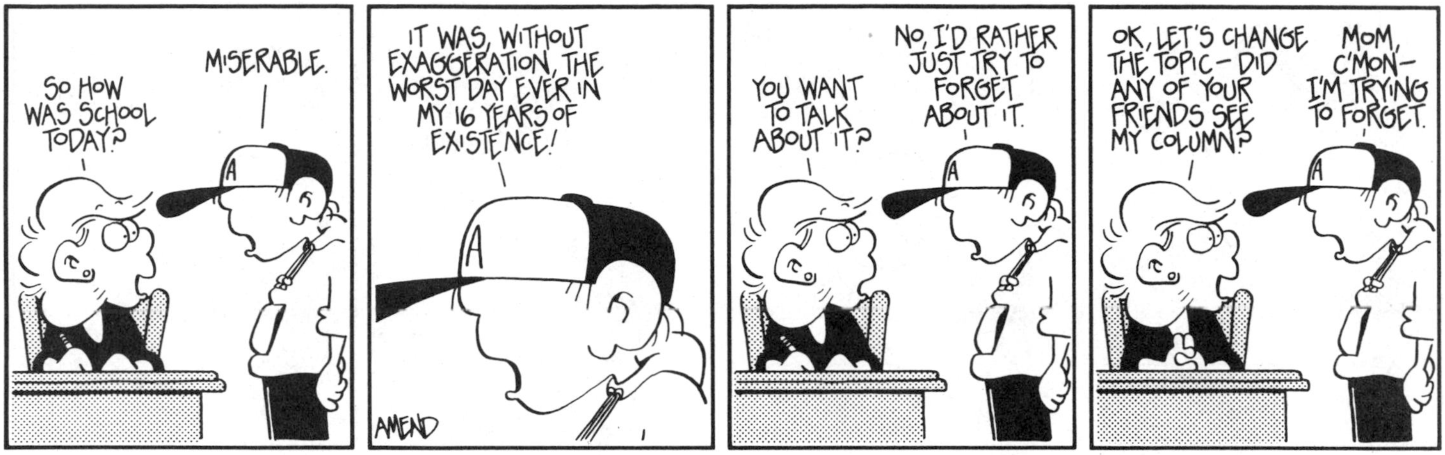

SO HOW WAS SCHOOL TODAY?
MISERABLE.
IT WAS, WITHOUT EXAGGERATION, THE WORST DAY EVER IN MY 16 YEARS OF EXISTENCE!
AMEND
YOU WANT TO TALK ABOUT IT?
NO, I'D RATHER JUST TRY TO FORGET ABOUT IT.
OK, LET'S CHANGE THE TOPIC - DID ANY OF YOUR FRIENDS SEE MY COLUMN?
MOM, C'MON- I'M TRYING TO FORGET.

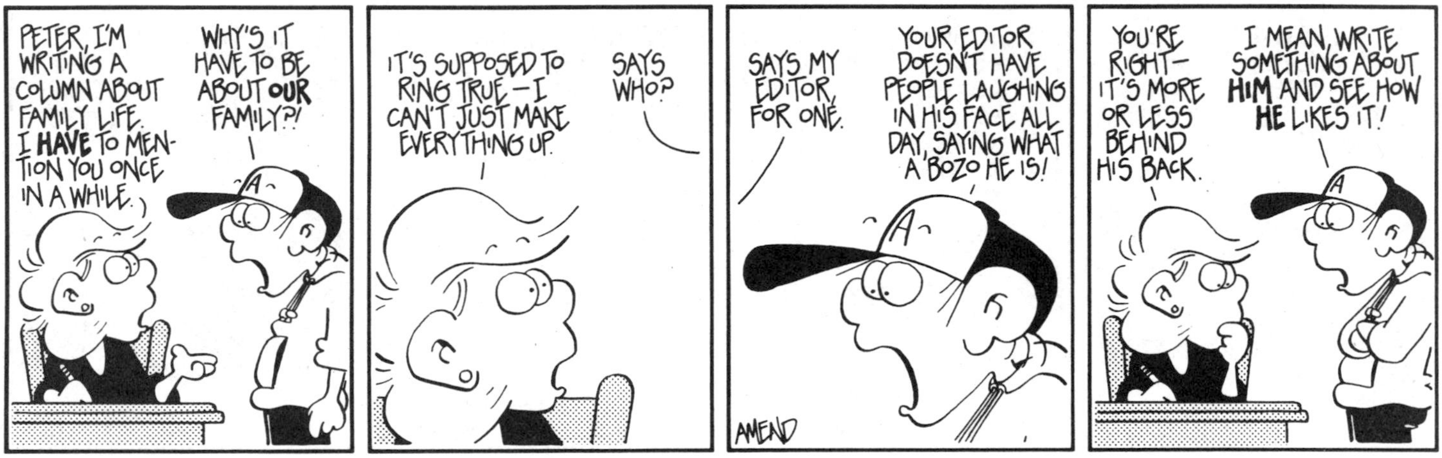

PETER, I'M WRITING A COLUMN ABOUT FAMILY LIFE. I **HAVE** TO MENTION YOU ONCE IN A WHILE.
WHY'S IT HAVE TO BE ABOUT **OUR** FAMILY?!
IT'S SUPPOSED TO RING TRUE - I CAN'T JUST MAKE EVERYTHING UP.
SAYS WHO?
SAYS MY EDITOR, FOR ONE.
YOUR EDITOR DOESN'T HAVE PEOPLE LAUGHING IN HIS FACE ALL DAY, SAYING WHAT A BOZO HE IS!
AMEND
YOU'RE RIGHT- IT'S MORE OR LESS BEHIND HIS BACK.
I MEAN, WRITE SOMETHING ABOUT **HIM** AND SEE HOW **HE** LIKES IT!

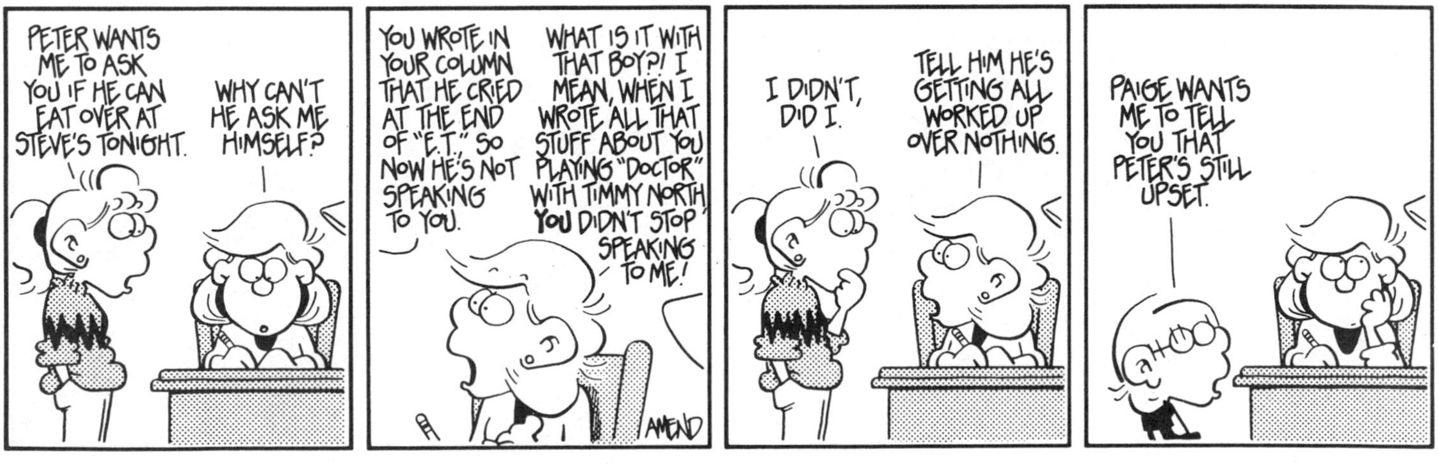

PETER WANTS ME TO ASK YOU IF HE CAN EAT OVER AT STEVE'S TONIGHT.
WHY CAN'T HE ASK ME HIMSELF?
YOU WROTE IN YOUR COLUMN THAT HE CRIED AT THE END OF "E.T.," SO NOW HE'S NOT SPEAKING TO YOU.
WHAT IS IT WITH THAT BOY?! I MEAN, WHEN I WROTE ALL THAT STUFF ABOUT YOU PLAYING "DOCTOR" WITH TIMMY NORTH **YOU** DIDN'T STOP SPEAKING TO ME!
AMEND
I DIDN'T, DID I.
TELL HIM HE'S GETTING ALL WORKED UP OVER NOTHING.
PAIGE WANTS ME TO TELL YOU THAT PETER'S STILL UPSET.

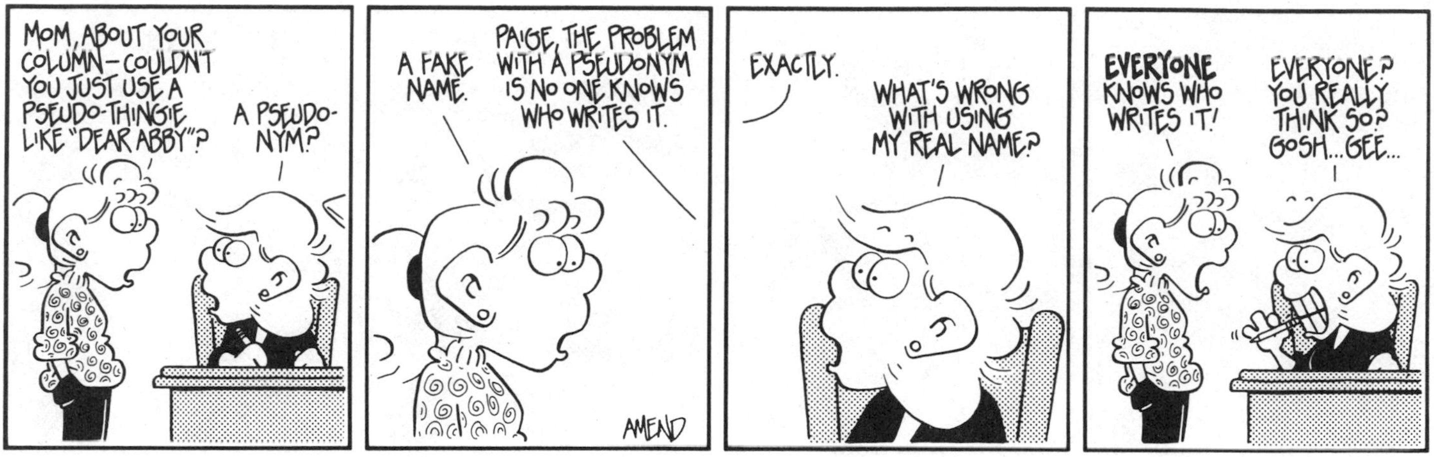
MOM, ABOUT YOUR COLUMN—COULDN'T YOU JUST USE A PSEUDO-THINGIE LIKE "DEAR ABBY"?
A PSEUDONYM?
A FAKE NAME.
PAIGE, THE PROBLEM WITH A PSEUDONYM IS NO ONE KNOWS WHO WRITES IT.
AMEND
EXACTLY.
WHAT'S WRONG WITH USING MY REAL NAME?
EVERYONE KNOWS WHO WRITES IT!
EVERYONE? YOU REALLY THINK SO? GOSH...GEE...

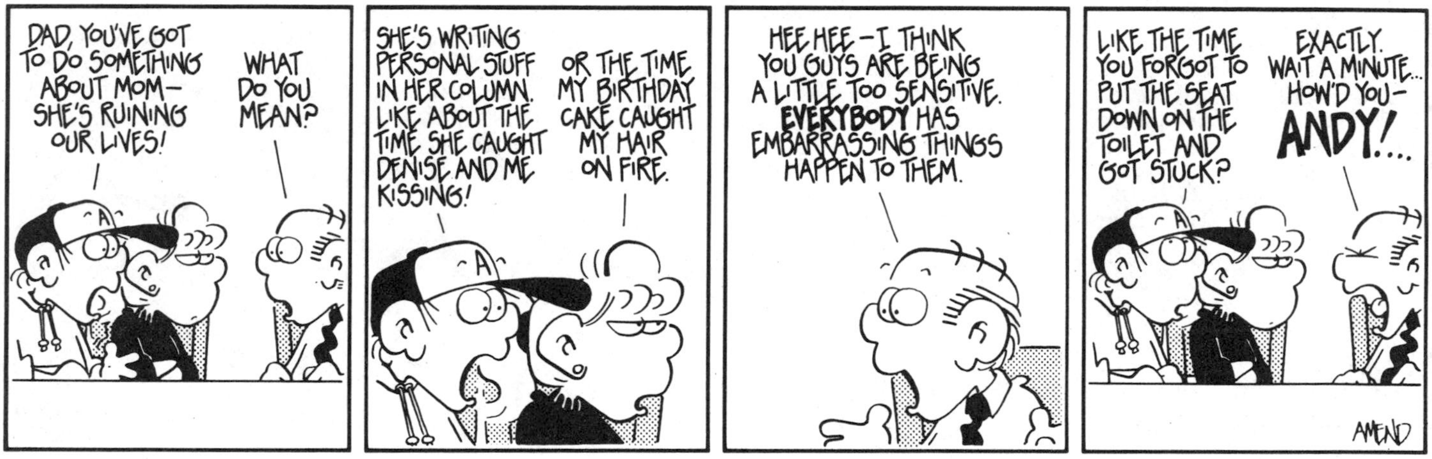
DAD, YOU'VE GOT TO DO SOMETHING ABOUT MOM—SHE'S RUINING OUR LIVES!
WHAT DO YOU MEAN?
SHE'S WRITING PERSONAL STUFF IN HER COLUMN. LIKE ABOUT THE TIME SHE CAUGHT DENISE AND ME KISSING!
OR THE TIME MY BIRTHDAY CAKE CAUGHT MY HAIR ON FIRE.
HEE HEE—I THINK YOU GUYS ARE BEING A LITTLE TOO SENSITIVE. EVERYBODY HAS EMBARRASSING THINGS HAPPEN TO THEM.
LIKE THE TIME YOU FORGOT TO PUT THE SEAT DOWN ON THE TOILET AND GOT STUCK?
EXACTLY. WAIT A MINUTE... HOW'D YOU—
ANDY!...
AMEND

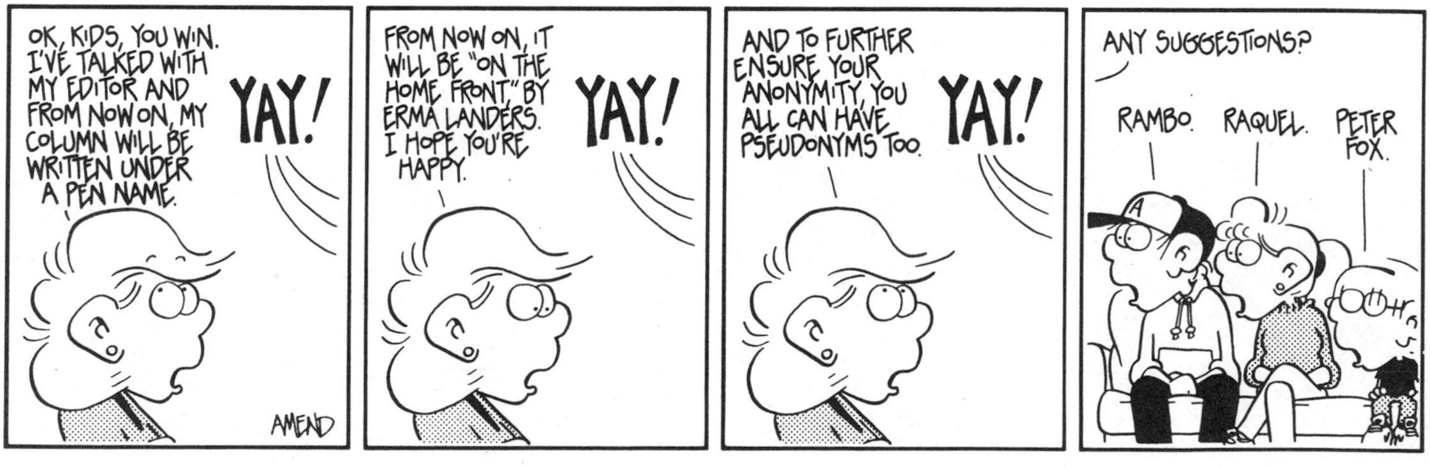
OK, KIDS, YOU WIN. I'VE TALKED WITH MY EDITOR AND FROM NOW ON, MY COLUMN WILL BE WRITTEN UNDER A PEN NAME.
YAY!
AMEND
FROM NOW ON, IT WILL BE "ON THE HOME FRONT," BY ERMA LANDERS. I HOPE YOU'RE HAPPY.
YAY!
AND TO FURTHER ENSURE YOUR ANONYMITY, YOU ALL CAN HAVE PSEUDONYMS TOO.
YAY!
ANY SUGGESTIONS?
RAMBO.
RAQUEL.
PETER FOX.

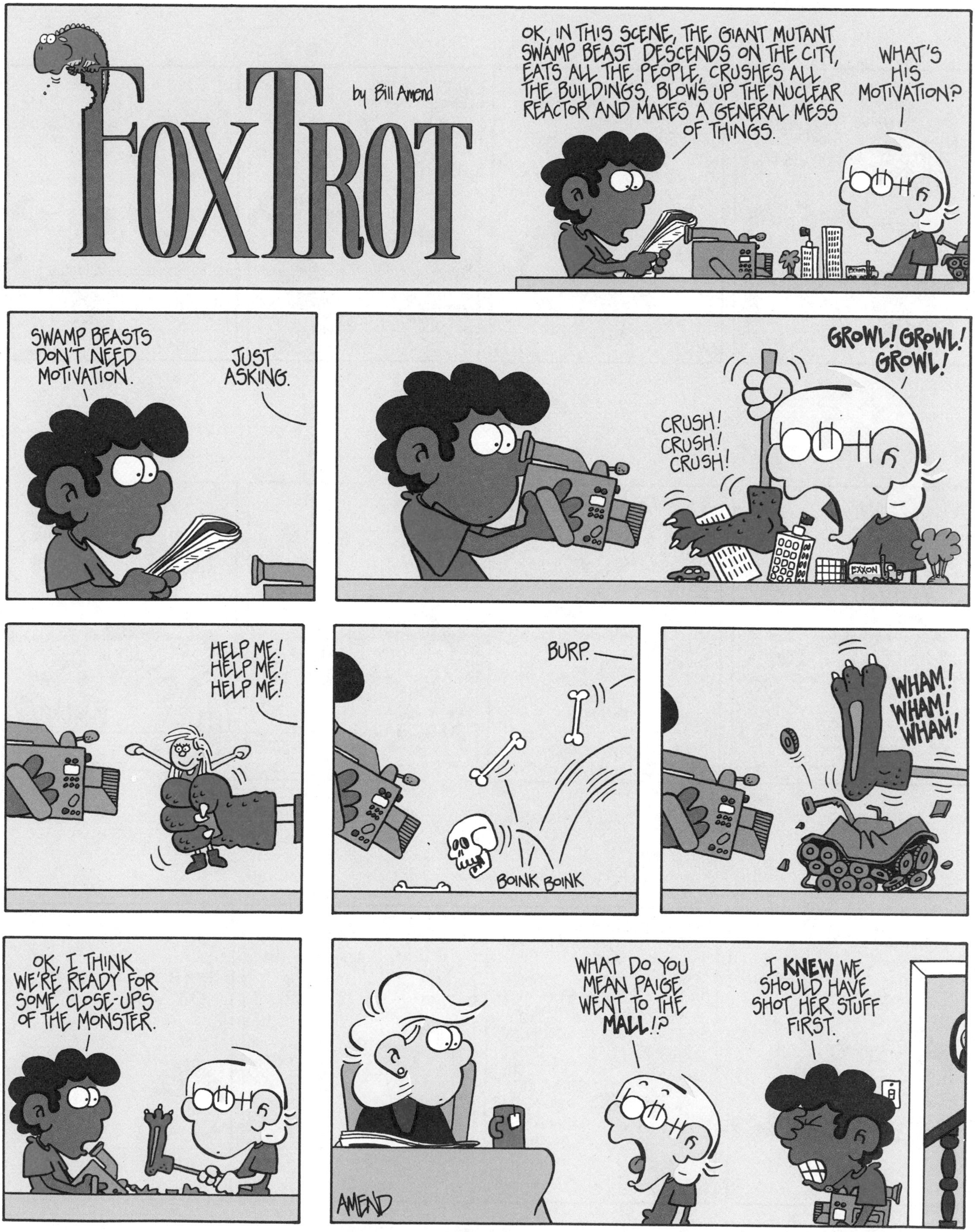
FoxTrot
by Bill Amend
OK, IN THIS SCENE, THE GIANT MUTANT SWAMP BEAST DESCENDS ON THE CITY, EATS ALL THE PEOPLE, CRUSHES ALL THE BUILDINGS, BLOWS UP THE NUCLEAR REACTOR AND MAKES A GENERAL MESS OF THINGS.
WHAT'S HIS MOTIVATION?
SWAMP BEASTS DON'T NEED MOTIVATION.
JUST ASKING.
GROWL! GROWL! GROWL!
CRUSH! CRUSH! CRUSH!
EXXON
HELP ME! HELP ME! HELP ME!
BURP.
BOINK BOINK
WHAM! WHAM! WHAM!
OK, I THINK WE'RE READY FOR SOME CLOSE-UPS OF THE MONSTER.
WHAT DO YOU MEAN PAIGE WENT TO THE MALL!?
I KNEW WE SHOULD HAVE SHOT HER STUFF FIRST.
AMEND

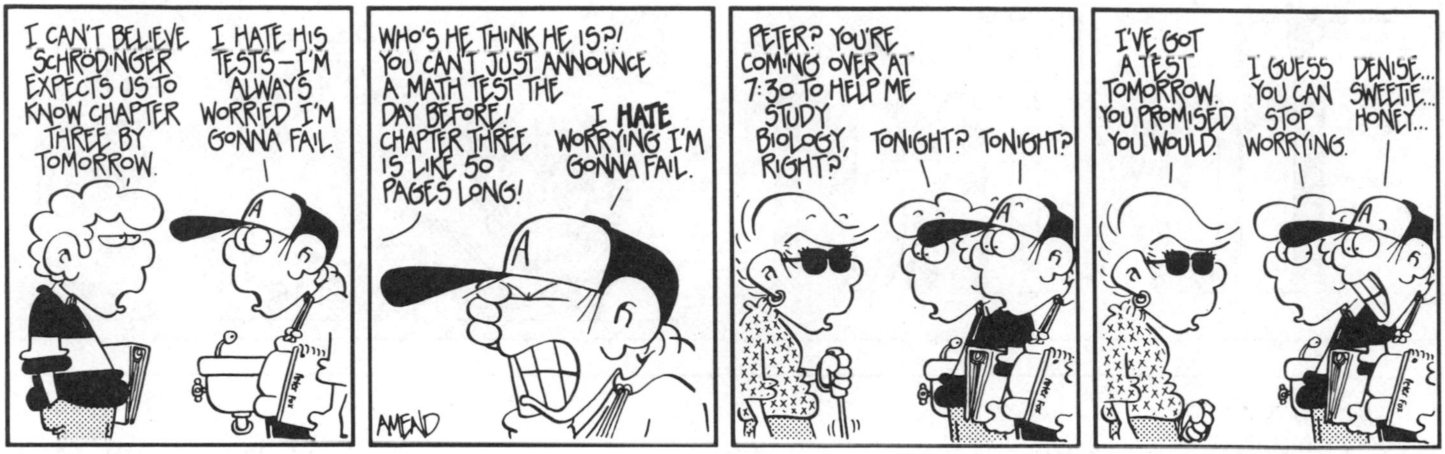
I CAN'T BELIEVE SCHRÖDINGER EXPECTS US TO KNOW CHAPTER THREE BY TOMORROW.
I HATE HIS TESTS—I'M ALWAYS WORRIED I'M GONNA FAIL.
WHO'S HE THINK HE IS?! YOU CAN'T JUST ANNOUNCE A MATH TEST THE DAY BEFORE! CHAPTER THREE IS LIKE 50 PAGES LONG!
I **HATE** WORRYING I'M GONNA FAIL.
AMEND
PETER? YOU'RE COMING OVER AT 7:30 TO HELP ME STUDY BIOLOGY, RIGHT?
TONIGHT?
TONIGHT?
I'VE GOT A TEST TOMORROW. YOU PROMISED YOU WOULD.
I GUESS YOU CAN STOP WORRYING.
DENISE... SWEETIE... HONEY...

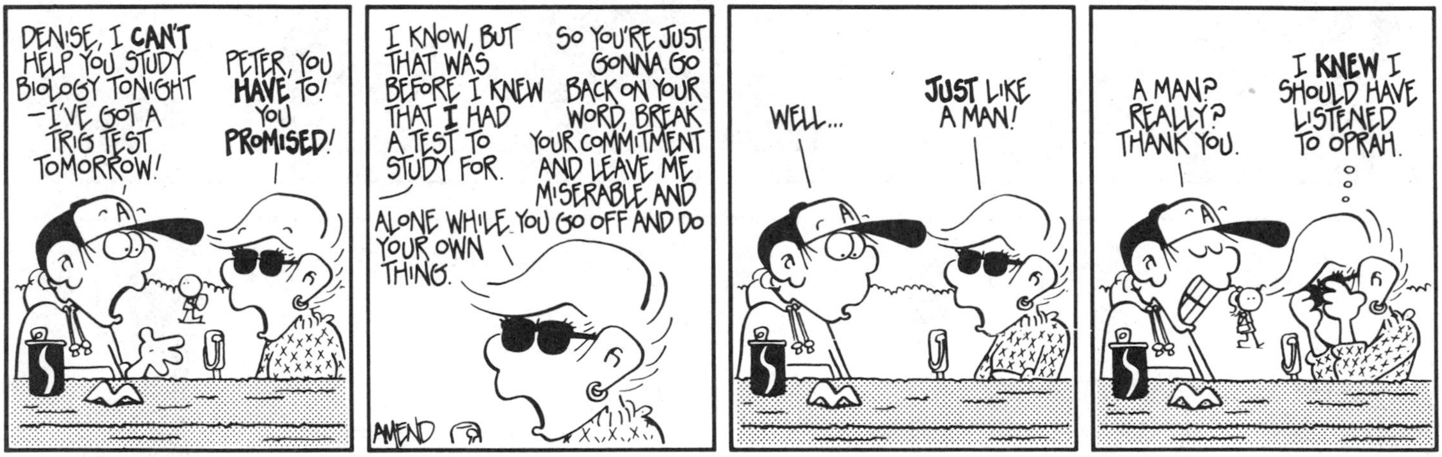
DENISE, I **CAN'T** HELP YOU STUDY BIOLOGY TONIGHT —I'VE GOT A TRIG TEST TOMORROW!
PETER, YOU **HAVE** TO! YOU **PROMISED**!
I KNOW, BUT THAT WAS BEFORE I KNEW THAT **I** HAD A TEST TO STUDY FOR.
SO YOU'RE JUST GONNA GO BACK ON YOUR WORD, BREAK YOUR COMMITMENT AND LEAVE ME MISERABLE AND ALONE WHILE YOU GO OFF AND DO YOUR OWN THING.
AMEND
WELL...
JUST LIKE A MAN!
A MAN? REALLY? THANK YOU.
I **KNEW** I SHOULD HAVE LISTENED TO OPRAH.

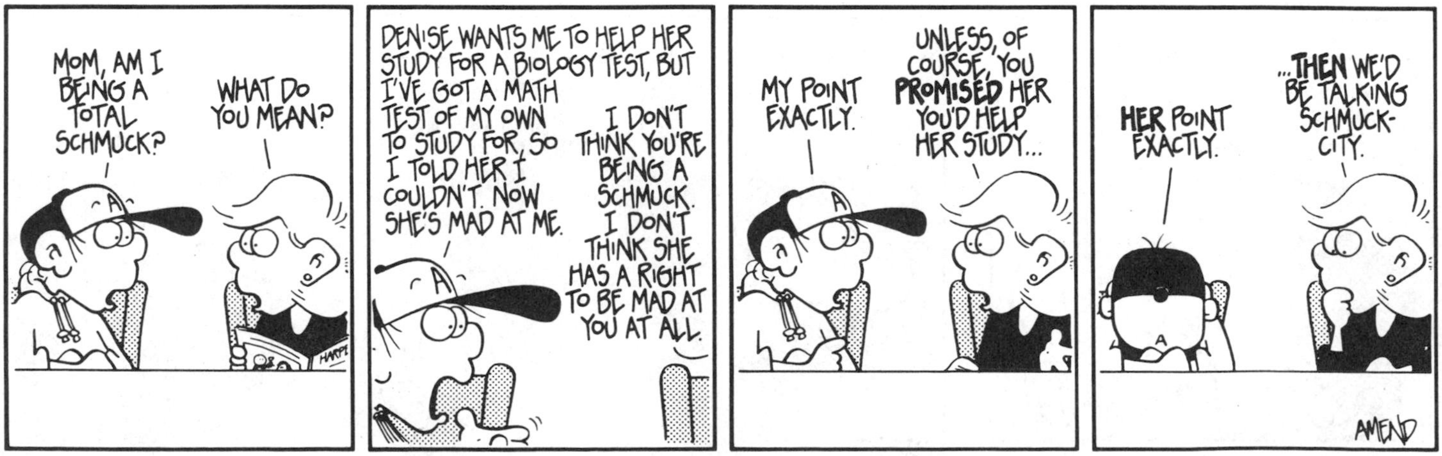
MOM, AM I BEING A TOTAL SCHMUCK?
WHAT DO YOU MEAN?
DENISE WANTS ME TO HELP HER STUDY FOR A BIOLOGY TEST, BUT I'VE GOT A MATH TEST OF MY OWN TO STUDY FOR, SO I TOLD HER I COULDN'T. NOW SHE'S MAD AT ME.
I DON'T THINK YOU'RE BEING A SCHMUCK. I DON'T THINK SHE HAS A RIGHT TO BE MAD AT YOU AT ALL.
MY POINT EXACTLY.
UNLESS, OF COURSE, YOU **PROMISED** HER YOU'D HELP HER STUDY...
HER POINT EXACTLY.
...**THEN** WE'D BE TALKING SCHMUCK-CITY.
AMEND

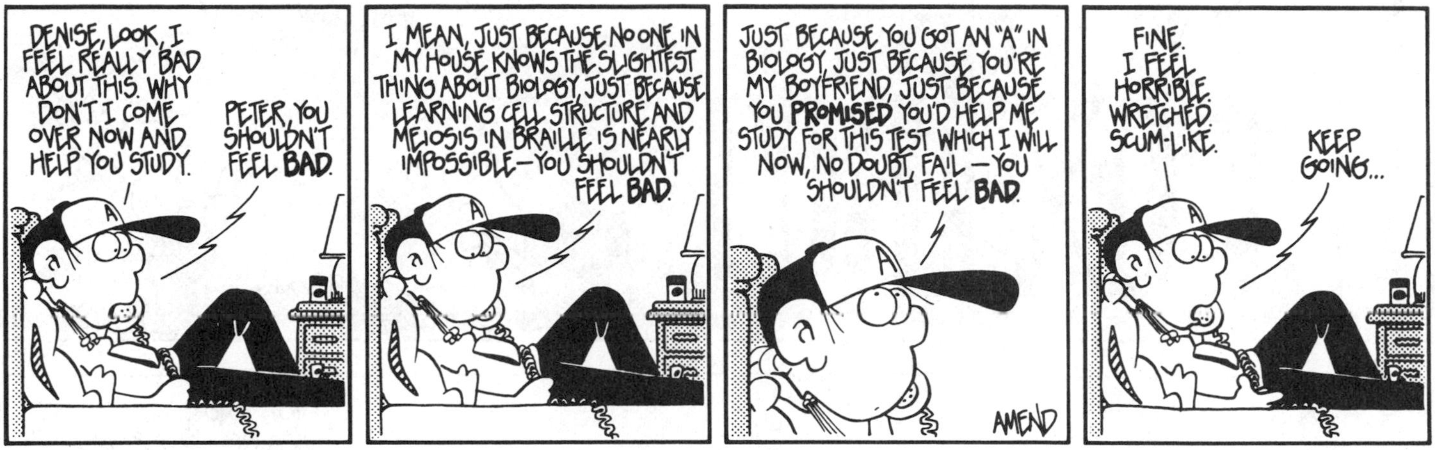
DENISE, LOOK, I FEEL REALLY BAD ABOUT THIS. WHY DON'T I COME OVER NOW AND HELP YOU STUDY.
PETER, YOU SHOULDN'T FEEL **BAD**.
I MEAN, JUST BECAUSE NO ONE IN MY HOUSE KNOWS THE SLIGHTEST THING ABOUT BIOLOGY, JUST BECAUSE LEARNING CELL STRUCTURE AND MEIOSIS IN BRAILLE IS NEARLY IMPOSSIBLE—YOU SHOULDN'T FEEL **BAD**.
JUST BECAUSE YOU GOT AN "A" IN BIOLOGY, JUST BECAUSE YOU'RE MY BOYFRIEND, JUST BECAUSE YOU **PROMISED** YOU'D HELP ME STUDY FOR THIS TEST WHICH I WILL NOW, NO DOUBT, FAIL — YOU SHOULDN'T FEEL **BAD**.
AMEND
FINE. I FEEL HORRIBLE. WRETCHED. SCUM-LIKE.
KEEP GOING...

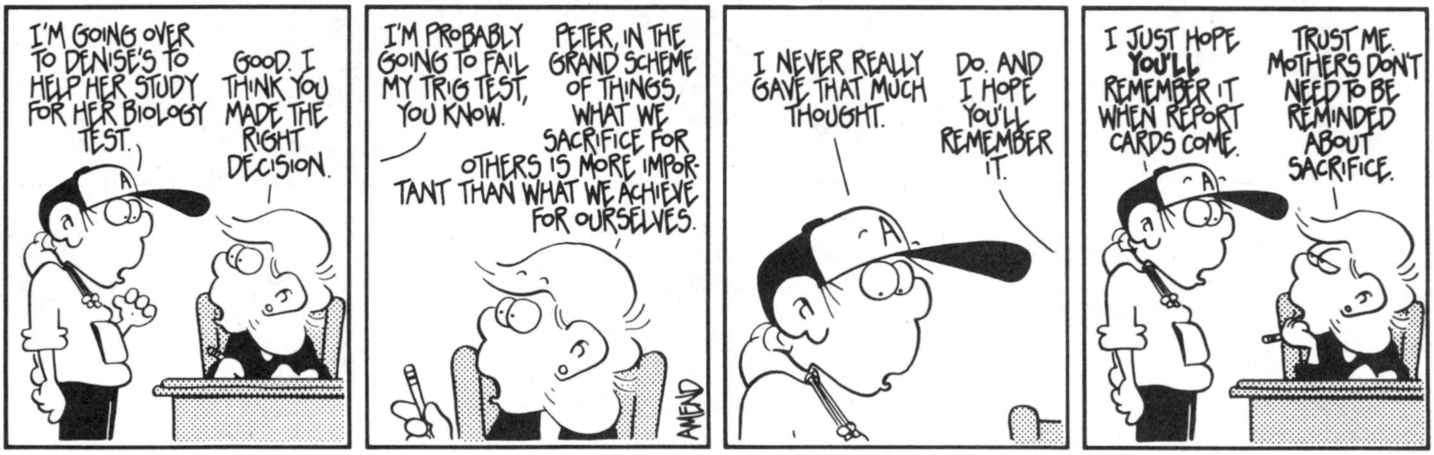
I'M GOING OVER TO DENISE'S TO HELP HER STUDY FOR HER BIOLOGY TEST.
GOOD. I THINK YOU MADE THE RIGHT DECISION.
I'M PROBABLY GOING TO FAIL MY TRIG TEST, YOU KNOW.
PETER, IN THE GRAND SCHEME OF THINGS, WHAT WE SACRIFICE FOR OTHERS IS MORE IMPORTANT THAN WHAT WE ACHIEVE FOR OURSELVES.
AMEND
I NEVER REALLY GAVE THAT MUCH THOUGHT.
DO. AND I HOPE YOU'LL REMEMBER IT.
I JUST HOPE **YOU'LL** REMEMBER IT WHEN REPORT CARDS COME.
TRUST ME. MOTHERS DON'T NEED TO BE REMINDED ABOUT SACRIFICE.

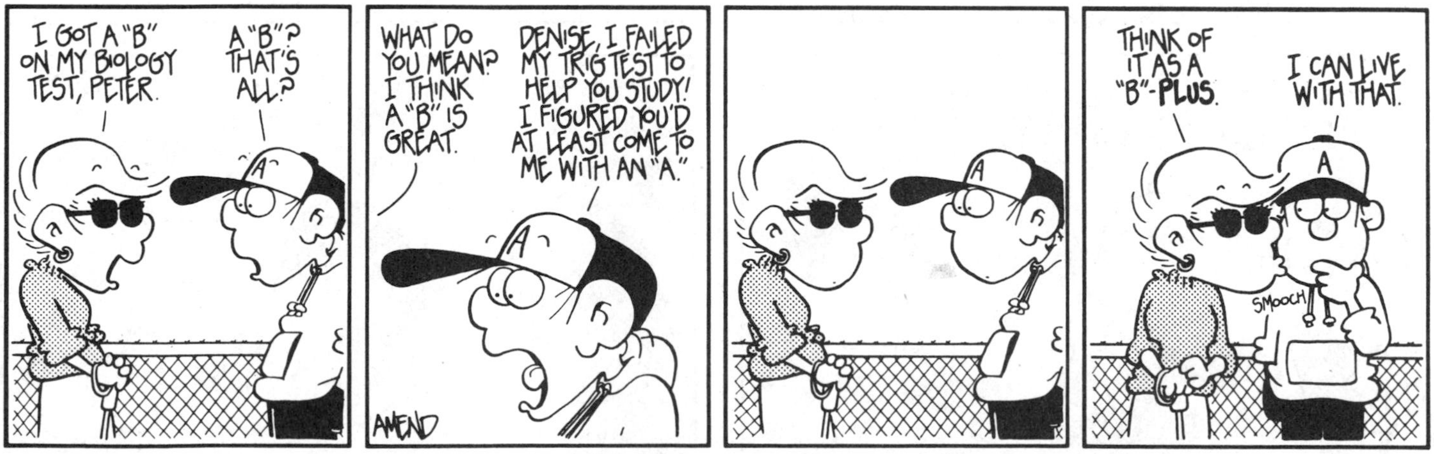
I GOT A "B" ON MY BIOLOGY TEST, PETER.
A "B"? THAT'S ALL?
WHAT DO YOU MEAN? I THINK A "B" IS GREAT.
DENISE, I FAILED MY TRIG TEST TO HELP YOU STUDY! I FIGURED YOU'D AT LEAST COME TO ME WITH AN "A."
AMEND
THINK OF IT AS A "B"-**PLUS**.
I CAN LIVE WITH THAT.
SMOOCH

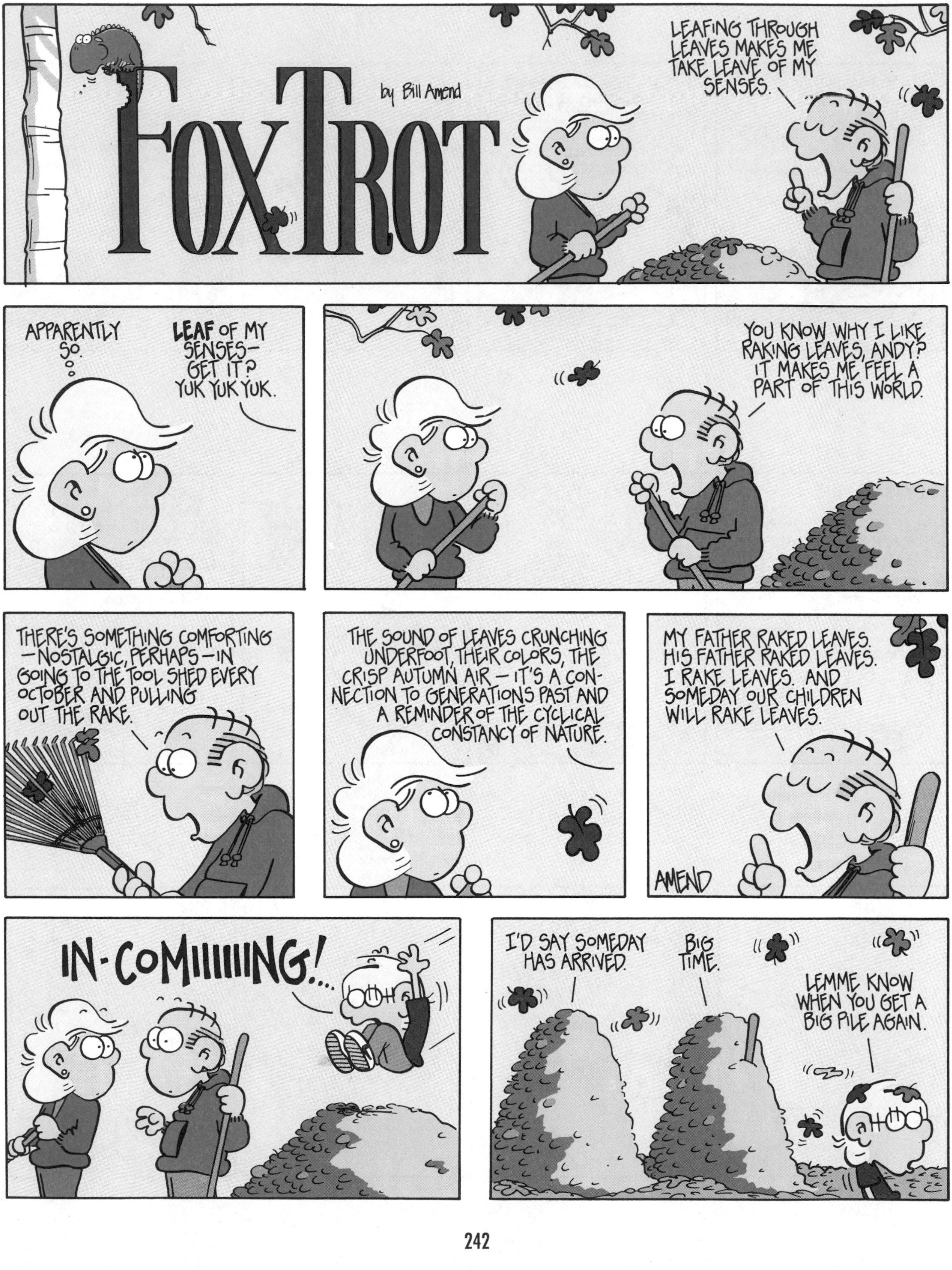
FoxTrot
by Bill Amend
LEAFING THROUGH LEAVES MAKES ME TAKE LEAVE OF MY SENSES.
APPARENTLY SO.
LEAF OF MY SENSES— GET IT? YUK YUK YUK.
YOU KNOW WHY I LIKE RAKING LEAVES, ANDY? IT MAKES ME FEEL A PART OF THIS WORLD.
THERE'S SOMETHING COMFORTING —NOSTALGIC, PERHAPS—IN GOING TO THE TOOL SHED EVERY OCTOBER AND PULLING OUT THE RAKE.
THE SOUND OF LEAVES CRUNCHING UNDERFOOT, THEIR COLORS, THE CRISP AUTUMN AIR — IT'S A CONNECTION TO GENERATIONS PAST AND A REMINDER OF THE CYCLICAL CONSTANCY OF NATURE.
MY FATHER RAKED LEAVES. HIS FATHER RAKED LEAVES. I RAKE LEAVES. AND SOMEDAY OUR CHILDREN WILL RAKE LEAVES.
AMEND
IN-COMIIIIIING!....
I'D SAY SOMEDAY HAS ARRIVED.
BIG TIME.
LEMME KNOW WHEN YOU GET A BIG PILE AGAIN.

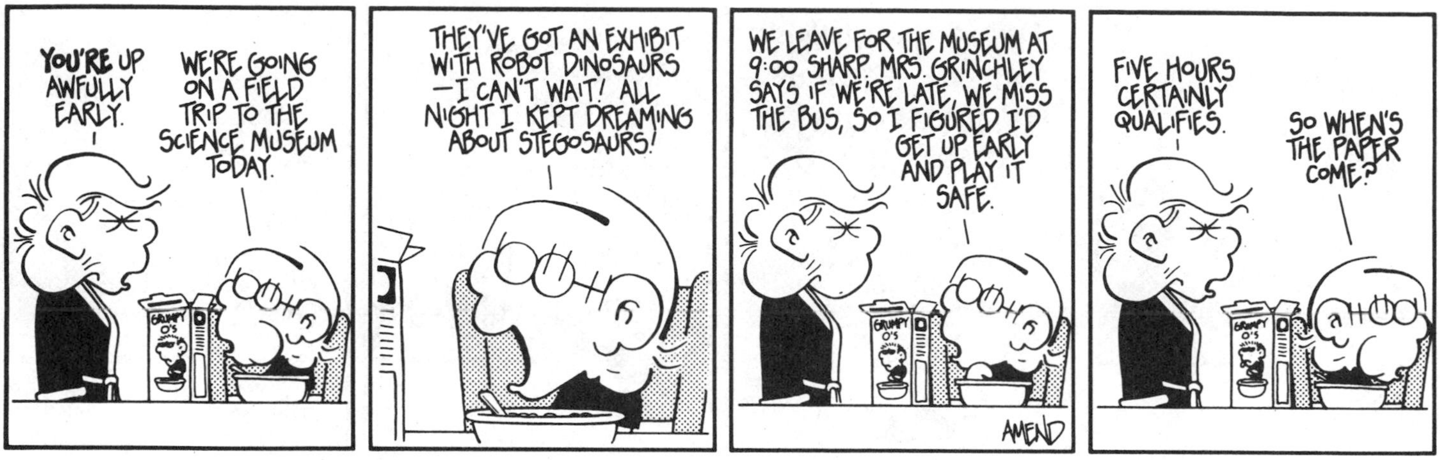
YOU'RE UP AWFULLY EARLY.
WE'RE GOING ON A FIELD TRIP TO THE SCIENCE MUSEUM TODAY.
THEY'VE GOT AN EXHIBIT WITH ROBOT DINOSAURS —I CAN'T WAIT! ALL NIGHT I KEPT DREAMING ABOUT STEGOSAURS!
WE LEAVE FOR THE MUSEUM AT 9:00 SHARP. MRS. GRINCHLEY SAYS IF WE'RE LATE, WE MISS THE BUS, SO I FIGURED I'D GET UP EARLY AND PLAY IT SAFE.
FIVE HOURS CERTAINLY QUALIFIES.
SO WHEN'S THE PAPER COME?
GRUMPY O'S
AMEND

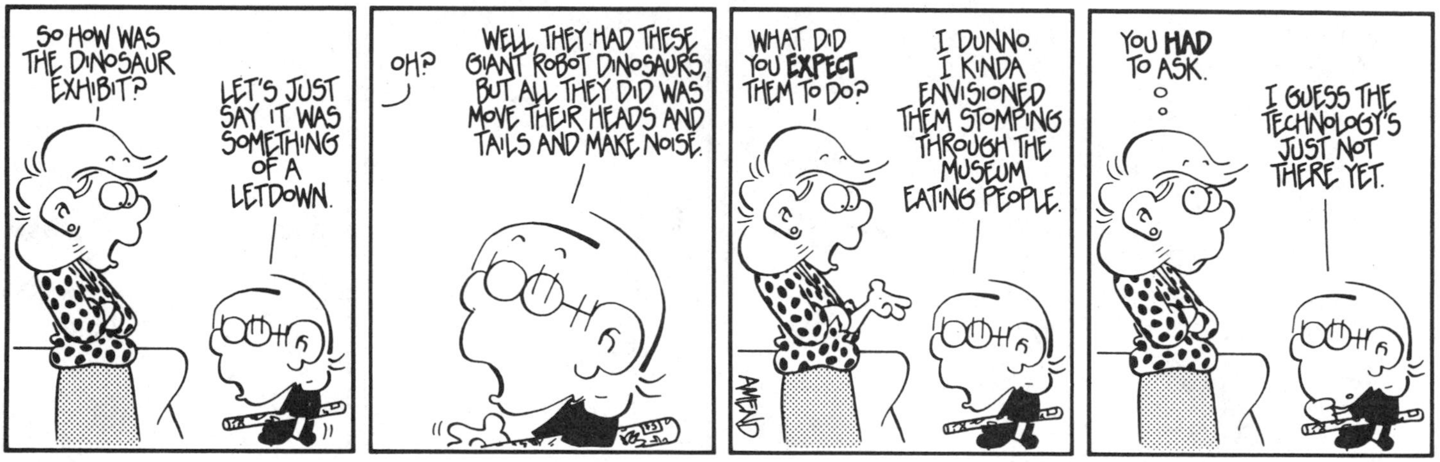
SO HOW WAS THE DINOSAUR EXHIBIT?
LET'S JUST SAY IT WAS SOMETHING OF A LETDOWN.
OH?
WELL, THEY HAD THESE GIANT ROBOT DINOSAURS, BUT ALL THEY DID WAS MOVE THEIR HEADS AND TAILS AND MAKE NOISE.
WHAT DID YOU EXPECT THEM TO DO?
I DUNNO. I KINDA ENVISIONED THEM STOMPING THROUGH THE MUSEUM EATING PEOPLE.
YOU HAD TO ASK.
I GUESS THE TECHNOLOGY'S JUST NOT THERE YET.
AMEND

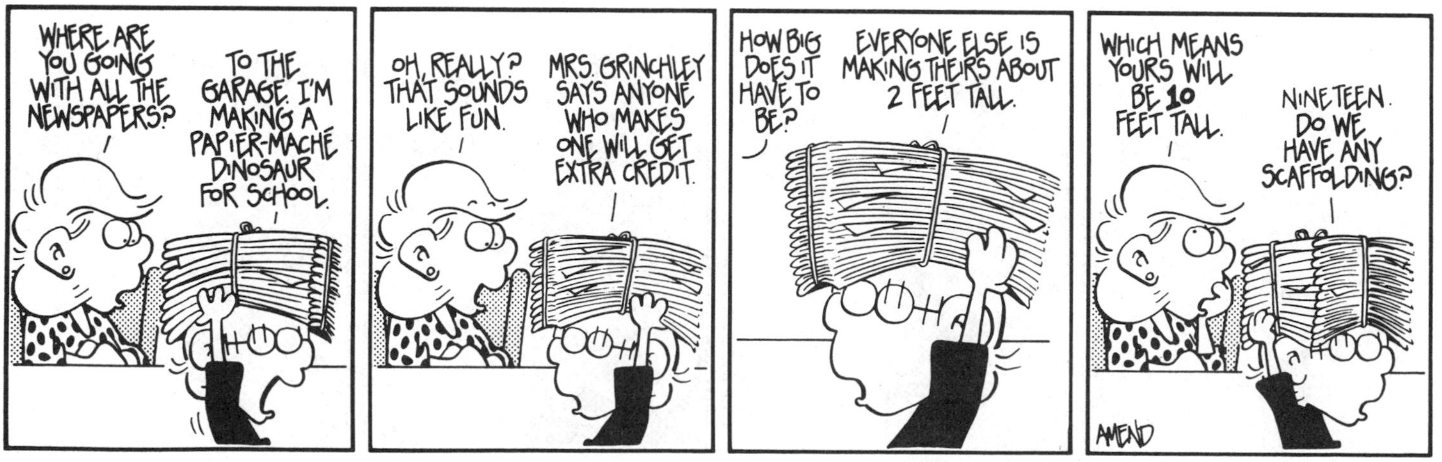
WHERE ARE YOU GOING WITH ALL THE NEWSPAPERS?
TO THE GARAGE. I'M MAKING A PAPIER-MACHE DINOSAUR FOR SCHOOL.
OH, REALLY? THAT SOUNDS LIKE FUN.
MRS. GRINCHLEY SAYS ANYONE WHO MAKES ONE WILL GET EXTRA CREDIT.
HOW BIG DOES IT HAVE TO BE?
EVERYONE ELSE IS MAKING THEIRS ABOUT 2 FEET TALL.
WHICH MEANS YOURS WILL BE 10 FEET TALL.
NINETEEN. DO WE HAVE ANY SCAFFOLDING?
AMEND

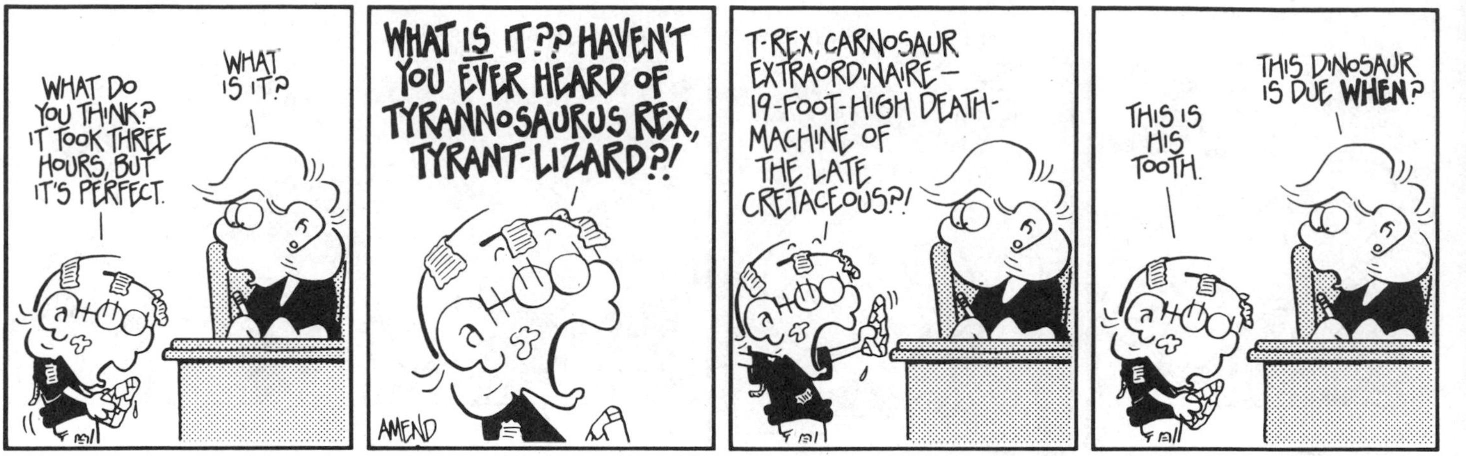
WHAT DO YOU THINK? IT TOOK THREE HOURS, BUT IT'S PERFECT.
WHAT IS IT?
WHAT IS IT?? HAVEN'T YOU EVER HEARD OF TYRANNOSAURUS REX, TYRANT-LIZARD?!
AMEND
T-REX, CARNOSAUR EXTRAORDINAIRE — 19-FOOT-HIGH DEATH-MACHINE OF THE LATE CRETACEOUS?!
THIS IS HIS TOOTH.
THIS DINOSAUR IS DUE **WHEN**?

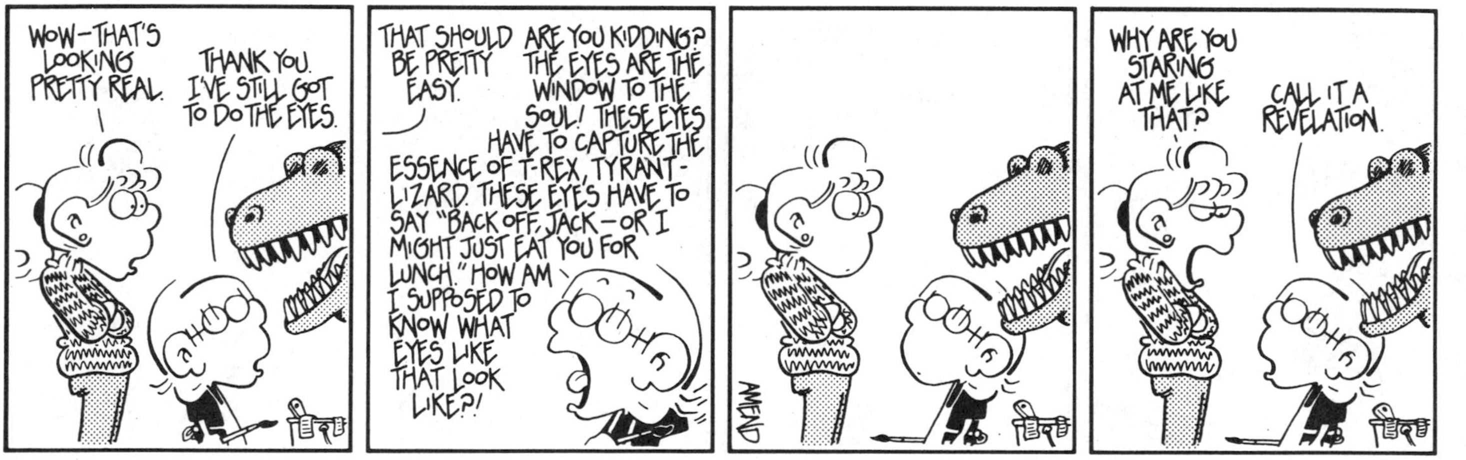
WOW—THAT'S LOOKING PRETTY REAL.
THANK YOU. I'VE STILL GOT TO DO THE EYES.
THAT SHOULD BE PRETTY EASY.
ARE YOU KIDDING? THE EYES ARE THE WINDOW TO THE SOUL! THESE EYES HAVE TO CAPTURE THE ESSENCE OF T-REX, TYRANT-LIZARD. THESE EYES HAVE TO SAY "BACK OFF, JACK—OR I MIGHT JUST EAT YOU FOR LUNCH." HOW AM I SUPPOSED TO KNOW WHAT EYES LIKE THAT LOOK LIKE?!
AMEND
WHY ARE YOU STARING AT ME LIKE THAT?
CALL IT A REVELATION.

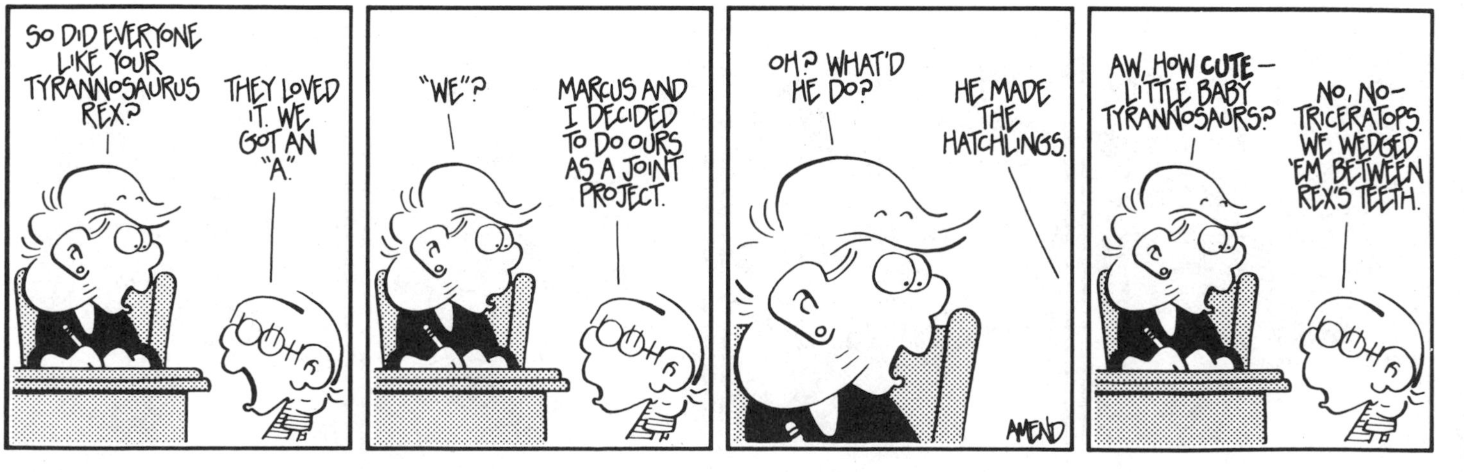
SO DID EVERYONE LIKE YOUR TYRANNOSAURUS REX?
THEY LOVED IT. WE GOT AN "A."
"WE"?
MARCUS AND I DECIDED TO DO OURS AS A JOINT PROJECT.
OH? WHAT'D HE DO?
HE MADE THE HATCHLINGS.
AMEND
AW, HOW **CUTE** — LITTLE BABY TYRANNOSAURS?
NO, NO—TRICERATOPS. WE WEDGED 'EM BETWEEN REX'S TEETH.

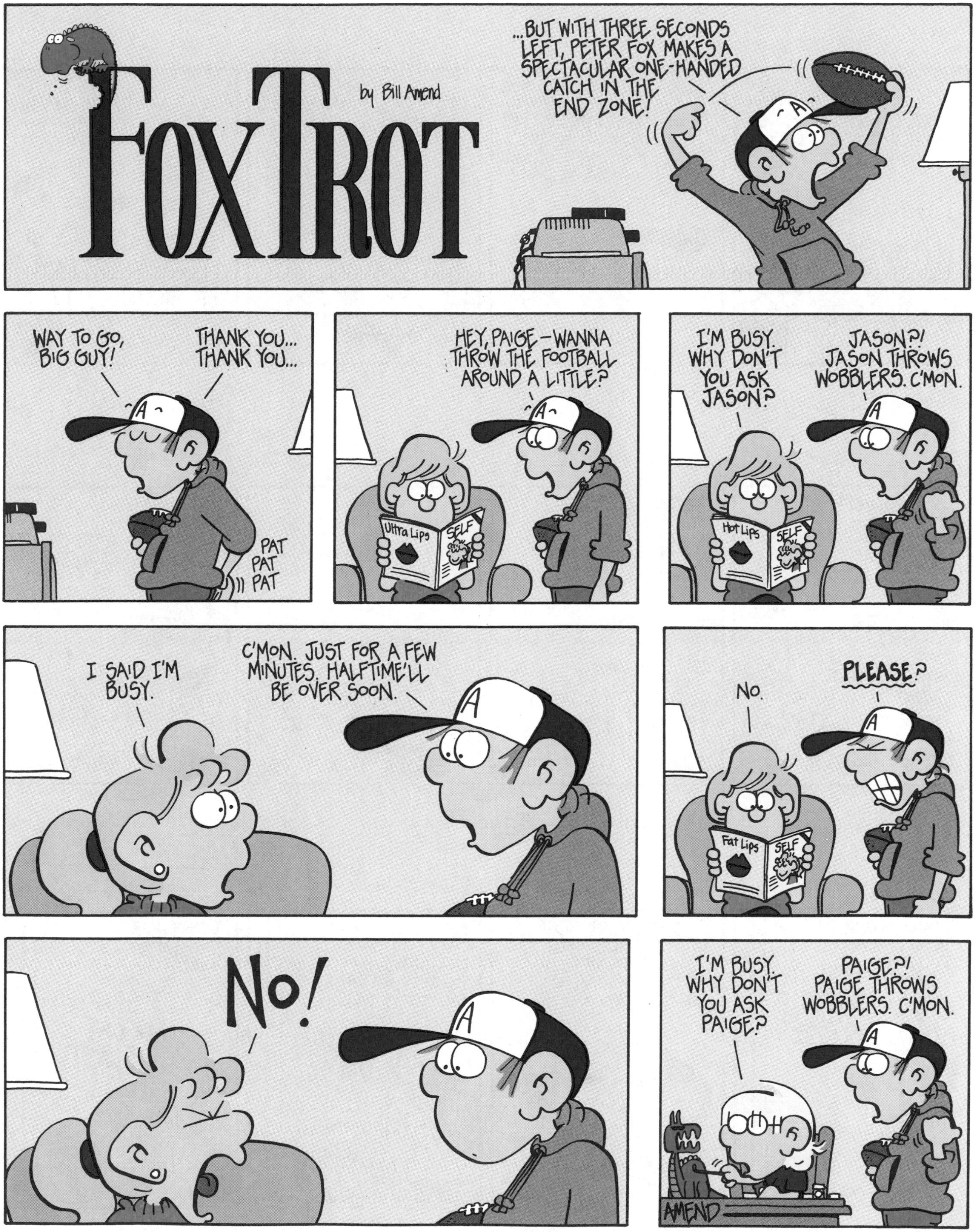
FoxTrot
by Bill Amend
...BUT WITH THREE SECONDS LEFT, PETER FOX MAKES A SPECTACULAR ONE-HANDED CATCH IN THE END ZONE!
WAY TO GO, BIG GUY!
THANK YOU... THANK YOU...
PAT PAT PAT
HEY, PAIGE—WANNA THROW THE FOOTBALL AROUND A LITTLE?
Ultra Lips
SELF
I'M BUSY. WHY DON'T YOU ASK JASON?
JASON?! JASON THROWS WOBBLERS. C'MON.
Hot Lips
SELF
I SAID I'M BUSY.
C'MON. JUST FOR A FEW MINUTES. HALFTIME'LL BE OVER SOON.
NO.
PLEASE?
Fat Lips
SELF
NO!
I'M BUSY. WHY DON'T YOU ASK PAIGE?
PAIGE?! PAIGE THROWS WOBBLERS. C'MON.
AMEND

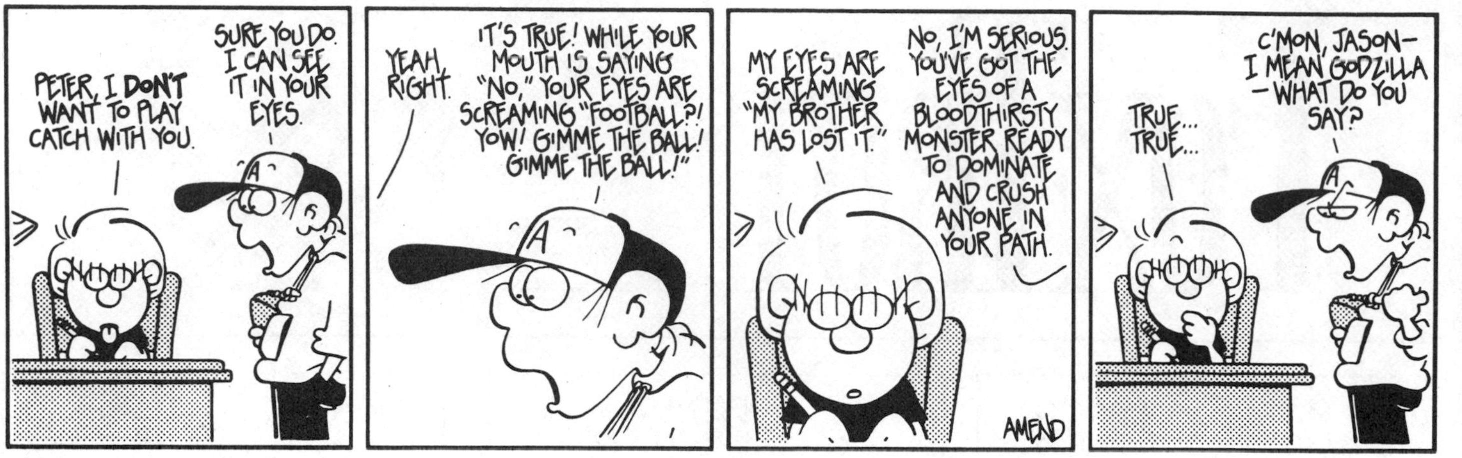
PETER, I DON'T WANT TO PLAY CATCH WITH YOU.
SURE YOU DO. I CAN SEE IT IN YOUR EYES.
YEAH, RIGHT.
IT'S TRUE! WHILE YOUR MOUTH IS SAYING "NO," YOUR EYES ARE SCREAMING "FOOTBALL?! YOW! GIMME THE BALL! GIMME THE BALL!"
MY EYES ARE SCREAMING "MY BROTHER HAS LOST IT."
NO, I'M SERIOUS. YOU'VE GOT THE EYES OF A BLOODTHIRSTY MONSTER READY TO DOMINATE AND CRUSH ANYONE IN YOUR PATH.
AMEND
TRUE... TRUE...
C'MON, JASON– I MEAN GODZILLA –WHAT DO YOU SAY?

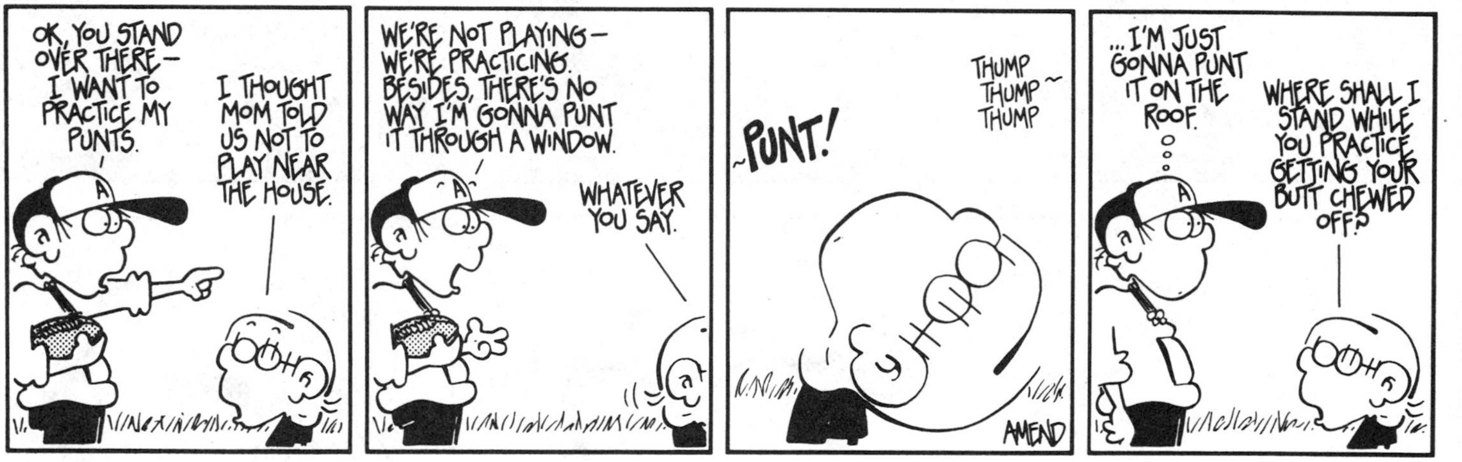
OK, YOU STAND OVER THERE– I WANT TO PRACTICE MY PUNTS.
I THOUGHT MOM TOLD US NOT TO PLAY NEAR THE HOUSE.
WE'RE NOT PLAYING– WE'RE PRACTICING. BESIDES, THERE'S NO WAY I'M GONNA PUNT IT THROUGH A WINDOW.
WHATEVER YOU SAY.
PUNT!
THUMP THUMP THUMP
AMEND
...I'M JUST GONNA PUNT IT ON THE ROOF.
WHERE SHALL I STAND WHILE YOU PRACTICE GETTING YOUR BUTT CHEWED OFF?

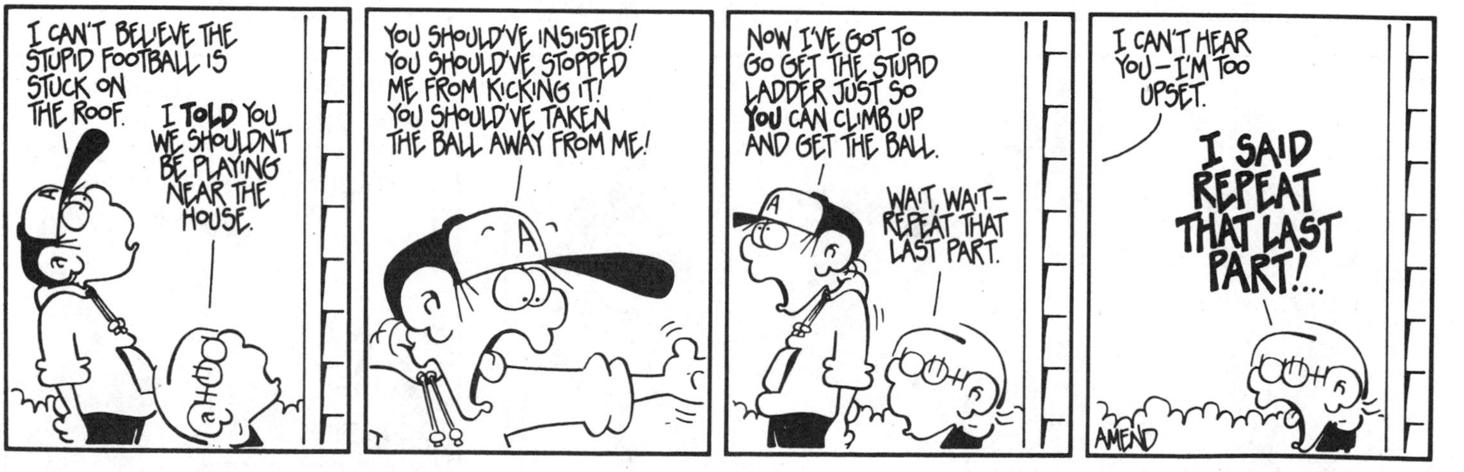
I CAN'T BELIEVE THE STUPID FOOTBALL IS STUCK ON THE ROOF.
I TOLD YOU WE SHOULDN'T BE PLAYING NEAR THE HOUSE.
YOU SHOULD'VE INSISTED! YOU SHOULD'VE STOPPED ME FROM KICKING IT! YOU SHOULD'VE TAKEN THE BALL AWAY FROM ME!
NOW I'VE GOT TO GO GET THE STUPID LADDER JUST SO YOU CAN CLIMB UP AND GET THE BALL.
WAIT, WAIT– REPEAT THAT LAST PART.
I CAN'T HEAR YOU–I'M TOO UPSET.
I SAID REPEAT THAT LAST PART!...
AMEND

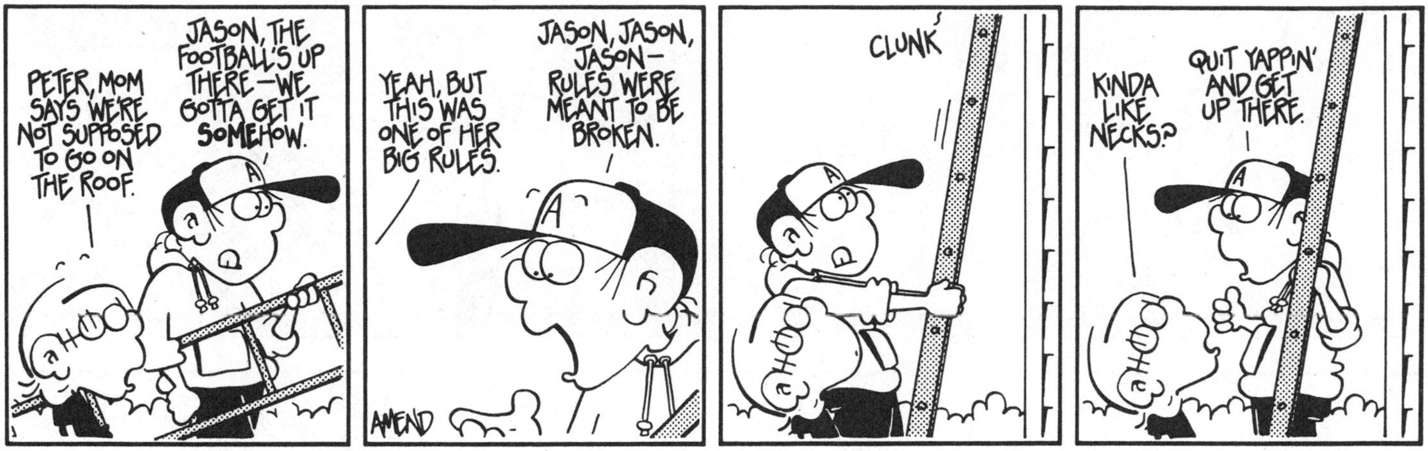
PETER, MOM SAYS WE'RE NOT SUPPOSED TO GO ON THE ROOF.
JASON, THE FOOTBALL'S UP THERE—WE GOTTA GET IT **SOMEHOW**.
YEAH, BUT THIS WAS ONE OF HER BIG RULES.
JASON, JASON, JASON—RULES WERE MEANT TO BE BROKEN.
AMEND
CLUNK
KINDA LIKE NECKS?
QUIT YAPPIN' AND GET UP THERE.

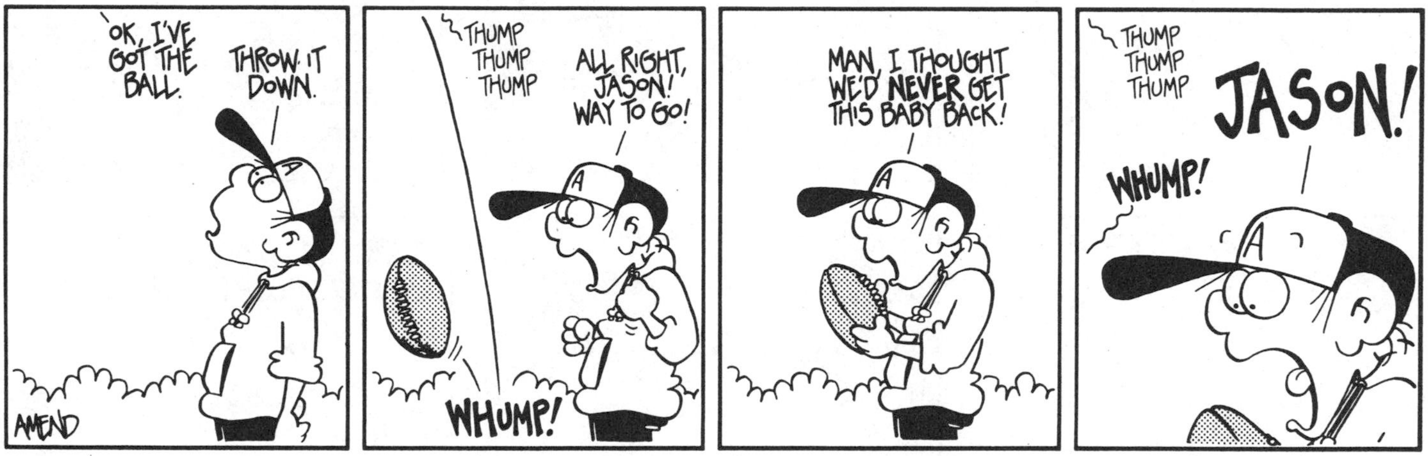
OK, I'VE GOT THE BALL.
THROW IT DOWN.
AMEND
THUMP THUMP THUMP
ALL RIGHT, JASON! WAY TO GO!
WHUMP!
MAN, I THOUGHT WE'D **NEVER** GET THIS BABY BACK!
THUMP THUMP THUMP
WHUMP!
JASON!

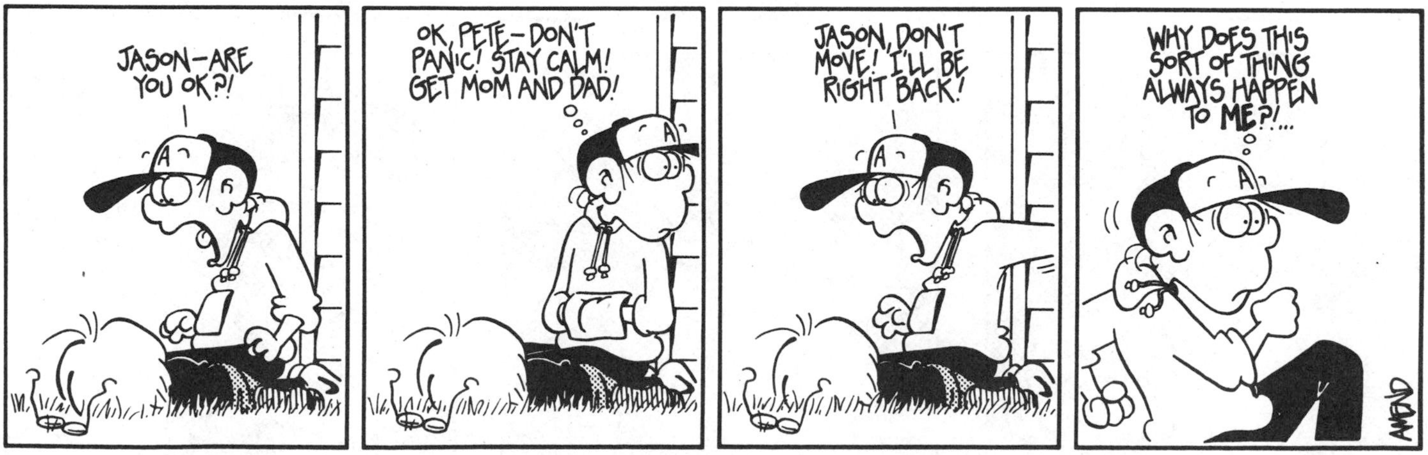
JASON—ARE YOU OK?!
OK, PETE—DON'T PANIC! STAY CALM! GET MOM AND DAD!
JASON, DON'T MOVE! I'LL BE RIGHT BACK!
WHY DOES THIS SORT OF THING ALWAYS HAPPEN TO **ME**?!...
AMEND

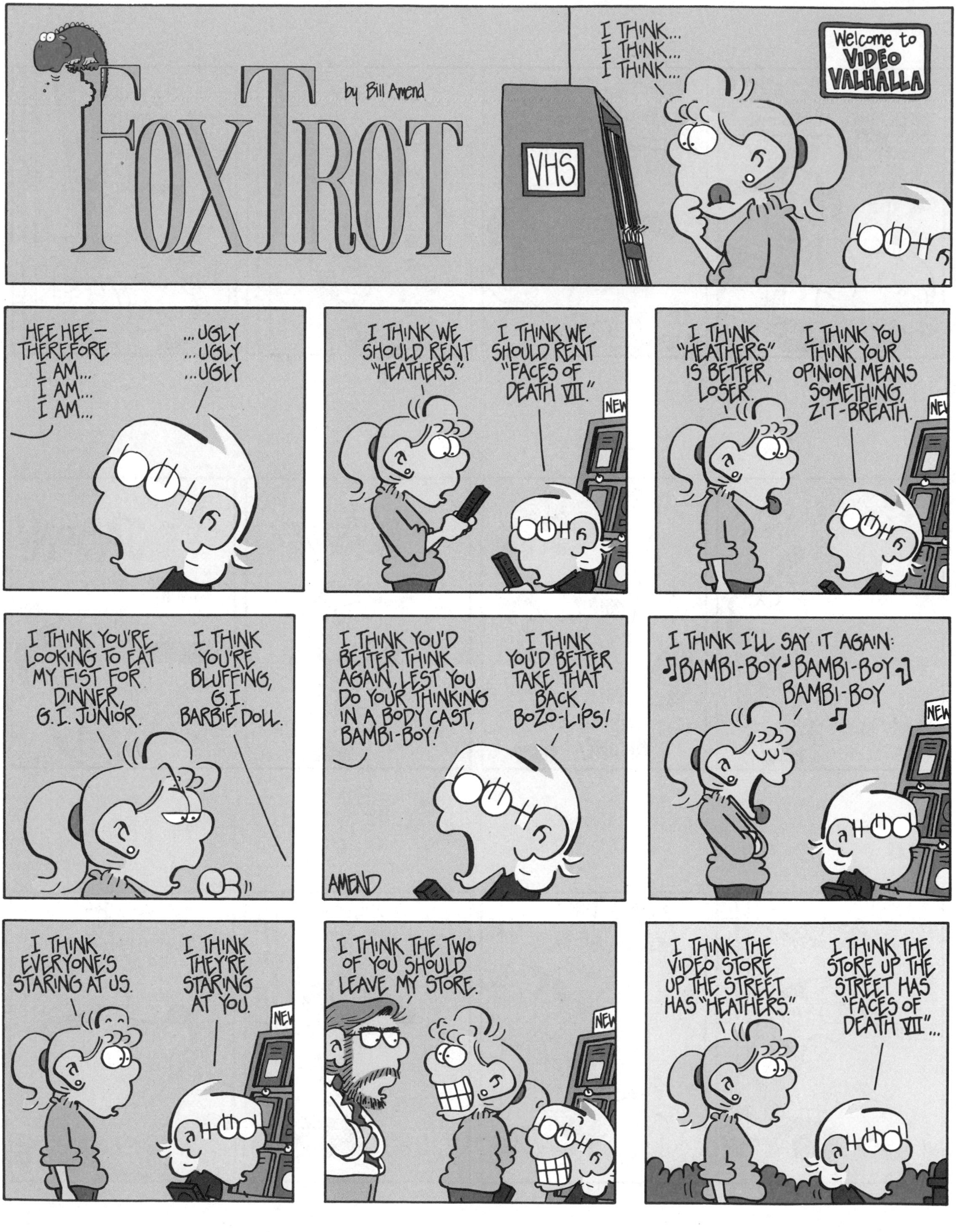
FoxTrot
by Bill Amend
I THINK...
I THINK...
I THINK...
Welcome to VIDEO VALHALLA
VHS
HEE HEE—
THEREFORE
I AM...
I AM...
I AM...
...UGLY
...UGLY
...UGLY
I THINK WE SHOULD RENT "HEATHERS."
I THINK WE SHOULD RENT "FACES OF DEATH VII."
NEW
I THINK "HEATHERS" IS BETTER, LOSER.
I THINK YOU THINK YOUR OPINION MEANS SOMETHING, ZIT-BREATH.
I THINK YOU'RE LOOKING TO EAT MY FIST FOR DINNER, G.I. JUNIOR.
I THINK YOU'RE BLUFFING, G.I. BARBIE DOLL.
I THINK YOU'D BETTER THINK AGAIN, LEST YOU DO YOUR THINKING IN A BODY CAST, BAMBI-BOY!
I THINK YOU'D BETTER TAKE THAT BACK, BOZO-LIPS!
AMEND
I THINK I'LL SAY IT AGAIN:
♫BAMBI-BOY♩BAMBI-BOY♫
BAMBI-BOY ♪
I THINK EVERYONE'S STARING AT US.
I THINK THEY'RE STARING AT YOU.
I THINK THE TWO OF YOU SHOULD LEAVE MY STORE.
I THINK THE VIDEO STORE UP THE STREET HAS "HEATHERS."
I THINK THE STORE UP THE STREET HAS "FACES OF DEATH VII"...

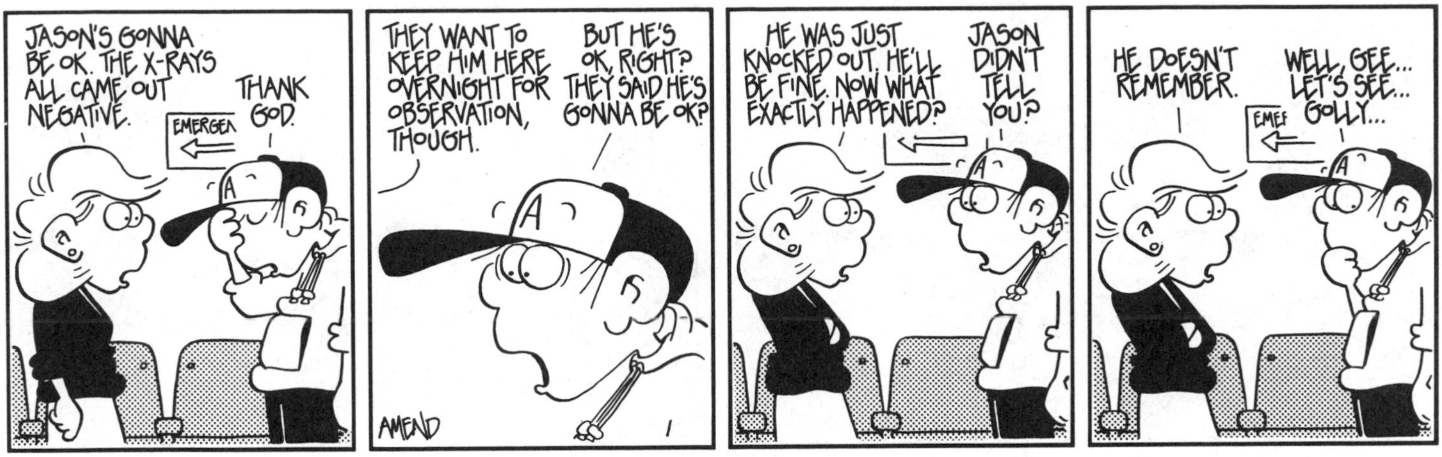
JASON'S GONNA BE OK. THE X-RAYS ALL CAME OUT NEGATIVE.
EMERGEN
THANK GOD.
THEY WANT TO KEEP HIM HERE OVERNIGHT FOR OBSERVATION, THOUGH.
BUT HE'S OK, RIGHT? THEY SAID HE'S GONNA BE OK?
AMEND
HE WAS JUST KNOCKED OUT. HE'LL BE FINE. NOW WHAT EXACTLY HAPPENED?
JASON DIDN'T TELL YOU?
HE DOESN'T REMEMBER.
EMEF
WELL, GEE... LET'S SEE... GOLLY...

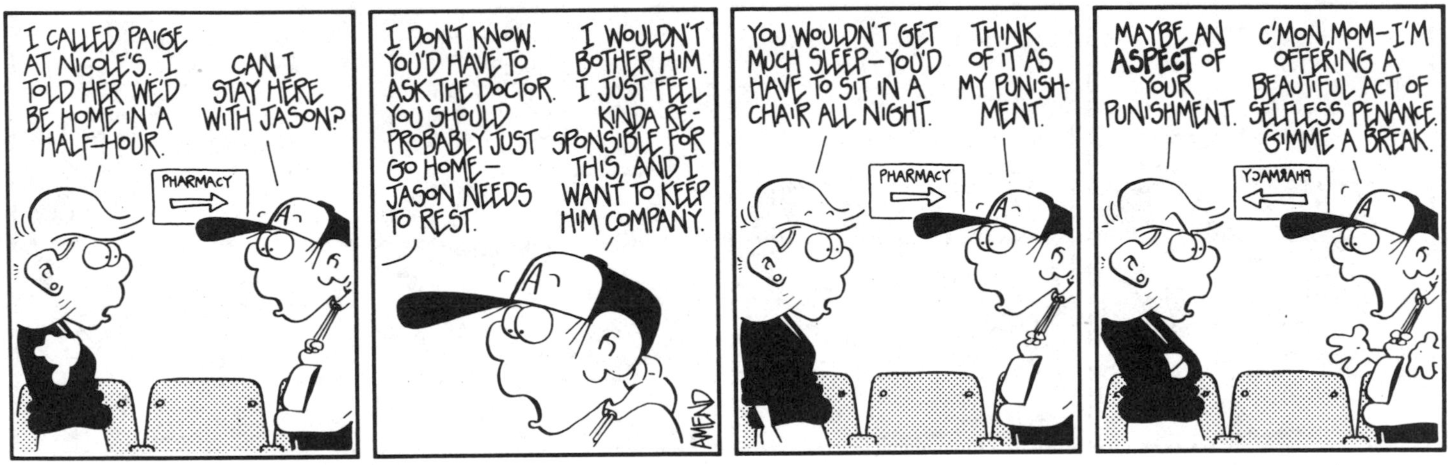
I CALLED PAIGE AT NICOLE'S. I TOLD HER WE'D BE HOME IN A HALF-HOUR.
PHARMACY
CAN I STAY HERE WITH JASON?
I DON'T KNOW. YOU'D HAVE TO ASK THE DOCTOR. YOU SHOULD PROBABLY JUST GO HOME— JASON NEEDS TO REST.
I WOULDN'T BOTHER HIM. I JUST FEEL KINDA RESPONSIBLE FOR THIS, AND I WANT TO KEEP HIM COMPANY.
AMEND
YOU WOULDN'T GET MUCH SLEEP—YOU'D HAVE TO SIT IN A CHAIR ALL NIGHT.
PHARMACY
THINK OF IT AS MY PUNISHMENT.
MAYBE AN **ASPECT** OF YOUR PUNISHMENT.
C'MON, MOM—I'M OFFERING A BEAUTIFUL ACT OF SELFLESS PENANCE. GIMME A BREAK.

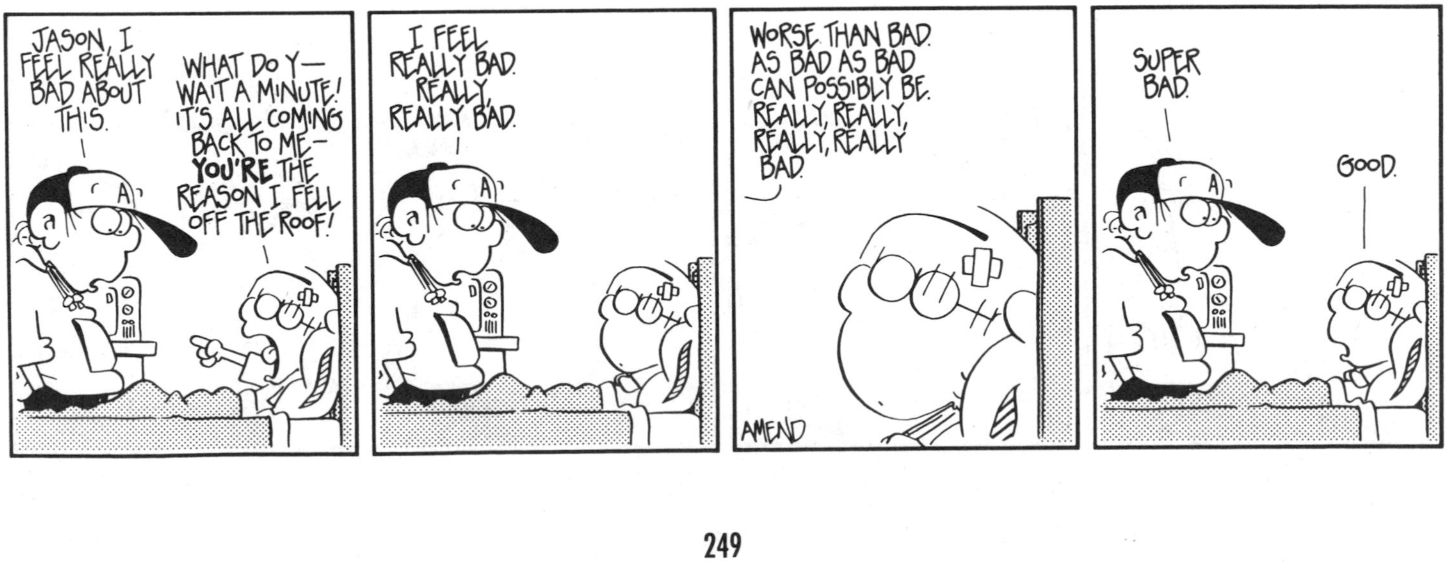
JASON, I FEEL REALLY BAD ABOUT THIS.
WHAT DO Y— WAIT A MINUTE! IT'S ALL COMING BACK TO ME— **YOU'RE** THE REASON I FELL OFF THE ROOF!
I FEEL REALLY BAD. REALLY, REALLY BAD.
WORSE THAN BAD. AS BAD AS BAD CAN POSSIBLY BE. REALLY, REALLY, REALLY, REALLY BAD.
AMEND
SUPER BAD.
GOOD.

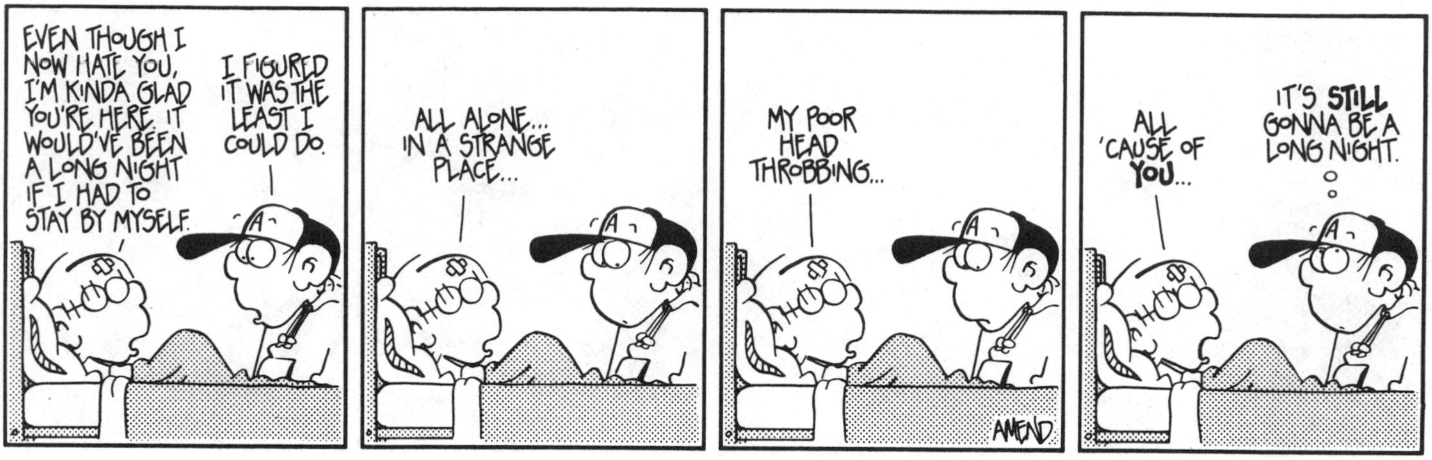
EVEN THOUGH I NOW HATE YOU, I'M KINDA GLAD YOU'RE HERE. IT WOULD'VE BEEN A LONG NIGHT IF I HAD TO STAY BY MYSELF.
I FIGURED IT WAS THE LEAST I COULD DO.
ALL ALONE... IN A STRANGE PLACE...
MY POOR HEAD THROBBING...
AMEND
ALL 'CAUSE OF YOU...
IT'S STILL GONNA BE A LONG NIGHT.

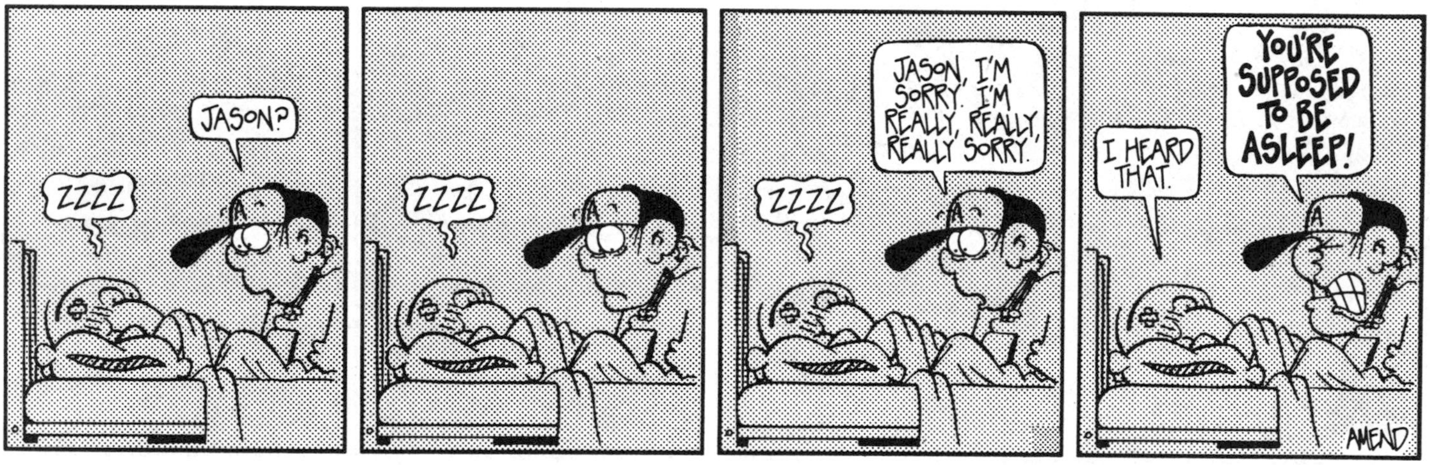
JASON?
ZZZZ
ZZZZ
JASON, I'M SORRY. I'M REALLY, REALLY, REALLY SORRY.
ZZZZ
I HEARD THAT.
YOU'RE SUPPOSED TO BE ASLEEP!
AMEND

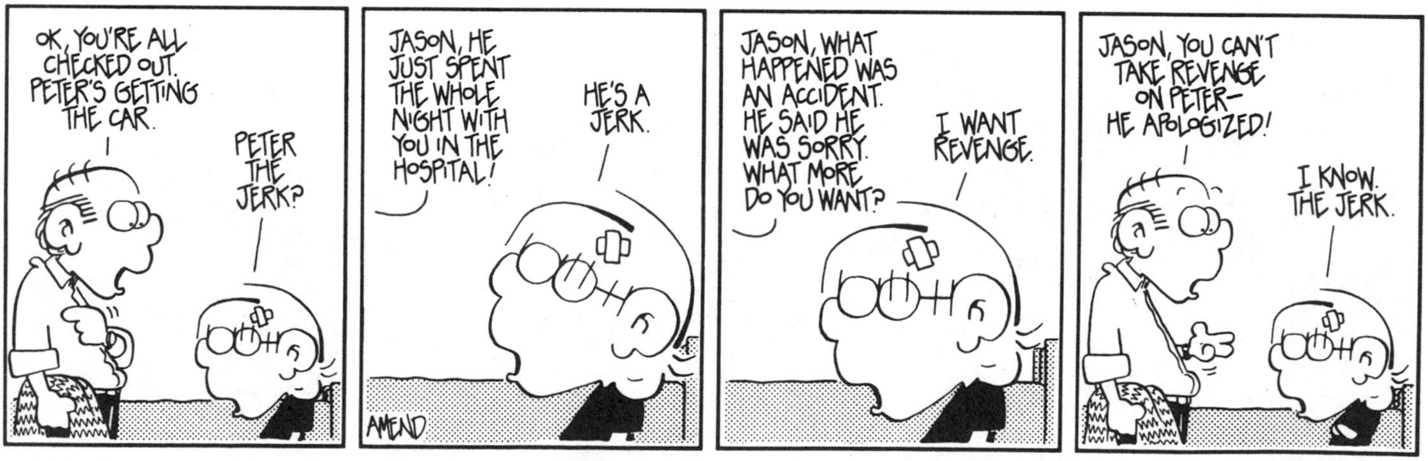
OK, YOU'RE ALL CHECKED OUT. PETER'S GETTING THE CAR.
PETER THE JERK?
JASON, HE JUST SPENT THE WHOLE NIGHT WITH YOU IN THE HOSPITAL!
HE'S A JERK.
AMEND
JASON, WHAT HAPPENED WAS AN ACCIDENT. HE SAID HE WAS SORRY. WHAT MORE DO YOU WANT?
I WANT REVENGE.
JASON, YOU CAN'T TAKE REVENGE ON PETER— HE APOLOGIZED!
I KNOW. THE JERK.

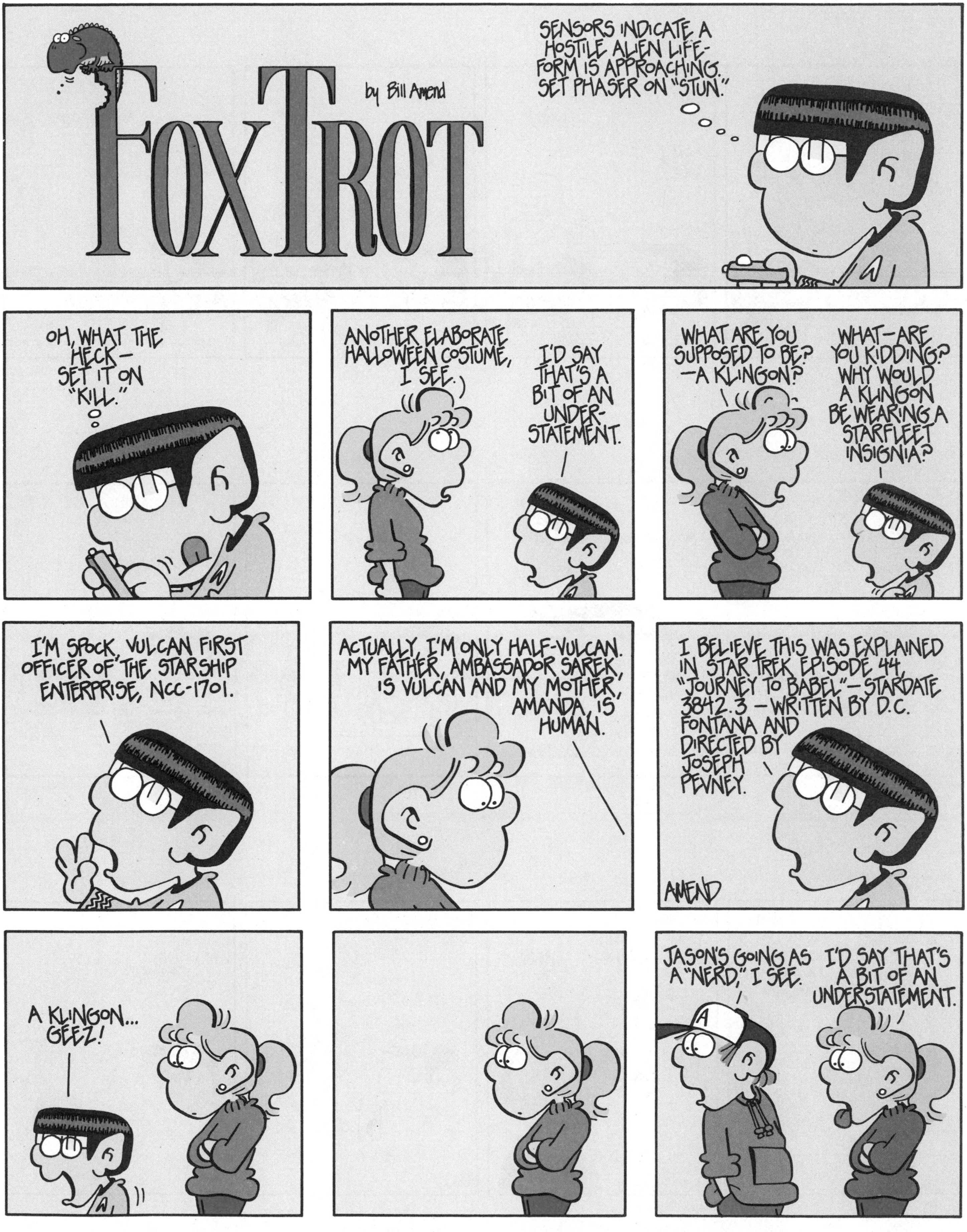
FoxTrot
by Bill Amend
SENSORS INDICATE A HOSTILE ALIEN LIFE-FORM IS APPROACHING. SET PHASER ON "STUN."
OH, WHAT THE HECK— SET IT ON "KILL."
ANOTHER ELABORATE HALLOWEEN COSTUME, I SEE.
I'D SAY THAT'S A BIT OF AN UNDER-STATEMENT.
WHAT ARE YOU SUPPOSED TO BE? —A KLINGON?
WHAT—ARE YOU KIDDING? WHY WOULD A KLINGON BE WEARING A STARFLEET INSIGNIA?
I'M SPOCK, VULCAN FIRST OFFICER OF THE STARSHIP ENTERPRISE, NCC-1701.
ACTUALLY, I'M ONLY HALF-VULCAN. MY FATHER, AMBASSADOR SAREK, IS VULCAN AND MY MOTHER, AMANDA, IS HUMAN.
I BELIEVE THIS WAS EXPLAINED IN STAR TREK EPISODE 44, "JOURNEY TO BABEL"—STARDATE 3842.3 — WRITTEN BY D.C. FONTANA AND DIRECTED BY JOSEPH PEVNEY.
AMEND
A KLINGON... GEEZ!
JASON'S GOING AS A "NERD," I SEE.
I'D SAY THAT'S A BIT OF AN UNDERSTATEMENT.

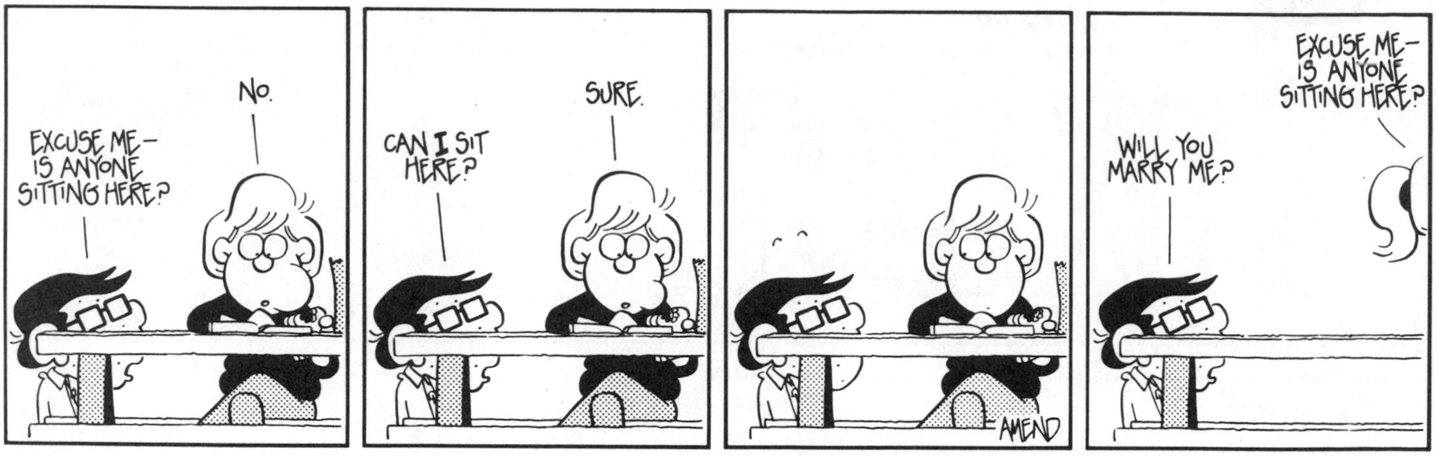
EXCUSE ME–
IS ANYONE
SITTING HERE?
NO.
CAN I SIT
HERE?
SURE.
WILL YOU
MARRY ME?
EXCUSE ME–
IS ANYONE
SITTING HERE?
AMEND

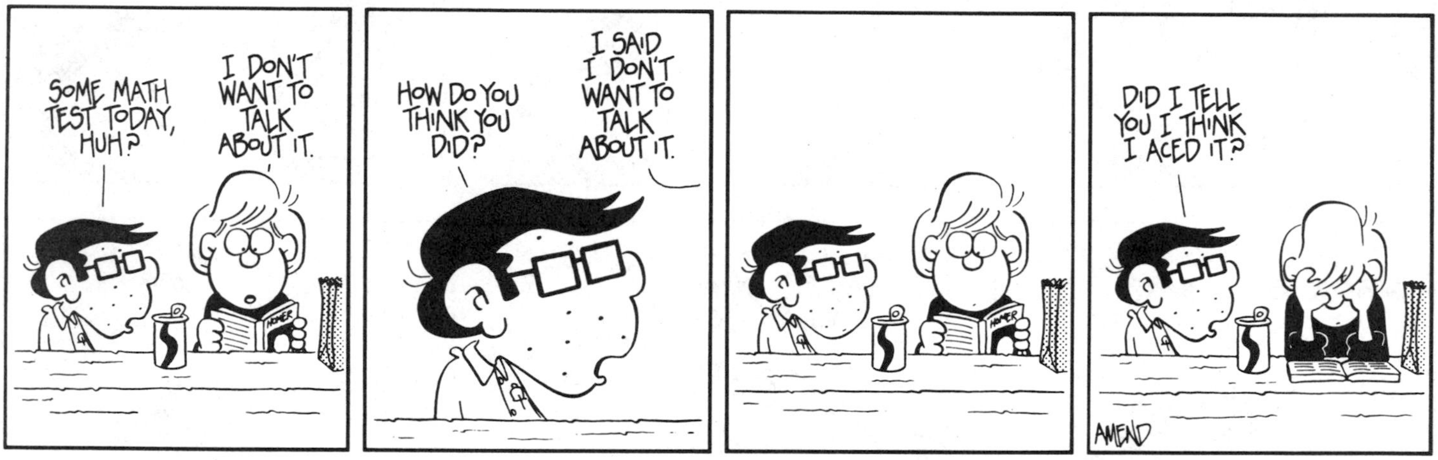
SOME MATH
TEST TODAY,
HUH?
I DON'T
WANT TO
TALK
ABOUT IT.
HOW DO YOU
THINK YOU
DID?
I SAID
I DON'T
WANT TO
TALK
ABOUT IT.
DID I TELL
YOU I THINK
I ACED IT?
AMEND

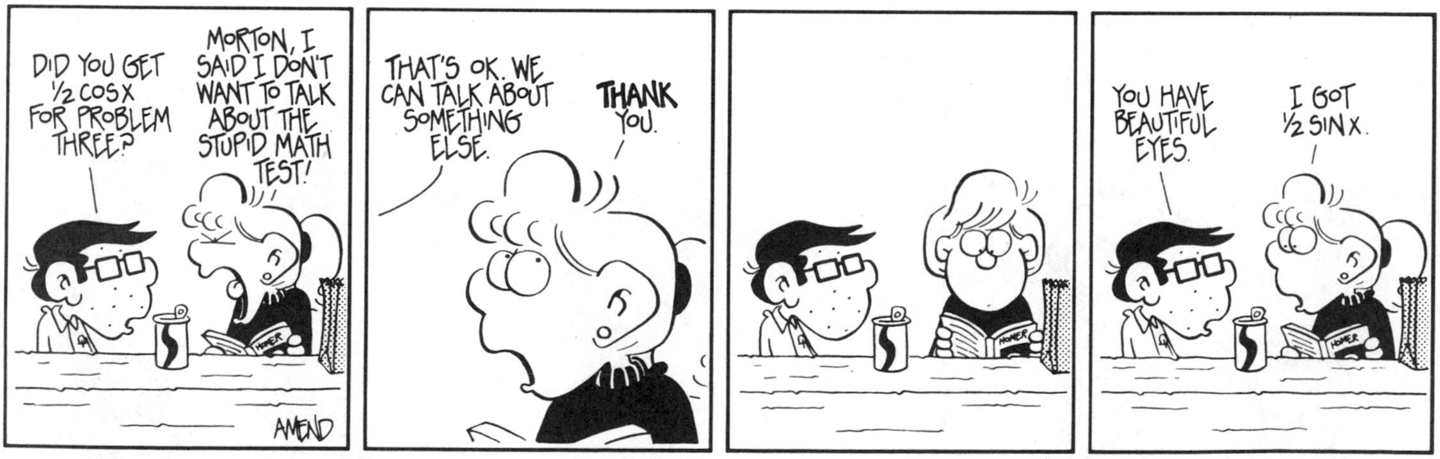
DID YOU GET
1/2 COS X
FOR PROBLEM
THREE?
MORTON, I
SAID I DON'T
WANT TO TALK
ABOUT THE
STUPID MATH
TEST!
AMEND
THAT'S OK. WE
CAN TALK ABOUT
SOMETHING
ELSE.
THANK
YOU.
YOU HAVE
BEAUTIFUL
EYES.
I GOT
1/2 SIN X.

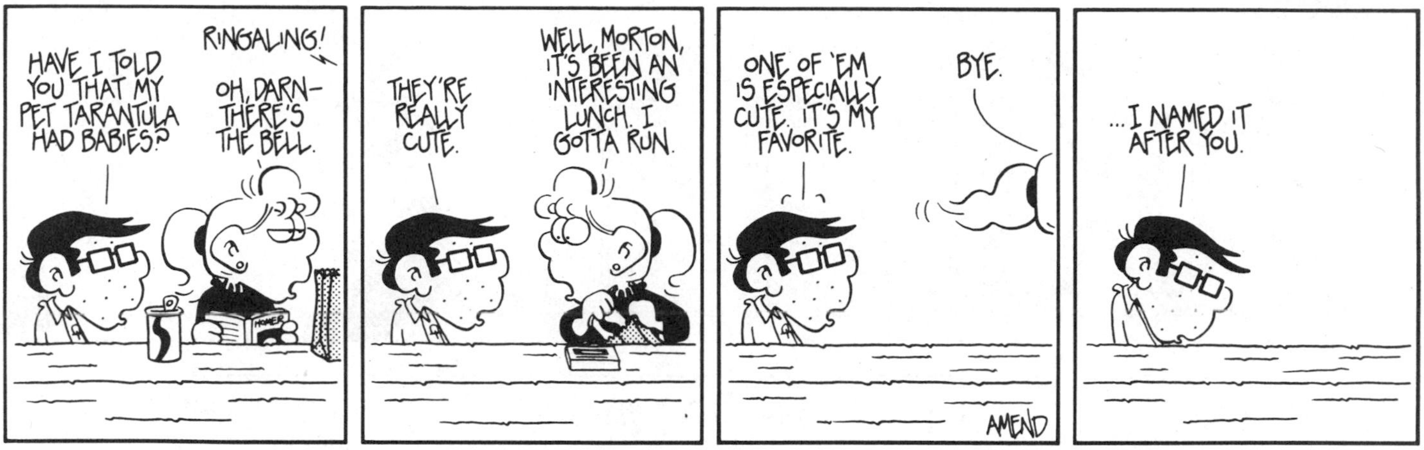
HAVE I TOLD YOU THAT MY PET TARANTULA HAD BABIES?
RINGALING!
OH, DARN- THERE'S THE BELL.
THEY'RE REALLY CUTE.
WELL, MORTON, IT'S BEEN AN INTERESTING LUNCH. I GOTTA RUN.
ONE OF 'EM IS ESPECIALLY CUTE. IT'S MY FAVORITE.
BYE.
AMEND
...I NAMED IT AFTER YOU.

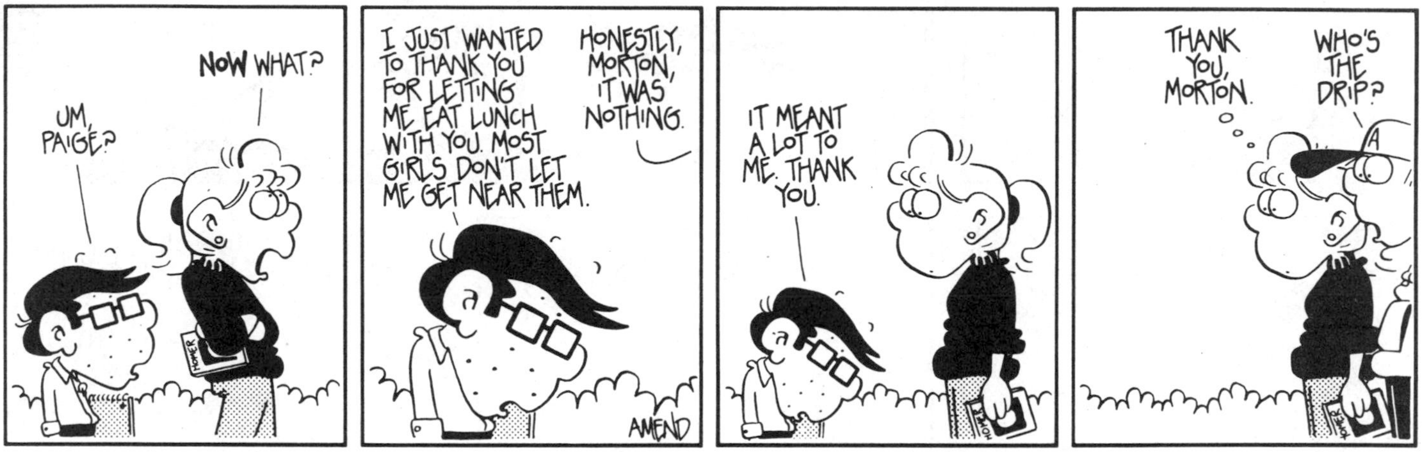
UM, PAIGE?
NOW WHAT?
I JUST WANTED TO THANK YOU FOR LETTING ME EAT LUNCH WITH YOU. MOST GIRLS DON'T LET ME GET NEAR THEM.
HONESTLY, MORTON, IT WAS NOTHING.
AMEND
IT MEANT A LOT TO ME. THANK YOU.
THANK YOU, MORTON.
WHO'S THE DRIP?

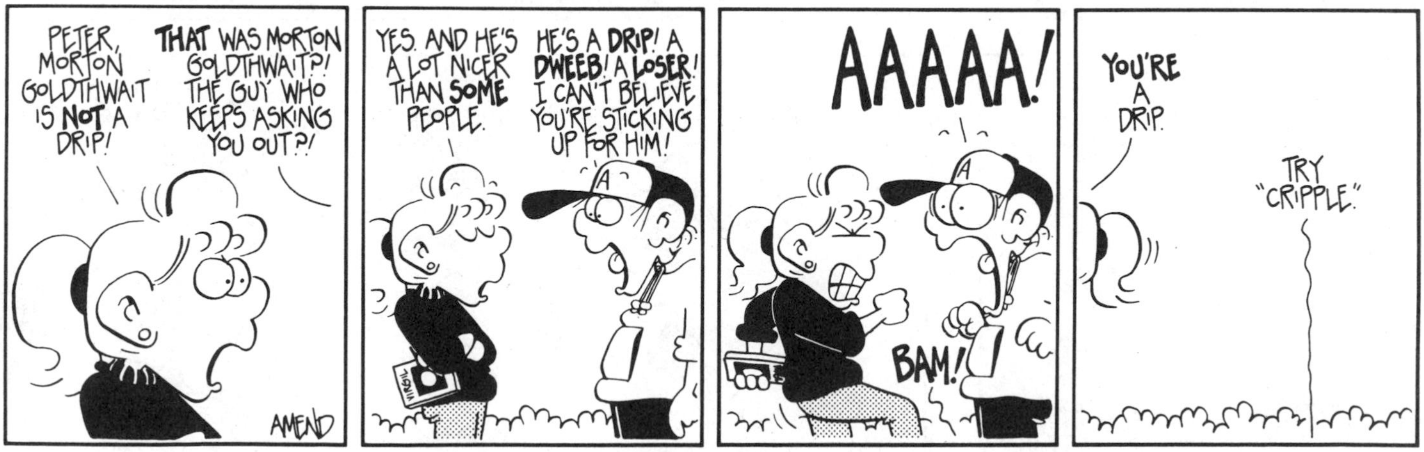
PETER, MORTON GOLDTHWAIT IS **NOT** A DRIP!
THAT WAS MORTON GOLDTHWAIT?! THE GUY WHO KEEPS ASKING YOU OUT?!
AMEND
YES. AND HE'S A LOT NICER THAN **SOME** PEOPLE.
HE'S A **DRIP**! A **DWEEB**! A **LOSER**! I CAN'T BELIEVE YOU'RE STICKING UP FOR HIM!
AAAAA!
BAM!
YOU'RE A DRIP.
TRY "CRIPPLE."

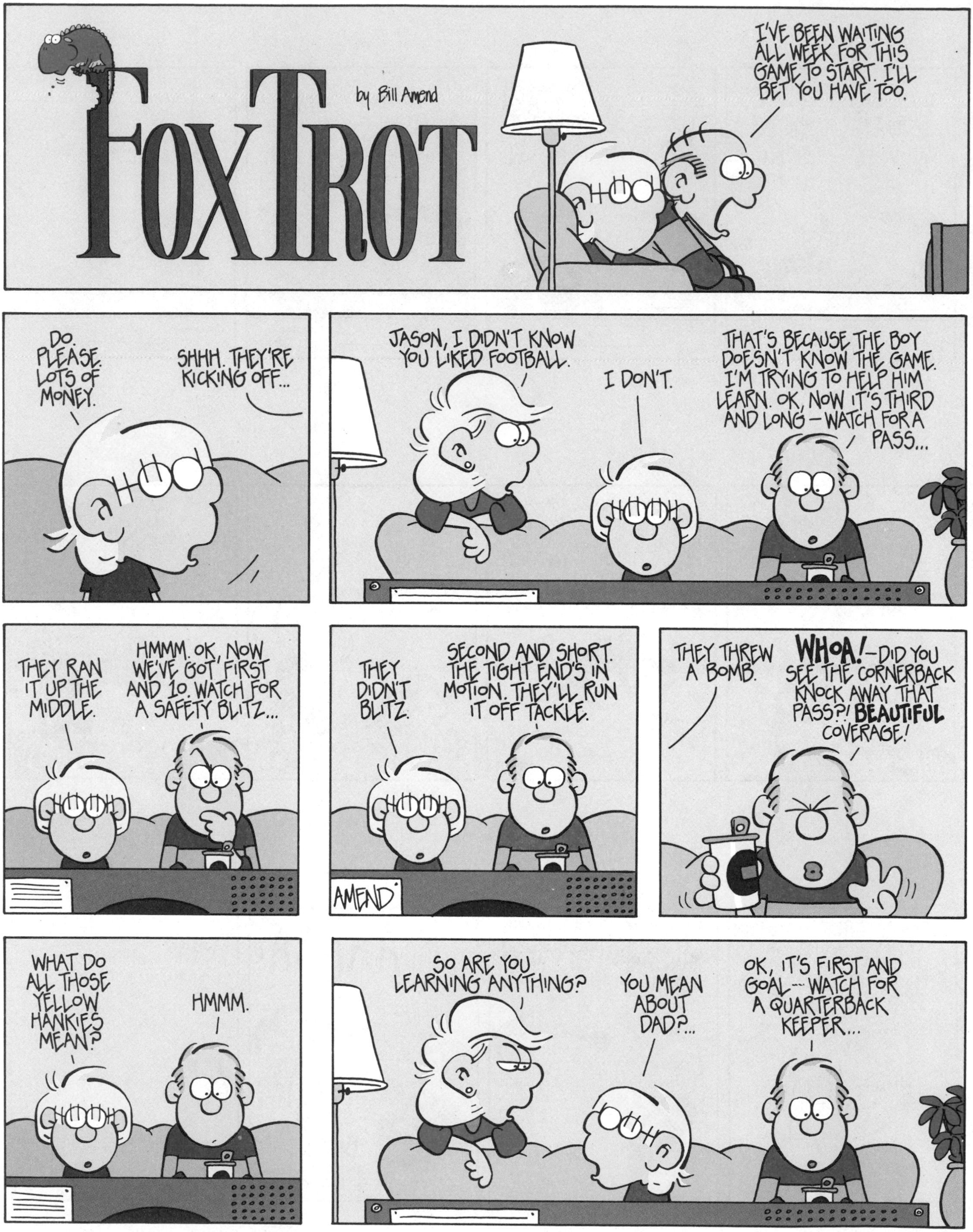
FoxTrot
by Bill Amend
I'VE BEEN WAITING ALL WEEK FOR THIS GAME TO START. I'LL BET YOU HAVE TOO.
DO. PLEASE. LOTS OF MONEY.
SHHH. THEY'RE KICKING OFF...
JASON, I DIDN'T KNOW YOU LIKED FOOTBALL.
I DON'T.
THAT'S BECAUSE THE BOY DOESN'T KNOW THE GAME. I'M TRYING TO HELP HIM LEARN. OK, NOW IT'S THIRD AND LONG – WATCH FOR A PASS...
THEY RAN IT UP THE MIDDLE.
HMMM. OK, NOW WE'VE GOT FIRST AND 10. WATCH FOR A SAFETY BLITZ...
THEY DIDN'T BLITZ.
SECOND AND SHORT. THE TIGHT END'S IN MOTION. THEY'LL RUN IT OFF TACKLE.
AMEND
THEY THREW A BOMB.
WHOA! – DID YOU SEE THE CORNERBACK KNOCK AWAY THAT PASS?! BEAUTIFUL COVERAGE!
WHAT DO ALL THOSE YELLOW HANKIES MEAN?
HMMM.
SO ARE YOU LEARNING ANYTHING?
YOU MEAN ABOUT DAD?...
OK, IT'S FIRST AND GOAL – WATCH FOR A QUARTERBACK KEEPER...